HIGHER
EDUCATION
LAW

IN AMERICA

Oakstone
Legal & Business Publishing
FORMERLY DATA RESEARCH, INC.

Oakstone Legal & Business Publishing, Inc.
11975 Portland Ave. S., Suite 110
Burnsville, Minnesota 55337

First edition 2000
Printed in the United States of America

> "This publication is designed to provide accurate and authoritative information in regard to the subject matter covered. It is sold with the understanding that the publisher is not engaged in rendering legal, accounting or other professional service. If legal advice or other expert assistance is required, the service of a competent professional person should be sought." *-from a Declaration of Principles jointly adopted by a Committee of the American Bar Association and a Committee of Publishers and associations.*

Library of Congress Cataloging-in Publication Data

Higher education law in America.
     p. cm.
    Includes index.
    ISBN 0-939675-95-1   (pbk.)
    1. Universities and colleges--Law and legislation--United States. I. Oakstone Legal & Business Publishing
    KF4225 .H54 2000
    378.73--dc21

                                           00-055074

ISBN 0-939675-95-1

Other Titles Published
By Oakstone Publishing:

Deskbook Encyclopedia of American School Law
Students with Disabilities and Special Education
U.S. Supreme Court Education Cases
Deskbook Encyclopedia of Public Employment Law
Deskbook Encyclopedia of Employment Law
U.S. Supreme Court Employment Cases
Federal Laws Prohibiting Employment Discrimination
Statutes, Regulations and Case Law Protecting Individuals with Disabilities
Deskbook Encyclopedia of American Insurance Law
Private School Law in America

TABLE OF CONTENTS

CHAPTER ONE
Student Rights

CHAPTER TWO
Discrimination Against Students

CHAPTER THREE
Athletics and Student Activities

CHAPTER FOUR
Freedom of Speech

TABLE OF CONTENTS

CHAPTER FIVE
Employment

TABLE OF CONTENTS

CHAPTER SIX
  Employment Discrimination

TABLE OF CONTENTS

TABLE OF CONTENTS

CHAPTER TEN
School Finance

APPENDIX A

APPENDIX B

INTRODUCTION

Our new deskbook, *Higher Education Law in America,* provides an encyclopedic compilation of federal and state court decisions in the area of college and university law. We have reviewed hundreds of federal and state court decisions involving higher education law and have included the most important ones in this deskbook. The chapters have been arranged topically, and the cases presented in an easy-to-use manner.

Each chapter contains explanatory passages at the beginning of each section to help you develop an overall understanding of the legal issues in that particular area. The case summaries have been written in everyday language, and at the start of each case is a brief note highlighting the holding or the significant issues discussed within. Further, the case summaries themselves contain boldface type to emphasize important facts, issues, and holdings.

We feel that *Higher Education Law in America* will help you to understand your rights and responsibilities under state and federal law. It has been designed with professional educators in mind, but also has tremendous value for lawyers. We hope you will use this book to protect yourself and to gain greater wisdom and understanding. Hopefully, we have succeeded in making the law accessible to you regardless of your level of understanding of the legal system.

Steve McEllistrem, Esq.
Editorial Director
Oakstone Legal & Business Publishing, Inc.

ABOUT THE EDITORS

Steve McEllistrem is the editorial director of Oakstone Legal & Business Publishing, Inc. He co-authored the Deskbook *Federal Laws Prohibiting Employment Discrimination* and is a former editor of *Private Education Law Report, Special Education Law Update* and *Legal Notes for Education*. He graduated *cum laude* from William Mitchell College of Law and received his undergraduate degree from the University of Minnesota. Mr. McEllistrem is admitted to the Minnesota Bar.

Patricia Grzywacz is the Managing Editor of Oakstone's Education Newsletters. She is the co-author of the deskbook *Students with Disabilities and Special Education*. Ms. Grzywacz graduated from Widener University School of Law and received her undergraduate degree from Villanova University. Prior to joining Oakstone, she was the Managing Editor of the *Individuals with Disabilities Education Law Report®* and authored the *1999 Special Educator Deskbook*, both published by LRP Publications. She is admitted to the Pennsylvania and New Jersey bars.

James A. Roth is the editor of the monthly newsletters *Legal Notes for Education* and *Special Education Law Update*. He also co-authored the deskbook *Statutes, Regulations and Case Law Protecting Individuals with Disabilities*. A graduate of the University of Minnesota and William Mitchell College of Law, Mr. Roth is admitted to the Minnesota Bar.

Kristina Whimpenny is the editor of *Higher Education Legal Alert* and *Private Education Law Report*. She received her B.A. in English from the University of Scranton, and is currently attending Immaculata College for her teacher certification. Ms. Whimpenny also writes several litigation reporters for Andrews Publications, a division of Oakstone Legal & Business Publishing.

How to Use Your Deskbook

We have designed *Higher Education Law in America* in an accessible format for both professional educators and attorneys to use as a research and reference tool toward prevention of legal problems.

Research Tool

As a research tool, our deskbook allows you to conduct your research on two different levels—by topics or cases.

Topic Research

♦ If you have a general interest in a particular **topic** area, our **table of contents** provides descriptive chapter headings containing detailed subheadings from each chapter.

➤ For your convenience, we also include the chapter table of contents at the beginning of each chapter.

Example:
For more information on sexual harassment in employment, the table of contents indicates that a discussion of sexual harassment takes place in Chapter Six, under Sex Discrimination, on page 228:

CHAPTER SIX
Employment Discrimination

How to Use Your Deskbook

♦ If you have a specific interest in a particular **issue**, our comprehensive **index** collects all of the relevant page references to particular issues.

Example:
For more information on sexual harassment, the index provides references to all of the cases dealing with sexual harassment instead of only those cases dealing with sexual harassment in the employment context:

Sex discrimination
    Against students, 64-68
    Defenses to different treatment, 218-222
    Equal Pay Act, 232-235
    Pregnancy, 235-236
    Procedural issues, 223-228
    Religious entanglement, 222-223
    Sexual orientation, 236-237
→ Sexual harassment
    Employee on employee, 228-231, 242-243
    Student on student, 36-37, 67, 69, 310-311
    Teacher on student, 69-72, 73, 74-75, 160-161, 178-179, 229, 298-300
    Title IX, 231-232
    Title VII, 228-231
Stalking, 305-306

Case Research

♦ If you know the **name** of a particular case, our **table of cases** will allow you to quickly reference the location of the case.

Example:
If someone mentioned a case named *Board of Regents v. Roth,* looking in the table of cases, which has been arranged alphabetically, the case would be listed under section "B" and would be found on p. 163 of the text.

B

Board of Curators v. Horowitz, 26
→ Board of Regents v. Roth, 163
Bob Jones University v. United States, 355
Boehm v. U. of Pa. Sch. of Vet. Med., 21
Bolton v. Tulane University of Louisiana, 191
Bonnell v. Lorenzo, 131

How to Use Your Deskbook

✓ Each of the cases summarized in the deskbook also contains the case citation which will allow you to access the full text of the case if you would like to learn more about it. *See, How to Read a Case Citation, p. 379.*

♦ If your interest lies in cases from a **particular state**, our **table of cases by state** will identify the cases from your state and direct you to their page numbers.

Example:
　　If cases from Wisconsin were of interest, the table of cases by state, arranged alphabetically, would list all of the case summaries contained in the deskbook from that state, including *Board of Regents v. Roth* on p. 163.

WISCONSIN

　　　　Bd. of Regents of Univ. of Wisconsin System
　　　　　　v. Southworth,　144
→　　　Board of Regents v. Roth,　163
　　　　Conroy v. Marquette Univ.,　283
　　　　Dilworth v. Dudley,　135
　　　　Duello v. Bd. of Regents of the Univ. of Wisconsin
　　　　　　System,　231

✓ Remember, the judicial system has two court systems—state and federal court—which generally function independently from each other. *See, The Judicial System, p. 375.* We have included the federal court cases in the table of cases by state according to the state in which the court resides. However, federal court decisions often impact other federal courts within that particular circuit. Therefore, it may be helpful to review cases from all of the states contained in a particular circuit.

Reference Tool

As a reference tool, we have highlighted important resources which provide the framework for many legal issues.

♦ If you would like to see specific wording of the **U.S. Constitution**, refer to **Appendix A**, which includes relevant provisions of the U.S. Constitution such as the First Amendment (Freedom of Speech and

Religion) and the Fourteenth Amendment (which contains the Equal Protection Clause and the Due Process Clause).

♦ If you would like to review **U.S. Supreme Court decisions** in a particular subject matter area, our topical list of U.S. Supreme Court case citations located in **Appendix B**, will be helpful.

The book also contains a glossary, which provides definitions of legal terms and descriptions ofcertain statutes. The Glossary can be found on p. 381.

We hope you benefit from the use of *Higher Education Law in America.* If you have any questions about how to use the deskbook, please contact Steve McEllistrem at 952-808-0550 or Patricia Grzywacz at 484-582-5050.

TABLE OF CASES

TABLE OF CASES

TABLE OF CASES

TABLE OF CASES

TABLE OF CASES

TABLE OF CASES

TABLE OF CASES

TABLE OF CASES BY STATE

TABLE OF CASES BY STATE

TABLE OF CASES BY STATE

TABLE OF CASES BY STATE

TABLE OF CASES BY STATE

TABLE OF CASES BY STATE

TABLE OF CASES BY STATE

TABLE OF CASES BY STATE

TABLE OF CASES BY STATE

CHAPTER ONE

Student Rights

I. THE CONTRACTUAL RELATIONSHIP

The relationship between students and colleges or universities is generally a contractual one, and the terms of the contract define the duties of both parties. Generally, when a contract has been breached, extra-contractual damages (like punitive damages) are not available. Only when there has been some egregious behavior, like fraud, will such damages be recoverable.

A. Breach of Contract

Courts generally hold that creation of a valid educational contract occurs upon acceptance of a student for admission. The contract terms exist in the tuition agreement, college catalogues or brochures and student handbooks. Both the institution and the student have obligations under the contract, and failure of either party to fulfill its obligations may result in a breach of contract claim.

♦ *The U.S. Supreme Court held that the doctrine of substantial performance— which allows a party who has substantially performed her promise under a contract to expect the other party to perform—applied to contracts in an academic setting. Moreover, the Court found that the doctrine applied even though one of the parties was a private educational institution.*

An overweight Rhode Island college student joined a nursing program in her sophomore year. During her junior year, the school began to pressure her to lose weight. The college tried to get her to sign a contract in which she would attend Weight Watchers. She refused to sign the contract, but attended Weight Watchers regularly without losing any significant weight. She obtained a failing grade in a clinical nursing course for reasons related to her weight and not her performance. Although expulsion was generally required for failing a clinical course, the school offered her another contract that required her to lose at least two pounds per week in order to remain in the program. She signed the contract but failed to lose two pounds per week, and was asked to voluntarily withdraw from the nursing program. She withdrew and transferred to another nursing program which caused her nursing education to last five years instead of the usual four. She sued the college in federal court, and was awarded damages for breach of contract. The school appealed to the U.S. Court of Appeals, First Circuit, which noted that the student-college relationship is essentially a contractual one, and that **as long as the student maintained good grades, paid tuition and abided by the disciplinary rules, the college was required to provide her with an education.** When the school forced her to withdraw because she was overweight and for no other reason, the school breached the contract.

The U.S. Supreme Court then heard the case and concluded that the court of appeals should have reviewed the case *de novo* (as if hearing it for the first time). It remanded the case with an order to review the district court's application of the substantial performance doctrine to the contract at issue. *Salve Regina College v. Russell*, 499 U.S. 225, 111 S.Ct. 1217, 113 L.Ed.2d 190 (1991). The doctrine of substantial performance allows a party who has substantially performed her promise under a contract to expect the other party to perform its promise. On remand, a jury found that **the student had substantially performed, and that the school had breached the contract** by not rendering its part of the exchange. The issue on appeal was whether the doctrine should have been applied to a contract in an academic setting. The college argued that the doctrine's application was limited, and urged certification to the Rhode Island Supreme Court to determine two issues: 1) whether a school can refuse enrollment in a course where the student has not met mutually established weight loss requirements, and 2) whether the doctrine of substantial performance applies to a dispute between a student and a private college. The court denied the school's request as inappropriate and unnecessary. It explained that **the doctrine was not precluded simply because one of the parties was a private educational institution**, and stated that "the instant case simply **does not implicate concerns of a school's academic integrity.**" The award of damages for the student was affirmed. *Russell v. Salve Regina College*, 938 F.2d 315 (1st Cir.1991).

◆   *A student's breach of contract claim could not succeed where she failed a required course.*

A nursing student at a Texas university passed the academic portion of a required nursing leadership/management course, but failed the clinical component when she was ordered off the hospital floor for compromising the safety of a patient. The university allowed her to complete the clinical component through an independent assessment, but she failed that as well. She sued the university and a number of officials for breach of contract, among other claims. A trial court ruled for the university, and the student appealed. The Texas Court of Appeals noted that a contractual relationship need not necessarily be inferred between a student and a public school. However, where, as here, the school was private, an implied contract existed. Nevertheless, **the student could not succeed on her breach of contract claim because she did not satisfy her obligations under the contract. She failed the clinical portion of a required class, and the court refused to second-guess the university's grading process.** *Southwell v. Univ. of the Incarnate Word*, 974 S.W.2d 351 (Tex.App.–San Antonio 1998).

◆   *By changing its procedure for selecting medical students from a university program, the school breached its contracts with the students.*

An Illinois university traditionally gave serious consideration to its applied physiology program students for entrance to its medical school where the students achieved a GPA of at least 3.0. However, **the university changed its policy to allow no more than 50 students from the physiology program into the medical school. It notified students of the change after they showed up for orientation even though it knew of the change two weeks earlier** and could have notified them before they sent their deposits to reserve their places. When a number of students who achieved a GPA of 3.0 or greater did not get into the medical school because of the 50-student limitation, they sued for breach of contract and fraud. A trial court found that because the purpose of the program was to allow students to get into medical school, the university had breached an implied contract with the students, but that it had not committed actionable fraud. The Appellate Court of Illinois affirmed. It stated that the school's unilateral change of the contract's terms amounted to a breach. However, the students failed to show actionable fraud under either the consumer protection act or the common law. *Yuan Chen v. Finch Univ. of Health Sciences*, 698 N.E.2d 257 (Ill.App.2d Dist.1998).

◆   *The First Circuit found that a student's breach of contract claim failed because he did not have a signed written offer of admission, which the school's graduate school catalog indicated was required to make an offer binding.*

A student applied for admission to a private university's graduate school, and was admitted as a probationary special student, which allowed the taking of graduate level courses but would not lead to a master's degree. An associate dean met with the student and explained to him that his admission was probationary because he lacked the requisite academic background or coursework in computer science. She told him that to be admitted to the degree program, he would need to successfully complete coursework in the computer science department and obtain a faculty advisor. However, **the university's graduate school catalog specifically provided that offers of admissions had binding force only when made by the school in writing.** The student obtained a letter from a professor which stated that he would be working under the professor's supervision for his master's project. Subsequently, the university informed the student that his special student status was discontinued and that he had not been admitted into the master's program. The student sued the university for breach of contract in a Rhode Island federal district court, and the judge granted judgment as a matter of law to the university.

The student appealed to the U.S. Court of Appeals, First Circuit, asserting that the district court judge had improperly taken the case from the jury. He asserted that he reasonably expected that if he satisfactorily performed his coursework and obtained a sponsor for his master's project, he would be admitted as a master's degree candidate based on the statement of the associate dean. The court, however, noted that **the graduate school catalog divested faculty members of any authority** to promise admission or to determine the necessary prerequisites for admissions. **Even if the associate dean had the authority to offer admission to the student, she could not do so except by a signed writing.** Further, the letter from the student's advisor did not qualify as a faculty recommendation. Accordingly, the student's breach of contract claim failed. The district court's decision was affirmed. *Mangla v. Brown Univ.*, 135 F.3d 80 (1st Cir.1998).

♦   *When an individual is induced to enroll in a college based upon an award for certain life experience credits, the institution may not thereafter revoke those credits.*

A detective enrolled in a master's degree program at a private college in Pennsylvania. He claimed that upon admission he was to be awarded certain **life experience credits**. In order to fulfill the requirements for his degree, the detective enrolled in a one-week course titled "Gender Stereotyping." As part of a classroom exercise, the instructor directed a classmate, whom the detective alleged to be a "known homosexual," to make physical advances toward the detective. The classmate complied by telling the detective he was attracted to him and by touching the detective above the knee. The detective rejected these advances and the instructor assigned that same classmate to act as a "facilitator" to deal with the detective's anger. The detective voiced his objections suggesting that the exercise was improper. The instructor then allegedly became openly critical of the detective's attitude and performance, and awarded him a "C" grade for the course. Thereafter, the instructor allegedly had himself appointed as the detective's academic adviser, and revoked and persuaded other instructors to revoke certain preapproved credits that had been granted upon admission. The detective filed suit claiming, among other things, breach of contract. The claims were dismissed by the trial court and the detective appealed to the Superior Court of Pennsylvania.

The appellate court began by reversing the trial court's order striking the detective's breach of contract claim. The court rejected the trial court's holding that the college was entitled to revoke credits previously granted for work performed out of school. The court noted that **an institution is not free to make a contractual obligation to a student and then later ignore it.** When an individual is induced to enroll in a college based upon an award for certain life experience credits, the institution may not thereafter revoke those credits. *Britt v. Chestnut Hill College*, 632 A.2d 557 (Pa.Super.1993).

♦   *A New Jersey appellate court found that a university's closure of a college did not constitute a breach of contract because the university acted fairly and in good faith pursuant to its reservation of rights in the graduate bulletin.*

A private university maintained a dental college in Hackensack, New Jersey. The university published an annual Graduate Studies Bulletin which detailed the programs offered, the curriculum, and the terms of acceptance, admission and continuation. **The bulletin contained a reservation of rights provision which allowed the university to eliminate a college, subject only to giving adequate notification to its students.** In 1989, the university's president met with the governor of New Jersey, who informed him that the dental college would receive no aid after the 1989-90 school year, and that aid would be reduced by 25% in that year. After losing $6.2 million, the president recommended to the board of trustees that the dental college be closed. The college set up a transfer program for its students and linked it with a tuition subsidy package funded by the New Jersey Department of Health and Education. Various dental students then brought suit against the board of trustees asserting that the university had breached a contract between the students and itself by closing the dental school.

The students argued that by paying their first year's tuition, they had entered into a complete and binding contract for the entire educational program. The board of trustees asserted that the court was required to give deference to university autonomy in academic decision making, and that its administrative decision to close the college was within the autonomous arena. The board further claimed that there was no contract with the students, and that, even if there was such a contract, the university had reserved the right to close the college upon adequate notice. The law division of the Superior Court of New Jersey determined that the "true" university-student "contract" was one of mutual obligations implied by law. Having decided that, it then became necessary to ascertain whether the university had acted in good faith and dealt fairly with its students. The court found that the **trustees had acted promptly and forthrightly as soon as they learned of the change in their financial circumstances.** Accordingly, the court ruled in favor of the board of trustees. *Beukas v. Board of Trustees of Fairleigh Dickenson Univ.*, 605 A.2d 776 (N.J.Super.L.1991).

The students then appealed to the Superior Court of New Jersey, Appellate Division, which affirmed the trial court's decision for substantially the same reasons as expressed by the trial court judge. However, the appellate court also noted that **even if an enforceable contract existed, the reservation of rights clause worked to defeat the students' claim because the university acted fairly and in good faith when it exercised its rights.** *Beukas v. Board of Trustees of Fairleigh Dickenson Univ.*, 605 A.2d 708 (N.J.Super.A.D.1992).

♦   *Although courts generally reject breach of contract claims based on the quality of a school's "educational experience," the Supreme Court of Colorado found that a breach of contract may occur where a school has failed to provide specifically promised educational services.*

Several Colorado residents enrolled in a private college which provided training for technical jobs in medical and dental careers. The students cited a variety of deficiencies which allegedly breached their enrollment agreements. Specifically, the students alleged that the college promised in their enrollment agreements and in the college catalogue to provide up-to-date equipment, qualified faculty, computer training, English language instruction and the ability to repeat courses with no additional fees. The students filed breach of contract claims in a Colorado district court. The district court held for the school, and the students appealed to the Court of Appeals of Colorado. The court of appeals reversed with respect to the breach of contract claim and the school appealed to the Supreme Court of Colorado.

The supreme court noted that **breach of contract claims which attack the quality of a school's "educational experience" are generally rejected.** These are essentially repackaged educational malpractice claims, and raise questions that must be answered by reference to principles of duty, standards of care, and reasonable conduct—things associated with the law of torts, not contract. However, **a breach of contract may occur where a school has failed to provide specifically promised educational services.** Here, the college allegedly failed to provide up-to-date equipment, qualified faculty, computer training and English language instruction. Thus, the students stated breach of contract claims to the extent that the alleged obligations to the students were educational services for which the students had already paid. The holding of the court of appeals was affirmed. *Cencor, Inc. v. Tolman*, 868 P.2d 396 (Colo.1994).

◆   *Students could not sue for breach of contract when a state closed a university campus.*

When the South Dakota legislature passed a law converting a university campus to a minimum security prison, it allowed students to complete the academic year and included other provisions to help the students acquire their degrees. A number of students sued the board of regents, asserting breach of contract, violations of their civil rights under 42 U.S.C. § 1983, and that the law was unconstitutional. A trial court granted summary judgment to the defendants, and the Supreme Court of South Dakota affirmed. It noted that **the students had no enforceable contract rights because their contract with the school was for the current term only.** It also held that the board of regents was not a person under § 1983, and that none of the students' constitutional rights were invaded by the closing of the school. *Aase v. State*, 400 N.W.2d 269 (S.D.1987).

◆   *An implied contract arises between a student and a school where the school promises to grant a degree upon completion of the terms outlined.*

Based on an advertisement published by the Teachers College of Columbia University, an undergraduate student with 60 credits became interested in the "Accel-A-Year" program offered by the college which would grant him a combined Bachelor of Science and Master of Arts degree. The combined degree could be obtained after an additional two years of study, thereby saving him one year toward the graduate degree. The student received an advisory statement from the college which referred to the prospective granting of his combined degree in this manner: "Application is in process to Albany for approval of this program as a *combined* degree program of B.S./M.A." The student checked the box marked "Master of Arts Degree" on his application for admission and the letter of acceptance from the college referred to his admission to a program leading to a Master of Arts degree. Oral statements by a college representative also indicated that the program would lead to a Master of Arts degree but that the application for the combined degree program had not yet been approved. When the student was notified that the application would not be approved in time for him to receive the combined degree he resumed his studies and received a Master of Arts degree in 1982 after three years of graduate study. The student sued the college for breach of contract and fraud in a New York trial court which ruled for the college. The student appealed to the New York Supreme Court, Appellate Division.

The court observed that an **implied contract** arises between a student and the school which states that if a student complies with the terms outlined by the school, he will obtain the degree. **The rights and obligations of the parties outlined in the college's bulletins, circulars and regulations become a part of the contract.** Because these documents merely stated that he was entering a program which would lead to a Master of Arts degree, the lower court properly dismissed his breach of contract claim. The student also contended that the college was liable for fraud. This claim was rejected because the student could not have justifiably relied on the statements in the advertisements and advisory statement to the effect that the program would result in a one-year saving in schooling. Any oral statements that the application was expected to be granted were merely predictions and were not misrepresentations. The trial court's decision in favor of the college was affirmed. *Vought v. Teachers College, Columbia Univ.*, 511 N.Y.S.2d 880 (A.D.2d Dept.1987).

B. Fraudulent Misrepresentation

Claims for fraudulent misrepresentation often accompany breach of contract claims. The claims usually involve the failure to provide promised services including qualified teachers and equipment or misrepresentations regarding enrollment and admissions.

◆   *Although educational malpractice claims cannot succeed in Minnesota, claims alleging consumer fraud or deceptive trade practices can be used where a school fails to perform on certain specific promises.*

A group of students filed a lawsuit against a for-profit, proprietary trade school, claiming fraud, misrepresentation, breach of contract and violation of the Minnesota consumer fraud and deceptive trade practices statutes in connection with a computer program offered by the school. A trial court characterized the students' claims as educational malpractice claims and granted the school's motion for pretrial judgment. The trial court further determined that neither the consumer fraud nor the deceptive trade practices statutes applied, and that neither of these statutes allowed damages.

The Minnesota Court of Appeals noted that **although educational malpractice claims were barred by public policy, claims for breach of contract, fraud or other intentional torts alleging the failure to provide promised educational services were actionable.** Under this analysis, the trial court correctly granted pretrial judgment to the school on the claims challenging the instructors and quality of education provided. The claims arising from the alleged failure to fulfill certain representations and promises were actionable; therefore, the trial court erred in granting pretrial judgment to the school on those claims. They were remanded to the trial court along with the claims based on the state consumer fraud statute (which allowed the recovery of money damages) and the state deceptive trade practices statute (which did not allow the recovery of money damages, but did allow for injunctive relief). *Alsides v. Brown Institute, Ltd.*, 592 N.W.2d 468 (Minn.Ct.App.1999).

♦   *A college was potentially liable for fraud and breach of contract where questions existed about representations it had made to incoming students.*

A college that specialized in psychology established a satellite campus in Alabama after acquiring the facilities of a psychotherapy institute. Four students enrolled in the college, seeking postgraduate degrees and eventually licensure. However, the school experienced financial difficulties and had to close before the students could complete their degrees. One of the reasons for its failure was its inability to get licensure for former students of the institute. This resulted in fewer students enrolling and less tuition revenue. The students sued the college for breach of contract and fraud, among other claims. A trial court granted pretrial judgment to the college, and the students appealed to the Court of Civil Appeals of Alabama.

The appellate court reversed, finding that **genuine issues of material fact existed as to whether the college had breached the contract or committed fraud.** First, the contract with the students was ambiguous, made up of a number of different documents and oral representations. There were questions as to whether the college had promised to do more than simply provide an education for each semester in exchange for tuition. Second, the students stated a potential fraud claim. In Alabama, a party can be liable for fraud even where a misrepresentation is "made by mistake and innocently" if another party acted on the misrepresentation and suffered harm. Because the college was potentially liable, the case had to be remanded for trial. *Craig v. Forest Institute of Professional Psychology*, 713 So.2d 967 (Ala.Civ.App.1997).

♦   *A federal district court held that recruiting vulnerable students and failing to provide promised services could support a fraud claim. However, New York law does not provide a cause of action based on negligent misrepresentation in the educational context.*

A New York corporation directing private business and data processing schools throughout the United States allegedly used unlicensed recruiters to entice persons with little or no education or income to enroll at the school. For example, the recruiters persuaded several persons without a high school diploma and who were dependent on public assistance to incur several thousand dollars in student loan debt to enroll in various programs. The school's published catalogue promised a high quality education provided by certified teachers. Instead, the students alleged that the teachers were frequently absent, unqualified or unlicensed and that the school failed to provide the specific courses promised in the catalogue. It also allegedly exaggerated the available curricula, instructional equipment, and placement services. The students filed suit in the U.S. District Court for the Eastern District of New York, alleging fraud, breach of contract, mail and wire fraud, and violations of the Higher Education Resources and Assistance Act (HEA). The school moved to dismiss all claims.

The district court first held that the allegations that the school had recruited vulnerable students and that it had failed to provide promised services pleaded fraud with adequate particularity. Because **the misrepresentations would influence a reasonable person's decision to attend the school,** they were "material" as required for pleading a fraud claim. Further, **the school had both a motive and a clear opportunity to commit fraud.** Government loans were readily available to vulnerable, uneducated persons from which the school stood to gain financially. The court noted that the students had adequately pleaded a cause of action for mail and wire fraud also, under the Civil Racketeer Influenced and Corrupt Organizations Act. However, the court held that New York law did not provide a cause of action based on negligent misrepresentation in the educational context. Nor did the HEA create a fiduciary duty between school and students sufficient to state a breach of fiduciary duty claim. *Moy v. Adelphi Institute, Inc.*, 866 F.Supp. 696 (E.D.N.Y.1994).

◆   *When a student possesses a right to cancel her contract, the student's misrepresentation claim may be based on postcontract-formation representations made during the cancellation period.*

After seeing several television commercials and newspaper advertisements, a prospective student contacted a business college to inquire about its program of study. She met with a representative of the school and signed an enrollment contract which called for a $500 down payment. The college catalogue was read aloud by the student to her mother that same evening. The catalogue made representations concerning the quality of its teachers, equipment, and training aids. It also stated that any student could cancel his or her contract within 72 hours of signing, and would receive a complete refund of the down payment. The student declined to cancel, but was greatly disappointed with the quality of education she received before eventually withdrawing. She contended that the college did not live up to the representations made in its catalogue and sued the school for violations of the Texas Deceptive Trade Practices Act. A jury awarded the student $28,000, and the school appealed to the Court of Appeals of Texas. The court held that **when a student possesses a right to cancel, the student's misrepresentation claim may be based on postcontract-formation representations made during the cancellation period.** The representative from the school, with whom the student originally spoke, gave testimony affirming that the catalogue had misrepresented the quality of teachers, equipment, and training aids. The court upheld the jury's findings that the student had suffered mental anguish as a result of the misrepresentations. However, it disagreed with the amount of attorney's fees which had been awarded. The award was modified and the decision was affirmed. *American Commercial Colleges, Inc. v. Davis*, 821 S.W.2d 450 (Tex.App.–Eastland 1991).

◆   *A college was not liable for a teacher's representations about the content of a course.*

Under a Washington law, one must satisfy both education and experience requirements to become a licensed real estate appraiser. A technical college developed a real estate appraising program and although the course fulfilled the educational requirements of the statute, the college made no statements that the course was designed to fulfill the licensure requirements. The course instructor represented to students that realistic training and experience would be provided, and that this would count toward the licensing requirements. However, the instructor was fired, and the new instructor stated that the program would not meet the experience requirements for licensure. All the students finished the course. They filed suit against the college in state court, alleging breach of contract and violation of the state Consumer Protection Act (CPA). The court found for the college and the students appealed to the Court of Appeals of Washington.

The students argued that they would not have taken the course had they known that it would not provide any work experience hours. The court of appeals noted that to show the existence of a contract, the students had to prove mutual assent between the contracting parties. **The court held that in all of the written materials regarding the program, the college stated that the course objective was to qualify students for entry-level employment in the appraising industry. It never stated that the program would meet the state licensure requirements.** The students argued that their first instructor was an agent of the college and that he orally represented that the program would provide work experience hours, but **the court found no authority stating that an instructor could create a contract between students and a school through oral representations.** The students also failed to show that the instructor had the authority to legally bind the school. Finally, the court held that the CPA did not apply to the college. Finding no contract between the students and the school, the court affirmed the trial court's decision. *Ottgen v. Clover Park Technical College*, 928 P.2d 1119 (Wash.App.Div.2 1996).

C. Tuition Issues

Courts generally enforce tuition contracts based on enrollment agreements, school handbooks or bulletins. Where a private school has breached its contractual obligations, courts will often award tuition refunds.

In addition to general contract considerations, post-secondary institutions have additional requirements under the Higher Education Act (HEA) and its amendments addressing the refunding of unearned tuition. Generally, the HEA requires schools to develop "fair and equitable" policies for refunding unearned tuition in the event the student fails to complete the enrollment period. Some of the regulations specify the order for reimbursement, while other regulations govern the calculation of the appropriate amount of the student's refund.

♦   *Under Department of Education regulations, institutions with cohort default rates of more than 25 percent for any of the three most recent fiscal years are disqualified from participation in Title IV programs.*

The Higher Education Act (HEA) requires that institutions develop "fair and equitable" policies for refunding unearned tuition. One provision states that refunds must be credited first to reimburse federal government programs, then other sources of aid, and last to the student. Formerly, institutions were not required to consider the student's scheduled, but not yet paid, cash payments in making their refund calculations. A new regulation required that after calculating the refund, the school subtract the student's unpaid charges from the amount it would otherwise retain. The HEA also provides that institutions with cohort default rates equal to or greater than 25 percent for each of the three most recent fiscal years will not be eligible to participate in Title IV programs. However, the Department of Education (DOE) passed regulations that disqualified institutions with cohort default rates of more than 25 percent for any of the three most recent fiscal years. Several institutions of higher education filed a lawsuit challenging the above regulations and several others, alleging that they violated the HEA. A U.S. district court granted summary judgment to the DOE, and the institutions appealed to the U.S. Court of Appeals, District of Columbia Circuit.

The institutions contended that the refund regulations impermissibly modified the definition of a fair and equitable refund policy as defined in the HEA. The court of appeals disagreed, holding that not including the unpaid amount, as under the prior regulations, had the effect of constructively refunding the amount to the student—at the expense of the federal government—and therefore crediting the refund to the student before the Title IV programs. **The present regulations properly put the risk of the student's default on the institution.** Moreover, because the DOE was expressly authorized to define administrative capability, the court held that it properly modified the 25 percent default rate criterion. *Career College Assn. v. Riley*, 74 F.3d 1265 (D.C.Cir.1996).

❖   *The Ninth Circuit enjoined implementation of a Department of Education regulation which effectively increased the required refund a school had to pay above the amount resulting from the statutory calculations.*

The Higher Education Amendments (HEA) of 1992 require post-secondary institutions that participate in Title IV programs to develop refund policies for students who do not complete the period of enrollment. The amendments require the institutions to refund the largest of the amounts provided under: 1) applicable state law, 2) the refund requirements of the institution's nationally recognized accrediting agency, or 3) the amount required under the *pro rata* refund calculation described in the HEA. In the present case, the largest of the statutory calculations would result under the *pro rata* or state regulations. The Department of Education (DOE) promulgated regulations requiring institutions to exclude "any unpaid amount of a scheduled cash payment" from the amount of earned institutional charges the school could retain. The regulation effectively increased the required refund a school had to pay above the amount resulting from the statutory calculations. An association of cosmetology schools brought an action in the U.S. District Court for the Central District of California seeking to enjoin implementation of the regulatory scheme.

The association contended that the payment of additional refunds pursuant to the regulation promulgated by the DOE violated the HEA. The court agreed and granted the association's motion for a preliminary injunction, ruling that the association established a strong likelihood of success on the merits. **The regulation arguably violated the enabling statute by requiring institutions to refund more money than the HEA deemed "fair and equitable."** Further, the mandated increase in refund payments could drive some small schools out of business and could saddle students with unexpected additional debt. Consequently, the court held that the association established the requisite likelihood of irreparable harm so as to justify injunctive relief. *California Cosmetology Coalition v. Riley*, 871 F.Supp. 1263 (C.D.Cal.1994). The Ninth Circuit Court of Appeals later granted the association summary judgment and issued a permanent injunction to enjoin implementation of the regulation. *California Cosmetology Coalition v. Riley*, 110 F.3d 1454 (9th Cir.1997).

D. Educational Malpractice

Claims for educational malpractice usually stem from accusations that a school has failed to evaluate and properly place a student, or failed to provide the educational services necessary to educate the student. However, courts have generally been extremely reluctant to recognize lawsuits based upon educational malpractice. In particular, claims for educational malpractice lack readily acceptable standards of care, cause or injury. The cause and nature of any damages to the student are also uncertain. Public policy considerations, such as an increase in litigation and embroiling courts in the day-to-day operations of schools, provide additional bases for denying an educational malpractice claim.

◆   *A student could not avoid the bar against educational malpractice claims by suing a school for constructive discharge.*
A dental student claimed to have witnessed rampant cheating that school officials refused to address. She asserted that this devalued her education and breached the university's promise to abide by its code of conduct. She also asserted that she had been constructively discharged from the dental program due to mistreatment by a faculty member. The faculty member in question had flunked her in a class, and she had subsequently failed the exam twice more. In her lawsuit against the university, a federal district court ruled in favor of the school. **It noted that her breach of contract claim was in essence a claim for educational malpractice, and that such a claim could not survive. The student failed to present specific promises that the school had breached.** Rather, she was asserting that the school had failed to provide an effective education. Further, the court refused to create a new cause of action for constructive discharge from a university. Doing so would undermine the public policy of leaving to professional educators decisions related to education, and would allow students to avoid the bar against educational malpractice claims. *Gally v. Columbia Univ.*, 22 F.Supp.2d 199 (S.D.N.Y.1998).

◆   *New York courts have declined to consider actions of educational malpractice because they require courts to make decisions as to the validity of broad educational policies such as the appropriateness of a textbook.*
Two New York residents registered for a Pascal computer programming course at an area private university. Prior to registration, they read the university's catalogue which encouraged students without a computer programming background to attend. They also read the class schedule which noted that there were no prerequisites for the Pascal course. Their advisor assured them that the course did not require an advanced math background and that their rudimentary high school math skills would suffice. They paid $855 to the university under its installment plan. The professor assigned readings from a course textbook

designed for computer science majors, scientists and engineers. He also assigned problems requiring an extensive math background. The students' advisor instructed them to keep working on the admittedly difficult problems. The professor attempted unsuccessfully to explain the problems during the first five class periods. The students then withdrew from the class in frustration. They were unable to contact their advisor for nearly three weeks, at which time they were no longer eligible for any type of tuition refund. The students filed suit against the school in a New York city court, seeking relief for breach of contract, rescission, breach of fiduciary duty, educational malpractice, and unfair and deceptive business practices.

The court held that the professor's use of an unsuitable textbook coupled with his inappropriate classroom examples intentionally drawn from math and science constituted breach of the college's educational contract with the students. Rescission of the contract was justified because it was unconscionable and because the students were induced to enter into the contract in reliance upon the college's gross misrepresentations. Further, the college assumed the obligations of a fiduciary when it assigned the students an advisor who made misrepresentations on which the students relied to their detriment. The court also held that the college was liable for educational malpractice, ruling that use of the improper textbook was a *per se* example of negligence, incompetence and malpractice. The school's actions also violated a New York law prohibiting deceptive business practices. The court ordered the school to reimburse the students and imposed punitive damages against it. *Andre v. Pace Univ.*, 618 N.Y.S.2d 975 (City Ct.1994).

The university appealed to the New York Supreme Court, Appellate Term, which noted that, as a matter of public policy, New York courts have declined to consider actions of educational malpractice because they require courts to make decisions as to the validity of broad educational policies. It noted that the claims asserted in this case entailed **an evaluation of the adequacy and quality of the textbook and the effectiveness of the teaching methods. These are determinations best left to the educational community** and the trial court erred by making them. The court also found that the trial court erroneously dismissed the university's counterclaim for the remainder of the tuition owed. The students were aware of the university's policy and did not present any evidence showing that their delay in requesting a refund was caused by the university. Thus, they were liable for the full tuition. The court reversed the trial court's decision and entered judgment for the university. *Andre v. Pace Univ.*, 655 N.Y.S.2d 777 (Sup.1996).

◆   *In rejecting an educational malpractice claim, the Seventh Circuit noted that the claim lacked a satisfactory standard of care, involved uncertainties about damages, created the potential for a flood of litigation, and embroiled courts in the day-to-day operations of schools.*

A Kansas high school basketball star was recruited by a private university in Nebraska to play on its team. The student was unprepared for a university education, but was assured that he would receive sufficient tutoring so that he would receive a meaningful education. During the student's four years at the university, his language and reading skills never rose to even a high school level. The university then made arrangements with an Illinois preparatory school for a year of remedial education. Afterwards, the student attended another university in Chicago, but had to withdraw for lack of funds. Following a depressive and destructive episode, the student sued the Nebraska university for negligence and breach of contract. The negligence claims were based on educational malpractice and negligent admission. A federal district court granted the university's motion to dismiss the complaint for failure to state a claim upon which relief could be granted. *Ross v. Creighton Univ.*, 740 F.Supp. 1319 (N.D.Ill.1990).

The student then appealed to the U.S. Court of Appeals, Seventh Circuit. The appellate court first looked at the educational malpractice claim. It noted that courts in at least eleven states have considered and rejected such claims. The main reasons given for rejecting educational malpractice claims are: 1) the **lack of a satisfactory standard of care** by which to evaluate an educator, 2) the inherent **uncertainties about the cause and nature of damages**, 3) the **potential for a flood of litigation** against schools, and 4) the threat of **embroiling courts in the day-to-day operations of schools.** With respect to the negligent admission complaint, the court applied many of the same reasons to reject the claim. On the breach of contract claim, the court found that a student would have to show more than that the education was not good enough. This would be nothing more than a repackaging of an educational malpractice claim. Instead, the student "must point to an identifiable contractual promise that the [university] failed to honor." Here, the student had alleged a breach of promise with respect to certain services, which effectively cut him off from *any* participation in and benefit from the university's academic program. The court thus affirmed in part the dismissal of the student's complaint, but allowed the breach of contract claim to proceed. *Ross v. Creighton Univ.*, 957 F.2d 410 (7th Cir.1992).

II. DISCIPLINARY ACTIONS

A. Due Process

Private schools have broad discretion in establishing disciplinary rules and procedures through their contractual relationships with students. Generally, the student is only entitled to procedural safeguards specifically provided for by the school in the enrollment agreement or student handbook or catalogue. Lawsuits often arise when a school fails to follow its rules and regulations or does not afford a student fundamental fairness by giving notice of the charges and a hearing.

1. Procedural Safeguards

◆   *Academic dismissals require less procedural protection than disciplinary dismissals; however, even an academic dismissal requires adequate notice.*

A graduate student at the University of Alaska Anchorage applied for and was accepted to an advanced practicum in special education. He worked with a host teacher at the school district to which he was assigned and was supervised by a university professor. After the host teacher notified the professor of problems with the student, the professor met with the student and attempted to rectify the problem. However, the school's principal later told the professor that things were worse than they had appeared at the previous meeting. The professor met with the principal and the host teacher before determining that the student should be removed from the practicum. The student was notified of his removal from the practicum, and was subsequently notified that he was being removed from the special education program. He appealed under the university's procedures, and the case ultimately reached the Supreme Court of Alaska. There, the court held that **the university had complied with its internal guidelines for dismissing a student from the practicum. However, an issue remained as to whether the student had been given proper notice that he was at risk of being removed from the special education program.** The court remanded the case. *Nickerson v. Univ. of Alaska Anchorage*, 975 P.2d 46 (Alaska 1999).

◆ *A student must be given notice and an opportunity to respond to charges that can lead to disciplinary action.*

A student at the University of Virginia got into a verbal altercation with a fellow student and punched him after being called a "fat ass." He pleaded guilty to a misdemeanor charge of assault and battery, served 21 days in jail, performed community service, attended anger management classes, and paid for the other student's medical expenses. The other student then initiated student disciplinary charges against him. **One day before the scheduled hearing against the student, he and his father asked the vice president of student affairs to postpone the hearing. The vice president allegedly agreed to do so, but the hearing proceeded as scheduled without the student's presence.** The judicial committee recommended the student's expulsion, and the student appealed. The vice president then scheduled a second hearing, at which the student appeared. After this hearing, it was recommended that the student be suspended for two semesters. This recommendation was forwarded to the university president, along with a letter from the student's representative asking that the penalty be decreased. Instead, the president increased the penalty to a two-year suspension, along with community service and participation in an anger and alcohol abuse program.

The student sued the university and a number of its officials, alleging that his due process rights had been violated by the refusal to postpone the first hearing (and thus depriving him of an opportunity to be heard), and by conducting a sham second hearing after which the president imposed a sanction in excess of the recommended one. A Virginia federal court considered the parties' motions and determined that **a fact question existed as to whether the student had received the opportunity to appear at the first hearing and respond to the charges against him.** However, with respect to the second hearing and the president's decision to increase the sanctions against the student, the court found that the defendants were entitled to a dismissal. The second hearing was not a sham hearing, and the president's decision to increase sanctions was not in violation of the student's due process rights. Part of the case would proceed to trial. *Smith v. Rector & Visitors of the Univ. of Virginia*, 1999 U.S. Dist. LEXIS 19517 (W.D.Va.1999).

◆ *Where a school substantially followed its published rules and regulations for academic dismissal, the student was without recourse.*

A third-year dental student received one F and two Ds. The student academic performance committee recommended his dismissal from the program, but the student was allowed to remediate his grades during a summer program. He was then promoted to his fourth year. However, the student performed even worse. He took an F in one course, unsatisfactory in three others, and had an unsatisfactory performance in four clinical departments. The committee again recommended his dismissal. Two administrative appeals by the student were unsuccessful and he was dismissed from the school. He sued, claiming that the student handbook created a contract that set forth pupil performance procedures and that the school had breached the contract. However, he did not specify how the school had breached the contract. The case reached the Superior Court of New Jersey, Appellate Division, which ruled in favor of the school. **The court refused to apply rigid contractual principles to university-student conflicts involving academic performance. It then noted that no evidence had been presented that the school had deviated from its published rules and regulations in some significant way.** The breach of contract claim could not succeed. *Mittra v. Univ. of Medicine & Dentistry of New Jersey*, 719 A.2d 693 (N.J.Super.A.D.1998).

♦   *A federal district court found that a private college student was not entitled to certain procedures which were not found in the college's regulations.*

A student at a private New York college received messages on his answering machine threatening him with physical violence because of his homosexuality. The student reported the incident and the college began an investigation. It played a tape of the messages throughout the campus and allegedly, a number of students stated that they thought another male student was one of the callers. The official conducting the investigation supposedly told others that she also thought that the student had made the calls. The student was later charged with harassment and a formal hearing was held. The student requested a voice analysis of the tapes but the college denied the request. Witnesses testified both for and against him and in the end, the hearing panel was unable to reach a conclusion on the charge. It stated that it found the student neither guilty nor innocent and that if the victimized student obtained any new evidence, the hearing would resume. However, the charged student would not be allowed to reopen the hearing with new evidence in his defense. He soon withdrew from the college, claiming mental and physical exhaustion from the experience and filed suit against the college in the U.S. District Court for the Southern District of New York. The college filed a motion to dismiss.

The student argued that the disciplinary proceedings against him were not conducted in accordance with the college's established rules. The college argued that because the student had not been expelled or suspended as a result of the proceeding, he could not assert this cause of action. The student responded that he had been constructively discharged since the school had made it impossible for him to continue there, but the court found no evidence of such conduct. The student also argued that the college violated its own procedures by denying his request for a voice analysis, by not preserving his confidentiality during the investigation, by not allowing all of his character witnesses to testify, by allowing the investigating official to testify and by not declaring him innocent once the hearing panel failed to find him guilty. The court found that none of these criteria were contained in the college's regulations as required procedures and that after the hearing, no sanctions had been imposed on the student. Because

the student failed to show that the college did not follow its established procedures, the motion to dismiss was granted. *Fraad-Wolff v. Vassar College,* 932 F.Supp. 88 (S.D.N.Y.1996).

◆   *Although a federal district court found that college students could not recover money damages in lawsuits based on college disciplinary actions, equitable relief could be requested to prevent irreparable injury which might otherwise lead to damage claims.*

Several students of a New York private college participated in an off-campus spree involving alcohol abuse. The students returned to the college where one allegedly engaged in sexual misconduct with another. A third took the abused student's undergarments and hid them in a wooded area. The students were questioned and were disciplined for giving inconsistent versions of the events. One student was allowed to voluntarily withdraw in lieu of expulsion while the other accepted disciplinary community service in lieu of suspension. Both filed suit in the U.S. District Court for the Southern District of New York, seeking injunctive relief and damages. Following settlement of the case, the court considered the appropriate role of the judiciary in student disciplinary matters.

The court held that college students could not recover money damages in lawsuits based on college disciplinary actions. Such actions would have a chilling effect on proper management of the institution, and might lead to abuse of the judicial process. However, equitable relief could be requested to prevent irreparable injury which might otherwise lead to damage claims. The court noted certain **informal procedures which might be implemented in order to minimize the risk of lawsuits.** They included: 1) use of **an impartial decisionmaker** chosen by the institution, 2) provision of **notice** as to the substance of the allegations against the student, 3) provision of an **opportunity to appear** in person before the decisionmaker, 4) permitting persons subject to discipline the **opportunity to suggest persons to whom questions would be addressed,** 5) **avoiding imposition of sanctions against persons requested to answer questions** based on the institution's disbelief of their responses, and 6) permitting an **opportunity for either voluntary acceptance of discipline or a ruling by the decisionmaker.** Although the above procedures were not mandatory, their adoption would help courts to decide whether to accept institutional disciplinary decisions. *A. v. C. College,* 863 F.Supp. 156 (S.D.N.Y.1994).

◆   *Because a college breached its contractual obligations to provide a student with notice of the nature of the charges against him, he was entitled to have the case reheard.*

A female student at a Vermont private college accused a male student of rape. After conducting an investigation, the county declined to prosecute the male student but the college pursued disciplinary steps against him as prescribed in the college handbook. The handbook provided that the student be given notice of the charges with "sufficient particularity to permit [him] to prepare to meet the charges." When asked to clarify the charges against him, the dean allegedly told the student to "concentrate on the issue of rape." The student was found not guilty of rape but guilty of engaging in inappropriate sexual activity with the female student. The College's Judicial Review Board upheld the ruling, and the student appealed to the U.S. District Court for the District of Vermont. The court held that **colleges are contractually bound to provide students with promised procedural safeguards**. However, the unique relationship between college and student with respect to disciplinary proceedings precluded rigid application of contract law. Here, the college had improperly deviated from its procedural obligations when it failed to notify the student prior to the hearing that there were two charges pending against him. He was never told that even if he was able to rebut the rape charge, he could still be found guilty of another charge. **Because the college did not state the nature of the charges with sufficient particularity to permit the student to meet the charges, the hearing had been fundamentally unfair.** However, since the inadequate notice provided the student was the only breach of the student-college contract, his case could be reheard after proper notice was given. *Fellheimer v. Middlebury College*, 869 F.Supp. 238 (D.Vt.1994).

2. Hearings

♦ *Where a student received notice and an opportunity to be heard, he could not claim due process violations.*

After spending twelve years as an engineer, a native of Iran enrolled in the College of Dentistry at the University of Tennessee. **He took exception to a policy promulgated by two of his professors—namely, that first-year students were not allowed to sit in the last row of their classrooms.** He claimed that he could see and hear better in the last row of the room. However, his professors refused to let him do so. One day, when there was a guest lecturer, the student refused to leave the last row, and finally left the classroom rather than move up one row. The academic standing committee convened a hearing for the purpose of determining whether the student's behavior warranted disciplinary action. The student was given notice of the hearing and an opportunity to be heard. He expressed his belief that the dispute over the last-row rule was really a power struggle between him and his professors. He indicated an intent not to comply with the rule. The committee determined that the student was guilty of misconduct, ordered that a letter of reprimand be placed in his file, ordered him to apologize, placed him on disciplinary probation, and warned that he would be dismissed for any other academic infractions. After losing an appeal, the student voluntarily withdrew from the college and sued.

He maintained that he was discriminated against on the basis of national origin and disability, and asserted numerous other claims, including violations of his free speech, due process and equal protection rights under the Constitution. A federal district court granted pretrial judgment to the defendants, and the student appealed to the Sixth Circuit Court of Appeals. The court of appeals affirmed the decision against the student. Here, **he presented no factual evidence of discrimination, and he was given notice and an opportunity to respond to the charges against him. Further, the pursuit of a power struggle against two professors did not amount to free speech under the First Amendment.** Accordingly, the student failed to show a constitutional violation. *Salehpour v. Univ. of Tennessee*, 159 F.3d 199 (6th Cir.1998).

◆   *Where numerous instances of dishonesty and failure to demonstrate profes-*
sional responsibility were presented at a hearing, the decision to dismiss a student
from medical school was upheld.

A student was accepted into a Wisconsin medical school. She deferred her
enrollment for one year, then withdrew during her first semester, and enrolled in
and withdrew from another medical college. She reapplied and was accepted
again but had a number of problems with taking examinations, and took a couple
of leaves from the school. After several semesters, the academic standing
committee warned her that she would have to take and pass the NBME to avoid
dismissal. However, when the exam was stolen, the NBME was cancelled for
everyone. The school then notified all students who had been scheduled to take
the examination that it would be offered three months later. The student failed to
take the NBME at that time. After a review of the student's status, **the academic
standing committee voted to conduct a dismissal hearing and notified the
student. She appeared at the hearing, at which evidence was presented of
dishonesty on her part.** Also, the hearing committee was presented with
evidence of her failure to demonstrate the expected level of professional responsibility by failing to take certain examinations, and evidence of her unwillingness
to accept responsibility for her actions. The academic standing committee then
voted to dismiss her from the school.

She sued, asserting numerous claims. A state trial court granted pretrial
judgment to the school, and the student appealed to the Court of Appeals of
Wisconsin. The court affirmed the decision in favor of the school, finding that **the
school had not breached a contract with the student because it had followed
the procedures and policies in place prior to dismissing the student. It
granted her a hearing before making its decision.** Further, none of the school
officials' actions was such as could support a claim for intentional infliction of
emotional distress. Their actions were not so extreme or outrageous that an
average member of the community would find them to be a complete denial of her
dignity. The court also held that the school's dismissal of the student was not
arbitrary and capricious. Finally, the other claims against the school had also been
properly dismissed. *Fernandez v. Medical College of Wisconsin, Inc.*, 549
N.W.2d 792 (Wis.App.1996).

◆   *Noting that private institutions have broad discretion in making rules*
and setting up procedures, an Ohio appellate court found that a private college
properly conducted a disciplinary hearing for a student's off-campus misconduct.

A female student claimed that a fellow student physically and sexually
assaulted her at his off-campus apartment. She filed a complaint with college
authorities alleging that he violated the student code of conduct. According to
school policy, a hearing was held before a judicial board to decide whether the
student had violated the student code and to recommend appropriate sanctions.
The board received evidence and found that the charges were justified. It
recommended that the student be indefinitely suspended and ineligible for
readmission for four years. The student appealed the decision and an appellate
board upheld the findings but reduced the suspension to just under two years. The
student filed suit against the college in state court, seeking to be reinstated as a

student. The college filed a motion to dismiss which the court granted. The student appealed to the Court of Appeals of Ohio.

On appeal, the student argued that the college violated a contractual obligation to provide him with a fair disciplinary hearing. He first stated that the college could not discipline him for an act that occurred off-campus. The court of appeals disagreed, finding that the college could discipline conduct which adversely affected its interests. The student also argued that members of the judicial board were inadequately trained and had conflicts of interest. The trial court found that **the board's actions were not arbitrary or capricious** and therefore upheld its decision. The court of appeals agreed with its findings, noting that private institutions have broad discretion in making rules and setting up procedures. Furthermore, **private schools must be allowed to meet their educational and doctrinal responsibilities**. Absent a clear abuse of discretion by the judicial board, the court could not interfere with its decision. Because the college's action was not an abuse of discretion, the trial court's decision was upheld. *Ray v. Wilmington College*, 667 N.E.2d 39 (Ohio App.12th Dist.1995).

◆   *A private university can formulate its own rules and implement its own punishment as applied to its students, staff and faculty subject to judicial review for arbitrary or capricious decisions.*

Two freshmen students (male and female) at a Louisiana private university left a local bar extremely inebriated. When the couple returned to the male student's dormitory, the female student told security that they had sex, that it was consensual, and that she did not need assistance. The security officer observed that she appeared coherent. The following morning, the female student filed a complaint with the campus police alleging that she had not consented to the intercourse. After two hearings with the hearing board and an appeal to the appellate committee, the male student as convicted of "causing harm or a reasonable apprehension of physical harm," in violation of the university's code of student conduct. The vice president of student affairs suspended the male student without academic credit for one semester, required him to attend a rape awareness program, and required him to write a letter to the female student. A Louisiana trial court enjoined the university from implementing the sanctions and ordered the university to reconsider the charges. The university appealed to the Court of Appeal of Louisiana, Fourth Circuit. The university contended that private schools could properly administer their own internal remedies. The court of appeal agreed. It first noted that **a private university could formulate its own rules and implement its own punishment as applied to its students, staff and faculty**. A trial court could only review a decision by a private university if it was deemed "arbitrary or capricious." Here, the university had arguably exceeded the process due even for public universities. The court reversed the trial court decision. *Ahlum v. Administrators of Tulane Educational Fund*, 617 So.2d 96 (La.App.4th Cir.1993).

◆   *Although the procedural safeguards afforded private school students rest on their contractual relationship with the school, private colleges still must afford their students fundamental fairness by giving notice of the charges and a hearing.*

Two Pennsylvania students at a private veterinarian school were accused of cheating and then notified of charges against them. The school held a hearing and the students were permitted to testify and examine adverse witnesses. The hearing panel found that the students were guilty of violating the school code by engaging in behavior suspicious of and compatible to cheating. The panel recommended probation but the dean of the school suspended the students for one year with additional sanctions. The students appealed to the school's appeals committee which upheld the dean's decision with some modifications. The students then filed a claim in a Pennsylvania trial court seeking injunctive relief. The trial court granted a preliminary injunction in favor of the students, and the school and the dean appealed to the Superior Court of Pennsylvania.

The superior court stated that while courts may take a broader view of sanctions imposed by public schools, the courts are more reluctant to interfere with sanctions given by a private school. **Because the relationship between a private college and its students is contractual in nature, the students are only entitled to the procedural safeguards which the school specifically provides for them.** The court then may only interfere if the private school does not comply with its own established safeguards. **However, private colleges must still afford their students fundamental fairness by giving notice of charges and a hearing.** The court held that the veterinarian school followed its own policies and afforded fairness by notifying the students of the charges against them and giving them a chance to appeal the decision. The superior court reversed the trial court's decision to interfere with the private school's sanctions and upheld the suspensions of the students. *Boehm v. University of Pa. Sch. of Vet. Med.*, 573 A.2d 575 (Pa.Super.1990).

♦   *Although a medical school's student handbook provided for a formal hearing before expulsion, it did not apply to a student who misrepresented his previous academic background to gain admission into the school.*

A New York medical school expelled a student based on his misrepresentations regarding the grades he previously received at another school. The student sought a formal hearing pursuant to a provision in the student handbook, but the college denied his request on the ground that the handbook was inapplicable to his situation. The student appealed to a New York trial court. The trial court directed the college to conduct a hearing concerning the student's alleged misrepresentations, and the college appealed to the New York Supreme Court, Appellate Division. The appellate division reversed, ruling that the college's decision was neither arbitrary nor capricious so as to warrant judicial intervention. **The handbook was aimed at misconduct committed by an individual while a student at the medical school, not to fraudulent acts committed prior to admission to the school.** Because the settled policy and practice of the school was to summarily dismiss any student who engaged in such misrepresentations, the school properly denied the student a formal hearing. The holding of the trial court was reversed. *Mitchell v. New York Medical College*, 617 N.Y.S.2d 894 (A.D.2d Dept.1994).

3. Search and Seizure

♦   *The pre-eminent search and seizure case in the school context is* New Jersey v. T.L.O. *Although it involved a high school student, the principles used to decide the case apply to colleges and universities also. In the case, the Supreme Court stated that a search by school officials need only be reasonable at its inception, and its scope may not exceed that which is necessary under the circumstances.*

A teacher at a New Jersey high school found two girls smoking in the lavatory in violation of school rules. She brought them to the assistant vice principal's office where one of the girls admitted to smoking in the lavatory. However, the other denied even being a smoker. The assistant vice principal then asked the latter girl to come to his private office where he opened her purse and found a pack of cigarettes. As he reached for them he noticed rolling papers and decided to thoroughly search the entire purse. He found marijuana, a pipe, empty plastic bags, a substantial number of one dollar bills and a list of "people who owe me money." He then turned her over to the police. A juvenile court hearing was held and the girl was adjudged delinquent. She appealed the juvenile court's determination, contending that her constitutional rights had been violated by the search of her purse. She argued that the evidence against her obtained in the search should have been excluded from the juvenile court proceeding.

The U.S. Supreme Court held that the search did not violate the Fourth Amendment prohibition against unreasonable search and seizure. **When police conduct a search, they have to meet the probable cause standard. However, school officials are held to a lower standard: reasonable suspicion.** Two considerations are relevant in determining the reasonableness of a search. First, the search must be justified initially by reasonable suspicion. Second, the scope and conduct of the search must be reasonably related to the circumstances which gave rise to the search, and school officials must take into account the student's age, sex and the nature of the offense. **The Court upheld the search of the student in this case because the initial search for cigarettes was supported by reasonable suspicion.** The discovery of the rolling papers then justified the further searching of the purse since such papers are commonly used to roll marijuana cigarettes. The "reasonableness" standard was met by school officials in these circumstances and thus the evidence against the girl was properly obtained. *New Jersey v. T.L.O.*, 469 U.S. 325, 105 S.Ct. 733, 83 L.Ed.2d 720 (1985).

♦   *Although the relationship between private colleges and local police may sometimes require application of Fourth Amendment protections, the Supreme Court of Tennessee found that a dormitory director's search of a student's room did not implicate the Fourth Amendment.*

A student at a private Tennessee college lived in a dormitory located on campus. As a condition to living in the dormitory, students had to consent to unannounced entries into their rooms for the purpose of maintaining order with respect to school policy. This policy was stated in the student handbook and was included in the housing contracts executed by the students. The contracts also prohibited the use of illegal substances in the dormitories. When the director of the dormitory received information that illegal drugs were located in the student's room, he went to the room, knocked on the door and, when no one answered, used his master key to get in. He found scales and a box containing a white, powdery substance. He called a police officer who acted as a liaison between the college and the police. The student was later arrested and convicted of possession of cocaine with intent to sell. The court of appeals affirmed and the student appealed to the Supreme Court of Tennessee.

The student argued that the director acted as an agent of the state by searching his room without a warrant, and therefore violated the Fourth Amendment protections against unreasonable searches and seizures. The court noted that the Fourth Amendment only limits governmental activities. **Evidence found by private persons (and, perhaps, by illegal means) need not be excluded from trial.** Two factors must be considered when determining whether a private person has acted as an agent or instrument of the state. The first factor is the government's knowledge and acquiescence to the search and the second factor is the intent of the party performing the search. Here, the court found that it was not the dormitory director's intent to act as an agent of the state. In searching the room, he was acting in furtherance of established school policy, not state policy. The court noted that sometimes the relationship between private colleges and local police can establish a sufficient link to create state action but it found that such a link was not present here. Because **the director was not acting as an agent of the state when he searched the student's room**, the search did not violate the Fourth Amendment. *State v. Burroughs*, 926 S.W.2d 243 (Tenn.1996).

◆   *A student who was searched because of a belief she was cheating had no recompense against the officials involved.*

A first-year veterinary student in Virginia began to suffer academic difficulties and fell below the grade point average necessary to continue her studies. She claimed that "test anxiety" caused her poor grades, and was allowed to retake her first year classes. She again experienced academic difficulties in her third-year studies and, after failing a urology class, obtained permission to re-take the test. During the exam, she went to the ladies' room. Because she was gone for a while, her professor sent a secretary to check up on her. The secretary saw notes arrayed on the floor and heard paper rustling when the student left one of the stalls. She reported this to the professor, who accused the student of cheating. **The professor and a dean directed the student to submit to a strip search by two female employees. No notes were found on the student; however, notes were found in the ladies' room and in the room where the student was taking the exam.** She was not allowed to finish the test. The student honor board found her guilty of cheating and suspended her for six weeks. She was then dismissed from the program because of her failing grade in urology. She sued various university officials in federal court, seeking damages for the strip search, and reinstatement. The court granted pretrial judgment to the officials, and the Fourth Circuit Court of Appeals affirmed. **The officials had reasonably believed that the student was cheating, and her ready acquiescence to the strip search led them to believe that she had impliedly consented to it.** *Carboni v. Meldrum*, No. 96-1236 (4th Cir.1996).

◆   *A regulation authorizing warrantless searches of dorm rooms was struck down in the following case.*

A student at Southern University was arrested when twelve bags of marijuana were found in his room during a dormitory sweep. The sweep was authorized by the campus housing agreement, which the student signed. After the student was expelled, he sued the university for unconstitutionally searching his dorm room. A state trial court held that **the regulation authorizing warrantless searches of rooms by university officials and police officers violated the Fourth Amendment.** The Court of Appeal of Louisiana affirmed. It differentiated this case from *State v. Hunter*, 831 P.2d 1033 (Utah App.1992), where a Utah State University regulation authorizing warrantless searches was upheld. In that case, university officials did not conduct their searches at the request of police officers or with the assistance of the police. Further, the stated purposes of the inspections at issue in *Hunter* were to maintain university property, the health and safety of students, and to preserve discipline in an educational atmosphere. However, the regulation at issue here allowed entry of dorm rooms accompanied by police without any stated purpose. **The court rejected the university's argument that its interest in eliminating weapons and drugs from the educational environment made its regulation constitutionally permissible.** Society shared that interest, yet was compelled to abide by the Fourth Amendment. The regulation was unconstitutional. *Devers v. Southern Univ.*, 712 So.2d 199 (La.App.1st Cir.1998).

◆   *All evidence obtained from an illegal search has to be suppressed.*

A maintenance worker at a state college in Massachusetts heard a cat inside a dormitory suite. He reported the noise to college officials who posted notices on the four bedrooms of the suite, informing the students of a possible violation of college policy, and alerting them that a "door to door check" would be conducted by 10 p.m. to ensure that the cat had been removed. When the officials inspected the individual bedrooms, they noticed a light behind one closet door. Fearing a fire hazard, they opened the door and found marijuana plants. **They summoned campus police who conducted a search and confiscated the plants without obtaining a warrant. In the criminal action that followed, the district court suppressed the evidence,** and the Supreme Judicial Court of Massachusetts affirmed. Although the initial search by the college officials was proper, the subsequent search and seizure by the campus police violated the Fourth Amendment. As a result, all evidence obtained from the illegal search had to be suppressed. *Commonwealth v. Neilson*, 666 N.E.2d 984 (Mass.1996).

B. Academic Dismissals

Courts generally distinguish between academic and nonacademic dismissals. In particular, courts usually grant schools greater deference regarding dismissal decisions based on academic deficiencies. Thus, so long as notice is provided, a hearing is not necessary, whereas for nonacademic dismissals, both notice and a hearing are required.

1. Poor Performance

◆ *Schools and universities are generally given a great deal of latitude by courts in making academic decisions. Their choices, however, must have some rational basis and not be arbitrary. Here, the Supreme Court upheld a university's decision to dismiss a student from an advanced academic program based on poor performance.*

A student was enrolled in the University of Michigan's "Inteflex" program, which is a special six-year course of study leading to both an undergraduate and medical degree. The student struggled with the curriculum for six years, completing only four years' worth of study and barely achieving minimal competence. Because he was given a grade of "incomplete" in several important classes and was forced to delay taking his examinations, he was placed on an irregular program. Finally, he completed the four years of basic study necessary to take the NBME Part I, a test administered by the National Board of Medical Examiners which is a prerequisite to the final two years of study under the Inteflex program. Unfortunately, the student failed the exam, receiving the lowest score ever in the brief history of the Inteflex program.

The university's medical school executive board reviewed the student's academic career, decided to drop him from registration in the program, and denied his request to retake NBME Part I. The executive board was not swayed by arguments that his failure on the exam was due to his mother's heart attack 18 months previously, the excessive amount of time he had spent on an essay contest which he had entered, and his breakup with his girlfriend. The student brought suit in federal court claiming breach of contract under state law and also alleging a violation of his due process rights under the U.S. Constitution.

At trial, the evidence showed that **the university had established a practice of allowing students who had failed the NBME Part I to retake the test one, two, three, or even four times. The student here was the only person ever refused permission to retake the test.** The district court ruled against him on the contract claim and further held that his dismissal was not violative of the Due Process Clause. The U.S. Court of Appeals, Sixth Circuit, reversed and held that the student had possessed a property interest in his continued participation in the Inteflex program, and that the university had arbitrarily deprived him of that property interest by singling him out as the only student ever denied permission to retake the NBME Part I.

The U.S. Supreme Court unanimously reversed the court of appeals' decision and reinstated the district court's ruling against the student. **The Due Process Clause was not offended because the university's liberal retesting custom gave rise to no state law entitlement to retake NBME Part I.** Furthermore, the university had based its decision to dismiss the student upon careful, clear and conscientious deliberation which took his entire academic career into account. The university had acted in good faith. The Supreme Court further observed that the discretion to determine, on academic grounds, who may be admitted to study is one of the "four essential freedoms" of a university. The Court thus held that the Due Process Clause was not violated by the student's dismissal. *Regents of the University of Michigan v. Ewing*, 474 U.S. 214, 106 S.Ct. 507, 88 L.Ed.2d 523 (1985).

♦   *Unlike dismissals for disciplinary reasons, dismissals for academic reasons do not require the procedural rigors as set down in* Goss v. Lopez, *a case involving suspensions of students for misconduct. In such situations, school officials must give the students notice of the charges against them and an opportunity to respond. School officials have a broader discretion in dealing with academic expulsions and suspensions than in disciplinary actions involving misconduct.*

The academic performance of students at the University of Missouri-Kansas City Medical School was assessed periodically by the Council of Evaluation, a faculty-student body with the power to recommend probation or dismissal subject to approval by a faculty committee and the dean. Several faculty members expressed dissatisfaction with the performance of a medical student. As a result, the Council of Evaluation recommended that she be advanced to her final year on a probationary status. Faculty complaints continued, and the Council warned the student that absent "radical improvement," she would be dismissed. She was allowed to take a set of oral and practical examinations as an "appeal" from the Council's decision.

The student spent a substantial portion of time with seven practicing physicians who supervised the examinations. Two recommended that she be allowed to graduate. Two recommended that she be dropped immediately from the school. The remaining three recommended that she not be allowed to graduate in June and be continued on probation pending further reports of her progress. Subsequent reports regarding the student were negative and she was dropped from the program following the Council's recommendation. The student sued, alleging that she had not been accorded due process prior to her dismissal. The district court determined that the student had been afforded due process. The U.S. Court of Appeals, Eighth Circuit, reversed.

On appeal, the U.S. Supreme Court held that **the student had been given due process as guaranteed by the Fourteenth Amendment.** The procedures leading to the student's dismissal, under which the student was fully informed of faculty dissatisfaction with her progress, and the consequent threat to the student's graduation and continued enrollment did not violate the Fourteenth Amendment. **Dismissals for academic reasons do not necessitate a hearing before the school's decision-making body.** *Board of Curators v. Horowitz,* 435 U.S. 78, 98 S.Ct. 948, 55 L.Ed.2d 124 (1978).

♦   *A university properly dismissed a student in the following case.*

A New York student was on academic probation while repeating his third year of medical school. After he failed written examinations in four of his clerkships, he was assigned four "conditional" grades. The academic promotions committee convened and provided him with an opportunity to appear and present evidence on his behalf. It then dismissed him from the school. In his lawsuit alleging that the decision to dismiss him was arbitrary and capricious, the Supreme Court, Appellate Division, held in favor of the university. **The decision to dismiss the student had been properly based upon academic considerations. It was neither arbitrary not capricious.** *Williams v. State Univ. of New York,* 674 N.Y.S.2d 702 (App.Div.2d Dept.1998).

♦   *Where a student received numerous warnings about her performance, and where the school's decision to dismiss her was not irrational or taken in bad faith, there was no due process violation.*

A graduate student in dentistry at a Nebraska university received evaluations that were substantially below those of the other students. Eight deficiencies were listed, and she was warned that she was in danger of dismissal from the program. She engaged in remediation efforts, but continued to have problems with her technical skills. Eventually, she was dismissed from the program. She sued the university in federal court, asserting that it had violated her due process rights and that it had discriminated against her on the basis of disability. The court found that, with respect to her disability (a vision problem), she never informed anyone at the university of it, other than to say that she had a depth perception problem, and she never asked for an accommodation. **With respect to her due process claims, the court found that she was given repeated warnings of the faculty's dissatisfaction. Further, there was no evidence that university officials had acted irrationally or in bad faith in dismissing the student.** The court ruled in favor of the university. *Rossomando v. Bd. of Regents of the Univ. of Nebraska*, 2 F.Supp.2d 1223 (D.Neb.1998).

♦   *A New York appellate court held that a school can expel a student for academic reasons in the exercise of its discretion as long as it does not act in an arbitrary or capricious manner or violate its rules and regulations.*

A student at a New York medical school had attended the school for four years but had not yet completed the second year requirements and failed to pass the only class he was taking in his current school year. An academic committee recommended his dismissal and he appealed to a faculty committee. He reached an agreement with the committee under which he was to pass the first step of the national medical licensing examination on his first attempt or withdraw from the college. When he failed to pass the first step of the exam, the college dismissed him. He filed suit against the college in state court to annul the college's decision. The trial court dismissed his petition and he appealed to the New York Supreme Court, Appellate Division. The appellate court noted that there are strong policy considerations against the intervention of courts in disputes relating to a school's judgment of a student's academic performance. **Absent any arbitrary behavior, a school can expel a student in the exercise of its discretion.** Since the student did not present any evidence that the college's decision was arbitrary or capricious or in violation of its rules and regulations, the trial court's decision was affirmed. *McDermott v. New York Medical College*, 644 N.Y.S.2d 834 (A.D.3d Dept.1996).

♦   *A student who failed to complete the requirements of her program was properly dismissed, since she failed to show that she was dismissed from the program because of her disability.*

A woman was enrolled in an occupational therapy program at a private New York college. To graduate, a student had to take the required number of credits and complete two placements. According to school policy, if a student left a placement without a supervisor's permission, he or she automatically failed the placement, and two failed field placements resulted in automatic termination from the program. During her final placement, the student had an argument with her supervisor, walked out and did not return. Two weeks later, she wrote a letter to the school stating that she was going to be evaluated for a learning disability and requesting accommodations. Because she had already failed a placement before walking out of her final placement, the school responded that she had been automatically terminated from the program. The student was later diagnosed with a mental disorder and requested that the college reconsider its decision. It refused and the student filed suit in the U.S. District Court for the Western District of New York, alleging violations of § 504 of the Rehabilitation Act and the Americans with Disabilities Act (ADA), among other claims. The college filed a motion to dismiss.

The court noted that to state a *prima facie* case of discrimination under § 504 the student had to show that she was disabled, that she was otherwise qualified for the program, that she was dismissed because of her disability and that the college received federal financial assistance. The court concentrated on the third element and found that **the student did not show that she was discharged because of her disability**. According to the evidence, she was automatically dismissed from the program when she walked out of her last placement. At this time, the college did not know that she had a disability and it was not informed of her disability until after her termination. The student argued that her letter informing the college that she was being evaluated for a possible disability was adequate notification but the court disagreed. The letter merely stated that she was going to be evaluated, not that she was disabled. The student also argued that once the college was informed, it was required to readmit her into the program. The court, however, found that **the college was not required to reconsider a nondiscriminatory decision.** Because the student could not show as a matter of law that she was dismissed from the program because of her disability, she was not able to make out a *prima facie* case of discrimination under § 504 or the ADA. The college's motion to dismiss was granted. *Goodwin v. Keuka College*, 929 F.Supp. 90 (W.D.N.Y.1995).

* *Academic dismissals made by educational institutions must be upheld unless arbitrary and capricious, irrational, made in bad faith, unconstitutional or contrary to statute.*

A student attending a New York private law school failed Civil Procedure in his first semester. The school informed him that it was dissatisfied with his progress. After he failed Constitutional Law and performed lower than average or failed to complete his other courses, he was dismissed for academic deficiency because his cumulative grade point average fell below 2.0. The school's Academic Policy Committee denied his request for probation in lieu of dismissal and he appealed to a New York trial court. The trial court ordered the school to hold another hearing on the issue, and the school appealed to the New York Supreme Court, Appellate Division. The court noted that terminations made by educational institutions must be upheld unless arbitrary and capricious, irrational, made in bad faith, unconstitutional or contrary to statute. The trial court had improperly vacated the school's decision. **The committee, as an expert evaluator of the cumulative information relating to the student's performance, was in a better position to determine whether or not he demonstrated a strong probability of future compliance with the school's academic standards.** The trial court's ruling was reversed and the case was dismissed. *Girsky v. Touro College, Fuchsberg Law Center*, 621 N.Y.S.2d 85 (A.D.2d Dept.1994).

◆   *An Illinois appellate court found that a Ph.D. candidate had no right to receive an additional two years to complete her dissertation. The university had properly enforced reasonable academic requirements, which were designed to ensure that the university students would safely serve the public as health care providers, in dismissing her.*

A candidate for a Ph.D degree in speech and language pathology at Northwestern University was required to prepare a prospectus, undertake creative research, complete a written dissertation, and pass an oral examination prior to graduation. Against the advice of her director, the candidate began working on a prospectus on apraxia. The director allegedly asked her out and told her that they should "be together." He and several other faculty members evaluated three different drafts of her prospectus and each time concluded that they were unacceptable for a variety of reasons. She began to work on a new topic but several professors again determined that it was not academically acceptable. The candidate alleged that the director had "usurped her ideas and surreptitiously utilized much of the information researched." She failed to complete her dissertation within the required five-year time frame. The university declined to grant the candidate a two-year extension, stating that she was unlikely to be able to research, prepare and defend a dissertation within a reasonable time. She filed suit against the university and director in an Illinois trial court, alleging breach of contract and tortious interference with contract. The trial court awarded the candidate a mandatory injunction to allow her an additional two years of study in which to complete her dissertation.

The court of appeal reversed, ruling that the trial court improperly granted injunctive relief absent a clearly ascertainable right to the two-year extension, a showing of irreparable harm or the inadequacy of legal remedies. The **college had properly enforced reasonable academic requirements** which were designed to ensure that the university students would safely serve the public as health care providers. Although the candidate had worked hard towards obtaining a degree at Northwestern, **the school's decision did not preclude her obtaining a degree at another institution**. Consequently, the harm was not irreparable. Further, Illinois law recognized the availability of monetary damages: an alternative legal remedy. Finally, **the candidate failed to establish evidence that the university's determination was arbitrary and capricious**. Rather, the professors' explanations showed a discernible rational basis for the university's decision. The trial court's injunction was reversed and the case was remanded for further proceedings. *Bilut v. Northwestern Univ.*, 645 N.E.2d 536 (Ill.App.1st Dist.1994).

The candidate appealed to the Supreme Court of Illinois, which denied her petition, and the case was then remanded to the circuit court. The university and director moved the court for summary judgment on grounds that the court of appeals had ruled as a matter of law that their actions were not arbitrary and capricious; thus, no factual issues existed for trial. The court entered summary judgment in their favor, but allowed the candidate to amend her complaint with charges of civil conspiracy, conversion of property and plagiarism. The court granted summary judgment to the university and the director on the grounds that the new claims were barred by the statute of limitations.

The candidate appealed to the state court of appeals, which found no merit to the civil conspiracy claim because the alleged conspirators were the university and its direct employees. Because of the principal-agent relationship existing between the university and director, they were legally incapable of conspiring with one another. The court also held that the amended complaint was barred by Illinois' five-year statute of limitations. The new claims pertained to conduct that had taken place at least seven years earlier. The candidate had no excuse for omitting them from her original complaint and the university and director were entitled to summary judgment. *Bilut v. Northwestern Univ.*, 692 N.E.2d 1327 (Ill.App.1st Dist.1998).

♦   *Where a school had properly based its expulsion decision on the totality of the evidence, the dismissal was neither arbitrary nor capricious and did not constitute a breach of contract.*

A phlebotomy student at an Illinois medical technology school received low scores on all but one of five examinations. As a result, she was placed on probation and notified that in order to graduate she would have to pass another exam, show marked improvement, better consider patient needs, handle patients more gently, and listen more closely to the instructor. She failed to achieve a passing score on the examination. **Her supervisor then described her treatment of patients as "brutal,"** noting instances where she: 1) failed to use proper procedures, 2) left an open dirty needle on top of a hazard box, and 3) left a urinal in a patient's bed. She also asked a patient who had undergone a double mastectomy "why she was in the hospital if she had just recently had a baby." The school expelled the student based on her performance, and she appealed to the U.S. District Court for the Northern District of Illinois.

The court employed a two-step analysis to determine whether the school had committed a breach of contract: 1) whether it breached a promise made either explicitly or through its academic bulletins or application forms; and 2) whether it acted arbitrarily, capriciously, and in bad faith. Because the school properly based its expulsion decision on the totality of the evidence, the dismissal was neither arbitrary nor capricious and did not constitute breach of contract. The student had failed to achieve the requisite score on her exam, had failed to improve her phlebotomy and communication skills, had failed to improve her handling of patients, and had failed to improve her ability to listen and to take constructive criticism. Even if the second term of her probation agreement obligated the instructor to review her performance, **her failure to achieve the other probationary conditions justified the expulsion.** *Haynes v. Hinsdale Hospital*, 872 F.Supp. 542 (N.D.Ill.1995).

♦   *Courts may review a grading policy that is arbitrary and capricious, irrational, made in bad faith or contrary to federal or state law.*

A New York Law School student performed below a 2.0, or "C," cumulative average. The law school rules required students to maintain a 2.0 or better, or be subject to academic dismissal by the Academic Status Committee. The student appeared before the committee to state her case, but the committee failed to be persuaded by the student's excuses and voted unanimously to dismiss her. The student asked the committee to reconsider its decision. When the committee declined, the student filed suit in a New York trial court challenging the committee's decision and the grades she received in three of her classes. The trial court dismissed all of the claims, but the appellate division reversed and remanded with respect to the student's grade in one of her classes to determine if the grade was a rational exercise of discretion. Both parties appealed to the Court of Appeals of New York.

The student claimed that when she met with the professor he indicated to her that she had received a zero on an essay question worth 30 percent of her grade because she had analyzed the problem under Delaware and New York law when only Delaware law was asked for. The student indicated that she analyzed the problem under New York law as well to get extra credit. The professor still refused to change her grade. The student contended that the grading policy was a matter for the court to adjudicate. **Courts have traditionally left grading policies to the special expertise of educators.** However, courts may review a grading policy that is arbitrary and capricious, irrational, made in bad faith or contrary to federal or state law. The court determined that **the student failed to meet this standard of review because the allegations went to the heart of the professor's evaluation of her academic performance.** The court dismissed the claim in its entirety. *Susan M. v. New York Law School*, 556 N.E.2d 1104 (N.Y.1990).

2. Cheating

♦   *An African-American student failed to demonstrate that his discharge for cheating was racially motivated.*

An economics professor, concerned about cheating, drafted two different exams, making only slight changes to the questions. He alternated the tests in a pile that a teaching assistant handed out in class. A student incorrectly answered several questions on his exam, but his answers were accurate responses to the corresponding questions in the other version of the exam. At his honor trial, the student jury found him guilty. The honor committee's appeal panel upheld the student jury's verdict. The student then sued the university in the U.S. District Court for the Western District of Virginia. Most of the claims were dismissed, except those alleging denial of equal protection of the laws, procedural due process violations and defamation.

To prove denial of equal protection, **the student used raw statistics to show that more minority students were prosecuted in similar situations compared to non-minority students, but the court found the actual evidence showed race was not a factor.** The court stated that statistics, standing alone, did not create a constitutional violation. In addition, three other students were charged with honor violations on the same exam. The case against the other African-American student was dropped for insufficient evidence, one of the white students was found not guilty and the other white student left the university after being formally accused. **The student's procedural due process claim also failed** because even though his honor advisor did not contact him until the following semester, the delay should not have resulted in his inability to recreate the seating arrangement on the test day, record the mental processes he used to come up with the answers he devised, and preserve the other students' papers and the honor committee files before they were destroyed. While having an honor advisor assigned during the pre-trial process may be beneficial, the due process clause does not *require* such assistance. The student's claim of defamation also failed because a letter that was circulated among persons within the university only went to persons who had a duty and interest in the subject matter. The university's motion for summary judgment was granted. *Cobb v. Rector and Visitors of Univ. of Virginia*, 84 F.Supp.2d 740 (W.D.Va.2000).

♦   *Where a student's teachers did not take allegations of cheating into account when they dismissed him from school, he had no cause of action against them.*

A graduate student in psychology received two grades of C that subjected him to possible expulsion. A number of his professors also knew of allegations against him for cheating. However, they asserted that they did not take the allegations into account when grading him. After the student's second C, he was placed in a remediation program. He then received two more Cs. He also failed two oral comprehensive examinations. A second, more demanding remediation plan was then drafted, calling for the student to enroll in a specific class. When he failed to do so, he was dismissed from the program because of his failure to comply with the program's academic requirements. He sued, claiming that the decision to dismiss him was tainted by the allegations of cheating and that he was not given a chance to address those allegations. A Texas federal court ruled in favor of the university, and the Fifth Circuit Court of Appeals affirmed. **Here, the dismissal had been for academic reasons, not disciplinary reasons. Thus, the protections available to the student were not as great. Further, even if the dismissal had been for disciplinary reasons, the student had essentially been given a hearing** when he went over the remediation plans with school personnel. It was only after he failed to meet the requirements of the second remediation plan that he was dismissed from the program. *Wheeler v. Miller*, 168 F.3d 241 (5th Cir.1999).

♦   *A loss of credit for two classes in which a student was found to have violated the honor code was a fair punishment.*

The University of Tennessee Board of Trustees' honor code created a violation for failure to report the giving or receiving of unauthorized aid on an examination. Four students reported observing a group of other students who apparently gave or received aid during several examinations. One of the accused students was charged with cheating on five examinations under the honor code. An administrative law judge found the student not guilty on three charges and guilty on two others. He imposed as a punishment one year of probation and the loss of credit for the two classes in which she was held in violation of the honor code. The student appealed the decision to a Tennessee trial court, stating that a 19-day delay by the administrative law judge in issuing his opinion caused her to delay retaking the two courses. The student nonetheless graduated. The court held for the university and the student appealed to the Court of Appeals of Tennessee. **The court of appeals found ample evidence in the record that the student had violated the honor code. There was evidence that the student had been looking at another person's examination papers.** The administrative law judge's delay did not violate state law and the court affirmed the trial court's judgment for the university. *Daley v. Univ. of Tennessee at Memphis*, 880 S.W.2d 693 (Tenn.App.1994).

♦   *A student who was dismissed for cheating was given due process because she received notice and an opportunity to be heard.*

An Indiana medical school student was observed copying another student's paper during a final examination. Two professors who monitored the test submitted the papers of both students to a statistician who determined that there was a significant probability of cheating based upon matching wrong answers. The professors assigned the student accused of cheating a failing grade and, **because she had received a prior failing grade, an informal conference was held to determine whether she should be dismissed from the school.** The decision to assign a failing grade was affirmed, and a formal dismissal hearing was held before an academic committee at which the student was represented by an attorney. The dean of the medical school adopted the committee's recommendation to dismiss the student, and she filed a lawsuit against school officials to challenge the action in an Indiana trial court. The court denied the student's motion for a preliminary order preventing dismissal, and she appealed to the Court of Appeals of Indiana.

The court rejected the student's claim that the medical school's procedures had violated her due process rights. In cases of academic dismissals, only minimal procedural protections are required. Where dismissal occurs for disciplinary reasons, due process requires only notice and an opportunity to be heard. **The student had received a hearing in this case which satisfied due process requirements under the standards for both academic and disciplinary dismissals.** She was not entitled to formally cross-examine the professors as she claimed. There was also no merit to her argument that the school's rules had violated her rights by allowing her dismissal for the "appearance of cheating." In this case, there was substantial evidence of cheating, and the court affirmed the trial court order. *Reilly v. Daly*, 666 N.E.2d 439 (Ind.App.1996).

C. Nonacademic Dismissals

Sometimes cheating is determined to be an academic dismissal. Other times it is considered a nonacademic dismissal. However, as long as the school follows reasonable procedures before dismissing a student accused of cheating, its decision is likely to be upheld. For example, notice and an opportunity to be heard (two basic due process protections) should be provided.

♦   *A university could expel a student for murdering a classmate even though he had completed all his degree requirements.*

A student enrolled at Johns Hopkins University and completed his degree requirements in three and a half years. However, because the university held its graduation ceremonies only once a year at the end of the spring semester, he had to wait to receive his diploma. During the spring semester, the dean of students contacted him about complaints of harassment filed by another student, and told him that he would have to notify her and campus security when he intended to be on campus. He informed the dean that he would be on campus on a particular date to attend a student organization meeting. As promised, he attended the meeting, where he got into a confrontation with the student who had accused him of harassment. He shot and killed the student, then pled guilty to murder. When the dean informed him that the university had expelled him and that he was not going to receive his diploma, he sued. A state trial court dismissed his action, and the Court of Special Appeals of Maryland affirmed. It did not matter that the student would have already received his diploma had the university conducted a fall graduation ceremony. What mattered was that the student had not yet been awarded his degree, and that he remained subject to the student handbook rules. **Since the student handbook required him to not only complete his coursework, but also to comply with the university's conduct code, and since murder was a violation of that code, the university was justified in expelling the student despite his completion of all degree requirements.** The student was not entitled to his diploma. *Harwood v. Johns Hopkins Univ.*, 747 A.2d 205 (Md.App.2000).

◆   *A student who tried to get drugs with a fraudulent prescription could be expelled.*

A nursing student at an Arkansas community college was arrested for attempting to obtain a controlled substance with a fraudulent prescription. She was suspended pending the police charges against her, and pleaded no contest to a misdemeanor offense. The college then expelled her from school. It later conducted a new hearing to give the student another opportunity to review all the evidence and participate in the hearing with the help of counsel. The college again upheld the decision to expel the student. She sued the college in a federal court under 42 U.S.C. § 1983, asserting that the college had violated her constitutionally protected due process rights. The court dismissed her lawsuit. The Eighth Circuit Court of Appeals affirmed the ruling in favor of the college. First, **the college's Standards of Conduct were not void for vagueness. They required students to obey all rules and regulations formulated by the college as well as all federal, state and local laws.** This was sufficient to notify the student that criminal conduct was not acceptable. Second, the student had been provided with adequate notice of the charges against her and an opportunity to present her side of the story. As a result, her claim against the college could not succeed. *Woodis v. Westark Community College*, 160 F.3d 435 (8th Cir.1998).

◆   *Where a university failed to follow proper procedures, it was found to have improperly expelled a student.*

A Texas medical school student took a National Board of Medical Examiners test in surgery. Two test proctors observed the student looking at another student's answer sheet. Eighteen days later, **the school advised the student by letter that he was accused of cheating on the test.** He denied wrongdoing but the school brought formal charges several weeks later and held a hearing on charges of academic dishonesty. The hearing officer and a school official viewed the test site during the hearing. The student was denied permission to view the room. The hearing officer recommended expulsion as well as changing the student's grade from a B to an F. A Texas district court held that the university had violated the student's due process rights, and the university appealed the adverse decision to the Court of Appeals of Texas, Houston.

The court of appeals observed that **the dismissal was for disciplinary reasons, which justified more stringent procedural protection than dismissal for academic reasons.** In this case, the university had deprived the student of a meaningful opportunity to respond to the charges against him. It had attempted to discourage him from obtaining legal counsel and had failed to inform him of the charges until it was too late for him to contact witnesses. The test proctors had failed to approach him and escort him outside the examination room and had thus violated university academic policies. The university's actions deprived the student of his procedural due process rights and the court of appeals affirmed the trial court's decision. *Univ. of Texas Med. School at Houston v. Than*, 874 S.W.2d 839 (Tex.App.–Houston 1994).

♦   *Courts are required to show great respect for the judgment of college faculty members and cannot override their decisions unless there is a showing of a substantial departure from accepted academic norms.*

An Iowa medical student attending an osteopathic medical college achieved superior grades on his examinations, but exhibited eccentric behavior, strong psychopathic tendencies and socially unacceptable behavior. Because of his unkempt appearance and lack of interpersonal skills, he failed his clinical assignment and was asked to withdraw from the college. He threatened to drive his car off a bridge and was briefly placed in a psychiatric ward. When he refused to withdraw from the program, the college dismissed him and he filed an unsuccessful appeal through the college. An Iowa trial court determined that the dismissal by the college violated its written procedures concerning the evaluation and remediation of clinical students and that college officials failed to exercise appropriate professional judgment. The college appealed the trial court's order to reinstate the student and to offer him an opportunity to repeat the clinic. The Supreme Court of Iowa determined that the trial court had applied an incorrect legal standard to evaluate the dismissal. **Courts were required to show great respect for the judgment of college faculty members and could not override their decisions unless there was a showing of a substantial departure from accepted academic norms.** The court rejected the student's characterization of the dismissal as "nonacademic." It also found that, contrary to the student's arguments, the school administration had shown great concern for him. The court reversed and remanded the judgment of the district court, dismissing the student's claims. *Lekutis v. Univ. of Osteopathic Medicine and Health Sciences*, 524 N.W.2d 410 (Iowa 1994).

♦   *Schools are generally accorded greater deference with respect to dismissals involving academic deficiency than for those involving nonacademic reasons.*

A student at a private college of osteopathic medicine failed several courses during his first year. He also failed his spring clinical rotations and a neurobiology class during his third year. However, he later passed the classes after retaking them. During his fourth year, the student refused the college's request to return from an internship in Minneapolis after problems arose there. He finally returned, was placed on probation, and then assigned to do his clinical rotations in Des

Moines. After serious attendance problems, two alleged incidents of unauthorized practice of medicine, and one alleged incident of forgery, the student was dismissed following a series of notices and hearings. The student challenged his dismissal in an Iowa trial court. The trial court held that the dismissal was arbitrary and capricious, but it denied reinstatement and awarded him the equivalent of four years' tuition. Both parties appealed their adverse rulings to the Supreme Court of Iowa. The court stated that **schools are generally accorded greater deference with respect to dismissals involving academic deficiency** than for those involving nonacademic reasons. Here, the school's admission at trial established that the student's dismissal was nonacademic. **Although professional training violations were academic matters, they were also considered nonacademic disciplinary violations.** However, even under the stricter burden applied to nonacademic disciplinary actions, the court held that the two incidents of unauthorized practice of medicine coupled with the events that led to his probation justified his dismissal. The holding of the district court was reversed. *Pflepsen v. Univ. of Osteopathic Medicine*, 519 N.W.2d 390 (Iowa 1994).

♦   *The Eighth Circuit upheld a school's refusal to reinstate a student who pleaded guilty to a criminal offense, even though the charge was eventually dismissed and his criminal record cleared.*

A law school student was arrested after attempting to use a stolen credit card. When authorities formally charged the student, he had only two semesters to complete before graduating. The student moved the court for a continuance until after his expected graduation date. Meanwhile, the law school faculty reviewed his criminal file and passed a resolution suspending any student indicted or charged with criminal conduct while the matter was pending in court. The faculty also suspended the student and notified him by letter. He then sued the school in an Iowa state court for an injunction which would compel the school to reinstate him the following semester. The court ruled against the student, who then pled guilty and was sentenced in the criminal case. A year later, the student completed probation, the charge was dismissed and his criminal record cleared. He then petitioned the school for reinstatement. The school rejected the petition. The student sued the school in an Iowa federal district court alleging violations of his constitutional rights and breach of contract. The court ruled for the school and the student appealed to the U.S. Court of Appeals, Eighth Circuit. The court ruled that the trial court had not been in error when it ruled that **the school's honor code, student handbook, and reservation of rights clause had formed a contract** between the school and the student. **Because the jury had not found that the school had breached the contract in any respect, the student could not now challenge the verdict** as a matter of law. The appeals court also affirmed the trial court's findings that the school had not been arbitrary, capricious or had acted in bad faith. *Warren v. Drake Univ.*, 886 F.2d 200 (8th Cir.1989).

♦   *A university followed its standards and procedures for disciplinary violations and properly expelled a student for violation of its harassment policy.*

An Illinois graduate student was expelled by a school disciplinary committee for violating the university's harassment policy. He appealed the committee's decision to a university review board arguing that the penalty was too harsh. When the board affirmed the committee's decision, the student brought a breach of contract action in federal court. He claimed that the university had expelled him arbitrarily, capriciously, and in bad faith, thus breaching the contract between himself and the university. He sought an injunction compelling the university to rescind his expulsion and to award him an M.B.A. retroactively. He also sought monetary damages for humiliation and financial losses. After a bench trial, the court determined that the relationship between the university and its students was a contractual one and was governed by the terms set forth in the university's catalogs and manuals. The university was obligated to follow its published standards and procedures when disciplining its students. However, the student was also obligated to abide by the university's rules of conduct. The court held that **the committee's determination that the student engaged in a "systematic, prolonged and premeditated pattern of harassment" against a fellow student was rationally based on the evidence**. The student argued that the faculty members on the disciplinary committee were biased against him because of professional and social contacts with the victim and her brother. However, the student failed to offer any credible evidence. The faculty committee was entitled to a presumption of impartiality. Also, the student had failed to establish that the school had breached its contractual obligations in conducting its disciplinary proceedings. The court entered judgment on behalf of the university. *Holert v. Univ. of Chicago*, 751 F.Supp. 1294 (N.D.Ill.1990).

◆   *A Pennsylvania court found that courts should not interfere with internal disciplinary matters unless the process has been found to be biased, prejudicial or lacking in due process.*

A student attending a private school operated by a Pennsylvania charitable foundation was suspended for one year after he repeatedly photographed and accosted visitors and scholars of the foundation. He was suspended for an additional two-year period after impersonating a foundation employee on three occasions in order to gain access to an area containing unique and priceless art. The student filed a lawsuit in a Pennsylvania trial court seeking a decree rescinding his suspension from the school. The trial court dismissed the lawsuit for lack of jurisdiction, and the student appealed to the Superior Court of Pennsylvania. The superior court held that because the student's lawsuit sounded in equity, the trial court had improperly declined to assert jurisdiction. However, pursuant to *Schulman v. Franklin & Marshall College*, 371 Pa.Super. 345, 538 A.2d 49 (1988), **courts should not interfere with internal disciplinary matters unless the process has been found to be biased, prejudicial or lacking in due process**. Here, the court held that the school reasonably suspended the student for his harassing behavior and unauthorized entries into areas containing priceless art. *In re Barnes Foundation*, 661 A.2d 889 (Pa.Super.1995).

III. STUDENT PRIVACY RIGHTS

Federal laws as well as the common law of most states provide for the protection of students' privacy interests, particularly in students' academic records. The laws provide guidelines as to the maintenance and disclosure of records as well as procedures for challenging the contents of the records.

A. The Family Educational Rights and Privacy Act

The Family Educational Rights and Privacy Act (FERPA) of 1974 [20 U.S.C. § 1232(g)], also called the Buckley Amendment (see Chapter 9, § VII), applies to any educational institution receiving federal funds. The act, along with U.S. Department of Education regulations (found at 34 C.F.R. Part 99), contains extremely detailed requirements regarding the maintaining and disclosing of student records. These requirements become applicable only upon a student's attendance at the school.

FERPA requires schools to allow parents the right of inspection and review with respect to their children's education records. When parents request access to their children's education records, schools must grant that access within a reasonable time, not to exceed 45 days. Parents must also be given the opportunity for a hearing to challenge the content of their children's education records, to insure that the records are not inaccurate, misleading, or otherwise in violation of the privacy or other rights of the students.

Education records include those records, files, documents and other materials that contain information directly related to a student and that are maintained by the school or by an agent of the school. Records maintained by a law enforcement agency of a school (for the purpose of law enforcement) do not constitute education records for purposes of FERPA. Schools cannot release, or provide access to, any personally identifiable information in education other than directory information without the parents' written consent. Violating FERPA results in a loss of federal funds.

At times, FERPA seems to come into conflict with other laws, like the 1990 Student Right-to-Know and Campus Security Act, 20 U.S.C. § 1092(f), which requires all institutions of higher education that participate in federal funding programs to prepare, publish and distribute to all current students and employees an annual campus security report. Because colleges and universities sometimes deal with student crime through disciplinary boards, rather than through campus police, there can be pressure to seal student disciplinary records (under FERPA) that would otherwise be public under the Campus Security Act.

Further, FERPA provides that a college or university can include in the education record of any student "appropriate information ... concerning disciplinary action taken against such student for conduct that posed a significant risk to the safety or well-being of that student, other students, or other members of the school community." [20 U.S.C. § 1232g(h).] Since schools often benefit more from designating a particular act a violation of the student code (and being able to keep the information private) rather than designating it a crime (and having to release the information to the public), reports on campus security are not always accurate.

♦   *Two universities violated the Family Educational Rights and Privacy Act (FERPA) by releasing disciplinary records containing personally identifiable information without the prior consent of the named students or their parents.*

In 1996, Miami University, Ohio, released copies of various disciplinary records to the school newspaper with the accused students' names, ages and sex excluded, as well as the date, time and location of the incidents. Dissatisfied with the amount of information provided in the redacted records, the newspaper requested full copies of the records with only the students' names and social security numbers deleted. The paper claimed it was entitled to full copies of the disciplinary records under the Ohio Public Records Act. The university maintained that the records it provided were in compliance with FERPA, which protects students' privacy interest in their educational records and generally prohibits the nonconsensual disclosure of personally identifiable information.

In 1997, the Ohio Supreme Court held that student disciplinary records were not "educational records" subject to FERPA because they "do not contain educationally related information, such as grades or other academic data, and are unrelated to academic performance, financial aid, or scholastic performance." Shortly thereafter, *The Chronicle of Higher Education*, a national weekly newspaper, requested disciplinary records from the university. The school notified the federal Department of Education that, due to the Ohio Public Records Act, it might be unable to comply with FERPA. The department responded that FERPA is applicable to disciplinary records. After the U.S. Supreme Court refused to review the state supreme court's decision, Miami University provided *The Chronicle* with full copies of its disciplinary records, less the students' names and social security numbers. The newspaper also obtained disciplinary records from Ohio State University.

The Department of Education sued to prevent the universities from providing *The Chronicle* with disciplinary records without the prior consent of the students or their parents. *The Chronicle* moved to dismiss the suit because the department lacked standing to bring the action. The court disagreed, finding that Congress had in fact given the department the authority to bring an action to enforce FERPA. It then held that university disciplinary records fell within the definition of "education records" under FERPA. **The court differentiated between disciplinary records and law enforcement records, which were not covered by FERPA. It granted the department's motion for summary judgment and permanently enjoined the universities from releasing student disciplinary records with personally identifiable information.** *United States v. Miami Univ.*, 2000 U.S. Dist. LEXIS 3345 (S.D.Ohio, 2000).

♦   *Parts of a statewide test that were owned by the state were public records and had to be disclosed to a student.*

The Ohio Department of Education (ODE) administers the Ohio Proficiency Test to high school seniors to ensure that they have requisite knowledge in selected academic areas. Ohio State University also administered a statewide test to high school students that was developed to accelerate the modernization of vocational education in the state. Part of that test was developed and owned by a private entity. Both tests used a new format each time a test was administered and the tests were owned in part by the state agencies which administered them. An

Ohio student who had taken both examinations requested access to the tests after they had been administered. The ODE refused to release test information for review unless the student signed a nondisclosure agreement. **The family refused to sign the agreement and instead commenced a state court action to compel state education officials to release relevant portions of both tests pursuant to the state Public Records Act.**

The Supreme Court of Ohio accepted jurisdiction over the case and found that **the state-owned parts of both tests were considered public records within the meaning of state law. Further, none of the exceptions to the state law presumption in favor of public disclosure applied.** The student sought release of the information for educational purposes and did not seek to use it for a commercial purpose. A state law that prohibits assisting a student in cheating on proficiency tests was not applicable to this case. The student was entitled to an order for disclosure of the requested information. However, the portion of the test devised by the private entity was not a public record and was not subject to release. *State ex rel. Rea v. Ohio Dept. of Educ.*, 81 Ohio St.3d 527, 692 N.E.2d 596 (1998).

♦   *Some student disciplinary records had to be disclosed to a university student newspaper because the records were not education records as defined by FERPA.*

An Ohio university student newspaper editor asked the university's student disciplinary board for certain student disciplinary records to develop a database and monitor crime on campus. The university denied the request, citing the state public records act. The editor made a written request for the records, requesting release of the data without identification such as names, social security numbers and student numbers. **The university released copies of disciplinary board records and deleted not only personal information such as identity, sex and age, but other data sought by the editors including the times and locations of the incidents leading to discipline.** The editors petitioned the Supreme Court of Ohio for an order requiring the release of the information.

The university argued that it had deleted the information in compliance with the confidentiality provisions of the Family Educational Rights and Privacy Act (FERPA), which provides for sanctions against education institutions that do not comply with its confidentiality requirements for education records. The court found that university disciplinary board records involved violations of student rules and regulations and some criminal matters. **Because the board's proceedings were not academic in nature, they contained no education-related information and were not education records as defined in FERPA.** The deletion of the general location of the violation, type of punishment and other relevant data deprived the public of important information that might compromise public safety. The court granted the order requested by the editors. *State ex rel. The Miami Student v. Miami Univ.*, 79 Ohio St.3d 168, 680 N.E.2d 956 (1997).

♦   *Although FERPA provides an opportunity for a hearing to challenge the content of a student's education record to ensure that it is accurate, a federal district court found that it does not permit challenges to the merit of testing procedures and substantive test answers.*

A Virginia medical student requested a one-year leave of absence and postponement of a pharmacology course. The school granted the request with the requirement that the student enroll in a similar course at another medical school and then pass a competency exam on the subject at his home school. The student agreed, took the required course but failed to pass the competency exam. He eventually enrolled in the course at his school and passed, but first, he protested his failing score on the competency exam. He argued that two of his answers that were found to be incorrect were actually correct. He also claimed that the school denied him the right to a formal hearing and the assistance of counsel to challenge the inaccurate grade, thereby violating his rights under the Family Educational Rights and Privacy Act (FERPA). He filed suit against the school in the U.S. District Court for the Eastern District of Virginia and the school filed a motion to dismiss.

The school argued that the student could not use FERPA to substantively challenge the correctness of answers on an exam. The court noted that the statute requires institutions receiving federal funds to provide an opportunity for a hearing to challenge the content of a student's education record to ensure that it is accurate. However, **the statute does not permit challenges to the merit of testing procedures and substantive test answers**. The student argued that the incorrectly graded answers resulted in a wrong test score which caused his education record to be inaccurate. The court found this argument unpersuasive. The student then argued that because the disputed answers were given for multiple choice questions, he could objectively verify that his answers were correct. The court, however, found that this would result in an **impermissible intervention in education since the student did not allege any technical or mathematical errors in the grading of the exam but rather attacked the substantive accuracy of the answers**. The motion to dismiss was granted. *Lewin v. Medical College of Hampton Roads*, 931 F.Supp. 443 (E.D.Va.1996).

♦ *Neither FERPA nor school policy provide a means by which a student may obtain information on how a particular grade was assigned.*

A Texas university student received a grade of C in a physics class. He was disappointed with the grade and sought to challenge the assignment of the grade in a federal district court, or in the alternative to strike it from the record. The university and the teacher moved to dismiss the case. The Family Educational Rights and Privacy Act of 1974 (FERPA) provides that no federal funds shall be made available to any educational agency or institution unless the parents of a student who has been in attendance at such institution are provided an opportunity for a hearing for the purpose of ensuring that the content of the student's education records are not inaccurate, misleading, or otherwise in violation of the privacy rights of the student. Neither FERPA nor school policy provide a means by which a student may obtain information on how a particular grade was assigned. The court ruled that **at most, the student was only entitled to know whether the assigned grade was recorded accurately** in the records. Therefore, the court granted the defendants' motion to dismiss the case. *Tarka v. Cunningham*, 741 F.Supp. 1281 (W.D.Tex.1990).

◆   *A New York federal court held that FERPA does not give rise to a private cause of action.*

A private New York university canceled an African-American student's registration, presumably because she had failed to make tuition payments. The student filed a variety of complaints against school officials including allegations that they refused to allow her access to records of actions taken against her. She also alleged that the officials had deprived her of an opportunity to file a formal sexual harassment complaint and had denied her a disciplinary hearing for an alleged infraction. Finally, the student alleged that the university illegally attempted to collect her debt after she had filed for bankruptcy under Chapter 7. One of the university's deans wrote a letter to the student which allegedly contained several false, malicious and libelous statements. The student filed a lawsuit against the university in a U.S. district court, alleging race discrimination under 42 U.S.C. § 1981, deprivation of her rights under the Family Educational Rights and Privacy Act (FERPA), a violation of the automatic bankruptcy stay, and defamation. The district court noted that § 1981 prohibits certain racially motivated and purposely discriminatory acts by state and private employers, including independent academic institutions. However, because the student was not treated differently than any similarly situated white student, the court dismissed her § 1981 claim. The student's FERPA claim was also dismissed because the statute did not give rise to a private cause of action. Moreover, **even if a FERPA claim could be enforced through 42 U.S.C § 1983, the university was a private institution and did not act under color of state law**. Finally, the court dismissed the alleged automatic stay violations and the defamation claims for lack of jurisdiction. *Odom v. Columbia Univ.*, 906 F.Supp. 188 (S.D.N.Y.1995).

◆   *A student newspaper had to be allowed to attend student Organization Court meetings and had to be granted access to the court's records.*

After the student newspaper at the University of Georgia was denied access to Organization Court records and proceedings involving hazing at fraternities, the newspaper sued, seeking access to records and disciplinary proceedings of the student Organization Court. The university claimed that the Buckley Amendment required it to keep confidential those records and proceedings. However, the Supreme Court of Georgia disagreed. It noted that even if the Buckley Amendment (which withdraws federal funding to institutions that have a policy or practice of permitting the release of education records) could be construed as prohibiting the release of education records, **the access being sought here was not access to "education records." What the newspaper was seeking was documentation of hazing charges against fraternities.** The court determined that the newspaper was entitled to the records of proceedings as well as to Organization Court proceedings under the state's Open Meetings Act. *Red & Black Publishing Co. v. Bd. of Regents*, 427 S.E.2d 257 (Ga.1993).

B. Implied Contractual Privacy Rights

Many states also recognize state or common law privacy claims based on contractual rights established through the student's enrollment contract with the private institution.

♦ *A student could sue a college for ordering an HIV test without his permission.*

A student in a Colorado college's medical assistant training program told his instructor that he had tested positive for HIV in an anonymous blood test. He asked the instructor to keep that information confidential. Shortly thereafter, the instructor informed the class that all students were required to be tested for rubella. **The student consented to the test with the understanding that his sample would be tested for rubella only. However, the instructor contacted the lab doing the testing and asked that the student's sample be tested for HIV.** She did not request such testing for any other student. After the sample tested positive, the lab reported the student's name, address and HIV status to the state department of health (as required by law) and informed the college of the results. The student sued the college for invasion of privacy, asserting two different causes of action— first, that the college had unreasonably disclosed private facts and, second, that the college had intruded upon his seclusion by having the test performed.

A court dismissed his second claim, but a jury found that he was entitled to damages for the college's unreasonable disclosure of private facts. When the student appealed the court's dismissal of his second claim, the Colorado Court of Appeals held in his favor. First, it stated that the two claims were not the same. **The claim for intrusion upon seclusion involved the college's authorization of a test that the student himself had not authorized, which was the improper appropriation of confidential information, whereas the claim for unreasonable disclosure of private facts involved the dissemination of that information.** That the student suffered harm because of the disclosure of information did not mean that he could not have suffered harm because of the improper appropriation of the information. The court reversed and remanded the case. *Doe v. High-Tech Institute, Inc.*, 972 P.2d 1060 (Colo.App.1998).

♦ *An Ohio appellate court found that the university's maintenance of a student's summer law program grades with his undergraduate grades was reasonable.*

A student enrolled in Ohio Northern University's summer law school qualification program. The program was designed for students who were not qualified for admission under regular criteria. Those who achieved a B- average would be admitted to the law school. The student failed to maintain the required grade point average and thus was not enrolled in the law school. Prior to enrollment in the summer program, the student had received an undergraduate engineering degree from the university. He sued the university in state court claiming that on at least two occasions it released his undergraduate transcript containing a record of his performance in the law school summer program. He sought a court order prohibiting the university from maintaining a record of his performance in the summer program and asking for money damages. An Ohio common pleas court ruled against him and he appealed. The appeals court held that **the student had failed to show that the maintaining of his summer law program grades together with his undergraduate record was unreasonable, arbitrary or in violation of any federal or state law.** Further, the court held that whether the student had been "admitted" to the law school or had merely been "participating" in the summer program was irrelevant. The important fact was that the student had attended courses at the law school. Accordingly, the university was entitled to maintain records of his law school attendance. The student's lawsuit against the university was dismissed. *Smith v. Ohio Northern Univ.*, 514 N.E.2d 142 (Ohio App.1986).

♦   *Alleging that a professor retaliated against him for giving the professor a poor student evaluation, an Illinois student failed to demonstrate sufficient evidence that his rights had been violated.*

An Illinois law school professor allegedly intercepted confidential teacher evaluations written by his students. One student made detailed critical comments about the professor. The student alleged that the professor identified his anonymous evaluation through handwriting comparison and retaliated against him by giving him a D for the course. The student also alleged that the professor accessed the student's file under false pretenses and violated his privacy. Following his graduation, the student sued the school and the professor in an Illinois trial court for breach of contract, breach of confidence, invasion of privacy, intentional infliction of emotional distress and other misconduct. The court ruled in favor of the school. Following the trial, the court requested the school to present a motion for sanctions against the student. The school did so and the court awarded over $12,000 to the school in fees and costs. The student appealed the trial court's decision to the Illinois Appellate Court, First District. The appellate court refused to award the student any damages for the D grade. The student failed to show any breach of contract, or that he had any privacy right in his school file. The conduct of the school and professor was not the extreme conduct required for tort claims. There was **no clear showing that the student's rights had been violated** and the court was unwilling to grant any injunctive relief or to award an damages. However, the trial court had erroneously ruled that the student must pay sanctions to the school for suing it. The appellate court affirmed the trial court's decision for the school, but reversed the order for sanctions. *Mucklow v. John Marshall Law School*, 531 N.E.2d 941 (Ill.App.1st Dist.1988).

♦   *An implied contract between the student and school exists which prevents a school from maliciously or in bad faith refusing to award a degree to a student who has fulfilled its requirements.*

A student attended an Illinois Christian College from September 1976 to March 1981. During his last semester the dean of students was told by another student that he might be gay. In reliance upon the college's assurances that he would graduate if he sought counseling, the student repeatedly traveled out of town to obtain counseling, and revealed many personal facts about his homosexuality. When the counselor reported the student's tendencies to the dean of students, the dean informed the student that the college would hold a hearing where he would be required to defend himself against the rumor that he was a homosexual. Afraid that the accusation of homosexuality on his transcript would destroy his career prospects, the student withdrew from the college. The hearing was held anyway and subsequently the dean informed the student's mother that her son was being dismissed because he was a homosexual. In November 1984, the student sued the college and the counselor in an Illinois circuit court. When the circuit court granted motions to dismiss the student's complaint, he appealed to the Appellate Court of Illinois.

The appellate court observed that the implied contract between a college and a student is legally enforceable. Because **a college cannot act maliciously or refuse in bad faith to award a degree to a student who fulfills its degree requirements**, the court concluded that the student's complaint stated a valid legal basis for breach of an implied contract. The court also ruled that if the student was later able to prove his factual allegations, the college would be judged to have violated **the Illinois Confidentiality Act**. It then concluded that the lower court was wrong in dismissing the student's claim that the college tortiously interfered with his contract with the counselor and that the counselor's disclosure of confidential information tortiously interfered with his contract with the college. These matters were remanded to the circuit court for further proceedings. *Johnson v. Lincoln Christian College*, 501 N.E.2d 1380 (Ill.App.4th Dist.1986).

IV. GRADING AND CURRICULUM

◆   *A student who waited more than two years to challenge an "incomplete" grade had her lawsuit dismissed.*

A disabled Georgia college student began a student teaching assignment during the spring quarter of 1994. She alleged that the classroom teacher discriminated against her because of her disability. In May 1994, the teacher issued the student a grade of "Unsatisfactory." On May 31 **college faculty changed her grade to an "Incomplete," which allowed her to repeat the student-teaching program the next year.** On June 6, the student received a letter from the same faculty members informing her that the May 31 decision would stand. On June 6, 1996, the student sued the college in the U.S. District Court for the Northern District of Georgia alleging violations of Title II of the Americans with Disabilities Act and the Rehabilitation Act. The college moved to dismiss her claims as time barred by a two-year state statute of limitations. The district court granted the motion for dismissal, and the student appealed to the U.S. Court of Appeals, Eleventh Circuit.

When a federal statute does not contain a limitations period, the courts should look to the most analogous state statute of limitations. Here, because Georgia had not passed a state law identical to the Rehabilitation Act, the trial court properly applied the state's two-year personal injury statute of limitations; civil rights actions are essentially personal injury claims. Because discrimination claims accrue when the plaintiff is informed of the discriminatory act, the court held that **the date the student first learned she would receive an "Incomplete," was when her claim began to accrue.** The letter of June 6, 1994, merely confirmed the faculty's May 31 decision, and at most only failed to undo prior discriminatory acts. Failure to remedy a prior discriminatory act does not constitute a new discriminatory act for the purpose of determining whether a claim is time barred. The lower court's judgment was affirmed. *Everett v. Cobb County School Dist.,* 138 F.3d 1407 (11th Cir.1998).

For additional cases involving disability discrimination against students, see Chapter Two, Section I.

◆   *A temporary grade reduction did not sufficiently injure a student such that he was entitled to damages.*

A Texas community college teacher responded to a tardiness problem in an 8:00 a.m. English class by stating that attendance would be taken and that those not present at the beginning of class would be counted absent. The department's attendance policy stated that students who were absent six days from a class were subject to a failing grade. However, when a student reached his sixth absence for the class, the teacher lowered his grade from an A to a B rather than issuing a failing grade. The student waited for one year to challenge the grade, and filed a complaint with the dean of the department. The teacher agreed to change the grade to an A but the student filed a lawsuit against the college and some of its employees in the U.S. District Court for the Northern District of Texas. The court dismissed the complaint and the student appealed to the U.S. Court of Appeals, Fifth Circuit.

The court found that the only injury claimed by the student was the reduction of the grade for approximately 12 months, which allegedly denied him an opportunity to compete for academic scholarships. **The student had failed to state that he actually applied for scholarships and thus failed to show that he was injured because of the grade reduction.** Any injury he suffered was purely speculative. Accordingly, the claim was frivolous and insufficient to invoke the jurisdiction of a federal court. The court affirmed the order to dismiss the lawsuit. *Dilworth v. Dallas County Comm. College Dist.*, 81 F.3d 616 (5th Cir.1996).

◆   *A grading complaint at a community college was deemed to be of an academic nature. Thus, the dean had final decisionmaking power in the area.*

Nursing students attending a Missouri community college complained that testing procedures in a required course caused them to fail the class. The claims included typographical errors, testing on materials not covered in classes and inability to review quizzes after grading. One of the students who failed the class met with the college dean to discuss retaking the final test, but her request was denied. The students complained to the state board of nursing, which conducted an investigation. The college responded by submitting a compliance proposal and offered the course again to the students. One of the failing students who subsequently retook and passed the class filed a lawsuit against the college and some of its officials in the U.S. District Court for the Eastern District of Missouri under 42 U.S.C. § 1983, alleging civil rights violations. The court granted summary judgment to the college and administrators and the student appealed to the U.S. Court of Appeals, Eighth Circuit.

The student claimed that she had suffered procedural due process violations when the college failed to follow its handbook grievance procedure for resolving grading disputes and that administrators used arbitrary and capricious administrative methods. She also complained of substantive due process violations in the college curriculum requirements and claimed that college administrators were motivated by bad faith. The court stated that the student's complaint was related to an academic matter for which the dean held final decisionmaking power. The court rejected the student's assertion that her complaint was a procedural and not an academic matter. **The alleged procedural irregularities did not rise to the level of a constitutional violation or bring the question of grading outside the realm of academics.** The administrators had appropriately responded to complaints and rescheduled the next course offering to an earlier semester. The court affirmed the district court decision. *Disesa v. St. Louis Community College*, 79 F.3d 92 (8th Cir.1996).

♦   *Academic freedom could be used as a defense to a claim brought under the Establishment Clause.*

A New York resident audited a community college course titled "Family Life and Human Sexuality" and claimed that it promoted Eastern religions and disparaged traditional Jewish and Christian teachings on marriage, procreation and adultery. He re-enrolled in the course the following semester and joined a number of New York taxpayers in filing a lawsuit against the community college, its administrators and board in the U.S. District Court for the Eastern District of New York, seeking declaratory and injunctive relief that the course offering violated the state and federal constitutions and New York law. The court considered several preliminary motions by the parties.

The court rejected the college and officials' dismissal motion based upon their claim that their right to academic freedom barred the plaintiffs from challenging college policies, activities and course materials. **Although the principles of academic freedom could provide a defense to the claims, they did not bar the claims altogether.** The court observed that the individual taking the course did not have a viable claim because the class would have ended before the litigation did. Taxpayer status alone was insufficient to confer standing to allow a free exercise claim, and these claims were dismissed. The court was unable to construe a New York law requiring course offerings in college catalogues to be plainly disclosed, and this claim was dismissed. It was also unwilling to grant the requested order prohibiting the college from offering the course the following semester. However, **the court denied pretrial dismissal of the remaining taxpayers' claim that the course offering violated the Establishment Clause of the Constitution or the New York Constitution.** It dismissed the other claims, allowing only the Establishment Clause claim to survive. *Mincone v. Nassau County Community College*, 923 F.Supp. 398 (E.D.N.Y.1996).

For additional cases involving academic freedom, please see Chapter Four, Section I.D.

♦   *A grade of F was properly assigned where a student turned in his assignments late.*

After being dismissed for academic reasons, a student was readmitted to a medical school in South Dakota. He then received a grade of F in internal medicine and was again dismissed from the school. He sued in federal court, asserting that the grade he received should have been I (incomplete), because although he failed to do all the requisite work before the end of the semester, he did complete the work shortly after the next semester began. He maintained that the professor had stated that incompletes would be given where a student failed to get all the work done on time, and he allegedly relied on that statement. He asserted that the grade of F in place of I was arbitrary and capricious conduct in violation of his substantive due process rights. A federal court granted pretrial judgment to the school, and the student appealed. The Eighth Circuit Court of Appeals held that there was no genuine issue of material fact as to whether the grade of F was arbitrary. **The student had failed the final written examination, failed to properly present patients during rounds, and failed to turn in required work on time. Thus, the grade was justified.** There had been no substantive due process violation, and the student had been properly dismissed from the school. The lower court's decision was affirmed. *Hines v. Rinker*, 667 F.2d 699 (8th Cir.1981).

CHAPTER TWO

Discrimination Against Students

I. DISABILITY DISCRIMINATION

Colleges and universities are subject to two important federal statutes that prohibit discrimination against individuals on the basis of disability. The Americans with Disabilities Act of 1990 (ADA), 42 U.S.C. § 12101 et seq., states that no qualified individual with a disability shall, by reason of such disability, be excluded from participation in or be denied the benefit of services, programs, or activities of a public entity, place of public accommodation or other covered entity. The ADA is based on the anti-discrimination principles of § 504 of the Rehabilitation Act of 1973, 29 U.S.C. § 794, but expands the coverage of § 504, which applies only to recipients of federal funding. Colleges and universities are also subject to the coverage of state anti-discrimination statutes, many of which use the same or similar language as the ADA and § 504.

A. Colleges and Universities

◆ *The U.S. Supreme Court held that a school can only be required to make minor curricular modifications to accommodate a disability. This means that schools do not have to make accommodations that fundamentally alter the nature of the programs offered.*

The U.S. Supreme Court's ruling in *Southeastern Community College v. Davis* set the standard for evaluating § 504 claims. In that case, a nursing school applicant, who was severely hearing impaired, claimed that the school's denial of her admission violated § 504 of the Rehabilitation Act. Section 504 states that an "otherwise qualified individual with a disability" may not be excluded from a federally funded program "solely by reason of her or his disability." In refusing to admit the applicant, the nursing school explained that the hearing disability made it unsafe for her to practice as a registered nurse. The school pointed out that even with a hearing aid the applicant had to rely on her lip-reading skills. It argued that patient safety demanded that she be able to understand speech without reliance on lip-reading. Agreeing with the school, the Supreme Court held that the term "otherwise qualified individual with a disability" meant an individual who is qualified in spite of his or her disability. The applicant's contention that her disability should be disregarded for purposes of determining whether she was otherwise qualified was rejected, as was her contention that § 504 imposed an obligation on the school to undertake affirmative action to modify its curriculum to accommodate her disability. **While a school may be required in certain cases to make minor curricular modifications to accommodate a disability, the applicant here was physically able to take only academic courses and no accommodations were required since clinical study would be foreclosed due to patient safety concerns.** The Court held that § 504 did not require a major curricular modification such as allowing the applicant to bypass clinical study. The school's denial of admission was upheld. *Southeastern Comm. College v. Davis*, 442 U.S. 397, 99 S.Ct. 2361, 60 L.Ed.2d 980 (1979).

♦   *The Supreme Court determined that a lower court had failed to consider a public university's argument that it should not have to pay for a handicapped student's special educational requirements in a case filed under § 504.*

   A deaf graduate student at a Texas university requested a sign language interpreter. The university refused to pay for an interpreter because the student did not meet university financial assistance guidelines. The student then sued the university in a federal district court under § 504 of the Rehabilitation Act, which forbids federal funding recipients from discriminating against otherwise qualified individuals with disabilities. He sought an order requiring the appointment of an interpreter at the university's expense for as long as he remained there. The court granted his request for a preliminary order requiring the university to pay for the interpreter. However, the court stayed further consideration of the case pending a final administrative ruling by a federal education agency.

   The university appealed to the U.S. Court of Appeals, Fifth Circuit, which affirmed the preliminary order, but vacated the stay pending administrative action. The university complied with the order by paying for the interpreter. The student completed his graduate program. The U.S. Supreme Court granted review to address the university's argument that the lower courts should make a final ruling on who was to pay for the interpreter. The student argued that the case was now moot in view of his graduation. The Supreme Court vacated the appeals court's decision and remanded the case for a trial on the merits to allow the university a full opportunity to argue for recoupment of its payments for the interpreter. *University of Texas v. Camenisch*, 451 U.S. 390, 101 S.Ct. 1830, 68 L.Ed.2d 175 (1981).

♦   *A private university's refusal to allow course substitutions for its foreign language requirement as an accommodation for learning-disabled students did not violate the ADA or the Rehabilitation Act.*

   Several learning-disabled students at a private Massachusetts university initiated a class action suit against the university in a federal district court, alleging that its policies violated the Americans with Disabilities Act (ADA), the Rehabilitation Act and state law. The university had established a policy under which learning-disabled students were not allowed to make course substitutions for the foreign language requirement.

The court found that **the university did not violate the ADA or the Rehabilitation Act.** The university committee that decided whether course substitutions would be acceptable was comprised of eminent members of the college faculty who deliberated the issue over a two-month period. The committee had vigorous discussions of the "unique qualities" of the foreign language requirement and its importance to the liberal arts curriculum. Finally, the committee's meeting minutes indicated that alternatives were discussed and the conclusion reached that **no content course taught in English could serve as a substitution.** The college had existing accommodations for learning disabled students and offered all students a variety of programs to assist in fulfilling the language requirement. *Guckenberger v. Boston Univ.,* 8 F.Supp.2d 82 (D.Mass.1998).

♦ *Where a student refused to be tested for a learning disability, a school could not be held liable for failing to reasonably accommodate him. Students cannot require schools to provide accommodations unless they can show that they have a disability that is covered by statute.*

A student was enrolled in a physician assistant program at a private West Virginia college that maintained a written policy outlining the process by which a learning disabled student could obtain academic accommodations. The policy required a student to take a specific intelligence test and to be evaluated by a professional. The student alleged that he suffered from a learning disability and the college referred him to a specialist. Because the student refused to take the required test, the evaluators were not able to diagnose a specific learning disability. The college allowed the student to continue his studies with certain accommodations on the condition that he take the required test by the next semester. It was also agreed that it was the student's responsibility to discuss accommodation options with his instructors. However, he did not discuss these options with his instructors, did not take the required test and was never formally diagnosed with a specific learning disability. He was later suspended from the program. He sued the college in a West Virginia federal court, asserting that it failed to reasonably accommodate him in violation of the ADA, § 504 of the Rehabilitation Act and a state statute and that it breached its agreement to provide certain accommodations. The college filed a motion to dismiss.

The court noted that under the ADA and § 504, a disability is defined as a physical or mental impairment which includes any mental or psychological disorder such as "specific learning disabilities." It noted that **at no time was the student diagnosed with a specific learning disability and furthermore, he failed to take the required test to determine if he had such a disability.** The court also found that the accommodations granted to him were not rescinded; rather, the student failed to take full advantage of them. He did not speak to his instructors at the beginning of the semester to arrange accommodations but waited until he had already missed assignments or had failed a test. The college argued that **to provide further accommodations in these situations would result in**

the lowering of the standards of the program, and the court agreed. Finding that the student failed to show that he suffered from a specific learning disability, that the college failed to reasonably accommodate him or that it breached its agreement to provide certain accommodations, the court granted the motion to dismiss. *Dubois v. Alderson-Broaddus College, Inc.*, 950 F.Supp. 754 (N.D.W.Va.1997).

◆ *A student who was disabled was nonetheless not entitled to the protections of the ADA and the Rehabilitation Act because he was not qualified to meet the school's requirements.*

A man was accepted into a University of Virginia Medical School program designed for economically disadvantaged and minority students. The students were guaranteed admission to the medical school if they completed the program with a minimum GPA of 2.75, received no grade below a C and met performance standards as determined by a faculty committee. The student failed to meet the grading requirements and was tested for a learning disability. He was not diagnosed with a specific impairment, but the evaluation center recommended that he be given double the usual time to take his exams. Although his grades improved with this accommodation, he nonetheless failed to achieve the required GPA and the faculty committee rescinded its offer of admission for the current year. He was offered admission for the following year on different terms but he refused and sued the university in a Virginia federal court, alleging violations of the ADA and § 504 of the Rehabilitation Act, among other claims. He requested preliminary and permanent injunctive relief, requiring the university to reinstate him for the current school year.

The court noted that a one-year delay in obtaining admission to medical school does not usually warrant injunctive relief in the absence of extraordinary circumstances. The student argued that he would be irreparably harmed because the program was being discontinued the following year, but the court noted that he had already been offered admission for that year with considerably relaxed requirements. Analyzing the disability discrimination claims, the court noted that the student most likely had a disability based on the evaluation center's findings and the accommodations granted by the university. It also noted that he was **denied admission to the university because of his poor performance** which resulted from his learning problems. However, the court found that the student was not qualified to meet the subjective requirements and the court stated that it was not qualified to evaluate his performance. Finding that **the university did not act with the purpose of denying education to disabled individuals,** the court denied the student's motion for preliminary injunctive relief. *Betts v. Rector & Visitors of Univ. of Virginia*, 939 F.Supp. 461 (W.D.Va.1996).

◆ *A medical school could deny admission to a blind applicant. Allowing her to enroll would require the school to waive its requirements and fundamentally alter the program.*

An Ohio woman became completely blind during her third year at a university. With accommodation, she was able to complete her academic program and graduate, cum laude, with a degree in chemistry. She then applied to the university's medical school. Although she was academically qualified, the university denied her application. This decision was in part based on standards issued by a medical association stating that candidates must be able to accurately observe patients. Faculty members also stated that she would not be able to look through a microscope, perform a visual diagnosis or insert an IV, all requirements for graduation. The university believed that no reasonable accommodations could enable the student to complete these requirements. The university considered the experience of another blind student who received his medical degree at a different school a number of years earlier. His success, however, depended on the efforts of the faculty and other students to spend extra time with him. The student here filed a complaint with the Ohio Civil Rights Commission (OCRC) which conducted a hearing. The examiner found that the university did not discriminate against her, but the OCRC disagreed and ordered the university to admit the student. The court of appeals reversed the order and the OCRC appealed to the Supreme Court of Ohio.

The court noted that to find a case of discrimination in education under the state statute an individual must show that he or she is a handicapped person, was otherwise qualified to participate in the program and was excluded from the program on the basis of a handicap. At issue here was whether the student was otherwise qualified. The court found that the student needed to show that she could safely and substantially perform the program's essential requirements with reasonable accommodation. It also stated that **an accommodation is not reasonable if it requires fundamental alterations in the essential nature of the program or imposes an undue financial or administrative burden.** Despite the experience of the previous blind student, the court found that the evidence did not demonstrate that the student in this case would be able to perform the requirements of this program. The decision to deny the application was an academic decision which the court was ill-equipped to evaluate. The application was not denied because of an intent to deny education to the student but because acceptance would require a waiver of the university's requirements and fundamentally alter the program. The court of appeals' decision was affirmed. *Ohio Civil Rights Comm'n v. Case Western Reserve Univ.*, 666 N.E.2d 1376 (Ohio 1996).

♦   *Disability discrimination claims are becoming increasingly common, as students who are unable to perform sue to obtain accommodations that will allow them to continue in their chosen course of study.*

A medical student at a private Rhode Island university experienced psychological problems associated with chronic fatigue syndrome during her first year of medical school but failed to notify any college official that she suffered from this condition. However, she obtained special accommodations from several instructors, including extra time for exams and a separate room in which to take them. After the student refused the dean's request that she either submit to a psychiatric examination or appear before the Impaired Medical Students Committee, he placed her on a leave of absence because of her emotional instability. The student remained enrolled but encountered further difficulties as a result of the above incidents, including problems with her loan package and denials of honors. She filed a lawsuit against the university in a Rhode Island federal court, alleging violations of the ADA, the Due Process Clause, and various state laws. The court dismissed the ADA claim, noting that **the act did not apply**

retroactively to events, such as the leave of absence, preceding its passage. The student contended that the school's activity following passage of the ADA, such as the loan problems and denials of honors, evidenced a continuing violation and that such conduct was actionable under the ADA. The court disagreed, ruling that **ADA claimants cannot use the continuing violation theory to resurrect claims about discrimination concluded in the past, even though its effects continued to persist.** Moreover, the student's vague allegations could not support an ADA claim. After dismissing the due process claim for lack of government action, the court declined to assert jurisdiction over the student's pendent state law claims. *Boyle v. Brown University*, 881 F.Supp. 747 (D.R.I.1995).

♦   *Where a school went out of its way to provide a disabled student with accommodations, it did not have to lower its standards or make fundamental changes to its program.*

While working as a paramedic, an Illinois man suffered a "spinal injury" catching a patient who was falling off a gurney. The paramedic later applied to a medical school, which accepted him. He then had difficulty passing his classes and sought a number of accommodations (like a reclining chair in the lecture hall and the library, and elevated placement of his microscope in the lab). The school granted his requests, but he continued to struggle academically. Eventually, he passed all his first and second-year classes. When he took the Step 1 United States Medical Licensing Exam, he asked for and received more accommodations. Nevertheless, he failed the exam twice. The school then allowed him to take the exam a third time, and he finally passed. Subsequently, he began his clerkships and requested more accommodations, which the school granted him. Finally, however, his lack of progress caused the school to dismiss him from the program. He sued under the ADA. **A federal court held that the school had gone out of its way to provide the student with every opportunity to meet its academic requirements. It was not required to lower its standards or make fundamental changes to its program.** Because it had made reasonable accommodations for the student, the school was entitled to pretrial judgment in its favor. *Herdman v. Univ. of Illinois*, 1998 U.S. Dist. LEXIS 17447 (N.D.Ill.1998).

♦   *Sometimes, even the provision of reasonable accommodations will be insufficient to allow a student to succeed. However, there is a limit on how far schools must go to accommodate under the ADA and the Rehabilitation Act.*

A student at a California medical school experienced difficulty in her classes and was referred for testing for a learning disability. When the test came back positive, the student was offered a number of accommodations: double time on exams, note-taking services, textbooks on audio cassettes, the option of retaking courses and the option to proceed on a decelerated schedule. However, she continued to have trouble with her classes. Eventually, she completed the pre-clinical portion of her schooling and took the USMLE, Part 1, which she failed. She then retested and passed. Again, though, she had trouble in school, this time with her clinical work. After being placed on academic probation, she was dismissed from the program. She sued the school under the ADA and the Rehabilitation Act. A California federal court ruled in the school's favor, and the student appealed. The Ninth Circuit Court of Appeals affirmed, finding that the school had offered the student reasonable accommodations. To accommodate her any further would require the school to fundamentally alter the nature of its program and lower its academic standards. Neither the ADA nor the Rehabilitation Act required this. *Zukle v. Regents of the Univ. of California*, 166 F.3d 1041 (9th Cir.1999).

◆ *A college reasonably accommodated a learning disabled student by offering her a number of specific accommodations. When she still failed a class, the college had the right to dismiss her from school.*

The student enrolled in a college of podiatric medicine through a standard four-year curriculum. Shortly thereafter, she suspected that she had a learning disability and notified an academic counselor of her belief. The counselor referred her for testing and evaluation where it was determined that the student did not have a learning disability but that she should be given some assistance with study skills. However, **the student did not seek any accommodations from the college until after the second semester, when she had failed two courses and been dismissed from the program.** At that time, she obtained reports from two psychologists who concluded that she had a learning disorder and listed eleven recommended accommodations for her. The college reinstated the student to its five-year program for students with special needs and offered her nine of the 11 recommended accommodations.

The student again failed biochemistry and was dismissed from the program a second time. She sued the college under the Rehabilitation Act, the Americans with Disabilities Act and the Ohio Civil Rights Act, alleging disability discrimination. The Ohio federal court granted pretrial judgment to the college, and the student appealed to the U.S. Court of Appeals, Sixth Circuit. The court of appeals affirmed, finding that the college had not discriminated against the student. **Educational institutions are not required to lower or effect substantial modifications of standards to accommodate persons with disabilities.** Here, the college had provided almost all the recommended accommodations. Further, its decision not to lower its standards was entitled to deference. *Kaltenberger v. Ohio College of Podiatric Medicine*, 162 F.3d 432 (6th Cir.1998).

◆ *A student with test anxieties in two subjects was not disabled under the ADA.*

A student at a New Mexico medical school suffered from "chemistry and mathematics anxiety." However, he had managed to overcome his anxiety while an undergraduate and while a graduate student. He informed his basic biochemistry professor of his anxiety, but stated that he needed no test-taking accommodations. After receiving marginal grades in two first-year courses, he was notified that he would have to repeat the first year. Instead, he sued the medical school for disability discrimination under the ADA. The court granted pretrial judgment to the school, and the student appealed. The U.S. Court of Appeals, Tenth Circuit, affirmed the lower court's decision. Here, **the student failed to show that his math and chemistry anxiety substantially limited him in the major life activity of learning. As a result, he was not a disabled person within the meaning of the ADA.** Further, even if was, he could not demand an unreasonable accommodation from the school. Requiring the school to advance the student to the next level would require an unreasonable accommodation. *McGuinness v. Univ. of New Mexico School of Medicine*, 170 F.3d 974 (10th Cir.1998).

◆   *The inability to turn in work that has not been plagiarized is a valid reason for expelling a student with a disability.*

A graduate student at Virginia Commonwealth University suffered from dysgraphia and/or other broad written language disabilities. He was charged with cheating and plagiarism—both violations of the student honor code—and was expelled. He sued under the ADA and the Rehabilitation Act, asserting that his disability affected and impaired his ability to reproduce or transcribe written language, and that the university failed to reasonable accommodate him. The U.S. District Court for the Eastern District of Virginia granted pretrial judgment to the university. **It found that fulfilling the terms of the university's honor code was an essential function of being a graduate student, and that the student could not meet this requirement even with a reasonable accommodation.** Accordingly, the university did not violate the ADA or the Rehabilitation Act by expelling the student. *Childress v. Clement*, 5 F.Supp.2d 384 (E.D.Va.1998).

◆   *Students with attention deficit hyperactivity disorder were not substantially limited in the major life activity of learning.*

Three students completed two years of medical school, and were required to pass Step I of the U.S. Medical Licensing Examination, administered by the National Board of Medical Examiners (Board). Each of the students was diagnosed with attention deficit hyperactivity disorder (ADHD), and two of the three students were diagnosed with specific learning disabilities. **The students sent applications to the Board requesting additional time in private rooms while taking the examination.** The Board submitted their applications to experts in the fields of ADHD and learning disabilities, but later denied the request and asserted that the students' alleged impairments did not significantly restrict one or more of their major life activities. The students brought suit against the Board in the U.S. District Court for the Southern District of West Virginia, seeking to compel the Board to grant their request.

In order to qualify as persons with a disability under the ADA, these claiming specific learning disabilities must show that they are substantially limited in one or more major life functions. The students and the Board both agreed that ADHD and specific learning disabilities were mental impairments for purposes of the ADA, and also agreed that these disorders affect the major life activity of learning. However, the parties disagreed on whether the students' alleged disorders "substantially limited" their ability to learn. The legislative history of the ADA shows that impairments must restrict an individual's major life activity as to the "conditions, manner, or duration under which the activity can be performed in comparison to most people." "Most people" can be reasonably interpreted to mean that the individual is restricted to a greater degree than a majority of people. **A learning disability does not always qualify as a disability under the ADA. The court found that none of the three students exhibited a pattern of substantial academic difficulties.** They were all able to graduate from high school and undergraduate school without any accommodations for their alleged disabilities. The court further found that each of the students had an average or greater than average ability to learn. Because the students' disabilities did not substantially limit their ability to learn in comparison with most people, the court denied their requests. *Price v. National Bd. of Medical Examiners*, 966 F.Supp. 419 (S.D.W.Va.1997).

◆ *A state violated the National Voter Registration Act when it failed to provide college campus voter registration sites at its public colleges and universities.*

An organization for students with disabilities filed an action in the U.S. District Court for the Eastern District of Virginia asserting that the state's failure to provide voting registration services at state universities and colleges violated the National Voter Registration Act (NVRA) and the Americans with Disabilities Act (ADA). The organization asserted that the state colleges and universities should have provided voter registration services on campus for students with disabilities. The state moved for summary judgment, and the court considered the NVRA and the ADA in determining whether to grant the motion. It first noted that the NVRA requires each state to designate as voter registration agencies "all offices in the State that provide State-funded programs primarily engaged in providing services to persons with disabilities."

The court then held that the state had not violated the NVRA because the primary purpose of Virginia's state colleges and universities was to provide a collegiate curriculum to confer degrees and to direct the activities of professors, teachers, staff members and agents. The institutions were not primarily engaged in serving disabled persons despite the fact that they had offices which provided support services for students with disabilities. The court then found that the state had not violated the ADA because that act does not require entities to expand the scope of their activities so as to provide services for disabled persons which are not provided to others. Here, since the colleges and universities did not provide voting registration services for any of their students, they were not required to provide such services for their disabled students under the ADA. The court granted pretrial judgment to the state.

The organization appealed the NVRA ruling to the Fourth Circuit Court of Appeals, which held that **the district court had improperly ruled that the colleges and universities did not have to provide the voter registration sites.** Of the three schools involved in the lawsuit, all had offices primarily engaged in serving persons with disabilities, and two of those offices were state funded. With respect to George Mason University, however, the office that assisted students with disabilities was funded by student activity fees. Accordingly, there was a question of fact as to whether that office was state funded and thus required to comply with the NVRA. If the university exercised control over the funds, they would be state funds (*Student Gov't Assn. v. Bd. of Trustees of the Univ. of Mass.*, 868 F.2d 473 [1st Cir.1989]). If, however, the funds were administered by students and kept separate from other university funds, they would not be state funds (*Rosenberger v. Rector and Visitors of the Univ. of Virginia*, 515 U.S. 819, 115 S.Ct. 2510, 132 L.Ed.2d 700 [1995]). This question had to be resolved on remand. The court reversed the lower court's grant of pretrial judgment to the state. *National Coalition for Students with Disabilities Educ. and Legal Defense Fund v. Allen*, 152 F.3d 283 (4th Cir.1998).

◆   *A student with a disability could sue his school for breach of the implied duty of good faith and fair dealing.*

An incomplete paraplegic attended a Wyoming technical institute, but later withdrew, alleging that his disability was not accommodated. The student asserted that the institute did not provide him with sufficient handicapped parking, accessible restrooms, or the equipment necessary to safely perform his assigned tasks. As a result, he suffered various injuries while in attendance there. The student filed suit against the institute in the U.S. District Court for the District of Wyoming, alleging, among several causes of action, breach of an implied duty of good faith and fair dealing. The student argued that his enrollment at the institute formed a contract between the parties that contained an implied covenant to act in fairness and good faith. The institute argued that such actions were limited to the insurer-insured and employer-employee contexts.

The court found that **a cause of action for breach of an implied duty of good faith and fair dealing existed in every contract in which a special relationship of trust and reliance exists between the parties.** Here, a special relationship existed because the student had a statutory right under the Rehabilitation Act and the Americans with Disabilities Act not to be discriminated against or unlawfully precluded from participation in the institute's programs based on his disability. Because a statutory right is sufficient to establish the requisite special relationship between a student and a school, **the duty of good faith and fair dealing gave rise to tort liability.** However, the actual determination of whether the institute had failed to act in good faith was an issue for the jury to decide. The school's motion for pretrial judgment on the ADA claim was denied. *Powers v. MJB Acquisition Corp.*, 993 F.Supp. 861 (D.Wyo.1998).

◆   *Where proposed accommodations would alter the fundamental nature of a training program, they did not have to be implemented.*

A Virginia trucking school received an application from a potential student with a severe hearing impairment. The school employees took the applicant on a tour of the facilities and advised him to return later and meet with an instructor to recommend accommodations for his impairment. He did not return. The school determined that the applicant could not be reasonably accommodated during the public road-training portion of the course. It rejected his application, and he sued the school in the U.S. District Court for the Eastern District of Virginia, claiming that the school's actions violated the ADA. At trial, a doctor who testified on behalf of the applicant stated that the applicant could be safely accommodated with an earphone amplification system while driving trucks. He also stated that the school could accommodate the student through expanded in-class training and increased truck driving simulator use. An instructor at the school testified that the proposed accommodations were no substitute for the road-driving portion of the course and would be unsafe, fundamental alterations of the training program.

The court stated that the ADA prohibits discrimination by providers of public accommodations on the basis of disability, but does not require them to fundamentally alter their programs to accommodate disabled individuals. In this case, **the applicant's proposed accommodations would have fundamentally altered the nature of the over-the-road instructional program.** Training in the class or in a simulator did not substitute for over-the-road training, and the use of an amplification device or an interpreter in the cab of a tractor posed a direct threat to the safety of the applicant, the instructor and the public. Because the proposed accommodations could not be implemented without fundamentally altering the program, the school's rejection of the applicant did not violate the ADA. *Breece v. Alliance Tractor-Trailer Training II, Inc.*, 824 F.Supp. 576 (E.D.Va.1993).

B. Outside Entities

*   *In* Traynor v. Turnage, *a case involving G.I. Bill educational assistance, the U.S. Supreme Court determined that a Veterans' Administration regulation defining alcoholism was not invalid under the Rehabilitation Act.*

Two honorably discharged veterans who were recovering alcoholics sought an extension of the 10-year Veterans' Administration (VA) limitation for receipt of educational assistance under the G.I. Bill. The 10-year limitation on educational benefits can be extended by the VA if the veteran can show he was prevented from using his benefits earlier because of "physical or mental disability which was not the result of ... [his] own willful misconduct." VA regulations state that the deliberate drinking of alcohol is considered willful misconduct. Both veterans requested an extension of benefits after expiration of their respective 10-year limitation periods. These requests were based on grounds that they were disabled by alcoholism. **The VA denied their requests, stating that their alcoholism had been willful misconduct.** One veteran sued the VA in a New York federal court. The other veteran sought review in a D.C. federal court. The New York court held for the VA, but its decision was reversed by the Second Circuit Court of Appeals. The D.C. court ruled that the VA regulation was contrary to the Rehabilitation Act, but the D.C. Court of Appeals reversed that decision.

Noting the disagreement between the two federal appeals courts, the U.S. Supreme Court granted review and heard the cases together. The Court held that the Rehabilitation Act does not preclude an action against the VA. The Court noted that Congress had changed the time limit for benefits several times, most recently in 1977. The Rehabilitation Act of 1978 did not repeal the "willful misconduct" provision of the 1977 regulations. Accordingly, **Congress had the right to establish the allocation priorities for veterans' benefits.** The D.C. Court of Appeals decision was affirmed and the Second Circuit Court of Appeals decision was reversed. The VA prevailed in both matters. *Traynor v. Turnage*, 485 U.S. 535, 108 S.Ct. 1372, 99 L.Ed.2d 618 (1988).

*   *In a Rehabilitation Act lawsuit brought by a former student against the U.S. Merchant Marine Academy, the Supreme Court held that Congress had not waived the government's sovereign immunity against monetary damages awards for violations of § 504(a).*

A first-year student at the U.S. Merchant Marine Academy was diagnosed with diabetes. He was separated from the Academy on the grounds that his diabetes was a disqualifying condition. He filed suit in federal district court against the Secretary of the Department of Transportation and others, alleging that they violated § 504(a) of the Rehabilitation Act (Act). He requested reinstatement, compensatory damages, attorneys' fees and costs. The district court granted the student summary judgment, finding that his separation from the Academy violated the Act, and ordered him reinstated.

The government disputed the compensatory damages award, contending that it was protected by sovereign immunity. The district court disagreed and found that the student was entitled to damages. Soon after, the U.S. Court of Appeals, District of Columbia Circuit, held in another case that the government had not waived its immunity against monetary damages for violations of § 504(a). The district court then vacated part of its prior decision and denied compensatory damages. The student appealed and the D.C. Circuit Court of Appeals granted the government's motion for summary judgment.

The U.S. Supreme Court granted review to determine **whether Congress has waived the government's sovereign immunity against monetary damage awards for violations of § 504(a).** The Court found that a waiver of sovereign immunity must be clearly expressed in the statutory text. The Court found no such language in the text of § 504(a). The student argued that § 505(a)(2) of the Act states that the remedies set forth in Title VI of the Civil Rights Act of 1964 are "available to any person aggrieved by any act ... by any recipient of Federal assistance or Federal provider of such assistance under [§ 504]." Because Title VI provides for monetary damages, the student claimed that read together, § 505(a)(2) and § 504(a) establish a waiver of the government's immunity against monetary damages.

The Court, however, found that this was not an unequivocal expression of a waiver of immunity. It also found that the Department of Transportation is not a provider of financial assistance to the Academy because it manages the Academy. **Because there is no clear expression of the government's intent to waive its sovereign immunity, monetary damage awards are not allowed under § 504(a) of the Act.** The court of appeals' decision was affirmed. *Lane v. Pena,* 518 U.S. 187, 116 S.Ct. 2092, 135 L.Ed.2d 486 (1996).

♦   *A law school graduate with dyslexia would have to be given reasonable accommodations when she took the New York bar exam if she was ultimately determined to be disabled.*

A law school graduate with dyslexia applied and requested accommodations for the July 1991 New York State Bar Examination. Because she had missed the deadline for requesting accommodations, her request was denied. She took and failed four consecutive bar exams. Several months later, she applied for the July 1993 examination, and again requested accommodations. After her request for accommodations was denied, she submitted her application for reconsideration, but was still allowed no accommodations. The applicant then brought suit against the State Board of Law Examiners and its members in the U.S. District Court for the Southern District of New York, alleging violations of the Americans with Disabilities Act (ADA) and the Rehabilitation Act. She sued for injunctive and other relief under several theories.

The court noted that the issue to be decided was whether the applicant was substantially limited in one or more major life activities. The applicant claimed that she was impaired in the major life activities of learning, reading and working, and **the court found that she was substantially limited in the major life activity of working.** It noted that the relevant comparison group was the average person having comparable training, skills and abilities. When compared to the average law school student, her reading skills were well below normal. The court therefore held that her inability to read and take the bar examination as compared to other law school graduates had the effect of impeding her entry into a "class of jobs," as the concept was understood under the ADA. The court concluded that the applicant was excluded from performing any and all jobs that comprised the practice of law. Because the graduate was disabled and was denied reasonable accommodations in taking the bar examination even though she was otherwise qualified, her rights under the ADA and the Rehabilitation Act were violated. The court awarded the applicant compensatory damages in the amount of $12,500, and ordered that she receive several reasonable accommodations should she decide to retake the examination.

On appeal, **the Second Circuit Court of Appeals affirmed the decision that the applicant was disabled, but for different reasons. It held that she was substantially limited in the major life activities of reading and learning.** Further, the board received federal funds, and thus was subject to the dictates of the Rehabilitation Act in addition to the ADA. The court also affirmed that the applicant was entitled to compensatory damages for the discrimination against her, but remanded the case for a determination of the proper amount. She was only entitled to be reimbursed for those exams she had taken where she had sought a reasonable accommodation and been denied one. *Bartlett v. New York State Bd. of Law Examiners*, 156 F.3d 321 (2d Cir.1998).

On further appeal, the U.S. Supreme Court vacated and remanded the case for consideration in light of *Sutton v. United Air Lines, Inc.*, 527 U.S. —, 119 S.Ct. 1752, 143 L.Ed.2d 785 (1999), *Murphy v. UPS*, 119 S.Ct. 2133 (1999), and *Albertsons, Inc. v. Kirkingburg*, 119 S.Ct. 2162 (1999), all decided on the same day, in which the Court held that **mitigating measures must be taken into account in determining whether a person is disabled.** Here, because the applicant had a history of self-accommodation that allowed her to achieve roughly average reading skills (on some measures) when compared to the general population, there was a question as to whether she was disabled under the *Sutton* and *Murphy* standard. *New York State Bd. of Law Examiners v. Bartlett*, 119 S.Ct. 2388, 144 L.Ed.2d 790 (1999).

♦ *A student's lawsuit against the National Board of Medical Examiners failed where he was unable to show that he was disabled under the ADA.*

A student at a Michigan medical school passed his first two years, then took the NBME Step 1 exam. He claimed to have a learning disability and asked for more time to take the exam as an accommodation from the National Board of Medical Examiners. The board denied his request, and he failed the exam twice. He then sued the board under Title III of the ADA, seeking a preliminary injunction that would force it to allow him twice the allotted time to take the exam. The question before the court was **whether the student's learning disability (slowness in language processing) amounted to a disability under the ADA. The court found that it did not. Even though some of the tests administered to the student indicated that he scored on the lower range of average, his verbal IQ was within the average range.** Further, his performance IQ was in the high average to superior range. As compared to the general population, the student's scores were overwhelmingly average to superior. Thus, he failed to demonstrate that he suffered from an ADA-defined disability that substantially limited him in a major life activity. The court ruled in favor of the board. *Gonzalez v. National Bd. of Medical Examiners*, 60 F.Supp.2d 703 (E.D.Mich.1999).

♦   *A bar applicant's request to average out exam scores was held not to be a reasonable accommodation.*

A Florida bar applicant with attention deficit disorder requested and was granted an accommodation of 25 percent more time on all portions of the bar exam. With this accommodation, the applicant had taken the bar exam several times, but had been unable to earn a passing score. The applicant then petitioned the Board of Bar Examiners for admission to the bar by requesting, as a reasonable accommodation of her disability, that her scores on parts A and B, taken at separate administrations, be averaged. The board denied her request and the applicant petitioned the Florida Supreme Court for relief. Assuming that the applicant was disabled under the Americans with Disabilities Act, the court found that the board had reasonably accommodated her by allowing her more time on the bar exam. However, the court found that **the applicant's request to average her exam scores was not an accommodation in the administration of the exam, but an accommodation in the scoring of the exam. This was not a reasonable accommodation.** A modification in the scoring of the exam would fundamentally alter the measurement of skills or knowledge the exam is intended to test. The court rejected the applicant's contention that averaging the score of her exam as though she took parts A and B at the same time would put her on equal footing with nondisabled applicants. This would give her an unfair advantage. The court denied her petition for relief. *Florida Bd. of Bar Examiners Re S.G.*, 707 So.2d 323 (Fla.1998).

♦   *Inquiries made into applicants' mental health by a state board of bar examiners violated Title II of the ADA.*

Four women who applied to be admitted to the Florida bar claimed that certain questions on the application violated the ADA. Specifically, there were questions on the application asking whether an applicant had ever sought treatment for nervous, mental or emotional conditions, had ever been diagnosed as having such a condition, or had ever taken any psychotropic drugs. The application also contained a consent form that released any of the applicant's mental health records to the Board of Bar Examiners. They sued under Title II of the ADA, and the board sought to dismiss the lawsuit. A federal court denied the motion to dismiss, noting that regulations issued under Title II made clear that **the inquiries here discriminated against the applicants by subjecting them to additional burdens based on their disabilities.** *Ellen S. v. Florida Bd. of Bar Examiners*, 859 F.Supp. 1489 (S.D.Fla.1994).

♦   *A student denied tuition assistance to attend law school could not sue under Title I of the Rehabilitation Act.*

A disabled Wisconsin student attended college under **Title I of the Rehabilitation Act** (Act) and received book and tuition assistance for classes through the Wisconsin Division of Vocational Rehabilitation (DVR). When he requested assistance under the Act to attend law school, the DVR declined to provide further tuition assistance and closed his file. He sued the DVR in the U.S. District Court for the Eastern District of Wisconsin under the Act. The DVR moved for pretrial judgment which was granted by the court. The student appealed to the U.S. Court of Appeals for the Seventh Circuit. The purpose of Title I is to provide disabled individuals with certain benefits and rights that will enable such persons to become gainfully employed. To this end, the person and a vocational counselor develop a written plan to which both agree. The Act provides specific administrative processes to address grievances but no private rights of action in a court. Because Congress only provided administrative remedies, the court determined that **Congress neither intended to create nor expressly implied a private cause of action under the Act. Nor did the Act guarantee an individual the right to tuition assistance at an institution of higher education.** The court affirmed the lower court's judgment. *Mallett v. Wisconsin Division of Vocational Rehabilitation*, 130 F.3d 1245 (7th Cir.1997)

♦ *A student was not entitled to receive a full ride to law school under the Rehabilitation Act because the Act does not require the maximizing of people's abilities.*

A profoundly deaf Florida student sought educational assistance from the state Division of Vocational Rehabilitation (DVR) so that he could attend college. The DVR certified the student as disabled and developed an individualized written rehabilitation plan which called for him to obtain a psychology degree. It then funded the student's attendance at several universities. After graduating, the student asked the DVR to pay for him to attend law school. The DVR refused to do so. The student sued it in the U.S. District Court for the Middle District of Florida, asserting that it had discriminated against him in violation of § 504 of the Rehabilitation Act. A magistrate judge ruled in favor of the DVR, and the student appealed to the U.S. Court of Appeals, Eleventh Circuit.

The appellate court held that **the student's claim failed. He was unable to show that he had been treated differently than anyone else when he was denied a full scholarship to law school. Section 504 is not designed to maximize abilities, but rather to maximize "meaningful" employment.** By paying for the student's college degree and offering him a job as a counselor for the deaf, the DVR had assisted the student in obtaining meaningful employment. It was not required to do more. *Berg v. Florida Dept. of Labor and Employment Security, Div. of Vocational Rehabilitation*, 163 F.3d 1251 (11th Cir.1998).

II. SEX DISCRIMINATION AND HARASSMENT

College and university students have the same rights as elementary and secondary school students to be free of sex discrimination, including sexual harassment. In the context of sex discrimination, Title IX applies to recipients of federal funding but also provides a specific exception which allows private undergraduate institutions to discriminate on the basis of sex in admissions (20 U.S.C. § 1681(a)(1)). However, private graduate institutions may not. Private professional schools affiliated with a single-sex undergraduate institution may exclude students based upon sex.

A. Discrimination

♦   *The U.S. Supreme Court held that the categorical exclusion of women from the Virginia Military Institute—a public school—denied equal protection to women despite the fact that the state offered them a parallel program at a private college.*

The U.S. Attorney General's office filed a complaint against the Commonwealth of Virginia and Virginia Military Institute (VMI) on behalf of a female high school student seeking admission to the male-only college. The U.S. District Court for the Western District of Virginia found that because single-gender education conferred substantial benefits on students and preserved the unique military training offered at VMI, the exclusion of women did not violate the Equal Protection Clause. The U.S. Court of Appeals, Fourth Circuit, vacated the district court judgment, ruling that **Virginia had failed to state an adequate policy justifying the men-only program.**

On remand, the district court found that the institution of coeducational methods at VMI would materially affect its program. It approved the commonwealth plan for instituting a parallel program for women even though the program differed substantially from VMI in its academic offerings, educational methods and financial resources. The court of appeals affirmed the district court decision, and the attorney general's office appealed to the U.S. Supreme Court.

The Court stated that parties seeking to defend gender-based government action must demonstrate an exceedingly persuasive justification that is genuine and not invented as a response to litigation. Virginia had failed to show an exceedingly persuasive justification for excluding women from VMI. There was evidence that some women would be able to participate at VMI, and the court of appeals had improperly relied on the district court judgment that most women would not gain from the adversative method employed by the college. **The remedy proposed by Virginia left its exclusionary policy intact and afforded women no opportunity to experience the rigorous military training offered at VMI.** The parallel women's program was substantially limited in its course offerings, and participants would not gain the benefits of association with VMI's faculty, stature, funding, prestige and alumni support. The proposal did not remedy the constitutional violation, and the Court reversed and remanded the case. *U.S. v. Virginia*, 518 U.S. 515, 116 S.Ct. 2264, 135 L.Ed.2d 735 (1996).

♦   *Although federal law or regulations may prohibit certain actions, it is not always clear whether Congress intends to allow private citizens to bring lawsuits for violations of those laws or regulations. Many times a cessation of federal funding or other punitive measure is intended to be the sole remedy for violation, depriving the private citizen of standing to bring suit. In this case, the Supreme Court upheld a woman's right to bring suit under federal education law despite the fact that the law created no express cause of action in the person injured.*

Section 901(a) of Title IX of the Education Amendments of 1972 prohibits any educational program or activity receiving federal funds from discriminating on the basis of sex. After being denied admission to two medical schools, a woman sued in federal court alleging that she had been excluded from participation in the private university programs on the basis of her gender, and that the universities were receiving federal funding at the time of this exclusion. The district court granted the universities' motion to dismiss since Title IX did not expressly authorize a private right of action by a person injured by a violation of § 901. The court also held that no private remedy should be inferred.

The U.S. Court of Appeals for the Seventh Circuit agreed. The court of appeals concluded that Congress intended the remedy of § 902, which allowed termination of federal funding, to be the exclusive means of enforcement, and that Title VI of the Civil Rights Act of 1964 did not include an implied private cause of action. On appeal, **the U.S. Supreme Court reversed, holding that the woman could maintain her lawsuit despite the lack of any express authorization in Title IX.**

The Court stated that before concluding that Congress intended to make a remedy available to a special class of litigants the following four factors must be analyzed: 1) whether the statute was enacted for the benefit of a special group of which the plaintiff is a member; 2) whether there is any indication of legislative intent to create a private remedy; 3) whether implication of such remedy is consistent with the underlying purposes of the legislative scheme; and 4) whether implying a federal remedy is inappropriate because the subject matter is basically a concern of the states. The Court stated that all four factors were satisfied here. **Title IX expressly conferred a benefit on those discriminated against on the basis of sex, and the woman clearly fell into that class.** Title IX was patterned after Title VI, which had been construed to create a private remedy. Implying a private remedy was consistent with the legislative scheme since it provided better protection against discrimination. And since the Civil War, the federal government has been the primary protector of citizens from discrimination of any sort. *Cannon v. University of Chicago*, 441 U.S. 677, 99 S.Ct. 1946, 60 L.Ed.2d 560 (1979).

◆   *Gender-based distinctions in academic fields will generally not withstand constitutional scrutiny. Here, the Supreme Court held that a Mississippi university for women could not justify a policy that denied men the opportunity to enroll for credit.*

The policy of the Mississippi University for Women, a state-supported university, was to limit its enrollment to women. The university denied otherwise qualified males the right to enroll for credit in its School of Nursing. One male, who was denied admission, sued in federal court claiming that the university's policy violated the Fourteenth Amendment's Equal Protection Clause. The lower federal courts agreed and the school appealed to the U.S. Supreme Court. In the view of the Supreme Court, **the university's discriminatory admission policy against men was not substantially and directly related to an important governmental objective.** The school argued that women enrolled in its School of Nursing would be adversely affected by the presence of men. However, the record showed that the nursing school allowed men to attend classes in the school as auditors, thus fatally undermining the school's claim that admission of men would adversely affect women students. The Court held that the policy of the university, which limited enrollment to women, violated the Equal Protection Clause. *Mississippi University for Women v. Hogan*, 458 U.S. 718, 102 S.Ct. 3331, 73 L.Ed.2d 1090 (1982).

♦   *A federal district court found that Title IX protected a biological male who was subjected to discriminatory conduct while being perceived as being a female.*

A transsexual student brought suit in federal court against a New York university for violations of Title IX. The student, a biological male, had undergone hormone treatments for breast augmentation but had not yet had sex-reassignment surgery at the time she was admitted to a graduate studies program in musicology. The student lodged a written complaint against a professor, alleging that he made unwelcome sexual advances during one-on-one tutorial sessions, fondled her, forcibly attempted to kiss her and repeatedly propositioned her for a sexual relationship. The university served a written reprimand upon the professor, but permitted him to continue teaching at the graduate and undergraduate levels. The student also claimed that she was treated in a hostile fashion by professors and administrators after the formal grievance proceedings. She left the doctoral program and sued the university for violating Title IX, which provides that no person in the United States shall, on the basis of sex, be subjected to discrimination under any education program or activity receiving federal financial assistance. The issue before the court was whether Title IX protected a biological male who was subjected to discriminatory conduct while perceived as being a female. The court held that the student was entitled to Title IX's protections. **It rejected the university's argument that the student was not among the class of persons whom Title IX was intended to protect.** The court denied the university's motion for summary judgment. *Miles v. New York Univ.,* 979 F.Supp. 248 (S.D.N.Y.1997).

♦   *A private religious college's policy against premarital sex did not constitute sex discrimination despite the potential for a disparate impact on women.*

A Tennessee woman attended a private college associated with the Church of God. According to school policy, as stated in the student handbook, students were prohibited from engaging in premarital sex. Violation of this policy would result in suspension or expulsion. However, if suspended, a student could apply for readmission the following semester. While unmarried and attending the college, the student became pregnant and gave birth to a child. The college took no action against her. One year later, the student became pregnant again. This came to the attention of school officials who spoke with her to determine that she was unmarried and pregnant and to discuss the school policy against premarital sex. When it was determined that she had violated the policy, she was suspended. She was not allowed to finish the semester, but following the birth of her child, she reentered the college the next semester and graduated later that year. She filed suit against the college in the U.S. District Court for the Eastern District of Tennessee, alleging gender discrimination in violation of Title IX.

The court found that on its face, the policy was not discriminatory. It applied to both sexes and evidence was presented that it had been equally enforced against both males and females. The court also found that it was a longstanding policy resulting from the college's religious beliefs and that women whose pregnancies resulted from rape had been allowed to stay in school. The court acknowledged that in practice, the policy might have a disparate impact on women since their violation of the policy could become known through pregnancy but a man's violation could remain secret. However, since no evidence was presented on this issue, the court held that the policy was not discriminatory. The court also noted that **no evidence was presented that the college took action against women because of pregnancy rather than because of their violation of the policy**. It found that the pregnant students who were allowed to remain in school were not treated any differently than other students. Finding that the **student failed to present any evidence of pregnancy discrimination**, the court held in favor of the college. *Hall v. Lee College, Inc.*, 932 F.Supp. 1027 (E.D.Tenn.1996).

◆   *A private college student presented sufficient facts that sex discrimination tainted the outcome of his school disciplinary proceeding.*

A student from Bangladesh enrolled at a New York private college. His Caucasian roommate allegedly attacked him, causing physical injuries. The Caucasian student was arrested by the local police department and was given a "suspended suspension" by college officials. He was permitted to remain in school until he graduated the following semester. The Caucasian student's girlfriend then filed sexual harassment charges against the student from Bangladesh, allegedly in retaliation for his pursuit of criminal prosecution against the Caucasian student. Following a hearing, the student from Bangladesh was found guilty of sexual harassment. Among other penalties, he was suspended from May 20, 1992, until the spring of 1993. The Dean of Student Life affirmed the decision, and the student filed a Title IX gender and race discrimination lawsuit against the college in the U.S. District Court for the Southern District of New York. The district court dismissed both claims, and the student appealed the gender discrimination ruling to the U.S. Court of Appeals, Second Circuit.

The court of appeals noted that the student's gender bias claim was based both on his allegation that he was wrongly found to have committed the offense and on the school's alleged selective enforcement. The selective enforcement claim asserted that the severity of the penalty was affected by the student's gender. The court held that the student had alleged facts sufficient to cast doubt on the disciplinary proceeding. He also alleged **circumstances suggesting that gender bias was a motivating factor** behind the erroneous finding. Specifically, **he alleged that: 1) a false and stale sexual harassment charge was made in retaliation for his criminal prosecution; 2) he was on good terms with the complainant until this time; 3) actions of the disciplinary tribunal prevented him from fully defending himself; and 4) males were systematically found guilty of sexual harassment without an evidentiary basis.** Because the student alleged provable facts which would allow a trier of fact to find that gender discrimination tainted the outcome of the disciplinary proceeding, the case was reversed and remanded for further proceedings. *Yusuf v. Vassar College*, 35 F.3d 709 (2d Cir.1994).

◆   *A female student who was barred from selective clubs which were connected to a university could sue for sex discrimination under state law.*

A New Jersey female was admitted to Princeton University. When she became a sophomore she went through the process of trying to join one of the selective eating clubs at Princeton. These clubs, which consisted only of men, could be joined by invitation only by juniors and seniors. Those who wanted to join went through a procedure during their sophomore year and then the clubs handed out invitations. The woman was not given an invitation to join any of the clubs. She filed a complaint with the Division of Civil Rights. After various administrative hearings held by the Division and an administrative law judge, it was decided that the Division had jurisdiction over the clubs because they were not distinctly private, and that gender discrimination did exist. The clubs appealed to the New Jersey Appellate Division. The appellate division partially reversed the decision, holding that there were material facts in dispute and thus, the division should have held a full hearing before determining jurisdiction. The woman appealed to the Supreme Court of New Jersey. The supreme court stated that both parties had many opportunities to be heard and many hearings to present their arguments. Further, the clubs knew the Division was going to make a jurisdictional determination and had the opportunity to rebut the decision. It also stated that no disputed facts existed in the record and that **the relationship between the university and the clubs was of mutual benefit and integral connection.** Thus, the clubs were under the jurisdiction of the Division and subject to New Jersey's Law Against Discrimination since they were not distinctively private and were connected to the school. The court stated that it was clear the clubs discriminated on the basis of gender. The supreme court reversed the decision of the appellate division and affirmed the Division's decision that gender discrimination was prohibited in the clubs. *Frank v. Ivy Club*, 576 A.2d 241 (N.J.1990).

♦   *New York could not use SAT scores only in awarding certain scholarships where doing so discriminated against female students.*

Ten high school students in New York sued the state department of education under Title IX and the Equal Protection Clause of the Fourteenth Amendment, asserting that the state's exclusive reliance on Scholastic Aptitude Test scores to determine eligibility for prestigious Empire and Regents scholarships discriminated against female students. They sought a preliminary injunction to stop the practice, alleging that although the policy of using only SAT scores was neutral on its face, it had a discriminatory impact on female students. A federal court agreed. It rejected the state's argument that the policy satisfied an educational necessity. In fact, the state could not even show a rational relationship between the policy and its purpose of recognizing and rewarding academic achievement in high school. Further, **the students had offered a much better alternative for awarding scholarships—a combination of grade point averages and SAT scores. The court ordered the state to stop using SAT scores as the sole determinant in awarding scholarships.** *Sharif v. New York State Educ. Dep't*, 709 F.Supp. 345 (S.D.N.Y.1989).

B. Harassment

The Supreme Court decided two cases recently involving sexual harassment in schools: *Gebser v. Lago Vista School Dist.*, 524 U.S. 274, 118 S.Ct. 1989, 141 L.Ed.2d 277 (1998), and *Davis v. Monroe County Bd. of Educ.*, 119 S.Ct. 1661, 143 L.Ed.2d 839 (1999). Although the cases did not involve colleges or universities, they are instructive because the standards used to determine liability can be applied in the higher education setting.

Those decisions (which follow) were built on the foundation of an earlier Supreme Court case: *Franklin v. Gwinnett County Public Schools*, 503 U.S. 60, 112 S.Ct. 1028, 117 L.Ed.2d 208 (1992). In *Franklin*, a high school student had been repeatedly harassed and sexually abused by a teacher. She sued the school under Title IX, and a federal court dismissed the action, finding that Title IX does not allow an award of money damages. The case eventually reached the U.S. Supreme Court, which held that money damages could be recovered under Title IX in cases involving a teacher's sexual harassment of a student. The Court reversed the dismissal of the student's lawsuit.

◆ *The U.S. Supreme Court determined that schools may be held liable for incidents of peer sexual harassment under Title IX of the Education Amendments of 1972.*

The case involved a fifth-grade Georgia student who claimed that a classmate subjected her to unwanted sexual comments, physical abuse and ongoing harassment for about five months. She complained to her teacher and the school's principal, but claimed that they did nothing in response. When the case reached the Supreme Court, it held that **a recipient of federal funds may be held liable for student-on-student sexual harassment under Title IX where the funding recipient is deliberately indifferent to known student sexual harassment and the harasser is under the recipient's disciplinary authority.** The Court additionally held that in order to make a finding of deliberate indifference, the recipient's response to harassment must be clearly unreasonable in light of the known circumstances. In order to create Title IX liability, the harassment must be so severe, pervasive and objectively offensive that it deprives the victim of access to the funding recipient's educational opportunities or benefits. *Davis v. Monroe County Bd. of Educ.*, 119 S.Ct. 1661, 143 L.Ed.2d 839 (S.Ct.1999).

◆ *The U.S. Supreme Court found that an award of damages would be inappropriate in a Title IX case unless an official with the authority to address the discrimination failed to act despite actual knowledge of it, in a manner amounting to deliberate indifference to discrimination.*

In 1998, the U.S. Supreme Court examined the potential liability of a Texas school district in a case involving a student who had a sexual relationship with a teacher. The Court rejected the liability standard advocated by the student and by the U.S. government, which resembled *respondeat superior* liability under Title VII. Title IX contains an administrative enforcement mechanism that assumes actual notice has been provided to officials prior to the imposition of enforcement remedies. An award of damages would be inappropriate in a Title IX case unless an official with the authority to address the discrimination failed to act despite actual knowledge of it, in a manner amounting to deliberate indifference to discrimination. Here, **there was insufficient evidence that a school official should have known about the relationship so as to impose liability on the school district.** *Gebser v. Lago Vista Indep. School Dist.*, 524 U.S. 274, 118 S.Ct. 1989, 141 L.Ed.2d 277 (1998).

◆   *Where a school allegedly conducted a "sham" investigation into charges of sexual harassment by a coach, there was an issue as to whether school officials had shown deliberate indifference to misconduct.*

Two former members of the Syracuse University women's tennis team, together with their parents, sued their former coach under Title IX for sexually harassing them over a three-year period. They also sued the university and several of its employees and agents, alleging that the defendants had concocted a "sham" investigatory proceeding to conceal the extent of the coach's misconduct, which they claimed went back more than 20 years.

A New York federal court held that under *Gebser v. Lago Vista Indep. School Dist.*, 118 S.Ct. 1989, 141 L.Ed.2d 277 (1998), where a school official has actual knowledge of sexual harassment against a student and is deliberately indifferent to that misconduct, the student can sue the school under Title IX. **Here, there were issues of fact to be resolved as to whether the defendants had been deliberately indifferent to the alleged misconduct.** The defendants' motion to dismiss the case was denied. *Erickson v. Syracuse Univ.*, 1999 WL 33467, No. 98 Civ. 3435(JSR) (S.D.N.Y.1999).

◆   *A student who was allegedly threatened with deportation if she did not submit to a professor's advances could sue the professor but not the school.*

After applying for and receiving an F-1 student visa, a graduate student from Taiwan entered the graduate program in history at Providence College. Subsequently, she encountered several visa problems and was directed to a professor who served as the college's international student advisor. She alleged that he sexually harassed her, threatening her with deportation to force her into a sexual relationship. She sued the college and the professor for sexual harassment. A Rhode Island federal court held that **the college could not be held liable for the professor's actions,** citing *Gebser*, above. **Here, there was no college official (with the authority to address the harassment) who had knowledge of the harassment and failed to take action to prevent it.** However, the professor could be liable under the civil remedies provision of the Violence Against Women Act (the Civil Rights Remedies for Gender Motivated Violence Act). The student also stated claims against him under the Rhode Island Civil Rights Act and the state Privacy Act. The court dismissed the college from the lawsuit but allowed the claims against the professor to proceed. *Liu v. Striuli*, 36 F.Supp.2d 452 (D.R.I.1999).

◆   *Allegations of a number of harassment incidents prevented a university from having a Title IX suit dismissed.*

A tenured professor at an Indiana university allegedly harassed a female graduate student, attempting to enter into a sexual relationship with her. The university issued the professor a written reprimand, warning him that another incident could lead to his firing. He then allegedly touched a visiting high school student on the buttocks. The university then referred him to a psychiatrist, but after learning that he had visited the doctor, did not follow up to determine the results of his counseling. The professor's supervisor, however, allegedly knew that a number of female students were uncomfortable in the professor's presence. Approximately five years later, the professor allegedly made inappropriate remarks to another student and put his arm around her a few times. The director of student services allegedly knew about this incident but did nothing other than warn the professor to "clean up his act." Two years later, the professor allegedly groped and kissed a student against her will. The university then instituted proceedings against the professor, who chose to resign with full benefits. When the student sued the university for harassment under Title IX, the university sought to dismiss the lawsuit. The court denied the university's motion. It noted that **a reasonable jury could find that the university had been deliberately indifferent to the professor's misconduct.** Rather than firing him after the second incident, it had only required counseling, and had not followed up to determine its effectiveness. Further, it had done nothing after the third incident. Thus, **factual issues existed as to whether the university was liable under Title IX because of deliberate indifference to harassment.** *Chontos v. Rhea*, 29 F.Supp.2d 931 (N.D.Ind.1998).

◆   *Where university officials took steps to keep an assistant coach away from a student he had sought to date, the university could not be held liable for sexual harassment.*

A student at Ohio State University participated on the track and cross-country teams. After her eligibility expired, an assistant coach allegedly offered to let her continue to train with the team and become a volunteer assistant coach. He then asked her out on two occasions. She refused to date him and allegedly was unable to continue training with the teams as a result of her refusal. She sued the university, the assistant coach and the athletic director under Title IX and 42 U.S.C. § 1983. The defendants moved to dismiss the lawsuit. The U.S. District Court for the Southern District of Ohio dismissed the case against the university, finding that **once the student informed school officials of the assistant coach's actions, they took prompt action to ensure that the "harassing" behavior, which had already ceased, would not recur.** However, the court found that a genuine issue of fact remained as to whether the assistant coach's actions in asking the student out amounted to a request for sexual favors. Accordingly, the case against the assistant coach could not be dismissed. *Klemencic v. Ohio State Univ.*, 10 F.Supp.2d 911 (S.D.Ohio 1998).

◆   *In a sexual harassment case under Title IX, a student must show actual notice of the harassment and deliberate indifference by school officials.*

Two days before graduating from a private college, a student filed a sexual harassment complaint against one of her professors. Her complaint was processed and, less than two months later, she signed off on an informal grievance procedure notifying the professor that his conduct amounted to sexual harassment. Two years later, she sued the college under Title IX. An Ohio federal court ruled in favor of the college, finding that the student could not show that the college had been deliberately indifferent to her situation after receiving actual notice of her complaint. **The U.S. Supreme Court has held that both deliberate indifference and actual notice are required for liability to attach under Title IX.** Pretrial judgment in favor of the college was granted. *Burtner v. Hiram College*, 9 F.Supp.2d 852 (N.D.Ohio 1998).

• *If a professor has a supervisory relationship over a student, and capitalizes on that relationship to further the harassment, the college is liable for the professor's conduct under Title IX. However, if the professor does not use his authority, the college will be liable only if it provided no reasonable avenue for complaint, or if it knew, or should have known about the harassment, yet failed to take appropriate remedial action.*

A student attending a New York private college entered an English professor's office to protest a failing grade on a paper. The professor allegedly locked the door and ordered her to read pornographic poetry, inquired about her sexual experiences, and told her that he could imagine her naked. He also made sexually explicit comments to an English graduate student and assigned her sexually explicit reading material. The professor later wrote a letter apologizing to the graduate student and no further action was taken in that matter. The undergraduate student filed a formal sexual harassment complaint pursuant to the college's sexual harassment policy. Both students then filed a Title IX sexual harassment lawsuit against the college in federal court, seeking monetary damages. The district court dismissed the lawsuit, and held that the college had taken the appropriate remedial action upon learning of the students' sexual harassment allegations. The students appealed to the U.S. Court of Appeals, Second Circuit.

The court noted that Title IX prohibits educational institutions receiving federal financial assistance from discriminating against students or employees on the basis of sex. **An educational institution may be held liable under standards similar to those applied in cases brought under Title VII.** Therefore, the court held that if a professor has a supervisory relationship over a student, and capitalizes on that relationship to further the harassment, the college is liable for the professor's conduct. If, however, the professor does not rely upon his authority to carry out the harassment, the college will be liable only if it provided no reasonable avenue for complaint, or if it knew, or should have known about the harassment, yet failed to take appropriate remedial action. Here, **there was evidence to suggest that the professor used his supervisory authority to harass the students, and that the college knew of the hostile environment, but failed to take appropriate remedial action**. The court remanded the case for further proceedings. *Kracunas v. Iona College*, 119 F.3d 80 (2d Cir.1997).

• *A rape victim's lawsuit under § 13981 of the VAWA had to be dismissed where Congress exceeded its authority in enacting that section of the law.*

A Virginia university student alleged that she was raped by two members of the school football team. Based on her report, a university judicial committee obtained a confession by one of the perpetrators at a hearing, and suspended him for two semesters. Two university officials later advised the victim that another hearing would be held based on their belief that the perpetrator who admitted guilt had been charged under a new student handbook policy that had not yet been widely disseminated to students. A second hearing was held, after which university officials deferred the perpetrator's suspension until after his graduation. The officials did not notify the victim of the altered discipline, and the perpetrator kept his full athletic scholarship. The victim quit school after reading a newspaper report of the reduced discipline and filed a federal district court action against the university and perpetrators under Title IX and the Violence Against Women Act of 1994 (VAWA). VAWA is a comprehensive federal law that creates a cause of action for victims of violent crimes motivated by gender.

The court dismissed the action, and the U.S. Court of Appeals, Fourth Circuit, affirmed the judgment. It held that **although the alleged conduct came within the act's language, the VAWA violated the Commerce Clause because Congress lacked the authority to enact the civil remedy provisions of the VAWA (42 U.S.C. § 13981).** The U.S. Supreme Court affirmed. It noted that Congress could not regulate noneconomic, violent criminal conduct based solely on the conduct's aggregate effect on interstate commerce. Further, § 13981 could not be justified by the enforcement provision of the Fourteenth Amendment because the Fourteenth Amendment prohibits only state conduct, not private conduct. The Supreme Court stated that the victim's remedy had to be provided by state courts under state law. *United States (Brzonkala) v. Morrison*, 120 S.Ct. 1740, 146 L.Ed.2d 658 (2000).

♦ *A federal court held that Title IX does not authorize a cause of action against individuals.*

A 28-year-old female student-employee at a Pennsylvania university accused her supervisor, an administrative level employee, of sexually harassing her on several different occasions. The university suspended the administrator and he allegedly retaliated against the student by defaming her and by filing a civil complaint against her. The student filed a Title IX sexual harassment lawsuit against the administrator in the U.S. District Court for the Eastern District of Pennsylvania. The district court dismissed the claim, holding that Title IX does not authorize a cause of action against individuals. A 1986 amendment to Title IX bolstered this conclusion since only remedies against "public or private entities" were mentioned. The court also noted that the full body of regulations promulgated under Title IX, found at 28 C.F.R. Part 106, suggested that **only "owners or operators" of independent educational programs or activities, rather than individual employees of the operator, were subject to Title IX lawsuits**. *Nelson v. Temple Univ.*, 920 F.Supp. 633 (E.D.Pa.1996).

♦ *An educational institution may be held liable under standards similar to those applied in cases under Title VII where an employer is culpable when it "knew or should have known of the conduct." In this case, the student's complaint failed to allege that the university's agents "should have known" about the continued harassment.*

A second year New York university student was allegedly harassed by a clinic patient between the fall of 1992 and the summer of 1993. The patient made unwanted advances and professions of love to the student, continually stared at her, and repeatedly followed her to her apartment. The chief of the dental clinic warned the patient to cease the offensive behavior after another student filed a complaint. The chief's admonitions were unavailing, and after further harassment, the student asked a clinic doctor for assistance with the patient. He told her to "grow up" and deal with the problem herself. The student failed six classes and received an incomplete in four. In September of 1993, the academic standing committee recommended that she repeat the second-year curriculum. Her appeal, based on the harassment which allegedly caused her poor academic performance, was dismissed. The student filed a Title IX gender discrimination lawsuit against the university in a U.S. district court. The district court granted the university's motion to dismiss, and the student appealed to the U.S. Court of Appeals, Second Circuit.

The court of appeals noted that in a Title IX lawsuit for gender discrimination based on sexual harassment of a student, an educational institution may be held liable under standards similar to those applied in cases under Title VII. An employer is culpable under Title VII where it "knew or should have known of the conduct." However, even under this standard, which the court declined to apply in the present case, **the student's complaint failed to allege that the university's agents "should have known" about the continued harassment.** The student never informed the clinic chief that the harassing behavior continued following the chief's warning to the patient nor did she inform the doctor that the "problem" involved ongoing sexual harassment. The court also noted that **the university had not selectively enforced its academic standards** and that the academic committee's decision had been made before the student informed them of the sexual harassment. *Murray v. New York Univ. College of Dentistry*, 57 F.3d 243 (2d Cir.1995).

♦   *A federal district court applied Title VII sexual harassment law to a student's claim brought under Title IX and found that the owners of the school could be held liable for the school administrator's sexual harassment.*

An administrator at a private cosmetology school allegedly subjected a student to continued unwanted and uninvited sexual comments, questions, phone calls and threats. The administrator had sole decisionmaking authority over the school's day-to-day operations. He had entered into a "lease with purchase option" with the owners of the school. The lease with purchase option provided that the administrator would assume liability for all claims arising from the use of the premises. The owners agreed to retain title to the school's assets and, since the school's license was not transferable, the owners agreed to maintain the license for the benefit of the administrator. The student filed a Title IX sexual harassment suit against the owners based on the administrator's alleged acts in the U.S. District Court for the District of Kansas.

The student contended that the owners of the school were liable for the school administrator's alleged sexual harassment. In holding that the student stated a valid Title IX sexual harassment claim, the court applied the well-developed body of Title VII sexual harassment law. Specifically, the court determined that **the owners might be liable for the administrator's harassment if: 1) the administrator acted within the scope of his employment; 2) the owners negligently or recklessly failed to take remedial action; or 3) the owners' agency relationship with the administrator aided the administrator's harassment.** The court rejected the first two bases for liability because the harassment did not occur within the scope of the administrator's duties and the owners could not reasonably have known about the alleged harassment. However, the owners arguably assisted the harassing administrator by holding the cosmetology license in their name and by allowing him to operate the school. Thus, genuine issues of material fact precluded summary judgment as to the Title IX sexual harassment claim. *Hastings v. Hancock*, 842 F.Supp. 1315 (D.Kan.1993).

◆   *A federal court allowed a claim of retaliation under Title IX to proceed.*

A student brought discrimination charges against a private university before the U.S. Department of Education, Office for Civil Rights. She alleged that she then suffered adverse action by being evaluated and treated unfairly. She also maintained that the university denied her access to instructors who could serve as references for jobs, and denied her the opportunity to pursue a graduate degree. **The U.S. District Court of the Northern District of Illinois found an implied right of action for retaliation in Section 106.1 of the Title IX regulations.** Section 106.1 prohibits retaliation against "any individual who has made a complaint, testified, or participated in any manner in an investigation into alleged noncompliance with Title IX." The court also found that the pleading standard for retaliation in a Title IX suit is the same as under Title VII. To state a claim of retaliation under Title VII, a claimant must allege that: 1) she engaged in a statutorily protected activity; 2) she suffered an adverse action; and 3) there was a causal link between the protected activity and the adverse action. Here, because the student's complaint properly alleged retaliation by the university, the court refused to dismiss the case. *Adams v. Lewis Univ.*, 1999 WL 162762, No. 97 C 7636 (N.D.Ill.1999).

III. RACE DISCRIMINATION

◆   *While achieving a diverse student body may be a worthy goal, the means chosen to achieve that goal must comport with the Equal Protection Clause. In this case, the U.S. Supreme Court held that a special admissions program which reserved close to one-sixth of the available spots in a medical school each year for minority students was unnecessary to achieve that goal and violated the Equal Protection Clause.*

The Medical School of the University of California at Davis had two admission programs for its entering class of 100 students. Under the regular procedure, candidates whose overall undergraduate grade point averages fell below 2.5 on a scale of 4.0 were summarily rejected. The special admissions policy, designed to assist minority or other disadvantaged applicants, reserved 16 of the 100 openings each year for medical school admission based upon criteria other than that used in the general admissions program. Special admission applicants did not need to meet the 2.5 or better grade point average of the general admission group nor were their Medical College Admission Test scores measured against general admission candidates.

A white male brought suit to compel his admission to medical school after he was twice rejected for admission even though candidates with lower grade point averages and lower test score results were being admitted under the special admissions program. The plaintiff alleged that **the special admissions excluded him from medical school on the basis of his race** in violation of the Equal Protection Clause of the Fourteenth Amendment, the California Constitution and Title VI of the 1964 Civil Rights Act. Title VI of the Civil Rights Act provides that no person shall on the ground of race or color be excluded from participating in any program receiving federal financial assistance. The Equal Protection Clause states that no state shall deny to any person within its jurisdiction the equal protection of the law. The California Supreme Court concluded that the special admissions program was not the least intrusive means of achieving the state's goals of integrating the medical profession under a strict scrutiny standard.

On appeal to the U.S. Supreme Court, the Court ruled that **while the goal of achieving a diverse student body is sufficiently compelling to justify considerations of race in admissions decisions under some circumstances, the special admissions program, which foreclosed consideration to persons such as the plaintiff, was unnecessary to achieve this compelling goal and was therefore invalid under the Equal Protection Clause.** Since the school could not prove that the plaintiff would not have been admitted even if there had been no special admissions program, the Court ordered that he be admitted to the medical school. *Regents of the University of California v. Bakke*, 438 U.S. 265, 98 S.Ct. 2733, 57 L.Ed.2d 750 (1978).

◆   *The Supreme Court held that a university could avoid liability for a race-based admission policy if it could show that the applicant would have been denied admission absent the policy.*

An African immigrant of Caucasian descent applied for admission to the Ph.D. program in counseling psychology at a Texas public university. The university considered the race of its applicants at some stage of the review process and denied admission to the applicant. He sued for money damages and injunctive relief, asserting that the race-conscious admission policy violated the Equal Protection Clause. The university moved for summary judgment, arguing that even if it had not used race-based criteria, it would not have admitted the applicant because of his GPA and his GRE score. A federal court granted summary judgment to the university, but the Fifth Circuit Court of Appeals reversed. The case reached the U.S. Supreme Court, which noted that its decision in *Mt. Healthy City Bd. of Educ. v. Doyle*, 429 U.S. 274, 97 S.Ct. 568, 50 L.Ed.2d 471 (1977), made clear that **if the government has considered an impermissible criterion in making an adverse decision to the plaintiff, it can nevertheless avoid liability by demonstrating that it would have made the same decision absent the forbidden consideration.** Therefore, if the state could show that it would have made the decision to deny admission to the applicant absent the race-based policy, it would be entitled to summary judgment on the claim for damages. With respect to the claim for injunctive relief, it appeared that the university had stopped using a race-based admissions policy. However, that issue had to be decided on remand. *Texas v. Lesage*, 120 S.Ct. 467, 145 L.Ed.2d 347 (1999).

◆   *The NCAA could not be sued under Title VI on the grounds that Proposition 16 had a disparate impact on African-American students.*

A number of African-American high school student athletes graduated with GPAs that exceeded the NCAA's requirements. However, they all scored lower than the minimum SAT score required for participation in Division I collegiate athletics as freshmen. They sued the NCAA, asserting that the minimum SAT score requirement of Proposition 16 had a disparate impact on African-American athletes in violation of Title VI. Essentially, they claimed that Proposition 16 was neutral on its face, but that its impact was to discriminate against African-American students. They also claimed that the NCAA was a program or activity that received federal financial assistance and that, under Title VI, it could not discriminate on the basis of race, color or national origin. The NCAA maintained that it was not subject to Title VI because it did not receive direct financial assistance, but rather received money from colleges and universities that received federal financial assistance. A Pennsylvania federal court found that the NCAA was subject to suit under Title VI, and that Proposition 16 had a disparate impact on African-Americans.

The NCAA appealed, and the Third Circuit Court of Appeals reversed. It assumed without deciding that the NCAA received federal financial assistance. However, it then stated that **Title VI was intended to be program specific. In other words, it only prohibited discrimination in the programs or activities that received federal funds.** Further, even though Congress had enacted the Civil Rights Restoration Act to broaden the protections of Title VI and Title IX, the Department of Education had not yet enacted regulations to implement that statute. Further, it was unclear whether those regulations could prohibit neutral actions that had a discriminatory effect (disparate impact discrimination) or whether they could only prohibit intentional (disparate treatment) discrimination. As a result, **the NCAA did not come under the umbrella of Title VI. It was not a direct recipient of federal funds and did not exert sufficient authority over its member institutions to make it liable under Title VI.** *Cureton v. NCAA*, 198 F.3d 107 (3d Cir.1999).

◆   *A graduate student's dismissal for failure to complete academic program requirements was found permissible by a federal district court because the school did not exhibit any discriminatory intent or assert pretextual reasons for the dismissal.*

A Hispanic graduate student at Duke University received five incomplete grades in his second semester, two of which were converted to failures which led to his dismissal. The student later gained readmission. At the time of his readmission, the deadline requirements for the completion of a research project and departmental examination had changed from two years to one-and-one-half years. After his topic proposal for the exam was rejected, he failed to submit another topic proposal or complete the exam despite having been give two warnings of the deadline. He was again dismissed. The student then alleged that the guidelines published in the university bulletin upon his original admission granted two years time to complete the exam, and constituted a binding contract. He further argued that the two-year time deadline should be measured from the date of his readmittance. The student lastly contended that he was dismissed because of his race. A lawsuit was brought in a federal district court, and the school made a motion for summary judgment.

On the contractual claim, the court found that the university bulletin did not create a binding contract. The discrimination claim was brought under Title VI of the Education Amendments of 1972, which uses an analysis similar to the analysis used in Title VII employment cases. The court noted that **the exam requirement applied to all students, regardless of race.** The Hispanic student showed that at least one white female student was granted a one-semester extension. However, the school showed that the complainant had been offered the same option, but refused to exercise it. The court found **no discriminatory intent on the part of the school or pretextual reasons for dismissal**. It stated that absent proof of intentional discrimination the court has neither the insight nor the expertise to make decisions concerning student termination. *Love v. Duke Univ.*, 776 F.Supp. 1070 (M.D.N.C.1991).

◆   *Although a university's use of racial preferences for admissions to law school was unconstitutional, four students failed to show that they would have been admitted to the school absent the discrimination.*

Four white students applied for admission to the University of Texas School of Law. After they were denied admission, they sued under Title VI of the Civil Rights Act of 1964 and 42 U.S.C. §§ 1981 and 1983, asserting that the law school's use of racial preferences for the purpose of achieving a diverse student body violated those laws. A federal court found that although the government had a compelling interest in achieving a diverse student body, and a compelling interest in overcoming the present effects of past race discrimination, the law school's use of separate admissions procedures for minority and nonminority students was not narrowly tailored to achieve those compelling interests. The court then held that the students had the ultimate burden to prove that they would have been admitted to the law school absent the unconstitutional procedures used by the university. It found that they failed to meet that burden. On appeal, the Fifth Circuit held that **the law school's use of racial preferences served no compelling state interests** and that the burden should have been on the law school to show that under a constitutional admissions procedure, the students would not have been admitted. On remand, the district court held that **the university had shown that the students would not have been admitted even if its procedures had been constitutional.** They all fell within the discretionary screening zone and were just four of 3,500 applicants, including 1,500 Texas residents, who were denied admission to the school. The university had to have the freedom to make the necessary difficult choices about who should be admitted to its law school. *Hopwood v. Texas*, 999 F.Supp. 872 (W.D.Tex.1998).

◆   *Applicants to law school were not in a protected class just because their family law firm often associated with minorities.*

In a Kansas case, two sisters and their brother, unsuccessful applicants to the Washburn University School of Law, filed suit against the school and individual members of the admissions committee alleging that they had been denied admission in retaliation for their family's association with civil rights causes through the family law firm. They argued that because their family's law firm often associated with minorities (a protected class), they were also a protected class under 42 U.S.C. § 1981. They also argued that they had a protected "property interest" in admission to the law school. A U.S. district court observed that there was no evidence of any bias against the family's law firm when their applications were reviewed by the admissions committee. Moreover, the court noted the strong civil rights interests of the individual members of the admissions committee, some of whom were minority group members. **Merely because their family's law firm associated with blacks and civil rights causes, the students were not a protected class under § 1981. Furthermore, even if they were a protected class, they did not have a legitimate property interest in admission to the law school.** Ruling that the evidence showed no hint of discriminatory conduct by the admissions committee, the court dismissed the case. *Phelps v. Washburn Univ. of Topeka*, 634 F.Supp. 556 (D.Kan.1986).

* *A university could use race as a component in a laboratory elementary school to research urban education. This was a compelling state interest that justified discrimination on the basis of race.*

The University of California, Los Angeles, Graduate School of Education and Information Studies operates a laboratory elementary school to research urban education. In order to conduct credible research, the laboratory school used racial criteria in its admission policy to obtain an adequate cross sample of the general population attending urban California schools. The admission policy contained non-racial components and the school admitted a limited number of students by discretion of the dean. The parents of one student who was denied admission by the school asserted that the use of racial and ethnic admission criteria violated her equal protection rights and Title VI of the Civil Rights Act of 1964. They filed a federal district court action against university regents, claiming that the use of racial criteria could not be justified since there was no prior history of discrimination by the school.

The court conducted a trial and agreed with the parents that the use of racial classifications called for the imposition of strict judicial scrutiny, requiring the school to advance a compelling government interest. However, **the court agreed with the school that the state had a compelling interest in research on effective urban education strategies, and that the criteria used by the school were narrowly tailored to serve this government interest.** There was strong evidence that a representative racial balance was required in the laboratory school to support the credibility of the educational research conducted there. The remediation of past discrimination by a state entity is not the only compelling interest which may justify racial classifications by the state. Accordingly, the university regents were entitled to judgment. *Hunter by Brandt v. Regents of the Univ. of California*, 971 F.Supp. 1316 (C.D.Cal.1997).

* *A Ph.D. candidate was unable to show that discrimination resulted in her inability to pass qualifying examinations.*

An African-American Ph.D. candidate received a fellowship for minority students in the University of Maryland's applied mathematics program. Only 40 to 50 percent of students enrolled in the program eventually received a Ph.D. Doctoral candidates were required to pass qualifying exams in three subject areas. The African-American candidate failed qualifying examinations nine times and was dismissed from the program. She filed a federal district court action against the university and certain university officials, claiming race and sex discrimination in violation of federal laws including Title IX of the Education Amendments of 1972, Title VI of the Civil Rights Act of 1964 and 42 U.S.C. §§ 1981 and 1983. The court considered summary judgment motions by the university and officials.

The candidate claimed that a teaching assistant and a professor had made racially biased remarks concerning the academic ability of African-American students and had established more difficult testing conditions than those experienced by male students. **The court found that there was no link between these incidents and the candidate's failure to pass the qualifying examinations.**

It is impermissible to base a lawsuit brought under federal antidiscrimination laws on speculation and belief, especially where the incidents are unrelated to a central issue, such as failure to pass qualifying tests. Because the candidate had failed to demonstrate that she was qualified to continue in the program, the court granted summary judgment to the university and officials. *Middlebrooks v. Univ. of Maryland at College Park*, 980 F.Supp. 824 (D.Md.1997).

◆ *Although several black football players boycotted practices because they believed that they were being treated in a racially discriminatory manner, a federal district court found that the school did not breach its scholarship agreement by removing the students from the team.*

Several black football players who attended Washburn University in Kansas on athletic scholarships alleged that they were being treated in a racially discriminatory manner by university officials. After the players boycotted team practices, the officials removed them from the team. The players then sued the university in a U.S. district court, claiming that it had infringed upon their free speech, liberty and property rights in violation of the Civil Rights Act. They argued that they held a property interest in contractual rights to play football for the university and that by removing them from the team the university had deprived them of a property right without due process of law. They also contended that their removal infringed upon their liberty interests in pursuing a college football career. The players also claimed that the university violated their First Amendment right to free speech by removing them from the team after they protested alleged racial mistreatment. Lastly, they alleged that the university breached their scholarship contracts.

The court held for the university on all but the free speech claim. **The players had no contractual rights under the scholarship agreements to play football. They only had property rights in the scholarship funds themselves**. A due process liberty interest claim is made out only if there is a protectable liberty interest under the Constitution. The players offered no reason why pursuit of collegiate athletic careers should be afforded liberty interest status. The university did not breach the scholarship contracts because it met all of its financial obligations. The scholarship agreements did not promise that the players would play football for the university. The free speech allegations would proceed to trial because a university official admitted that if a player missed practice due to protesting alleged racial mistreatment the absence would be excused. *Hysaw v. Washburn Univ. of Topeka*, 690 F.Supp. 940 (D.Kan.1987).

IV. AGE DISCRIMINATION

In addition to state laws, the Age Discrimination Act of 1975 (42 U.S.C. § 6101, et seq.) provides the basis for claims of age discrimination by students. Similar to Title IX claims, however, the Age Discrimination Act applies only to programs or activities receiving federal funding. Since the Age Discrimination in Employment Act (ADEA) is a broader statute (albeit only in employment), the Age Discrimination Act is not used very often, but its protections should be noted.

♦ *Only where federal funding is received will the Age Discrimination Act apply.*

In February 1983, a man sued Yale University alleging that Yale had discriminated against him on the basis of both handicap and age. Yale had dismissed him as a student in the graduate English department in 1967 and denied him readmission in 1975 and 1981. The issue before a U.S. district court was whether Yale discriminated against the man in violation of the Rehabilitation Act of 1973 and the Age Discrimination Act of 1975 when it denied him readmission. The court observed that a July 1986 evidentiary hearing revealed that the Yale English department received no federal funding which would trigger the application of the Acts. **The fact that a few of the English department's professors participated in Yale's summer program, which was federally funded, did not trigger the application of the Acts** since the seminars did not involve Yale graduate students. The summer program office administered the federal grants relating to the English department professors. The man could not meet his threshold burden that the specific program which allegedly discriminated against him, in this case the English department, received federal financial assistance. The man was not protected by the Acts and therefore his case was dismissed. *Stephanidis v. Yale Univ.*, 652 F.Supp. 110 (D.Conn.1986).

♦ *An older student's claim of age discrimination failed where he could not show that he was qualified for entrance into a medical school's class.*

A 53-year-old psychologist applied to be a member of a first-year medical class at the Albert Einstein College of Medicine. The psychologist was called for an interview, and recommended for acceptance by the interviewer. However, the psychologist was not accepted. He alleged age discrimination in violation of New York Education Law and filed suit in a state court. The complaint alleged that faculty members indicated that the problem was not with the psychologist's qualifications, but with his age. The school contended that the psychologist's qualifications clearly precluded him, and that it had followed its established and published admittance regulations. The school was granted a dismissal and the psychologist appealed to the New York Supreme Court, Appellate Division. The issue in this case was whether the psychologist was otherwise qualified for admittance, ignoring his age. A court's review of a school's policies is limited to determining whether it acted in good faith or irrationally and arbitrarily. The school showed that the psychologist's grades, in both science classes and overall grade point average, were clearly unacceptable. It also alleged that his Medical College Aptitude Test score was lower than any student accepted. The psychologist pointed out that he was called for an interview and not summarily dismissed. He also noted his accomplishments in his current field, which included having hosted a weekly television show on mental health. The court ruled that **the psychologist was trying to create his own entrance standards, which the court had no power to allow.** The dismissal of claims was affirmed. *Brown v. Albert Einstein College of Medicine*, 568 N.Y.S.2d 61 (A.D.1st Dept.1991).

◆   *A student's Age Discrimination Act claim failed where he was unable to show that his age had anything to do with the denial of his readmission to medical school.*

A student at Thomas Jefferson University Medical School who was also a practicing attorney sued the school for age discrimination after he was denied readmission to the school. Asserting a claim under the Age Discrimination Act (among other claims), **the student averred that he was treated differently because he was older than his classmates.** He maintained that he was improperly failed in Family Medicine, that he was given less than average evaluations in Pediatrics, that his request for transfer of his Internal Medicine clerkship was denied, and that his application for readmission to the school was denied after his withdrawal. He further claimed that he had been fraudulently induced to sign an agreement withdrawing from the school and that he had signed the agreement under duress. He also contended that the school's attorney induced him to sign the agreement by stating that he had received a failing grade in his Family Medicine written examination when in fact the exam had not yet been graded. However, the student had drafted the agreement himself. It specified that if he were allowed to resign from the school in good standing, he would agree to withdraw an age discrimination complaint he had filed with the U.S. Department of Health and Human Services.

A Pennsylvania federal court noted that the student was an experienced attorney. **It rejected his age discrimination claim, noting that younger students had also failed courses under similar circumstances and had received evaluations based on the same criteria as were used to evaluate him.** Since he was the one who had drafted the agreement, and since the agreement had been drafted before the conversation with the school's attorney took place, the student could not show that the school's attorney fraudulently induced him to sign the agreement. The court further held that the school did not have to make extraordinary efforts to enable the student to practice law and study medicine at the same time. The court ruled for the school. *Petock v. Thomas Jefferson Univ.*, 630 F.Supp. 187 (E.D.Pa.1986).

CHAPTER THREE

Athletics and Student Activities

I. ATHLETIC PROGRAMS

College athletics are big business. As a result, lawsuits in this area have risen greatly in recent years. This section focuses on students' issues rather than coaching issues.

A. Eligibility of Participants

In *Vernonia School District 47J v. Acton,* 515 U.S. 646, 115 S.Ct. 2386, 132 L.Ed.2d 564 (1995), the U.S. Supreme Court noted that students have a lesser expectation of privacy than the general populace, and that student-athletes have an even lower expectation of privacy in the locker room. The Court upheld a random drug-testing program imposed by an Oregon public school district because the insignificant invasion of student privacy was outweighed by the school's interest in addressing drug use by students who risked physical harm while playing sports. Similarly, drug-testing programs applicable to private schools have been upheld under the notion that student-athletes have a lower expectation of privacy.

♦   *Student-athletes have a lower expectation of privacy than the general student population and the NCAA has an interest in protecting the health and safety of student-athletes involved in NCAA-regulated competition.*

In 1986, the National Collegiate Athletic Association (NCAA) instituted a drug-testing program for six categories of banned drugs including steroids and street drugs. Under the program, the drug tests took place at championship competitions. In order to participate, all students had to sign a consent form at the start of each school year allowing the drug tests. Two Stanford athletes instituted this action in a California trial court alleging that the drug-testing program violated their right to privacy. The trial court granted a preliminary injunction prohibiting the NCAA from enforcing its drug-testing program against Stanford or its students, except in the sports of football and men's basketball. After a full trial on the merits, the court permanently enjoined the NCAA from enforcing any aspect of its drug-testing program against Stanford or its students, including those involved in football and basketball. The NCAA appealed to the Court of Appeal of California, which affirmed the trial court decision.

The NCAA appealed to the Supreme Court of California. The supreme court reversed the decisions of the lower tribunals, noting that student-athletes had a lower expectation of privacy than the general student population. Observation of urination obviously implicated privacy interests. However, by its nature, participation in highly competitive post-season championship events involves close regulation and scrutiny of the physical fitness and bodily condition of student athletes. **Required physical examinations (including urinalysis) and the special regulation of sleep habits, diet, fitness and other activities that intrude significantly on privacy interests are routine aspects of a college athlete's life not shared by other students or the population at large.** Further, the court noted that drug-testing programs involving student-athletes have routinely survived Fourth Amendment privacy challenges. The court concluded that the NCAA had an interest in protecting the health and safety of student-athletes involved in NCAA-regulated competition. *Hill v. NCAA*, 26 Cal.Rptr.2d 834 (Cal.1994).

♦   *A drug-testing program was struck down where it was not voluntary, and where the college athletes did not have a diminished expectation of privacy.*

The University of Colorado conducted a drug-testing program for intercollegiate athletes that entailed a urine test at each annual physical with random tests thereafter. A program amendment substituted random rapid eye examinations for urinalysis, and the university prohibited any athlete refusing to consent to the testing from participating in intercollegiate athletics. The program called for progressive sanctions ranging from required participation in rehabilitation programs to permanent suspension from athletics. A group of athletes filed a class-action suit against the university in a Colorado trial court seeking declaratory and injunctive relief. The court ruled for the athletes. The Colorado Court of Appeals affirmed this decision, and the university appealed to the Supreme Court of Colorado. The supreme court observed that the program did not ensure confidentiality and was mandatory inasmuch as refusal to participate disqualified students from participating in university athletic programs. **The university was unable to articulate an important governmental interest for the program. Unlike cases involving high school athletes, college students did not have a diminished expectation of privacy under the Fourth Amendment that justified government searches in the absence of an important governmental interest.**

Random, suspicionless urinalysis was unconstitutional. University student athletes did not consent to participation in the program because there could be no
voluntary consent where the failure to consent resulted in denial of a governmental
benefit. The court affirmed the lower courts' decisions for the athletes. *Univ. of
Colorado v. Derdeyn*, 863 P.2d 929 (Colo.1993).

◆   *The Supreme Court held that the NCAA is not a state actor in the
following case.*

Following a lengthy investigation of allegedly improper recruiting practices
by the University of Nevada, Las Vegas (UNLV), the NCAA found 38 violations,
including 10 by the school's head basketball coach. The NCAA proposed a
number of sanctions and threatened to impose more if the coach was not
suspended. Facing an enormous pay cut, the coach sued the NCAA under 42
U.S.C. § 1983 for violating his due process rights. The Nevada Supreme Court
held that the NCAA's conduct constituted state action for constitutional purposes.
It upheld a Nevada trial court's dismissal of the suspension and award of
attorney's fees. The NCAA appealed to **the U.S. Supreme Court, which held
that the NCAA's participation in the events that led to the suspension did
not constitute state action within the meaning of § 1983. The NCAA was not
a state actor** on the theory that it misused the power it possessed under state law.
UNLV's decision to suspend the coach in compliance with the NCAA's rules and
recommendations did not turn the NCAA's conduct into state action. This was
because UNLV retained the power to withdraw from the NCAA and establish its
own standards. The NCAA could not directly discipline the coach, but could
threaten to impose additional sanctions against the school. It was the school's
decision and not the NCAA's to suspend the coach. *NCAA v. Tarkanian*, 488 U.S.
179, 109 S.Ct. 454, 102 L.Ed.2d 469 (1988).

◆   *A wrestler who transferred from the University of Nebraska to Brown
University had to sit out for one year because he was not in good academic
standing.*

A student at Brown University spent his first two semesters of college at the
University of Nebraska. The student, a talented wrestler, failed a course during his
first semester at Nebraska and did not repeat the course. The NCAA notified him
that he would be prohibited from wrestling during the following academic year
because he had not successfully repeated the course. The student sued in federal
court seeking an injunction to restrain the NCAA from preventing him from
wrestling. The federal district court denied the injunction since the student was not
likely to succeed on the merits of his case. **NCAA regulations prevent athletic
participation for one year after transfer. There is an exception to the one-
year abstinence rule for students in good academic standing who would have
been eligible to participate had they remained at their previous institution.**
Since he had failed the course, he would have been ineligible at Nebraska, so he
was ineligible at Brown. In addition, the student could not bring constitutional
claims since the NCAA is a private actor, not a state agent. *Collier v. NCAA*, 783
F.Supp. 1576 (D.R.I.1992).

♦   *The Massachusetts Civil Rights Act did not apply to prohibit a university's drug-testing policy which required varsity student-athletes to sign a drug-testing consent form.*

A private Massachusetts university required its varsity athletes to sign an NCAA student-athlete statement which included a drug-testing consent form. The university also required its athletes to sign a university drug-testing consent form as a condition for participating in varsity athletics. The university's program required student-athletes to be tested once each year for specific drugs and also authorized random testing throughout the year. Testing was required for all athletes before NCAA post-season competition. In practice, the university only tested its athletes prior to post-season competition. Students had the right to appeal to the university's review board at any time. A student who had participated in the university's track and field and cross-country teams signed the consent forms. Later he revoked them by letter and refused to sign either the university or NCAA drug-testing consent forms. The university declared the student ineligible for varsity sports. The student was otherwise eligible to participate. Claiming that the university's program violated the Massachusetts Civil Rights Act, the student sued the university in a Massachusetts trial court. The court ruled in favor of the student and the university appealed to the Massachusetts Supreme Judicial Court.

The supreme judicial court ruled that in order to prove a case under the state civil rights act, the complaining party must prove that a right guaranteed by the Constitution or laws of the U.S. or Massachusetts had been interfered with by threats, intimidation or coercion. The civil rights act was intended to provide a remedy for victims of racial harassment. According to the court, the state legislature did not intend to create a vast constitutional tort. **The act's application was limited to situations in which actual threats, intimidation or coercion were present.** The student had not proven that these conditions were present in the university's program. The court reversed the trial court's decision in favor of the student. *Bally v. Northeastern Univ.*, 532 N.E.2d 49 (Mass.1989).

B. Students with Disabilities

♦   *The performance of a specific activity, such as playing basketball, did not constitute a major life activity and the student was not a qualified individual entitled to protection under § 504 of the Rehabilitation Act.*

A high school student suffered sudden cardiac death while playing basketball. He was resuscitated and a defibrillator was implanted in his body to restart his heart in case it stopped again. He had been recruited to play basketball by an Illinois university which stated that it would honor his scholarship despite his medical condition. He was later found medically ineligible to play and although he maintained his scholarship and his place on the team, he could not compete or practice. He filed suit against the university in federal district court, alleging a violation of § 504 of the Rehabilitation Act and requesting an injunction allowing him to play. The court found that playing basketball was a major life activity for the student and by not allowing him to play, the university violated § 504. The court granted the injunction. The university appealed to the U.S. Court of Appeals, Seventh Circuit.

The court of appeals found that **participating in intercollegiate athletics is not a major life activity.** In the regulations interpreting § 504, a major life activity is defined as a basic life function such as caring for one's self, walking, breathing or speaking. The court held that performing a specific activity, such as playing basketball, does not fit in with this list. It also held that the student's impairment did not prevent him from obtaining an adequate education and therefore did not limit his major life activity of learning. The court then found that as a matter of law, **the student was not a qualified individual.** To be qualified to play college basketball, the student had to meet all of the university's technical and physical requirements. The court found that her the student's risk of potential injury was too great. Although some level of risk is inherent in all athletic activities, the student in this case faced the possibility of death. Because the university rationally and reasonably reviewed all of the medical evidence before making its decision, the court held that it had the right to find the student ineligible to play. The court reversed the district court's decision and denied the injunction. *Knapp v. Northwestern Univ.*, 101 F.3d 473 (7th Cir.1996).

♦   *A college football player with a disability could be prohibited from continuing to play without violating the Rehabilitation Act.*

A University of Kansas student who was on a football scholarship experienced an episode of transient quadriplegia during a scrimmage. The team physician discovered that the student had a congenital condition that put him at an extremely high risk for suffering severe and potentially permanent neurological injuries, including quadriplegia. **The university disqualified the student from participating in intercollegiate football.** Although he obtained opinions from three other doctors stating that his risk of injury was no greater than any other player's, the university denied his request to rejoin the football team. He filed a lawsuit against the university in the U.S. District Court for the District of Kansas, claiming that it had violated § 504 of the Rehabilitation Act of 1973. Section 504 prohibits discrimination by recipients of federal funding against individuals on the basis of disability, if the individual is otherwise qualified to participate in the recipient's programs or activities. The court denied the university's motion to dismiss the lawsuit, and the student filed a motion for a preliminary order to allow his reinstatement to the football team.

Because § 504's definition of a person with a disability involves a consideration of whether the individual is impaired in some major life activity, the court considered whether intercollegiate athletic participation was a major life activity. The university argued that it was not, because the general population cannot participate in college athletics. The student argued that his grades improved and he gained many other opportunities for personal development by playing on the team. **The court agreed that playing football was related to the major life activity of learning, but held that his disqualification was not a substantial limitation on his continuing ability to learn.** The university had not revoked the student's athletic scholarship and he retained the opportunity to participate in the football program in a role other than player. The court accepted the conclusion of the university's physicians that there was a reasonable basis for his exclusion from the team that did not violate § 504. The court denied the student's motion. *Pahulu v. Univ. of Kansas*, 897 F.Supp. 1387 (D.Kan.1995).

+   *A student with a learning disability who was labeled a nonqualifier by the NCAA could sue for disability discrimination.*

A New Jersey high school student was heavily recruited by several Division I colleges and universities to play football at the collegiate level. Because of a learning disability, the student received special education and related services while in high school. In 1995, the student paid an $18 fee to ACT (a nonprofit corporation which contracted with the NCAA to establish the NCAA Clearinghouse and enforce the initial eligibility requirements set forth by the NCAA) to evaluate his initial eligibility application.

The NCAA Clearinghouse determines initial eligibility by looking at grades in 13 core courses, SAT scores, and, for special education students, it looks at whether the student is expected to acquire the same knowledge, quantitatively and qualitatively, as students in other core courses. There are three possible initial eligibility statuses: "qualifier," "partial qualifier" and "nonqualifier." Depending on status, a student may not be able to practice or play with the team, and may not even be eligible for an academic scholarship. In 1996, **the Clearinghouse notified the student of its final determination that he was a nonqualifier despite receiving information from the student's principal that he was expected to acquire the same knowledge as students in other core courses.** The Clearinghouse only gave the student credit for three core courses.

The student filed suit against the NCAA, ACT, the Clearinghouse and several colleges, asserting breach of contract and claims under the Americans with Disabilities Act and the Rehabilitation Act, among other claims. The defendants sought to dismiss the actions against them, and the U.S. District Court for the District of New Jersey granted the motions in part. However, it held that the defendants might have discriminated against the student because of disability, and that they might have breached a contract with him. These issues would have to be decided at trial. *Bowers v. NCAA*, 9 F.Supp.2d 460 (D.N.J.1998).

C. Academic Restrictions

Some associations, such as the National Collegiate Athletic Association, impose academic requirements on student-athletes. The academic requirements may include specific course requirements or designated grade point averages.

+   *Where a student's scholarship was withdrawn after a university learned that she was a nonqualifier, she could not sue the university because of the Eleventh Amendment.*

A student was offered an NCAA-approved track scholarship at Kansas State University that covered tuition, fees, room, board and books. However, after she enrolled, the university withdrew the scholarship. It learned that **the NCAA Initial-Eligibility Clearinghouse had failed to certify the student because she was a "nonqualifier," having failed two high school classes.** The Clearinghouse report was not produced until after the student had enrolled. When the college sought to recover tuition and other expenses for the fall semester, the student and her father sued it for breach of contract and fraud. They also sued several university officials, including the track coach. A New York federal court held that the university was immune to suit under the Eleventh Amendment (which prohibits a suit by a private party against a state in federal court). Since the university had not consented to be sued, the student and her father could not maintain their action against it. Further, the officials had been acting in their official capacities; thus, they were also entitled to Eleventh Amendment immunity. *Adams v. Kansas State Univ.*, 27 F.Supp.2d 469 (S.D.N.Y.1998).

♦   *An Illinois appellate court found that a student's religious courses and computer classes did not constitute "core courses" under the NCAA academic eligibility requirements.*

The NCAA sets eligibility requirements for Division I competition which mandate that students take at least 13 high school "core courses," and that students achieve a specified minimum grade point average in those courses, as well as a specified minimum score on either the SAT or ACT. The higher a student's test score, the lower the required GPA needed. An 18-year-old black student who excelled at basketball graduated from a private Catholic high school and enrolled in a private university. He had been heavily recruited by a number of colleges and universities before his decision to enroll at the private university. The NCAA made a determination that the student was not qualified to compete in Division I play during his freshman season, and the student sued the NCAA in an Illinois federal district court seeking a preliminary injunction to allow him to play during his freshman year.

The student asserted that the NCAA had improperly found him to be ineligible by, among other things, excluding from the "core course" requirements two religion and two computer classes. The court examined the religion courses and determined that **they were taught from a particular religious point of view—based on a Christian ideology.** The court also determined that, based on the syllabi **for the computer classes, at least 50 percent of the course instruction included keyboarding or word processing,** which took the classes outside core status. As a result, the student did not have even a negligible chance of success on the merits of his claim, and he was not entitled to injunctive relief. Further, the student's claims of breach of contract and misrepresentation likewise had a very slim chance of success. The court refused to overrule the NCAA's eligibility determination, and the student was not allowed to play basketball during his freshman season. *Hall v. NCAA*, 985 F.Supp. 782 (N.D.Ill.1997).

♦   *Although the NCAA denied a student academic eligibility waiver arbitrarily, bad faith required a finding of a dishonest purpose.*

A high school senior intended to attend a private university under a basketball scholarship. However, the National Collegiate Athletic Association (NCAA) determined that the student failed to complete the minimum of 13 "core courses" required under the NCAA's eligibility standards. It notified the student that he was ineligible under NCAA guidelines to play college basketball for or receive financial aid from the university. The university sought a waiver of the eligibility requirements, which the NCAA denied on the ground that there were neither exceptional circumstances present nor independent evidence of the student's academic qualifications that warranted granting relief. The student sought a preliminary injunction from the U.S. District Court for the District of Connecticut to prevent the NCAA from further interfering with his opportunity to attend the university and play basketball for its team. The district court granted the motion for an injunction, reasoning that the student would suffer irreparable harm if the injunction were denied, and that he was likely to prevail on his argument that the NCAA breached its duty to the student by arbitrarily refusing to grant him a waiver of its eligibility requirements. The NCAA appealed to the U.S. Court of Appeals, Second Circuit.

The court of appeals first determined that the injunction in this case was prohibitory in nature rather than mandatory. Accordingly, its terms would preserve the status quo by restraining the NCAA from acting to interfere with the university's decision to award the student a scholarship and to allow him to play basketball. As a result, the student and the university did not have to meet a heightened standard to obtain injunctive relief. However, the court then held that the district court had erred in finding that the NCAA had exhibited bad faith simply by acting arbitrarily. Under Connecticut law, bad faith means more than mere negligence; it involves a dishonest purpose. Here, **despite determining that the NCAA had arbitrarily refused to grant the student a waiver because it had granted waivers in similar cases in the past, the court failed to make a factual finding of bad intent.** The court of appeals remanded the case and left the injunction intact. However, it conditioned the maintenance of the injunction upon commencement of a trial on the merits within four months. *Phillip v. Fairfield Univ.*, 118 F.3d 131 (2d Cir.1997).

D. Eligibility of Schools

♦   *The Fifth Circuit found that the NCAA's suspension of all athletic programs at a private university did not violate any property interests.*

An alumnus of Southern Methodist University (SMU) filed a class-action suit against the National Collegiate Athletic Association (NCAA) in a federal district court on behalf of SMU. The lawsuit was brought in response to the NCAA's suspension of all 1987 SMU athletic programs. The lawsuit was also brought on behalf of other SMU graduates and current SMU students, football team members and cheerleaders. The complaint alleged that the NCAA had violated federal antitrust laws by restricting compensation to college football players. This allegedly violated price-fixing restraints under the Sherman Anti-Trust Act. The SMU suspension allegedly constituted a "group boycott" by NCAA members. The complaint also contained civil rights claims which alleged that the suspension destroyed the careers of SMU football players and caused the cheerleaders emotional distress. The NCAA allegedly imposed these penalties on SMU repeatedly in a manner which violated due process of law. The lawsuit requested an order preventing the suspension as well as the payment of monetary damages in excess of $200 million.

The federal district court dismissed the lawsuit. The alumnus appealed to the U.S. Court of Appeals, Fifth Circuit, which noted that SMU had failed to represent itself in the lawsuit. The alumnus could not properly bring a suit on SMU's behalf and the complaint failed to state any legal grounds. **No property interests were violated by the NCAA suspension and the damages were insufficient to support an antitrust lawsuit.** According to the court, **NCAA eligibility rules were reasonable and did not constitute price-fixing.** They were an appropriate means to integrate athletics with academics. Enforcement of the rules did not constitute an illegal group boycott. The district court had properly dismissed the civil rights claims. State participation in a private entity such as the NCAA does not make the entity a state actor unless the entity enforces state laws. Because no state action existed in the enforcement of NCAA rules, there was no basis for the federal civil rights complaint. *McCormack v. NCAA*, 845 F.2d 1338 (5th Cir. 1988).

◆ *Although a private university was prevented from participating in the championship playoffs, the court refused to grant an injunction to allow its participation since the other schools would have suffered harm if displaced by the university.*

Howard University's football team compiled a regular season record of nine wins and one loss in 1987. This was one of the best records for all National Collegiate Athletic Association (NCAA) Division I-AA schools and Howard won the championship of its conference, the Mid-Eastern Athletic Conference (MEAC). All of the MEAC schools including Howard are known as traditionally black institutions. Despite its fine season, Howard was excluded from the Division I-AA championship. Howard brought an antitrust action in federal district court, seeking to prevent the NCAA from holding its championship playoffs until a decision by the district court was issued. The district court noted that in order to obtain the injunction sought, Howard would have to show that it was likely to prevail in its case, that it would be irreparably harmed without the injunction, that other parties would not suffer substantial harm and that the public interest would be served. While noting that Howard's low ranking by the committee ran contrary to logic, the possibility that Howard would suffer irreparable harm was balanced by the potential that any of the other 16 teams already in the playoffs would suffer equal harm if displaced by Howard. Because **the playoff games were already set and scheduled with television arrangements**, the district court was unwilling to delay the playoff schedule. **Any delay of the playoff games would be disruptive and cause severe hardships to the teams already selected.** Howard's interest was outweighed by that of the general public, and the games would commence as scheduled. *Howard Univ. v. NCAA*, 675 F.Supp. 652 (D.D.C. 1987).

E. Discrimination

Title IX (20 U.S.C. § 1681 et seq.) addresses sex discrimination in school athletics. It applies only to athletic programs that receive federal financial assistance. One of the most important Title IX implementing regulations provides as follows:

A recipient which operates or sponsors interscholastic, intercollegiate, club or intramural athletics shall provide equal athletic opportunity for members of both sexes. In determining whether equal opportunities are available the Director will consider, among other factors:

(1) Whether the selection of sports and levels of competition effectively accommodate the interests and abilities of members of both sexes;

(2) The provision of equipment and supplies;

(3) Scheduling of games and practice time;

(4) Travel and per diem allowance;

(5) Opportunity to receive coaching and academic tutoring;

(6) Assignment and compensation of coaches and tutors;

(7) Provision of locker rooms, practice and competitive facilities;

(8) Provision of medical and training facilities and services;

(9) Provision of housing and dining facilities and services;

(10) Publicity.

Unequal aggregate expenditures for members of each sex or unequal expenditures for male and female teams if a recipient operates or sponsors separate teams will not constitute noncompliance with this section, but the Assistant Secretary may consider the failure to provide necessary funds for teams for one sex in assessing equality of opportunity for members of each sex. [34 CFR § 106.41(c).]

◆   *The U.S. Supreme Court has held that the NCAA is not a recipient of federal funds and is therefore not subject to suit under Title IX of the Education Amendments of 1972.*

The case was filed by a college graduate who had played two years of intercollegiate volleyball at a private college before enrolling in postgraduate programs at two other colleges. Because she had exhausted only two years of her eligibility, she sought a waiver from the NCAA's Postbaccalaureate Bylaw, which allows postgraduate student-athletes to compete in intercollegiate sports only at the institution where they received an undergraduate degree. The student sued the NCAA in a Pennsylvania federal court after it denied her requests for a waiver. She claimed that the NCAA discriminated against her on the basis of gender in violation of Title IX, which prohibits sex-based discrimination by any education program or activity that receives federal funding. The complaint asserted that the NCAA granted more waivers to male postgraduate students than it did to females.

The case reached the U.S. Supreme Court, which noted that Title IX covers entities that receive federal financial assistance—whether direct or indirect—whereas those entities that only benefit economically from federal financial assistance are not covered. **Because the NCAA only benefited economically from institutions that received federal financial assistance, it could not be sued under Title IX.** *NCAA v. Smith*, 525 U.S. 459, 119 S.Ct. 924, 142 L.Ed.2d 929 (1999).

◆   *The Fifth Circuit held that discrimination under Title IX was intentional even where it was motivated by chauvinistic notions rather than by enmity.*

A number of female undergraduate students at Louisiana State University brought separate lawsuits under Title IX, alleging that the university discriminated against women in the provision of facilities and teams for intercollegiate athletic competition. A federal district court held that LSU had violated and continued to violate Title IX, but determined that it had not intentionally violated the statute. As a result, the female students were not entitled to monetary damages. On appeal, the Fifth Circuit Court of Appeals determined that LSU had intentionally violated Title IX. The court stated that paternalism and stereotypical assumptions about female students' abilities and interests led to the decision not to provide equal facilities and teams for female students. **It did not matter that LSU had no intention to discriminate against women. What mattered was that it intended to treat women differently. By holding onto archaic assumptions about women in sports, LSU perpetuated a grossly discriminatory athletics system.** The court reversed the district court's decision, finding that LSU intentionally discriminated against female students in violation of Title IX. *Pederson v. Louisiana State Univ.*, 2000 U.S. App. LEXIS 990 (5th Cir.2000).

◆   *Where a university allowed a woman to try out for the football team, it could not later discriminate against her in violation of Title IX by dropping her from the team because of her sex.*

The student sued the university, alleging discrimination in violation of Title IX when the football coach refused to allow her to participate in summer camps, games, and practices, and made offensive comments to her regarding her attempts to participate in the football program. After being dropped from the team, the student sued in a North Carolina federal court. The district court dismissed the Title IX portion of the complaint, and the student appealed to the Fourth Circuit Court of Appeals, which reinstated the Title IX claims. The court concluded that once the student was allowed to try out for football, the university could not discriminate against her based on her sex. **Although Title IX regulations made a distinction between contact and non-contact sports operated for members of one sex, the court concluded that this distinction vanished once a member of the opposite sex was allowed to try out for a single-sex contact sport team.** Since the student was a member of the university's male football team at one point, her allegations of discrimination under Title IX stated a cause of action. The district court decision was reversed and remanded. *Mercer v. Duke University,* 190 F.3d 643 (4th Cir.1999).

◆   *The Ninth Circuit held that a university could reduce athletic opportunities for male students in order to come into compliance with Title IX.*

A California university with a high percentage of female students, but low participation rates in female interscholastic athletics, could reduce the size of male athletic teams without violating Title IX, according to the U.S. Court of Appeals, Ninth Circuit. Female students constituted 64 percent of the university's student population, but only 39 percent of athletic team rosters. Female teams received only 32 percent of available athletic scholarship money, prompting a lawsuit by the National Organization of Women. The matter was settled under a consent decree mandating target percentages for female athletic participation. The decree was patterned after the first part of the Title IX compliance test published by the U.S. Department of Education Office for Civil Rights.

The university attempted to comply with the decree by reducing the size of male athletic teams. After the men's wrestling team roster was capped at 25, team members filed a federal district court lawsuit alleging gender discrimination in violation of Title IX and the Equal Protection Clause. The case reached the Ninth Circuit Court of Appeals, which noted that Congress enacted Title IX with the understanding that male athletes had an enormous head start over female athletes for athletic resources. **The intent of the act was to level the playing field and** encourage female athletic participation. **Title IX permits universities to reduce athletic opportunities for male athletes in order to bring participation into line with lower opportunities available for females.** The court reversed the judgment and vacated the preliminary injunction for the team members. *Neal v. Bd. of Trustees of California State Universities*, No. 99-15316, 1999 WL 1144948 (9th Cir.1999).

◆   *Like the court in the case above, the Seventh Circuit held that eliminating athletic opportunities for men was not a violation of Title IX.*

The U.S. Court of Appeals, Seventh Circuit, held that Illinois State University could respond to disproportionate athletic participation rates and budget concerns by dropping men's wrestling and soccer programs, adjusting men's team rosters, adding a women's soccer program and adjusting grants in aid for both sexes. Male enrollment at Illinois State was only 45 percent, but the athletic participation rate for male students was 66 percent. A university gender equity commission concluded that the disparity was inequitable to females and the university considered 10 options to achieve Title IX compliance. The university decided to focus on the goal of substantial proportionality in athletic participation as a means of complying with Title IX policy interpretations published by the Office for Civil Rights. After the university decided to make these adjustments, the female athletic participation rate rose to almost 52 percent, while the male rate slipped to 48.

Former members of the men's soccer and wrestling teams sued university regents in a federal district court, asserting that elimination of their programs under the gender equity plan had been based on their sex and therefore violated Title IX. They also asserted constitutional rights violations. The court awarded summary judgment to the university on the Title IX claim, and found that the constitutional claims were preempted by the availability of a cause of action under Title IX. The male student-athletes appealed to the Seventh Circuit, which **rejected their argument that the university could not eliminate male programs when the decision was motivated by sex-based considerations.** The Office for Civil Rights policy interpretations were entitled to deference, and clearly stated that Title IX compliance may be shown where there is proof that female athletic participation is substantially proportionate to female enrollment. **After the male programs had been eliminated, male athletic participation remained within three percentage points of male enrollment.** This interpretation of Title IX did not violate the Equal Protection Clause. The court affirmed the district court decision for the university regents. *Boulahanis v. Bd. of Regents, Illinois State Univ.*, No. 99-1561, 1999 U.S. App. LEXIS 31969 (7th Cir.1999).

◆   *A university was allowed to spend more money on scholarships for female student-athletes, even though male athletes represented the majority of athletes at the university, in order to meet its requirements under Title IX regulations.*

A strategic planning commission for an Iowa private university recommended that the school terminate its wrestling program based on budgetary constraints. The director of athletics was not informed of this decision and told newly recruited wrestlers about the school's "total commitment" to the program, although he never promised that it would be retained indefinitely. The undergraduate student body during the 1992-1993 school year was 57.2 percent female and 42.8 percent male but 75.3 percent of the athletes were men. The school spent 47 percent of its total athletic scholarship budget on male athletes and spent 53 percent of its budget on females. The wrestlers brought suit, and their motion for a preliminary injunction was denied by the U.S. District Court for the Southern District of Iowa. The court then addressed the merits of the wrestlers' Title IX and constitutional claims.

The court noted that one Title IX regulation, 34 C.F.R. § 106.37(c)(1), required universities to award scholarships "in proportion to the number of students of each sex participating in ... athletics." However, another regulation, 34 C.F.R. § 106.41(c)(1), required universities to provide "equal athletic opportunity for members of both sexes." The wrestlers argued that compliance with § 106.37 did not preclude liability under § 106.41. The court disagreed, ruling that such a holding would arguably lock scholarships in at the current participation ratio and possibly perpetuate the under-representation of women in university athletics. It also held that **restricting universities from eliminating men's scholarship sports under § 106.37 while requiring them to expand athletics under § 106.41 would improperly restrain their spending decisions.** Because § 106.37 served the remedial purposes of Title IX more effectively than § 106.41, the court granted summary judgment to the university on this claim. The court also dismissed the federal Equal Protection Clause challenge to Title IX as applied to the wrestlers, ruling that mere disadvantage to males did not support such a constitutional challenge. Moreover, since no state action was involved, the court dismissed the wrestlers' constitutional claim against the university based on 42 U.S.C. § 1983. *Gonyo v. Drake Univ.*, 879 F.Supp. 1000 (S.D.Iowa 1995).

♦   *Liability under Title IX requires a showing of under-representation, ineffective accommodations and a lack of responsiveness to the under-represented.*

A Rhode Island private university reduced the women's gymnastics and volleyball teams to intercollegiate club status. They not only lost university funding, but they also lost admissions preferences, a recruiting budget and the coaches' salaries. They were permitted to participate in intercollegiate competition provided that they raised all their own operating funds from private sources. The female athletes filed a class action lawsuit in a U.S. district court alleging violations of Title IX of the Education Amendments of 1972. At the time of the lawsuit, the university had 63 percent male athletes and 37 percent female athletes. The university population itself was comprised of 52 percent male students and 48 percent female students. Since the 1970s, the female undergraduate enrollment had hovered around 48 percent to 49 percent while the athletic program had been approximately 37 percent female. Additionally, only two women's teams had been added since 1977. The district court granted the female athletes' motion for a preliminary injunction, reinstating the women's gymnastics and volleyball teams to full varsity status. A federal court of appeals affirmed the district court's ruling and remanded the case for a trial on the merits.

The district court applied the final policy interpretation implemented by the U.S. Department of Education pursuant to Title IX, ruling that **the university's athletic program did not comply with gender equity guidelines.** First, the court noted that the gender balance of the university's program was far from substantially proportionate to its student environment. The college maintained a

13 percent disparity between female participation in intercollegiate athletics and female student enrollment. Second, although the university had an impressive history of program expansion, it had added only two women's sports since 1977. This was not a continuing practice of program expansion as required by the policy interpretation. Finally, the court held that the university's demotion of two women's sports to "donor-funded" varsity status precluded a finding that the university "effectively accommodated the interest and ability of the underrepresented sex to the extent necessary to provide equal [athletic] opportunity." The court noted that the spirit and meaning of Title IX would be circumvented if a university could fully and effectively accommodate the underrepresented sex by creating a second-class varsity status. Moreover, because far more male athletes than female athletes were university funded, the program violated the "treatment" aspect of the regulation. Consequently, the court ordered the university to balance its program to provide equal opportunities for both sexes but left the means of such Title IX compliance to the discretion of the university. *Cohen v. Brown Univ.*, 879 F.Supp. 185 (D.R.I.1995).

The district court later held that the subsequently proposed plan failed to comply with Title IX. In an attempt to avoid protracted litigation and to expedite the appeal on the issue of liability, the district court then ordered specific relief in place of the compliance plan. The university appealed both the district court's finding for the plaintiffs and its order of specific relief to the U.S. Court of Appeals, First Circuit. The university argued that the district court should not have given controlling weight to the regulations and policy interpretations of the statute, but the court of appeals disagreed. **The guidelines were consistent with the statute and required showings of under-representation, ineffective accommodations and a lack of responsiveness to the under-represented gender before liability could be imposed.** The court also rejected the university's argument that the disparity in athletic opportunities for women was not a result of discrimination, but the result of a lack of interest on the part of its female students. Finally, the court found that the district court erred by substituting the order of specific relief in place of the university's compliance plan. Although the court agreed that the plan was ineffective and did not meet the requirements of Title IX, it also noted that, in accordance with academic freedom, places of higher education must be given as much freedom as possible in conducting their own affairs. The university was given another opportunity to submit a plan in compliance with Title IX, and the case was affirmed in part, reversed in part and remanded for further proceedings. *Cohen v. Brown Univ.*, 101 F.3d 155 (1st Cir.1996).

♦   *Although a private cause of action to redress violations of Title IX exists, Title IX cannot be applied to individuals such as school administrators and employees.*

The women's basketball coach at a private Texas university complained about the disparate allocation of resources among the men's and women's athletic programs. Specifically, she noted inequities between the terms of her employment contract and those of the men's basketball coach. She was discharged three years later, allegedly for violations of National Collegiate Athletic Association (NCAA) and Southwest Conference rules. She filed a complaint with the U.S. Department of Education's Office of Civil Rights and was reinstated on the same terms under which she had been previously employed. Because she failed to achieve a winning record as required by the contract, her employment was again terminated. The coach filed a Title IX lawsuit against the university and various officials in a U.S. district court, alleging gender discrimination in its allocation of funds to university athletic programs. The university and officials moved to dismiss the suit. The coach contended that **an employee of a private school which receives federal funds has a private cause of action against that school for damages under Title IX.** The court agreed, noting that the U.S. Supreme Court has created such an implied cause of action with respect to monetary damages for students who are sexually harassed in public schools. It has also held that those directly benefiting from federal grants, loans or contracts clearly fall within Title IX. Although the court found that there is a private cause of action to redress violations of Title IX, **Title IX could not be applied to individuals,** and the lawsuit against the school administrators and employees was dismissed. The lawsuit against the university was allowed to continue. *Bowers v. Baylor Univ.*, 862 F.Supp. 142 (W.D.Tex.1994).

◆   *A university could eliminate a men's sports program without eliminating a women's program in order to comply with Title IX.*

The **University of Illinois eliminated four varsity athletic programs, including men's swimming, in response to a $600,000 budget shortfall.** The decision was in part motivated by the need to comply with Title IX, which prohibits discrimination on the basis of sex by recipients of federal financial assistance. Participation in women's intercollegiate athletics at the university was disproportionate to female undergraduate enrollment; therefore, **the university did not eliminate the women's swimming program.** Members of the men's swim team sued the university and its board of trustees in the U.S. District Court for the Central District of Illinois, alleging violations of Title IX and their equal protection rights. The court granted pretrial judgment to the university and board, and the complaining parties appealed to the U.S. Court of Appeals, Seventh Circuit. The court of appeals observed that **elimination of the women's swimming program could have exposed the university to further Title IX violations because of the great disparity between female enrollment and women's sports participation.** The university's response to budget constraints had been reasonable and Title IX did not require parallel teams to ensure compliance. The university action also did not violate any equal protection rights because it furthered the important governmental objective of removing sex discrimination. *Kelley v. Bd. of Trustees, Univ. of Illinois*, 35 F.3d 265 (7th Cir.1994).

◆   *A university violated Title IX by eliminating the women's softball program.*

A Colorado university terminated its women's varsity softball team. Former members of the team then sued the university, seeking reinstatement of the team and money damages. They asserted that the university had violated Title IX. Alternatively, they claimed that the termination was the perpetuation of an already existing violation of Title IX by the university. Title IX requires recipients of federal financial assistance who operate or sponsor interscholastic, intercollegiate, club or intramural athletics to provide equal athletic opportunity for members of both sexes. In determining whether equal opportunities are available, one of the considerations is whether the selection of sports and the levels of competition effectively accommodate the interests and abilities of members of both sexes. The U.S. District Court for the District of Colorado ruled that **the decision to terminate the women's softball team violated Title IX.** In the last 12 years, women's participation opportunities declined by approximately 34 percent while men's participation opportunities declined by only 20 percent. Finally, the court noted that **the university had not demonstrated that the interests and abilities of women were being fully and effectively accommodated by the university's present athletic program. It had eliminated varsity athletic opportunities for women in a sport where there was significant interest and talent.** The court issued a permanent injunction against the university requiring it to reinstate the women's softball team. *Roberts v. Colorado State Univ.*, 814 F.Supp. 1507 (D.Colo.1993).

◆   *A university violated Title IX by eliminating women's gymnastics and field hockey, and it could not come into compliance by substituting women's soccer for gymnastics.*

A Pennsylvania university with an undergraduate population that was 56 percent female fielded an equal number of male and female varsity athletic teams. However, male teams had more athletes and were better funded. The university cut men's tennis and soccer and women's gymnastics and field hockey teams because of budget problems. Three female athletes sued the university in the U.S. District Court for the Western District of Pennsylvania under Title IX of the 1972 Education Amendments, seeking an order to force the university to reduce the disparity between men's and women's varsity athletics, and to reinstate women's gymnastics and field hockey. The court granted a preliminary injunction and certified a class. **It then held that the university was not in compliance with Title IX regulations and ordered reinstatement of the gymnastics and field hockey programs. The university filed a motion to modify the injunction to allow replacement of the gymnastics team with a women's soccer team. The court refused to modify the injunction** and the university appealed to the U.S. Court of Appeals, Third Circuit. The court observed that modification of an injunction is appropriate only when there has been a change of circumstances making the original order inequitable. There was no such change in circumstances in this case. The district court had not abused its discretion in ordering the temporary preservation of athletic programs. The university's proposal for a women's soccer program as a replacement for the women's gymnastic team would result in a net reduction in funding for women's athletics that was in contravention of Title IX goals. *Favia v. Indiana Univ. of Pennsylvania*, 7 F.3d 332 (3d Cir.1993).

◆   *In spite of the financial hardship, a federal district court determined that limited university resources had to be reallocated more equitably between men's and women's athletic programs requiring "equal opportunity" but not necessarily "equal funding."*

A private New York university had a competitive men's varsity ice hockey team. Hockey was an "emphasized sport" and received special support. The team was a strong member of the Eastern Collegiate Athletic Conference (ECAC) and had recently challenged for the Division I NCAA title. Conversely, women's ice hockey was run as an informal club team. The women's requests for varsity status were repeatedly denied by the university's Committee on Athletics. Members of the women's hockey team filed suit against the university in a U.S. district court alleging that the university's denial of varsity status violated Title IX. The court stated that under Title IX the interests and abilities of both sexes must be accommodated. In order to determine whether discrimination had occurred, the court utilized the Title VII burden-shifting analysis of *McDonnell Douglas Corp. v. Green,* 411 U.S. 792, 93 S.Ct. 1817, 36 L.Ed.2d 668 (1973). To prove a *prima facie* case of discrimination, the women had to establish that the university was subject to Title IX and that the women were entitled to its protection. Also, the women had to prove that they had not been given "equal athletic opportunities." Next, the university had to offer legitimate nondiscriminatory reasons for refusing to grant the women varsity status. Finally, if there were reasons, the women would have to show them to be pretextual.

The court noted that both parties agreed that the women were entitled to the protection of Title IX. Further, the women had provided ample evidence indicating unequal treatment. Foremost was the extreme disparity in the university's allocation of funds between the men and women. The men's funding was 50 times that of the women. As a result, the women had inferior equipment, facilities, travel accommodations, and coaching. The court then addressed the university's alleged nondiscriminatory reasons for the unequal treatment. First, **the court rejected the university's argument that there was insufficient interest in women's hockey and that there were too few female high school hockey players to justify recruitment efforts.** On the contrary, thousands of girls in both the United States and Canada played hockey on high school teams. Also, many women had shown interest in the university club team. Second, the university contended that the women lacked the ability expected of a varsity level team. The court determined that, given the lack of university support, **the women had a sufficiently solid foundation to justify varsity status.** Finally, the court noted that despite the expense of funding a varsity women's hockey program, **"financial concerns alone could not justify gender discrimination."** The court determined that limited university resources had to be reallocated more equitably between men's and women's athletic programs. It ordered the university to grant the women varsity status with "equal opportunity" but not necessarily "equal funding." *Cook v. Colgate Univ.,* 802 F.Supp. 737 (N.D.N.Y.1992). On further appeal, the Second Circuit Court of Appeals held that the action was mooted by the end of the hockey season and the graduation of the last of the students bringing the action. *Cook v. Colgate Univ.,* 992 F.2d 17 (2d Cir.1993).

F. Injuries

Under common law, athletes were held to assume the risks inherent in participating in school athletics; consequently, most lawsuits by injured individuals were unsuccessful. However, in many states the doctrine of assumption of risk has been eliminated or replaced with comparative negligence, which allows at least partial recovery of damages upon proof of negligence.

◆   *A university could not be held liable for injuries a student suffered when he was punched in the face during an intramural soccer game.*

A student at a California university was punched in the face by a member of the opposing team while playing in an intramural soccer game. He sued the university for negligent supervision. The university asserted that it had no duty to the student and that, even if it had, it fulfilled that duty by providing referees for the game. It also asserted that a statute immunized it from liability because the student had engaged in a hazardous recreational activity. A trial court found that the university had no duty to the student, and dismissed the case. The California Court of Appeal affirmed, noting that **the university had no general duty of care toward the student** by virtue of *in loco parentis* (a doctrine that places an entity in the place of the parents) because the student was not a child. Further, there existed no special relationship between the student and the university such that the university had to protect the student from the criminal act of a third party. Finally, **because soccer is an intensely physical game, fraught with risk of serious injury, the student's participation in the game amounted to a "hazardous recreational activity" for purposes of the immunizing statute.** *Ochoa v. California State Univ., Sacramento*, 85 Cal.Rptr.2d 768 (Ct.App.3d Dist.1999).

◆   *A student injured while playing rugby could not recover from the state where he assumed the risk of injury.*

A student at a New York public university was a member of the school's rugby club, which was not a varsity sport. The club received funding from the student association, but did not receive state money. It did have a faculty advisor. On the day of the first practice, the student, who had been playing the sport for three years as a fullback and wingman, volunteered to play the hooker position, at which he was generally inexperienced. During the second scrumdown, the scrums moved prior to the call to engage and the student's head became lodged against the opposing hooker's body. As the student's scrum moved to the low side of the field, he was lifted off the ground. Although he yelled, "Stop!" before the players complied, the upward force of the players behind him broke his neck, rendering him a quadriplegic.

The student sued the state for failing to properly supervise the practice, for furnishing an unsafe field and for negligence in training and instructing the rugby players. The court of claims dismissed his action, and the New York Supreme Court, Appellate Division, affirmed. Here, **the student had assumed the risk of injury by participating in a sport that carried the potential for serious injuries. He had previously played rugby on the same field and under the same conditions; thus, he was aware of the dangers of the sport.** He also was unable to show that the slope of the field was a legal cause of his injury. Accordingly, the state could not be held liable. *Regan v. State of New York*, 654 N.Y.S.2d 488 (App.Div.3d Dep't1997).

◆   *A Georgia appellate court found that an injured student presented sufficient facts demonstrating that the college's gross negligence caused his injuries and that his waiver did not encompass assumption of the risk relative to the college's gross negligence.*

While practicing for a collegiate rowing regatta in Augusta, Ga., a member of a private college's men's varsity team was injured when he was struck in the back by another boat operated by members of the women's varsity team. The usual traffic pattern for boats on the river was the right-hand rule. However, on the day of the injury, the traffic pattern was changed to a left-hand rule to enable boats to practice on the actual course. The coach of the men's team, who was also the supervisor of the entire rowing program, notified the team that the left-hand rule was in effect. However, it was uncertain whether the coach of the women's team informed his team of the changed traffic pattern, or whether he was aware of the change on that day. After the accident, the injured rower brought suit against the college and the coaches, among others, asserting that their gross negligence caused his injuries. The college and coaches maintained that at worst they were negligent and that, because the rower had signed a release document releasing all participants from any claims except those arising out of gross negligence, the case should not even go to the jury. The court denied their motion for a directed verdict, and the jury returned a verdict in favor of the rower. The college and coaches appealed to the Court of Appeals of Georgia.

The court of appeals noted that **there were sufficient facts presented to the jury to show gross negligence.** The jury could have concluded that the coach of the women's team was grossly negligent in failing to advise the team of the change in the traffic pattern, in failing to be aware of the change himself and in failing to be on the water supervising his team at the time of the accident. The jury could also have concluded that the men's coach was grossly negligent in failing to stop the men's boat when he became aware of the women's boat on the course, and in failing to ensure that the women's team was advised of the traffic pattern change. The question had therefore been properly given to the jury and it had concluded, within reason, that the defendants were grossly negligent. **With respect to the release form, even though the rower was aware of and assumed the general risks inherent in rowing, it could not be said that he had assumed the particular risk to which he was subjected** as a result of the defendants' gross negligence. The court upheld the lower court's verdict in favor of the rower. *Trustees of Trinity College v. Ferris*, 491 S.E.2d 909 (Ga.App.1997).

◆   *It is only the risk which results in the harm that must be reasonably foreseeable, held a Massachusetts court, not the precise manner of the accident or the extent of the harm.*

A senior at the Massachusetts Institute of Technology (MIT) majored in aeronautical engineering and was also a member of the men's track and field team. He had been pole vaulting since his freshman year. While practicing under his coach's direct supervision, the student was injured after vaulting when he fell backward and struck his head on the hard track surface. Although the NCAA recommended a length of 16 feet for the pole-vaulting pit, the pit at MIT was only 13 feet in length. The coach had witnessed, or was at least aware of, a vaulter bouncing off the pit mattress, resulting in the vaulter sustaining second-impact injuries. On the day of the accident, there were no pads at the back or sides of the pit. After noticing that the student was running too fast, the coach failed to instruct him to slow down or abort his vault. The student was later diagnosed as having sustained a skull fracture with associated contusions to the brain. He brought suit against the university and two of its track and field coaches in the Superior Court of Massachusetts for injuries sustained in the accident. The court entered judgment upon the jury verdict for the student and denied the defendants' motions for judgment notwithstanding the verdicts or for a new trial. The defendants appealed to the Appeals Court of Massachusetts.

On appeal, the defendants argued that there was no evidence to support a finding that they should have reasonably foreseen that the student would land beyond the back of the pit and hit his head on the track surface. However, the court stated that **it is only the risk which results in the harm that must be reasonably foreseeable, not the precise manner of the accident or the extent of the harm.** The court held that from the evidence, the student's accident was reasonably foreseeable by the defendants. The length of the landing pit and its location near a hard surface did not provide a safe environment for pole-vaulters. Accordingly, their motions were properly denied. *Moose v. Mass. Institute of Technology*, 683 N.E.2d 706 (Mass.App.Ct.1997).

◆   *Although some risks are inherent to activities like weightlifting, the risk of a spotter intentionally failing to provide necessary assistance is not.*

A scholarship player on an Ohio university basketball team was required by the university to lift weights to improve as a player. While lifting weights at the university's gym, the student attempted to bench-press a 365-pound weight. The weight fell on the student, injuring him. He claimed that a university employee agreed to act as a spotter for him, though the employee claimed that he had not done so. The student sued the employee and the university for his injuries, claiming that the employee's reckless and wanton misconduct had caused his injuries. The trial court held that the employee was at most negligent, and granted pretrial dismissal to the defendants.

The Court of Appeals of Ohio noted that **where individuals are engaged in recreational or sports activities, they assume the ordinary risks of the activities and cannot recover for any injury unless they can show that their injury resulted from reckless or intentional conduct.** Here, it was undisputed that the student was engaged in a recreational activity at the time he was injured. However, there was a dispute over whether the employee had agreed to perform as a spotter for the student. As a result, the action should have gone to trial. The court reversed and remanded the case. *Sicard v. Univ. of Dayton*, 660 N.E.2d 1241 (Ohio App.1995).

◆   *A college was found to have a duty to provide prompt medical attention to all students participating in sports that presented a risk of severe injury.*

A Pennsylvania college student wished to play lacrosse and was examined by his family physician and the college's doctor, who both determined that the student was healthy and able to participate in physical activity. During an off-season lacrosse practice, the student collapsed. All attempts to resuscitate him were unsuccessful. He died of a cardiac arrest. Post-mortem examinations could not detect the reason for the student's fatal arrythmia. The student's parents then filed suit against the college in a federal district court, asserting that the college's negligence caused their son's death. The court granted the college summary judgment, and the student's parents appealed to the U.S. Court of Appeals, Third Circuit.

Both parties disputed the amount of time lapse between the dispatch of the students and the arrival of medical aid. The student's parents contended that the college had a duty to take preventive measures which would assure that student-athletes who engaged in intercollegiate athletics received prompt medical attention for their injuries. The court of appeals agreed. **The college had a special relationship with the student and therefore a duty of care toward him.** Other student-athletes had died while competing in athletics, and lacrosse was considered a relatively dangerous contact sport. Consequently, not having qualified trainers at the practice site posed a risk of life which was both foreseeable and unreasonable. **Although no athlete had previously suffered a cardiac arrest, the injury was one of a "broadly definable class of events."** The presence of foreseeability and consequent duty to care for the student was not "dependent on the foreseeability of a specific event." Therefore, the college had a duty to provide prompt medical attention to all students participating in sports that presented a risk of severe injury. The court of appeals reversed the holding of the district court on this issue. It remanded the case for a determination of whether prompt emergency medical service was actually given to the student. *Kleinknecht v. Gettysburg College*, 989 F.2d 1360 (3d Cir.1993).

◆   *The doctrine of express assumption of the risk did not bar a student's claim; rather, a jury had to determine the comparative fault of the student and the school.*

A cheerleader for a Florida private university severely injured her foot during practice after the coach failed to provide adequate spotters for a stunt. She filed a negligence lawsuit against the university in a Florida circuit court, alleging that the coach had failed to adequately supervise the students. The trial court held for the cheerleader, and the university appealed to the District Court of Appeal of Florida, Fourth District. The university contended that the doctrine of express assumption of risk barred the cheerleader's negligence claim. The court of appeal disagreed, ruling that although the cheerleader may have been foolish to attempt the stunt without spotters, her unreasonable conduct did not absolve the university from liability. The case was correctly submitted to a jury on comparative fault principles. It was the **jury's duty to weigh the reasonableness of her activity against the school's negligence.** Thus, the doctrine of express assumption of risk did not bar the cheerleader's claim. Finally, the court determined that the trial court had correctly denied the university's motion for a continuance until the cheerleader's foot was healed. Sufficient expert testimony existed from which a determination of future damages could be made. The holding of the trial court was affirmed. *Nova Univ. v. Katz*, 636 So.2d 729 (Fla.App.4th Dist.1993).

II. STUDENT ACTIVITIES

Colleges and universities must respect individual rights to free religious exercise and association as well as state and federal civil rights laws. However, schools may limit official recognition of particular organizations and impose restrictions on them. Liability for student organizations also becomes a concern for schools, particularly in relation to fraternities and sororities.

A. Student Associations and Activities

Most schools have a wide variety of student associations and activities for their students. While some associations receive school sponsorship and funding, many only receive official recognition of their association. Lawsuits often arise when schools attempt to impose restrictions on the associations that impact their constitutional rights of expression or limit access to school facilities.

1. Freedom of Expression

◆   *The U.S. Supreme Court held that because a state university had opened a limited public forum by paying other third-party contractors on behalf of student groups, it could not deny a religious group's claim for funds on the basis of its viewpoint.*

A group of students who published a Christian publication sought financing from a state university student activity fund. Their request was denied by the student council and two university tribunals. Although political and religious organizations could qualify as approved student groups, they could not receive student activity funds. The student group filed a lawsuit in the U.S. District Court for the Western District of Virginia. The court granted summary judgment to the university and the students appealed to the U.S. Court of Appeals, Fourth Circuit. The court of appeals affirmed, and the students appealed to the U.S. Supreme Court. **The Supreme Court held that because the university had opened a limited public forum by paying other third-party contractors on behalf of student groups, it could not deny the religious group's claim for funds on the basis of its viewpoint.** Allowing the payment of the group's printing costs amounted to a policy of government neutrality for different viewpoints. The Court reversed the lower court decisions, ruling that access to public school facilities on a neutral basis does not violate the Establishment Clause of the First Amendment. *Rosenberger v. Rector and Visitors of Univ. of Virginia*, 515 U.S. 819, 115 S.Ct. 2510, 132 L.Ed.2d 700 (1995).

◆   *A university's funding system created a limited public forum under which it could not discriminate against speech on the basis of its viewpoint.*

The University of South Alabama encouraged a wide variety of activities through the establishment of student organizations which were eligible for certain benefits, including the use of campus banking services and funding from the student government association. A gay and lesbian group was denied the banking privileges and certain funding by the university because it believed such action would violate a state statute. The statute prohibited any college or university from using public funds or facilities to support any organization that promoted a lifestyle that was prohibited by the state sexual misconduct laws. The student group filed suit against the state attorney general and university officials in federal district court, alleging that the statute constituted impermissible viewpoint discrimination in violation of the First Amendment and that it was invalid on its face. The court found for the student group and the attorney general appealed to the U.S. Court of Appeals, Eleventh Circuit.

The attorney general argued that the speech covered by the statute was not protected speech because it advocated the violation of sexual misconduct laws, but the court of appeals disagreed, noting that the First Amendment protects advocacy to violate a law. The only exception is when such advocacy is directed to incite imminent lawless action and is likely to produce such action. The court then noted that the university's funding system created a limited public forum under which it could not discriminate against speech on the basis of its viewpoint. **Because the university funded groups that advocated compliance with the sexual misconduct laws, it could not discriminate on the basis of viewpoint and refuse to fund groups which advocated the violation of these laws.** The court then held that facial invalidation is a drastic remedy and should only be used when the statute's interpretation cannot be narrowed to make it constitutionally permissible. Finding that the statute here was overbroad and not susceptible to a narrowing interpretation, the court found it facially invalid and affirmed the district court's decision. *Gay Lesbian Bisexual Alliance v. Pryor*, 110 F.3d 1543 (11th Cir.1997).

2. Facilities and Services

◆ *Although a university's Free Exercise Clause rights would be burdened to some extent by being forced to provide facilities and services to gay student groups, that burden was outweighed by the government's important goal of eradicating discrimination based upon sexual orientation.*

Georgetown University, a Jesuit-controlled Roman Catholic institution, was sued in a District of Columbia superior court by two gay rights groups when it refused to extend full university recognition to the groups as student organizations. The gay student groups claimed that the university's refusal to recognize them violated the District of Columbia Human Rights Act. The Act provided in part that educational institutions could not deny access to their "facilities and services" on the basis of sexual orientation. The university countered that the First Amendment's Free Exercise Clause protected it from violating the tenets of its religious heritage by recognizing student groups whose goals were at odds with the university's religious affiliation. The superior court upheld Georgetown's free exercise defense and ruled that it did not have to recognize the gay student groups. The gay student groups appealed. A three-judge panel of the District of Columbia Court of Appeals reversed the panel's ruling and the case was held over for consideration by the entire court.

Modifying the three-judge panel's decision, the court of appeals held that the university had to provide the gay student groups with all the "facilities and services" afforded to groups that had attained university recognition. However, the university was not required to endorse the gay student groups' goals by officially recognizing them. Although the university's Free Exercise Clause rights would be burdened to some extent by being forced to provide facilities and services to the gay student groups, that burden was outweighed by the government's important goal of eradicating discrimination based upon sexual orientation. **The university was ordered to provide the groups with facilities and services but was not required to actually recognize the groups.** *Gay Rights Coalition v. Georgetown Univ.*, 536 A.2d 1 (D.C.App.1987).

+ *The Third Circuit found that a state commission on human relations could not prevent a university from making its placement service available to the military for recruitment even though it discriminated on the basis of sexual orientation.*

The Temple University School of Law operated a placement service that arranged interviews between employers and students. One of the potential employers was the Judge Advocate General (JAG) Corps of the U.S. Army, Navy and Marines. These branches did not employ homosexuals. After being notified of the practice, the Pennsylvania Commission on Human Relations issued a complaint against the law school, alleging that it had violated the Philadelphia Fair Practices Ordinance in permitting the JAG Corps to interview at the law school. The commission claimed that the law school had violated the ordinance when referring persons to the JAG Corps knowing that it was discriminatory in its hiring practices. A U.S. district court ruled in favor of the law school and the commission appealed. The U.S. Court of Appeals, Third Circuit, observed that all parties were in agreement that the commission could not directly keep the military from recruiting persons on whatever terms it deemed appropriate. However, the parties sharply disagreed as to whether the commission could prevent the school from making its placement service available to the JAG Corps for recruitment when it discriminated on the basis of sexual orientation. In ruling in favor of the JAG Corps and the law school, the court of appeals referred to the federal Department of Defense Authorization Act of 1973, in which Congress declared that access to college and university employment facilities was of paramount importance. The court observed that in the above-mentioned act (and others similar to it) the government had shown **that recruitment on a variety of campuses is essential to having a broad scope of skilled personnel in the U.S. military.** The court ruled that to uphold the commission's complaint would potentially frustrate effective military recruiting in the area. The Philadelphia Fair Practices Ordinance was in direct conflict with federal legislative policy, and the court ruled that federal law took precedence. The local ordinance therefore could not be enforced against the law school. *U.S. v. City of Philadelphia*, 798 F.2d 81 (3d Cir.1986).

B. Fraternities and Sororities

Many colleges and universities allow fraternities and sororities on their campuses. Some of the fraternities and sororities represent chapters of national fraternities and sororities, while others may be local in nature. Lawsuits arise concerning the operation of the organizations, as well as liability for members' actions. Many lawsuits seek to hold both the organization and the school liable for misconduct.

1. Operation and School Supervision

+ *A university's residential policy, which required all students to live in college-owned facilities, may constitute a violation of the Sherman Act.*

A New York private college announced a policy requiring all students to live in college-owned facilities and to purchase college-sponsored meal plans. Four college fraternities brought an action against the college and its president in the

U.S. District Court for the Northern District of New York, alleging that the residential policy violated the Sherman Act by unlawfully monopolizing the market for residential services in the city where the college was located. The district court held that the residential policy was not "trade or commerce" and that it lacked a substantial connection to interstate commerce. The court dismissed the complaint, and the fraternities appealed to the U.S. Court of Appeals, Second Circuit. On appeal, the fraternities argued that the residential plan had the commercial purpose of eliminating competition in the provision of residential services in order to raise revenues. The college maintained that its purpose was to create an academic environment that was more appealing to female applicants who were unable to enjoy the privileges of fraternity life. The court of appeals noted that the Sherman Act would apply only if the residential policy constituted trade or commerce. It then stated that in determining whether particular conduct was commerce, the principal focus had to be on the nature of the activity, rather than the form or objectives of the organization. Here, **the fraternities had provided facts to support a connection between the residential policy and interstate commerce.** The college collected approximately $4 million in room and board fees from students who came from outside New York state. Further, **the fraternities and other private landlords in the city would lose approximately $1 million per year as a result of the new policy,** a substantial portion of which would have been collected from out-of-state residents. Because the allegations were sufficient to survive dismissal, the court reversed and remanded the case. *Hamilton Chapter of Alpha Delta Phi, Inc. v. Hamilton College,* 128 F.3d 59 (2d Cir.1997).

◆ *A court's role in due process actions concerning a private institution, absent state involvement, was limited to determining whether the school had substantially complied with its own disciplinary guidelines.*

A fraternity at a private university was burglarized and records of the fraternity's activities were stolen. Portions of these records later appeared in the university's newspapers, and were mailed to the university's officials. The published records alleged violations of the school's anti-hazing policy as well as other infractions. The dean of the university then conducted an investigation of the fraternity, which resulted in several penalties. The fraternity brought suit against the school in a state court, and alleged that its members' Fourteenth Amendment due process rights had been violated. A New York trial court dismissed the claim, and the fraternity appealed to the Supreme Court, Appellate Division. **Private school students cannot allege violations of constitutionally protected due process rights absent a showing of state involvement in the university activity.** Here, no such state involvement was shown. A court's role in due process actions concerning a private institution, absent state involvement, is limited to determining whether the school had substantially complied with its own disciplinary guidelines. The court reviewed the record concerning the university's regulations and actions, and affirmed the dismissal of the claim. *Mu Chapter Delta Kappa Epsilon v. Colgate,* 578 N.Y.S.2d 713 (A.D.3d Dept.1992).

◆ *A college's decision to withdraw recognition from all fraternities was a legitimate exercise of the college's supervisory authority.*

A Maine private college decided to withdraw recognition from all fraternities on the campus in 1984. A realty company, on behalf of a fraternity, sued the college for breach of contract in a state superior court. The court ruled in favor of the college and the realty company appealed to the Supreme Judicial Court of Maine. The dispute arose over a Memorandum of Agreement executed in 1951 between the realty company and the college. Section III(e) of that agreement stated that the college could cancel the agreement only in the following circumstances: "In the event the ZETA PSI Fraternity ceases to have a chapter at Colby College, or in the event the Chapter is suspended or expelled for reason either by the College or the National Fraternity...." The college maintained that the "expelled for reason" phrase should be construed according to its common meaning, *i.e.*, a "rational justification," a definition which would preclude only arbitrary or capricious actions by the college. The supreme court agreed, ruling that the college rationally justified its decision to oust all fraternities from the campus as a move to more fully "integrate the housing units into the academic program of the college." It observed that **the president and trustees of the college had the right and responsibility to periodically evaluate and change policies for the purpose of achieving certain educational goals.** The court ruled that the 1984 decision by the college president and trustees to eliminate fraternity chapters at the college was a legitimate exercise of the college's supervisory authority. The college, therefore, properly ended its relationship with the realtor and fraternity under the 1951 lease agreement. The decision of the superior court in favor of the college was affirmed. *Chi Realty Corp. v. Colby College*, 513 A.2d 866 (Me.1986).

2.   Organizational Liability

◆   *A national fraternity could not be held liable for a student's injuries because it was not in a position to control the actions of its chapters on a day-to-day basis and had no knowledge of any hazing activity.*

A student at a private university in Louisiana was accepted into a fraternity. During the intake process, he was physically beaten and abused by several members of the fraternity while they were conducting hazing activities. The student and his parents filed suit against the national fraternity, among others, to recover damages for the injuries sustained as a result of the hazing. A Louisiana trial court granted summary judgment to the national fraternity, and the student and his parents appealed to the Court of Appeal of Louisiana, First Circuit. They argued on appeal that the national fraternity should be personally or vicariously liable for the actions of its chapter members because it had a duty to prevent injury to new members. They also asserted that the national fraternity's action in forbidding hazing activities showed a clear knowledge and former approval of those activities. The court, however, noted that the national executive director of the fraternity had stated by affidavit that he had no knowledge of any hazing activity at the local chapter and that the **national fraternity took numerous steps to inform local chapters and members that hazing activities were clearly prohibited.** Further, deposition testimony by several local chapter members indicated that **any hazing activity that occurred was purposely hidden from the national fraternity.** Because the national fraternity was not in a position to control the actions of its chapters on a day-to-day basis, and because it had no knowledge of any hazing activity, it could not be held liable for the student's injuries. The trial court decision was affirmed. *Walker v. Phi Beta Sigma Fraternity (RHO Chapter)*, 706 So.2d 525 (La.App.1st Cir.1997).

◆   *A student's negligence claim against a fraternity as a result of a member's alleged assault and rape of her failed, in part, because the fraternity never assumed a duty to provide security to the student.*

A college student in Ohio alleged that she was assaulted and raped by a fraternity member. After the fraternity member was arrested and charged with rape, the student filed a civil complaint against the fraternity for negligence as well as intentional and negligent infliction of emotional distress. She alleged that the fraternity breached its duty to provide security for guests and members and that it decided to wage a campaign against her by ostracizing her as revenge for her decision to file rape charges against one of its members. The trial court granted summary judgment to the fraternity, and the student appealed to the Court of Appeals of Ohio, Sixth District. On appeal, the court noted that the **fraternity never assumed a duty to provide security to the student.** Nor could the student demonstrate that she had relied on the fraternity's security program (which had been set up to provide members with transportation home from local bars) to protect her. Accordingly, the negligence claim failed. The court also noted that the student's assertion that the fraternity's members had called her names and otherwise harassed her did not amount to extreme and outrageous conduct so as to make the fraternity liable for intentional infliction of emotional distress. Further, the student presented no admissible evidence to show that the fraternity ordered its members to engage in such conduct. The court also stated that the negligent infliction of emotional distress claim failed because the student had not shown that she was in fear of real physical danger from the fraternity members as a result of their actions—a necessary element of such a cause of action in Ohio. Accordingly, the lower court's grant of summary judgment to the fraternity was affirmed. *Rine v. Sabo*, 680 N.E.2d 647 (Ohio App.6th Dist.1996).

◆   *Although the university had a substantial interest in maintaining an appropriate learning environment, it would have to do so without restricting expression based upon its content.*

Fraternity members who attended a Virginia university staged an **"ugly woman contest"** which was objected to by other university students as racist and sexist. The university determined that the behavior created a hostile learning environment for women and blacks which was incompatible with the university's mission. It suspended the fraternity from many school activities, and the fraternity filed a civil rights lawsuit in a federal district court. The U.S. Court of Appeals, Fourth Circuit, affirmed the district court's summary judgment motion for the fraternity, ruling that **the contest was protected by the First Amendment.** This was because the contest was expressive conduct intended to convey a message. Although the university had a substantial interest in maintaining an appropriate learning environment, it would have to do so without restricting expression based upon its content. *IOTA XI Chapter of Sigma Chi Fraternity v. George Mason Univ.*, 993 F.2d 386 (4th Cir.1993).

3. Injuries

♦ *Fraternity sponsors of a "paint ball" game could be liable for a player's injuries if their actions were negligent. They were not entitled to assert that the game was inherently dangerous.*

A prospective pledge at a fraternity participated in a "war game," wherein players shot paint balls at each other. During the game, the student's goggles were snagged by a tree limb and lifted away from his eyes. When he stood and fired another round without replacing them, a paint ball hit him, permanently blinding him in one eye. He sued the fraternity, the chapter that had sponsored the war game and the chapter president, alleging that they had sponsored an unreasonably dangerous activity, that they had provided inadequate supervision and equipment, and that they had failed to train him properly. A trial court granted summary judgment to the defendants, finding that the student had engaged in a competitive contact sport, thereby assuming the risk of injury. The student appealed to the Texas Court of Appeals, contending that **sponsors of an event cannot assert the "competitive contact sports" doctrine because they are not participants.** The court agreed. Participants in a competitive contact sport are judged under the intentional or reckless conduct standard because they are caught up in the spirit of the contest. Sponsors, however, have the benefit of time to reflect before they act. Thus, they are to be judged by concepts of ordinary negligence. The court reversed and remanded the case for further proceedings. *Moore v. Phi Delta Theta Co.*, 976 S.W.2d 738 (Tex.App.–Houston 1998).

♦ *A college had no legal duty to shield its students from their own dangerous activities.*

A student at a private New York university was a member of a fraternity. He lived at the fraternity house and his room had a window which was centered over a portico that covered the front entrance of the house. Although the student had no recollection of a fall and there were no witnesses to his actions, he was found one morning lying on the ground near the entrance of the house, unconscious and bleeding profusely. His blood alcohol level was .18 percent. He filed suit in state court against the university, the fraternity and the owner of the house, seeking to recover damages for his personal injuries. The defendants filed a motion to dismiss. The court granted the motion with regard to the university and the fraternity and partially granted the motion with regard to the owner of the house. The student appealed to the New York Supreme Court, Appellate Division, on the claims against the university and the owner of the house.

The student argued that the university assumed the duty to control the conduct of students in fraternity houses when it stated in the student handbook that all roofs and porticos were off limits and that underage drinking was prohibited. He argued that the university knew or should have known that students at fraternity houses routinely violated these provisions, and therefore its failure to enforce its own rules should result in liability for his injuries. The appellate court disagreed, finding that colleges have no legal duty to shield their students from their own dangerous activities. **Despite the handbook provisions, the college did not assume any duty to take affirmative steps to supervise students and to prevent them from engaging in prohibited conduct.** Also, since the university did not own or control the fraternity house, it was not required to install safety features to prevent the prohibited activity. The court affirmed the dismissal of the complaint against the university but held that an issue of fact existed as to whether the owner of the house maintained it in a reasonably safe condition. *Rothbard v. Colgate Univ.*, 652 N.Y.S.2d 146 (A.D.3d Dep't1997).

◆   *A college and national fraternity did not owe students a special duty of care to prevent underage drinking which violated the college's alcohol policy.*

A minor freshman student in Pennsylvania was socializing at a fraternity house early in the afternoon prior to a large homecoming party scheduled for that evening. Kegs of beer arrived shortly after noon and the students decided to tap them earlier than allowed by school policy. While the minor student socialized at the fraternity house, he sat in a hot tub provided for the party and drank beer. The student left the house hours later on his motorcycle, which had a dim or burnt out headlight. While driving down a local highway, he attempted to pass a car in front of him. A fatal head-on collision resulted and a subsequent analysis revealed that the minor was legally intoxicated at the time he was killed. The administratrix of the minor's estate filed suit against the college and the national fraternity. She alleged that the college's alcohol policy and lack of adult supervision impliedly sanctioned underage drinking on campus, that the college was negligent for these reasons, and that the college's policies and inaction were a direct cause of the minor's fatal collision. The administratrix also alleged that the national fraternity was responsible for control of the actions of its members. A Pennsylvania trial court granted summary judgment in favor of both the college and the fraternity and the administratrix appealed to the Superior Court of Pennsylvania. On appeal, the court noted that **both the college and the national fraternity counseled against the use of alcohol, and neither defendant owed the student a special duty of care which had been breached.** The holding in favor of both defendants was affirmed. *Cooperstein v. Liberty Mutual*, 611 A.2d 721 (Pa.Super.1992).

◆   *A university had no duty to protect a student from fraternity members who had been drinking.*

A student at a private university was in her dormitory room when a fraternity member called her to the lobby. When she arrived, the fraternity member grabbed her, then threw her over his shoulder and ran out of the building. The student asserted that as the fraternity member ran, he fell, crushing her underneath him on the sidewalk. She claimed that as a result of a head injury she received in the fall she completely lost her sense of smell and also suffered hearing loss. The student filed a lawsuit against the fraternity member, the fraternity and the private university seeking monetary damages for doctors' bills, surgical treatments, medicine and nursing care. She also sought compensatory damages for a reduction in her earning capacity. The student claimed that the fraternity member had gone to the dormitory after a fraternity party at which members of the fraternity drank alcohol. The student claimed that the university had failed to control the on-campus activities of the fraternity and its members. The student also asserted that by installing safety devices in the dormitory the university assumed the duty of protecting dormitory residents and that this duty was breached. The university sought a dismissal of the case before trial. An Illinois appellate court noted that although college students were once considered minors subject to control by colleges and universities, they are now generally considered adults. **Universities are educational rather than custodial institutions, and requiring the university to babysit each student would be inappropriate.** The university had no duty to protect the student from fraternity members who had been drinking. *Rabel v. Illinois Wesleyan Univ.*, 514 N.E.2d 552 (Ill.App.4th Dist.1987).

4. Hazing

♦ *Corps of Cadets officials at Texas A&M were entitled to immunity in the following hazing case.*

The Texas A&M Corps of Cadets is a voluntary student military training organization consisting of approximately 2,000 students (about 5 percent of the student population). Members of the Corps live together, drill together, stand for inspections and physically train on a daily basis. A freshman student enrolled as a member of the Corps and joined a precision rifle drill team. **During "hell week," he was allegedly subjected to numerous hazing incidents by the drill team advisors, including having his head taped like a mummy, and enduring several beatings.** He was also allegedly beaten after the drill team lost a competition to another school's team. He never reported the incidents to school authorities; however, he did tell his parents, who then informed school authorities that hazing was occurring. When asked about hazing by the faculty advisor, the student downplayed the seriousness of it. Near the end of his first year, he went to a "hound interview" (seeking to become an advisor to the drill team) where he was beaten and forced to cut himself with a knife. He and his parents then met with the Commandant of the Corps, who took them to the university police to file criminal charges. All the drill team advisors were then expelled or suspended for hazing.

He sued a number of Corps officials under 42 U.S.C. § 1983 and Texas' hazing statute, alleging that the officials' failure to supervise the Corps' activities demonstrated a deliberate indifference to his constitutional rights. The U.S. District Court for the Southern District of Texas held that **the actions of the Corps officials in educating students about the illegality of hazing were reasonable.** They disseminated brochures and other materials to students what hazing was and how to prevent it. They met with students and their parents to discuss hazing and to encourage parents to report it if they saw evidence of it, and they reasonably believed that their efforts were sufficient to prevent constitutional violations. **As a result, the court found that the officials were entitled to qualified immunity from suit.** On appeal, the Fifth Circuit Court of Appeals affirmed the grant of immunity to the officials. The student failed to show that the officials were deliberately indifferent to his constitutional rights. *Alton v. Hopgood*, 168 F.3d 196 (5th Cir.1999).

♦ *A university could not be held liable for a student's hazing where it had no reason to know that hazing was going on.*

A student transferred to Cornell University after spending his first two years at other institutions. He was accepted to pledge a fraternity, the national organization of which prohibited hazing, as did Cornell. After allegedly enduring beatings and torture, psychological coercion, and embarrassment, the student sued Cornell for negligent supervision, premises liability and breach of an implied contract to protect him. Before the U.S. District Court for the Northern District of New York, Cornell sought to dismiss the action. The court granted its motion, finding that there was no special relationship between the university and the student, and that the university published information about the dangers of hazing and its prohibition on campus. **Further, the university did not have sufficient reason to believe that hazing activities were going on; and once it became aware of the hazing, it took disciplinary action against the perpetrators.** Finally, the court could find no evidence of any specific promises by the university that could be deemed part of an implied contract. The university was not liable for the hazing of the student. *Lloyd v. Alpha Phi Alpha Fraternity*, 1999 U.S. Dist. LEXIS 906 (N.D.N.Y.1999).

◆   *Fraternity members could be sued for negligence and for violating an anti-hazing statute in the following case.*

A 17-year-old college freshman was invited to pledge a fraternity and died after consuming excessive amounts of alcohol during a hazing ritual. His parents sued several members of the fraternity for negligence, and also asserted claims under two New York statutes. The fraternity members sought to have two of the causes of action against them dismissed, and the case reached the Supreme Court, Appellate Division. The appellate court held that the fraternity members were not entitled to dismissal. Here, **the parents had alleged that their son's intoxication was not entirely voluntary and had also asserted careless acts by the fraternity members that went beyond the mere furnishing of intoxicants.** Accordingly, the action against the fraternity members could proceed. *Oja v. Grand Chapter of Theta Chi Fraternity*, 684 N.Y.S.2d 344 (App.Div.1999).

◆   *A university that knew about prior instances of hazing had a duty to protect a student from such behavior.*

Four or five members of a fraternity at a Nebraska university kidnapped a pledge, handcuffed him to a radiator and gave him a large quantity of alcohol. After the pledge became ill from his intoxication, he was taken to a third-floor restroom where he was handcuffed to a toilet pipe. The pledge escaped from the handcuffs and attempted to escape by exiting a restroom window and sliding down a drainpipe. However, he fell and suffered severe injuries. He sued the university, claiming that it had acted negligently in failing to enforce prohibitions against acts of hazing, the consumption of alcohol, and acts of physical abuse, when it knew or should have known that the fraternity was in violation of those prohibitions. The university moved for a pretrial judgment, asserting that it owed the pledge no duty to supervise the fraternity and protect the pledge from harm. The court granted the university's motion, and appeal was taken to the Supreme Court of Nebraska. The supreme court held that **the university could be liable to the pledge as an invitee on its property. Because the university knew of two prior instances of hazing at fraternities on campus, and because the university was aware of several incidents involving members of that fraternity, the acts taken against the pledge were reasonably foreseeable and the university owed him a duty to protect.** Whether it breached that duty was a question of fact that had to be decided at trial. The court reversed the pretrial judgment in favor of the university. *Knoll v. Bd. of Regents of the Univ. of Nebraska*, 601 N.W.2d 757 (Neb.1999).

◆   *Where the consumption of alcohol is coerced by social pressure or otherwise, it may not be voluntary, and liability may result.*

A Missouri university student was invited to become a member of a campus organization that was responsible for organizing the annual St. Pat's festivities. To gain membership to the organization, the student had to undergo an initiation that allegedly consisted of the coerced chugging and excessive consumption of alcohol, as well as other physical and verbal abuse. Members of the organization allegedly forced the student to consume a heated preparation of grain alcohol and green peas until he became unconscious, then left him unattended despite knowing that a participant in the initiation had died three years earlier. The student died two days later, and his parents filed a wrongful death lawsuit against the organization and the individual members who had conducted the initiation, as well as the fraternities on whose property the initiation took place. The trial court dismissed the action, and the parents appealed to the Court of Appeals of Missouri. The court of appeals reversed and remanded the case. **Here, despite the apparently voluntary consumption of alcohol by the student, there may have been great social pressure to drink. That coercion may have overcome any decision the student might have made about whether he should consume alcohol and, if so, how much he should consume.** The case should not have been dismissed. *Nisbet v. Bucher*, 949 S.W.2d 111 (Mo.App.1997).

◆   *A university was liable to a student for hazing injuries where it knew or should have known that hazing was going on.*

After receiving a full football scholarship, a student at the University of Delaware decided to join a fraternity and began his pledge period. The university prohibited hazing, as did the national organization. However, hazing continued. At the end of the pledge period—on "hell night"—the student was subjected to physical and emotional abuse as part of the hazing process. The night culminated with a lye-based liquid oven cleaner being poured over his back and neck. He suffered first- and second-degree chemical burns, withdrew from the university and relinquished his scholarship. The national organization revoked the local fraternity's charter, but the university, due to a lack of cooperation, was unable to discipline students after the incident. The student sued the university, the fraternity and the perpetrator who poured the lye on him, and a jury awarded him $30,000, apportioning 93 percent of the liability against the university and 7 percent against the perpetrating student. The court then overturned the jury verdict against the university.

On appeal to the Supreme Court of Delaware, the court held that the student could be deemed an invitee of the university. Accordingly, once the university knew or had reason to know that a third party's actions could cause harm to the student, it had a duty to protect him. **The court found that there was sufficient evidence before the university that hazing activities were still taking place, and that the university thus had a duty to protect the student.** Further, the university's anti-hazing and security regulations indicated that the university had control over the premises sufficient to justify the award of damages against it. The court reversed the lower court's decision to overturn the jury verdict. *Furek v. Univ. of Delaware*, 594 A.2d 506 (Del.1991).

♦   *A fraternity member was convicted under a hazing statute after the death of a pledge. His challenge to the constitutionality of the statute failed.*

A fraternity member at a university in Missouri subjected pledges to repeated physical abuse, including kicks, punches, caning of the soles of the feet and other forms of beating. As a result of the abuse, one of the pledges blacked out. He never regained consciousness, and died the following afternoon. An autopsy revealed that he had broken ribs, a lacerated kidney, a lacerated liver, upper body bruises and a subdural hematoma of the brain, which proved fatal. The fraternity member was charged with five counts of hazing and, after his conviction, was sentenced to six months imprisonment for each count. He appealed to the Supreme Court of Missouri, asserting that the hazing statute violated the First Amendment's right to associate, as well as the Fifth and Fourteenth Amendments' rights to due process and equal protection. The supreme court disagreed. It found that **the hazing statute did not prevent fraternity members from meeting at any time and place they might choose. Further, the statute did not infringe upon constitutional rights once the fraternity members met. It merely prohibited recklessly endangering the mental or physical health or safety of a prospective member as a condition of admission into or preservation of membership in the fraternity.** Accordingly, the statute did not violate the First, Fifth or Fourteenth Amendments, and the fraternity member's conviction was affirmed. *State v. Allen*, 905 S.W.2d 874 (Mo.1995).

CHAPTER FOUR

Freedom of Speech

I. EMPLOYEES

The First Amendment guarantees freedom of speech by prohibiting the government from abridging that freedom. This does not mean that the freedom to speak is absolute. Certain kinds of speech are entitled to more protections than others. For example, the Supreme Court has held that obscenity is not protected by the First Amendment.

Where speech addresses a matter of public concern, rather than a purely private matter, courts will balance the interests of the individual whose speech is being curtailed against the interests of the government in prohibiting that speech. Where the governmental interests outweigh the individual's interests, the right to speak is lost. Where the individual's right to speak prevails, the speech is protected by the First Amendment.

The balancing test utilized in First Amendment cases comes from the Supreme Court case of *Pickering v. Bd. of Educ.*, below. Other important Supreme Court cases that help define free speech rights include *Mt. Healthy City School Dist. v. Doyle*, below; *Connick v. Myers*, 461 U.S. 138, 103 S.Ct. 1684, 75 L.Ed.2d 708 (1983), where the Court held that a public employee's speech upon matters of purely personal interest is not afforded constitutional protection; and *Rankin v. McPherson*, 483 U.S. 378, 107 S.Ct. 2891, 97 L.Ed.2d 315 (1987), where the Court held that whether an employee's speech addresses a matter of public concern must be determined by the **content, form and context** of a given statement as revealed by the entire record.

It is important to note that free speech protections do not exist in the private sector. The First Amendment generally prohibits only governmental action against an individual's right to speak. Where the entity infringing on speech rights is private, the First Amendment does not protect against censorship. Thus, free speech issues tend to be much more prevalent in the context of public college and university law.

It is also important to note that prior restraint—prohibiting a person from speaking before they can do so—is especially frowned upon. Courts presume that prior restraint is constitutionally invalid. Thus, the government must meet a very heavy burden to show that such restraint is necessary. The government's interest must be compelling and there must be no less restrictive means of achieving that governmental interest.

A. Protected Speech

♦   *When an employee speaks on a matter of public concern, and is then disciplined, courts will use a balancing test to determine whether the employee's right to speak outweighs the employer's right to prohibit that speech (e.g., to promote an efficient workplace).*

An Illinois school district fired a high school teacher for sending a letter to the editor of the local newspaper. The letter criticized the board and district superintendent for their handling of school funding methods. The letter particularly criticized the board's handling of a bond issue and allocation of funding between school educational and athletic programs. The teacher also charged the superintendent with attempting to stifle opposing views on the subject. The board held a hearing at which it charged the teacher with publishing a defamatory letter. The board then fired the teacher for making false statements. An Illinois court affirmed the board's action, finding substantial evidence that publication of the letter was detrimental to the district's interest. The Illinois Supreme Court affirmed the dismissal, ruling that the teacher's speech was unprotected by the First Amendment because his teaching position required him to refrain from statements about school operations.

The U.S. Supreme Court found no support for the state supreme court's view that public employment subjected the teacher to deprivation of his constitutional rights. The **state interest in regulating employee speech was to be balanced with individual rights.** The Court outlined a general analysis for evaluating public employee speech, ruling that **employees are entitled to constitutional protection to comment on matters of public concern.** The public interest in free speech and debate on matters of public concern was so great that it barred public officials from recovering damages for defamatory statements unless they were made with reckless disregard for their truth. Because there was no evidence presented that the letter damaged any board member's professional reputation, **the teacher's comments were not detrimental to the school system, but only constituted a difference of opinion.** Since there was no proof of reckless disregard for the truth by the teacher and the matter concerned the public interest, the board could not constitutionally terminate his employment. The Court reversed and remanded the state court decision. *Pickering v. Bd. of Educ.,* 391 U.S. 563, 88 S.Ct. 1731, 20 L.Ed.2d 811 (1968).

♦   *Where employees can be disciplined or discharged for legitimate reasons, the First Amendment will not protect them from the adverse action unless the action was taken in response to protected speech.*

An untenured teacher was not rehired after a number of incidents which led the school board to conclude that he lacked tactfulness in handling professional matters. After the board decided not to reemploy the teacher, he asked for and received a list of the reasons for the board's decision. The board gave general reasons for its failure to rehire the teacher and noted that he had made an obscene gesture and had given an on-air opinion about school dress codes at a local radio station. The teacher sued for reinstatement on the grounds that his discussion with the radio station was protected by the First Amendment and that to refuse reemployment was a violation of his free speech rights. An Ohio federal court and later a court of appeals agreed and ordered reinstatement with backpay. The school board appealed to the U.S. Supreme Court.

The Court first rejected the school board's argument that the Eleventh Amendment barred private lawsuits against local political subdivisions such as a school district. City and county governments were not "states" within the meaning of the Eleventh Amendment. However, the Court overturned the court of appeals and district court decisions, holding that apart from the actions for which the teacher might claim First Amendment protection, the board could have chosen not to rehire him on the basis of several other incidents. The radio station incident, while clearly implicating a protected right, was not the substantial reason for nonrenewal. The board could have reached the same decision had the teacher not engaged in constitutionally protected conduct. **A marginal employee should not be able to prevent dismissal by engaging in constitutionally protected activity and then hiding under a constitutional shield as protection from all other actions that were not constitutionally protected.** The lower courts were instructed to determine whether the board's decision could have been reached absent the constitutionally protected activity of phoning the radio station, and, if such a decision could have been reached, whether remedial action to correct the constitutional violation would be necessary. *Mt. Healthy City School Dist. v. Doyle,* 429 U.S. 274, 97 S.Ct. 568, 50 L.Ed.2d 471 (1977).

♦   *A university violated a professor's First Amendment rights by denying him a promotion after he publicly denounced the large amount of feminist literature in the curriculum.*

A tenured professor who taught American literature courses at Portland State University **spoke out publicly against feminist criticism of male writers in American literature and against the increase of non-traditional, feminist-oriented courses being offered in the English department.** He alleged that two colleagues opposed and delayed his promotion to full professor and that they and other members of the department recommended that he not receive merit pay increases and salary raises proportionate to his qualifications. He also alleged that the defendants sought to eliminate the American Literature and Culture courses he taught and succeeded in reducing the extent of the course offering and that they had ridiculed, harassed and humiliated him.

In his 42 U.S.C. § 1983 lawsuit against his colleagues, a federal court granted summary judgment to the defendants. The U.S. Court of Appeals, Ninth Circuit, noted that a college professor cannot be arbitrarily disciplined for speaking freely. The court added that **any member of a college faculty would know that denying a staff member a promotion because of his speech on educational policy would violate his constitutional rights.** The allegations of denial of promotion and discrimination in pay constituted denials of government benefits redressable by § 1983. However, the allegations that the defendants limited his course offerings and denied him a position on a search committee were not covered by § 1983. Professors do not have property rights to the units assigned their courses, the length of courses or their place on a college search committee. The court reversed in part the lower court's decision and remanded the case. *Hollister v. Tuttle*, 2000 U.S. App. LEXIS 5631 (9th Cir., 2000).

◆　*In a case involving Internet access, the Fourth Circuit held that state officials could limit employee access to sexually explicit materials.*

Six employees of Virginia public higher education institutions sued various state officials in a federal district court, challenging the constitutionality of a state statute barring public employees from using agency owned or leased computers to access, download, print or store sexually explicit material without the written approval of the agency head. The employees claimed that the restrictions on their use of state-owned or leased equipment violated their right of free expression under the First Amendment. The court agreed, and the state officials appealed to the Fourth Circuit.

The court observed that the law provided an avenue for employees to obtain permission from agency heads when access was required for a legitimate research project and did not prohibit all access by state employees to sexually explicit materials. Employees remained free to access any materials from their personal computers. The court balanced the employee interest in expression against the agency interest in promoting efficient public services. The Virginia law only regulated the speech of public employees while they acted within their capacity as employees. **Because the state retained the ability to control the manner in which employees performed their work and to direct employee activities, the court reversed the district court judgment and upheld the law.** *Urofsky v. Gilmore*, 167 F.3d 191 (4th Cir.1999).

◆　*University professors could not be barred from testifying against the state in various lawsuits.*

A Texas state university policy and a state law prohibited university professors and state employees from taking employment as consultants or expert witnesses in litigation against the state, or when doing so would create a conflict with the state's interests. A number of professors sued to have the policy and the law struck down as unconstitutional. They asserted that their free speech and equal protection rights were being violated. A federal court granted the professors a preliminary injunction, and the state appealed. The Fifth Circuit Court of Appeals affirmed, finding that the policy and the law were impermissibly overbroad under the First Amendment. **The professors' rights to testify (whether for a fee or not) on a matter of public concern outweighed the state's right to prevent its employees from creating a conflict by testifying against it.** Although the court acknowledged that there could be times when the state's interest would outweigh the interests of the professors, the policy and the law at issue here prohibited all speech, even that which would not adversely affect the state's interest in the efficient delivery of public services. The court further noted that although some of the professors were being paid as expert witnesses or consultants, their speech did not qualify as commercial speech, for which less protection would be available. The policy and the law were struck down. *Hoover v. Morales*, 164 F.3d 221 (5th Cir.1998).

◆   *Where a university allowed the history department to use a display case, it could not regulate the type of expression employed.*
The history department of a Minnesota university maintained a display case in a university building hallway. Two student members of the university history club proposed that professors pose in photographs depicting their areas of historical interest for a display in the case. Eleven professors posed in period costumes and their pictures were displayed with their written comments. **The university's affirmative action officer observed that two of the photographs showed professors posed with weapons and declared them insensitive and inappropriate.** The university chancellor agreed to remove the pictures, and the students and professors filed a federal district court action against the chancellor and university, asserting constitutional violations. The court granted the university's summary judgment motion. However, the court denied summary judgment to the chancellor on the issue of qualified immunity, finding that his actions violated the clearly established First Amendment rights of the professors and students.
The chancellor appealed to the U.S. Court of Appeals, Eighth Circuit, which reversed the district court decision, but later granted a petition to review the matter. On review, **the court found that the history display was an appropriate use of the display case and that once the university recognized the use of the case by the history department, it could not discriminate against different types of speech being expressed there.** The chancellor's decision to discriminate against the viewpoint expressed by the professors and students violated clearly established First Amendment rights. Because there was no valid reason for curtailing this expression, the district court had correctly denied the chancellor's summary judgment motion for qualified immunity. *Burnham v. Ianni*, 119 F.3d 668 (8th Cir.1997).

◆   *In* Waters v. Churchill, *511 U.S. 661 (1994), the Supreme Court held that where a reasonable belief of workplace disruption motivates an adverse employment decision, that can be enough to outweigh a speaker's rights under the First Amendment.*
The chairman of the Black Studies department at City College of New York gave a speech proclaiming bias in the state public school curriculum. His remarks included derogatory statements against Jews. The college board of trustees then voted to limit his term as department chair to one year instead of the usual three. The professor sued the college, its board of trustees and individual trustees in the U.S. District Court for the Southern District of New York for violating his First Amendment rights. **The court conducted a jury trial and determined that the professor had been demoted because of his speech, even though the speech did not disrupt department operations.** The jury also determined that the

trustees had been motivated by a reasonable expectation that the speech would cause disruption and that some of the trustees had acted with malicious intent to violate his constitutional rights. The court ordered reinstatement and awarded punitive damages to the professor. The U.S. Court of Appeals, Second Circuit, affirmed the decision in part and remanded the case for correction of some inconsistencies in the damage award. However, the U.S. Supreme Court vacated and remanded the case for reconsideration.

On remand, the court of appeals reviewed the case in light of *Waters v. Churchill*, 511 U.S. 661, 114 S.Ct. 1878, 128 L.Ed.2d 686 (1994), a Supreme Court decision that reduced the burden on a government employer to demonstrate the actual disruptiveness of an employee's speech. *Waters* held that employment termination was permitted where only a likelihood of disruption existed. It was unnecessary to demonstrate an actual disruption if termination was based on the employer's reasonable belief that a disruption could occur. **Because the jury had found that the professor's speech had a reasonable potential for interfering with college operations, the demotion had not been improperly motivated.** The trustees had not violated the professor's First Amendment rights, and the district court's judgment was reversed and remanded. *Jeffries v. Harleston*, 52 F.3d 9 (2d Cir.1995).

◆   *Prior to* Waters v. Churchill, *511 U.S. 661 (1994), courts required actual harm to an employer's operations before governmental interest would outweigh an employee's interest.*

A Wisconsin man worked for a government-sponsored survey research laboratory as an interviewer. Interviewers were required to sign and abide by a pledge of confidentiality. The employee was assigned to conduct a survey of shoppers' attitudes toward group activities and demonstrations in shopping centers. The employee expressed displeasure that the laboratory was conducting the survey. He explained that there was litigation concerning the free speech rights of individuals and groups in shopping malls pending in a local circuit court. He did not further participate in the survey. He contacted a newspaper which published the survey questions. The survey was stopped after the article appeared. The employee was then fired. He sued his employer, alleging that he was fired in retaliation for exercising his First Amendment rights. The trial court found for the employee and the appellate court affirmed. The employer appealed to the Wisconsin Supreme Court.

On appeal, the court noted that courts have emphasized that the public employer must show actual, material and substantial harm to its operations as a result of the employee's speech. The employer may justify discharging an employee by showing, as it did here, that the employee's speech will have a substantial and detrimental impact on its long-term operations and viability. The court found that **the employee's speech threatened the laboratory's viability and profitability as a research organization because if the laboratory developed a reputation for disclosing survey questions before the completion of a survey, present and future clients would go elsewhere and the laboratory's very existence would be threatened.** The court found for the employer. *Barnhill v. Bd. of Regents*, 479 N.W.2d 917 (Wis.1992).

+ *Where a coach used a racially derogatory term, he could be fired even though he meant the term in a positive way. However, the school's anti-harassment policy violated the First Amendment.*

The head basketball coach of Central Michigan University used the word "nigger" during a team locker room meeting. He later stated that he had used the word in a positive sense to inspire the team to play harder. He maintained that the players used the word themselves "to connote a person who is fearless, mentally strong and tough." A player complained to the CMU affirmative action officer about the incident, and she recommended discipline for violating the university's anti-harassment policy. The incident became widely publicized and the university athletic director advised the coach that he would not be retained. The coach filed a lawsuit against CMU in the U.S. District Court for the Eastern District of Michigan claiming wrongful termination and violation of his First Amendment rights. Some members of the basketball team joined the lawsuit alleging that the anti-harassment policy violated their First Amendment rights. The court agreed with the students, ruling that the policy was unconstitutionally vague and overbroad. However, the court granted summary judgment to CMU on the employment claim.

The U.S. Court of Appeals, Sixth Circuit, reviewed the policy, which prohibited "racial and ethnic harassment." This was defined as any physical, verbal or nonverbal behavior that intimidated an individual or created a hostile, offensive environment. **Because the policy would allow CMU to violate the First Amendment rights of many individuals without regard for the speaker's intent, it was unconstitutionally overbroad. It was also unconstitutionally vague** because it deprived speakers of fair notice of acceptable standards of conduct. Accordingly, the court affirmed the district court's decision concerning the speech policy. The district court had also properly determined that the use of racial epithets by the coach was not constitutionally protected and served no academic purpose. *Dambrot v. Central Michigan Univ.*, 55 F.3d 1177 (6th Cir.1995).

B. Religion and Free Speech

The First Amendment, in addition to providing free speech rights, contains the Establishment Clause (which prohibits Congress from making any law respecting the establishment of religion), and the Free Exercise Clause (which bars Congress from making any law that prohibits the free exercise of religion).

However, like the free speech provisions of the First Amendment, the religion clauses target governmental action. Thus, they do not apply to private schools except where those schools are dealing with governmental entities.

+ *A college course on sexuality that examined religious views toward the subject did not impermissibly endorse religion in violation of the First Amendment.*

A New York community college offered a physical education course titled "Family Living and Human Sexuality" as an elective since the 1960s. Textbooks for the course referred to religion: one compared the approaches of Eastern and Western religions to sexuality, and another expressed support for the gay rights movement. Course instructors encouraged students to re-examine their attitudes toward sexuality, and openly discussed abortion, contraception and sexual acts. **A taxpayer group sought an order from a federal district court stating that the course violated the U.S. Constitution** because it subjected "impressionable students to a barrage of dogmatic pronouncements against the Judeo-Christian sexual ethic and in favor of Eastern spirituality." The court dismissed most of the claims advanced by the taxpayers, including those based on New York law and the Free Exercise Clauses of the New York and U.S. constitutions. The college then requested summary judgment on the remaining Establishment Clause claim.

The court determined that the course did not involve state endorsement of or entanglement with religion, finding no evidence that curriculum committee members had any dealings with religious organizations. There was no legitimate state interest in protecting taxpayers from views they found distasteful. The course covered a wide variety of subjects, and the course materials were designed to teach students about human sexuality, not religion. **In the court's view, adopting the taxpayers' position would lead to a constitutional violation since it would allow one group to dictate the content of a public college's curriculum.** Summary judgment was awarded in favor of the college. *Gheta v. Nassau County Community College,* 33 F. Supp.2d 179 (E.D.N.Y.1999).

◆ *If a public college or university creates a public forum for speech, it cannot prohibit religious speech. However, where no public forum is created, reasonable restrictions can be imposed.*

A physiology professor at the University of Alabama occasionally mentioned his religious beliefs during classes. He also scheduled an after-class discussion group titled "Evidence of God in Human Physiology," which several of his students attended. Although he stated that his remarks were his own personal bias, a group of his students complained to the head of the physiology department. **The department head, after meeting with the dean and the school's attorney, drafted a memo directing the professor to stop interjecting his personal religious beliefs in class and not to hold the optional classes.** The professor petitioned the president of the university for a rescission of the order, but the president affirmed the restrictions. The professor filed suit in federal court under 42 U.S.C. § 1983 seeking an injunction lifting the restrictions placed on his speech. The professor moved for summary judgment. **The trial court determined that the university had created a public forum for the exchange of ideas, and that the university's interests were not sufficient to justify restricting the professor's freedom of speech.** The court granted summary judgment in favor of the professor. The university appealed to the U.S. Court of Appeals, Eleventh Circuit.

The appeals court rejected the district court's determination that a classroom constituted a public forum. It relied on the U.S. Supreme Court's decision in *Hazelwood School Dist. v. Kuhlmeier,* 484 U.S. 261, 108 S.Ct. 562, 98 L.Ed.2d 592 (1988), in which the Court stated that "school facilities may be deemed to be public forums only if school authorities have ... opened those facilities for indiscriminate use by the general public." If the facilities, as in this case, have been reserved for other intended purposes, no public forum has been created. **Where no public forum exists, school officials may impose reasonable** restrictions on the speech rights of students and teachers. **Accordingly, the appeals court held that the professor's classroom was not a public forum and the university could reasonably regulate his speech.** In addition, the university could prohibit the professor from promoting and scheduling optional classes. The court reversed the district court's judgment. *Bishop v. Aronov*, 926 F.2d 1066 (11th Cir.1991).

◆   *The Supreme Court ruled that the act of certifying a union by the National Labor Relations Board would infringe upon a Catholic school's religious freedom rights under the First Amendment.*

The right of employees of a Catholic school system to join together and be recognized as a bargaining unit was successfully challenged in a case decided by the U.S. Supreme Court. In this case, the unions were certified by the NLRB as bargaining units but the diocese refused to bargain. The court said that the religion clauses of the U.S. Constitution, which require religious organizations to finance their educational systems without governmental aid, also free the religious organizations of the obviously inhibiting effect and impact of unionization of their teachers. The court agreed with the employer's contention that **the very threshold act of certification of the union by the NLRB would necessarily alter and infringe upon the religious character of parochial schools,** since this would mean that the bishop would no longer be the sole repository of authority as required by church law. Instead, he would have to share some decision making with the union. This, said the Court, violated the religion clauses of the U.S. Constitution. *NLRB v. Catholic Bishop of Chicago*, 440 U.S. 490, 99 S.Ct. 1313, 59 L.Ed.2d 533 (1979).

◆   *Where two nuns were hired to perform secular services and then fired, they could bring a breach-of-contract action against the university.*

Two Ursuline nuns applied to a private Catholic university for professorial positions in the computer science department. The university offered them probationary positions under a contract which had no religious conditions and which was used for both lay and clerical faculty. There was no contractual provision that called for permission by their religious superiors. Both nuns eventually accepted the employment. During their second year, doubts were voiced by other faculty members and the administration as to whether the nuns were qualified to do the job. The university determined that the nuns were a "disruptive influence" and that they should be dismissed. However, instead of following proper procedures, university officials consulted a Marist brother who was also an administrator for the university. He conferred with the nuns' Ursuline superiors who refused the nuns permission to renew their contracts. The university dismissed the nuns under Roman Catholic canon law which prohibited "accepting duties outside the institute without permission of the legitimate superior." A district court found for the nuns on a breach-of-contract claim. The court of appeals reversed. The nuns appealed to the New Jersey Supreme Court.

The issue on appeal was **whether there were matters of religion that precluded a civil court action under the First Amendment Free Exercise Clause.** First, the supreme court distinguished between religious institution employees who "spread the faith" and those with "secular obligations." It then determined that the "ministerial function test" prohibited court intervention only when the employment activity involved some sort of direct participation in religious activities. Other jurisdictions had concluded that ministerial functions "did not depend upon ordination but upon the function of the position." The nuns had not counseled students as to spiritual affairs or moral matters and had performed primarily secular tasks. The court concluded that **the nuns had not performed any "ministerial functions." They had been hired for their valuable computer related skills, not for their clerical value.** Further, there had been no indication by either party that the contract was to be governed by canon law. The supreme court held that the courts had jurisdiction and reversed the holding of the court of appeals. *Welter v. Seton Hall University*, 608 A.2d 206 (N.J.1992).

C. Loyalty Oaths

◆   *A loyalty oath could not be administered to two applicants who objected to it on religious grounds.*

Two Jehovah's Witnesses applied for positions with the California Community College District. As part of state-mandated pre-employment procedures, the district required the applicants to sign an oath swearing "true faith and allegiance" and to "support and defend" the United States and California constitutions. The applicants refused to take the oath due to their religious beliefs, and the district rejected their applications. The applicants filed suit against the district under the Religious Freedom Restoration Act of 1993 (RFRA), challenging the validity of the loyalty oath as a condition precedent for employment. The U.S. District Court for the Eastern District of California held that the RFRA applied retroactively, that the applicants had timely filed their claim within California's catch-all three-year statute of limitations and that the community college district was not qualifiedly immune from suit. Next, the court held that **requiring the applicants to take an oath that violated their religious tenets placed an undue burden on their right to free exercise of religion.** The district failed to assert that the loyalty oath furthered a compelling government interest or was the least restrictive means of achieving that interest. Although employee loyalty was a compelling interest, the evidence failed to establish that a loyalty oath effectively achieved this goal. An alternative oath directed to an applicant's actions rather than his or her beliefs would be equally effective and less restrictive. Because the loyalty oath could not be justified under the compelling interest test articulated in the RFRA, the court enjoined the district from administering the loyalty oath to the applicants. *Bessard v. California Community Colleges*, 867 F. Supp. 1454 (E.D.Cal.1994).

[*Editor's Note*: The U.S. Supreme Court held that the RFRA was unconstitutional as applied to state actions in *City of Boerne, Texas v. Flores*, 521 U.S. 507, 117 S.Ct. 2157, 138 L.Ed.2d 624 (1997).]

◆   *In 1955, as McCarthyism waned, the Supreme Court invalidated a New York City charter provision which purported to deprive Communist Party members of their Fifth Amendment right against self-incrimination.*

Section 903 of New York City's charter provided that any city employee who used the Fifth Amendment's self-incrimination privilege to avoid

answering a question relating to official conduct would lose tenure and be ineligible for future city employment. An associate professor of German at Brooklyn College was called before the U.S. Senate Judiciary Committee's Internal Security Subcommittee to testify about subversive influences within the nation's educational system. The professor testified that he was not a member of the Communist party and was completely willing to answer questions about his political affiliation from 1941 to the present date. However, he refused to answer questions about his political beliefs during 1940 and 1941 on the grounds that his answers might incriminate him. After the professor testified, the college suspended him even though he had taught there 27 years and was entitled to tenure under New York state law. Three days later, his position was vacated in accordance with § 903. If not for § 903, because he was tenured, the professor would have been entitled to notice, a hearing and the opportunity to appeal an unfavorable decision, with discharge for just cause being the only appropriate result.

The professor sued, challenging the constitutionality of § 903. He argued that the section violated the Privileges and Immunities Clause of the Fourteenth Amendment since it effectively imposed a penalty on the exercise of a federally guaranteed right in a federal proceeding. He also argued that it violated his due process rights under the Fifth and Fourteenth Amendments because the statute did not provide a reasonable basis for his termination. The case reached the U.S. Supreme Court, which held that **the statute violated the Due Process Clause** and therefore did not rule on the Privileges and Immunities Clause claim. The Court also held that taking the self-incrimination privilege could not automatically be interpreted to mean that the teacher had been a Communist Party member. The Court held that such an arbitrary dismissal violated due process. *Slochower v. Board of Education*, 350 U.S. 551, 76 S.Ct. 637, 100 L.Ed. 692 (1955).

◆   *A state could not require teachers to file annual affidavits listing every organization they belonged to in the past five years.*

The Arkansas legislature established **a statute that required every teacher employed by a state-supported school or college to file an annual affidavit listing every organization to which he or she had belonged in the past five years.** A teacher who had worked for an Arkansas school system for 25 years and who was a member of the NAACP was told he would have to file such an affidavit before the start of the next school year. After he failed to do so, his contract for the next year was not renewed. He filed a class-action lawsuit against the school district in a federal district court. The court found that the teacher was not a member of the Communist Party, nor of any organization advocating the violent overthrow of the government. It upheld the statute, finding that the information requested by the school district was relevant. The Supreme Court of Arkansas had previously upheld the statute's constitutionality in a case brought in the state court system by other teachers. The U.S. Supreme Court agreed to hear both cases and consolidated them for a hearing. The Court noted that the state certainly had a right to investigate teachers, since education of youth was a vital public interest. It stated that the requirement of the affidavit was reasonably related to the state's interest. However, the Court held that **requiring teachers to name all their associations was an interference of teacher free speech and**

association rights. The Court ruled that because fundamental rights were involved, governmental screening of teachers was required to be narrowly tailored to the state's ends. Because the statute went beyond what was necessary to meet the state's inquiry into the fitness of its teachers, the Court ruled it unconstitutional. *Shelton v. Tucker,* 364 U.S. 479, 81 S.Ct. 247, 5 L.Ed.2d 231 (1960).

◆   *The Supreme Court struck down a Florida loyalty oath statute as unconstitutionally vague.*

A Florida law required all state employees to submit a written oath, certifying that they had never lent counsel, advised, aided or supported the Communist party. Failure to submit such an oath resulted in the employee's immediate termination. A teacher who had taught in the same Florida school district for nine years was dismissed when he refused to sign the oath. The teacher sought a declaration that the statute was unconstitutional and an injunction to prevent its enforcement. A Florida trial court refused to grant an injunction, and the Florida Supreme Court affirmed this decision. After determining that the case was based on federal law and was properly a matter in which it had jurisdiction, the U.S. Supreme Court struck the statute down as a violation of the Fourteenth Amendment's Due Process Clause. **The statute was too vague to pass constitutional standards.** It compelled state employees to take the oath or face immediate dismissal. Because the statute lacked objective standards, no employee could truthfully take the oath. Statutes which made persons of average intelligence guess at their possible meanings and applications violated the Due Process Clause because they did not constitute true rules or standards. The Court reversed the Florida court decision, ruling for the teacher. *Cramp v. Board of Public Instruction of Orange County,* 368 U.S. 278, 82 S.Ct. 275, 7 L.Ed.2d 285 (1961).

◆   *Likewise, a Washington statute aimed at prohibiting subversives from becoming teachers was too vague to be constitutional.*

Faculty members at the University of Washington brought a class-action suit to declare two state statutes unconstitutional. One statute required all state employees to take loyalty oaths, and the other required all teachers to take an oath as a condition of employment. Both oaths dealt with employee loyalty to the U.S. Constitution and to the government. The public employee statute applied to all public employees and defined a "subversive person" as one who conspired to overthrow the government. The Communist Party was also named as a subversive organization. Persons designated as subversives or Communist Party members were ineligible for public employment. The U.S. Supreme Court held that the statutes were vague and overbroad, and violated the Fourteenth Amendment's Due Process Clause. The statutes were too unspecific to provide sufficient notice of what conduct was prohibited. This constituted a denial of the teachers' due process rights. **The university could not require its teachers to take an oath that applied to some vague behavior in the future,** especially since there were First Amendment freedom of speech and association claims at stake. *Baggett v. Bullitt,* 377 U.S. 360, 84 S.Ct. 1316, 12 L.Ed.2d 377 (1963).

♦   *An Arizona statute that prohibited even associating with the Communist Party was struck down. The statute should have prohibited only those employees with a "specific intent" to do something illegal.*

An Arizona teacher who was a Quaker refused to take an oath required of all public employees under state law. The oath swore that the employees would support both the Arizona and the U.S. Constitutions as well as state laws. The legislation also stated that anyone who took the oath and supported the Communist party or the violent overthrow of government would be discharged from employment and charged with perjury. The teacher sued for declaratory relief in the Arizona courts, having decided she could not take the oath in good conscience because she did not know what it meant. The case eventually reached the U.S. Supreme Court which held that political groups may have both legal and illegal aims and that there should not be a blanket prohibition on all groups that might have both legal and illegal goals. Such a prohibition would threaten legitimate political expression and association. The Court held that mere association with a group cannot be prohibited without a showing of "specific intent" to carry out the group's illegal purpose. It went on to say that **the Arizona statute was constitutionally deficient because it was not confined to those employees with a "specific intent" to do something illegal.** The statute infringed employee rights to free association by not punishing specific behavior that yielded a clear and present danger to government. The statute was struck down as unconstitutional. *Elfbrandt v. Russell*, 384 U.S. 11, 86 S.Ct. 1238, 16 L.Ed.2d 321 (1965).

♦   *In 1967, the Supreme Court held that New York statutory prohibitions on treasonable and seditious speech by public employees were unconstitutionally vague. The statute might have allowed dismissal of employees who believed in such a doctrine, without actually advocating it.*

A group of faculty members were employed by the privately owned University of Buffalo in New York. They continued their employment when the university merged into a state-operated university. Because they became public employees, the faculty members were required to comply with a state plan that disqualified subversive persons from public employment. Four professors refused to sign a certificate that they were not Communists and that if they ever had been, they had notified the state university's president. One instructor was dismissed immediately for refusing to sign the certificate. Two more continued to teach until their contracts ran out. Another was dismissed after refusing to answer under oath whether he had ever been a Communist party member. The group sought injunctive and declaratory relief in a federal district court. The district court held that the state requirements were constitutional. The U.S. Supreme Court agreed to hear the case.

The Court examined the statute, which allowed the removal of public school teachers for "treasonable or seditious" utterances or acts. The Court held that such words were too vague to allow teachers to know the difference between seditious and nonseditious utterances or acts. In addition, another section of the statute allowed dismissal of any person who "by word of mouth or writing willfully and deliberately advocates, advises or teaches the doctrine" of the violent overthrow of government. The Court struck it down as too vague and sweeping, stating that it might allow dismissal of an employee who merely believes in such a doctrine, without actually advocating it. Because of such vague provisions, teachers would not know exactly what is prohibited and would stay away from all utterances or acts that might constitute treachery or sedition. Thus, **teachers' speech and association rights would be inhibited. Although the state has a legitimate interest in screening teachers, it must do so only in a manner that does not stifle fundamental personal rights. Public employment may not be conditioned upon the surrender of constitutional rights.** The Court reversed the district court's decision. *Keyishian v. Board of Regents*, 385 U.S. 589, 87 S.Ct. 675, 17 L.Ed.2d 629 (1967).

◆   *The Supreme Court held that the line between permissible and impermissible conduct must be clearly drawn in loyalty oaths.*

A teacher was offered a position with the University of Maryland. However, he refused to take a loyalty oath required by the university for its employees. The oath required the employee to swear that he was not engaged in any attempt to overthrow the government by force or violence. The teacher brought suit challenging the oath's constitutionality. The U.S. Supreme Court decided that the oath's constitutionality had to be considered in conjunction with the state statute allowing the university board of regents to establish the oath. In addition, free speech rights were implicated because the First Amendment protects controversial as well as conventional speech. The Court held that **the authorizing statute was unconstitutionally vague and overbroad. It falsely assumed that someone belonging to a subversive group also supported the violent overthrow of the government.** The statute also put continuous surveillance on teachers by imposing a perjury threat. Such a concept was hostile to academic freedom, limiting the free flow of ideas in places of learning. The Court ruled that the line between permissible and impermissible conduct must be clearly drawn. **Because the statute failed to clearly define prohibited behavior, it was unconstitutional.** *Whitehill v. Elkins*, 389 U.S. 54, 88 S.Ct. 184, 19 L.Ed.2d 228 (1967).

D. Academic Freedom

In *Sweezy v. New Hampshire*, 354 U.S. 234, 77 S.Ct. 1203, 1 L.Ed.2d 1311 (1957), the Supreme Court said about academic freedom that "the essentiality of freedom in the community of American universities is almost self-evident.... Scholarship cannot flourish in an atmosphere of suspicion and distrust. Teachers and students must always remain free to inquire, to study and evaluate, to gain new maturity and understanding; otherwise our civilization will stagnate and die." However, academic freedom is not an absolute principle. The teacher's right to speak on a given matter must be balanced against the college or university's right to forward legitimate pedagogical interests.

◆   *A college was held to have inappropriately fired a professor for conduct and comments he made during class.*

A former professor at a Colorado junior college sued the college for terminating his employment on the basis of allegedly inappropriate classroom conduct and speech. He claimed that the college violated his First Amendment and academic freedom rights. The case arose when **a number of students**

complained that the professor used an inappropriate teaching style and
made offensive comments during class. He allegedly discussed the presence of
tampons in a sewer plant while lecturing about animal parasites; referred to human
oral and anal sex and male orgasms during a lecture about the transmission of
parasites; used euphemisms to describe feces; implied that students were "dumb";
inappropriately referred to comments made in student evaluations; and discussed
matters unrelated to course content during class. A jury found in favor of the
professor, awarding him over $550,000 in damages. The college appealed.

The Tenth Circuit Court of Appeals affirmed the ruling for the professor. It
noted that teachers enjoy some First Amendment protection in their classroom
speech and cited to *Keyishian v. Board of Regents*, 385 U.S. 589 (*see* Section I.C.,
above), and *Tinker v. Des Moines Indep. Community School Dist.*, 393 U.S. 503
(1969), where the Supreme Court stated that **students and teachers do not shed
their constitutional rights to freedom of expression at the schoolhouse gate.**
Further, although not every word uttered by a teacher in class is protected by
academic freedom, the jury here had ruled that the professor's termination was not
reasonably related to legitimate pedagogical interests, and the college had failed
to object to having the jury decide that question. *Vanderhurst v. Colorado
Mountain College Dist.*, 208 F.3d 908 (10th Cir.2000).

♦   *A professor who used offensive language in the classroom for the purpose of
teaching his students could not be suspended.*
**A community college professor in English and literature used "all of the
English language" in his teaching style, employing words that some might
regard as offensive.** However, he encountered no complaints for over 30 years.
In 1998, a student complained of his profane language in the classroom. She
asserted that it was harassing even though it was not directed at any particular
student. A parent also complained about a handout the professor had distributed.
The college revised its sexual harassment policy and also distributed a memorandum which stated that "regular use of profane, vulgar or obscene speech which
is not germane to course content (and thus educational purpose) … will lead to the
imposition of discipline." A second student complaint was then filed against the
professor, who redacted the student's name and the course she was taking from
the complaint, and distributed it to his students (along with a memo on the First
Amendment) for a discussion of academic freedom. The college eventually
determined that the sexual harassment claim did not have merit, but suspended the
professor for three days because of his classroom language.

The college later indefinitely suspended the professor (with pay and benefits)
for redacting the student's name from the complaint and then distributing it to his
students. The professor sued various college officials in a Michigan federal court,
which held in his favor. It noted that the professor's redaction of the student's
identifying information prior to distributing the complaint and the memo did not
breach the duty of confidentiality or amount to retaliation against the complaining
student. Further, **his acts were protected by the First Amendment. The court
ordered the college to reinstate the professor.** *Bonnell v. Lorenzo*, 81 F.Supp.2d
777 (E.D.Mich.1999).

◆   *A professor fired for teaching pornography was able to survive a motion to dismiss his claim for violating his academic freedom rights.*

An adjunct assistant professor of humanities at a New York college was also hired to be an English instructor. **He conducted a lesson aimed at reducing the use of repetitive words and ideas in essay writing and allowed the students to choose the topic. They chose sex. He modified it to relationships/sex and warned the students against using sexually explicit terms,** as doing so would alienate readers. He wrote down ideas suggested by the students on the blackboard, but used initials to represent sexually explicit terms. Subsequently, he was fired for violating the college's sexual harassment policy and for teaching pornography. He sued under a number of theories, one of which was that the college had violated his academic freedom rights under the First Amendment. The court refused to dismiss the action, finding that the university had failed to properly move for dismissal on the claim. However, it indicated that he was unlikely to win on his claim. *Vega v. State Univ. of New York Bd. of Trustees*, 67 F.Supp.2d 324 (S.D.N.Y.1999).

◆   *A public university professor did not have a right to determine what would be taught in his classroom.*

A professor at a Pennsylvania university taught a course titled "Introduction to Educational Media." One of his students complained that he used the class to advance religious ideas. For example, his syllabus for at least one class included an emphasis on bias, censorship, religion and humanism, and listed numerous publications discussing those issues as required or recommended reading. The vice president for academic affairs wrote the professor, directing him to cease and desist from using "doctrinaire materials" of a religious nature. When **the new chair of the education department became concerned that the professor was still advancing religious issues,** he and the department faculty voted to reinstate an earlier syllabus, and he cancelled certain book orders. Eventually, the professor was suspended with pay, although he returned the next semester to teach several courses. When the professor sued the university for violating his free speech rights, the case reached the U.S. Court of Appeals, Third Circuit. The court of appeals held that **a public university professor does not have a First Amendment right to determine what will be taught in the classroom.** Outside the classroom, the professor had a right to advocate for the use of certain curriculum materials. However, inside the classroom, he did not have a right to use those materials without permission. The university was allowed to make content-based decisions when shaping its curriculum. *Edwards v. California Univ. of Pennsylvania*, 156 F.3d 488 (3d Cir.1998).

II. DEFAMATION

Defamation consists of an oral (slander) or written (libel) communication which injures a person's reputation. The defamatory material must have been disclosed to third parties who understand that the material refers to the plaintiff. Also, the plaintiff's reputation must have suffered in the minds of the third parties, and there must be a tangible (usually economic) injury. Several absolute defenses exist to a defamation lawsuit including truth, consent and opinion. Another defense, fair comment, also provides a conditional defense.

◆   *A newspaper could not repeat a defamatory statement without determining the truth of the statement.*

In a newspaper commentary written by a nonemployee, a professor was identified as having been reprimanded for numerous complaints of sexual harassment. The commentary also stated that, as revealed in recently unsealed court papers, the professor had been accused of masturbating during a faculty meeting, but that no sanctions were imposed for that offense. The professor sued the newspaper and the writer for defamation, conceding that he had been accused of masturbating but denying that the accusation was true. The newspaper defended the action by claiming the privilege of fair reporting of judicial proceedings and by asserting that the accusation was true. A trial court granted summary judgment to the defendants.

The Superior Court of New Jersey, Appellate Division, reversed. It noted that **the privilege was not available because the report was not full, fair and accurate. First, the report implied that the masturbation incident came after the reprimand for sexual harassment, when in fact the accusation had come some 10 years earlier.** Second, the report implied that the professor had been charged in the court action, which was not true. And third, by stating that the professor had not been sanctioned, the report implied that he had been found guilty or liable. The court also found that, **in order to assert the defense of truth, the newspaper had to show more than that the accusation had been made. It had to show that the accusation was true as well.** Otherwise, it could escape liability by merely repeating what someone else (perhaps an unreliable gossip) had said first. The defamation action could continue. *Fortenbaugh v. New Jersey Press, Inc.*, 722 A.2d 568 (N.J.Super.A.D.1999).

◆   *A university employee could not show defamation where he admitted the facts upon which the statement was based.*

The University of Kentucky hired a manager for its College of Engineering's machine shop. The dean of the college informed the manager that he could do private consulting work the equivalent of one day per week. The dean's understanding was that the machinist would not use shop machinists in his private consulting work. However, the manager believed that he could use shop facilities, materials and machinists. He contracted for outside work and used university machinists and materials for the jobs, but never reimbursed the university for the use of the machines, materials or the machinists' work. Subsequently, an audit was conducted. The report stated that it appeared that the manager had violated university policy as well as criminal law regarding theft and misapplication of property. The university fired the manager, who sued for wrongful discharge and defamation, among other claims.

A state court dismissed his claims and he appealed. The Court of Appeals of Kentucky affirmed, noting that **the manager could not show defamation because he had conceded that he used university machinists for his personal work.** Because truth is a defense to a defamation action, the manager could not show that the statement about him violating university policy was defamatory.

Further, a statement in the form of an opinion (like this one was) could be defamatory only if it implied the existence of undisclosed defamatory facts. **Here, the audit report stated the facts upon which the opinion was based and therefore did not imply the existence of undisclosed defamatory facts.** *Buchholtz v. Dugan*, 977 S.W.2d 24 (Ky.App.1998).

◆ *A supervisor's statements that an employee did not follow up on assignments and did not get along well with her co-workers was not defamatory.*

An Illinois woman worked as the director of corporate relations for a private university for nine years. She was then approached by an organization about a comparable position. She was interviewed by a number of people at the organization and was told that the interviews had gone well. She believed that she was the leading candidate for the position and after another interview, she was told that she was going to be recommended for the job. Before her final interviews, the organization's director spoke to her supervisor at the university who stated that she "did not follow up on assignments" and did not get along well with her co-workers. Her final interviews were then canceled. She sued the university for defamation and intentional interference with prospective economic advantage. The trial court dismissed the case. The appellate court reversed, and the university appealed to the Illinois Supreme Court.

The court held that to state a claim of intentional interference with prospective economic advantage, **the employee had to show that she had a reasonable expectancy of getting a position with the organization. Here, the employee had not completed all of the interviews and her beliefs that she was the leading candidate and that all of the interviews went well were completely subjective.** She did not attribute these assessments to anyone at the organization and did not support them with adequate evidence. Finding that the employee was nothing more than a candidate for the position with further interviews pending, the court held that she had no reasonable expectation of employment. The court also noted that the supervisor's statements could have been innocently construed to mean that the employee did not fit in with the university and did not perform well in that particular position. Since they were not necessarily comments on her lack of ability in her profession, they did not qualify as defamation *per se*. The court reversed the appellate court's decision. *Anderson v. Vanden Dorpel*, 667 N.E.2d 1296 (Ill.1996).

◆ *A professor who labeled an engineer a "crank" was found not liable for defamation.*

A mathematics professor employed by an Indiana private university wrote a book titled *Mathematical Cranks* in which he addressed a publication written by a Wisconsin engineer. The professor noted that the engineer's article read as if written by someone "whose mind will not be changed by anything" and labeled the engineer a "crank." The professor explained that the spectrum of mathematical cranks ran from the "slightly eccentric" to "people who are convinced that they have the truth, that it is revolutionary, and that mathematicians are engaged in a vast conspiracy to suppress it." The engineer filed a defamation lawsuit against the professor in a U.S. district court, alleging that the professor had acted with actual malice in writing the article. The district court granted the professor's motion to dismiss on the ground that the word "crank" was mere "rhetorical hyperbole," a well-recognized category of privileged defamation. The engineer appealed to the U.S. Court of Appeals, Seventh Circuit.

The court of appeals affirmed, holding that where one scholar calls another a "crank" for having taken a position that the first scholar considers patently wrong, the second does not have a remedy in defamation. **To call a person a "crank" is basically a colorful and insulting way of expressing disagreement with the owner's idea,** and it therefore belongs to the language of controversy rather than the language of defamation. This was especially clear where, as in the present case, the word was used in a work of scholarship. Scholars have their own remedies for unfair criticisms of their work. If the professor's criticisms of the engineer were unsound, the engineer could publish a rebuttal in the same journal in which he published the article that the professor attacked. *Dilworth v. Dudley*, 75 F.3d 307 (7th Cir.1996).

* *By making a statement that implied negative facts about a professor, a school's president set the school up for potential liability.*

A New York private school discharged an associate professor who was the chair of the liberal arts department. The president then distributed a memorandum informing the faculty that the chairman had been replaced. The memorandum also noted that he had been replaced because "there was no responsible alternative" and that the president was "confident that the department would improve under the new chairman." The discharged chairman filed suit against the school and its president in a New York trial court, alleging defamation and negligent hiring (presumably, of the president). The trial court denied the school's motion for summary judgment, and the school appealed to the New York Supreme Court, Appellate Division.

The appellate court affirmed, noting that the memorandum allegedly disparaging the chairman's professional ability was arguably libel *per se*. Whether the particular words were defamatory presented a legal question to be resolved by the trial court. **Although pure opinion was not actionable, the present memorandum implied the existence of undisclosed detrimental facts.** Consequently, the trial court had properly denied the school's motion for summary judgment with respect to the defamation claim. However, the professor's punitive damages and negligent hiring claims were dismissed. *Kovacs v. Briarcliffe School, Inc.*, 617 N.Y.S.2d 804 (A.D.2d Dept.1994).

* *A university was privileged to make otherwise defamatory statements in the following case.*

A New Jersey private university accepted the resignations of three department managers in the wake of their alleged diversion of university property for private gain. The university published a statement to members of the faculty and the administration that certain equipment had been used off campus on personal projects, that the estimated losses totaled approximately $10,000 and that three staff members had submitted their resignations. Reports in two university publications (for both students and alumni) expressly connected these three individuals with the alleged improprieties. The university declined to elaborate on any of the employees' cases or resignations and described them as "mutually arrived at decisions." One manager sued the university and certain officials, alleging that statements in the university publications were defamatory. The trial court granted the university's motion for pretrial judgment, and the manager appealed to the Superior Court of New Jersey, Appellate Division.

The court noted that **private corporations, including private universities, have a qualified privilege to communicate with contributors, employees and other persons involved in their activities regarding alleged employee wrongdoing.** It also noted that dissemination of information to the media may be the only method for such communication under some circumstances. Here, the university administration had an interest in informing the university community about the investigation rather than allowing it to remain the subject of vague and exaggerated rumors which could have damaged the university's reputation.

Because the university had tens of thousands of employees, students and alumni throughout the world, the publications utilized were the only effective method of disseminating the information. The court also held that the manager failed to establish that the university officials had made the statements with "reckless disregard of their truth or falsity." In fact, the officials had acted with circumspection in all their public comments regarding the investigation. The trial court ruling was affirmed. *Gallo v. Princeton University,* 656 A.2d 1267 (N.J.Super.A.D.1995).

♦   *Even though a school official's statements to a newspaper reporter were not published by the newspaper, they were "published" for purposes of defamation law and subjected the school to potential liability.*

The vice president of a private religious college spoke to a reporter from a local newspaper about a Missouri Department of Education evaluator's recent report concerning the college's teacher education program. He described the evaluator as "incompetent, out to get the college, prejudiced against the college, and opposed to church schools having education programs." The vice president also implied that the evaluator was a homosexual and that she was in a conspiracy with her housemate to effect a bad educational program evaluation of the college. However, **none of these statements were ever published by the newspaper.** The evaluator filed a defamation suit against the school and its vice president. A state trial court dismissed the lawsuit and the evaluator appealed to the Supreme Court of Missouri.

The school argued that the statements were never "published" in any form. The supreme court disagreed, ruling that **publication is merely communication to a third party** and hence the statements to the reporter constituted publication under state defamation law. The court then held that in all future Missouri defamation cases, a jury would be precluded from awarding damages unless actual damages were proven. Here, because the evaluator had stated in her complaint that she suffered injury to her business contacts and standing as a professional as well as loss of reputation and respect, resulting in a risk to her employment, the case had been wrongly dismissed. *Nazeri v. Missouri Valley College,* 860 S.W.2d 303 (Mo.Banc.1993).

III. STUDENTS

A. Religion and Free Speech

◆   *The Establishment Clause does not prevent private citizens from using public facilities for religious purposes. In fact, if a facility is made available to the public, religious groups cannot be excluded from using it also.*

The University of Missouri at Kansas City, a state university, made its facilities available for the general use of registered student groups. **A registered student religious group that had previously received permission to conduct its meetings in university facilities was informed that it could no longer do so because of a university regulation that prohibited use of its facilities for the purposes of religious worship or teaching**. Members of the group brought suit against the district in federal court, alleging that the regulation violated their First Amendment rights to free exercise of religion and freedom of speech. The court upheld the school's regulation, but the U.S. Court of Appeals, Eighth Circuit, reversed, stating that the regulation was discriminatory against religious speech and that the Establishment Clause does not bar a policy of equal access in which facilities are open to groups and speakers of all kinds.

The Supreme Court agreed with the court of appeals' assessment, stating **that the university policy violated the fundamental principle that state regulation of speech must be content-neutral**. It is obligatory upon the state to show that the regulation is necessary to serve a compelling state interest and that it is narrowly drawn to achieve that end. The state was unable to do that here. The state's interest in achieving greater separation of church and state than is already ensured under the Establishment Clause was not sufficiently "compelling" to justify content-based discrimination against religious speech of the student group in question. *Widmar v. Vincent*, 454 U.S. 263, 102 S.Ct. 269, 70 L.Ed.2d 400 (1981).

◆   *In* Rosenberger, *the Supreme Court held that the University of Virginia could not withhold authorization for payments to a printer on behalf of a Christian student organization. Because the university had opened a limited public forum by paying other third-party contractors on behalf of student groups, it could not deny payment to the printer on the grounds that the student organization's viewpoint was religious.*

The University of Virginia collected a mandatory $14 student activity fee from full-time students each semester. The fees supported extracurricular activities that were related to the educational purposes of the university. University-recognized student groups could apply for funding by the activities fund, although not all groups requested funds. University guidelines excluded religious groups from student funding as well as activities that could jeopardize the university's tax- exempt status. A university-recognized student group published a Christian newspaper for which it sought $5,862 from the activities fund for printing costs. The student council denied funding because the group's activities were deemed religious under university guidelines.

After exhausting appeals within the university, group members filed a lawsuit in the U.S. District Court for the Western District of Virginia, claiming constitutional rights violations. The court granted summary judgment to the university, and its decision was affirmed by the U.S. Court of Appeals, Fourth Circuit. The students appealed to the U.S. Supreme Court. The Court observed that **government entities must abstain from regulating speech on the basis of the speaker's opinion.** Upon establishing a limited public forum, state entities must respect the forum by refraining from the exclusion of speech based upon content.

Because the university had opened a limited public forum by paying other third-party contractors on behalf of student groups, it could not deny the religious group's claim for funds on the basis of its viewpoint. Allowing the payment of the group's printing costs amounted to a policy of government neutrality for different viewpoints. The Court distinguished the student fee from a general tax and placed emphasis on the indirect nature of the benefit. The Court reversed the lower court decisions, ruling that access to public school facilities on a neutral basis does not violate the Establishment Clause of the First Amendment. *Rosenberger v. Rector and Visitors of Univ. of Virginia*, 515 U.S. 819, 115 S.Ct. 2510, 132 L.Ed.2d 700 (1995).

◆   *Temporarily suspending the showing of a religious film did not result in liability.*

The Board of Regents of Oklahoma State University (OSU) temporarily suspended the showing by the university Student Union Activities Board (SUAB) of **"The Last Temptation of Christ,"** a film depicting Jesus descending from the cross to marry, father children and return to the cross. An association of students and faculty members advocating free speech rights filed a lawsuit in the U.S. District Court for the Northern District of Oklahoma, seeking declaratory relief. The regents lifted the suspension, and the film was shown as originally scheduled. The district court held that school officials could not be held liable for damages under 42 U.S.C. § 1983, and the association appealed to the U.S. Court of Appeals, Tenth Circuit. The court remanded the case to determine whether the association was entitled to nominal damages and whether the regents had qualified immunity from liability. The court determined that the association was not entitled to nominal damages and that the board enjoyed qualified immunity. The association filed a second appeal with the Tenth Circuit.

The court rejected the association's argument that the regents had violated the constitutional rights of its members by imposing content-based censorship. The regents had merely imposed a temporary suspension while obtaining a legal opinion concerning OSU's potential liability if it chose to allow the showing of the film. **The regents could not be held liable for violating any clearly established constitutional rights and the regents' action did not violate constitutional restraints on censorship.** Because the SUAB and OSU were closely related in funding and staffing, the regents had merely displayed caution in their decisionmaking process. The association was entitled to an award of attorney's fees for work done before the district court's initial order. *Cummins v. Campbell*, 44 F.3d 847 (10th Cir.1994).

◆   *Graduation prayers were allowed at Indiana University in the following case.*

In a case involving graduation prayers at Indiana University, the U.S. Court of Appeals, Seventh Circuit, distinguished the ceremonies from public school ceremonies involving younger students. **There was no element of coercion** requiring students to participate in the large, impersonal university commencement exercises, and many students and family members remained in their seats during the prayer. Adult students were unlikely to succumb to peer pressure and could choose not to attend the ceremony without suffering any severe consequences. The court agreed with the university that the prayers solemnized the ceremony, did not endorse any particular religion and allowed the university to continue a 155-year-old tradition. *Tanford v. Brand*, 104 F.3d 982 (7th Cir.1997).

B. Newspapers

♦   *Insulting statements that cannot be reasonably interpreted as stating facts cannot form the basis of a defamation action.*

A student newspaper at a Virginia university published an article describing the success of a student placement program. The article quoted a university official who facilitated student participation in the program and referred to her as "Director of Butt Licking." The official filed a Virginia circuit court action against the student newspaper for defamation and use of insulting words in violation of state law. The court held that the newspaper reference was void of any literal meaning and not reasonably susceptible to interpretation as containing factual information. The official appealed.

The Supreme Court of Virginia observed that statements that cannot reasonably be interpreted as stating facts about a person cannot form the basis of a defamation action. The court rejected the official's claim that she was entitled to present her case to a jury on grounds that literal interpretation of the offensive phrase imputed to her a criminal violation of the state sodomy statute and was defamatory. It also rejected her assertion that the statement injured her reputation and held her up to ridicule by implying that she lacked integrity. The court affirmed the judgment for the newspaper. *Yeagle v. Collegiate Times*, 497 S.E.2d 136 (Va.1998).

♦   *Where student editors refused to publish an advertisement they believed was defamatory, they could not be held liable under the First Amendment.*

An attorney wrote two articles that were highly critical of his law school, and which were published in his law school's newspaper. Subsequently, the attorney sought to have a classified advertisement placed in the paper, soliciting material that would discredit certain faculty and administrators at the school for the purpose of assisting him in a federal civil rights action against the school. He also sought in the ad to urge students who had been discriminatorily treated by the school's criminal defense clinic to join his Office of Civil Rights complaint against the clinic. When the paper's three student editors refused to publish the ad, fearing that it was defamatory and would expose them and the paper to litigation, the attorney sued the students and the school under the First Amendment. The U.S. District Court for the Eastern District of New York noted that the student editors were not state actors (a requirement for a claim brought under the First Amendment) and that the school did not exercise control over the newspaper. As a result, the attorney's claim could not succeed. The court dismissed the lawsuit. *Leeds v. Meltz*, 898 F.Supp. 146 (E.D.N.Y.1995).

◆   *Student journalists were entitled to receive campus arrest reports in the following case.*

A group of student journalists and an organization which promoted the rights of the student press brought a lawsuit against the U.S. Department of Education and the Secretary of Education. **They sought to enjoin the government from enforcing a provision of the Family Educational Rights and Privacy Act (FERPA), which allows the complete withdrawal of federal funding from any university that discloses personally identifiable student records.** The journalists alleged that this prohibition, as applied to campus security arrest reports, violated their First Amendment right to receive information. The journalists moved for an injunction in a federal district court to immediately halt enforcement of FERPA's prohibition. After resolving numerous procedural matters, the court examined the burdens imposed by FERPA and balanced them against the corresponding governmental interest. The journalists argued that the general arrest reports which are provided by local law enforcement officials do not distinguish which arrestees are students. Further, any attempt at matching those lists to student records is difficult and makes the effort to report campus crime ineffectual. The government maintained that the burden was trivial. **The court held that the government's position was "untenable," and that its interests were outweighed by the rights of the journalists.** A temporary injunction was issued which prevented the withdrawal of federal funding from any campus that disclosed its arrest reports. *Student Press Law Center v. Alexander*, 778 F. Supp. 321 (D.D.C.1991).

◆   *A university could not forbid some newspapers while allowing others to be distributed.*

Southwest Texas State University had a policy forbidding the distribution of newspapers that contained advertisements. The university did not regulate the distribution of newspapers or literature without advertisements. The regulation also did not apply to the student-run university newspaper, which contained many advertisements. Aside from these restrictions, the university fostered an environment of free expression. A group of students and a small, politically oriented, local newspaper that had attempted free distribution on campus sued the university, claiming that its "no solicitation" policy violated the First Amendment. A federal district court held for the university and the students appealed to the U.S. Court of Appeals, Fifth Circuit, which stated that **the university was a limited public forum. As such, its ability to regulate expressive conduct was limited.** There was no evidence that handing out free newspapers would affect the university's academic mission or crime rate. The regulation was not narrowly tailored to meet the privacy, litter or congestion interests of the university. Moreover, the fact that the university did not regulate publications without advertisements illustrated the tenuous nature of those arguments. The regulation was declared unconstitutional. *Hays County Guardian v. Supple*, 969 F.2d 111 (5th Cir.1992).

♦   *Following its ruling in* Healy v. James, *408 U.S. 169 (1972), the Supreme Court held that, at the collegiate level, the conduct of students and the dissemination of ideas—no matter how offensive—could not be curtailed based solely on the "conventions of decency."*

A graduate student at the University of Missouri was expelled for distributing on campus a newspaper that allegedly violated the bylaws of the university's curators since it contained forms of "indecent speech." The newspaper was found objectionable for two reasons. First, on the front cover was a political cartoon of policemen raping the Statue of Liberty and the Goddess of Justice with a caption that read "… with Liberty and Justice for All." Second, the issue contained an article titled "Mother Fucker Acquitted," which discussed the trial and acquittal on an assault charge of a New York youth. The expelled student sued the university in a federal district court, alleging that the university's action was improperly premised on activities protected by the First Amendment. The district court denied relief, and the Eighth Circuit Court of Appeals affirmed.

On further appeal, the U.S. Supreme Court held that the student should be reinstated to the university. The Court stated that **while a university has an undoubted prerogative to enforce reasonable rules governing student conduct, it is not immune from the sweep of the First Amendment.** The Court noted that *Healy v. James* (Section D, below) makes it clear that the mere dissemination of ideas—no matter how offensive to good taste—may not be shut off in the name of "conventions of decency" alone. *Papish v. University of Missouri*, 410 U.S. 667, 93 S.Ct. 1197, 35 L.Ed.2d 618 (1973).

C. Gay Rights

♦   *A university violated the speech rights of two organizations by prohibiting them from using facilities that they had reserved.*

A female graduate student at the University of Massachusetts sought to secure a classroom for two organizational meetings on two different nights. The meetings were sponsored by the Reproductive Rights Network and the Coalition for Lesbian and Gay Civil Rights, among other organizations. The student asked her professor for assistance in scheduling the space, and was authorized to call and reserve the room in the professor's name. A staff meeting was held on the morning of the first scheduled meeting, at which concerns were expressed about the effect of having the organizations meet on campus. **Officials were concerned that the university would be perceived as a sponsor, thus detrimentally affecting public and private fundraising.** However, the university allowed the first meeting to take place. None of the anticipated problems from allowing the meeting to occur came to pass. Nevertheless, the university closed the building where the second meeting was to take place, and 17 police officers prevented people from entering.

A trial court found that the university had violated the organizations' free speech rights, and entered an injunction to prevent the university from interfering with the organizations' rights to use university facilities for political speech. However, the court found that the university had not violated the Massachusetts Civil Rights Act. The Appeals Court of Massachusetts upheld the injunction, but also found that the university had violated the MCRA. **The university's failure**

to publish an explicit, content-neutral policy, containing objective standards on the use of university facilities, allowed it unbridled discretion to
deny use of its facilities to groups on the basis of the content of their speech.
Further, the use of numerous police officers to secure the building amounted to
"threats, intimidation or coercion" under the MCRA even though no physical
confrontation occurred. The court remanded the case for a determination of
reasonable attorney's fees and costs. *Reproductive Rights Network v. President
of the Univ. of Massachusetts*, 699 N.E.2d 829 (Mass.App.1998).

* *The military could be prohibited from recruiting on a school's campus
because of its discriminatory policies toward homosexuals.*

An unincorporated student organization representing gay and lesbian law
students attending the University of Connecticut School of Law opposed the
appearance of military recruiters at the school because of military policies that
discriminated on the basis of sexual orientation. **It filed a lawsuit against
university trustees in a state trial court, seeking a temporary order and
declaration that the state Gay Rights Law prohibited on-campus military
recruiting efforts**. The court issued a temporary order prohibiting law school
officials from permitting any organization that discriminated on the basis of sexual
orientation, including the military, from using on-campus employment recruiting
facilities. The law school and trustees appealed to the Supreme Court of
Connecticut.

The court first disposed of procedural and standing issues raised by the board
and law school, holding that the organization was entitled to advance claims on
behalf of the students. It observed that the state Gay Rights Law protected
members of the organization against discrimination. The school and trustees
argued that another statute which required institutions to treat all employment
recruiters alike required that they allow access to the military. The supreme court
disagreed, stating that the school had to provide equal access to the military, not
preferential treatment. **Because no civilian employer with discriminatory
practices would be allowed to recruit on campus, the military was prohibited
from on-campus appearances**. The court affirmed the trial court judgment for
the student organization. *Gay and Lesbian Law Students Ass'n v. Bd. of Trustees,
Univ. of Connecticut*, 236 Conn. 453, 673 A.2d 484 (1996).

* *A state university could not refuse to recognize gays, lesbians and bisexuals
when it recognized other student groups.*

An Alabama statute prohibits any college or university from spending public
funds or using facilities to sanction, recognize or support any group promoting
lifestyles or actions prohibited by state sodomy and sexual misconduct laws. It
also prohibits any group from permitting or encouraging persons to engage in
homosexual lifestyle and activity. **A university-recognized organization representing gay, lesbian and bisexual students attending the University of
South Alabama was denied access to funding**. It filed a lawsuit against the state
of Alabama claiming that the statute violated its members' rights under the First
Amendment to the U.S. Constitution. The organization sought a declaration that
the act was unconstitutional and an order that would forbid the university from
denying it access to university facilities.

The court commented that the First Amendment prohibits viewpoint discrimination and requires government entities to abstain from regulating speech based on the desire to restrict a speaker's opinion. **A state university making its facilities and funding available to different student organizations may not withhold access to persons holding a particular viewpoint without violating the First Amendment**. The statute clearly violated the First Amendment by targeting the gay student organization's speech and access to university funds. States cannot exclude particular viewpoints with respect to an idea even where a compelling state interest in the idea exists. The court issued the declaration sought by the organization but denied its application for an injunction as unnecessary. *Gay Lesbian Bisexual Alliance v. Sessions*, 917 F.Supp. 1548 (M.D.Ala.1996).

The attorney general then moved for a partial stay pending appeal to the U.S. Court of Appeals, Eleventh Circuit. The court denied the motion, observing the state's failure to adequately show a possibility of prevailing on the merits of the case. The court also denied the organization's motion for an injunction to enforce the declaratory judgment as unnecessary. *Gay Lesbian Bisexual Alliance v. Sessions*, 917 F.Supp. 1558 (M.D.Ala.1996).

D. Student Activity Fees

◆   *The U.S. Supreme Court held that the University of Wisconsin could assess a mandatory activity fee to fund student extracurricular programs, including student groups with controversial ideological positions.*

The University of Wisconsin required all students to pay the university a non-refundable activity fee to support registered student groups. While many did not engage in political or ideological speech, others did, including the International Socialist Organization, College Democrats, College Republicans and ACLU Campus Chapter. The university justified the fee as an enhancement to the educational experience of students by promoting extracurricular activity, stimulating advocacy and debate on diverse points of view, enabling student political participation and providing opportunities to develop social skills, consistent with the university's mission. In order to qualify for registered student organization status, students were required to organize as nonprofit organizations, limit membership primarily to students and agree to undertake activities related to student life on campus. During the year the lawsuit was commenced, 623 groups had registered student organization status, and the university charged a mandatory activity fee of $331.50 to each full-time student. Organizations could obtain funding from student government activity funds, general student services funds or by student referendum in which the student body could approve or disapprove assessment. The student government approved initial funding decisions under the first two methods and also approved the results of student referendums.

Students who objected to the collection and use of their student fees to support objectionable political and ideological expression sued university regents in a federal district court, asserting that the program violated their speech rights. The court held that the fee program compelled students to support political and ideological activity with which they disagreed in violation of the First Amendment. It prohibited the university from using student fees to fund registered student organizations engaged in such activity. The U.S. Court of Appeals,

Seventh Circuit, affirmed the decision in part, finding that the student activity fee program was not germane to the university's mission, did not further a vital university policy and burdened student speech.

The U.S. Supreme Court found that the university assessed the fee to facilitate the free and open exchange of ideas among students. Objecting students could insist upon certain safeguards regarding the compelled support of expressive activities. Even though the student activities fund was not a traditional public forum, the case was controlled by the standard from public forum cases. To insist upon germaneness to the university's mission would contravene the purpose of the program, which was to encourage a wide range of speech. The Court found it inevitable that the fees would subsidize some speech that students would find objectionable, and it declined to impose a constitutional requirement upon the university compelling it to refund fees to students. Viewpoint neutrality was the proper standard for the protection of the First Amendment rights of the objecting students, as set forth in the Court's decision in *Rosenberger v. Rector and Visitors of Univ. of Virginia*, 515 U.S. 819 (1995).

The Court held that the university could require students to support extracurricular speech of other students in a viewpoint-neutral manner, and observed that the parties had stipulated in this case that the program was viewpoint-neutral. The university had wide latitude to adjust its extracurricular speech programs to accommodate students. The Court reversed the Seventh Circuit's decision, and remanded the case for further proceedings on the issue of the student referendum. The record required further development on whether a referendum by students undermined constitutional protection for viewpoint neutrality. *Bd. of Regents of Univ. of Wisconsin System v. Southworth*, 120 S.Ct. 1346, 146 L.Ed.2d 193 (2000).

♦   *Oregon students could be required to pay fees that supported a nonpolitical public interest research group.*

The University of Oregon required students, as a condition of matriculation, to pay incidental fees that contributed to the support of the Oregon Student Public Interest Research Group (OSPIRG) Education Fund. A number of students sued to have the fees declared unconstitutional. The Ninth Circuit Court of Appeals first held that the university and the state board of higher education were immune from liability under the Eleventh Amendment. However, the officials responsible for the administration of the fees could be sued. The court then held that the fees were not unconstitutional. **This was not a case of compelled membership in an objectionable organization. Students were not required to join the OSPIRG Education Fund.** Nor did the fees go to an organization that did political lobbying because the OSPIRG Education Fund was separate from the OSPIRG (the political arm of the group). Here, the fees were allocated among scores of campus organizations representing many diverse viewpoints. Further, the OSPIRG Education Fund provided college students with hands-on experience in recognizing, researching and solving the problems of society. This furthered the university's educational mission. *Rounds v. Oregon State Bd. of Higher Educ.*, 166 F.3d 1032 (9th Cir.1999).

◆   *A California university could require students to pay student fees that funded political activities.*

The Associated Students of the University of California (ASUC) administers student government and extracurricular activities at the University of California, Berkeley. The ASUC senate conducts student government through 30 elected student representatives. During the school year, the senate meets weekly and sometimes debates controversial public issues including gay and lesbian rights, gun control, and marijuana legalization. A group of students and student organizations challenged the mandatory collection of student fees of which a part funded ASUC senate political activities. They filed a lawsuit against university regents in a California superior court. The court held for the regents, and the Court of Appeal of California affirmed the judgment. However, the Supreme Court of California remanded the case for a determination of whether senate activities violated the speech and association rights of dissenting students by using their fees to support certain ideological and political views.

The superior court again held for the regents, and the dissenting students appealed to the court of appeal. The court reviewed trial court findings that the financial burden on the dissenting students was minimal and that senate activities accounted for only four percent of total ASUC expenditures. The senate's primary function was to administer and govern ASUC activities and the senate was not dedicated to achieving a particular political or ideological outlook. **The expenditure of mandatory fees did not violate the test described by the supreme court since the educational benefits provided by the ASUC senate outweighed the advancement of political and ideological interests** and was not merely incidental to those interests. The court affirmed the judgment for the regents. *Smith v. Regents of the Univ. of California*, 65 Cal.Rptr.2d 813 (Cal.App.1st Dist.1997).

◆   *In the following case, the Supreme Court held that students' rights to freedom of association may not be disregarded, nor may those rights be limited solely on the basis of the philosophy underlying the students' desire to associate.*

A group of students desired to form a local chapter of Students for a Democratic Society (SDS) at a state-supported college. They were, however, denied recognition as a campus organization. Recognition would have allowed the student organization to use campus facilities for meetings and to use the campus bulletin board and school newspaper. The president had denied recognition because he was not satisfied that the group was independent of the national SDS, which he concluded had a philosophy of disruption and violence in conflict with the college's declaration of student rights. The students sued for declaratory and injunctive relief.

The district court first ordered an additional administrative hearing, at which the college president reaffirmed his prior decision. It then held that the students had failed to show that they could function independently of the national SDS and that the college's refusal to recognize the group, in light of the disruptive and violent nature of the national organization, was justifiable. The U.S. Court of Appeals for the Second Circuit affirmed, stating that the students had failed to avail themselves of the due process of law accorded to them and had failed to meet their burden of complying with the prevailing standards for recognition.

The U.S. Supreme Court held that **the lower courts erred in disregarding the First Amendment interest in freedom of association that the students had in furthering their personal beliefs.** It also held that putting the burden on the students (to show entitlement to recognition) rather than on the president (to justify nonrecognition) was also in error. The Court stated that insofar as the denial of recognition was based on the group's affiliation with the national SDS, or as a result of disagreement with the group's philosophy, the president's decision violated the students' First Amendment rights. A proper basis for nonrecognition might have been that the group refused to comply with a rule requiring them to abide by reasonable campus regulations. Since it was not clear that the college had such a rule, and whether the students intended to observe it, the case was remanded to the district court for resolution. *Healy v. James,* 408 U.S. 169, 92 S.Ct. 2338, 33 L.Ed.2d 266 (1972).

E. Commercial Speech

♦ *The Supreme Court has held that restrictions on commercial free speech need not be subjected to as rigorous an analysis to determine the restrictions' reasonableness. As long as the restriction is reasonable, it will be upheld.*

The State University of New York (SUNY) prohibited private commercial enterprises from operating in SUNY facilities. Campus police prevented a housewares manufacturer from demonstrating and selling its products at a party hosted in a student dormitory. The manufacturer and a group of students sued SUNY in a federal district court, stating that the policy violated the First Amendment. The court held for SUNY, stating that the student dormitories did not constitute a public forum for purposes of commercial activity, and that the restrictions were reasonable in light of the dormitories' purpose. The manufacturer dropped out of the lawsuit and the students appealed to the U.S. Court of Appeals, Second Circuit. The court of appeals reversed, stating that it was unclear whether the policy directly advanced SUNY's interest and whether it was the least restrictive means of achieving that interest. The court of appeals remanded the case to the district court, but the U.S. Supreme Court granted review of the case.

The Supreme Court stated that the court of appeals erred in requiring the district court to apply a least restrictive means test. The Court stated that **regulations on commercial speech require only a reasonable "fit" between the government's ends and the means chosen to accomplish those ends.** The Supreme Court reversed and remanded the case. *Bd. of Trustees of the State Univ. of New York v. Fox,* 492 U.S. 469, 109 S.Ct. 3028, 106 L.Ed.2d 388 (1989).

♦ *A university's radio station did not have to allow the KKK to underwrite a program.*

A not-for-profit public broadcast radio station operated by the University of Missouri (and a member of National Public Radio) received a request from the state coordinator for the Knights of the Ku Klux Klan, Realm of Missouri, to underwrite a number of 15-second spots on the station's "All Things Considered" program. This would require the station to acknowledge the gift by reading a message from the Klan stating that it was a white Christian organization standing up for the rights and values of white Christians and giving contact information.

Although this did not violate any of the station's enhanced underwriting guidelines, the station's general manager asked the university's chancellor what to do. The chancellor decided that allowing the underwriting would result in a loss of revenue to the station of at least $5 million from donor support and lost tuition, and she rejected the offer. The state coordinator and the Klan sued the station manager, asserting that the station could not reject the offer because it was a public forum, and could not discriminate on the basis of viewpoint.

The U.S. District Court for the Eastern District of Missouri held that **the station did not have to accept the Klan's offer to underwrite "All Things Considered." The station's employees had the discretion to choose which underwriting offers to accept, and the underwriting program could not be deemed a public forum.** Further, the decision to reject the offer was not based on viewpoint but on business considerations. The court granted pretrial judgment to the station manager. The Eighth Circuit Court of Appeals affirmed. It noted that the underwriting spots constituted governmental speech and that the government could exercise discretion over what it chose to say. Since the station had the right to reject the proposed spots, the Klan's lawsuit could not succeed. *KKK v. Bennett*, 203 F.3d 1085 (8th Cir.2000).

♦   *A college dean could not restrict a student editor from accepting an advertisement from a strip club and bar.*

A Michigan student held the position of editor-in-chief of her community college newspaper. She printed an advertisement of a Canadian bar where the drinking age was only 19 and the dancers were nude. When the school's dean prohibited her from printing any more of the bar's advertisements, the student sued the school in a federal court, alleging violations of her free speech rights and intentional infliction of emotional distress. The court noted that if the editor had the authority to run the newspaper, the school would have to have a compelling interest in restricting her speech in it. **Where commercial speech is lawful and not misleading, and where the governmental interest in restricting that speech is substantial, then the government may restrict the speech where the means it employs are narrowly tailored to meet its objective.** Here, the newspaper was independent of the school because the editor-in-chief had the full authority to decide its content, policies and personnel. The dean's policy of exerting final control over what could be published in the newspaper was not narrowly tailored to achieve the government's interests. It burdened substantially more speech than was necessary and violated the student's free speech rights. *Lueth v. St. Clair County Comm. College*, 732 F.Supp. 1410 (E.D.Mich.1990).

CHAPTER FIVE

Employment

I. WRONGFUL TERMINATION AND BREACH OF CONTRACT

The at-will employment doctrine refers to an employment contract without a specific term that may be terminated at any time by either party. Under the doctrine, either the employer or employee may terminate the employment relationship without cause or notice unless otherwise stipulated in an employment contract or unless contrary to public policy. Claims for breach of contract, tortious wrongful discharge and First Amendment challenges attempt to circumvent the at-will doctrine.

A. Breach of Contract

Breach of contract claims arise from written contracts; academic custom and usage, including faculty handbooks; First Amendment issues based on the use of religious criteria in employment decisions; application of the American Association of University Professors (AAUP) guidelines; and reliance on oral statements implying or modifying an employment contract.

1. Written Contracts

◆   *A New Mexico public university was not immune to suit in an action brought under a written contract.*

A tenured professor in pediatric medicine at the University of New Mexico began serving as the director of the division of developmental disabilities under a written contract that provided $5,000 for his administrative duties. After the professor helped the university obtain a grant to establish a center for training and research in developmental disabilities, he became the director of the center and his administrative salary increased to $10,000. A few years later, after a review of the center, the dean of the medical school informed the professor that his directorship would be on probation for the rest of the year. The following year, he was removed as director of the center, and the year after that, his administrative salary returned to $5,000. The professor sued the university for breach of contract, and a state trial court denied the university's claim of governmental immunity. The Supreme Court of New Mexico affirmed that decision, noting that **the professor's action against the university was based on a written contract.** It further noted that **a New Mexico statute provided that governmental entities were immune from actions based on unwritten contracts, thereby implying that the government could be sued under valid written contracts.** *Handmaker v. Henney,* 1999 N.M. LEXIS 343 (N.M.1999).

◆   *A liquidated damages clause in a coach's contract was valid and enforceable where the amount of harm caused by the coach's early departure was difficult to ascertain, and where the amount chosen as liquidated damages was reasonable.*

After a Vanderbilt University football coach joined another school, a Tennessee federal court awarded Vanderbilt $281,886.43 under the employment contract. The sum included a liquidated damages amount for the two-year time period covered by a contract extension the coach had earlier signed. The coach appealed, alleging that the liquidated damages provision was unenforceable as a penalty and that the contract extension was not binding upon him. The U.S. Court of Appeals, Sixth Circuit, reversed and remanded, **holding that the liquidated damages clause was not a penalty and that it was enforceable. By leaving early, the coach would harm Vanderbilt more than by just the cost of replacing him.**

However, a question of fact existed as to whether the two-year contract extension was enforceable. Although the coach had signed the contract, he had told the athletic director that the extension would not be "final" until his attorney-brother looked at it. The court remanded the case for a determination as to whether the brother had to approve the contract extension before the coach could be held bound under its terms for damages and, if so, whether the brother's failure to object to the contract's language constituted *de facto* approval. *Vanderbilt Univ. v. DiNardo*, 174 F.3d 751 (6th Cir.1999).

♦ *A coach had no cause of action under a contract in the following case because he was paid through the term of the contract despite having his duties taken away.*

The head football coach at a private Pennsylvania college was sent a letter each year offering him employment for the following year. To accept, he would sign and return a copy of the letter to the president of the college. After an unsuccessful football season, a number of football players wrote to college officials, expressing their dissatisfaction with the coach. The officials began an investigation and met with the coach to share their findings. They laid out new terms and conditions for his employment the following year. When he did not respond, he was informed that his employment would not be continued after the academic year. **He was paid for the rest of the year pursuant to his contract but was relieved of all duties.** The coach sued the college and three of his players for breach of contract and intentional interference with employment relations. The case reached the Superior Court of Pennsylvania.

The court found that the coach was not an employee at will because he had been issued successive one-year contracts. The coach argued that his employment was governed by the college's personnel manual which contained "just cause" and conflict resolution provisions. The court, however, found no evidence that the manual was intended to contradict the terms of his annual contract and held that **a reasonable person would not have interpreted the provisions as converting his contracts into permanent employment.** The court also found that the players did not intentionally interfere with the coach's employment contract. Students should not be discouraged from voicing their opinions, even when these opinions are based on unverified facts. They cannot be burdened with the possibility of liability for expressing their thoughts. The coach's case was dismissed. *Small v. Juniata College*, 682 A.2d 350 (Pa.Super.1996).

♦ *Transferring a professor to a non-teaching staff position was not a breach of contract where there was no reduction in pay and where the contract called for the professor to teach and/or serve the college.*

A professor employed by a Georgia private art college developed personality conflicts with several colleagues in the video department. His colleagues complained and requested that the college transfer the professor out of the department. The college complied with the request, reassigning the professor to a non-teaching "staff" position in an ancillary video production unit with no reduction in salary. The new position was consistent with his training and experience. The professor wanted to teach, but refused to accept the college's offer to place him as a visiting teacher in a county public school system. He filed a lawsuit in a Georgia trial court, alleging breach of contract and seeking damages. The trial court granted summary judgment to the professor. The college appealed to the Court of Appeals of Georgia. The court of appeals held that the professor's contract, which required him to devote his time "to teaching and/or service to the college," recognized the flexibility necessary in the effective administration of a college. The trial court's reliance on the professor's transfer from "faculty" to "staff" as the basis for its ruling was misplaced. **Considering the nature of the new position, as opposed to its classification, the court held that the transfer was not a breach of contract.** *Johnson v. Savannah College of Art*, 460 S.E.2d 308 (Ga.App.1995).

◆   *Professors who were contractually entitled to the rank of professor for life were not entitled to lifetime employment where they signed annual employment contracts.*

Two faculty members at a Pennsylvania private university were promoted to professor in 1965. The contracts provided that "the distinctive rank of professor is an appointment for life." However, the contract also provided that they would receive a salary for the following academic year only. Between 1965 and 1990 both professors entered into similar annual contracts with the university, except that the appointment for life clause was deleted. In 1982, the university modified its retirement policy to make retirement mandatory for tenured faculty members who reached the age of 70. Pursuant to this policy, both professors were retired from active faculty status. The professors challenged the mandatory retirements in court, and the case eventually reached the Superior Court of Pennsylvania.

The university contended that **while the rank of professor was a lifetime rank, employment as a member of the faculty was year by year.** The superior court agreed, noting that employment relationships are generally terminable at will. In holding for the university, the superior court noted its reluctance to interpret employment contracts as guaranteeing employment for life. Rather, it gave effect to the intent of the parties as reasonably manifested by the language of their written agreement. Here, the language of the contract clearly entitled the professors to retain their rank for the remainder of their life. However, the faculty members were not guaranteed employment for life. The duration of each employment contract was for a period of one academic year only. *Halpin v. LaSalle University*, 639 A.2d 37 (Pa.Super.1994).

2. Handbooks

◆   *Even though a college failed to provide a professor with written evaluations as required by the faculty handbook, it did not have to renew the professor's contract.*

A private college in New York employed a nontenured probationary assistant professor in its accounting department under a series of one-year contracts. The faculty handbook called for written evaluations to be provided each teacher, but the college failed to provide them. After the professor organized and participated in a student protest aimed at the accounting department's curriculum, the college sent him a letter along with his proposed contract notifying him that upon expiration of the contract, it would not be renewed. The letter indicated that **the basis for nonrenewal was the impaired collegiality and confidence between the professor and the accounting department.** The professor signed the one-year, nonrenewable contract that accompanied the letter and became unemployed at the end of the year. He sued the college for breach of contract in a state trial court where summary judgment was granted to the college. The New York Supreme Court, Appellate Division, affirmed the lower court decision in favor of the college. It noted that the nonrenewal of the professor's contract was solely related to his failure to get along with his colleagues and was not related to his teaching skills, which the college conceded were excellent. Also, even though the college failed to provide written evaluations as called for in the faculty handbook, **there was no duty to automatically renew the professor's contract if he was found to be an excellent teacher.** The college's decision not to renew the professor's contract did not amount to breach of contract. *DeSimone v. Siena College*, 663 N.Y.S.2d 701 (A.D.3rd Dept.1997).

◆   *Where a professor failed to follow the procedures outlined for challenging his discharge, his lawsuit for breach of contract failed.*

Several allegations of plagiarism were leveled against a private college professor regarding a book he published in 1983. The college proposed to reduce the professor in rank and pay, but he filed a grievance against it and was reinstated to a full professorship. However, at the same time, he was notified that he would be fired at the end of the year. A grievance committee and the president of the college upheld the termination and dismissed the professor's grievance. The professor failed to commence an article 78 proceeding to review the president's determination. Instead, he brought suit in a New York trial court for breach of contract. The court dismissed the breach of contract action, stating that the professor should have brought an article 78 proceeding to challenge the validity of the grievance decision. On appeal to the New York Supreme Court, Appellate Division, the court noted that **the college had followed the procedures provided in the handbook governing employment termination.** The professor's sole remedy if he was dissatisfied with his discharge was to commence an article 78 proceeding. Accordingly, the trial court had properly dismissed the breach of contract claim. *Klinge v. Ithaca College*, 663 N.Y.S.2d 735 (A.D.3d Dept.1997).

◆   *Where a professor maintained that a handbook created a contract, and that the university breached that contract, her claim failed because the university followed the procedures outlined in it.*

A woman was hired as a part-time lecturer on graphic design by a private Iowa university. She was later given a faculty position under a one year contract and told that she would be evaluated annually. She received excellent reviews and eventually became a tenure-track faculty member. Before becoming eligible for tenure, the professor began to have difficulties with the art department's new chairperson concerning the submission of her work for review as part of her annual evaluation. The professor objected to the lack of stated criteria and noted that her graphic design work, often created in a commercial setting, did not easily fit into the category "scholarly and artistic development" used in her evaluation. Consequently, the chairperson found her work insufficient in this area. After being given three more annual appointments she was fired. She challenged this decision before an academic committee, stating that she was denied her procedural rights, but the committee disagreed. The professor sued the university for breach of contract, and the case reached the Supreme Court of Iowa.

The court found that although the professor was employed under a series of one-year contracts, she was more than an at-will employee. In order for the professor to prove that her faculty handbook was an enforceable employment contract, she had to show that it was sufficiently definite in its terms to create an offer, that it was communicated and accepted by her so as to create acceptance and that she continued working, so as to provide consideration. The court found that here, **the handbook created an enforceable contract but also found that the university did not breach that contract.** The handbook did not state that any particular criteria should be used to evaluate the professor's work and it did not allow her to demand that the university use more or different criteria than what was currently used. Furthermore, **all the grievance procedures described in the handbook were given to the professor.** She was given adequate warning, told she could remedy the situation by providing sufficient documentation of her commercial work and given full access to the appeals process. *Taggart v. Drake Univ.*, 549 N.W.2d 796 (Iowa 1996).

◆ *Where a handbook's language clearly indicated an intent not to create a contract, none was formed.*

A carpenter foreman at a Pennsylvania private college was discharged, allegedly for abuse of college time and materials and for submitting false time sheets. However, the foreman alleged that the college had a longstanding policy and practice of allowing its employees to use scrap materials and allowing them to perform personal projects during "nonbusy" work time. The employee handbook outlined the four disciplinary steps, ranging from an oral warning to discharge, but stated that the steps were merely intended as a guide to both supervisors and employees. The handbook also contained an introductory letter from the college president which stated that the handbook was "intended to serve as an introduction and guide to expectations at the college." The foreman filed suit in a Pennsylvania federal court, alleging breach of contract and detrimental reliance. He contended that the employee handbook and the college policies constituted a binding contract which entitled him to continued employment. The district court disagreed, ruling that the foreman was an at-will employee subject to discharge with or without cause. Here the foreman failed to overcome the at-will presumption. **The president's disclaimer in his introductory statement and the precatory language in the handbook clearly indicated an intent not to create an employment contract.** The court dismissed the breach of contract and detrimental reliance claims. *Raines v. Haverford College*, 849 F.Supp. 1009 (E.D.Pa.1994).

◆ *Where a handbook provided that it was subject to modification at any time, it did not provide contractual rights over and above those existing in the at-will relationship.*

A Massachusetts resident was hired as an associate director of admissions at a Rhode Island private university. He later became a member of the university president's advisory council. A new president took office and "philosophical differences" developed between the two men. The university informed the associate director that he would be replaced, but that he would be appointed to a new position through the summer of the following year. The university's personnel policy manual provided that employees with over 10 years of service would be given severance pay and that all employees would receive a written warning prior to termination. However, **the manual was subject to modification at any time.** The associate director allegedly declined a position at another university in reliance on the manual's severance pay provision. He did, however, obtain positions with two other private universities following his termination. The associate director filed suit against the university in federal court, alleging breach of contract, breach of an implied covenant of good faith, and wrongful termination. The university moved to dismiss the claims.

The associate director first contended that the university failed to observe its employment contract pursuant to the employment manual which provided that he receive severance pay and adequate notice prior to his termination. The district court disagreed, noting that **employment manuals that can be modified at any time do not provide additional contractual rights to at-will employees.** Nor, given the express revocation provision within the manual, had the employee detrimentally relied on the provisions in the manual. Further, the court noted that absent a violation of an express statutory standard, an employer of an at-will employee is not subject to an implied covenant of good faith. Similarly, wrongful termination claims by at-will employees fail unless the employer violates a statute. Since neither claim alleged a statutory violation, both were dismissed. *Dunfey v. Roger Williams University*, 824 F.Supp. 18 (D.Mass.1993).

* *Where a college failed to follow procedures in a handbook on achieving tenure, it was required to conduct another tenure review.*

A New York private college hired an art history professor for a newly created tenure-track position. According to the faculty manual, once a professor was hired, consideration for tenure was governed by procedures set forth in the manual. The evaluation subcommittee and the advisory committee recommended that tenure be granted. However, the dean gave a negative recommendation based on declining enrollment in art history courses. During the tenure review, the president's participation was limited to his consultation with the dean in contravention of express provisions in the faculty manual. The board of trustees voted to deny tenure to the professor. A New York trial court vacated the denial and directed the college to conduct another tenure review. The college appealed.

The New York Supreme Court, Appellate Division, affirmed, holding that the college had failed to follow its own procedures in conducting the professor's tenure review. **The college did not adhere to the process set forth in the faculty manual** insofar as that process contemplated an active role for the president of the college. The court also held that the college had failed to apply its own substantive criteria in evaluating the professor for tenure. Student involvement, the crucial factor in the dean's negative recommendation, was not among the enumerated criteria in the faculty manual. While enrollment could be an appropriate consideration in the decision whether to create or continue a tenure-track position, it was not an appropriate consideration in the tenure review of a particular faculty member. The appellate division court affirmed the order requiring the college to conduct another tenure review. *Bennett v. Wells College*, 641 N.Y.S.2d 929 (A.D.4th Dept.1996).

3. AAUP Guidelines

♦   *A professor could not use the AAUP guidelines, which had been incorporated into his contract, to modify the intent of the contract.*

A professor and a New Jersey private university entered into five separate employment contracts, each of which incorporated the terms of the university's collective bargaining agreement with the American Association of University Professors (AAUP) guidelines. However, the professor's applications for tenure were denied due to his lack of a doctorate degree and his failure to publish. His contract for a sixth academic year stated that his associate professor position was a "non-tenured position." In the following year, he was appointed as an associate dean but continued to teach three credits per semester without additional compensation. He was fired several years later because his overall performance was found to be "significantly below expectations." The professor filed a lawsuit in a New Jersey superior court, alleging that he had acquired *de facto* tenure under the provisions of the AAUP contract. The AAUP contract required that faculty members who had taught for 14 continuous academic semesters be granted tenure. The superior court held for the university, and the professor appealed to the New Jersey Superior Court, Appellate Division.

The appellate division court noted that **the provision requiring tenure for faculty members teaching 14 continuous semesters was a subsidiary provision that should not be interpreted so as to conflict with the principal purpose of the contract.** The court rejected the professor's disproportionate emphasis on the provision to support his tenure claim. The interpretation of the probationary appointments provision urged by the professor unlawfully conflicted with the principal purpose of the university's formal tenure policy, which placed substantive and procedural prerequisites on the acquisition of tenure. The superior court ruling was affirmed. *Healy v. Fairleigh Dickinson University*, 671 A.2d 182 (N.J.Super.A.D.1996).

♦   *A seminary breached a professor's employment contract by refusing to follow its own regulations.*

The executive committee of a seminary's board of trustees ordered the president of the seminary to reduce the budget by at least $50,000. As a result, a 62-year-old tenured faculty member, who had taught there for 31 years, was fired. The faculty member sued for breach of contract. The seminary agreed that the contract was subject to the AAUP Recommended Institutional Regulations on Academic Freedom and Tenure. This document, along with the faculty promotion and tenure policy of the seminary, contained provisions governing the firing of a tenured faculty member. The seminary claimed that the document did not require it to allow the fired teacher to participate in "any way at any stage" of the proceedings. The court observed, however, that **the regulations required any**

faculty member facing termination to be allowed to participate in the dismissal proceedings before a faculty group and the governing board. It noted that without an opportunity to be heard, the faculty member had no opportunity to have pertinent issues reviewed and discussed in a meaningful way. The court therefore ruled that the seminary failed to follow its own regulations since the language of the document clearly expressed that an aggrieved faculty member had a "contractual right to request a review of his termination." In this case, the discharged faculty member was denied that opportunity, which meant that the seminary had breached his employment contract. *Linn v. Andover-Newton Theological Sch.*, 638 F.Supp. 1114 (D.Mass.1986).

◆ *Where a part of the AAUP guidelines was excluded from an employment contract, the university did not have to follow the procedures listed in that part.*

A private Louisiana university dismissed a tenured professor because of her alleged professional incompetence. She sued the university seeking reinstatement of tenure and employment. She argued that the university, after agreeing to modify her existing employment contract, failed to apply Paragraph Seven of the AAUP guidelines, which provide procedures for the termination of a tenured professor. The trial court held that the college had no obligation to comply with Paragraph Seven. The professor appealed to the Louisiana Court of Appeal, Fourth Circuit. On appeal, the professor argued that Paragraph Seven of the AAUP guidelines was an implied provision in her employment contract. Her contract incorporated the provisions listed in the university's faculty handbook, which provided procedures for the termination of faculty appointments. The appellate court held that **the faculty handbook and the contract clearly excluded Paragraph Seven of the AAUP guidelines. As a result, the paragraph did not apply to any procedures established by the university for the termination of tenured professors.** The appellate court further stated that there was no merit to the professor's argument that the college agreed to modify her original employment contract. The appellate court affirmed the trial court's decision. *Olivier v. Xavier Univ.*, 553 So.2d 1004 (La.App.4th Cir.1989).

◆ *The AAUP guidelines were held not to apply in a case where teachers' contracts were not terminated but rather not renewed.*

Three teachers were employed at Talladega College under employment contracts with a term of one year from August 1984 to August 1985. In May 1985, each received a letter from the college president notifying them that their employment with the college would end in August 1985. The teachers sued the college in an Alabama circuit court for breach of contract. The court ruled for the college, and the teachers appealed to the Alabama Supreme Court. They claimed that the *Procedural Standards in Faculty Dismissal Proceedings* published by the American Association of University Professors (AAUP) were incorporated within their employment contracts. The teachers filed a breach of contract and wrongful termination lawsuit, alleging that the AAUP standards favored them because the standards applied to any nontenured teacher "whose term appointment has not expired."

The supreme court stated that although the AAUP standards were neither expressly nor impliedly a part of the teachers' contracts, it would apply the standards for purposes of the appeal. The court concluded that the title of the publication and the publication's provisions indicated that the standards applied only to dismissals of college faculty members. **The standards did not apply here since the teachers' contracts were not cancelled prior to their completion.** The teachers completed their performance through August 1985, and were paid for the entire term. They had no valid claims since they were not dismissed but rather were simply not reemployed for the next year. One of the teachers claimed that he had achieved *de facto* tenure status since he had been employed for over seven years. The court disagreed, noting that the faculty handbook required that permanent tenure be extended only to persons specifically elected by the board of trustees and that the "acquisition of tenure ... is not automatic after seven years of teaching...." The circuit court's decision in favor of the college was affirmed. *Hill v. Talladega Col.*, 502 So.2d 735 (Ala.1987).

4. Implied Contracts

♦   *A written contract that did not specify an exact term of employment did not alter the at-will employment relationship.*

A Texas Baptist college hired an administrator in 1969 pursuant to a written contract which did not specify an exact term of employment. Throughout the early years of the administrator's 23-year term of employment, the college's president allegedly assured him that his job was secure as long as his work was satisfactory. However, in 1992, the administrator resigned in lieu of termination. He then filed a constructive discharge lawsuit, alleging breach of contract and that the college's new president had tortiously interfered with his employment contract. A Texas trial court granted summary judgment to the college and the president, and the administrator appealed to the Court of Appeals of Texas. The court of appeals held that **the contract, without a specified term of employment, did not alter the administrator's at-will status.** Moreover, even assuming that oral promises of lifetime employment were made and that the president had authority to make them, the administrator's breach of contract action based on this oral representation was barred by the statute of frauds. Finally, because the president was an agent of the college and an agent could not be personally liable for tortious interference with its principal's contracts, this claim had also been properly dismissed. The trial court ruling was affirmed. *Massey v. Houston Baptist University*, 902 S.W.2d 81 (Tex.App.–Houston 1995).

♦   *Where written and oral evidence was too vague to support an implied contract, the employment remained at will.*

An Oklahoma junior college was dissatisfied with its new president's job performance and offered suggestions for improvement. After he failed to make the requisite improvements, his employment with the college was terminated. He filed breach of contract, wrongful discharge and intentional infliction of emotional distress (IIED) claims against the college in an Oklahoma trial court. At trial, the president introduced a standard rejection letter from the college, a college manual highlighting suggested termination procedures, and evidence of oral assurances of "lengthy employment." However, both parties acknowledged that either could have terminated the employment relationship at any time. The trial court entered summary judgment in favor of the college, and the president appealed to the Court of Appeals of Oklahoma. The court noted that **factors indicating an implied contract of job security include evidence of additional consideration, longevity of employment, employee handbooks, detrimental reliance on oral assurances, and promotions or commendations.** Here, the written and oral evidence was too vague to support an implied contract. Further, because the employee was never asked to perform illegal acts and was never prohibited from discussing employment matters, his wrongful discharge claim was dismissed. Finally, the dismissal of his breach of contract and wrongful discharge lawsuits precluded the IIED claim. The district court's ruling was affirmed. *Beck v. Phillips Colleges, Inc.*, 883 P.2d 1283 (Okla.App.1994).

◆   *The statute of frauds provides that contracts extending beyond one year must be in writing to be enforceable.*

An Illinois private school contracted to pay its football coach $30,000 annually for three years. The contract was modified to give annual salary increases. The parties allegedly entered an oral contract for coaching services for a fourth year, and later extended this oral contract for another two years. However, the coach with more than a year left on the extended contract. He filed suit in an Illinois court, alleging that the school had breached the oral extension of his employment contract. The court dismissed the case and the coach appealed to the Appellate Court of Illinois. On appeal, the coach supplied a written memorandum from the school which documented his salary increase effective for the season in which he had been discharged. He also included a newspaper article announcing that he had been awarded a two-year contract extension.

The school contended that the oral contract violated the statute of frauds. The court of appeals agreed, ruling that the newspaper article was no more than a "written notation of [the parties'] oral statements," and was therefore merely evidence of an oral agreement. Neither writing was enforceable under the statute of frauds. Next, since the coach had initially pursued legal remedies (monetary damages), the court held that he could not now raise the partial performance exception to the statute of frauds and obtain reinstatement, an equitable remedy. **The court also refused to imply a contract under promissory estoppel based on the school's alleged promises to the coach.** Such an exception would make the statute of frauds ineffectual. Finally, no precedent had exempted oral extensions of written contracts and the court refused to do so here. Therefore, no exceptions to the statute of frauds applied to preclude its application in the present case. The holding of the circuit court was affirmed. *Dickens v. Quincy College*, 615 N.E.2d 381 (Ill.App.4th Dist.1993).

◆   *Negotiations and documentation were sufficient to constitute a two-year contract in the following case.*

A private university conducted a federally funded research project in collaboration with the government of Ecuador. The research project involved the appointment of a field sociologist who was to live in Ecuador for two years. **The university selected a sociologist but the parties never signed a contract.** The sociologist accepted a temporary appointment and commenced working even before he was placed on the university's payroll. He traveled to Ecuador with some of his staff for three months to do preliminary research and obtain housing for his family. When the sociologist returned to the U.S. to arrange his move to Ecuador, a dispute arose between him and the staff over research methodology. **The university staff decided not to appoint the sociologist** and gave him a written notice that he would not be hired. When the university claimed that no employment contract existed, the sociologist sued, seeking general damages of over $111,000 and punitive damages of over $335,000. The trial court held that the university had hired the sociologist for a period of two years for a salary of $30,000 per year but that no contractual breach had occurred. The court awarded damages of $22,379 to the sociologist. The reduced damages reflected mitigation for his acceptance of employment at another institution. A New York appellate division court affirmed the trial court decision, finding that the negotiations and the documentation constituted a two-year employment contract. *Merschrod v. Cornell Univ.*, 527 N.Y.S.2d 109 (A.D.3d Dept.1988).

◆ *By proposing a new contract, a teacher was offering to rescind the original contract, and he could not complain when the college president asked him to resign.*

After four months, an Iowa teacher met with his college's president to discuss his duties and salary because he was disappointed with his original employment contract. At this meeting, the teacher proposed a new employment contract on a form the college had used for his prior contract. The unsigned contract provided for an increase in his annual salary for the remaining eight months on his original contract. The following day the parties met again and the college president asked the teacher to resign. The teacher refused, relying on his original employment contract. Subsequently, the teacher received a letter from the president which indicated that his position was to be declared open. The teacher left his job and sued the college in an Iowa trial court for breach of contract. The trial court held that the teacher's proposed employment contract, prepared on the college's form, showed an intent to terminate the parties' original contract. The court entered judgment for the college, and the teacher appealed to the Court of Appeals of Iowa. The appellate court held that **when the teacher presented the new employment contract, it was an offer to rescind the original contract. The president accepted this rescission** in the letter the teacher received declaring that his position was open. As a result, neither party had any obligation under the rescinded contract. The court affirmed the trial court ruling. *Wiysel v. William Penn College*, 448 N.W.2d 712 (Iowa App.1989).

B. Employee Misconduct

Employee misconduct includes a variety of actions such as inappropriate, unethical, or criminal behavior. In addressing such actions, educational institutions may be bound by faculty handbooks or requirements for hearings.

◆ *A university did not violate an instructor's property or liberty rights by refusing to rehire him for the following year.*

After an anonymous written complaint of sexual harassment against an instructor at the University of Mississippi Medical Center, an investigation revealed no violation of the school's sexual harassment policy. However, it was determined that the instructor's conduct amounted to inappropriate behavior. The report indicated that the instructor had touched a student's breast while answering her question on mammograms, although the instructor denied that he had touched her breast. He was issued a written reprimand, and documentation of the investigation (including the reprimand) was placed in his personnel file. The university then informed him that it was not going to renew his contract for the following year. After his administrative appeals failed, he sued, asserting that he had been denied substantive due process by the university's failure to follow its internal procedures in conducting an unauthorized investigation.

The case reached the Supreme Court of Mississippi, which held that **the instructor did not have a property interest in continued employment with the university.** Because he was not a tenured professor, he did not have a legitimate expectation of, nor entitlement to, continued employment beyond the term of his one-year contract. **He did have a liberty interest in his reputation; however, the university did not violate that interest by merely refusing to rehire him for the following year.** No stigmatizing or defamatory statements or implications were made that would foreclose him from further employment opportunities. The court ruled in favor of the university. However, it did find that the investigatory materials should not have been placed in the instructor's personnel file. Instead, they should be kept in the confidential investigation file kept by the university police. *Hall v. Bd. of Trustees of State Institutions of Higher Learning*, 712 So.2d 312 (Miss.1998).

◆ *Where an employee refused to discuss matters relating to a grievance she had filed, she could not be discharged for insubordination.*

An administrative employee and her supervisor at the University of Alaska did not get along. The supervisor delivered a memorandum to the employee requiring her to meet regarding problems in the office. The employee attended the meeting. The supervisor then delivered a second memorandum which gave the employee three months to improve her performance and which required a written response. The employee notified her supervisor that the information contained in the second memorandum was inaccurate and that she was going to file a grievance. She then refused to discuss any matters relating to the grievance. The next day, the supervisor delivered a third memorandum which placed the employee on unpaid leave and scheduled a pre-termination hearing. After the hearing, the employee was discharged. She sought a review of the decision, and the case reached the Supreme Court of Alaska.

The supreme court found insufficient evidence that the employee had been insubordinate so as to justify her discharge. She had provided a written response to the second memorandum in the form of a grievance letter, and **her refusal to talk with her supervisor about matters relating to the grievance was not insubordination.** Further, even if, as the university contended, the employee refused to communicate at all with her supervisor, that refusal resulted from an ambiguous and unclear order. **Because the employee reasonably believed that the supervisor was asking her to discuss grievance-related matters, she was entitled to refuse to do so.** The court found the termination unjustified. *Nyberg v. Univ. of Alaska*, 954 P.2d 1376 (Alaska 1998).

◆   *Where a handbook provided that dismissal was the only form of discipline for misconduct, a college should not have imposed a lesser punishment.*

A New York college faculty handbook provided that dismissal was the only expressly authorized punishment for misconduct and that tenured professors remained subject to annual renewal. Each professor's offer of renewal was delivered on a single sheet of paper containing a footnote which incorporated the college faculty handbook by reference. An associate professor received a promotion after he published a book in 1985. Upon review, the dean and the provost concluded that the professor was guilty of plagiarism and demoted him from full professor to associate professor, reduced his salary, and restricted his academic duties in the 1993-1994 school year. His offer of renewal did not contain the footnote but the cover letter noted that the appointment was subject to the terms of the faculty handbook. The professor reluctantly accepted the demotion and filed a lawsuit against the college in a New York trial court, alleging breach of contract and intentional infliction of emotional distress (IIED).

The court held that, given the unequivocal assurance found in the cover letter, the contract continued to incorporate the handbook provisions on tenure renewal and faculty discipline for the 1993-1994 school year. Here, **a jury could find that the college properly imposed a punishment, in the form of demotion, for the misconduct of the professor without following the rule mandated in the handbook.** The provost arguably imposed a limited punishment, in the form of a punitive renewal contract which was not clearly contemplated by the handbook, rather than the sanction of termination expressly authorized. The court then dismissed the IIED claim, holding that the college's actions were not sufficiently outrageous to state such a claim. However, the court held that the professor stated an emotional injury claim against two of the professors who may have needlessly and indiscriminately disclosed false and defamatory plagiarism charges to members of the campus community in violation of college rules. *Klinge v. Ithaca College*, 634 N.Y.S.2d 1000 (Sup.1995).

◆   *Where a student teacher was properly dismissed for misconduct, her lawsuit against the school failed.*

A student pursuing a teaching degree at a California private college exhibited erratic and sometimes disturbing episodes of unprofessional behavior as a student teacher in a public school district. For example, she repeatedly left young students unattended, was inappropriately harsh with students due to her frequent mood swings and emotional problems, took out her frustrations on the students by being angry and abrupt, and was unable to perform many routine teaching duties. On one occasion, she verbally abused a student's grandmother for her failure to bring a particular pair of shoes for a school play. On another occasion, she disrupted a number of different classes by going room-to-room looking for students whose skin color was "dark enough" to be in a play she wrote about Martin Luther King, Jr. After she resorted to physical violence against a student and used excessive classroom time discussing a lurid murder which had occurred in the area, the college dismissed her from the program. The student filed suit against the college in a California trial court, alleging wrongful dismissal and other related claims. The trial court granted summary judgment to the college, and the student appealed to the Court of Appeal of California, First District.

The court utilized a highly deferential standard and held that **the college had properly enforced reasonable academic requirements that were designed to protect young children.** The student had failed to present evidence of fraud, breach of contract, interference with prospective economic advantage, defamation or intentional infliction of emotional distress. In fact, her appeal—based on an unauthenticated hearsay letter and tape recording, irrelevant deposition testimony, and her own perceptions that she was competent—failed to create genuine issues of material fact that she had been wrongfully dismissed. Moreover, the student's "vexatious and harassing" lawsuit warranted the imposition of severe monetary sanctions against her. The trial court ruling was affirmed. *Banks v. Dominican College,* 42 Cal.Rptr.2d 110 (Cal.App.1st Dist.1995).

◆ *An instructor who made no voluntary attempt to repay a student loan was properly terminated.*

An instructor at a North Carolina technical institute was notified by her employer that it believed she was in violation of North Carolina law regarding repayment of her state-funded student loans. At a hearing, she testified that there was a clerical error on the part of the lender. Shortly thereafter her employer determined that there was no clerical error, nor any voluntary attempt to pay the state. She was fired. The instructor alleged wrongful termination and brought suit against the college in a state court. After two adverse rulings, the instructor appealed to the Court of Appeals of North Carolina. North Carolina law provides that "employees of the state who owe money to the state must make full restitution of the full amount as a condition for continued employment." **Without deciding whether the repeated garnishment of income tax amounted to "repayment," the court agreed that the lack of a voluntary attempt at repayment justified the termination.** *Battle v. Nash Technical College,* 404 S.E.2d 703 (N.C.App.1991).

C. Tenure and Promotion Denials

State tenure laws create property rights in public employment that vest school employees with certain procedural rights. These rights vary from state to state according to the type of personnel action. In cases of employment termination, tenured school employees are generally entitled to notice and an opportunity to respond to the charges, a hearing with the right to confront and cross-examine witnesses, and the right to be represented by counsel. These and other related procedural protections are referred to as due process rights. Absent a state statute specifically governing tenure at private educational institutions or a claim of discrimination, tenure disputes at private schools rest on principles of contract law.

1. Supreme Court Decisions

◆ *Two U.S. Supreme Court decisions,* Board of Regents v. Roth, *408 U.S. 564, 92 S.Ct. 2701, 33 L.Ed.2d 548 (1972), and* Perry v. Sindermann, *408 U.S. 593, 92 S.Ct. 2694, 33 L.Ed.2d 570 (1972), help define the due process rights of teachers.*

The *Roth* case explained that **in order for a teacher to be entitled to due process, the teacher must have a "liberty" or "property" interest at stake.** The teacher in *Roth* was hired at a Wisconsin university for a fixed contract term of one year. At the end of the year, he was informed that he would not be rehired. No hearing was provided and no reason was given for the decision not to rehire. In dismissing the teacher's due process claims, the Supreme Court stated that no liberty interest was implicated because in declining to rehire the teacher, the university had not made any charge against him such as incompetence or immorality. Such a charge would have made it difficult for the teacher to gain employment elsewhere and thus would have deprived him of liberty. As no reason was given for the nonrenewal of his contract, the teacher's liberty interest in future employment was not impaired and he was not entitled to a hearing on these grounds.

The Court declared that because the teacher had not acquired tenure he possessed no property interest in continued employment at the university. To be sure, the teacher had a property interest in employment during the term of his one-year contract, but upon its expiration the teacher's property interest ceased to exist. The Court stated: **"To have a property interest in a benefit, a person clearly must have more than an abstract need or desire for it. He must have more than a unilateral expectation of it. He must, instead, have a legitimate claim of entitlement to it."**

The *Sindermann* case involved a teacher employed at a Texas university for four years under a series of one-year contracts. When he was not rehired for a fifth year, he brought suit contending that due process required a dismissal hearing. The Supreme Court held that "a person's interest in a benefit is a 'property' interest for due process purposes if there are such rules and mutually explicit understandings that support his claim of entitlement to the benefit that he may invoke at a hearing." Because the teacher had been employed at the university for four years, the Court felt that he may have acquired a protectible property interest in continued employment. The case was remanded to the trial court to determine whether there was an unwritten "common law" of tenure at the university. If so, the teacher would be entitled to a dismissal hearing.

Roth and *Sindermann* emphasize, first, that there must be an independent source for a liberty or property interest to exist. Such interests are not created by the Constitution, but arise by employment contract or by operation of state tenure laws. Second, if a liberty or property interest is not established, no requirement of due process exists under the Fourteenth Amendment. Third, **if a teacher possesses a liberty or property interest in employment, then due process is required and the teacher may not be dismissed without a hearing.** A tenured teacher, or an untenured teacher during the term of his or her contract, possesses a property interest in continued employment. An untenured teacher who is not rehired after expiration of his or her contract is entitled to a due process hearing if the decision not to rehire is accompanied by a finding of incompetence or immorality, because the teacher's liberty of employment would be impaired by such a finding. However, probationary employees or at-will employees generally do not enjoy the due process protections.

2. Claims of Discrimination

♦   *Where a professor obtained tenure through an internal grievance process, she was not subjected to discrimination in violation of Title VII.*

Despite a departmental recommendation to grant tenure to a professor of philosophy employed by Vanderbilt University, the acting dean of the relevant college informed the professor that her employment with the university would end the following year. The professor filed a grievance with the professional ethics committee, which concluded that irregularities had occurred and forwarded the matter to the promotion and tenure committee. Meanwhile, the professor sued the college in a Tennessee federal court for national origin and gender discrimination in violation of Title VII.

However, before the court considered the case, the tenure committee awarded the professor tenure, and granted her an award of back pay. The professor claimed the back pay award was insufficient to compensate her for the emotional distress and damage to her reputation, but the district court granted pretrial judgment to the university. The U.S. Court of Appeals, Sixth Circuit, affirmed, holding that **because the professor successfully obtained tenure through the university's internal grievance process, no adverse employment action ever occurred.** Accordingly, no violation of Title VII was committed. *Dobbs-Weinstein v. Vanderbilt University,* Nos. 98-5266/5268, 1999 WL 455388 (6th Cir.1999).

♦   *Where legitimate reasons existed for denying tenure to an instructor, her age discrimination claim failed.*

A 58-year-old instructor at a private Illinois university applied for tenure. Two tenure committees recommended against granting tenure, and the university denied her application. The instructor filed charges of age discrimination with the EEOC and an internal grievance with a faculty appeals committee. Due to procedural problems, the appeals committee recommended that the university give the instructor another year to apply for tenure. The next year, the tenure committees unanimously rejected her application. The instructor again filed an internal grievance, and the appeals committee found procedural errors. However, the university upheld the decision to deny her tenure. After the university rejected her appeal, she filed suit in federal court. The court granted the university pretrial judgment, and appeal was taken to the Seventh Circuit Court of Appeals.

The court of appeals found that the university had met its burden of articulating a legitimate, nondiscriminatory reason for its decision to deny the instructor's second application for tenure. Its decision was based on the unanimous view of the two tenure committees that **the instructor failed to demonstrate the "high level of performance expected of a tenure applicant,"** which included: 1) a significant level of involvement in curriculum innovation, instructional research and programmatic design that would be expected of a tenure candidate; 2) significant service to the institution; and 3) an exhibited commitment to the university in terms of significant leadership or contribution in areas of institutional importance. One of the committees also noted a lack of reference letters from her colleagues and little evidence of significant scholarly presentations. Although the instructor presented some evidence of decisions disfavoring older employees, she failed to supplement the information by engaging in a detailed comparison of her own qualifications (or those of the other older candidates denied tenure) to those of younger candidates who were granted tenure. The judgment of the lower court was affirmed. *Vanasco v. National-Louis Univ.*, 137 F.3d 962 (7th Cir.1998).

3. Collegiality and Animosity

♦   *Even though collegiality was not listed as a specific factor for tenure or promotion review, a university could consider it when evaluating a teacher.*

A teacher at a Maryland university sought an early review for tenure and a promotion. When both were denied, she sued the university for breach of contract, asserting that it had improperly considered collegiality (defined by the court as "the capacity to relate well and constructively to the comparatively small bank of scholars on whom the ultimate fate of the university rests" and as "the relationship of colleagues") in its decision-making process. She claimed that the university could only evaluate teaching, research and service. The university claimed that although nothing in the contract mentioned collegiality, it was inherently a part of the contract and therefore a proper consideration in both tenure and promotion decisions.

The Court of Special Appeals of Maryland ruled in favor of the university, finding that **collegiality was a proper factor for review.** It noted that the American Association of University Professors had even contemplated as much in its Statement on Professional Ethics. **Collegiality plays an important role in both teaching and service.** Finding insufficient evidence that the university breached either the contract or its implied covenant of good faith and fair dealing, the court ruled that the teacher's claim could not succeed. *Univ. of Baltimore v. Iz*, 716 A.2d 1107 (Md.App.1998).

♦   *While a university professor may have been denied tenure because of personal animosity, the law could offer him no remedy.*

An English and drama professor sued Wesley College for wrongfully denying him tenure. The professor claimed that the president of the college held such personal animosity towards him that he intentionally undermined his tenure application by providing misleading materials to the Board of Trustees. The Trustees, after assessing negative financial figures for the college and a lack of students interested in the degree program for drama, denied the professor tenure. Without tenure, the college would only renew the professor's employment contract for one additional year.

The Court of Chancery of Delaware ruled in favor of the Trustees. Because the college faced a $300,000 operating deficit and was in danger of facing financial insolvency, the Trustees could properly adopt plans to eliminate the budget deficit, including personnel cutbacks. Even though the professor presented evidence of personal animosity toward him, he did not present evidence that the president lied to the trustees. Finally, the court held that **personal animosity, in and of itself, could not constitute the foundation of a lawsuit.** *Hudson v. Wesley College, Inc.*, 1998 WL 939712, No. 1211 (Del.Ch.1998).

◆ *A university could deny tenure to a professor based on lack of collegiality.*

A professor employed part-time by a Louisiana private university was promoted to full-time probationary faculty status in 1987. He was again promoted to associate professor in 1991 and entered into a series of one-year contracts with the university. Each contract constituted a new appointment with the university for that respective year. The faculty handbook provided that "each non-tenured member of the ordinary faculty is considered to be on probation" but that "tenured faculty contracts may not be terminated except for cause." Although the faculty exercised the primary right of determination in matters of faculty status, the university conciliation committee could request reconsideration of tenure decisions. The faculty ultimately denied the professor's application for tenure based on his alleged lack of "collegiality" and refused the conciliation committee's request for reconsideration. The professor filed suit in a Louisiana trial court, alleging breach of contract. The trial court held for the university, and the professor appealed to the Court of Appeal of Louisiana. The court of appeal held that **any ambiguity with regard to the employment relationship should be construed in favor of employment-at-will. The professor was a non-tenured employee who could be terminated at the expiration of his annual contract without cause.** Consequently, he was permissibly denied tenure based on lack of collegiality. A contrary ruling would improperly destroy the distinction between probationary and tenured faculty. The holding of the trial court was affirmed. *Schalow v. Loyola Univ. of New Orleans*, 646 So.2d 502 (La.App.4th Cir.1994).

4. Handbooks and Procedures

◆ *A university did not have to grant tenure to an assistant professor merely because a handbook described tenure procedures.*

A Louisiana man was hired by a private university as an assistant professor. His position was classified as a probationary regular appointment, with the prospect of tenure. The faculty handbook explained that appointments during the probationary period were made for periods of one year, with written notification of reappointment made annually, and further explained that tenure-track professors were eligible for tenure if they met the university's expectations for tenured faculty. During the professor's third year review, he was informed that he had a low number of publications. During his sixth year review, the provost rejected all recommendations that he be given tenure. The professor appealed the provost's decision, but a committee determined that the provost had not acted improperly. Thereafter, the professor filed suit against the university for breach of contract in a state trial court, which granted the university's motion for summary judgment. The professor appealed to the Court of Appeal of Louisiana, Fourth Circuit.

On appeal, the professor argued that the university had breached its contract of employment with him by denying him promotion and tenure. In contrast, the university argued that there was no factual support for his claim that a contract existed that promised him tenure. The professor asserted that a contract was formed by the parties mutually agreeing to be bound by certain terms and conditions described in the faculty handbook. However, a handbook is a unilateral expression of company policy, and the publishing of that policy does not evidence a meeting of the minds. **Here, the professor did not claim that he was**

promised tenure, he claimed that he understood that the faculty handbook constituted such a promise because each party mutually agreed to be bound by the terms and conditions set forth therein. Because there was no proof that there was a contract between the parties, the trial court had correctly found that the university was entitled to judgment in its favor. *Schwarz v. Administrators of the Tulane Educational Fund*, 699 So.2d 895 (La.App.4th Cir.1997).

♦ *A handbook designed as a guide for the faculty did not create a property right to tenure.*

After five years of employment, an assistant German professor at a Texas university was notified that his contract would not be renewed for financial reasons. The professor asked that he be allowed to undergo the tenure approval process so he could tell potential employers he was being considered for tenure. According to the faculty handbook, he was eligible for tenure consideration. He was not, however, granted tenure. He sued the university in a federal district court, claiming he was denied due process of law in being refused tenure and in being fired. A jury agreed, but the judge overturned the jury's decision. The professor appealed to the U.S. Court of Appeals, Fifth Circuit. The court of appeals stated that **the handbook was a guide for the faculty and not a self-contained policy document. It did not create a constitutionally protected property right in continued employment or an assurance of tenure. The handbook was not a contract.** The only process due to the professor was the exercise of professional judgment in a nonarbitrary fashion. Since there was evidence to support the termination, it was not arbitrary. *Spuler v. Pickar*, 958 F.2d 103 (5th Cir.1992).

♦ *A probationary professor did not have a property interest in being granted tenure.*

A probationary professor at the University of Oklahoma was denied tenure despite the unanimous recommendation of the members of her department. The tenure committee had denied tenure because it felt her research was deficient. Claiming that the tenure committee breached university procedures by performing an independent evaluation of her scholarship, the professor sued the university in a state court, arguing that she had a property interest in being granted tenure. The Court of Appeals of Oklahoma disagreed. The court stated that **there was no evidence to suggest that tenure was meant to be granted routinely or that it could be withheld only "for cause." Once tenure was granted, a property interest would arise, but not until then.** In addition, it was within the power of the committee to perform an independent evaluation of the teacher's scholarship. *Stern v. Univ. of Oklahoma Bd. of Regents*, 841 P.2d 1168 (Okla.App.1992).

♦ *Even though a university offered one-year contracts to a teacher for more than seven years, she was not entitled to tenure by default.*

A nontenured assistant professor at a Georgia university was given a series of one-year contracts for each academic year. Although university policy stated that no regular eighth-year contract should be given unless an award of tenure had already been made, the university offered the professor an eighth one-year contract without offering her tenure. It then offered her a final contract for her ninth year. She sued, asserting that since she had taught at the university for eight years, she was either entitled to tenure or had already acquired tenure by default (tenure *de facto*). A federal court granted summary judgment to the university, and the Eleventh Circuit Court of Appeals affirmed. First, **the university's policy of allowing contracts for nontenured professors for only seven years did not create an entitlement to tenure** where the university offered a teacher an eighth year of employment. Second, the professor could not show that she had been tenured *de facto* where she failed to show that a past practice of the university allowed for automatic tenure. She presented no evidence that tenure *de facto* had ever occurred at the university. She was not entitled to tenure. *Gray v. Bd. of Regents of the Univ. System of Georgia*, 150 F.3d 1347 (11th Cir.1998).

♦ *A Georgia appellate court held that the decision to deny tenure did not have to be unanimous in order for the denial to be effective.*

A university employed a professor under a series of annual contracts. Each contract incorporated portions of the university's faculty handbook but made no explicit references to the faculty handbook tenure section. University policy was to discharge tenure-track faculty members if they remained untenured upon completing their seventh annual contract. The university denied the professor tenure in his fifth, sixth and seventh years of employment. He claimed that the university deviated from its faculty handbook procedures. He also claimed that tenure decisions required a joint determination by the dean and appropriate chairpersons, and a specific recommendation to the university with supporting data. In his final unsuccessful attempt at gaining tenure, **the dean and division chairperson had disagreed on whether to grant tenure. The professor claimed that the handbook required a unanimous decision by the dean and chairperson in order to effectively deny tenure.** The professor sued the university in a Georgia trial court, which ruled in the university's favor. The professor appealed to the Georgia Court of Appeals which affirmed the trial court's decision. The court agreed that the faculty handbook tenure provisions formed a part of the professor's employment contract. However, it found no merit to his claim that tenure recommendations from the dean and division chairperson must be unanimous. While supporting data should have been provided, failure to do so did not injure the professor. Nothing in the employment contract or faculty handbook indicated the right to a board of trustees review. The professor had already received three opportunities to obtain tenure and no further consideration was due. *Moffie v. Oglethorpe Univ.*, 367 S.E.2d 112 (Ga.App.1988).

5. Other Tenure and Promotion Cases

♦ *Where a university conducted a fair review of a professor's record before denying tenure, the professor could not succeed in his lawsuit against it.*

Washington State University hired a professor with eight years' teaching experience and promised to review him for tenure after three years instead of six. However, at the review, his research record revealed that he had been a co-author on all his publications, and they were not in top-tier journals. He had also received poor teaching scores. After he was denied tenure, he sued the university for breach of contract, discrimination and misrepresentation. The case reached the Supreme Court of Washington, which ruled in favor of the university. **The court found** that the university had considered the professor's full teaching and publication record, and that the procedure used had been fair. None of the professor's claims could survive. *Trimble v. Washington State Univ.*, 993 P.2d 259 (Wash.2000).

♦   *A professor's position as associate dean was not a protected property interest preserved by her tenured faculty position.*

The University of North Dakota hired a professor in the School of Communication. She was also given administrative duties as the director of the School of Communication and as the associate dean of the College of Fine Arts and Communication. In 1995, she was told by her senior administrators to improve her administrative performance. Eventually, she was dismissed from her administrative duties, but remained a faculty member. She sued in federal court, alleging that her discharge from the administrative positions violated her protected property interests under tenure. The court dismissed her claim that she had a protected property interest in her administrative positions. Citing the North Dakota State Board of Higher Education Policy Manual, which was included in her employment contract, the district court noted that tenure does not extend to administrative positions.

The Eighth Circuit Court of Appeals agreed, noting that the professor's administrative position was at will, which does not evoke a protected property interest. In fact, the letter of understanding supplementing her employment contract stated, "Associate Deans have no specific term, but rather serve at the pleasure of the Dean." The circuit court found that the professor's position as director of the School of Communication included a three-year contract, but **her protected property interest had been satisfied because the university had fully compensated her for the salary associated with the position even though she did not serve out the full term.** *Rakow v. State of North Dakota*, 2000 U.S. App. LEXIS 2691 (8th Cir., 2000).

♦   *A university could deny tenure to a professor with electronic publications on the ground that her work was not published in refereed journals.*

An associate professor at a New York university went before a tenure review committee and received a 3-2 vote in her favor. Nevertheless, the dean of the school of education recommended to the university president that she be denied tenure because of her lack of publications in peer-reviewed, scholarly (refereed) journals. The professor specialized in computer applications in occupational therapy and had developed a number of computer applications. **Her work had been published electronically or in non-print media.** After tenure was denied, she claimed that the review process had been flawed and that she had not been allowed to demonstrate her computer materials to the committee. The case reached the New York Supreme Court, Appellate Division, which held that there was no record of the review being arbitrary, capricious or tainted by bad faith. Here, the dean had recommended against tenure because she believed that the professor needed to theoretically justify and validate through research the computer applications she had developed. However, **the university had conducted the review process in substantial compliance with its procedures.**

As a result, the court refused to overturn the university's decision to deny tenure. *Loebl v. New York Univ.*, 680 N.Y.S.2d 495 (App.Div.1st Dept.1998).

♦ *A university was liable for breach of contract where it failed to deliver on a promised raise.*

A professor and his wife, both employed at a Florida university, were offered jobs at a Texas university. The professor met with his supervisors and discussed the offer, at which time the dean of the college of social sciences promised him that he would match the offer within three years. The professor and his wife decided to stay in Florida. When the university failed to raise the professor's salary to the agreed-upon level, the professor sued the university for fraud and breach of contract. A jury awarded him $65,000 for breach of contract and $86,450 for the fraudulent misrepresentations made by university officials. The trial court overturned the jury's verdict, finding that sovereign immunity barred both the fraud and breach of contract claims. The Court of Appeal of Florida agreed that the fraud claim was barred by sovereign immunity. However, it held that **the breach of contract claim survived. Because the dean was acting within the scope of his employment when he entered into the contract with the professor, the court reinstated the jury's verdict on the breach of contract claim.** *Parker v. State of Florida Bd. of Regents*, 724 So.2d 163 (Fla.App.1st Dist.1998).

♦ *An associate professor could not sue a university for denying him a promotion where he was found to have withdrawn his request for the promotion.*

An assistant professor of anesthesiology at the University of West Virginia's School of Medicine attained tenure and a promotion to associate under guidelines that called for him to demonstrate "excellence" in teaching and service, and a level of "satisfactory" in the area of research. Subsequently the university modified the guidelines to require "excellence" in research. When the associate professor applied for the position of professor, he was informed that he would be evaluated under the new guidelines and that he did not qualify for promotion under them. **He then wrote two letters, informing the university that he declined to be evaluated under the new guidelines,** and filed an administrative grievance, requesting that the old guidelines be used in evaluating him for promotion. He also asserted that the university was retaliating against him for two earlier grievances he had filed in which he had obtained substantial dollar amounts. An administrative law judge (ALJ) determined that the associate professor had withdrawn his request for promotion, and the case reached the Supreme Court of Appeals of West Virginia. **The court agreed with the ALJ that the associate professor had withdrawn his request for promotion.** Even though his letters stated that he declined to be evaluated under the new guidelines, and there was some question as to whether this meant that he was withdrawing his promotion request, the ALJ had concluded that the letters were a withdrawal. Since this determination was not clearly wrong, it could not be reversed The associate professor's claim had to be dismissed. *Graf v. Univ. of West Virginia Bd. of Trustees*, 504 S.E.2d 654 (W.Va.1998).

♦ *A university did not have a duty to avoid making negligent misrepresentations to a teacher.*

A man worked as a professor at an Oregon community college. He took a leave of absence to work as a visiting professor at a nearby university and at the end of the year, applied for a permanent tenure-track position there. He was offered the position but before accepting, he received his student evaluations. They were well below those of the average teacher at the university and the professor asked a dean whether the poor evaluations would affect his chances of obtaining tenure. The dean told him that the evaluations would not be a problem and the professor resigned his position at the community college and accepted the job at the university. Over the next year, **his student evaluations did not improve, and the following year he was offered a nonrenewable one-year contract.** The professor filed suit against the university in state court, alleging that the dean negligently misrepresented to him that the evaluations would not affect his prospects of receiving tenure. A jury found for the professor, and the university appealed. The court of appeals reversed, finding that the university did not owe the professor a duty to exercise due care regarding the representations it made. The professor appealed to the Supreme Court of Oregon.

The supreme court noted that the determining issue was whether the university owed the professor a duty to avoid making negligent misrepresentations. The court found that there was no such duty here. The parties were in a contractual relationship and both were acting on their own behalf. The court also held that **the university's employee handbook did not require the university to provide employees with information regarding their job security,** so as to create a duty to avoid making negligent misrepresentations. Finally, the court held that the employer-employee relationship does not create a special duty of care. Finding that the university had no duty to avoid making negligent misrepresentations, the court affirmed the decision for the university. *Conway v. Pacific Univ.*, 924 P.2d 818 (Or.1996).

♦   *Even though two physicians had an understanding that tenure would be a formality, a university was not required to grant it.*

A private Maryland university recruited two physicians to join its pediatric cardiology department. Both were tenured professors at different universities and dealt primarily with the department director in their negotiations. After interviews with other university officials, the physicians were offered professor positions. The physicians began to have difficulties in the department. Other doctors and staff complained that they were difficult to get along with, had poor management skills and failed to adequately monitor research projects. Because the physicians had not yet been approved for tenure, the university terminated their employment. They filed suit against the university in state court for breach of contract, alleging that the director had orally assured them that the approval process was a formality and that they would receive tenure. The jury found that the physicians had accepted contracts for tenured professorships and that the university did not have just cause to fire them. The university appealed to the Court of Special Appeals of Maryland.

The university argued that the contract was embodied entirely in the exchange of letters between the physicians and the director which specifically stated that no offers of tenure were being made. The physicians argued that based on the director's statements and the general practice within the academic community, they believed that the approval process was a mere formality. Considering the director's statements, the court of appeals held that the jury could have properly found that the approval process was a formality and that the physicians' tenured positions were assured. However, the court then found that **the director did not have the authority to bind the university to a guarantee of tenure since the university never told him that the physicians could bypass the approval process.** Although the director may have believed that the physicians would have little difficulty obtaining tenure, there was no indication that the tenure committees shared this belief. Finding that the director had no authority to guarantee tenure to the physicians, the court reversed the trial court's decision. *Johns Hopkins Univ. v. Ritter*, 689 A.2d 91 (Md.App.1996).

◆   *A college could not dismiss tenured professors for financial reasons where the board of trustees did not declare a state of financial exigency.*

An Illinois college entered into contracts with tenured faculty members which provided that they could be discharged if the board of directors declared that the college was in a state of financial exigency. The college encountered severe financial difficulty, and signed an agreement to become part of an Illinois university, but the board never declared a state of financial exigency. The parties signed an indemnification agreement and the university promised to give tenured appointments to at least 26 members of the college's tenured faculty. It then offered 11 five-year contracts, and dismissed three professors with two years' salary. Two of the three dismissed professors sued the university for breach of their tenure contracts. The trial court granted pretrial judgment to the university, and the professors appealed to the Appellate Court of Illinois.

The appellate court reversed, ruling that **the financial distress of the college leading to the affiliation with the university did not extinguish the college's obligations under the faculty manual.** Because the board of trustees had improperly failed to declare a state of financial exigency and no other contractual provision justified their dismissal, the professors' tenure rights had not expired. Neither the college nor its contractual obligations were extinguished when it became part of the university. Although the American Association of University Professors' guidelines caution against portable or transferable tenure, the court held that whether the parties intended that tenure be extinguished if the college affiliated with another university was a question of fact to be determined at trial. The trial court ruling was reversed and the case was remanded for further proceedings. *Gray v. Loyola University of Chicago*, 652 N.E.2d 1306 (Ill.App.1st Dist.1995).

◆   *A college president could issue a positive letter of recommendation about an instructor and still deny him tenure.*

A full-time faculty member of the dance and theater department at a New York college underwent a tenure review by the status committee, provost and president. The committee voted 4-1 for tenure but noted a concern "with the lack of interdisciplinary dance/theater productions." The provost and president noted that the instructor had difficulty working with colleagues in a collaborative manner which gave rise to doubts about his leadership potential. However, the president had earlier praised the faculty member in a letter of recommendation to prospective employers. After the president denied his application for tenure, the instructor challenged the decision in the U.S. District Court for the Southern District of New York. The court held for the college, ruling that intrusions into tenure decisions would improperly substitute judicial evaluation of teaching effectiveness for the judgment of those charged with that function by the college. It **rejected the faculty member's argument that "precise terms and conditions of every appointment" be specified prior to the tenure decision. Such a conclusion would prevent consideration of sometimes critical but more subjective factors.** Further, the court held that the president's letter was not inconsistent with his negative tenure decision when the different audiences and circumstances were taken into account. On reconsideration, after allowing the faculty member time for discovery, the court adhered to its prior decision. There had been neither breach of contract nor bad faith on the part of the college. The district court granted summary judgment to the college. *Bresnick v. Manhattanville College*, 864 F.Supp. 327 (S.D.N.Y.1994).

D. Letters of Intent

A letter or statement of intent regarding future employment is generally not enforceable against an employer unless the letter evinces a bilateral understanding that employment will be forthcoming. A unilateral, subjective expectation on the part of an employee (or future employee) is insufficient to subject an employer to liability.

◆   *Where an employee received a letter that only confirmed his compensation, and not the duration of the employment, he could be discharged during the school year.*

A manager employed by a Missouri university received letters each year confirming his reappointment and compensation for the following school year. Ten years after his initial hiring, he received a letter that confirmed only his proposed compensation. The school discharged him in November of that same year. The manager filed a wrongful discharge lawsuit against the university in a Missouri trial court. The trial court dismissed the claim, and the manager appealed to the Missouri Court of Appeals.

The court of appeals held that the compensation letter sent to the manager was insufficient to establish a contract. The court noted that **a statement of duration was an essential element of an employment contract.** An indefinite hiring at a set amount per year was a hiring at will and could be terminated by either party at any time. Moreover, even if the letters received from the university in prior years formed a series of one-year contracts, the university purposely excluded the language "reappointing" the manager for another year. Any previous contract the manager had with the university had expired by the time he was discharged, and the university was not under any obligation to rehire him. *Clark v. Washington University*, 906 S.W.2d 789 (Mo.App.E.D.1995).

◆   *A letter addressing the use of laboratory facilities at a university did not amount to a contract requiring the university to provide such facilities.*

A Northwestern University medical school professor sued the university, claiming that it had harassed him into resigning from his tenured position. He alleged that the university had failed to assign him new patients for research and removed him from the patient rotation hospital calendars. He filed a lawsuit against the university in an Illinois circuit court, which held in his favor. The court issued a temporary restraining order preventing the university from changing the professor's research practices. On appeal, an appellate court reversed the circuit court decision and remanded the case for additional proceedings.

On remand, the circuit court enjoined the university from evicting the professor from his laboratory facilities. It based its decision on a partially written agreement allegedly requiring the university to provide the professor with adequate facilities to continue and expand his research. The university sought a reversal of the circuit court's injunction. The university's request was denied and it again appealed to an Illinois appellate court. The appellate court reversed the circuit court decision. **Although the agreement mentioned the laboratory facilities, it did not clearly reflect an agreement between the university and the professor for his continued use of the facilities.** The professor was not entitled to the injunction allowing him continued use of the laboratory facilities. *Williams v. Northwestern Univ.*, 523 N.E.2d 1045 (Ill.App.1st Dist.1988).

E. Investigations, Hearings and Procedural Disputes

Several substantive and procedural rights surround employment decisions, particularly when an employee has a property interest in employment. The rights afforded to the employee may include administrative remedies, collective bargaining grievance procedures and state or federal court actions.

1. Investigations

When administrative agencies attempt to investigate discrimination charges, they frequently issue subpoenas for school employment records and may seek testimony from school officials regarding employment decisions. Schools are often reluctant to provide such information because of two factors: 1) the First Amendment's assurance that the government will not entangle itself in religious affairs (applicable only to religious schools) and 2) the perceived need to protect the integrity of the peer review process (applicable regardless of religious affiliation). While the lower courts are split on whether to allow broad inquiries by federal authorities into private school employment records, the U.S. Supreme Court has ruled that investigations by state agencies should be allowed to proceed unhampered by the federal courts.

◆   *A private college had to disclose certain records to the EEOC in the following case.*

A professor, who had been employed at a Pennsylvania private college for three years, was denied tenure after he was reviewed by the school's Professional Standards Committee. The committee, composed of the dean and five faculty members, recommended that tenure not be granted to the professor. The committee's recommendation was also reaffirmed by the college's grievance committee. The professor then filed a complaint with the EEOC alleging discrimination based on his French national origin. The EEOC issued a subpoena for the committee's records. Although the EEOC offered to accept the records with names deleted, the school refused to disclose them. The EEOC then filed suit in federal district court to compel the college to comply with the subpoena. The district court ordered disclosure of the records and the college appealed. The court of appeals affirmed, holding that **although the disclosure might burden the tenure process or invade the privacy of other professors, the records had to be disclosed because they were "relevant" to the EEOC's case.** The college appealed to the U.S. Supreme Court, but its petition for review was denied. *Franklin & Marshall College v. EEOC*, 476 U.S. 1163, 106 S.Ct. 2288, 90 L.Ed.2d 729 (1986).

◆ *The U.S. Supreme Court required a university to comply with an EEOC subpoena seeking peer-review information.*

After the University of Pennsylvania, a private institution, denied tenure to an associate professor, she filed a charge with the EEOC alleging discrimination based on race, sex and national origin in violation of Title VII. During its investigation, the EEOC issued a subpoena seeking disclosure of the professor's tenure-review file and the tenure files of five male faculty members identified as having received more favorable treatment. The university refused to produce a number of the tenure-file documents and asked the EEOC to modify the subpoena to exclude "confidential peer review information." The EEOC refused and successfully sought enforcement of its subpoena through a federal district court. The U.S. Court of Appeals, Third Circuit, affirmed and rejected the university's claim that policy considerations and First Amendment principles of academic freedom required recognition of a qualified privilege or the adoption of a balancing approach that would require the EEOC to demonstrate a showing of need to obtain peer review materials. The U.S. Supreme Court then held that **a university does not enjoy a special privilege requiring a judicial finding of necessity prior to access of peer review materials.** The Court was reluctant to add such a privilege to protect "academic autonomy" when Congress had failed to do so in Title VII. The Court also stated that "academic freedom" could not be used as the basis for such a privilege. The Court affirmed the lower court decisions. *Univ. of Pennsylvania v. EEOC*, 493 U.S. 182, 110 S.Ct. 577, 107 L.Ed.2d 571 (1990).

2. Hearings and Procedural Disputes

◆ *When a property right to employment exists, due process requires that the employee receive notice and an opportunity to be heard before being dismissed.*

In two consolidated cases, the U.S. Supreme Court considered what pretermination process must be afforded a public employee who can be discharged only for cause. In the first case, a security guard hired by a school board stated on his job application that he had never been convicted of a felony. Upon discovering that he had in fact been convicted of grand larceny, the school board summarily dismissed him for dishonesty in filling out the job application. He was not afforded an opportunity to respond to the dishonesty charge or to challenge the dismissal until nine months later. In the second case, a school bus mechanic was fired because he had failed an eye examination. The mechanic appealed his dismissal after the fact because he had not been afforded a pretermination hearing. The Supreme Court held that **because the employees possessed a property right in their employment, they were entitled to a pretermination opportunity to at least respond to the charges against them.** The pretermination hearing need not fully resolve the propriety of the discharge, but should be a check against mistaken decisions. The Court held that in this case the employees were entitled to a pretermination opportunity to respond, coupled with a full-blown administrative hearing at a later time. *Cleveland Bd. of Educ. v. Loudermill,* 470 U.S. 532, 105 S.Ct. 1487, 84 L.Ed.2d 494 (1985).

◆   *When the disciplinary action is something less than termination, the protections afforded by due process are not the same as required in* Loudermill.

A police officer employed by a Pennsylvania state university was arrested in a drug raid and charged with several felony counts related to marijuana possession and distribution. State police notified the university of the arrest and charges, and the university's human resources director immediately suspended the officer without pay pursuant to a state executive order requiring such action where a state employee is formally charged with a felony. Although the criminal charges were dismissed, university officials demoted the officer because of the felony charges. The university did not inform the officer that it had obtained his confession from police records and he was thus unable to fully respond to damaging statements in the police reports. **He filed a federal district court action against university officials for failing to provide him with notice and an opportunity to be heard before his suspension without pay.** The court granted summary judgment to the officials, but the U.S. Court of Appeals, Third Circuit, reversed and remanded the case.

The U.S. Supreme Court agreed to review the case, and stated that the court of appeals had improperly held that a suspended public employee must always receive a paid suspension under *Cleveland Bd. of Educ. v. Loudermill,* above. The Court held that **the university did not violate due process by refusing to pay a suspended employee charged with a felony pending a hearing.** It accepted the officials' argument that the Pennsylvania executive order made any pre-suspension hearing useless, since the filing of charges established an independent basis for believing that the officer had committed a felony. The Court noted that **the officer here faced only a temporary suspension without pay, and not employment termination as in *Loudermill.*** The Court reversed and remanded the court of appeals' judgment for consideration of the officer's arguments concerning a post-suspension hearing. *Gilbert v. Homar,* 520 U.S. 924, 117 S.Ct. 1807, 138 L.Ed.2d 120 (1997).

◆   *Where a state university violated a professor's procedural due process rights, but no proof of actual injury was shown, the professor was only entitled to $1.00 in nominal damages.*

A tenured professor at a West Virginia university was issued a letter of reprimand by a dean, who cited a number of deficiencies, including that the professor's second job with Dupont was interfering with his duties. The professor replied that the letter lacked specifics and was without a basis in fact. Subsequently, the university discharged him by letter. He appealed through the university's appeal system. After a hearing, it was determined that the discharge had been for just cause, but that the failure to hold a pre-termination hearing required the university to pay the professor back pay. The university appealed. The Supreme Court of Appeals of West Virginia held that **the university had improperly terminated the professor without providing him an opportunity to respond. This was a violation of his due process rights.** However, the court then found that the termination was proper and that no proof of actual injury had been shown from the denial of procedural due process. As a result, the award of back pay was reversed, and the university only had to pay nominal damages of $1.00. *Barazi v. West Virginia State College*, 498 S.E.2d 720 (W.Va.1997).

♦   *A college could not violate a professor's due process rights where the state was not involved and the college was entirely private.*

A tenured professor at a New York private college was fired. He filed suit against the college in state court, alleging that his discharge violated due process. After the court dismissed the case, he appealed to the New York Supreme Court, Appellate Division. The appellate court noted that students and **instructors at private colleges have no right to due process in the colleges' proceedings unless they can show that the state was involved in the challenged activity.** The professor argued that all private colleges and universities in New York are included in the University of the State of New York and are subject to regulation and inspection by the Board of Regents. The court, however, found that **mere regulation is not enough to show state involvement.** Rather, there must be a sufficiently close relationship between the state and the action of the entity so that the action can be regarded as an activity of the state itself. Because that was not the case here, the court found that the professor had no due process rights and it affirmed the trial court's decision. *Moghimzadeh v. College of Saint Rose*, 653 N.Y.S.2d 198 (A.D.3d Dept.1997).

♦   *A professor who was fired following a sexual harassment complaint failed to show a due process violation.*

A Vermont private college ended its "presumptive tenure" plan pursuant to measures undertaken to downsize the school. Professors with presumptive tenure were entitled to five-year contract extensions absent misconduct or exigent circumstances. A male student at the college filed a complaint with the sexual harassment committee under an interim policy, alleging that a professor forced him to have sexual relations with him. The interim policy was more comprehensive than the older policy with respect to the informal and formal procedures in cases alleging sexual harassment. The professor received notice of the complaint and a hearing, but was told that only witnesses with potential direct knowledge of the incident would be permitted to testify. After extensive deliberations, the committee unanimously recommended termination of the professor's employment. The president dismissed his appeal, and the professor filed a breach of contract lawsuit against the college in a U.S. district court. He also asserted that the college had violated his due process rights. A jury awarded substantial damages, and the college appealed to the U.S. Court of Appeals, Second Circuit.

The court of appeals noted that the jury had reasonably interpreted the handbook as constituting a contract of employment between the professor and the college. However, the court held that there was insufficient evidence in the record for a reasonable jury to find that the college adopted the interim policy in violation of handbook procedures. The professor failed to present any evidence establishing that he was discharged without cause; he had merely asserted his innocence in a conclusory manner. There was also insufficient evidence to find for the professor on his claim that the college had breached its duty of good faith and fair dealing. **The committee's conduct did not deprive the professor of any substantive or procedural rights he had under his employment contract.** *Logan v. Bennington College Corp.*, 72 F.3d 1017 (2d Cir.1995).

◆   *A professor was not entitled to an injunction allowing him to remain in his position.*

A California private university established an accredited department of emergency medicine. The university appointed a professor of surgery with limited experience in emergency medicine as the chairman of the department. However, the university removed the professor from his position after the Accreditation Council announced its intention to withdraw accreditation of the program based on his lack of experience. The professor sought a preliminary injunction in a state trial court, alleging violations of his due process rights and civil service rules. The trial court granted the professor a preliminary injunction, and the university appealed to the California Court of Appeal.

The professor contended that his removal from the position required application of predisciplinary protections mandated by county civil service rules. The court of appeal disagreed, holding that the university bylaws vested such decisions in the president. Because the professor was not likely to prevail on the merits of the claim, and because the university was more likely to be harmed by the injunction than the professor, the court reversed the order granting the injunction. Finally, the court of appeal held that **the alleged improprieties surrounding the professor's dismissal did not allege state action necessary to implicate due process protections.** The university was a private institution and the professor's position was not governmental. *Shoemaker v. County of Los Angeles*, 43 Cal.Rptr.2d 774 (Cal.App.2d Dist.1995).

◆   *A federal appeals court could remand a case to state court after dismissing the federal cause of action. It did not have to dismiss the case—thereby defeating the plaintiff's claims because of the statute of limitations.*

An employee of Carnegie-Mellon University (CMU) filed a lawsuit in a Pennsylvania trial court charging that CMU violated the federal Age Discrimination in Employment Act (ADEA). He also alleged violations of state laws. CMU was allowed to remove the case from state court to a U.S. district court because the alleged violation of the ADEA gave federal court jurisdiction over the entire lawsuit. The employee subsequently discovered that the federal claim could not be successful because he had failed to file a timely age discrimination charge with a federal or state agency. He requested that the federal claim be deleted and that the case be remanded to state court. The federal court granted this request. CMU then requested that the U.S. Court of Appeals, Third Circuit, order the lower court not to remand the case to the state court. The court of appeals denied that request and CMU appealed to the U.S. Supreme Court.

The Supreme Court noted that when a case is removed from state to federal court because it contains a federal claim, the federal court can exercise jurisdiction over the entire case, including claims arising under state law. However, the federal and state law claims must arise from the same "operative fact," in this case the employee's dismissal. In cases where the federal claim is dropped from the lawsuit after removal, a federal court has discretion to dismiss the case and let the plaintiff start over again in state court. The question in this case, however, was **whether the federal court has discretion to remand the case to the state court, thereby preserving state law claims that would otherwise be lost if state statutes of limitation have run before the plaintiff can start again in state court.** The Supreme Court asserted that federal courts have such discretion and ruled that the employee's case could be remanded to the Pennsylvania trial court in which it was filed, thus preserving his state law claims. *Carnegie-Mellon Univ. v. Cohill*, 484 U.S. 343, 108 S.Ct. 614, 98 L.Ed.2d 720 (1988).

◆　*After a finding in favor of a university on labor relations issues, a civil rights lawsuit on discrimination could be heard.*

A Pennsylvania private university discharged five minority advisors who were working in its minority educational program. They claimed that they were discharged because they had criticized the university's minority education program and had filed collective bargaining grievances. The advisors' labor union filed an unfair labor practice charge with the Pennsylvania Labor Relations Board (PLRB) claiming that the advisors were terminated in violation of the Pennsylvania Public Employee Relations Act. The university stated that the advisors were terminated for legitimate educational purposes. The PLRB ruled in the university's favor. The advisors then filed a civil rights lawsuit against the university in a federal district court. The university argued that the PLRB's findings were binding and that they precluded the advisors from bringing any federal claims. The court disagreed, finding **dissimilar issues in the PLRB action and the civil rights lawsuit.** The advisors deserved consideration because they were raising race and national origin discrimination issues for the first time. The court denied the university's motion to dismiss the race discrimination portion of the advisors' complaint but dismissed all issues dealing with the PLRB decision. The lawsuit could continue in federal court as a discrimination case. *Stokes v. Bd. of Trustees of Temple Univ.*, 683 F.Supp. 498 (E.D.Pa.1988).

◆　*An employee could not invoke the grievance procedures of a staff handbook because he was a high-level managerial employee.*

A Louisiana man worked for Tulane University for more than 30 years as the director of the university's physical plant department. He was eventually discharged for poor job performance and because he and his immediate supervisor were unable to resolve their differences. Upon his discharge, the director sought to invoke the grievance procedures outlined in the university's staff handbook. The university responded that the grievance procedures were unavailable to high-level managerial employees. He then sued the university. After a federal court determined that the employee was an at-will employee and had no contractual right to a grievance proceeding, the director appealed to the U.S. Court of Appeals, Fifth Circuit. The court first noted that **because the handbook was not an employment contract, and because the university had not entered into an oral contract with the director concerning the handbook's grievance proceedings, the director had no right to invoke its protections.** The court also held that the director could not show that he had justifiably relied on the availability of the grievance procedures. The appellate court affirmed the decision in favor of the university. *Gilbert v. Tulane Univ.*, 909 F.2d 124 (5th Cir.1990).

F. Wrongful Termination

Generally, an at-will employee may be discharged at any time without cause unless an agreement exists that limits the employer's right to terminate employment. Public policy also restricts an employer's right to discharge an employee.

◆ *A public university was entitled to immunity in a wrongful refusal to hire case.*

A New York mathematical physicist sought employment at the Lawrence Livermore National Laboratory, which is operated by the University of California pursuant to a contract with the federal government. He sued university regents in a federal district court, claiming breach of contract because the university agreed to employ him but then wrongfully refused to hire him when he could not obtain a required security clearance from the U.S. Department of Energy (DOE). The court held that the Eleventh Amendment, which provides for state immunity from lawsuits, barred his breach of contract action. The U.S. Court of Appeals, Ninth Circuit, reversed the decision and the U.S. Supreme Court agreed to review the case. On appeal, the physicist contended that the Eleventh Amendment was inapplicable in this case because any award of damages would be paid by the DOE and not the state of California. The Supreme Court rejected this argument, finding that **an entity's potential legal liability, not its ability to discharge the liability or to require a third party to reimburse it, was the relevant inquiry when determining the immunity issue. The Eleventh Amendment protects a state from the risk of adverse judgments even though the state may be indemnified by a third party.** The Court reversed the court of appeals' judgment. *Regents of Univ. of California v. Doe,* 519 U.S. 337, 117 S.Ct. 900, 137 L.Ed.2d 55 (1997).

◆ *An employee alleging retaliatory discharge was entitled to a trial.*

While conducting a study on the interaction between passive smoking and contact with radioactive materials for the University of Chicago, **an employee noticed that human test subjects had been exposed to dangerously high levels of radiation. After insisting that the matter be reported to the federal government, the employee was fired.** The employee filed suit, claiming that his termination was retaliatory, but a trial court dismissed the case because the employee did not allege that a criminal statute, state law or actual violation was involved. The Illinois Appellate Court reversed and remanded the case. It held that the employee merely had to allege that he had a good-faith belief that a violation of public policy occurred in order for the case to go to trial. *Stebbings v. University of Chicago*, 2000 Ill. App. LEXIS 152 (Ill.App., 2000).

• *When a junior college attempted to discharge a teacher for writing anony-mous letters critical of the college district's president, she brought a variety of claims against it.*

When anonymous letters critical of the president of a junior college district were distributed, the president took action to determine who had written them. He authorized the search of personnel files and data from employees' computers. The governing board later concluded that a teacher had written the letters and issued her a notice that it intended to dismiss her. She sued, denying that she had written the letters, and obtained a temporary restraining order that put her on paid administrative leave. Subsequently, the governing board withdrew the charges against her, but reserved the right to reinstate them. A California federal court examined her claims.

It first found that the Eleventh Amendment prevented her lawsuit for money damages against the junior college district and its governing board. It then held that the teacher did not have a reasonable expectation of privacy in the material on her computer or in her personnel file such that the search could be ruled unconstitutional under the Fourth Amendment. However, **she stated a valid claim under the First Amendment even though she claimed not to have written the letters. If the attempted discharge was due to the belief that she had written the letters, then it did not matter if she did not write them. She would still have a claim under the First Amendment.** The court dismissed most of her claims, but held that she could re-file in state court. *Wasson v. Sonoma County Junior College Dist.*, 4 F.Supp.2d 893 (N.D.Cal.1998).

• *An employee's wrongful discharge claim failed where she could not show that her firing had been related to her reports of theft in the office.*

A Massachusetts private college employee reported the apparent theft of funds from the office in which she worked. She was employed at will and after her reports of theft, she was discharged. She brought suit against the college and her former supervisor in the superior court, claiming wrongful discharge and inten-tional interference with her employment contract. The court granted summary judgment in favor of the college and her former supervisor. She appealed unsuccessfully to the Appeals Court, then appealed to the Supreme Judicial Court of Massachusetts.

The lower court had held that as an at-will employee, she could not obtain redress from her former employer when it discharged her for reporting the theft of funds. In certain circumstances, however, an at-will employee may maintain an action against her former employer for wrongful discharge. Public policy is violated when an employer discharges an employee for reporting criminal activity even if the reports were made only within the employing units. Here, there was no dispute that the woman was an at-will employee. She therefore had an obligation to support her claim that she was discharged for reporting criminal conduct to her superiors. However, **she had no facts to support her claim, and the record contained nothing showing that the college discharged her for a reason contrary to a well-established public policy.** Further, she failed to show that her supervisor intentionally interfered with her employment contract because she was unable to prove that he knowingly induced the college to break the contract, that his interference, in addition to being intentional, was improper in motive or means, and that she was harmed by his actions. Rather, the record stated several examples of problems she was having on the job. Therefore, the court affirmed the grant of summary judgment for the college and the supervisor. *Shea v. Emmanuel College*, 682 N.E.2d 1348 (Mass.1997).

✦   *An employee was allowed to proceed in his lawsuit against a college for retaliation.*

A security officer employed by a Vermont private college sought workers' compensation benefits after he was injured while working overtime during commencement events. The college denied his claim but the Department of Labor and Industry reversed and granted him benefits. The security officer alleged that during and after the period in which he applied for and received the benefits, the college discriminated against him by badgering him to come back to work, changing his employment duties and responsibilities, requiring him to work night shifts in breach of a previous agreement, changing his work hours, giving him unfairly low job evaluations, and challenging his right to receive workers' compensation benefits. He was also demoted and placed on probation for six months based on a student's complaint. The security officer did not return to work following his demotion, allegedly because his stress-induced depression prevented him from working. The security officer was fired after his short-term disability benefits ran out, and he filed a lawsuit against the college in a Vermont superior court, alleging retaliatory discrimination and intentional infliction of emotional distress. The superior court granted summary judgment to the college, and the officer appealed to the Supreme Court of Vermont.

The supreme court held that **employees have a private right of action under the workers' compensation act when an employer allegedly discharges them or discriminates against them for filing a workers' compensation claim.** Although the college articulated a legitimate, nondiscriminatory reason for the officer's discipline, the court held that genuine issues of material fact remained concerning whether he was discriminated against for filing a workers' compensation claim, and whether the severity of the disciplinary action resulting from the student's complaint was the result of discriminatory treatment. Finally, the court dismissed the officer's intentional infliction of emotional distress claim, holding that mere insults and indignities in the workplace were not sufficiently outrageous to prevail on this claim. *Murray v. St. Michael's College*, 667 A.2d 294 (Vt.1995).

✦   *A wrongful discharge claim failed where the employee was paid through the end of his contract.*

A licensed veterinarian contracted with a Missouri private university to work for its animal facilities department from July 1989 through June 1990. The interim director ultimately notified him that his services would not be needed in 1990 but that he would remain on the payroll until the expiration of his current contract. The veterinarian filed a wrongful discharge lawsuit in a Missouri trial court, alleging that he had been discharged in retaliation for reporting infractions of the federal Animal Welfare Act. The trial court granted pretrial judgment to the university, and the court of appeals transferred the case to the Supreme Court of Missouri.

The supreme court affirmed, ruling that only discharged at-will employees may state a wrongful discharge cause of action. Here, **because the veterinarian**

had not been discharged (his contract had expired), his claim had been properly dismissed. Given the significant differences between employees at will and contractual employees, the court rejected the veterinarian's contention that the failure to renew an employment contract should be treated the same as the discharge of an employee at will. The court declined to consider whether a separate (as yet unrecognized) tort or theory of damages should have been alleged in place of the wrongful discharge claim. Whether liability exists for wrongful failures to renew contracts or what type of damages may be recovered for a breach of contract in "whistleblower" situations were still open questions. *Luethans v. Washington University*, 894 S.W.2d 169 (Mo.banc 1995).

◆   *A discharge that violates public policy will generally yield liability for wrongful discharge.*

An African-American director of admissions at a Virginia private college felt that the college discouraged African-American students from enrolling, discriminated against African-American job applicants, improperly tried to force her to fire African-American employees, and tolerated racially derogatory remarks and jokes about African-Americans. She refused to participate in such practices and reported the allegedly discriminatory acts to her superiors. As a result, she was demoted from director of admissions to senior admissions representative. The director then reported the alleged violations to the NAACP. Shortly thereafter, she was given an unsatisfactory job performance evaluation and was discharged even though allegedly less productive white employees were retained. The director filed suit in state court claiming that her discharge was racially motivated. The court dismissed the case, holding that Virginia did not recognize a cause of action for this type of wrongful discharge. The director appealed to the Supreme Court of Virginia.

The director contended that her discharge was improperly motivated by race and was in retaliation for her opposition to the college's allegedly discriminatory practices and policies. The supreme court agreed. Although private college employees could generally be discharged at any time and for any reason pursuant to the state's employment-at-will doctrine, discharges that violate Virginia public policy are excepted from this general rule. Here, the state legislature had declared its strong public policy against employment discrimination based upon race or gender in the Virginia Human Rights Act. **Racially motivated discharges fell within the narrow exception to the employment-at-will doctrine. The employee could not be discharged for reporting racially discriminatory practices.** The case was reversed and remanded for further proceedings. *Lockhart v. Commonwealth Educ. Systems Corp.*, 439 S.E.2d 328 (Va.1994).

II. EMPLOYEE BENEFITS

Like their counterparts in the public sector, many private schools offer a broad range of employment benefits to employees. These benefit programs are subject to federal civil rights laws such as Title VII and the Equal Pay Act as well as income tax laws. Employer-employee disputes concerning benefits will generally be resolved according to contract law rules (see Section I).

A. Retirement Benefits

◆   *Where a university reasonably modified a retirement plan, it was not liable for violating ERISA.*

A professor employed by a New York private university retired in 1977 and began receiving benefits under the school's contributory retirement plan. The board of trustees amended the plan periodically to provide cost of living adjustments (COLAs) to plan members or their beneficiaries. Subsequently, the retirement committee amended the COLA and the board of trustees amended the plan again to provide that "the retirement committee shall have exclusive authority and discretion to construe any disputed term." After the retirement committee denied the professor's claim for additional benefits, he filed suit against the retirement plan and the university under the Employee Retirement Income Security Act (ERISA) in a state trial court. The case was ultimately transferred to a U.S. Magistrate Judge. The magistrate judge granted the university's motion for summary judgment, and the professor appealed to the U.S. Court of Appeals, Second Circuit.

The retirement committee contended that it had properly modified the earlier increases by calculating what each retiree's monthly benefit would have been under the amended COLA, subtracting the value of increases actually given, and adding the difference to each retiree's monthly benefits. The professor contended that the base figure to which the above formula would be applied should include all prior COLAs. The court ruled that **the retirement committee had discretion to construe any uncertain or disputed term.** Consequently, the court applied the arbitrary and capricious standard of review. Because the retirement committee's interpretation of the statute was reasonable, the court affirmed the magistrate judge's ruling in favor of the university. *Jordan v. Retirement Committee of Rensselaer Poly. Inst.,* 46 F.3d 1264 (2d Cir.1995).

◆   *A professor was entitled to sue after a college improperly fired him and terminated his retirement benefits.*

A Wisconsin professor was promoted to president of a private college. He signed an employment agreement for a three-year term with the understanding that the agreement could be terminated by either party with one year's notice. **The professor also entered into a retirement agreement with the school which provided him with four payments of $30,000 over the three-year term, as long as he did not retire or terminate his employment.** The college terminated his employment, without the required one-year notice, after two retirement payments had been made. The professor sued the college for the payments and for the wages he would have earned from the time of termination to the time the contract was to have expired. The trial court ruled in favor of the college, stating that the statute of limitations had tolled and there was no consideration for the retirement payments. The professor appealed to the Wisconsin Court of Appeals.

The professor argued that the statute of limitations had not run because he was suing for wages unearned. The court of appeals agreed, stating that the statute of limitations is shorter when suing for wages earned than when suing for wages unearned. Further, it stated that there was consideration for the retirement payments. Continuation of employment may consist of a detriment to the promissee or a benefit to the promissor. For the professor to receive retirement benefits, he was required to remain at the college and not retire or accept other employment. Thus, he gave up exercising a legal right which is valid consideration. The court of appeals reversed the trial court's decision. *Lovett v. Mt. Senario College, Inc.*, 454 N.W.2d 356 (Wis.App.1990).

B. Welfare Benefits

♦   *An employee welfare benefit plan established by an association of Christian schools was not entitled to tax-exempt status.*

The American Association of Christian Schools (AACS), a tax-exempt association of Christian schools located in all 50 states, established a "welfare plan" providing health, disability, and life insurance as well as other benefits to employees of member schools. The welfare plan, which was a separate legal entity, sued the Internal Revenue Service in a U.S. district court seeking a tax refund for fiscal years ending July 31, 1982, and 1983. It contended that it was exempt from paying federal income taxes under §§ 501(c)(3), (4) and (9) of the Internal Revenue Code. The court observed that under § 501(c)(3), groups organized and operated exclusively for religious purposes were exempt from paying federal income taxes. The court concluded that the welfare plan did not meet the operational test of the provision because **it could not show that it was operated exclusively for a tax- exempt religious purpose.** Here, the welfare plan essentially sold insurance coverage. It extended insurance benefits in return for premiums based on the risk assumed by the welfare plan's insurance company. Further, an administrative staff collected insurance premiums, maintained files, accepted claims and issued benefits. **Because the welfare plan had a significant nonexempt purpose, the court held that the welfare plan was not exempt under § 501(c)(3).** The presence of a significant non-exempt purpose also prevented the welfare plan from being eligible for § 501(c)(4)'s "social welfare" exemption.

The welfare plan also argued that it was exempt from federal taxation because it was a voluntary employees' beneficiary association (VEBA) under § 501(c)(9). The court observed that one of the requirements for being a VEBA is that the organization be controlled by either its membership, an independent trustee or a board of trustees, at least some of whom were designated by, or on behalf of, the employees themselves. Here, because the AACS welfare plan board was self-perpetuating, it failed to meet any one of these criteria. Even though school employees had some say in selecting the pastors of the churches, the court noted that when an employee selected a pastor who served on the board of trustees of the welfare plan, he or she was acting as a church member and not as an employee of the school. The welfare plan was not tax exempt and its request for a refund was denied. On appeal, the decision was affirmed. *American Ass'n of Christian Schs. Voluntary Employees Beneficiary Ass'n Welfare Plan Trust v. U.S.*, 850 F.2d 1510 (11th Cir.1988).

♦   *A school was forced to reinstate health insurance for an employee who failed to pay her premium after becoming mentally incompetent.*

A school offered a health plan which was governed by the Employee Retirement Income Security Act (ERISA) and the Consolidated Omnibus Budget

Reconciliation Act (COBRA). An employee suffered from cerebral atrophy and became hospitalized and mentally incompetent. She failed to pay a premium, and her insurance was canceled. A representative notified her employer of her incompetency. Following the representative's judicial empowerment as legal guardian, he paid the premiums which would have come due. However, her employer contended that it could not be forced to reinstate coverage. The guardian sought reinstatement in a federal district court. The school filed a motion to dismiss. Although ERISA and COBRA speak to the nonpayment of premiums, neither directly speak to nonpayment of premiums due to incompetency. The court held that judicial consideration of the issue could thus go beyond the statutory language and consider common law and public policy. The court then considered the policies underscoring the statutes, which included "the continued well being and security of employees." Common law provides that the actions of an incompetent are disregarded. It followed that an incompetent's inaction should also be disregarded. Further, an earlier case ruled that an insured is not bound to give notice of a disability when made unable to do so by the disability insured against. **The employee in the case at hand was rendered unable to appreciate the fact that her premium was due. The court held that the school could be required to accept the premium and reinstate coverage.** The motion for dismissal was denied and the case was allowed to proceed to trial. *Sirkin v. Phillips Colleges, Inc.*, 779 F.Supp. 751 (D.N.J.1991).

C. Discrimination

◆   *A private education institute could not stop paying disability benefits to an employee who turned 65 because the employee was not receiving pension benefits.*

A man was employed as a research scientist at a California research and education institute. He was diagnosed with Parkinson's disease and took a medical leave of absence. He eventually became eligible to receive long-term disability benefits through the institute's insurance plan but he retained his employee status and his right to return to work if his health improved. While still receiving his disability benefits, he turned 65 years old and became eligible for retirement. Had he chosen to retire, his pension benefits would have been slightly more than his disability benefits. **Although he did not retire (and thus did not receive pension benefits), the institute offset his disability benefits with the amount of pension benefits he would have received by retiring, thereby reducing his income to zero.** He filed suit against the institute in state court, alleging violations of the Age Discrimination in Employment Act (ADEA) and a state statute. The institute cross-claimed for the amount of disability benefits it had inadvertently paid him after he turned 65, removed the case to federal court and filed a motion to dismiss. The motion was granted and the employee appealed to the U.S. Court of Appeals, Ninth Circuit.

The court of appeals noted that this was not a case of double-dipping which the ADEA was designed to prevent. In order to preclude employees from receiving both long-term disability benefits and pension benefits for which the employee is eligible, the ADEA allows employers to offset the amount of disability benefits with the amount of pension benefits. The institute argued that since the employee was eligible to retire, he was eligible to receive the pension benefits, and therefore it could offset them. The court disagreed. **Because the employee had not retired, he was not receiving any pension benefits.** The court also noted that the ADEA expressly prohibits any employee benefit plan from requiring or permitting involuntary retirement. The primary effect of the institute's policy was to leave an employee without an income unless he or she retired, and the court held that a reasonable person in the employee's position would feel that he had no choice but to retire. Finding that **the offsetting of long-term disability benefits is only allowed when pension benefits are being paid concurrently,** the court found that the institute's disability plan violated the ADEA. The district court's decision was reversed. *Kalvinskas v. California Institute of Technology*, 96 F.3d 1305 (9th Cir.1996).

D. Income Tax Laws

◆ *A religious school was not entitled to a refund of federal income taxes paid on behalf of employees who were getting fringe benefits in lieu of a higher salary.*

Marquette University, a tax-exempt educational institution, provided certain fringe benefits to its employees from 1973 to 1978 with commensurate salary reductions, but did not withhold federal income tax on the amounts by which the salaries of participating employees were reduced. The university paid taxes on those amounts after they were assessed by the IRS and then sued the government in U.S. district court seeking a refund. The Internal Revenue Code defines gross income as "all income from whatever source... including... compensation for services...." The district court observed that this included income obtained in any form, whether services or property, and that the university would be obligated to locate a specific statutory section which allowed it to exclude the questionable amounts from "gross income." **The three benefits at issue were parking spaces, recreation center memberships and tuition payments by the university for certain employees' children at area high schools.**

The university claimed that the tuition payments remitted to the area high schools were scholarships and therefore were exempt from taxation. The district court ruled, however, that the tuition payments were not scholarships since the payments had been deducted from the salaries of the employees and remitted to the high schools by the university and were therefore to be considered part of the employees' taxable gross income. The university also contended that waived parking fees and recreation center memberships were not taxable income. The district court observed that "entertainment, medical services, or so called 'courtesy' discounts furnished by an employer to his employee generally are not considered as wages subject to withholding if such facilities or privileges are of relatively small value and are offered by the employer merely as a means of promoting the health, goodwill, contentment, or efficiency of its employees." However, the court concluded that the benefits here did not meet the criteria since they were considered significant enough to be deducted from the employee's wages and were only available to employees who agreed to the salary reduction in return for the benefits. **The university's attempt to recover the taxes paid was rejected by the court.** *Marquette Univ. v. U.S.*, 645 F.Supp. 1007 (E.D.Wis.1986).

◆ *Although wage cuts used to purchase annuity contracts were not taxable as income, they were subject to social security taxation.*

John Carroll University is a not-for-profit institution exempt from federal income taxes under §§ 501(a) and 501(c)(3) of the Internal Revenue Code. The university established a retirement annuity plan for employees in which participating employees agreed to take salary cuts in exchange for contributions by the university on their behalf toward the purchase of annuity contracts. The university's contributions were excludable from the employees' gross income for federal income tax purposes. When the university filed claims for refunds of FICA taxes paid for certain years, the IRS denied the university's claim for one year and failed to rule on the claims for two other years. The university sued the IRS in U.S. district court seeking a refund of FICA taxes for the years in question totaling $79,147 plus interest.

At issue was whether taxpayers acting pursuant to salary reduction agreements are exempt from FICA taxes paid on amounts contributed prior to Jan. 1, 1984, toward the purchase of retirement annuities. The court observed that in 1965, the IRS decided that amounts withheld because of a salary cut agreement are to be included in the employee's taxable wage base for FICA tax purposes, even though the amounts withheld are excluded from gross income for federal income tax purposes. The court reasoned that if retirement annuity contributions were not included in the FICA wage base, individuals could control which part of their wage was to be included in the FICA wage base. In denying the university's claim, the court also referred to a 1981 U.S. Supreme Court decision in which the court held that **"the term 'wages' must be interpreted consistently for purposes of both income tax withholding and FICA."** The district court also concluded that a 1984 Act of Congress, which applied FICA taxation to remuneration paid on or before March 4, 1983, made retroactive taxation possible. **The contributions of the university to the annuity plans were therefore subject to FICA taxes** and the university's claim was dismissed. *John Carroll Univ. v. U.S.*, 643 F.Supp. 675 (N.D.Ohio 1986).

III. UNEMPLOYMENT AND WORKERS' COMPENSATION

A. Unemployment Benefits

The Federal Unemployment Tax Act (FUTA), 26 U.S.C. § 3301 et seq., establishes a federal program to compensate persons temporarily unemployed. Although the federal Department of Labor oversees the program, states meeting specific criteria administer the program. A major exemption from coverage, in § 3309(b)(1) of the Act, states: "This section shall not apply to service performed ... in the employ of (A) a church or convention or association of churches, or (B) an organization which is operated primarily for religious purposes and which is operated, supervised, controlled, or principally supported by a church or convention or association of churches."

◆ *A student worker who lost his job was not entitled to unemployment benefits because the job was deemed incidental to his studies.*

A university graduate student in cinema-television obtained a job in the School of Business Administration at the University of Southern California. His job category was student worker even though it was described as "faculty assistant" by the business school. It was a "nonbenefits position" available only to students. This meant that the university did not provide a funding pool for unemployment benefits for the position. The student ultimately lost his job and was denied unemployment compensation pursuant to California Unemployment Insurance Code § 642. This section provides that "employment" (for unemployment insurance purposes) does not include services performed for a school by an enrolled student who is regularly attending classes. However, regulations promulgated pursuant to this statute provide that "if the course of study is incidental to the employment, the exemption shall not apply." The case reached the California Court of Appeal, Second District, where the student contended that his studies were incidental to his employment. Specifically, **he alleged that his job in the business school was not exempt from unemployment compensation benefits because it did not directly further his course of study. The court of appeal disagreed,** noting that the student was employed in a position available only to students regularly enrolled at the university. Consequently, even though the position was in a different department, it was incidental to his studies. *Davenport v. Cal. Unemp. Ins. Appeals,* 30 Cal.Rptr.2d 214 (Cal.App.2d Dist.1994).

B. Workers' Compensation

◆   *After sustaining injuries in an automobile accident, an assistant coach was limited to collecting workers' compensation benefits.*

A Louisiana private university hired a female assistant basketball coach. Her duties included recruitment of new basketball players, which required some travel. The coaches arranged for an official visit from a high school senior from Mississippi. After returning the senior to her home following a recruiting visit, another assistant coach fell asleep at the wheel and caused an accident in which the first assistant coach sustained severe injuries, including a broken neck. The university paid workers' compensation benefits in addition to many of her medical expenses. Thereafter, she filed a negligence action against several defendants including the driver of the vehicle, the university, and the university's insurer. The defendants filed motions for summary judgment, and the coach filed a cross motion for summary judgment against the university. Summary judgment was entered against the coach and she appealed to the Court of Appeal of Louisiana, Fourth Circuit.

The court noted that an employee's exclusive remedy against an employer for an injury occurring within the course and scope of her employment is workers' compensation benefits. The court often looks at the following factors to determine the course and scope of employment: the time, place and purpose of the act; the relationship between the employee's act and the employer's business; and the reasonable expectation of the employer that the employee would perform the act. The court held that **the risk that caused the car accident arose out of her employment duties and occurred during the time of her employment at a place contemplated by her employer. Therefore, the court held that the coach was within the course and scope of her employment at the time of the**

accident. The court held that her sole remedy against the defendants was under the provisions of the workers' compensation statutes. *Bolton v. Tulane University of Louisiana*, 692 So.2d 1113 (La.App.4th Cir.1997).

◆   *An employee who was also a union representative was not entitled to workers' compensation benefits when she slipped and fell on her way back to work from a union meeting.*

A Connecticut woman worked for a private university. She was also a local union representative and while returning to work after a union meeting during her lunch break, she fell on a sidewalk not under the control of the university and injured her arm. The meeting had been a weekly meeting and not a grievance or negotiating session. Her employer was not allowed to attend the meeting and her attendance was voluntary. She filed a claim for workers' compensation benefits and after a hearing, the workers' compensation commissioner found that her injury was compensable because the coming and going to the meeting was part of her employment or incidental to it. He noted that the meeting had been for the mutual benefit of the employee and the university. The university appealed to a workers' compensation review board which reversed the commissioner's decision. The employee appealed to the Supreme Court of Connecticut.

The supreme court noted that when employees leave work for lunch or for other functions not related to work, they are outside the scope of their employment if they are injured. However, if the activity is work-related, the employee can fall within the workers' compensation act's coverage if he or she can show that the activity benefited the employer. **Traditionally, attendance at union meetings has been held not to benefit employers, but more recent decisions have looked at the particular nature of the union activity. For example, grievance hearings and negotiation settlements have been held to benefit employers.** Because the employee here was only attending a weekly meeting, the court found that she was not acting within the scope of her employment or performing an activity that benefited her employer. The court held that the commissioner's decision was unreasonably drawn from the facts and it affirmed the board's decision. *Spatafore v. Yale Univ.*, 684 A.2d 1155 (Conn.1996).

◆   *An employee hospitalized for job stress was entitled to compensation because her disability was an "occupational injury" rather than an "occupational disease."*

A Pacific University office manager had surgery in 1977 to repair a ruptured brain aneurysm, and subsequently suffered headaches, nausea and high blood pressure. In 1986, she was informed that her job title was changed. She viewed this as a demotion, and was later suspended because of alleged mismanagement. She was very upset and left immediately for home. She became confused and disoriented and her apartment manager took her to a hospital. She was hospitalized for one week complaining of nausea, a severe headache and lethargy. She filed for workers' compensation benefits for job stress which caused her disability. The Workers' Compensation Board held that her condition was an occupational disease rather than an occupational injury, and that she had not proven that her work activities were a major contributing cause of her disability. Thus, her disability was not a compensable occupational injury. She appealed to the Court of Appeals of Oregon.

The appellate court held that her disability was an occupational injury rather than an occupational disease. **Her disability was unexpected and sudden, reflecting an injury rather than a disease.** Although she did suffer from stress and high blood pressure, there was no evidence that these conditions were inherent in her work. Also, since her brain surgery, she had sought no medical treatment for those conditions. Thus, her disability was unexpected and sudden and established a compensable occupational injury. The appellate court reversed and remanded the Workers' Compensation Board decision in order for the board to determine whether her job was a material contributing cause of her disability. *Morrow v. Pacific Univ.*, 785 P.2d 787 (Or.App.1990).

♦   *A janitor was entitled to benefits after an injury on school grounds.*

A janitor at a private Georgia law school commonly rode to work on his bicycle. One morning, while on property owned by the law school, he had an accident while riding his bicycle to a building in order to sign in and obtain keys necessary for his job. Although the street on which he was injured was open to travel by the public, it was owned and patrolled by the university. The university denied workers' compensation coverage. An administrative law judge awarded benefits but the full board reversed the decision. The Court of Appeals of Georgia held that the "ingress and egress" rule applied. Under this rule, **the worker's employment period included a reasonable time while he traveled to and from work on his employer's premises.** The "employer's premises" was considered all property owned, maintained or controlled by the employer. Here, the janitor was on his "employer's premises," he was traveling to work and was performing a function directly related to his job. The court deemed it insignificant that the street on which the employee was injured was open to the public and held that the janitor was entitled to workers' compensation benefits. The holding of the board was reversed. *Peoples v. Emory University*, 424 S.E.2d 874 (Ga.App.1992).

♦   *An employee exposed to chemicals at work was entitled to benefits for her continuing problems.*

An administrative assistant was exposed to fumes during the repair of an air conditioning unit. The assistant later developed flu-like symptoms and was only able to work "off and on." She did not connect her symptoms to her exposure. A physician prescribed antibiotics, which intensified the symptoms. She also visited numerous other physicians who were unable to help. The off-and-on work schedule continued for approximately five months, during which the school changed its workers' compensation insurer. The assistant then received a leave of absence and began seeing an environmental specialist. She later returned to work for one day approximately one year after the original exposure but was only able to work for 45 minutes. The employee then connected her symptoms to her chemical exposure, and the theory was confirmed by her doctor. She was determined to be totally disabled due to a dysfunctioning immune system and organic brain damage. The assistant was forced to undertake extensive environmental changes both in and out of her home. A referee awarded workers' compensation benefits against the original insurer and the board affirmed. The school and its insurer then appealed to a Pennsylvania trial court.

The trial court first ruled that the statute of limitations began to run when the injury was connected to the exposure. Next, the court explained that **an original insurer is liable for a recurrence of symptoms, and a subsequent insurer is liable for aggravation of work related conditions.** The court held that the assistant suffered from both an occupational injury and a disease. Because the symptoms were never fully absent, the later exposures were a recurrence. The court affirmed the finding of the original insurer's liability. *Temple Univ. and PNA v. Workers Compensation Appeal Bd.,* 588 A.2d 63 (Pa.Cmmw.1990).

IV. LABOR RELATIONS

The National Labor Relations Act (NLRA), as amended by the Labor Management Relations Act (LMRA), 29 U.S.C. § 141 et seq., governs unionization and collective bargaining matters in all aspects of the private sector, including private education. States are also subject to the dictates of the act. The NLRA was passed to protect the rights of employees to organize, or to choose not to organize, and to ensure that commerce is not interrupted by labor disputes.

A. Managerial Employees

Managerial employees are not protected by the National Labor Relations Act.

◆ *In certain circumstances, faculty members at private educational institutions can be considered managerial employees.*

Yeshiva University's faculty association had petitioned the National Labor Relations Board seeking certification as bargaining agent for all faculty members. The NLRB granted certification but the university refused to bargain. After the U.S. Court of Appeals declined to enforce the NLRB's order that the university bargain with the union, the NLRB appealed to the U.S. Supreme Court, which upheld the appeals court. The Supreme Court's ruling was based on its conclusion that Yeshiva's faculty were managerial employees. It stated:

> The controlling consideration in this case is that the faculty of Yeshiva University exercise authority which in any other context unquestionably would be managerial. **Their authority in academic matters is absolute.** They decide what courses will be offered, when they will be scheduled, and to whom they will be taught. They debate and determine teaching methods, grading policies, and matriculation standards. They effectively decide which students will be admitted, retained, and graduated. On occasion their views have determined the size of the student body, the tuition to be charged, and the location of a school. When one considers the function of a university, it is difficult to imagine decisions more managerial than these. To the extent the industrial analogy applies, the faculty determines within each school the product to be produced, the terms upon which it will be offered, and the customers who will be served.

The Court noted that its decision applied only to schools that were "like Yeshiva" and not to schools where the faculty exercised less control. **Schools where faculty do not exercise binding managerial discretion do not fall within the scope of the managerial employee exclusion.** *NLRB v.Yeshiva Univ.*, 444 U.S. 672, 100 S.Ct. 856, 63 L.Ed.2d 115 (1980).

◆   *There must be a broad measure of control for faculty to be considered management.*

The faculty of Florida Memorial College, a private, nonprofit four-year liberal arts college, established a union pursuant to a NLRB directive. The college filed a petition with the NLRB claiming that under the U.S. Supreme Court's decision in *NLRB v. Yeshiva University*, above, the faculty should be prevented from forming a union due to its managerial/supervisory status. After the NLRB dismissed the college's petition, the college continued in its refusal to bargain with the union. The NLRB asked the U.S. Court of Appeals, Eleventh Circuit, to enforce the NLRB order.

The court of appeals observed that the college faculty here was not managerial or supervisory. Unlike *Yeshiva's* faculty, **the faculty in this case asserted insufficient control in almost every one of the areas examined by the Supreme Court in *Yeshiva*.** Among other things, the Florida Memorial College faculty lacked a comprehensive governing organization which provided meaningful input as to administrative and academic matters. Although faculty members sat on various administrative committees at the college, their influence was diluted since they were appointed by college administrators and because the committees included a number of administrators and students. Further, the faculty had no effective control over curriculum, student policies, faculty hiring, tenure or termination. Also, the fact that there was an absence of tenure at the college indicated that the faculty was nonmanagerial. The court of appeals ordered the college to comply with the NLRB's collective bargaining order. *NLRB v. Florida Memorial College*, 820 F.2d 1182 (11th Cir.1987).

◆   *Where faculty had little control over management decisions, they could not be deemed managerial employees.*

The Cooper Union for the Advancement of Science and Art, a private institution of higher education located in Manhattan, had an enrollment of 900 to 1,000 students and employed 55 to 60 full-time faculty members. In 1974, the Cooper Union Federation of College Teachers was certified to represent a bargaining unit of full-time faculty members and librarians. In 1980, however, after the U.S. Supreme Court's decision in *NLRB v. Yeshiva University*, the school withdrew its recognition of the bargaining unit and refused to bargain with it. The U.S. Court of Appeals, Second Circuit, noted several distinctions between Cooper Union and Yeshiva. Cooper Union's **faculty had no "effective recommendation or control" of management decisions,** and lacked the authority possessed by the Yeshiva faculty. Also, the Cooper Union faculty had little or no authority over financial concerns and other nonacademic matters and merely had restricted access to ordinary office supplies. In addition, the authority of Cooper Union's faculty over academic matters was relatively weak. In light of these differences, the court ruled that the holding of the *Yeshiva* case could not be applied to Cooper Union. Therefore, the Cooper Union faculty was held to be nonmanagerial and was entitled to the protection of the NLRA. The court affirmed the decision of the NLRB and ordered Cooper Union to bargain with the faculty bargaining unit. *NLRB v. Cooper Union for the Advancement of Science & Art*, 783 F.2d 29 (2d Cir.1986).

* *An exclusive bargaining representative that is duly elected by school employees should have the sole voice in discussing employment-related matters with the employer.*

In a U.S. Supreme Court case, Minnesota community college faculty members brought suit against the State Board for Community Colleges. **The faculty alleged that a state statute requiring public employers to engage in official exchanges of views only with their professional employees' exclusive representatives on certain policy questions violated their First Amendment rights.** Under the statute, public employers were required to bargain only with the employees' exclusive bargaining representative. The statute gave professional employees, such as college faculty members, the right to "meet and confer" with the employer on matters outside the scope of the collective bargaining agreement. The faculty members objected to the "meet and confer" provision, saying that rights of professional employees within the bargaining unit who were not members of the exclusive representative were violated. The Supreme Court held that the "meet and confer" provision did not violate the faculty members' constitutional rights. **There was no constitutional right to force public employers to listen to the members' views.** The fact that an academic setting was involved did not give them any special constitutional right to a voice in the employer's policymaking decisions. Further, the state had a legitimate interest in ensuring that its public employer heard one voice presenting the majority view of its professional employees on employment related policy questions. *Minnesota Comm. College Assn. v. Knight*, 465 U.S. 271, 104 S.Ct. 1058, 79 L.Ed.2d 299 (1984).

* *In 1999, the Supreme Court held that public university regents could set standards for faculty instructional workloads for the purpose of emphasizing undergraduate instruction, and that such standards could be removed from the collective bargaining table.*

The Ohio Legislature passed a statute requiring state universities to adopt faculty workload policies and made them an inappropriate subject for collective bargaining. The law was enacted to address the decline in the amount of time faculty spent teaching, as opposed to time spent on research. Any university policy prevailed over the contrary provisions of collective bargaining agreements. One university adopted a workload policy pursuant to the law and notified the collective bargaining agent that it would not bargain over the policy. As a result, **the professors' union filed a state court action, seeking an order that the statute violated public employee equal protection rights.** The Supreme Court of Ohio struck down the statute, finding the collective bargaining exemption was not rationally related to the state's interest of encouraging public university professors to spend less time researching at the expense of undergraduate teaching. The U.S. Supreme Court accepted the university's appeal.

According to the Supreme Court, the state supreme court had not applied the correct standard of review under the Equal Protection Clause. In equal protection clause cases that do not involve fundamental rights or suspect classifications, there need only be a rational relationship between disparity of treatment and some legitimate government purpose. In this case, the disputed statute met the rational relationship standard. Ohio could reasonably conclude that the policy would be undercut if it were subjected to collective bargaining. **The state legislature could properly determine that collective bargaining would interfere with the legitimate goal of achieving uniformity in faculty workloads.** The Ohio Supreme Court decision was reversed and remanded. *Central State Univ. v. American Ass'n of Univ. Professors, Central State Univ. Chapter,* 119 S.Ct. 1162, 143 L.Ed.2d 227 (1999).

◆   *Compelled agency fees cannot be used to support political viewpoints.*

In 1977, the U.S. Supreme Court held that the First Amendment prohibited states from compelling teachers to pay union dues or agency fees where their labor unions used the fees for purposes that were unrelated to collective bargaining. Compelled support of collective bargaining representatives implicated free speech, freedom of association, and freedom of religion concerns. However, some constitutional infringement on those rights was justified in the interest of peaceful labor relations. Thus, as long as the union acted to promote the cause of its membership, individual members were not free to withdraw their financial support. However, **compelled agency fees could not be used to support political views and ideological causes which were unrelated to collective bargaining issues.** *Abood v. Detroit Bd. of Educ.,* 431 U.S. 209, 97 S.Ct. 1782, 52 L.Ed.2d 261 (1977). This decision built on two earlier Supreme Court cases dealing with these issues in the private sector: *Railway Employees' Dep't v. Hanson,* 351 U.S. 225 (1956), and *Machinists v. Street,* 367 U.S. 740 (1961).

◆   *In order to justify agency fees, the activities for which the fees are collected must be germane to collective bargaining activity, be justified by the government's interest in labor peace (and the avoidance of free riders), and present only an insignificant burden on employee speech.*

The exclusive bargaining representative of the faculty at a state college in Michigan entered into an agency-shop arrangement with the college requiring nonunion bargaining unit employees to pay a service or agency fee equivalent to a union member's dues. Employees who objected to particular uses by the unions of their service fee brought suit under 42 U.S.C. § 1983, claiming that using the fees for purposes other than negotiating and administering the collective bargaining agreement violated their First and Fourteenth Amendment rights. A federal district court held that certain collective bargaining expenses were chargeable to the dissenting employees, the U.S. Court of Appeals for the Sixth Circuit affirmed and the U.S. Supreme Court granted *certiorari.* The Court first noted that chargeable activities must be "germane" to collective bargaining activity and be justified by the policy interest of avoiding "free riders" who benefit from union efforts without paying for union services. It then stated that **the local union could charge the objecting employees for their *pro rata* share of costs associated with chargeable activities of its state and national affiliates, even if those** activities did not directly benefit the local bargaining unit. **The local could even charge the dissenters for expenses incident to preparation for a strike which would be illegal under Michigan law.** However, lobbying activities and public relations efforts were not chargeable to the objecting employees. The Court affirmed in part and reversed in part the lower courts' decisions and remanded the case. *Lehnert v. Ferris Faculty Ass'n,* 500 U.S. 507, 111 S.Ct. 1950, 114 L.Ed.2d 572 (1991).

B. Collective Bargaining Agreements

◆   *Where a no-smoking policy was not included in a collective bargaining agreement, a university did not have to bargain over the policy.*

The University of Alaska's Board of Regents adopted a policy that excluded smoking from university facilities open to the public. It later amended the policy to prohibit smoking in motor vehicles. Prior to the adoption of the policy, the union representing certain university employees formally requested bargaining. One union member learned of the revised smoking policy but continued to smoke in the vehicle assigned to him. He was censured for smoking in the vehicle and circulated a petition signed by 30 union members asking the union to negotiate the non-smoking policy. The union presented the proposal to the university, which refused to bargain, asserting that the policy was a permissive subject for which it had no obligation to bargain. **The parties reached a collective bargaining agreement that was ratified by the union membership containing no express reference to the no-smoking policy.** The agreement contained a reservation of rights clause stating that bargaining unit members agreed to follow all university policies not specified in the agreement and reserving the right to change university policies.

The union filed an unfair labor practice against the university, asserting that the no-smoking policy was a mandatory subject of bargaining. The state labor relations agency determined that the policy was a mandatory subject of bargaining, but that the union had contractually waived it by executing the collective bargaining agreement. On appeal, the Supreme Court of Alaska observed that **because the collective bargaining agreement contained no specific reference to the no-smoking policy, the union had contractually waived its right to bargain on that issue** by agreeing to the contract. The union could also be deemed to have waived its right to bargain under the reservation of rights section of the agreement. The court affirmed the agency ruling that the union had waived bargaining on the policy by entering into the agreement. *University of Alaska v. Univ. of Alaska Classified Employees Ass'n,* 952 P.2d 1182 (Alaska 1998).

◆   *A law requiring Massachusetts employees to take days off or to work for deferred pay violated the Contract Clause of the Constitution by substantially impairing the state's obligations under the collective bargaining agreements. Such impairment was neither reasonable nor necessary.*

In the face of a perceived fiscal crisis, **Massachusetts implemented a mandatory furlough program for almost all state employees.** Under the program, employees could take unpaid days off, work without pay and receive bonus paid vacation days after the beginning of the next fiscal year, or work without pay and receive a lump-sum payment upon terminating employment with the state. The amount of mandated days off increased with the amount of compensation an employee earned. After faculty and various professional staff at several of the state's community colleges, and unions representing employees in the state college system challenged the program, the case reached the Supreme Judicial Court of Massachusetts.

The supreme court found that **the program violated the Contract Clause of the U.S. Constitution by substantially impairing the state's obligation to pay compensation to the various affected employees under their collective bargaining agreements.** Further, the state was unable to show that the impairment was both reasonable and necessary to serve an important state purpose. Because the increasing fiscal deficit problems were reasonably foreseeable at the time the state entered into the collective bargaining agreements with the employees, the substantial impairment of the employees' rights under those contracts (after the contracts were signed) could not be reasonable. The court struck down the mandatory furlough program. *Massachusetts Community College Council v. Commonwealth*, 649 N.E.2d 708 (Mass.1995).

◆ *A law allowing Hawaii to postpone employees' pay by a few days was unconstitutional.*

To remedy a budget crisis, Hawaii passed a law authorizing the state to postpone by a few days, at six different times, the dates on which state employees were to be paid. It also declared that the postponements were "not subject to negotiation" by the state employees' unions. University of Hawaii faculty members and their union sued in federal district court to stop the state from implementing the act, and the district court granted the injunction. The case then reached the Ninth Circuit Court of Appeals, which affirmed. It held that **the law violated the U.S. Constitution's Contract Clause by substantially impairing the state's obligation to honor its collective bargaining agreements with the unions.** The law not only changed the employees' pay dates, but also removed "the whole subject from the bargaining table." It could not be justified as reasonable and necessary because there were less drastic ways to reduce the state's financial obligations. *University of Hawaii Professional Assembly v. Cayetano*, 183 F.3d 1096 (9th Cir.1999).

◆ *Florida could not renege on a contract that promised pay raises to public employees.*

During the collective bargaining process, unions representing public employees in Florida reached an impasse with the state. The legislature resolved the impasse by authorizing a 3 percent pay raise, which the unions ratified. Subsequently, state officials projected a shortfall in public revenues, causing the legislature to convene a special session and postpone the pay raises. Several months later, the legislature responded to continuing revenue shortfalls by eliminating the pay raises altogether. When the unions sued, a state trial court ruled in their favor, and the state appealed. The Supreme Court of Florida affirmed the ruling against the state. **Here, the state had a fully enforceable agreement with the unions that it could not break unless there existed no other reasonable alternative means of preserving the contract, in whole or in part.**

The state could not nullify the pay raises simply because that was the most expedient solution. By appropriating public money to fund the pay raises, the state and all its branches became bound by the agreement. The court ordered the state to take the necessary steps to implement the pay raises. *Chiles v. United Faculty of Florida*, 615 So.2d 671 (Fla.1993).

V. STATE ACTION

Section 1983 of the Civil Rights Act forbids action taken under the color of state law that deprives any person of federal constitutional or statutory rights. However, the U.S. Supreme Court has sharply limited the circumstances in which an ostensibly private institution can be found to be acting "under the color of state law."

A. 42 U.S.C. § 1983

◆ *State funding and state regulation are not sufficient to amount to state action.*

The Fourteenth Amendment prohibits any state action which deprives any person within that state's jurisdiction of any rights, privileges or immunities secured by the U.S. Constitution. When a privately operated school in Massachusetts fired a teacher for speaking out against school policy, she sued under the Civil Rights Act of 1871 (42 U.S.C. § 1983) on the grounds that the state, acting through the private school, had abridged her First Amendment right to free speech. As evidence of the control the state had over the private school, she cited the fact that: 1) the school issued diplomas approved by the local school districts whose special students the private school contracted to teach; 2) the private school received 99 percent of its funding from state sources; and 3) her position on the private school staff had been created and funded by a state agency. The U.S. Supreme Court ruled that **even though all of her examples of state control and funding were true, these factors in themselves were not sufficient to show that the state had created an agency or so controlled the private school as to make the school's actions its own.** Absent a showing of actual control by the state, any deprivations of constitutional rights claimed by the teacher were matters between her and another private party. Such complaints between private parties are not within the scope of the 1871 Civil Rights Act. Her dismissal was allowed to stand. *Rendell-Baker v. Kohn*, 457 U.S. 830, 102 S.Ct. 2764, 73 L.Ed.2d 418 (1982).

◆ *A private university was not a state actor by virtue of an affiliation agreement with a city university.*

In 1967, a not-for-profit university in New York entered into an affiliation agreement with the Board of Higher Education in the city of New York. The agreement provided for a common academic calendar and combined academic programs, and further gave the city university the responsibility and authority to approve appointments, promotions, designation of persons as department chairpersons and the granting of tenure to certain faculty members. The private university hired a professor in 1980 and granted him tenure in 1990. He began to have problems with the chief of his division, and alleged that he was subjected to harassment in violation of his First, Fifth and Fourteenth Amendment rights, and 42 U.S.C. § 1983. He also maintained that he was constructively discharged by virtue of having his salary cut. He sued the university in a New York federal district court. The university moved to dismiss the case.

The court first determined that the affiliation agreement between the university and the board of higher education was not sufficient to convert the university into a state actor so as to allow the professor's § 1983 and constitutional rights violations claims. Here, the professor was unable to show that the state played any role in the actions which were the subject of this complaint. **The fact that the state provided some funding, and the state approval of courses, faculty appointments and grants of tenure did not establish a connection between the harassing activity, including the salary cut, and the state support or regulation.** The court held that the university was not a state actor. *Tavoloni v. Mount Sinai Medical Center*, 984 F.Supp. 196 (S.D.N.Y.1997).

* *Using state disciplinary rules is not sufficient to show state action.*

Private college students held a sit-in in their college president's building to protest the college's refusal to divest itself of South African investments. The college suspended the students when they refused to halt their sit-in. The students sued the college president under § 1983 for violating their constitutional due process rights. They argued that their suspension was in accordance with state-prescribed rules of conduct by state officers. The district court dismissed the lawsuit and the students appealed to the U.S. Court of Appeals, Second Circuit. The circuit court ruled that **the private college's adoption of its disciplinary rules pursuant to the New York code did not qualify as "state action."** There was no basis for suing the college or any of its officials under § 1983. The court noted that nothing in the state law or the college rules required suspension. The state of New York never actually compelled schools to enforce its rules and did not even inquire about enforcement. The New York statute was not mandatory. The students could show no evidence that the college had adopted the New York statute in the belief that it was enforcing state law. The full court vacated the previous panel decision of the circuit court. *Albert v. Carovano*, 851 F.2d 561 (2d Cir.1988).

B. Privacy Rights

* *The distribution and reading of a memo to a professor's colleagues was not an invasion of privacy, but could be defamation.*

An assistant professor in the School of Education at a Connecticut university received "commendable" annual evaluations in the areas of teaching, publication and service to the university. When she became eligible for promotion to the rank of associate professor and for tenure, the president of the university granted her the promotion but denied her tenure, allegedly solely for budgetary reasons. Subsequently, the professor was chosen by her colleagues to serve as the chair of the department's appointments committee. The dean of the School of Education asked her to resign from that position, and **wrote a memo to her colleagues and members of the department,** disclosing that she was in the process of leaving the university and that she had been "nonrenewed," recommending that she be removed as chair, and stating that there was rancor in the department. A fellow professor read portions of the memo aloud at a departmental meeting without stating that the only reason for the tenure denial was because of budgetary concerns.

The professor sued the dean and the fellow professor for invasion of privacy and defamation, asserting that the memo was defamatory and that distributing it and reading parts of it aloud invaded her privacy because their actions allowed the inference that she had been denied tenure for other than budgetary reasons. The defendants moved for pretrial judgment, denying that the facts in the memo were private facts, that the memo was defamatory, and that distributing and reading the memo placed the professor in a false light before the public. The Superior Court of Connecticut held that **the claim for invasion of privacy had to be dismissed because, while the facts in the memo may have been private, the distribution and reading of the memo did not amount to the giving of publicity. Since the communication of the professor's tenure status was made only to 10 members of her department in a business-related communication, it was not certain to reach the public at large.** However, the court refused to dismiss the defamation action, finding that there were questions of fact as to whether the communication in the memo could be interpreted as defamatory, and as to whether the persons receiving the memo had a valid business reason to receive it. *Handler v. Arends*, 1995 Conn. Super. LEXIS 660 (Conn.Super.1995).

◆   *A teacher and a professor were held not to have violated the Electronic Communications Privacy Act in the following case.*

A private college in Delaware employed a computer programmer who alleged that the president of the college often mistakenly printed out e-mail message in the office where the programmer worked, and that he would either return them to the president's assistant, or place them in a folder beside the printer. After the programmer was discharged, he told a paralegal teacher that the college was foolish to fire him, as he had "seen things" on the computer screens. He also mentioned that he had seen an e-mail relating to an English professor's breach of contract lawsuit against the college. The paralegal teacher then called the English professor and recounted the conversation she had with the programmer. Neither the paralegal teacher nor the professor saw any e-mail until a lawsuit was filed against them and the programmer by the college. The college alleged violations of the federal Electronic Communications Privacy Act (ECPA) as well as state statutes. The teacher and the professor moved for summary judgment.

The U.S. District Court for the District of Delaware noted that Title I of the ECPA prohibits people from intentionally intercepting, endeavoring to intercept, or procuring another to intercept any electronic communication. The court found that **a reasonable factfinder could not conclude that the teacher or professor took affirmative steps to intercept or access the president's e-mail,** because there was no evidence that they possessed the capability to take those steps or join forces with someone who did. Title I also prohibits any person from using or disclosing to any other person the contents of any electronic communication while knowing or having reason to know that the information was obtained through the illegal interception of an electronic communication. The court held that there was insufficient evidence to conclude that the teacher and professor should have known that the programmer intercepted the e-mail in violation of the ECPA. Also, the college had not shown that the programmer had acquired the e-mails while they were being transmitted. He could have merely seen them on the screen. This would not violate the ECPA. Fact issues precluded summary judgment with respect to the programmer. However, the court granted the teacher's and professor's motions for summary judgment. *Wesley College v. Pitts*, 974 F.Supp. 375 (D.Del.1997).

◆ *A coach was not liable to a former player for defamation or contract interference where there was no showing of damages.*

The head basketball coach and women's athletic director at the University of Wisconsin-Madison accused a standout women's player of forming an inappropriate relationship with an assistant coach. The head coach called a team meeting to announce the suspension of the assistant coach, and when the player interrupted the meeting, the head coach stated that she was a "disgrace" to the team and university. The player resigned from the team. She later agreed to share an apartment with another player for the following year. **The head coach discouraged the player from living with the former teammate, and the former player filed a lawsuit against the head coach** in a Wisconsin trial court for defamation, invasion of privacy, tortious interference with the apartment sharing agreement, and intentional infliction of emotional distress. The court granted the coach's summary judgment motion for the defamation and contract interference claim. Following a jury trial, the court entered judgment for the coach on the remaining claims. The former player appealed dismissal of the defamation and contract interference claims to the Court of Appeals of Wisconsin. **The court agreed with the trial court's decision, finding no evidence of special damages that might justify the defamation claim. There was also no showing of an inability to locate another roommate.** Because there was no showing of extreme emotional distress, the trial court had properly dismissed the claims against the coach. *Bauer v. Murphy*, 530 N.W.2d 1 (Wis.App.1995).

VI. LEAVES OF ABSENCE

*The Family and Medical Leave Act of 1993 (FMLA), 29 U.S.C. §§ 2601–2654, makes available to eligible employees up to 12 weeks of unpaid leave per year: 1) because of the birth of a son or daughter of the employee and in order to care for such son or daughter; 2) because of the placement of a son or daughter with the employee for adoption or foster care; 3) in order to care for the spouse, or a son, daughter or parent, of the employee, if such spouse, son, daughter or parent has a serious health condition; or 4) because of a **serious health condition** that makes the employee unable to perform the functions of the position of such employee. 29 U.S.C. § 2612.*

The FMLA exempts small businesses and limits coverage of private employers to those engaged in commerce or in activities affecting commerce and who employ 50 or more employees for each working day during each of 20 or more calendar workweeks in the current or preceding calendar year. 29 U.S.C. § 2611.

To be eligible for leave, an employee must have been employed by the covered employer for at least 12 months, and must have worked at least 1,250 hours during the 12 month period preceding the commencement of the leave. 29 U.S.C. § 2611.

If the employer provides paid leave for which the employee is eligible, the employee may elect, or the employer may require the employee, to substitute the paid leave for any part of the 12 weeks of leave to which the employee is entitled under the act. 29 U.S.C. § 2612. When the need for leave is foreseeable, the employee must provide reasonable prior notice (generally, at least 30 days for birth or placement of a child, and at least 30 days for planned medical treatment, unless the employee does not have 30 days in which to provide notice). 29 U.S.C. § 2612. The employee must also make efforts to schedule the leave so as not to unduly disrupt the employer's operations. Further, where spouses are employed by the same employer, they can be limited to a total of 12 weeks of leave for the birth or adoption of a child or for the care of a sick parent. 29 U.S.C. § 2612.

An employer may require medical certification to support a claim for leave for an employee's own serious health condition or to care for a seriously ill child, spouse or parent. If the certification is for the employee's health condition, it must contain a statement that the employee is unable to perform the functions of his or her position. 29 U.S.C. § 2613. If the certification is for a child, spouse or parent, it must include an estimate of the amount of time the employee is needed to care for the family member.

Further, an employer may require, at its own expense, a second opinion. 29 U.S.C. § 2613. An employer may also require an employee on leave to report periodically to the employer on his or her leave status and intention to return to work. 29 U.S.C. § 2614. The regulations implementing the FMLA (29 C.F.R. Part 825) define "serious health condition" to include treatment two or more times by a health care provider, and a period of absence to receive multiple treatments "for a condition that would likely result in a period of incapacity of more than three consecutive calendar days in the absence of medical intervention or treatment." 29 C.R.F. § 825.114.

An employee needing leave for a serious health condition may, if medically necessary, take leave intermittently or on a reduced leave schedule that reduces the employee's usual number of hours per workweek or per workday. However, if an employee requests leave on such a basis, the employer may require the employee to transfer temporarily to an alternative position that better accommodates the intermittent or reduced leave, provided that the position has equivalent pay and benefits. 29 U.S.C. § 2613.

During leave, any pre-existing health benefits provided to the employee by the employer must be maintained. However, **the employer is under no obligation to allow the employee to accrue seniority or other employment benefits during the leave period.** 29 U.S.C. § 2614. Upon return from leave, the employee must be restored to the same or an equivalent position. 29 U.S.C. § 2614.

However, the statute contains an exemption for certain highly compensated employees, allowing an employer to deny restoration if: 1) such denial is necessary to prevent substantial and grievous economic injury to the operations of the employer; 2) the employer notifies the employee of its intent to deny restoration on such basis at the time the employer determines that such injury would occur; and 3) in any case in which the leave has commenced, the employee elects not to return to employment after receiving such notice. 29 U.S.C. § 2614.

It is unlawful for an employer to interfere with, restrain, or deny the exercise of or the attempt to exercise, any right provided under the FMLA. 29 U.S.C. § 2615. It is also unlawful for an employer to discharge or in any other matter discriminate against any individual for opposing a practice made unlawful under the act, or for participating in any inquiry or proceeding relating to rights established under the act. 29 U.S.C. § 2615.

Rights established under the FMLA are enforceable through civil actions. An employer who violates § 2615 will be liable for money damages resulting from the violation, and an additional amount equal to the actual damages as liquidated damages. The employer may also be required to provide equitable relief, including employment, reinstatement or promotion. 29 U.S.C. § 2617. Where an employer can prove to the satisfaction of the court that it acted in good faith and had reasonable grounds to believe that its acts or omissions were not a violation, the court may, in its discretion, limit the employer's damages liability to the actual damages and refuse to award liquidated damages. 29 U.S.C. § 2617. The prevailing plaintiff in an action under the FMLA is also entitled to reasonable attorneys' fees, expert witness fees and other costs of the action.

Actions brought under the FMLA must be brought not later than two years after the date of the last event constituting the alleged violation for which the action is brought, or within the last three years of the last event if the violation is wilful. 29 U.S.C. § 2617. An employee's right to bring a civil action terminates if the Secretary of Labor files an action seeking relief with respect to that employee. 29 U.S.C. § 2617.

The FMLA sets forth special rules for employees of local educational agencies who are employed principally in an instructional capacity. These rules apply to the scheduling of intermittent leave based on planned medical treatment, and leave beginning or ending during the five-week period prior to the end of an academic term. 29 U.S.C. § 2618.

The FMLA further provides that it does not modify or affect any federal or state law prohibiting discrimination on the basis of race, religion, color, national origin, sex, age or disability. 29 U.S.C. § 2651. It also states that nothing in the act shall be construed to supersede any provision of any state or local law that provides greater family or medical leave rights than the rights established under the FMLA or any amendment to it. 29 U.S.C. § 2651. Further, **nothing in the FMLA is to be construed to diminish the obligation of an employer to comply with any collective bargaining agreement or any employment benefit plan or**

program that provides greater family or medical leave rights to employees than the rights established under the FMLA. 29 U.S.C. § 2652. Nor shall rights established for employees under the FMLA be diminished by any collective bargaining agreement or by any employment benefit plan or program. 29 U.S.C. § 2652.

◆   *A college may have violated the FMLA when it refused to renew an employee's contract shortly after she returned from a medical leave.*

A New York woman began working for a college as an assistant dean of admissions with the responsibility of recruiting and evaluating applicants for admission to the college. She was required to travel at times for college fairs in her assigned geographic region. While traveling to Florida for the college, she sustained a back injury and obtained workers' compensation benefits for her expenses associated with the injury. The college continued to pay her salary. **In a performance evaluation, she was rated as meeting or exceeding expectations in every category.** The college then reappointed her for another one-year term. By that winter, the employee's back injury developed into severe fibromyalgia. Her doctor recommended that she take a medical leave, but because she was in the busy season, the employee did not ask for a leave.

When a new president took the helm of the college, he appointed an associate dean to the position of dean of admissions. The new dean then expressed to the president that she was concerned about the employee's performance, even though she had been one of the supervisors to sign off on the employee's evaluation. Later, the employee notified the dean that her doctor had again recommended a medical leave, but that she would stay until a there was better time to take it. When the employee asked the college's director of personnel for a leave, the director promised to discuss the matter with the college president. She then notified the employee that her leave request had been denied. The employee contacted an attorney who wrote the college a letter stating that the employee was entitled to leave under the Family and Medical Leave Act (FMLA). The college then granted her leave request.

When the employee returned from her leave, she perceived the atmosphere to be hostile. She obtained her personnel file from the dean's office, and copied its contents. She also copied some performance evaluations of other staff members and a blank evaluation form. Subsequently, **the college refused to renew her contract, or to grant her requests for a final performance evaluation and severance benefits. She sued the college under the FMLA, asserting that it had retaliated against her for exercising her statutory rights.** The college moved for pretrial judgment. A New York federal court denied the college's motion. It found that issues of fact existed as to whether it had violated the FMLA.

First, it noted that the employee had presented a *prima facie* case of retaliation under the FMLA because she had suffered an adverse employment action after engaging in a protected activity under the statute. Next, although the college asserted that she could not show a causal connection between taking the leave and the nonrenewal of her contract, the court found that issues of fact existed here. During discovery, several of the documents the employee had copied from her file were missing from the college's file on her. One of those documents contained references to both the employee's leave and to not renewing her contract. Further, **the college's asserted reasons for the nonrenewal—poor performance, poor attitude and unreliable attendance—could be construed as a pretext, especially because the decision came within a month of the employee's return from leave, and because the employee's evaluation showed that she met or exceeded the college's expectations** in every category.

Finally, with respect to the after-acquired evidence of wrongdoing (the employee's copying of her file and the copying of others' evaluations), there was also an issue of fact as to whether the college would have dismissed her for that action. Here, the dean allegedly failed to produce certain documents during discovery; yet she had not been fired. As a result, the court determined that a trial would have to be held to determine if the FMLA had been violated. *Hillman v. Hamilton College*, 1998 U.S. Dist. LEXIS 5064 (N.D.N.Y.1998).

CHAPTER SIX

Employment Discrimination

I.   RACE AND NATIONAL ORIGIN DISCRIMINATION

*Title VII of the Civil Rights Act of 1964, later amended in 1991, 42 U.S.C. §
2000e et seq., prohibits discrimination in employment based upon race, color,
sex, religion or national origin. It applies to any institution, affecting commerce,
which has 15 or more employees. Title VII exempts employment decisions based
on religion, sex or national origin where these characteristics are "bona fide
occupational qualifications reasonably necessary to the operations of that
particular business or enterprise." The First Amendment may also preclude
consideration of such claims against religious schools. However, no such
exemptions exist for race-based discrimination. Other federal statutes cover
discrimination based upon age and disability.*

*The prohibition against race and national origin discrimination in employ-
ment extends to all "terms or conditions of employment," including hiring and
firing decisions, promotions, salary, seniority, benefits, and work assignments.
Reverse discrimination claims are also recognized under Title VII. Title VII
applies to both public and private institutions of higher education.*

A.   Race Discrimination

◆   *An Ohio community college did not commit race or gender discrimination
when it passed over a female minority employee for a promotion. The school was
not bound by its affirmative-action policy to promote the employee over a more
qualified applicant.*

An African-American woman held several positions at the college during her
20 years of employment there, before taking the position of district director III for
curriculum management. Her immediate supervisor was supportive of her work
and went so far as to recommend her for the ACE Fellowship Program, a year-long
academic program. In 1995, the director requested an independent compensation
study of the salaries of two of her white co-workers whom she felt were paid more
than her because of their race. A study by an independent consulting firm,
demonstrated that her compensation was in line with her job responsibilities, and
that her co-workers were being properly compensated because their positions
were more important to the college's success.

At the end of 1995, the supervisor recommended the creation of a new
position: assistant vice president of academic and student affairs. Out of 40
candidates, the director was one of three who made it past the initial review
process. However, her supervisor ultimately hired a white male, who had the
professional experience needed for the position. Immediately after learning she
had not been selected for the position, the director resigned. She sued the college,
claiming race and gender discrimination along with constructive discharge. A
trial court granted summary judgment to the college.

The Ohio Court of Appeals noted that **the college's affirmative-action plan
did not require it to pass over a more qualified candidate to hire a less
qualified one.** Further, the affirmative-action plan profile reflected that 40.7
percent of middle-management positions at Tri-C were held by women, and that
29.6 percent of those positions were held by minorities. The availability of women
and minorities in the county to fill such positions was 42.7 percent and 16.1

percent, the court noted. **Although the director was a minority female who arguably could have been considered for the new position, the supervisor asserted that the other candidate was the most qualified applicant. The director failed to prove that the supervisor's reasons for not hiring her were based on her gender or race.** The court also rejected the director's claim that the college committed race discrimination by paying her less than two white employees in similar positions. The independently conducted compensation study found legitimate and non-discriminatory reasons for the director's lower salary. *Minter v. Cuyahoga Community College*, 2000 Ohio App. LEXIS 598 (Ohio App., 2000).

◆   *An affirmative action plan did not violate Title VII where it was not based strictly on racial quotas.*

The University of Nevada hired minority faculty members under an unwritten affirmative action policy to rectify an imbalance in the faculty's racial composition. A white female applicant was hired for $5,000 less than an African-American male applicant in a similar position. The pay gap widened due to merit increases and she filed a complaint against the state university system in a Nevada district court for violation of the Equal Pay Act and Title VII. After a jury ruled that the applicant was entitled to $40,000 in damages, the court denied a motion to set aside the award. The university system appealed to the Supreme Court of Nevada.

The supreme court observed the tension between affirmative action goals and Title VII's prohibition on discriminatory employment practices. It cited U.S. Supreme Court cases approving of voluntary affirmative action plans which further Title VII's purposes through temporary measures that do not unnecessarily harm the rights of white employees and that avoid racial quotas. **The university's affirmative action plan did not violate Title VII because it was not strictly based upon race but allowed the university to make employment decisions on criteria including educational background, publishing history, teaching experience and areas of specialization.** The plan did not violate the Equal Pay Act because the university demonstrated a legitimate business reason for the wage disparity between the two employees—obtaining a culturally diverse faculty. The court reversed the district court judgment. *Univ. and Community College System of Nevada v. Farmer*, 930 P.2d 730 (Nev.1997).

◆   *Where an affirmative action plan was not adopted to remedy an imbalance in the workforce, it was held unlawful.*

Illinois State University (ISU) required employment applicants to pass a civil service examination, and its employment policies were regulated by the state universities' civil service system. A veterans' preference program awarded veterans points that could be added to their civil service test scores. This resulted in many veterans reaching the top of the ISU hiring register with higher than perfect scores. Minority applicants composed only 4.3 percent of the local labor force, and most of the veterans on the hiring register were white males. ISU adopted a "learner program" to diversify its workforce by hiring short-term apprentices as building service workers. White males were excluded from the learner program even though ISU's minority hiring rate was two to three times the local minority population. The EEOC prosecuted a discrimination charge on behalf of a white male applicant excluded from the program, forcing ISU to accept the applicant and other white males. The EEOC also brought an action in federal court, asserting Title VII violations.

The court held that ISU had adopted the learner program solely to defeat the effect of the veterans' preference program. This constituted a pattern or practice of discrimination on the basis of race in violation of Title VII. **Because an affirmative action policy that is inconsistent with Title VII is impermissible, and because ISU was not required to hire more minorities to achieve racial balance, the program violated Title VII.** Although women were underrepresented as employees of ISU, the learner program had not been adopted to eliminate the imbalance, but to circumvent a lawful veterans' preference program. The court prohibited the exclusion of white males from the learner program. *U.S. v. Bd. of Trustees of Illinois State Univ.*, 944 F.Supp. 714 (C.D.Ill.1996).

◆ *Different treatment because of personality conflicts is not discrimination in violation of Title VII.*

An African-American man who had been born in Barbados became employed as an environmental research analyst for a private university in Massachusetts. After receiving a promotion to another analyst position, the employee was given an inconsistent performance rating. When he asked for documentation, the written account was even more negative than the oral review. Subsequently, the employee initiated an internal grievance procedure alleging discrimination by his supervisor. A grievance committee was convened and it made several recommendations among which was relieving the supervisor of his supervisory duties and allowing the employee to report to another superior. When the employee was later fired, he sued the university under Title VII and state law. The case reached the U.S. Court of Appeals, First Circuit.

The court of appeals looked to the report made by the committee, and concluded that it did not provide the required inference of bias behind the university's actions. Rather, it concluded that the employee was being treated differently from other professional staff, probably because of personality conflicts, and that the supervisor's behavior left the employee with the perception that he had been discriminated against. This perception was not enough. Since **the employee had failed to present any evidence to allow a reasonable juror to infer discrimination,** his race and national origin discrimination claims failed. *Pilgrim v. Trustees of Tufts College*, 118 F.3d 864 (1st Cir.1997).

◆ *Retaining a white professor while letting a black professor go was not discriminatory where the two professors were not similarly situated.*

A Virginia private college hired a black professor from the West Indies, despite his barely adequate credentials, in order to increase the number of blacks on its faculty. His appointment to a tenure track position was expressly contingent upon his receiving a doctoral degree by a certain date. He received two substandard evaluations by the college and numerous negative student evaluations. The college conducted a third evaluation and issued the professor a one-year contract instead of allowing him to remain in the tenure track position. The college's decision was based on his consistently poor student evaluations, his failure to obtain a doctoral degree, and his failure to produce scholarly work. **The professor** appealed the college's decision to a U.S. district court, alleging race and national origin discrimination. At trial, several students submitted letters in support of the professor which hinted that the poor evaluations were the result of a racist collaboration among the student population. The district court entered judgment in favor of the professor, and the college appealed to the U.S. Court of Appeals, Fourth Circuit.

The court of appeals reversed, ruling that the letters in support of the professor were far too vague, speculative and insubstantial to give rise to an inference of collusive discrimination. The court also held that the trial court had improperly failed to consider the negative student evaluations. The professor's failure to obtain his doctorate by the mutually agreed upon date also justified the college's actions. The college's retention of a white professor who had not obtained his doctorate did not prove that it inconsistently applied the tenure standards. **Not only did the white professor receive superior student evaluations, but having an advanced degree was not an explicit requirement for his promotion** when he was hired. Consequently, the court rejected the professor's contention that his failure to obtain a doctorate was a pretext for race or national origin discrimination. *Jiminez v. Mary Washington College*, 57 F.3d 369 (4th Cir.1995).

♦ *Despite evidence that two black employees had stolen from a college, they could not be discharged if a white supervisor had not been discharged for stealing.*

Two African-American maintenance workers at a Pennsylvania private college were discharged, allegedly for abuse of college time and materials and for submitting false timesheets. The Caucasian director of the college's physical plant was allegedly aware of this behavior and had allegedly misused college time and materials as well. The employees alleged that the college had a long-standing policy and practice of allowing them to use scrap materials and allowing them to perform personal projects during "nonbusy" work time. They filed suit in the U.S. District Court for the Eastern District of Pennsylvania, alleging breach of contract, detrimental reliance and race discrimination. The court dismissed the breach of contract and detrimental reliance claims. In a separate action, the court considered the college's motion for summary judgment with respect to the discrimination claims.

The court determined that the employees' continuous employment by the college for more than a decade coupled with their good reviews and commensurate salary increases established that they were qualified for their positions. Although neither employee was replaced by someone not in a protected class, the Caucasian physical director was arguably treated more favorably than the African-American employees. The physical plant director had allegedly known about the misuse of college funds and even misused funds himself to a lesser degree, yet he was not fired. The court also ruled that the college's nondiscriminatory reasons for the discharges were arguably pretextual. **The plant director was arguably treated better and held to lower standards than the African-American employees because of his race.** Thus, in spite of the substantial evidence of massive theft from the college that personally benefited the African-American employees, the alleged disparate treatment arguably established pretext. The college's motion for summary judgment was denied. *Anderson v. Haverford College*, 868 F.Supp. 741 (E.D.Pa.1994).

B. National Origin Discrimination

♦ *Where genuine issues of fact existed as to whether the reason for denying tenure was a pretext for discrimination, a university was not entitled to pretrial dismissal of a professor's lawsuit.*

An Ohio university employed an Iranian-born Muslim as a tenure track assistant professor. He was promoted to an associate professor and given his third year pre-tenure peer review. Although his review was largely positive, it also contained suggestions for improvement. Typically, faculty members on a pre-tenure track received a sixth year review in addition to the third year review. However, the professor did not receive his sixth year review because the chairman of the department failed to notify the department that the review was due. A university grievance panel found that the professor should receive a proper review, but the university continued to deny him tenure on three different occasions. When the professor sued the university for **national origin and religious discrimination,** the university moved for pretrial judgment.

The court noted that although the professor was a member of a protected class and suffered an adverse employment action, genuine issues of material fact existed as to whether he was qualified to receive tenure. The evidence showed that the professor's research, publications, collaborative work, and service were adequate for tenure in the opinion of outside reviewers. Additionally, **some evidence existed that nonprotected employees were treated differently.** Moreover, a material issue existed as to whether the university's proffered reasons for the denial of tenure were pretextual. The professor alleged that he met all university expectations prior to the chairman's membership in the faculty, and provided evidence that the chairman gave preference to American-born or Jewish employees. Thus, the court denied pretrial judgment to the university. *Amini v. Case Western Reserve Univ.*, 5 F.Supp.2d 563 (N.D.Ohio 1998).

♦ *A tenure review committee did not demonstrate a discriminatory bias against a professor when it denied her tenure.*

A Pakistani Muslim was hired as an associate professor at a New York university. Upon review of her publications and reference letters for tenure, the history department personnel committee almost unanimously recommended her for tenure. However, the nondepartmental *ad hoc* committee unanimously denied tenure. The professor sued the university in federal court, asserting **national origin and religious bias** on the part of certain members such as the chairperson.

The professor conceded that no discussion of her national origin or religion occurred during the committee's deliberations, but inferred that the chairperson was able to affect the outcome of the committee vote by means of her negative, but facially nondiscriminatory comments. The district court found that **the professor failed to show discriminatory animus on the part of the chairperson. The chairperson had not influenced the committee's decision** because of the mere fact that she participated in deliberations. Each member of the committee had grave reservations about the quality of the professor's work before the *ad hoc* committee meeting, and those conclusions were reached without any substantive input from the chairperson. Furthermore, the chairperson did not contribute at all to the hostile questioning of the professor's witnesses. As a result, the court granted the university pretrial judgment. *Jalal v. Columbia Univ. in the City of New York*, 4 F.Supp.2d 224 (S.D.N.Y.1998).

◆   *It was permissible for a university to promote more qualified white employees over a lesser-qualified black employee even though all the employees were technically qualified for the job.*

A private university in New York passed over for promotion a clerical employee of African-American descent. The reason given was her failure to obtain a college degree. It instead hired a white male employee with a management and accounting degree. However, the clerical employee met all of the minimum requirements necessary to fill the position. The university passed over the clerical employee twice more under similar circumstances. When her performance evaluations began to decline, she filed a federal district court action against the university, alleging race and gender discrimination in violation of Title VII and Title IX. The university moved to dismiss the complaint.

The court held that the employee had stated a *prima facie* case for adverse employment action since she was a member of a protected class, had applied for the promotional positions and was passed over in favor of a white male despite her qualification for the positions. However, the university successfully rebutted the inference of discrimination created by the employee since **it had legitimate, nondiscriminatory reasons for hiring the white males, who were more experienced in the relevant areas and had managerial experience.** The court rejected the employee's claim that the decline in her evaluations was the result of race discrimination, as it appeared to be the result of personal animosity between the employee and manager. Because the employee failed to demonstrate that the employer created a hostile work environment, the claims under Title VII and Title IX were dismissed. *Carter v. Cornell Univ.*, 976 F.Supp. 224 (S.D.N.Y.1997).

◆   *A university may have committed national origin discrimination against a white professor by hiring a Hispanic professor as the director of its Spanish language program.*

A white male professor at a private university in New York served as the acting director of the university's Spanish language program. When the university decided that a fulltime director should be hired, despite his strong credentials and recommendations, the professor was passed over in favor of a Hispanic male. He sued the university for national origin discrimination in violation of Title VII, and a federal district court granted summary judgment to the university. It stated that although the professor had presented sufficient evidence to establish a *prima facie* case, it would not second-guess the nondiscriminatory reason proffered by the university for the selection of the chosen candidate—that he was a better classroom teacher.

On appeal to the U.S. Court of Appeals, Second Circuit, the professor reiterated that his qualifications were superior to those of the selected candidate, that the university had deviated from its own prescribed practices in seeking to fill the position, and that university officials had indicated that he would not be seriously considered for the position because of their desire to find a minority candidate. **The evidence he presented was sufficient to support a finding that the university's reason for rejecting him was pretextual,** and the district court should not have granted summary judgment to the university. *Stern v. Trustees of Columbia Univ.*, 131 F.3d 305 (2d Cir.1997).

◆ *A College was allowed to deny a sabbatical to a qualified Filipino priest while granting it to an unqualified nursing instructor.*

The priest worked for a South Dakota Catholic college which denied him a paid sabbatical leave. However, the college granted a nursing instructor's requested leave for a two-year period to complete her Ph.D. even though she lacked the requisite seniority. As the reason for its decision, the college noted that it was seeking accreditation for a four-year bachelor's degree nursing program which required faculty members to upgrade their credentials by obtaining Ph.D. degrees. The college also noted that the priest's application was not sufficiently focused and did not fit the needs of the college. The priest resigned and filed suit against the college in the U.S. District Court for the District of South Dakota, alleging race, national origin, gender, and age discrimination in violation of Title VII and the Age Discrimination in Employment Act. The college moved for summary judgment. The court held that although the priest established a *prima facie* case, **the college had successfully articulated legitimate, non-discriminatory reasons for the denial of his sabbatical application.** Consequently, the college's motion for summary judgment with respect to the discrimination claims was granted. The court also dismissed the priest's constructive discharge claim, ruling that he failed to produce any evidence that he quit as a reasonably foreseeable consequence of the college's allegedly harassing actions. *Roxas v. Presentation College*, 885 F.Supp. 1323 (D.S.D.1995). On appeal, the Eighth Circuit affirmed the district court's decision. 90 F.3d 310 (8th Cir.1996).

◆ *A university's different treatment with respect to tenure applicants created a presumption of unfair treatment in the following case.*

A female math professor of Indian descent was denied tenure by a District of Columbia private university based in part on her allegedly serious mathematical errors in several papers published by Indian math journals. The university handbook provided that an applicant for tenure be judged in four areas: research and scholarly publications, teaching, service to the university, and community and professional development. The professor alleged that male, nonIndian professors were treated more favorably in the tenure application process. For example, she alleged that the chairman appointed members to the tenure review subcommittee who were unfamiliar with her work but appointed friends of other tenure applicants. The professor filed suit in the U.S. District Court for the District of Columbia, alleging Title VII sex and national origin discrimination, and breach of contract. The university moved for pretrial judgment.

The court rejected the university's motion, ruling that issues of fact existed regarding the professor's qualifications. Several outside evaluators had recommended that the professor be awarded tenure. Moreover, the alleged errors in her published papers and the accuracy of the chairman's highly critical reports were questions of fact for a jury. Because a male, nonIndian professor was ultimately promoted to tenure during the same period of time, the court held that the professor stated a *prima facie* case of sex and national origin discrimination. The court also held that **the university's different treatment with respect to the tenure applicants allegedly proved the university's nondiscriminatory reasons to be pretextual.** Finally, the court held that issues of fact precluded pretrial judgment with respect to the breach of contract claim. Arguably, the tenure policy was not applied uniformly, the university failed to give careful and continued evaluation to the professor's application, the four criteria were not adequately considered, and the subcommittee was not competent to judge the professor's work. The district court denied the university's motion for pretrial judgment. *Nayar v. Howard Univ.*, 881 F.Supp. 15 (D.D.C.1995).

C. Individual Liability

◆   *In the following case, a federal court explained the reasoning behind why, in most jurisdictions, individuals cannot be held liable under Title VII.*

A white, Jewish, New Jersey woman worked as an assistant professor in the theater department of a private university. She alleged that the chairman of the department, a black, male professor, conspired with the dean and the president to deny her tenure. She further alleged that the chairman discriminated against her in numerous other ways. She filed a complaint with the EEOC which issued her a right to sue letter. She then sued the university, the chairman and the two officials in the U.S. District Court for the District of New Jersey, alleging racial, gender and religious discrimination in violation of Title VII of the Civil Rights Act of 1964, among other claims. The defendants filed a motion to dismiss.

The defendants argued that the chairman of the department and the two officials could not be held individually liable under Title VII. Under Title VII, it is unlawful for an employer to discriminate against an employee with respect to race, religion or sex. An employer is defined as "a person engaged in an industry affecting commerce who has 15 or more employees and any agent of such a person." The court noted that courts disagree over whether this provision allows individual liability, but it followed those courts that have held that the language imputes liability only on the employer and not on the employer's agents. It stated that **the statute does not cover businesses with less than 15 employees** in an attempt to protect small entities from the costly burdens of discrimination claims. Therefore, it would be logical to assume that the statute would also protect individuals from these burdens. Further, in the Civil Rights Act of 1991, **damage awards are calibrated with regard to how many employees an employer has.** Because similar damages are not calibrated with regard to individuals, the court held that Congress had no intention of imposing individual liability. The court dismissed the claims against the chairman and the two university officials. *Schanzer v. Rutgers Univ.*, 934 F.Supp. 669 (D.N.J.1996).

◆   *A temporary employee who was denied a permanent position failed in her claim of discrimination in the following case.*

A private college in New Hampshire hired a black woman as a temporary employee in its dining service program. When she applied for a permanent position, her application was rejected, ostensibly because she had accrued too many absences during her temporary employment. During that temporary employment, one of her supervisors made several comments that were derogatory and of a racial nature. The employee filed a charge of race discrimination with the Equal Employment Opportunity Commission (EEOC), then brought suit against the college and certain supervisors in the U.S. District Court for the District of New Hampshire alleging both sex and race discrimination in violation of Title VII and Title IX, among other claims.

The college and the supervisors moved for judgment on the pleadings, arguing that the Title VII claim should be dismissed to the extent that it alleged sex discrimination because the employee failed to make a specific allegation of discrimination on the basis of sex to the EEOC. The court granted this motion because **the employee failed to exhaust her administrative remedies** by claiming only race discrimination in the charge to the EEOC. Accordingly, only the Title VII race discrimination claim could proceed. The court also granted the supervisors' motion to dismiss because **there was no individual liability under Title VII in New Hampshire.** The court then dismissed the Title IX claim because the dining service program was not an education program or activity within the meaning of Title IX even though the dining service employed some students who were enrolled in federal work-study programs. **The employee did not allege that she was a student; thus, her Title IX claim failed.** The court dismissed in part the claims against the college and the supervisors. *Preyer v. Dartmouth College*, 968 F.Supp. 20 (D.N.H.1997).

D. 42 U.S.C. § 1981

Section 1981 of the Civil Rights Act makes it unlawful for any person or entity to discriminate on the basis of race in the making and enforcement of contracts, therefore providing an alternative basis for race discrimination claims. Section 1981 applies not only at the initiation of contracts, but also at any time during the life of the contract.

◆   *The U.S. Supreme Court has held that persons of Arab descent are protected from racial discrimination under § 1981 of the federal Civil Rights Act of 1866.*

The case involved an Arab-American Muslim professor who sued St. Francis College in a U.S. district court after St. Francis denied his tenure request. The Pennsylvania district court ruled that § 1981, which forbids racial discrimination in the making and enforcement of any contract, does not reach claims of discrimination based on Arab ancestry. It held that Arabs were Caucasians, and that since § 1981 was not enacted to protect whites, the Arab professor could not rely upon that statute. The professor appealed. The U.S. Court of Appeals, Third Circuit, reversed in favor of the professor, and St. Francis appealed to the U.S. Supreme Court.

Section 1981 states that "[a]ll persons shall have the same right to make and enforce contracts ... as is enjoyed by white citizens...." In affirming the court of appeals' decision, the Supreme Court noted that although § 1981 does not use the word "race," the Court has construed the statute to forbid all racial discrimination in the making of private as well as public contracts. It observed that all who might be thought of as Caucasian today were not thought to be of the same race at the time § 1981 became law. The Court cited several sources to support its decision that **for the purposes of § 1981, Arabs, Englishmen, Germans and certain other ethnic groups are not to be considered a single race.** If the professor could prove that he was subjected to intentional discrimination because he was an Arab, rather than solely because of his place of origin or his religion, he would be entitled to relief under § 1981. The court of appeals' decision in favor of the professor was affirmed and the case was remanded for trial. *St. Francis College v. Al-Khazraji*, 481 U.S. 604, 107 S.Ct. 2022, 97 L.Ed.2d 749 (1987).

♦   *Where an employee failed to prove that the discrimination against her was intentional, her lawsuit under § 1981 could not succeed. However, she stated a possible claim for retaliation.*

An African-American woman was employed by a private university in the District of Columbia for 13 years. After being appointed the acting dean of students and serving in that capacity for over two years, she applied for the permanent position of dean of students. The university considered her application but eventually selected a white male for the job. The employee then returned to her previous position as director of student services and held that position until the university laid her off as part of a budget reduction. She sued the university in federal court, asserting discrimination under 42 U.S.C. § 1981. The court noted that **to make out a claim under § 1981, the employee had to show that the university had intentionally or purposefully discriminated against her.** Here, although the employee had made out a *prima facie* case by demonstrating that she was a member of a protected class, that she was qualified for the position, that she was not hired, and that someone outside the protected class received the job, the university had proffered legitimate, nondiscriminatory reasons for hiring some-one else. After it ruled for the university, the employee appealed to the District of Columbia Circuit Court of Appeals. That court affirmed in part, finding that the employee had presented insufficient evidence that discrimination motivated either adverse decision. However, there was an issue of fact as to whether the university had retaliated against her. *Carney v. American Univ.*, 151 F.3d 1090 (D.C.Cir.1998).

II. SEX DISCRIMINATION

Sex discrimination is prohibited by Title VII, the Equal Pay Act, and by state statutes. These laws apply equally to public and private institutions of higher education. Colleges and universities may not engage in sexually discriminatory employment practices unless the employee's gender is a bona fide occupational qualification. The First Amendment may also preclude sex discrimination claims against religious schools where the position involved is a religious one.

A. Different Treatment

♦   *After a university began providing salary increases for female faculty, a male professor sued claiming sex discrimination. His lawsuit could not be dismissed.*

The University of Minnesota entered into a consent decree to settle a sex discrimination class action lawsuit that began in the 1970s. The decree provided for the distribution of $3 million in salary increases to female faculty members. Subsequently, a male professor sued, asserting that the regression analysis used by the university to provide the salary increases amounted to unlawful sex discrimination by failing to take into account rank and market value. A federal court granted pretrial judgment to the university, and the professor appealed. The Eighth Circuit Court of Appeals reversed in part, vacated in part and remanded the case for trial. Here, **the professor had presented a genuine issue of material fact as to whether there was a salary imbalance based on gender that justified the salary increases.** Accordingly, the lower court should have conducted a trial. *Maitland v. Univ. of Minnesota*, 155 F.3d 1013 (8th Cir.1998).

◆ *Even though some colleges do not rely on student evaluations, it was permissible for a college to do so in the following promotion denial case.*

An African-American woman was a tenured associate professor at a New York college. Although she worked at the college for 25 years, she was denied promotion to full professor in 1989 and again in 1994. After the second denial, she filed a complaint with the EEOC, which issued a right-to-sue letter. She sued the college in a New York federal court alleging, among other claims, race and gender discrimination under Title VII. The college argued that the professor was not promoted to full professor because **she had not demonstrated marked distinction in scholarship or teaching and, therefore, did not meet the college's stated qualifications for promotion to full professor.** Among other evidence, the college relied on the results of Course Evaluation Questionnaires (CEQs) submitted anonymously by students which revealed that the professor's CEQs were poor and getting poorer. The court noted that the college had the right to rely on the bad CEQs as an actual objective record even if other institutions tended to discount such evidence. The district court concluded that on the totality of the evidence no reasonable juror could find that the stated grounds for the decision were pretextual. The college was granted summary judgment. The Second Circuit Court of Appeals affirmed. It agreed that the professor did not present sufficient rebuttal evidence from which a rational trier of fact could infer that, more likely than not, the college had intentionally discriminated against her on the basis of race or sex. *Bickerstaff v. Vassar College*, 196 F.3d 435 (2d Cir.1999).

1. Defenses to Different Treatment

◆ *There was no discrimination where poor job performance provided a legitimate reason for an adverse employment action.*

Louisiana State University opened the position of admissions counselor for applications. A female university employee with a poor job performance history decided not to apply because she was led to believe that the position required frequent travel when in fact it did not. Approximately six months later, the employee was notified that she would be fired in 90 days because of poor job performance unless her work skills improved. After a dispute with her supervisor, the employee met with an Equal Opportunity Compliance officer and complained of alleged misrepresentations regarding the admissions counselor position as well as maternity leave harassment. A few days later, she received notice that she would be fired, and she resigned. The employee sued the university for gender discrimination and retaliatory discharge under Title VII. The university moved for pretrial judgment.

Although the employee was a member of a protected class and was not hired for the admissions counselor job, she failed to establish that she was qualified for the position because of her previous performance problems. Even if she had established a *prima facie* case of gender discrimination, the university offered a legitimate nondiscriminatory reason for why she wasn't hired—poor job performance. The employee did not offer any evidence that the university's proffered reason was pretextual. The court also rejected the employee's claim of retaliatory discharge. Even though her meeting with the Equal Opportunity Compliance officer was a protected activity, she failed to establish a causal connection between the meeting and the adverse employment decision. The court granted the university's motion for summary judgment. *Keenan v. State of Louisiana*, 985 F.Supp. 658 (M.D.La.1997).

♦   *Where a graduate student lost a teaching position because of an incomplete grade, there was no discrimination.*

An Ohio university graduate student enrolled in a two-year master's degree program in psychology. She received a full scholarship and a graduate student assistant stipend under three separate contracts. The university advised her in writing that her current grade average was lower than was permissible for the doctoral program and that her practicum performance was only average. She advised her supervisor that she was expecting a child and requested leave from her clinical practicum cases for one semester. She also asked to forgo employment as a graduate assistant for the entire school year. Her supervisor admonished her, stating his belief that she would neglect her duties. The following semester, the student received an incomplete grade for one class and poor evaluations for her practicum. Although the student's grades later improved and she was able to successfully defend her master's thesis, the incomplete grade caused her to lose her graduate assistant position. She sued the university in federal court, alleging violations of Title VII and Title IX.

The court held that the student was an employee for purposes of federal antidiscrimination laws despite her status as a student. The fact that she received a stipend under contract bolstered the reasoning for considering her an employee. **Although her advisor's comments were blatantly discriminatory, the university had articulated a legitimate nondiscriminatory reason for assigning the student an incomplete grade.** The student had been unable to show that this reason was a pretext for discrimination. The evidence indicated that the grading was caused by her poor performance. Accordingly, the court granted the university's summary judgment motion. *Ivan v. Kent State Univ.*, 863 F.Supp. 581 (N.D.Ohio 1994).

♦   *Where a fair process was used to hire an athletic director, a claim of sex discrimination failed. The applicant who was not hired could not state a claim under Title IX.*

A female assistant athletic director for a private Rhode Island university served as the acting athletic director while a search committee conducted a nationwide search for a qualified athletic director. The assistant applied for the position, but a male applicant from outside the university was hired. The assistant then returned to her original duties. She began to have increasing difficulty working with the new athletic director, and received reprimands. Eventually, she was fired. The dean of students investigated her allegations of sex discrimination, but concluded that no factual basis existed to support them. The assistant then sued the university under Title IX.

The court determined that a private cause of action existed under Title IX for employment discrimination against a federally funded education program. However, the assistant failed to produce sufficient evidence to support her claim. **The search committee had conducted a nationwide search, ranked applicants on a point system, and then held interviews.** Once the committee had narrowed the number of applicants, it submitted the top three applicants for review. The applicant ultimately hired had been ranked first, while the assistant had been ranked fourth. The conduct and composition of the search committee also reasonably suggested a gender-neutral approach toward the hiring of the new athletic director. There was an effort to include women on the search committee, and sufficient evidence demonstrated that **the assistant's application had been fully reviewed.** The court held for the university. *Bedard v. Roger Williams Univ.*, 989 F.Supp. 94 (D.R.I.1997).

♦   *Denial of tenure because of insufficient merit to the quality of scholarship was held not to be a pretext for discrimination.*

A female associate professor at a private Illinois university twice applied for tenure and was twice denied. In each instance, a male professor was granted tenure. Under the university's tenure process, an *ad hoc* committee recommended that tenure be denied or granted based on materials created by the candidate and letters from scholars in the candidate's particular field. A faculty review committee then either accepted or rejected the *ad hoc* committee's recommendations and the dean would deny or recommend tenure to the provost. In both of her applications for tenure, the *ad hoc* committee recommended a denial of tenure. After the second denial, the professor appealed to a university appeals panel, alleging sex discrimination. While the appeal was pending, the professor filed a charge with the EEOC. Her appeal was denied and she filed suit against the university for sex discrimination and retaliation.

The professor presented a *prima facie* case of discrimination by showing that she was a member of a protected class, she was qualified for tenure, and individuals not in the protected class were granted tenure. **The university then offered a legitimate and nondiscriminatory reason for denying tenure by stating that the quality of her scholarship was not of sufficient merit.** The professor had to show that this reason was a pretext for discrimination. To determine this issue, the court only had to find that the reason given by the university was invalid. It did not need to consider any evidence of the professor's qualifications but rather only had to look for evidence contradicting the university's assertion. After considering all of the evidence, the court found no indications that the university's reason was pretextual. The court also failed to find a causal link between the provost's denial of her appeal and her charge with the EEOC. The court found for the university on both the sex discrimination and retaliation claims. *Schneider v. Northwestern Univ.*, 925 F.Supp. 1347 (N.D.Ill.1996).

◆   *A private university in Rhode Island did not discriminate when it reopened a position, rather than offering it to a female candidate, after two male candidates turned it down.*

A Rhode Island university opened a search for a position and narrowed the field to two male candidates and one female candidate. The position was offered to the first two choices, both men. After they turned down the job, the university did not offer the female applicant the job, but instead reopened the search. The applicant sued the university in a federal district court alleging sex discrimination. The court held for the university, ruling that there had never been unanimous support for the applicant's nomination and that **the applicant did not meet the unique requirements of the position in terms of accomplishments and peer recognition.** The U.S. Court of Appeals, First Circuit, held that the university had not discriminated against the applicant. Rather it had stated legitimate, nondiscriminatory reasons for reopening the search. The university had proven by clear and convincing evidence that its reasons were valid. Because **the applicant was significantly less qualified than the two men,** the university properly decided it should reopen the search rather than appoint the applicant. The court of appeals affirmed the district court's decision. *Lamphere v. Brown Univ.*, 875 F.2d 916 (1st Cir.1989).

◆   *Discriminating on the basis of sex is allowed where gender is a bona fide occupational qualification, as shown by the following case where a male janitor was not allowed to work in a women's dormitory.*

A male custodian at a Minnesota private university worked in a women's dormitory on campus. He had held this position for nearly six years. The university reorganized its custodial operations and, pursuant to recommendations from a consulting firm, adopted a new gender policy for custodians. In effect, the new policy prohibited custodians from working in dormitories where students of the opposite sex resided. During the reassignment process, the custodian bid for his old position in the women's dormitory. The university refused and assigned him to another position where the "same sex policy" was not in effect. The custodian filed suit in the U.S. District Court for the District of Minnesota, alleging that sex was not a bona fide occupational qualification (BFOQ) for custodial work in a women's dormitory.

The district court stated that **sex could be a BFOQ if an essential part of the custodian's job intruded upon the students' legitimate privacy interests.** To justify the change in policy, the previous gender policy must have undermined the "central mission" of the university. The university did not need to establish that the policy resulted in a loss of students from the dormitory. "Qualitative issues" as well as "quantitative results" could affect the central mission of the university. The court noted a number of qualitative issues raised by the university. First, the male custodian had to schedule his work in the women's dormitory within certain admissible hours. Time was lost both at the beginning and end of the day for this reason. Second, female residents frequently interrupted the custodian while he was working in the dormitory bathrooms.

Finally, "peeping incidents" on campus and the embarrassment and inconvenience to female residents due to the bathroom closings brought up legitimate privacy concerns. Thus, the policy change was justified. *Hernandez v. Univ. of St. Thomas*, 793 F.Supp. 214 (D.Minn.1992).

2. Religious Entanglement

♦ *A Wisconsin civil rights act provided no protection to a female teacher whose contract with a seminary was not renewed. Because the position involved was a religious one, the statute did not apply.*

A part-time female teacher employed by a Wisconsin Roman Catholic theological seminary was selected to organize, develop, and lead the newly implemented department of field education. The purpose of the department was to increase seminary students' pastoral development outside the classroom. The Catholic church promulgated an administrative policy requiring that directors of field education be experienced priests. Based on these policy guidelines, the seminary declined to renew the director's contract. The director challenged the seminary's action with the Labor Industry Review Commission, alleging sex discrimination in violation of the Wisconsin Fair Employment Act (WFEA). At a hearing, an administrative law judge determined that the seminary was wholly sectarian in purpose and ruled that the Equal Employment Opportunity Commission lacked subject matter jurisdiction over religious institutions such as the seminary. A Wisconsin trial court affirmed, and the director appealed to the Court of Appeals of Wisconsin.

The court of appeals held that the department could constitutionally investigate employment discrimination complaints but **could not enforce employment discrimination laws against religious associations when the employment position at issue served a "ministerial" or "ecclesiastical" function.** As a general rule, if the employee's primary duties consist of teaching, spreading the faith, church governance, supervision of a religious order, or supervision or participation in religious ritual and worship, he or she should be considered ministerial or ecclesiastical. Because the director performed several of these duties, the department was constitutionally precluded from enforcing the WFEA against the seminary. *Jocz v. Labor and Industry Review Comm'n*, 538 N.W.2d 588 (Wis.App.1995).

♦ *An EEOC investigation and lawsuit resulted in an impermissible entanglement with religious decisionmaking where they interfered with the church's ability to select and train its clergy.*

A Catholic nun received a doctorate degree in canon law from a Catholic university and was hired as an associate professor. She applied for tenure, which required approval by three academic bodies and ecclesiastical authorities. After a number of rejections, the professor's application was presented to the third academic body. It rejected her application and she appealed to a school committee, alleging differential treatment. The university responded that her scholarship, measured primarily by her publications, was not up to its standards. She filed a complaint with the EEOC, which filed suit on her behalf in federal district court against the university, alleging sex discrimination and retaliatory conduct. The trial judge dismissed the case, finding that the application of Title VII to the case would violate the Free Exercise and Establishment Clauses. The professor appealed to the U.S. Court of Appeals, District of Columbia Circuit.

The professor argued that the district court improperly used **the ministerial exception which exempts the selection of clergy from Title VII,** and similar statutes. The court of appeals found that the exception did apply since the professor's duties included spreading the faith and participation in religious worship. The court held that the EEOC's investigation and lawsuit violated the First Amendment since they resulted in an impermissible entanglement with religious decisionmaking and interfered with a procedure of critical importance to the Catholic church, its ability to select and train its clergy. The university's interest in employing faculty of its choice outweighed the government's interest in eliminating discrimination and therefore, the professor's claims were barred by the Free Exercise and Establishment Clauses. The district court's decision was affirmed. *EEOC v. Catholic Univ. of America,* 83 F.3d 455 (D.C.Cir.1996).

◆   *A female professor's liberal views on abortion could legitimately be considered in a hiring decision by a religious university.*

A female professor at Marquette University was repeatedly denied a position as associate professor of theology. The professor sued Marquette under Title VII of the Civil Rights Act of 1964, alleging that it had refused to hire her because she was a woman. She also claimed that Marquette had discriminated against her on the basis of her religious views, *i.e.,* her liberal views on abortion. The district court ruled against the professor, holding that the First Amendment prohibited any court from considering her claim since Marquette's interest in the integrity of its theology department was an overriding factor. The court of appeals concluded that the professor's Title VII claim failed as a matter of law because **the record clearly indicated that she would not have been granted the associate position even if she were a man.** It agreed with the district court's observation that Marquette was exempt from Title VII under the provision which permits a university to hire and employ employees of a particular religion if it is owned by that religion. The professor's liberal abortion views could legitimately be considered in whether the professor ought to be hired as an associate professor. The district court's decision was upheld. *Maguire v. Marquette Univ.,* 814 F.2d 1213 (7th Cir.1987).

3. Procedural Issues

◆   *In a 1980 employment case brought under Title VII, the Supreme Court concluded that the statute of limitations began to run on the date the teacher was denied tenure, rather than on his final employment date.*

A black Liberian teacher taught at a state-supported Delaware college which was attended predominantly by blacks. The faculty committee on tenure recommended that he not be given tenure, and the college faculty senate and board of trustees adhered to this recommendation. The teacher then filed a grievance with the board's grievance committee, which took the case under advisement. The college offered him a one-year "terminal contract" in accordance with state policy. After the teacher had signed the terminal contract without objection, the grievance committee denied his grievance. The teacher then attempted to file a complaint with the Equal Employment Opportunity Commission (EEOC). However, he was notified that he would first have to exhaust state administrative remedies if he wanted to file a claim under Title VII of the 1964 Civil Rights Act. After the appropriate state agency waived its jurisdiction, the EEOC issued a right-to-sue letter.

The teacher then filed a lawsuit in a federal district court, alleging that the college had discriminated against him on the basis of his national origin in violation of Title VII and 42 U.S.C. § 1981. The district court dismissed the teacher's claims as untimely because the Title VII complaint had not been filed with the EEOC within 180 days and the § 1981 claim had not been filed in federal court within three years. The U.S. Court of Appeals, Third Circuit, reversed, holding that the limitations on Title VII and § 1981 did not begin to run until the teacher's terminal contract expired. It reasoned that a terminated employee should not have to file suit until termination had actually occurred. The U.S. Supreme Court granted review.

The Court reversed the court of appeals' decision, finding that **both the Title VII and § 1981 claims were untimely. Statutes of limitations exist to ensure that plaintiffs promptly assert their rights and to protect employers from the burden of defending stale actions.** The teacher's complaint did not state that the college discriminated against him on the basis of national origin, it simply concentrated on the college's denial of tenure. The teacher had failed to make out a *prima facie* case of employment discrimination under Title VII, because he had stated no continuing violation of his civil rights. The Court noted that, in fact, the teacher had received essentially the same treatment accorded to other teachers who were denied tenure. The statute of limitations began to run when the teacher was denied tenure, specifically, on the date when the college had offered him a terminal contract. As the district court was correct in that holding, the Court upheld its decision. *Delaware State College v. Ricks*, 449 U.S. 250, 101 S.Ct. 498, 66 L.Ed.2d 431 (1980).

♦   *The Supreme Court compelled a private college to disclose employment records in an administrative proceeding before the Equal Employment Opportunity Commission (EEOC). The EEOC enforces Title VII and other antidiscrimination laws.*

The U.S. Supreme Court refused to intervene in *EEOC v. Franklin & Marshall College*, 775 F.2d 110 (3d Cir.1985). The case arose when a professor, who had been employed at a private school in Pennsylvania for three years, was denied tenure. The school's professional standards committee, composed of the dean and five faculty members, recommended that tenure not be granted to the professor. The committee's recommendation was reaffirmed by the college's grievance committee. The professor then filed a complaint with the EEOC, alleging discrimination based on his French national origin. The EEOC issued a subpoena for the committee's records. Although the EEOC offered to accept the records with names deleted, the school refused to disclose them. The EEOC then filed suit in federal district court to compel the college to comply with the subpoena.

The district court ordered disclosure of the records and the college appealed. Before the court of appeals, the college argued that "the quality of a college and ... academic freedom, which has a constitutional dimension, is inextricably intertwined with a confidential peer review process." The court of appeals held that **although the disclosure might burden the tenure process or invade the privacy of other professors, the records had to be disclosed because they were "relevant" to the EEOC's case. The records were ordered disclosed to the EEOC.** The college appealed to the U.S. Supreme Court, but its petition for review was denied. *Franklin & Marshall College v. EEOC*, 476 U.S. 1163, 106 S.Ct. 2288, 90 L.Ed.2d 729 (1986).

◆   *The Supreme Court ruled that a state administrative proceeding on a Title VII discrimination claim filed in state court could be appealed to the federal court system when the state administrative proceeding remained unreviewed by state courts.*

The University of Tennessee Agricultural Extension Service discharged a black employee, allegedly for inadequate work and misconduct on the job. The employee requested a hearing under the state Uniform Administrative Procedures Act to contest his termination. Before his administrative hearing took place the employee also filed a claim in a U.S. district court under federal civil rights laws, alleging that his dismissal had been racially motivated. The district court entered a temporary restraining order halting the state administrative hearing, but it later allowed the hearing to go forward. The hearing officer determined that the dismissal had not been racially motivated. The university moved to dismiss the employee's federal court lawsuit because it had already been resolved in the administrative hearing. The district court agreed and dismissed the case, holding that it would not afford the employee a chance to relitigate the same case in federal court.

The U.S. Court of Appeals, Sixth Circuit, reversed the decision and allowed the case to remain in federal court. The university appealed the decision to the U.S. Supreme Court, which held that the case should be heard by the district court. The Court ruled that **a state administrative proceeding on a Title VII claim not reviewed by a higher state board could be heard in federal court.** Since the decision made at the employee's administrative hearing was not reviewed by the state courts, it had no preclusive effect. The employee had the right to introduce his claim anew. *University of Tennessee v. Elliot*, 478 U.S. 788, 106 S.Ct. 3220, 92 L.Ed.2d 635 (1986).

◆   *In an employment discrimination lawsuit filed under Title VII, the aggrieved party bears the burden of proving that the employer's refusal to hire is a pretext for unlawful discrimination.*

In an employment discrimination case against a state college, a federal district court ruled that the college had discriminated against a professor on the basis of sex. The U.S. Court of Appeals, Fifth Circuit, affirmed the decision, ruling that Title VII of the 1964 Civil Rights Act, 42 U.S.C. § 2000e *et seq.*, required the college to prove absence of discriminatory motive. In a per curiam opinion, the U.S. Supreme Court held that this burden was too great. It ruled that **in an employment discrimination case, the employer need only "articulate some**

legitimate, nondiscriminatory reason for the employee's rejection." In other words, the employee has the burden of proving that the reason for the employee's rejection was a mere pretext. The Court vacated the court of appeals' decision and remanded the case for reconsideration under the lesser standard. *Trustees of Keene State College v. Sweeney,* 439 U.S. 24, 99 S.Ct. 295, 58 L.Ed.2d 216 (1978).

◆ *The U.S. Supreme Court issued a ruling affecting the right of a former private university employee to have his case returned to state court rather than dismissed at the federal court level.*

A private university employee sued the university in a Pennsylvania trial court, claiming that the school had violated the federal Age Discrimination in Employment Act (ADEA). He also brought state law claims for wrongful discharge, breach of contract and other violations. The employee was allowed to remove the case from state court to a federal district court because the alleged violation of the ADEA gave federal court jurisdiction over the entire lawsuit. The employee then discovered that he had failed to file a timely age discrimination charge with a federal or state agency. He requested that the federal claim be deleted and that the case be remanded to the Pennsylvania trial court in which it was filed. The U.S. district court granted this request. The university then requested that the U.S. Court of Appeals, Third Circuit, order the U.S. district court not to remand the case to the state court. The court of appeals denied the request and the university asked the U.S. Supreme Court to review that decision.

The Supreme Court noted that when a case is removed from state to federal court because it contains a federal claim, the federal court has jurisdiction over the entire case, including claims arising under state law. The federal and state law claims must arise from the same "operative facts." In cases where the federal claim is dropped from the lawsuit after removal, a federal court has discretion to dismiss the case and let the plaintiff start over again in state court. The question in this case, however, was whether the federal court has discretion to remand the case to the state court, thereby preserving state law claims that would otherwise be lost if state statutes of limitation have run before the plaintiff can start again in state court. The Supreme Court concluded that **federal courts had discretion to remand a case which had been removed from state court back to state court if such action would best accommodate the values of economy, convenience, fairness and comity.** The Court ruled that the employee's case could be remanded to the Pennsylvania trial court in which it was filed. *Carnegie-Mellon University v. Cohill,* 484 U.S. 343, 108 S.Ct. 614, 98 L.Ed.2d 720 (1988).

◆ *Providing false and pretextual reasons for denying tenure did not amount to discrimination in violation of Title VII, the Second Circuit held.*

A married female associate professor of biology was denied tenure by a New York private college, allegedly because she did not demonstrate the "outstanding quality" required by the college promotion guidelines. The biology department, the dean, the Faculty Appointments and Salary Committee and the president all refused to discuss the decision with the professor. She filed suit in the U.S. District Court for the Southern District of New York, alleging Title VII sex discrimination and violations of the Equal Pay Act.

The court held that **discrimination based on marital status qualifies as sex discrimination under Title VII.** Here, the court determined that the professor was in a protected class (a married woman), she was qualified for the position and she had demonstrated that the circumstances of her rejection gave rise to an inference of unlawful discrimination. Specifically, the court observed that all the other tenure candidates had less impressive qualifications and that the department had never tenured a married woman. Further, since married women received smaller salaries than less qualified men and single women, the college had violated the Equal Pay Act.

On appeal, the U.S. Court of Appeals, Second Circuit, reversed, finding that **although the college had provided false and pretextual reasons for its decisions, it had not committed sex discrimination.** Further, the professor had failed to show sufficiently that she had been paid less than male employees performing similar work. Upon a rehearing in banc, the court of appeals stated that **a finding of discrimination, like any other determination of fact, is reviewable upon appeal for clear error.** It concluded that the panel of the court of appeals was within its powers in reviewing the district court's finding of discrimination for clear error. Accordingly, it directed the district court to dismiss the instructor's lawsuit. *Fisher v. Vassar College*, 114 F.3d 1332 (2d Cir.1997).

◆   *Where tenure denial was held discriminatory, the First Circuit held that a federal court could order tenure to be granted.*

A Boston University professor of English Literature who had taught for six years became eligible for tenure review. During the sixth year, she was evaluated in three areas: scholarship, teaching and service to the university. Excellence had to be demonstrated in two of the three areas. She had published one book and three essays, and had received a grant to write another book. She had also advised 15 to 20 undergraduate students in scheduling their classes, had conducted a "women's literature discussion group," and had served on various university committees. Her department, the tenure committee and the dean all recommended that she be tenured. However, the assistant provost, the provost and the president recommended against tenure to the trustees, who denied tenure. She then sued the university for sex discrimination. A jury found that the professor had been denied tenure because of her sex, and the district court granted the professor tenure. The university appealed to the U.S. Court of Appeals, First Circuit.

The court of appeals first noted that the evidence introduced by the professor as to her qualifications had been properly admitted. Thus, the court decided that it had been reasonable for a jury to determine that tenure denial had been discriminatory here. **Although a court order to grant tenure was a rarity, the court held that such an order was appropriate where it was simply attempting to make the professor "whole."** The trial court ruling granting the professor tenure was affirmed. *Brown v. Trustees of Boston Univ.*, 891 F.2d 337 (1st Cir.1989).

◆   *The burden is on the plaintiff to show that gender bias exists.*

A female associate professor at Harvard University requested that certain faculty be excluded from her tenure review committee. One of the professors she wanted excluded was alleged to be gender biased. Although this type of request was usually granted, he was not excluded from the committee. All members of the committee, with the exception of the allegedly gender biased professor, agreed that the associate professor merited tenure and had met the scholastic requirements by publishing a book. The allegedly biased professor did not feel that the book met the scholastic criteria, but he still recommended the associate professor for tenure. However, when all the tenured faculty met to discuss her tenure, the faculty was split. The school extended the associate professor's appointment for three years, at which time another vote was taken and only a small minority were in favor of granting her tenure. She sued the school in a federal district court alleging gender bias. The district court ruled in favor of the school, and she appealed to the U.S. Court of Appeals, First Circuit, arguing that but for the gender bias, she would have been granted tenure. The court of appeals stated that **the associate professor did not present any direct evidence of gender bias,** nor had she established that her request to exclude certain faculty from the tenure committee was denied because she was a woman. The court affirmed the lower court's decision. *Jackson v. Harvard Univ.*, 900 F.2d 464 (1st Cir.1990).

B. Harassment

Sexual harassment is a form of sex discrimination prohibited by Title VII of the Civil Rights Act of 1964 and by Title IX of the Education Amendments of 1972. However, to be actionable under Title VII, the harassment must be severe or pervasive, and it must be based on gender.

In 1998, the U.S. Supreme Court held that in Title VII sexual harassment suits, employers may have a defense available where no tangible adverse action is taken against the employee. In such cases, the employer can avoid liability by showing that it exercised reasonable care to prevent and promptly correct any harassing behavior, and that the employee unreasonably failed to use those procedures or otherwise avoid harm.

1. Title VII

♦ *An Indiana federal court held that a single instance of harassing conduct could create a hostile work environment if the conduct was severe enough.*

A female employee of an Indiana university **alleged that she was lured to a supervisor's office where the supervisor grabbed her, kissed her, and reached inside her blouse and groped her.** She managed to get away from him and immediately went to the restroom where she vomited. However, she did not report the incident until three months later. At that time, a university official said, "Oh no, not again." The university conducted an investigation that resulted in the supervisor's resignation. When the employee sued for sexual harassment under Title VII, the university sought to dismiss the action, maintaining that one instance of harassment was not enough to create a hostile work environment, that it had acted promptly in its investigation, and that the employee had waited too long to report the incident. The court refused to dismiss the case. It noted that **the alleged incident was severe enough to create a hostile work environment.** Further, although the university acted promptly once it learned of the incident, it arguably had knowledge of previous instances of misconduct by the supervisor. Thus, there was an issue of fact as to whether the university should have taken action to prevent the attack. Finally, the court could not say that a delay of three months in reporting the assault was unreasonable. The case would have to proceed to trial. *Fall v. Indiana Univ. Bd. of Trustees*, 12 F.Supp.2d 870 (N.D.Ind.1998).

◆ *A university could be sued for discharging an employee after she complained of sexual harassment, even though the harassment did not rise to the level necessary under Title VII.*

A woman worked for a private New Hampshire university bookstore as a buyer. She made a number of complaints to her superiors about harassing comments made by the shipping room manager. Afterwards, the buyer received a letter of reprimand for being present during and encouraging a coworker who tore down one of the shipping room manager's "girlie" posters. The buyer signed the letter, but denied encouraging the conduct. Two months later, the bookstore discharged the buyer. She sued the bookstore in the U.S. District Court for the District of New Hampshire, alleging age and sex discrimination in the form of harassment, and **retaliation.** The bookstore moved for summary judgment.

The court noted that the severity of the conduct referred to did not rise to the level of sexual harassment and granted the bookstore summary judgment on the sexual harassment and age harassment claims. The court noted that to make a *prima facie* showing of retaliation, the buyer did not have to prove that the conduct complained of amounted to a Title VII violation; it was enough that the buyer had a reasonable, good-faith belief that a violation of Title VII occurred, that she had acted on it, and that she suffered an adverse employment action. Here, **the buyer's repeated complaints to management about the shipping room manager's conduct were motivated by a reasonable, good-faith belief that a violation of Title VII had occurred.** Therefore, the court denied the bookstore's motion for summary judgment on her retaliation claim. *McKeown v. Dartmouth Bookstore, Inc.*, 975 F.Supp. 403 (D.N.H.1997).

◆ *A medical school student was allowed to proceed with a claim of sexual harassment where questions of fact precluded dismissal of the case.*

An anesthesiology resident at a private university's hospital and medical school sued the university under Title VII in a Missouri federal district court. She alleged that because of her gender the chairman of the anesthesiology department repeatedly spoke to her in a derogatory manner. And that after she complained to the dean of student affairs, the chairman gave negative reviews about her to two prospective employers. The district court granted summary judgment to the university, and the resident appealed to the U.S. Court of Appeals, Eighth Circuit. The court of appeals reversed and remanded the case. It noted that **the resident had presented enough evidence to raise a genuine issue of material fact as to whether the university's four-month response time to her complaint was proper remedial action.** There were also questions surrounding the university's decision to put the chairman in charge of stopping the harassment even though the resident had alleged that he was the principal malefactor. Finally, the giving of negative job references could amount to retaliation for the complaint of harassment, and summary judgment on that issue had been improper. *Smith v. St. Louis Univ.*, 109 F.3d 1261 (8th Cir.1997).

◆　*The president of a college could, without specific endorsement by the trustees, promulgate a sexual harassment policy that bound the faculty.*

A private New York college board of trustees adopted an equal opportunity/ affirmative action statement. The college president then promulgated a sexual harassment policy without specific endorsement by the trustees. During this time, a tenured instructor was warned by the president that his sexual innuendoes and allusions in the classroom were considered a violation of the sexual harassment policy. Upon additional written complaints by female students, the college investigated and an affirmative action officer sustained the harassment charges. A remediation plan was devised. However, the instructor failed to abide by the remediation plan, refused to discuss the findings with the dean and the provost, and was fired. The instructor then filed suit against the college in the New York Supreme Court, alleging various contract and tort claims.

The court rejected the instructor's argument that the sexual harassment policy, which was promulgated by the president, was not binding upon the faculty. The policy had been adopted not by a subordinate academic unit which lacked any explicit authority to adopt rules, but by the president who, under the by-laws, was the chief executive officer of the institution and was directly responsible to the board of trustees. Moreover, **the president's authority to issue the policy could be traced to the equal opportunity/affirmative action policy statement adopted by the trustees.** Although not directly anointed by the governing board, the policy fell within the delegated powers of the president and implemented the trustees' statement. Therefore, the president acted within the scope of his delegated powers by promulgating the policy and the college had the right to terminate the tenured instructor for cause. The court dismissed the instructor's complaint. *Holm v. Ithaca College*, 669 N.Y.S.2d 483 (Sup.1998).

◆　*An employee's Title VII sexual harassment claim against a university was allowed to proceed where a high-level supervisor committed the alleged harassment, even if the university had no notice of his actions.*

A Columbia University employee was allegedly coerced into a violent sexual relationship by her supervisor. The employee acquiesced to the relationship because she feared for her job. She informed two university counselors about the relationship but requested that her statements remain confidential. She then applied for and was promoted to project director. She again contacted university officials about the allegedly violent relationship but this time gave them permission to speak to others. In response, the university forced the supervisor to resign, closed the fundraising office, and laid off the employee. The employee filed a Title VII sex discrimination lawsuit in a U.S. district court. The district court granted pretrial judgment to the university, and the employee appealed to the U.S. Court of Appeals, Second Circuit.

The court of appeals held that both threatened economic loss (threatened loss of employment or benefits) and tangible economic loss (actual loss of employment or benefits) will successfully establish *quid pro quo* sexual harassment. In so holding, the court determined that those who submit to the harassment and thereby avoid the threatened economic loss should be able to successfully assert this claim. Next, the court noted that although employers are not always liable for hostile environments created by their employees, a high level supervisor's actions may be imputed to the employer. Here, a high level supervisor allegedly created a hostile work environment via his apparent authority delegated to him by the university. On remand, if the trial court accepted the employee's allegations, the university would be liable. Thus, **the employee was not required to demonstrate tangible economic harm to establish *quid pro quo* sexual harassment.** Nor was she required to establish that the university had notice of the harassment or that it had failed to establish a reasonable avenue for making complaints. The holdings of the district court were reversed and the case was remanded for further proceedings. *Karibian v. Columbia Univ.*, 14 F.3d 773 (2d Cir.1994).

2. Title IX

◆   *A Wisconsin court held that Title VII preempted Title IX with respect to sex discrimination claims in the employment setting.*

A professor at a Wisconsin university brought suit under Title IX and the Equal Pay Act, alleging that the university had paid her less than male professors with comparable experience and substantially similar duties. The court dismissed her Title IX claim, but a jury found in her favor on the Equal Pay Act claim. It also found that the university had committed a willful violation of the Act, and awarded her double damages as a result. She appealed the dismissal of her Title IX claim to the Court of Appeals of Wisconsin, which affirmed. **It noted that Title VII was a comprehensive legislative scheme that targeted employment-related discrimination. Title IX was enacted in part to provide relief for victims of discrimination who had no recourse under Title VII.** Since the professor could have pursued her rights under Title VII, she was not one of those for whom the statute was meant to provide protection. Although Title VII requires the complainant to follow certain procedures (like filing a claim with the EEOC prior to instigating a lawsuit), it was the exclusive remedy available for claims of sex discrimination in the workplace. *Duello v. Bd. of Regents of the Univ. of Wisconsin System*, 583 N.W.2d 863 (Wis.App.1998).

◆   *A professor's claim that Title IX was violated when a college fired him for sexual harassment failed.*

A Minnesota man working as a professor at a private college was accused of violating the college's sexual harassment policy because of his sexual contact with a student. He was later fired and the student filed suit against the professor and the college. She later settled these claims but the professor counterclaimed against the college and its president in the U.S. District Court for the District of Minnesota, alleging a violation of Title IX, breach of contract, defamation and tortious interference with contract. Both sides filed for summary judgment.

The court noted that Title IX prohibits sex discrimination by educational programs that receive federal funds. Although courts have recognized a cause of action under the act on behalf of students who are discriminated against by these programs, few courts have found that employees of educational institutions have a cause of action for damages under Title IX. Because Title VII provides a comprehensive system for redressing employment discrimination, courts have refused to infer one in Title IX. The professor argued that Title IX requires educational recipients of federal funding to establish grievance procedures for handling sexual harassment claims which would be for the benefit of both the accused and the accusers. The court disagreed, finding that **there is no statutory right to due process in grievance proceedings under Title IX separate from the general discrimination prohibition.** The court held that the professor had no cause of action under Title IX and dismissed this claim, as well as his other claims. However, it noted that the college did not follow the sexual harassment procedures contained in the faculty manual and therefore issues of fact existed on the breach of contract claim. The professor's motion was denied and the college's motion was granted in part and denied in part. *Cooper v. Gustavus Adolphus College,* 957 F.Supp. 191 (D.Minn.1997).

♦ *A lawsuit against a university for harassment by a supervisor could not be dismissed where fact issues were in doubt as to what the university knew.*

A male supervisor at a Maryland private university allegedly sexually harassed two female employees. When they reported the incidents, they alleged that no action was taken and that one of them was assigned to a less desirable position. They also maintained that the university failed to distribute to them its policy manual prohibiting sexual harassment. They filed Title IX hostile work environment claims against the university in a Maryland federal court.

The court examined the university's motion for summary judgment and determined that claims brought under Title IX for abusive work environments should be analyzed under Title VII standards. It then found that the alleged conduct was severe and pervasive enough to warrant a trial on the facts. Here, **the university arguably had actual or constructive notice of the harassment,** and a jury would have to decide whether liability should be imputed to the university. *Ward v. Johns Hopkins Univ.,* 861 F.Supp. 367 (D.Md.1994).

C. Equal Pay Act

Enacted by Congress in 1963, the Equal Pay Act (EPA) requires that employers pay males and females the same wages for equal work. The EPA applies only to sex discrimination in pay, and thus racially-based equal pay claims must be litigated under the more general provisions of Title VII. Because the EPA is part of the Fair Labor Standards Act, employees are protected by the EPA as long as the employer is engaged in an enterprise affecting interstate commerce (contrast Title VII's 15 employee minimum for triggering coverage). The employee's burden of proof under the EPA has been interpreted by the courts to require only that the jobs under comparison be "substantially" equal. Strict equality of the jobs under comparison is not required. The EPA requires equal pay for jobs involving "equal skill, effort, and responsibility, and which are performed under similar working conditions, except where such payment is made pursuant to (i) a seniority system; (ii) a merit system; (iii) a system which measures earnings by quantity or quality of production; or (iv) a differential based on any other factor other than sex."

♦ *Where a university was found to have willfully violated the Equal Pay Act, a coach was entitled to double damages.*

The women's basketball coach at a New York university also held the position of women's sports administrator. She received $42,000 and $44,000 in the two years at issue, while the men's basketball coach made $40,000 and $42,000, and the men's sports administrator made $69,000 and $70,000. Because **she was paid significantly less than the two men who held equivalent positions in the men's athletic department,** she sued the university under the Equal Pay Act. A jury ruled in her favor, and the university moved for a post-verdict ruling on its behalf. In the alternative, it sought a new trial. It maintained that the female coach did not have comparable work experience to either of the male employees. The court denied the university's motions, finding substantial evidence that the university had committed a willful violation of the Act. **The female coach's duties and responsibilities were substantially the same as those of the two male employees.** As a result, the coach was entitled to back wages of over $134,000 and an equal amount in liquidated damages. The coach was also entitled to prejudgment interest and attorney's fees. *Perdue v. City Univ. of New York*, 13 F.Supp.2d 326 (E.D.N.Y.1998).

♦   *In the following case, a professor was able to show a violation of the Equal Pay Act; however, she could not prove discriminatory intent so as to succeed on her Title VII wage discrimination claim.*

A professor of political science at a New York private school was granted tenure in 1966, and promoted to full professor in 1976. She twice served as chair of the political science department but was paid a salary lower than the salaries of five male teachers who were comparable to her. When the professor turned 70, she was forced to retire at the end of the academic year. Her request to stay on in her tenured position was denied but she was offered an adjunct position as senior lecturer teaching two courses per year. She accepted the position under protest and sued the school for violating Title VII and the Equal Pay Act. A jury found in her favor and made the additional finding that the Equal Pay Act violation was willful or reckless. The district court awarded the professor 19 years of backpay, and the school appealed to the U.S. Court of Appeals, Second Circuit.

The court of appeals noted that a claim under the Equal Pay Act must be commenced within three years if the violation is willful. Here, over several years, the professor had complained to school decisionmakers about discrepancies between her salary and the salaries of male professors. Although the school was aware of the discrepancies, it continued to pay her less than comparable male teachers. This was sufficient to support the jury's finding of **a reckless or willful violation of the Equal Pay Act.** However, because of the statute of limitations, the professor was limited to receiving three years' backpay for the violations rather than the 19 years awarded by the jury. The court did **award her double her compensatory damages under the liquidated damages provision** of the Fair Labor Standards Act. With respect to the Title VII claim, the court noted that the professor was unable to prove discriminatory intent on the part of the school. Its decision to grant her only part-time, adjunct, nontenured employment upon her attainment of the age of 70 was not shown to be intentional discrimination based on gender. The court affirmed in part and reversed in part the lower court decision. *Pollis v. New School for Social Research*, 132 F.3d 115 (2d Cir.1997).

◆   *A federal court held that individuals could be held liable under the Equal Pay Act.*

An employee of a private college in Massachusetts sued the college and various officials alleging that they discriminated against her on the basis of sex in setting her rate of pay. She claimed violations of Title VII, the federal Equal Pay Act and the Massachusetts Equal Pay Act. She also asserted that the college and its officials violated the statutes by retaliating against her for pursuing rights guaranteed by the laws. The officials moved to dismiss the complaints against them. The U.S. District Court for the District of Massachusetts noted that eight circuit courts had addressed the issue of individual liability under Title VII, and that seven had rejected the idea. It agreed with the majority in finding that although a literal reading of the statute allows the imposition of liability on individual employees, Congress likely did not intend to impose individual liability under Title VII. However, under both the federal and state Equal Pay Acts, the **individual defendants could qualify as employers by virtue of their involvement in decisions affecting the employee's employment terms, conditions and compensation, and their relative operational control in the workplace.** Accordingly, the court denied the motions to dismiss the Equal Pay Act claims against the individual defendants. *Danio v. Emerson College*, 963 F.Supp. 61 (D.Mass.1997).

◆   *An Equal Pay Act claim failed where a fair process resulted in a determination that a professor's pay was appropriate.*

A female professor at a Texas private university filed repeated grievances with the English department arguing that her salary was not comparable to that of her male colleagues. She alleged that she was not given adequate consideration for positions that would have increased her compensation. She complained that these inequities were perpetuated by a subjective promotion process controlled by males. After scholars outside the university critiqued her work, the university concluded that the professor's pay was adequate. The professor filed suit in a U.S. district court alleging that the university's promotion process violated the Equal Pay Act (EPA) and Title IX of the Education Amendments of 1972 (which prohibits gender discrimination in educational programs receiving federal financial assistance). The district court held in favor of the university, and the professor appealed to the U.S. Court of Appeals, Fifth Circuit.

The court of appeals determined that **comparably skilled female professors were not paid less than their male counterparts.** There was no intentional discrimination amounting to a Title IX violation Nor was there an EPA violation. The university's commission on women and other objective evaluators had concluded that the professor's salary was not unreasonably low. In fact, the professor's credentials were less impressive than many of her male colleagues, which indicated that the wage disparities were justified. Thus, since there was no violation of the EPA or Title IX, the court affirmed the holding in favor of the university. *Chance v. Rice Univ.*, 984 F.2d 151 (5th Cir.1993).

◆   *Where a previous lawsuit under Title VII ended in favor of a college, a later lawsuit under the Equal Pay Act and the Age Discrimination in Employment Act also ended in the college's favor because the later lawsuits involved the same facts as the earlier one.*

An assistant professor employed by a Maryland private college was denied tenure, allegedly because she was unqualified. The board of trustees upheld the decision and the assistant professor sued the college in a U.S. district court. She alleged that the college had violated her rights under Title VII, the Equal Pay Act (EPA), and the Age Discrimination in Employment Act (ADEA). The district court dismissed her EPA and ADEA claims without considering them, and then ruled for the college on the Title VII claim, concluding that the assistant professor was not qualified for tenure. The U.S. Court of Appeals, Fourth Circuit, upheld the Title VII decision but remanded the EPA and ADEA claims to the district court for reconsideration because the claims "did not present a significant risk of infringement upon the First Amendment rights" of the college. The district court subsequently ruled for the college on the EPA and ADEA claims. In so ruling, **the court relied on its previous Title VII decision that the assistan professor had failed to demonstrate that she was qualified for tenure at the college.** She appealed once again to the U.S. Court of Appeals. The question before the court was whether the district court's initial Title VII decision favoring the college should prevent the retrial of the same facts before a jury on the remanded EPA and ADEA lawsuits. Using a legal doctrine called "collateral estoppel," which prevents the relitigation of issues already decided by a court, the court of appeals affirmed the ruling against the assistant professor. *Ritter v. Mount St. Mary's College*, 814 F.2d 986 (4th Cir.1987).

D. Pregnancy Discrimination

Pregnancy discrimination is prohibited by Title VII of the Civil Rights Act of 1964. However, a religious school can discipline employees for failing to comply with religious teachings. Thus, where sex outside of wedlock is prohibited, for example, a teacher can be discharged for such activity. The school must merely ensure that it treats men and women alike.

◆   *A pregnancy discrimination case could not be dismissed where the employee presented evidence that her pregnancy was the reason for her termination.*

A community college hired an Illinois woman as a secretary. A few months later, her supervisors informed her that her work was not satisfactory and that she would have to improve if she wanted to keep her job. Over the next two months her work improved. She then learned that she was pregnant and informed her supervisors of that fact. Ten days later, they informed her that they were recommending that she be fired. Rather than appeal that recommendation internally, she hired an attorney and, after her employment was terminated, sued the college and various college officials for pregnancy discrimination. The defendants sought to dismiss the lawsuit. The court noted that where an indirect method of proving discrimination is employed, the employee must prove that she was doing her job well enough to meet her employer's legitimate expectations. However, **where, as here, the direct method of proof is used, even an employee who cannot prove that she was satisfying her employer's legitimate expectations is protected by Title VII, though evidence about the employee's job**

performance may play an important role in the court's assessment of the direct case. Because there was a question of fact as to whether the discharge was because of pregnancy, the court refused to dismiss the case. *Suarez v. Illinois Valley Community College*, 688 F.Supp. 376 (N.D.Ill.1988).

• *There was no pregnancy discrimination where a marginal employee was denied additional leave beyond what she was owed.*

A twenty-year old woman worked for the University of Tennessee Press from January until August 1981 as a clerk-typist and receptionist. Although her work was good initially, her supervisors became increasingly dissatisfied with it. She also experienced some attendance problems. After exhausting all her sick and annual leave time, and several days leave without pay, she discovered that she was pregnant. She suffered from nausea related to the pregnancy and asked for a two-week unpaid leave. Her supervisors granted her request on the condition that she return to work by August 17. However, when she did so, she still felt ill. She sought an additional week of unpaid leave, but her supervisors turned her down. She then resigned and sued under the Pregnancy Discrimination Act. A federal court held for the employer, finding that **a legitimate explanation for the supervisors' refusal to grant additional leave had been provided:** namely, the employee's short tenure, her work record, her past absentee record and the need for a permanent secretary-receptionist in the office. **Because the employer had granted pregnancy related leave to employees with more tenure or better work records, the court found that the refusal to grant additional leave was not based on pregnancy.** *Connors v. Univ. of Tennessee Press*, 558 F.Supp. 38 (E.D.Tenn.1982).

E. Sexual Orientation

• *The denial of health care benefits to same sex partners of employees was held to violate the Alaska Human Rights Act.*

The University of Alaska denied health insurance benefits to the domestic partners of two employees because the domestic partners were neither spouses nor dependents. The employees sued the university for violating the state Human Rights Act, and the case reached the Supreme Court of Alaska. The university conceded that it had discriminated against the employees on the basis of their marital status, but asserted that providing lower health care benefits to single employees did not violate the Human Rights Act because the legislature did not intend to prohibit the kind of discrimination it was practicing. **Noting that the Human Rights Act prohibits discrimination on the basis of marital status, the supreme court held that the university had violated the Act.** *Univ. of Alaska v. Tumeo*, 933 P.2d 1147 (Alaska 1997).

• *Denying health care benefits to domestic partners of gay and lesbian state university employees violated Oregon's Constitution.*

The Oregon Court of Appeals determined that a public health sciences university violated the state constitution's privileges and immunities clause by maintaining **a practice of denying health insurance coverage to the domestic partners of its homosexual employees.** The case arose after three university nurses applied for insurance coverage for their domestic partners. The benefits manager refused to process the application because the university provided health insurance to spouses, not unmarried partners. After the state employee benefits board upheld the denial of benefits, the nurses sued in state court.

The court of appeals stated that Oregon's employment discrimination statute protected the nurses on the basis of their sexual orientation. However, the university did not violate that statute. Rather, the university violated the state constitution's privileges and immunities clause (which requires governmental entities to make benefits available on equal terms to all Oregon citizens). **Because homosexuals cannot marry under Oregon law, the university's health insurance benefits were made available on terms that, for gay and lesbian couples, were a legal impossibility.** *Tanner v. Oregon Health Sciences Univ.,* 971 P.2d 435 (Or.App.1998).

III. RELIGIOUS DISCRIMINATION

Title VII generally prohibits religious discrimination. However, religious preferences are permitted if the institution is substantially "owned, supported, controlled, or managed" by a religious organization or if the curriculum "is directed toward the propagation of a particular religion." As a result, there are times when discrimination on the basis of religion is allowed, but generally only by religious schools seeking to fill religious positions.

◆ *A religious college could fire a lesbian employee who worked closely with students.*

A Baptist college in Tennessee offered baccalaureate degrees in nursing and health sciences. It did not offer any religion degrees and required only one three-hour course in religion for its degree programs. It also did not require its faculty, staff members or students to be Baptists. The college hired a student services specialist to work with students in planning activities of various campus student organizations. Subsequently, the college learned that the employee was a lesbian, who was also a minister at a Christian church that advertised itself as being open to gays and lesbians. Because the college's Southern Baptist constituency believed homosexuality to be sinful, the college asked for the employee's resignation. When she refused to provide it, she was fired. She sued the college and its parent corporation for religious discrimination under Title VII, claiming that she was fired because of her different religious beliefs.

The U.S. District Court for the Western District of Tennessee granted summary judgment to the defendants. It noted that **religious organizations may discriminate on the basis of religion in certain circumstances** (for example, where an educational institution employs individuals of a particular religion to perform work connected with the carrying on by such institution of its activities). Here, the court found that the college qualified as a religious educational institution even though it did not offer any degrees in religion or theology. Further, even if it were not exempted from Title VII, it did not discriminate against the employee. **Its reason for firing her—that she had assumed a leadership role in an organization espousing beliefs diametrically opposed to its own—was**

not a pretext for discrimination. The employee's claim could not succeed. *Hall v. Baptist Memorial Health Care Corp.*, 27 F.Supp.2d 1029 (W.D.Tenn.1998).

♦   *A Christian college could fire a Catholic teacher without violating Title VII.*

A Catholic faculty member at a Presbyterian college conducted a survey of fellow faculty members. Subsequently, the dean instructed him to stop the survey. He alleged that he then failed to receive raises or received less than average raises for seven years, after which he was fired. He sued the college for discrimination on the basis of religion and for retaliation. A Missouri federal court dismissed his lawsuit. It stated that the college (as a Christian college) was exempt from Title VII's prohibition against religious discrimination. Further, **even though the employee—as a Catholic—was a Christian, the college could still disagree with his religious views. Therefore, if the college in fact discharged him because of his religious views, it could lawfully do so under Title VII.** With respect to the retaliation claim, the court noted that the employee had not been engaged in protected activity under Title VII. As a result, he could not prove that the college had retaliated against him in violation of that statute even if it took adverse action against him because of the survey. *Wirth v. College of the Ozarks*, 26 F.Supp.2d 1185 (W.D.Mo.1998).

♦   *A private university which had established a divinity school qualified as a religious educational institution under Title VII.*

An Alabama private university received a bequest to establish a divinity school and entered into a contract with a professor to teach in both the divinity school and the undergraduate departments of religion and English at the university. Because the professor and the dean of the divinity school did not share the same theological views, the university eventually removed the professor from the divinity school teaching schedule. He filed a Title VII claim of religious discrimination against the university in the U.S. District Court for the Northern District of Alabama. The university sought summary judgment on the grounds that it qualified for a religious exemption under the statute. The district court granted the motion, and the professor appealed to the U.S. Court of Appeals, Eleventh Circuit.

The court of appeals first held that the university qualified for the religious educational institution exemption under § 702(a) of Title VII. The university received approximately seven percent of its annual budget (over $4 million) from the Alabama Baptist Convention. Further, both the Internal Revenue Service and the U.S. Department of Education recognized the university as a religious educational institution and granted it exemptions on that basis. The court then examined § 703(e)(2) of **Title VII which grants an exemption to schools, colleges, universities and other educational institutions that are owned, supported, controlled or managed in whole or substantial part by a religious association.** Here, the university's receipt of seven percent of its budget from the convention amounted to substantial support. Accordingly, as an alternative to the court's § 702 holding, the university qualified as an educational institution which was in substantial part supported by a religious association and was thus protected by the exemptions in Title VII. The court affirmed the district court's decision. *Killinger v. Samford Univ.*, 113 F.3d 196 (11th Cir.1997).

+   *State human rights laws mirror Title VII. They generally prohibit religious discrimination except by religious organizations.*

A Jewish vice-president at a New York Catholic university was discharged, allegedly because of poor job performance. He filed suit in a New York trial court, alleging that he was subjected to increased scrutiny and then discharged because of his Jewish faith in violation of the Human Rights Law. The trial court granted summary judgment to the university, and the vice-president appealed to the New York Supreme Court, Appellate Division. The appellate division affirmed, ruling that the university was exempt from the prohibition against religiously motivated discharges. The vice-president appealed to the Court of Appeals of New York.

The court of appeals noted that the New York Human Rights Law permits religious organizations to "giv[e] preference to persons of the same religion" or "to promote the religious principles for which it is established or maintained." **However, the court held that the university could not "discriminate against the vice-president for reasons having nothing to do with the free exercise of religion and then invoke the religious exemption as a shield against its unlawful conduct."** Here, disputed issues of fact as to whether the university engaged in unlawful discrimination precluded summary judgment in its favor. The holding of the appellate division was reversed. *Scheiber v. St. John's Univ.*, 84 N.Y.2d 120, 615 N.Y.S.2d 332 (Ct.App.1994).

IV. AGE DISCRIMINATION

The Age Discrimination in Employment Act (ADEA), 29 U.S.C. § 621 et seq., prohibits age discrimination against individuals at least 40 years of age. As part of the Fair Labor Standards Act, it applies to institutions with 20 or more employees and which affect interstate commerce. Although state employees can no longer sue under the ADEA (see Kimel, below), state statutes and the Equal Protection Clause can provide relief. With respect to private employers, the ADEA remains in force.

A. ADEA

+   *Recently, the Supreme Court held that state employees could not sue their employers under the ADEA.*

Two associate professors at the University of Montevallo sued the university in an Alabama federal court under the ADEA. They alleged that the university had discriminated against them on the basis of their age, that it had retaliated against them for filing charges with the EEOC, and that its College of Business, where they were employed, used an evaluation system that had a disparate impact on older faculty members. The university sought to dismiss the action on the grounds of Eleventh Amendment immunity, and the district court agreed, finding that the ADEA did not eliminate the state's immunity.

Subsequently, a group of current and former faculty and librarians of Florida State University and Florida International University filed suit against the Florida Board of Regents under the ADEA, alleging that the board refused to require the two state universities to allocate funds to provide previously agreed upon market adjustments to the salaries of eligible university employees. They maintained that this failure had a disparate impact on the base pay of employees with a longer record of service, most of whom were older. The board sought to dismiss the action under the Eleventh Amendment, but the court refused to do so.

On appeal to the Eleventh Circuit, the court of appeals consolidated the cases and held that the ADEA did not abrogate (do away with) the states' Eleventh Amendment immunity. The U.S. Supreme Court then agreed to review the case and affirmed the court of appeals' decision. It noted that **although the ADEA contains a clear statement of Congress' intent to eliminate the states' immunity under the Eleventh Amendment, such action exceeded Congress' authority under § 5 of the Fourteenth Amendment** (which grants Congress the power to enact laws under the Equal Protection Clause). The Court observed that although state employees cannot sue their employers for discrimination under the ADEA, they are not without remedies. Every state has age discrimination statutes, and almost all of them allow the recovery of money damages from state employers. *Kimel v. Florida Board of Regents*, 120 S.Ct. 631, 145 L.Ed.2d 522 (2000).

1. Applicability to Religious Schools

◆ *The ADEA was held not to apply in the following case involving a seminary.*

A Missouri seminary allegedly dismissed an employee because of his age. He sued the seminary in a federal district court under the ADEA. The seminary brought a motion for pretrial judgment, stating that the ADEA was inapplicable because the institution was pervasively religious. The court agreed. It considered the U.S. Supreme Court's decision in *NLRB v Catholic Bishop of Chicago*, 440 U.S. 490, 99 S.Ct. 1313, 59 L.Ed.2d 533 (1979), in which the Court held the National Labor Relations Act inapplicable to church-operated schools. The court ruled that although the ADEA was a remedial statute rather than a regulatory statute such as the NLRA, the ruling in *Catholic Bishop* applied here. Because application of the ADEA could implicate enforcement by the EEOC, government regulatory powers were involved. Thus, **since the potential existed for impinging the seminary's religious freedoms, the court ruled that the ADEA was inapplicable.** It granted the seminary's motion for pretrial judgment. *Cochran v. St. Louis Preparatory Seminary*, 717 F.Supp. 1413 (E.D.Mo.1989).

◆ *However, an Ohio federal court held that the ADEA could be applied to a religious institution.*

An employee at Xavier University, an institution operated by the Order of Jesuits, sued the university under the ADEA in an Ohio federal court. The university asserted that the court had no authority to rule on the case because the university, as a religious institution, was exempt from the ADEA's provisions. The court observed that because the ADEA gave no indication that religious institutions were exempt from its provisions, the issue became whether application of the ADEA to the university would violate the Free Exercise and Establishment Clauses of the First Amendment. It then held for the employee, noting that the Fourth Circuit (covering West Virginia, Maryland, Virginia, South Carolina and North Carolina) had held in *Ritter v. Mount St. Mary's College*, 814 F.2d 986 (4th Cir.1987), that **application of the ADEA to a religious institution did not**

present a significant risk of infringement on the institution's First
Amendment rights. Here, the facts gave no indication that enforcement of
the ADEA would violate the religion clauses of the First Amendment.
Accordingly, the university was not entitled to a dismissal of the case. *Soriano v.
Xavier Univ. Corp.*, 687 F.Supp. 1188 (S.D.Ohio 1988).

2. Releases and Settlements

◆   *The Seventh Circuit held that an instructor could not challenge a release
agreement as violative of the OWBPA because he kept the money he received
under the agreement. However, in 1998, the U.S. Supreme Court, in* Oubre v.
Entergy Operations, Inc.*, 118 S.Ct. 838, held that where an employer failed to
comply with the OWBPA (an amendment to the Age Discrimination in Employment Act) by having an employee sign a release that did not comply with the
requirements of the statute, the employee could sue even though she kept the
money. The release was invalid and could not be enforced.*

An artist in residence/instructor employed by a New York private college on
a year-to-year, nontenure basis performed a variety of tasks for the visual arts
department. The college faced financial difficulties, and the president told the
instructor that he could retire or have his position eliminated in six months.
However, if he did not retire promptly, he would not be eligible for post-retirement
medical benefits. He resigned in exchange for a variety of benefits including
tuition assistance for his children, lifetime medical benefits, $5,000 in severance
pay and art studio space at no charge. The college hired several younger part-time
replacements and saved approximately $56,000 per year. The instructor filed and
withdrew an age discrimination charge with the EEOC and ultimately filed suit
in a Maryland federal court, alleging violations of the ADEA. The district court
held that the release agreement did not comply with the Older Workers Benefit
Protection Act (OWBPA) and that the professor had not waived his ADEA claim,
but found that he failed to state a *prima facie* case of age discrimination. The
professor appealed to the U.S. Court of Appeals, Fourth Circuit.

The court of appeals held that by accepting the benefits of the agreement, with
full awareness that it did not meet the requirements of the OWBPA, the professor
ratified it and thereby waived any claim under the ADEA. The court of appeals
also held that the professor failed to state a *prima facie* claim of age discrimination. Although **forced early retirement to prevent the reduction of benefits
could, under some circumstances,** give rise to a constructive discharge claim,
**the withdrawal of gratuitous benefits could never render continued employ-
ment so intolerable that an employee would reasonably be compelled to
resign.** Finally, the court noted that the professor was not replaced by someone
outside the protected class. The district court dismissal of the ADEA claim was
affirmed. *Blistein v. St. John's College*, 74 F.3d 1459 (4th Cir.1996).

◆   *A private university could require a former employee to withdraw her EEOC
claim in order to obtain a settlement award.*

A Tennessee woman who worked for a private university received a letter of
reprimand and filed two grievances against her supervisors as a result. Subsequently, the head of the department and another supervisor asked her to sign a

voluntary resignation letter and when she refused, she was discharged. Eight days later, she filed an age discrimination charge with the EEOC. The university conducted a grievance hearing before the associate dean of students who found no evidence of age discrimination or harassment. However, she recommended that the employee be placed on paid administrative leave for six months with a reasonable letter of recommendation to help her find another position within the university system. The university informed the employee that it would accept the recommendation of the hearing officer subject to the employee's agreement to withdraw her EEOC charge. When the employee refused to do so, the university declined to implement the recommended resolution. The employee then sued the university in the U.S. District Court for the Middle District of Tennessee alleging retaliation in violation of the ADEA.

The court noted that not only does the ADEA prohibit discrimination in employment on the basis of age, but it specifically prohibits employers from retaliating against employees who have filed charges with the EEOC. Here, the question was whether the university took an adverse employment action against the employee by declining to place her on paid administrative leave for six months when she refused to withdraw her EEOC charge. The court found that the university had not taken an adverse employment action against the employee. **Requiring an employee to withdraw an EEOC claim in order to have a recommended settlement award implemented is not an adverse employment action.** The university could not be expected to award the employee compensation and to receive nothing in return. Accordingly, the university was entitled to judgment as a matter of law. *Hansen v. Vanderbilt University*, 961 F.Supp. 1149 (M.D.Tenn.1997).

3. Defenses

♦   *An employee's age discrimination lawsuit failed where the university that fired him offered a legitimate nondiscriminatory reason for so doing—sexual harassment by the employee.*

A 43-year-old man was employed as a carpenter in the physical plant department at a private Illinois university. He began writing letters to the office manager, who was six months pregnant with her first child. He continued to write personal letters to her and began bringing gifts for her and the baby. After complaining to another manager about the letters and gifts, the office manager spoke to the carpenter and asked him to stop writing her. However, the carpenter continued to write and send her gifts. After the manager returned from maternity leave, she again complained to the other manager and her supervisor about the carpenter's continued behavior. That same day, the carpenter was summoned to a meeting with his supervisors, who told him about the manager's complaints. After he refused to resign, his employment was terminated for sexual harassment. Shortly thereafter, he was replaced by a 32-year-old man. The carpenter sued the university in an Illinois federal court, alleging that his discharge violated the ADEA. The court ruled for the university, and the carpenter appealed to the U.S. Court of Appeals, Seventh Circuit.

The court noted that the university had articulated a legitimate, nondiscriminatory reason for the discharge—sexual harassment. Therefore, the only remaining issue was whether the reason given by the university was pretextual. Here, **the carpenter produced no evidence to support his claim of age discrimination.** He had been requested by the manager to stop sending her letters, but continued to do so. Upon his refusal to resign, he was told that he was being discharged for sexual harassment. Therefore, the court affirmed the ruling in favor of the university. *O'Connor v. DePaul University*, 123 F.3d 665 (7th Cir.1997).

♦   *A professor was not entitled to a promotion simply because he received satisfactory evaluations as an assistant professor.*

An assistant professor employed by an Indiana private university retired after having been denied a promotion to associate professor. The promotion and tenure committee stated as reasons for the rejection that his work as a teacher was not superior, his service to the university community was limited, and that he had not achieved distinction in performance. The professor countered that he was viewed as a satisfactory member of the faculty, and that he would have been promoted to associate professor on several earlier occasions but for his lack of a Ph.D. and budgetary shortfalls. The professor also observed that a younger person was promoted to associate professor in 1991-92. The professor filed an age discrimination lawsuit against the university in a U.S. district court which granted summary judgment to the university. The professor appealed to the U.S. Court of Appeals, Seventh Circuit. The court of appeals held that **the professor's argument failed to distinguish between competent and superior achievement. Satisfactory performance as an assistant professor did not entitle him to the promotion.** Nor could he court find discrimination based on a single incident of alleged disparate treatment. The professor should have subjected all of the employer's decisions to statistical analysis to find out whether age made a difference. Without knowing how many people of what age were not promoted, the court could not decide which party's proposed inference was superior. Because nothing in the record supported an inference of discrimination, the district court holding in favor of the university was affirmed. *Kuhn v. Ball State Univ.*, 78 F.3d 330 (7th Cir.1996).

4. Evidence of Discrimination

♦   *An age discrimination claim failed where a 55-year-old applicant made it to the stage of finalist.*

A Wisconsin technical college advertised for an instructor of psychology, listing the minimum criteria as a masters' degree in psychology with a sociology minor preferred. The college received 29 applications, of which the top ten were numerically rated. Only the three highest-rated candidates received interviews. The fifth-rated applicant was a 55-year-old male with a doctorate degree in teaching with a psychology minor and relatively little teaching experience. He claimed that the college's hiring practices were biased in favor of young women, observing that the three top-ranked candidates were all women and that only one was over 40. He sued the college in a federal district court for age discrimination. The court entered pretrial judgment for the college, and the applicant appealed to the U.S. Court of Appeals, Seventh Circuit. The court agreed with the applicant that it was only necessary for him to show some evidence that the college's reasons for rejecting his application were pretextual. However, **his presence among the job finalists undermined his age discrimination theory, and although there were irregularities in the college's hiring policies, there was no evidence of discrimination.** The court affirmed the summary judgment order for the college. *Senner v. Northcentral Technical College*, 113 F.3d 750 (7th Cir.1997).

♦ *Paying employees by their market value did not violate the ADEA.*

In 1985, the faculty at an Illinois university entered into a collective bargaining agreement whereby each faculty member's salary would be determined at the time he or she was hired, but thereafter a faculty member could only obtain an individual raise by presenting a bona fide offer of employment from another employer. A 58-year-old professor sued the university, claiming that the compensation system discriminated on the basis of age. The U.S. Court of Appeals, Seventh Circuit, noted that although the ADEA forbids discrimination on the basis of age, it does not require employers to pay older employees higher salaries than younger employees. **Since the university's salary increase policy depended on outside offers of employment, each professor's salary was determined by his value in the employment market.** The court of appeals affirmed the trial court's dismissal of the case. *Davidson v. Bd. of Governors of State Colleges and Universities for Western Illinois Univ.*, 920 F.2d 441 (7th Cir.1990).

♦ *After a jury found that a college discriminated against a professor, the court stated that it would not issue an order placing the professor in the job. Instead, it awarded front pay to the professor.*

A professor employed by a Pennsylvania private college applied for a tenure-track position in Biblical Studies. The dean allegedly agreed to support her appointment at the associate level if she was selected for the tenure track position. However, the faculty of the Religious Studies Department voted to select another candidate. The professor sued for age discrimination. A jury found for the professor on the ADEA claim and a Pennsylvania federal court then **sought to determine the appropriate remedy.** The professor requested instatement to the Biblical Studies position or a comparable position, but the college argued that an award of front pay was the only appropriate remedy. Although instatement or reinstatement is the preferred remedy to avoid future lost earnings, the court noted that it is not feasible when the relationship between the parties has been irreparably damaged or when there is no position in which to instate the plaintiff.

The professor argued that the college could either bump the newly-hired professor and give her the position or give her the position being vacated by the chairman of the department. The court noted that **few courts have held that innocent third parties should be bumped in order to instate aggrieved parties.** The few courts that have done so have determined that a balance of the equities required such action. For example, when an employer is on notice of past discrimination or has exhibited bad faith behavior, bumping has been allowed. It has also been allowed when an employer has acted intentionally or wilfully or when the harm to the bumped employee could be minimized. Since none of these factors were present here, the court refused to bump the newly-hired professor. It also found that the chairman taught classes in a field in which the professor was not trained. Finding that a comparable position did not exist at the college, the court refused to grant instatement and instead awarded front pay. *Kraemer v. Franklin and Marshall College*, 941 F.Supp. 479 (E.D.Pa.1996).

◆   *No discrimination was found in the following case even though the department head had referred to a teacher as too old.*

A 61-year-old professor at a North Carolina technical college had trouble adapting to a new curriculum designed by the Electrical Engineering Department Chair. The department chair repeatedly admonished the professor to discontinue teaching the outmoded curriculum. After one confrontation within earshot of students, the professor challenged the department chair to a fist fight. The department chair subsequently stated that the college needed "new blood," because the professor was "outdated, too old, behind the times and unable to teach at the pace required." The college declined to extend the professor's contract beyond the following summer. A younger applicant was hired in his place. The college also denied the request for a hearing although the personnel policy provided for review of all contractual decisions. The professor sued the college under the ADEA in a North Carolina federal court.

The district court first held that the department chair's statements did not constitute direct evidence of discrimination. Here, the only arguably discriminatory statement was the department chair's reference to the professor as "too old." The other comments merely reflected the college's desire that older employees remain current in their job knowledge. Further, such allegedly discriminatory comments were unlawful only if acted upon. Although the college replaced the professor with a younger employee, **there was a lack of direct evidence establishing discriminatory intent. The professor also failed to establish that the college's nondiscriminatory reasons (his teaching of outmoded material and his confrontation with the department chair) were pretextual.** Moreover, there was not enough statistical evidence to support a finding of disparate impact on older employees. Finally, the court held that neither the professor's contractual expectations nor the college's personnel policy established a property interest in his employment. Consequently, the professor was not entitled to a due process hearing. *Fisher v. Asheville-Buncombe Technical Community College*, 857 F.Supp. 465 (W.D.N.C.1993).

◆   *A private university was held to have discriminated against an employee who was five years away from mandatory retirement.*

A 60-year-old Washington, D.C. private university employee was promoted to assistant director. He had extensive university experience and had 25 years of managerial experience in the U.S. Air Force. He also had an M.B.A. In 1983, the director resigned and recommended that the assistant director replace him. The position required a college degree but an M.B.A. was preferred. The university imposed mandatory retirement on employees at age 65. In spite of the assistant director's many credentials and the director's recommendations, the university transferred the assistant director to an inferior position. It also imposed a "hiring freeze," ostensibly for financial reasons, which included the director position. However, the university reinstituted the position when another preselected individual finished his college degree. Contrary to university hiring procedures, the assistant director was not given the opportunity to apply for the position. He sued the university in the U.S. District Court for the District of Columbia, alleging that its failure to promote him violated the ADEA.

The court determined that **the university's failure to promote the assistant director was age discrimination.** Since the assistant director was within the protected age group, was qualified, was not promoted, and a substantially younger individual was hired, he stated a *prima facie* case of age discrimination. Further, the university's alleged legitimate business reasons for its failure to promote him were pretextual. **Its "clear anti-age animus" reflected in its employment and retirement policies "directly affected" its decision not to promote the assistant director.** Finally, given the early mandatory retirement age, the court inferred that employees close to this age were not given serious consideration for promotions. Therefore, the university discriminated against the assistant director when it hired a less qualified and substantially younger individual for the director position. *Ware v. Howard Univ.*, 816 F.Supp. 737 (D.D.C.1993).

◆   *An insurer had to reimburse a private school that had violated the ADEA because the school had not acted with the specific intent of violating the ADEA.*

A private school terminated an older tenured professor in order to meet budgetary requirements. The professor sought and obtained damages for the school's violation of the ADEA. The school then filed suit against its insurer for reimbursement. A Massachusetts federal court granted pretrial judgment to the insurer, and the appeals court reversed. On remand, the insurer was required to prove that the school knowingly violated the ADEA in order to avoid payment of the reimbursement costs under a policy exclusion. The district court found for the school. Both parties appealed to the U.S. Court of Appeals, First Circuit. The main issue on appeal was **whether an actor of an intentionally committed wrongful act must also have had a "specific intent" to do something against the law in order to invoke the policy exclusion and thus preclude insurance coverage** for damages arising from a violation of the ADEA. Here, the court held that "specific intent" was absent, and the insurer was obliged to reimburse the school for its loss. Since the dean of the school was not familiar with the ADEA, he could not possibly have acted with the requisite "specific intent." Thus, the holding of the district court was not clearly erroneous and was affirmed. *Andover Newton Theological School v. Continental Cas. Co.*, 964 F.2d 1237 (1st Cir.1992).

B. Mandatory Retirement

◆   *A professor who was subjected to mandatory retirement was not entitled to an injunction prohibiting her retirement.*

A world-renowned professor at a New York private university turned 70 years of age in 1993. As a fulltime tenured professor, she had a student assistant, full use of the library and computer facilities, and was responsible for advising graduate students. The university informed her that she would be retired from her tenured position when she reached the age of 70 pursuant to its mandatory retirement policy. The professor rejected a part-time position as an adjunct professor after she retired and then filed suit in the U.S. District Court for the

Southern District of New York, alleging age and sex discrimination and seeking an injunction prohibiting her retirement from her tenured position.

Although the mandatory retirement age was permissible under an exemption in the ADEA, the professor contended that it did not apply because the college's tenure policies did not strictly comply with the 1940 Principles on Academic Freedom and Tenure. The district court disagreed, ruling that the college's substantial compliance with the 1940 principles was sufficient to fall within the ADEA § 12(d) exemption. Consequently, **the college's mandatory retirement of the professor was permissible.** The court then held that the professor stated a valid Title VII sex discrimination claim. However, the court noted that the professor failed to establish the requisite "irreparable harm" necessary to justify a preliminary injunction prohibiting her removal from the tenured position (until resolution of the Title VII claim). The professor was not being placed in severe financial difficulty nor was she being "isolated" or "academically deprived." Rather, she merely faced reductions and limitations. Thus, the mandatory retirement did not violate the ADEA and the professor was not entitled to a preliminary injunction. *Pollis v. New School for Social Research*, 829 F.Supp. 584 (S.D.N.Y.1993). For discussion of the sex discrimination claims, see Section II.C.

♦   *Where a retired security guard did not sue for age discrimination until ten years after the mandatory retirement policy was changed, he could not succeed.*

A man was hired in 1966 by Columbia University as a resident hall security guard and worked in that position for 22 years until retiring at the age of 65. The guard believed that he was required to retire because of his age. Ten years later, he learned that the mandatory retirement age was being changed at the time of his retirement. He claimed that this change should have applied to him. He sued the university and his former union. The university moved for pretrial judgment, and the union moved for dismissal. The question in this case was whether the guard's actions were barred by the applicable statute of limitations. The normal time limit for these claims is six months from when the claimant could successfully have brought the claims. In some cases, this is interpreted as meaning either **when the claimant knew, or should have known, about the action.** The guard argued that the claims against the union should include a failure to notify him of the change in retirement age. However, the court held that his action against both the school and the union had accrued upon the execution of the change of mandatory retirement age, and that **the guard should have known about the claim at that time.** The facts which persuaded the court included ongoing negotiations at the time the guard retired, the union holding monthly meetings which the guard failed to attend, and the negotiations being well-publicized. The court dismissed the claims as being time-barred. *Walker v. Columbia Univ. in City of New York*, 756 F.Supp. 149 (S.D.N.Y.1991).

C. State Statutes

♦   *Where an employee was not qualified for a position, she could not success-fully sue for discrimination.*

An Ohio private college hired a female applicant to implement and develop a new degree completion program in organizational management. She signed a one-year contract for the period September 1992 to August 1993. Her supervisor notified her five months later that her contract would not be renewed because she had allegedly failed to work closely with the faculty, failed to recruit program faculty, and failed to develop the organizational, communication and management skills which were necessary to perform the position. The college hired another female in her place. The employee filed suit in an Ohio trial court, alleging sex, age, and religious discrimination. At trial, the employee testified that her supervisor deliberately excluded her from committee meetings, acted differently toward women of her age, and appeared to be "more comfortable" in a male environment. The trial court granted pretrial judgment to the college, and the employee appealed to the Court of Appeals of Ohio.

The court held that because the employee had been replaced by another woman, she failed to establish an essential element of her sex discrimination claim. Moreover, with respect to her age and religious discrimination claims, even assuming that the employee could state a *prima facie* case as to each claim, there was insufficient evidence from which a rational trier of fact could conclude that the college's articulated reasons for the nonrenewal were pretextual. In fact, **not only did the employee lack the necessary skills, she acknowledged that communication problems existed between her and her supervisor.** Because there were no genuine issues of material fact, the trial court had properly granted the university's motion for pretrial judgment. *Doerter v. Bluffton College*, 647 N.E.2d 876 (Ohio.App.3d Dist.1994).

◆   *Five years after settling a discrimination claim against a college, a professor was allowed to sue the college despite a release she had signed in the settlement.*

An economics professor at a New York college initiated several state and federal lawsuits against the college alleging discrimination. She claimed the college was liable for age and sex discrimination because it reduced her employment status from fulltime to three-fourths status after she turned 65. Subsequently, the professor executed a settlement agreement with the college. In return, the college agreed to continue her employment as an adjunct professor teaching six courses per year until she turned 70. The agreement also stated that the professor released the college from: "any manner ... of [lawsuits] which now exist or may hereinafter arise...." College officials allegedly informed her that due to college policy, she would not be employed beyond her seventieth birthday. She then sued the college. A trial court held for the college, and the professor appealed. The issue before the appellate division court was **whether the settlement agreement precluded the professor from suing the college for age discrimination after she reached age 70.** The court observed that the settlement agreement released the college from the professor's original age discrimination lawsuit in exchange for its promise to employ her until she turned 70. It held that the new lawsuit was not barred by the settlement agreement. This was due to the fact that the college officials allegedly stated that the college had a policy of not hiring professors over 70 years of age. This presented **a fresh discrimination claim upon which the professor could sue.** The lower court decision was reversed. *Jochnowitz v. Russell Sage College*, 523 N.Y.S.2d 656 (A.D.3d Dept.1988).

◆   *Where a university provided adequate documentation to support its discharge decision, an age discrimination claim failed.*

A private university discharged a 61-year-old food service employee after 16 years of employment. In the months leading to the discharge, the university documented the employee's noncooperation and job deficiencies. The documentation included a memorandum written six months before the discharge which specifically explained the employee's failures and outlined necessary steps for improvement. The formal discharge notice was a two-page document describing his inability to cooperate. The Washington Supreme Court held that **the employee failed to prove an age discrimination claim because he could not overcome the university's evidence of performance deficiencies.** *Grimwood v. Univ. of Puget Sound*, 753 P.2d 517 (Wash.1988).

V. DISABILITY DISCRIMINATION

Section 504 of the Rehabilitation Act of 1973, 29 U.S.C. § 794, prohibits discrimination against qualified individuals with disabilities in programs or activities receiving federal financial assistance. The Americans with Disabilities Act of 1990 (ADA), 42 U.S.C. § 12101 et seq., extends protection to both private and public employees. It also prohibits discrimination against employees who are associated with disabled individuals (for example, an employee with a disabled son or daughter).

A. Liability

◆   *The Seventh Circuit held that a state university employee could not sue the university in a federal court under the ADA because of the Eleventh Amendment. However, the university still had to comply with the ADA, which was valid legislation.*

An employee at Northeastern Illinois University rose from the position of secretary to "program associate." She underwent medical care for her infertility, which was physically demanding and had side effects. Both the treatment and the circumstances that gave rise to it were emotionally draining. At times, the employee failed to show up for work or came to work late. Eventually, she was fired when she became distraught and stayed home for six working days. She sued the university under the ADA, alleging that it should have tolerated absences and tardiness from her that it would not have tolerated from nondisabled employees. The university moved to dismiss the case under the Eleventh Amendment, but the court denied the motion.

The U.S. Court of Appeals, Seventh Circuit, reversed. It noted that **the ADA did not "enforce" the Fourteenth Amendment because it went beyond the scope of what the Fourteenth Amendment prohibited.** Discrimination that was not prohibited by the Fourteenth Amendment was prohibited by the ADA. Also, the ADA required accommodation for disabilities. Noting in the Constitution requires employers to provide an accommodation for disabilities. Thus, **the employee could not sue the state in federal court because the Eleventh Amendment prohibits a party from suing a state in federal court without its consent.** The exception for legislation that "enforces" the Fourteenth Amendment did not apply. However, the state was still bound to follow the ADA because the statute was valid. The employee could sue the university in state court, or the federal government could sue the university in federal court. *Erickson v. Bd. of Governors of State Colleges & Universities for Northeastern Illinois Univ.*, 2000 U.S. App. LEXIS 5074 (7th Cir., 2000).

◆   *The Fifth Circuit decided that a teacher at a community college in Texas raised sufficient factual issues to bring his ADA case to a jury.*

A Texas bank employee suffered a head injury in 1975, following which he was left with impairments that included slurred speech, walking with a limp, a language communication disorder and partial paralysis of his right side. In 1988, he was hired by Palo Alto College to teach business administration classes and to coordinate a joint program sponsored by the American Institute of Banking (AIB). He never felt the need for or requested any accommodations.

In 1992, the then-president of the college transferred him to a full-time teaching position, stating in a letter that the banking program was not running well and that the instructor had a handicap that could have contributed to the problem. The next year, the instructor was informed that his contract was not going to be renewed, in spite of the recommendation of two separate committees that he be promoted and granted tenure. The reasons given for the transfer were that an allegation had been made that the instructor had been intoxicated while teaching, and a letter from the AIB, commenting that the banking program had improved since the instructor had been removed. An investigation had revealed that **the claim of intoxication had been based on the instructor's slurred speech and unsteady gait, both of which were due to his accident.**

The instructor sued, alleging that he had been discriminated against on the basis of a perceived disability. A magistrate judge disagreed, and entered judgment in favor of the college. The Fifth Circuit, however, determined that there were enough facts in dispute to entitle the instructor to bring his case to a jury. **There was evidence that the college perceived him to be disabled and transferred him to a full-time teaching position because of his limited speaking ability.** The court cited at least eight pieces of evidence which supported an inference that the instructor was discriminated against because of his perceived disability, and the inference was strong enough to require that the case be presented to a jury. *McInnis v. Alamo Community College Dist.*, 2000 U.S. App. LEXIS 4294 (5th Cir., 2000).

◆   *Discrimination based on either a record of a disability and/or the perception of disability are two types of discrimination prohibited by the ADA.*

A police officer at a Pennsylvania university suffered a work-related injury to his back, which prevented him from continuing in that position. The university offered him a job as a secretary, which he accepted. His insurer placed him on partial disability, classifying him as totally disabled for the duties of police officer, but able to perform secretarial duties. Later, the officer obtained a dispatcher position with the university. When his back improved, he applied for a police officer position. The university informed him that it would treat him as a new applicant, and would only consider him if he submitted a medical release (a condition not imposed on other applicants). When he submitted a release from his neurosurgeon, the university rejected it as inadequate. After another position opened up and his application was again denied, the officer sued the university under the ADA for disability discrimination, among other claims. The university moved to dismiss the claims. **The court refused to dismiss this part of the lawsuit, finding that the officer had alleged that the university had discriminated against him because he had a record of an impairment and because he was regarded as having an impairment.** *Fosburg v. Lehigh Univ.*, 1999 U.S. Dist. LEXIS 2833 (E.D.Pa.1999).

♦   *A university failed to make a reasonable accommodation where it refused to consider reassigning a disabled employee.*

A clerical employee of the University of Arizona had carpal tunnel syndrome and myofascial pain syndrome which prevented her from performing her heavy word processing duties. She became unable to perform her work despite accommodations provided by the university and requested reassignment to a position with less word processing work. The university considered the transfer request under its general personnel policy by requiring her to go through a competitive hiring process. She was not reassigned and the university fired her. She sued the university under the Americans with Disabilities Act (ADA), § 504 of the Rehabilitation Act and Arizona law. The court considered cross-motions for pretrial judgment by the parties, and rejected the university's claim that the ADA does not mandate affirmative action efforts by employers.

The court held that the ADA and § 504 are comprehensive antidiscrimination laws designed to prohibit discrimination on the basis of disability through the requirement of reasonable accommodation. Reasonable accommodation, contrary to the university's claim, requires employers to evaluate possible ways to structure work for individuals with disabilities. **The university had failed to demonstrate that it had conducted any analysis to determine whether reassignment of the employee was reasonable and whether it presented an undue hardship.** Because undue hardship was the university's only possible defense for failing to make a reasonable accommodation in this case, the employee was entitled to pretrial judgment. *Ransom v. State of Arizona Bd. of Regents*, 983 F.Supp. 895 (D.Ariz.1997).

♦   *An employee's claim under § 504 failed where the college had a legitimate reason for laying him off.*

A disabled part-time instructional aide at an Ohio community college experienced problems with his supervisor and coworkers. He stated that they demonstrated negative attitudes toward his disability, and he complained that one coworker called him names and made offensive statements about him to her class. The community college responded by transferring his supervisor to another office and admonishing the coworker against making derogatory comments. The community college had a policy of limiting its part-time employees to 1,040 hours of work during each fiscal year. The instructional aide and several coworkers were laid off after exceeding the hour limit. The aide filed a complaint with the U.S. Department of Education, Office for Civil Rights, which investigated the matter and determined that it was without merit. The aide nonetheless filed a lawsuit in a federal district court against the college under § 504 of the Rehabilitation Act of 1973.

The U.S. District Court for the Northern District of Ohio stated that in order to prevail in a discrimination claim for hostile work environment under the Rehabilitation Act, the complaining party must demonstrate repeated discriminatory conduct by a defendant that is tolerated and condoned by management. In this case, **the aide's supervisors had taken corrective measures in response to his complaints. Accordingly, there was insufficient evidence of a hostile work environment. The court also held that the layoff action had not been discriminatory** because there was evidence that the aide had exceeded the permitted number of hours for part-time employees and this was a legitimate reason for the layoff. The court granted pretrial judgment to the community college, and the U.S. Court of Appeals, Sixth Circuit, affirmed that decision. *Spells v. Cuyahoga Community College*, 51 F.3d 273 (6th Cir.1995).

◆   *A Wisconsin federal court held that a public employee could sue under Title II of the ADA without exhausting administrative remedies.*

A University of Wisconsin-Madison employee worked for over four years at the university's small business development center. The university advised him that it would not renew his employment contract for the upcoming year because of the conflict between his "personal needs," resulting from a disability and the school's objectives. The employee elected not to file an EEOC complaint, instead filing a lawsuit in federal court under the ADA. The university filed a motion to dismiss, claiming that the employee had failed to exhaust his administrative remedies as set forth under Department of Justice regulations arising under ADA Title I. The employee argued that by filing the lawsuit under ADA Title II, he was under no obligation to exhaust administrative remedies by filing an EEOC complaint.

The court compared Titles I and II of the ADA and found that only Title I contained the requirement to exhaust administrative remedies. ADA Title I applies broadly to employers with 15 or more employees, while Title II applies only to public entities and broadly prohibits discrimination, only incidentally referring to employment discrimination. **The court held that even though Title I was the ADA's primary means of combating employment discrimination, a complaint under Title II was expressly permitted and carried no requirement for exhausting administrative remedies.** Title II of the ADA was modeled after § 504 of the Rehabilitation Act, while Title I was patterned after Title VII of the Civil Rights Act of 1964, accounting for the different procedural requirements. The court denied the university's motion to dismiss the lawsuit. *Petersen v. Univ. of Wisconsin Bd. of Regents,* 818 F.Supp. 1276 (W.D.Wis.1993).

◆   *After a jury found that a college had discriminated against a professor, the college was ordered to reinstate the professor and pay her damages.*

A religious studies professor employed by a New Hampshire private college suffered from **morbid obesity.** Because of her condition, she had difficulty walking more than 500 yards and performing some of her daily activities. At a faculty meeting, the president of the college referred to the need to educate both the mind and the body and stated that the faculty needed to be an example to the students in this respect. The professor was later told that her contract would not be renewed for the following year. She filed suit against the college in the U.S.

District Court for the District of New Hampshire, alleging a violation of the ADA. The court denied the professor's motion for a preliminary injunction, finding that she was unlikely to succeed on the merits of her ADA claim and that her morbid obesity did not substantially impair her ability to walk or work. The college then filed a motion to dismiss which was denied. The jury returned a verdict on the ADA claim of $68,974, and $137,500 on the breach of contract claim, and the court directed the parties to address the issue of reinstatement. The court noted that a victim of discrimination is entitled to be made whole through the use of equitable remedies. Accordingly, the first choice is reinstatement of the employee. Because the professor succeeded on her ADA claim, **the court directed the college to reinstate her as a fulltime faculty member.** The court also found that the jury awards were duplicative, and limited her recovery to the larger award of $137,500. *Nedder v. Rivier College*, 972 F.Supp. 81 (D.N.H.1997).

B. Defenses

◆   *Where a professor suffered from a mental impairment that prohibited him from being able to teach, he was not entitled to the protections of the ADA.*

A man was hired by a Massachusetts university under a special appointment with teaching as his primary function. Several female students complained that the professor pressured them to attend a party at his house. The professor later took an underage student out to dinner, bought her a glass of wine and allegedly made suggestive remarks. He was given a formal reprimand and after another complaint by a female faculty member, he was notified that any further occurrences would result in his dismissal. Nonetheless, he later took another underage student off campus and purchased alcohol for her. The university began investigation and termination proceedings. The professor then asserted that he suffered from a depressive disorder which reduced his inhibitions. He requested that he be allowed to continue in his position with extra monitoring as a reasonable accommodation. The university fired him and he filed suit, alleging violations of the ADA and § 504 of the Rehabilitation Act.

The U.S. District Court for the District of Massachusetts noted that to be a qualified individual under the ADA, an individual must be able to perform the essential functions of his or her position. The professor admitted that in his present condition, he was not qualified to teach students because of his inability to conform his conduct to appropriate boundaries. However, **because teaching was an essential function of his position, he was not a qualified individual under the ADA.** Further, he could not assert a claim under Title III of the ADA which addresses disability discrimination in places of public accommodation. The court held that Title III was not designed to include employment practices and to hold otherwise would disrupt the balance created between Title III and Title I, which does cover disability discrimination in the workplace. Finding that the professor could not perform the essential functions of his position, the court granted the university's motion to dismiss the case. *Motzkin v. Trustees of Boston Univ.*, 938 F.Supp. 983 (D.Mass.1996).

◆   *An employee with an impairment was not covered under the ADA where the restrictions on his ability to walk were not significant.*

A Pennsylvania man who worked for a private university suffered an injury to his hip which caused him to limp. He was unable to walk more than a mile or so at a time and had to climb stairs at a slower pace while holding the rail. Six years later, when the employee was 68 years old, the university discharged him as part of its university-wide reduction in force. He sued the university in a Pennsylvania federal court, asserting age discrimination in violation of the ADEA and disability discrimination in violation of the ADA.

The court first determined that a supervisor's question to the employee concerning when he planned to retire, made approximately one year before the layoff, was merely a casual remark that resulted from the employee's child's graduation from college. The court next determined that **the employee's trouble in climbing stairs and his ability to walk only one mile without pain did not substantially limit his ability to walk under the ADA.** Further, even assuming that the employee had produced a *prima facie* case of disability discrimination, the university had asserted a legitimate, nondiscriminatory reason for its employment decision. The employee's supervisor had explained that he was required to reduce his budget by $30,000. Only by eliminating a position from the department could he meet that requirement. Further, the supervisor had permissibly considered the future adaptability of his employees upon the consolidation of two positions as a result of the reduction in force. Since **economic necessity was a legitimate, nondiscriminatory reason for the layoff,** the court granted the university's motion for pretrial judgment. *Kelly v. Drexel Univ.*, 907 F.Supp. 864 (E.D.Pa.1995).

On appeal to the U.S. Court of Appeals, Third Circuit, the court found that in order for his condition to qualify as a disability, it would have to significantly restrict his ability to walk as compared with an average person in the general population. However, he was able to walk and did not need a cane or crutches to aid him. Although his ability to walk was moderately restricted, the court found that he was not disabled. The court also refused to second-guess the university's assertion that economic necessity had led to the dismissal. Finding that the employee failed to state a claim of disability or age discrimination, the court affirmed the district court's decision. *Kelly v. Drexel Univ.*, 94 F.3d 102 (3d Cir.1996).

◆   *An instructor was not protected under the ADA where she was not able to meet the attendance requirements of the job.*

A part-time medical assistance instructor at a Virginia private college suffered from an autoimmune system disorder. She frequently missed work because of her condition and also missed work to take care of her son, who suffered from gastroesophageal reflux disease. The college permitted the instructor to take sick leave and to take breaks whenever she felt ill. It granted her requests for accommodation and permitted her to keep flexible hours. The instructor was also permitted to take a leave of absence to be with her son while he was undergoing surgery. However, her request for additional time off to take care of his postoperative problems was denied. The instructor resigned, and signed a report prepared by the college stating that her separation was "mutual." She then filed a lawsuit against the college in a U.S. district court, alleging discrimination under the Americans with Disabilities Act (ADA). The ADA proscribes actions taken based on an employer's mere belief that an employee would have to miss work to take care of a disabled person. The court entered summary judgment for the college, and the instructor appealed to the U.S. Court of Appeals, Fourth Circuit.

The court of appeals stated that **an employee who cannot meet the attendance requirements of a job is not protected by the ADA. The instructor's absences had rendered her unable to function effectively as a teacher.** Consequently, she was not a "qualified individual with a disability" under the ADA and was unable to avail herself of ADA protections. The court also rejected her claim that the discharge constituted discrimination based on her association with her disabled son. The ADA did not require the college to restructure the instructor's work schedule. The instructor was permissibly discharged based on her past absences and her statement that she would miss more work to take care of her son. This, coupled with the college's reasonable accommodations, established that disability was not a motivating factor in the dismissal. The district court decision was affirmed. *Tyndall v. National Education Centers*, 31 F.3d 209 (4th Cir.1994).

♦   *An alumni association may not be a private club and thus may have to comply with the ADA.*

A New York man was hired by the alumni association of the United States Military Academy to solicit contributions from alumni. His wife suffered from Lyme disease, chronic fatigue syndrome and depression, and consequently was unable to accompany her husband to various association social events. Allegedly because of this and other problems caused by his wife's illness, the employee was treated in a discriminatory manner by his superiors and was eventually fired. He and his wife filed suit against the association in the U.S. District Court for the Southern District of New York, alleging violation of the Americans with Disabilities Act (ADA) and state law. The association counterclaimed and both sides filed motions to dismiss.

The court dismissed the ADA claim asserted by the employee's wife, finding that she had no standing to sue the association for such discrimination. **The association then argued that it was a bona fide private membership club exempt from ADA coverage.** The court noted that to qualify for this exemption, the association had to show that it existed for recreational or social purposes, was legitimate and private, and required meaningful conditions for membership. The court found that the association's primary function was to raise money and not to involve itself with fraternal activities. Although a tax-exempt status is evidence of the private nature of a club, the court found that here it was granted because the association was so closely integrated with the academy. Finally, the court noted that the members of the association had no control over the membership pool. Finding that **a genuine issue of fact existed as to whether the association qualified as a private club,** the court denied the motion to dismiss the employee's ADA claim. *Willson v. Assn. of Graduates of U.S. Military Academy*, 946 F.Supp. 294 (S.D.N.Y.1996).

C. Contagious Diseases

In 1998, the U.S. Supreme Court held that a person with HIV was protected by the Americans with Disabilities Act despite the fact that she was not yet exhibiting any symptoms of the disease. Since the HIV infection substantially impaired her ability to reproduce, she could not be discriminated against unless her condition presented a direct threat to the health and safety of others. *Bragdon v. Abbott,* 524 U.S. 624, 118 S.Ct. 2196, 141 L.Ed.2d 540.

◆ *The Supreme Court held that a person with a contagious disease was entitled to the protections of the Rehabilitation Act.*

A Florida elementary school teacher was discharged because of her continued recurrence of tuberculosis. She sued the school board under § 504 of the Rehabilitation Act, which prohibits entities that receive federal funding from discriminating against individuals with disabilities. A federal court dismissed her suit, but the Eleventh Circuit reversed, holding that persons with contagious diseases fall within § 504's coverage. The case then reached the U.S. Supreme Court, which held that **tuberculosis was a disability under § 504.** The disease attacked the teacher's respiratory system and affected her ability to work. It would be unfair to allow an employer to distinguish between a disease's potential effect on others and its effect on the afflicted employee in order to justify discriminatory treatment. Accordingly, she was entitled to reinstatement or front pay if she could show that despite her disability, she was otherwise qualified for her job with or without a reasonable accommodation. *School Board of Nassau County v. Arline,* 480 U.S. 273, 107 S.Ct. 1123, 94 L.Ed.2d 307 (1987).

◆ *The transfer of an HIV-positive employee was not discriminatory where the employee had committed infractions that resulted in risks to others.*

A New York medical college employed a phlebotomist who was HIV positive. The college had a policy in place requiring employees to wear gloves on both hands when drawing blood. After the employee violated that policy on at least three occasions, the college reassigned her to the billing department. The employee brought suit against the college in a state trial court, alleging that it had discriminated against her based on her HIV-positive disability. The case was transferred to the New York Supreme Court, Appellate Division, which held that **the college did not discriminate against the employee by reassigning her.** The court noted that the employer was unaware of any similar infractions by any other employees. Thus, it had provided a legitimate, nondiscriminatory reason for the transfer which was supported by substantial evidence. *Friedel v. New York State Division of Human Rights,* 632 N.Y.S.2d 520 (A.D.1st Dept.1995).

VI. RETALIATION

Title VII prohibits an employer from taking action against an employee because the employee has filed, or has participated in the investigation of, a discrimination complaint. In 1997, the Supreme Court decided Robinson v. Shell Oil Co., *where it held that a **former employee** of a corporation could bring a retaliatory discrimination lawsuit against his former employer after he was given*

*a negative employment reference following his filing of an EEOC complaint.
Title VII protects not only current employees but also former employees from
retaliatory actions. See 519 U.S. 337, 117 S.Ct. 843, 136 L.Ed.2d 808.*

A. Former Employees

◆   *A college's actions were held not to be retaliatory because its allegedly
retaliatory actions did not "touch" an employment relationship. In other words,
because the conduct occurred after the employment relationship had ended, and
did not impact on the employee's future employment, the conduct could not give
rise to a retaliation claim.*

An African-American part-time gospel choir director employed by a New
Jersey private college was discharged after the position was eliminated for
budgetary reasons. After student protest, the college decided to fund the choir but
as an elective course for which students could receive academic credit. Because
all faculty members were required to have a college degree, the college rejected
the director's application for the new position in favor of a female African-
American candidate with a Master of Arts degree in music performance. In an
unrelated incident, the dean of students allegedly refused to accept a petty cash
voucher signed by the director, stating that unauthorized submissions were
"tantamount to stealing from the college." The director filed a race discrimination
charge with the EEOC, which was settled. Pursuant to the agreement, she entered
into a temporary contract with the college as a director of the extra-curricular
gospel choir. In spite of written admonitions that the college preapprove any
campus visits after the temporary contract expired, she attended a campus protest
and returned to lead a "Gospel Sing Fest." After the EEOC dismissed a second
discrimination complaint, the director filed suit in federal court, alleging unlawful
retaliation under Title VII, among other claims. The district court granted the
college's motion for pretrial judgment on the retaliation claim, and the director
appealed to the U.S. Court of Appeals, Third Circuit.

The director contended that actionable retaliation includes all conduct that
"arises out of the employment relation." The court of appeals disagreed, ruling
that **an employer's significant wrongful post-employment conduct must
"touch an employment relationship."** The university's requirement that the
director obtain its approval before entering its campus was not an "employment
practice" because the director was not the college's employee when the requirement was imposed. Neither the requirement nor the college's allegedly defamatory publications impacted on her actual or proposed employment anywhere else.
Consequently, the college's actions did not give rise to a retaliation claim. The
court affirmed the district court's decision. *Nelson v. Upsala College*, 51 F.3d 383
(3d Cir.1995).

◆   *Two former employees who brought retaliation claims against a college were
allowed to proceed with their lawsuit where issues of fact had to be resolved
regarding the college's true reason for the discharges.*

A Hispanic woman worked in the human resources department of a private
Texas college. She misplaced a file room key but did not tell anyone because she
was afraid that the director of the department would yell at her. She had previously

complained that the director treated her in a racially discriminatory manner. The employee contacted a secretary in another department to ask for assistance in obtaining a duplicate key. The secretary had also had problems with her supervisor and had previously complained that her supervisor treated her in a sexually discriminatory manner. She obtained a duplicate key and gave it to the employee. When their supervisors discovered that they did not follow the proper key replacement procedure, both employees were recommended for discharge and were fired by the college's president. They filed suit in federal district court, alleging Title VII claims for national origin and gender discrimination, based on theories of unlawful retaliation and hostile work environment. The college filed motions to dismiss which the trial court granted. The employees appealed to the U.S. Court of Appeals, Fifth Circuit.

The court noted that to show claims of unlawful retaliation, **the employees needed to show that they were engaged in activities protected by Title VII, that an adverse employment action occurred and that a causal link existed between the protected activities and the adverse employment action.** Because each employee presented evidence that she was treated differently because of either her national origin or her gender, the court found that they were subjected to conduct that violated Title VII. Since both employees were fired, they were subjected to an adverse employment action. Although they were fired by the college president, the court noted that they were recommended for discharge by their supervisors. Since the degree to which the president made the decision based on his own independent thinking was an issue of fact, the court found that, when taken in the light most favorable to the employees, there was a causal link between the protected activities and their dismissal. Although the college stated that the employees did not follow the correct key replacement procedure, the employees presented evidence that not every department followed the procedure and no one had ever been fired for violating the procedure in the past. Finding that the college's reason could be a pretext for unlawful retaliation, the district court's decision was reversed on this claim. *Long v. Eastfield College*, 88 F.3d 300 (5th Cir.1996).

B. Defenses

♦ *A retaliation claim failed in the following case where the professor could not show that it had occurred because of opposition to an unlawful employment practice.*

A professor employed by a private, Alabama university often supported his students when they complained of discrimination by the university. A female student informed him that because of her gender she was being discriminated against by the university. He directed her to the appropriate school officials and then personally notified a university dean and the provost. He was told by the officials to keep the matter private but in the next month, he informed a university trustee of his concerns about the situation. After this, his relationship with the university deteriorated significantly and he was given repeated warnings to forget the situation. He was then told that the university was not going to renew his contract because he had informed the trustee of the discrimination complaint. He sued the university and its officials, alleging violations of Title VII and Title IX.

The U.S. District Court for the Northern District of Alabama noted that Title VII permits suits only against employers. Therefore, specific persons sued either in their individual capacities or as agents of an employer are not proper defendants. The court also found no indication in Title IX that anyone other than an educational institute receiving federal funds can be named as a defendant. Therefore, the claims against the university officials were dismissed. In considering the professor's retaliation claim under Title VII, the court noted that he had to show that he was discriminated against because he opposed an unlawful employment practice. **Here, the student did not claim that she was discriminated against in employment and therefore, the professor's Title VII claim for retaliation failed. With regard to Title IX, the court found no express remedy for retaliation in the statute** and refused to imply one. Even if it could imply such a remedy, the court nonetheless found that because the professor himself was not alleging gender discrimination, his claim was too far removed from the coverage of Title IX. Because the court could envision no other way for the professor to reassert his claim and state a valid cause of action, it dismissed the case. *Holt v. Lewis*, 955 F.Supp. 1385 (N.D.Ala.1995), affirmed, 109 F.3d 771 (11th Cir.1997).

♦   *A retaliation claim failed in the following case because the university had proffered a legitimate nondiscriminatory reason for its nonrenewal of the professor's contract.*

A female assistant professor was denied tenure by a New York private university, allegedly because she lacked a Ph.D. and a sufficient record of scholarly research. The professor rejected several offers for part-time adjunct positions and filed a complaint against the university with the New York Human Rights Commission, alleging that she had been denied tenure on the basis of her sex. She was permitted to teach in adjunct status without a contract for an additional two years, despite the university's policy of not allowing persons to teach without signed contracts. During settlement negotiations, the university offered her a five-year adjunct contract with a 60 percent pay increase in exchange for her withdrawal of the sex discrimination complaint. The professor declined the offer, and the university unconditionally refused to consider her for additional available adjunct positions. The professor filed a second complaint with the commission, alleging that the university had retaliated against her for not withdrawing her sex discrimination complaint. The commission held that the university had retaliated against the professor but dismissed the discrimination claim. The case reached the Court of Appeals of New York.

The court of appeals held that **the record was devoid of evidence that the university had a subjective retaliatory motive for the nonrenewal.** The professor's failure to agree to any of the university's adjunct offers over the course of two years belied her assertion that the nonrenewal was in retaliation for her failure to withdraw the discrimination claim. Rather, her adjunct status was not renewed because of her protracted tactical decisions not to execute a series of adjunct contracts, in favor of her relying completely on her achieving full tenure in the pending discrimination proceeding. Moreover, the university's enforcement of its policy prohibiting adjuncts from teaching without a signed contract was a legitimate nondiscriminatory reason for the nonrenewal. *Pace Univ. v. N.Y. City Comm'n on Human Rights*, 623 N.Y.S.2d 765 (Ct.App.1995).

◆   *An employee who asserted that her supervisor gave other employees better assignments because they were involved in a homosexual relationship with her, and that she was discharged for complaining about it could not prove that the discharge had been retaliatory.*

An Associate Director of Nursing employed by a Washington, D.C. private university hospital frequently complained that the director showed partiality to two subordinate employees by granting them extensive overtime pay, choice working assignments, and lenient disciplinary action. She alleged that the director's behavior undermined her authority, contradicted hospital policy, and adversely affected department morale. She also believed, but never explicitly alleged, that the favoritism stemmed from the subordinates' homosexual relationships with the director. After the university fired the associate director, she filed suit in a District of Columbia trial court alleging retaliatory discharge in violation of the District of Columbia Human Rights Act.

At trial, the allegations of the employees' homosexual status were based on evidence that the director and the subordinates took shopping trips together, dined together and spent nights at each others' homes, and on personal facts about the women including their marital status and mode of dress, as well as other alleged homosexual stereotypes. The jury held for the associate director and awarded damages. The university filed a motion for judgment notwithstanding the verdict, but the court denied the motion. The university appealed to the District of Columbia Court of Appeals, which reversed, ruling that **the associate director failed to establish that she was engaged in a protected activity or that she opposed practices made unlawful by the human rights act. Allegations of cronyism or favoritism are generally insufficient to state a claim for retaliatory discharge.** The court rejected the associate director's assertion that, based on the work environment, university officials should have known a complaint of unlawful discrimination was being made. Because the associate director failed to state a *prima facie* retaliation claim, her action was dismissed and the trial court's ruling was reversed. *Howard Univ. v. Green*, 652 A.2d 41 (D.C.App.1994).

◆   *Where an employee had lied on her application, she was not entitled to any relief despite a university's discriminatory acts against her.*

A woman who had been in law enforcement for several years began working for a private university as its only female public security officer. She was placed on probationary status. During her first month on the job, she was cited for a uniform code violation. On her 30-day evaluation, she was given "marginal" ratings. Her supervisor made a reference to the uniform violation, but did not do so for a male officer who had been similarly cited. Her supervisor then reassigned her badge number to give her the one always assigned to women, and she was placed in a "meter maid" position by virtue of a shift transfer. When she complained about this treatment, her supervisor said, "You've got the lady's job. Don't you like it?" She then filed a complaint with the EEOC. Shortly thereafter, she was fired for spending too much time in the office and for not satisfactorily completing her probationary period. She brought suit against the university in federal court under Title VII, alleging sex discrimination and retaliation for filing an EEOC complaint. In preparing for trial, the university learned that the officer had omitted a prior DUI conviction from her employment application. The district court found this to be a material falsification. It also found that the university had violated Title VII. The court limited the officer's award to backpay, and appeal was taken to the U.S. Court of Appeals, Sixth Circuit. On appeal, the court held that **the employee's falsification on her employment application barred any relief to which she might be entitled.** Here, the university would have fired the employee if it knew of her misrepresentation on the application. Accordingly, the officer was not entitled to any relief, and the lower court decision was reversed. The court held for the university. *Milligan-Jensen v. Michigan Technological Univ.*, 975 F.2d 302 (6th Cir.1992).

C. Causal Connection

◆   *To succeed on a claim of retaliation under Title VII, an employee (or former employee) must show a causal connection between the protected activity and the adverse employment action.*

A Texas business school discharged an African-American admissions representative. The representative applied for another position with the U.S. Internal Revenue Service (IRS) which requested a reference from the school. The school responded that the representative was below average in the categories of quality of work, judgement, dependability and flexibility. It also noted that he was discharged due to his tardiness and insubordination. The school contended that the evaluation was based on observations of the representative during his employment. The representative filed a Title VII lawsuit against the school, alleging race discrimination and retaliation with respect to his discharge, the school's failure to promote him, and its allegedly false references to the IRS. The school moved for summary judgment.

The court held that the representative's failure to obtain a right to sue letter precluded his discrimination claim with respect to his discharge and denial of promotion. Next, the court noted that Title VII prohibits retaliation for an employee's past discrimination charges. However, although the representative could premise a Title VII retaliation claim on the school's post-employment retaliatory conduct, his self-serving, generalized testimony stating his subjective belief that discrimination had occurred was insufficient to show a causal connection between the protected activity and the adverse employment action. Further, **there was nothing in the record that could support a finding that the appraisal was motivated by malice or retaliatory intent,** or that the school's explanation of the appraisal was pretextual. The court granted the school's motion for summary judgment. *Fields v. Phillips School of Business & Technology*, 870 F.Supp. 149 (W.D.Tex.1994).

◆   *Multiple discrimination and retaliation claims failed in the following case involving a private college counselor.*

An African-American female was hired as a talent search counselor for a Mississippi private college to plan services and activities designed to encourage the retention of first-generation college students. A year later, she applied for the position of educational talent search coordinator. However, an African-American male was hired to fill this position. The counselor filed a written grievance in accordance with college procedure stating that the vacancy had not been properly posted and that she had been mistreated by her supervisor. The position became available again in 1992 but the college revised the job qualifications to require administrative supervisory experience. The counselor was again rejected, this time in favor of an African-American female who met the revised job qualifications. The counselor filed suit in a U.S. district court, alleging that the college retaliated against her for filing a sex discrimination grievance in violation of Title VII, 42 U.S.C. § 1981 and the Fourteenth Amendment. The college moved for pretrial judgment.

The district court held that the counselor failed to state a *prima facie* case under Title VII. Although she asserted an adverse employment action (failure to promote her), she failed to establish that she had engaged in statutorily protected expression or that any causal connection existed between the allegedly protected expression and the adverse employment action. Specifically, her grievance had merely asserted that the job vacancy was not properly noticed and that she had been treated unfairly by her supervisor. She had not complained of sex discrimination. Further, since the change in job qualifications occurred almost 16 months after she filed her grievance, **there was no causal connection between her grievance and the college's failure to promote her.** Next, because § 1981 does not apply to sex discrimination claims, the court dismissed this claim. Finally, an action taken by a private college (even funded by federal grants) failed to allege state action necessary to assert a Fourteenth Amendment claim. The district court granted summary judgment to the college and dismissed all the claims against it. *Aldridge v. Tougaloo College*, 847 F.Supp. 480 (S.D.Miss.1994).

CHAPTER SEVEN

Intellectual Property

I. INTRODUCTION

In determining who owns the patent rights to an invention, what is looked at is the nature of the relationship between the inventor and the employer. Where the inventor is hired to invent something, the employer retains all patent rights; and where the inventor is hired under a general contract of employment, the inventor will retain ownership rights. However, most cases fall somewhere in between these two: for example, where a university hires a professor or a graduate student to teach and do research. The ambiguity this creates has led colleges and universities to enter into pre-employment assignments of intellectual property rights that specifically lay out the rights of both parties. Sometimes this is done by written agreement—other times, by use of a faculty handbook.

Generally, copyright rights are treated more laxly than patent rights. Perhaps this is because of tradition but, whatever the reason, a professor who writes a book is likely to retain all ownership rights to the work. In contrast, the professor who invents a new printing press that will produce a better book likely will not own the rights to that work. However, copyright policies are becoming more common, due largely to the fact that computer programs, which are potentially very lucrative, are copyrightable.

With respect to patent rights, professors usually are required to assign creations and patent rights to the colleges and universities that employ them in exchange for a percentage of the royalties (at a minimum, usually 20 percent). The issue becomes trickier when dealing with graduate students. Some universities require graduate students to assign patent rights: others do not.

A number of states have enacted statutes to limit the extent to which employers can claim an interest in employee inventions. However, those statutes generally provide that if the employer provides resources, or if the invention relates to the employer's business, the employer can require assignment of intellectual property rights. It is only where the employer has no involvement at all that the employee can claim full rights to his or her invention.

This chapter focuses on a number of copyright and patent issues in the context of higher education.

II. COPYRIGHTS

Article I, Section 8 of the U.S. Constitution provides that Congress can secure for limited times to authors and inventors the exclusive right to their respective writings and discoveries. From this provision came the Copyright Act and the patent system.

Section 107 of the Copyright Act states:

17 U.S.C. § 107

"The fair use of a copyrighted work, including such use by reproduction in copies … for purposes such as criticism, comment, news reporting, teaching (including multiple copies for classroom use), scholarship, or research, is not an infringement of **copyright.** In determining whether the use made of a work in any particular case is a fair use the factors to be considered shall include—

(1) the purpose and character of the use, including whether such use is of a commercial nature or is for nonprofit educational purposes;
(2) the nature of the copyrighted work;
(3) the amount and substantiality of the portion used in relation to the copyrighted work as a whole; and
(4) the effect of the use upon the potential market for or value of the copyrighted work.

♦   *By refusing to pay permission fees to copyright holders, a copy shop violated the Copyright Act.*
A commercial copy shop reproduced substantial segments of copyrighted works and bound them into "coursepacks," which were sold to students so that they could fulfill reading assignments given by professors at the University of Michigan. The copy shop acted without the permission of the copyright holders, claiming that the fair use doctrine eliminated the need for it to obtain permission. The fair use doctrine states that the fair use of a copyrighted work for teaching, scholarship or research, among other uses, is not an infringement of copyright. In this case, a number of copyright holders sued the copy shop claiming that its reproduction of material was not fair use. A federal district court held that the usage was not fair and awarded damages against the copy shop. It also found that the infringement was willful.
On appeal, the U.S. Court of Appeals, Sixth Circuit noted that **by reproducing copies for students without paying the copyright holders the permission fees that other copy shops paid, the copy shop was reducing the potential market for or the value of the copyrighted works.** Since one of the potential

uses of a copyright is to grant a license to reproduce part of the work for use in a classroom, and since the copyright holders were willing to grant those licenses, by refusing to pay the permission fees, the copy shop violated the Copyright Act. The court also noted that the purpose and character of the use was of a commercial nature, that the material being reproduced was creative in nature, and that the amount and substantiality of the reproduced segments in relation to the works as a whole were quite large (between 5 and 30 percent). **The court affirmed the finding that the copy shop had infringed the copyright holders' rights. However, it refused to find that the infringement had been willful.** It remanded the case for reconsideration as to the damages that should be awarded. *Princeton Univ. Press v. Michigan Document Services*, 99 F.3d 1381 (6th Cir.1996).

◆ *A copy shop violated the Copyright Act by copying excerpts from books and putting them in course packets. This was not "fair use" under the act.*

Several New York publishers sued Kinko's for copyright infringement as a result of the store's policy of copying excerpts from books, compiling them into course "packets," and selling them to college students. Kinko's admitted that it copied the works, but asserted that doing so was a fair use under the Copyright Act, and that since it had been doing this type of copying for 20 years, the publishers could not now claim copyright infringement. A federal court held that Kinko's had infringed the copyrights. First, the usage was commercial in nature, rather than for nonprofit educational use. Second, the amount and substantiality of the copied works weighed against Kinko's because the portions copied were critical parts of the copyrighted works. Third, and most importantly, **the effect of the use on the value of and market for the works weighed against Kinko's. Thus, the copying did not amount to fair use under the Copyright Act.** Further, the court accepted the publishers' assertion that although they had known Kinko's was copying their works for 20 years, they did not know that Kinko's had been infringing on their copyrights all that time. It ordered Kinko's to obtain permission in the future, to pay any licensing fees required, and to pay $510,000 in statutory damages for past infringement. *Basic Books, Inc. v. Kinko's Graphics Corp.*, 758 F.Supp. 1522 (S.D.N.Y.1991).

◆ *New York's Standardized Testing Act requires testing agencies to file reports on standardized tests with the Commissioner of Education, and also requires the filing of copyrightable test questions.*

The American Association of Medical Colleges (AAMC), a nonprofit educational association, sponsors a medical school testing program, the central feature of which is the MCAT exam. The AAMC holds copyrights in the MCAT test forms, test questions, answer sheets, and reports. When the state of New York enacted the Standardized Testing Act, requiring disclosure of this copyrighted information, the AAMC sued to enjoin the application of the Act. It claimed that the Act was preempted by the federal Copyright Act and moved for pretrial judgment, which the court granted. The court found that the purpose and character of the use was non-commercial and educational, and that disclosure of the test questions would prevent their re-use.

The Second Circuit Court of Appeals reversed, finding that there were issues of fact that precluded a grant of pretrial judgment. If the disclosure of material were considered "fair use," then there would be no Copyright Act violation. However, if the state Act facilitated infringement, then the Copyright Act would preempt it. **Here, the state's goal of encouraging valid and objective tests was laudable, and there was a question of fact as to whether the test questions could be used again after being disclosed.** As a result, the fourth and most important fair use factor—the effect of the use upon the potential market for or value of the copyrighted work—did not necessarily weigh in favor of the AAMC. The court remanded the case for further proceedings. *Assn. of American Medical Colleges v. Cuomo*, 928 F.2d 519 (2d Cir.1991).

◆ *A federal district court agreed with four educational testing agencies, including the College Entrance Examination Board, that the required disclosure of test questions under a New York law violated federal copyright law. The court issued a preliminary injunction indicating a likelihood of success on the merits of the copyright infringement claim.*

New York education law requires college testing services to file copies of their test questions and statistical reports with the state education commissioner. A number of testing agencies claimed that the statute violated federal copyright law, and filed a lawsuit against the governor and other state officials in the U.S. District Court for the Northern District of New York. In view of the result in a similar case filed by the Association of American Medical Colleges, the parties entered into a stipulation under which the testing agencies disclosed questions for only some of the tests administered in the state and were allowed to administer a fixed number of undisclosed tests. The court then considered a motion by the agencies for temporary relief. The agencies argued that the compelled disclosure of the test questions violated federal copyright law and that disclosure to the state did not meet the fair use exception to federal copyright law. **The state argued that the public had an interest in ensuring the fairness and objectivity of standardized admission tests** and had a strong need to evaluate the scoring process. It also claimed that disclosure did not violate copyright laws because of the lack of any commercial purpose.

The court agreed with the testing agencies that the disclosure of test questions violated federal copyright law and issued a preliminary injunction indicating a likelihood of success on the merits of their copyright infringement claim. The court also found that the agencies were entitled to the presumption of irreparable injury that normally accompanies the showing of copyright infringement. However, because of the many factual issues existing in the case, the court issued an order preserving the status quo, under which only some tests administered in the state would be subject to the disclosure law pending further proceedings. *College Entrance Examination Bd. v. Pataki*, 889 F.Supp. 554 (N.D.N.Y.1995).

Three of the testing agencies moved the court for partial reconsideration of the order summarized above, requesting an order completely barring enforcement of the state law or alternative relief. A fourth agency submitted a statement indicating that it would comply with the order by disclosing three testing forms administered in New York during the test year and an additional form traditionally administered in the state in low-volume administrations.

The testing agencies asserted that the wording of the preliminary order would prevent the Graduate Record Examination (GRE) program from offering at least one administration in the state, and that the status quo provision of the order did not account for changing circumstances in testing from year to year. They further asserted that the preliminary order contravened **the principle in copyright infringement cases that the status quo sought to be preserved is the state of non-infringement**.

The court held that the preliminary order struck the correct balance between competing interests, including that of the students who would take the examinations. There was no need in this case to strictly comply with the rule that the status quo to be preserved is a state of non-infringement, since the parties had agreed by stipulation to provide for limited disclosure of test forms. The court modified the preliminary order to accommodate the GRE program's phase-out of paper and pencil administrations. *College Entrance Examination Bd. v. Pataki*, 893 F.Supp. 152 (N.D.N.Y.1995).

♦   *A Michigan fine arts student received permission to proceed with her claim against a professor for breach of fiduciary duty, based on her claim that the professor allowed the unauthorized reproduction of her work. However, her other state law claims were dismissed prior to a trial because they were preempted by federal copyright law.*

A fine arts student enrolled in a masters program at a Michigan university agreed to create background art for display by an automaker at the 1997 North American Auto Show. The automaker also prepared a brochure promoting the exhibit, which featured student-prepared artwork. The student received $1,400 for her efforts and was offered a paid trip to Spain to continue the exhibit, which she declined. She claimed that the automaker reproduced three of her paintings in the brochure without permission, and that it printed one of them upside down. In addition, she claimed that her professor refused to take any action to stop the unauthorized reproduction of her work.

The student brought a federal district court action against the university, professor and automaker for copyright infringement under the Copyright and Lanham Acts, and for state law claims such as breach of fiduciary duty, intentional infliction of emotional distress and unjust enrichment. She sought injunctive relief to prevent further reproduction and distribution of her paintings, and monetary damages, including a share of the profits acquired by the automaker resulting from the infringement. The defendants moved to dismiss the state law claims on grounds that they were preempted by federal copyright law.

The court stated that under 17 U.S.C. § 106, a copyright owner has the exclusive right to reproduce the copyrighted work, prepare derivative works, distribute copies of the work and perform or display the work publicly. **The key to determining whether the state claim is preempted by federal copyright law is the presence of an "extra element" beyond the acts of reproduction, performance, distribution or display protected by § 106**. The court analyzed whether the state causes of action granted or destroyed equivalent rights to the exclusive rights of copyright law to each of the student's claims for breach of fiduciary duty, intentional infliction of emotional distress and unjust enrichment.

The claim against the professor for breach of fiduciary duty required a showing that a position of influence has been acquired, and abuse. These were extra elements beyond the protection of § 106 and were not preempted by the Copyright Act. The claim for intentional infliction of emotional distress required proof of extreme and outrageous conduct arising from the unauthorized reproduction of her work. Similarly, the claim for unjust enrichment alleged that the automaker benefited from the unauthorized copying of artwork. Since the claims for intentional infliction of emotional distress and unjust enrichment relied on conduct that would be protected by copyright law, both claims failed and the defendants were entitled to summary judgment.

The student's claim that she was entitled to a share of the automaker's profits was speculative, because there was no showing that any such profits were attributable to the alleged copyright infringement. Her claim for a share of indirect profits also lacked sufficient proof, since the brochures benefited the automaker only indirectly in the form of good will. There was no way to reasonably calculate indirect profits arising from copyright infringement, and summary judgment was appropriate. The student would be limited to claims for actual and statutory damages in the event that she prevailed on any of her claims in further proceedings. *Rainey v. Wayne State Univ.*, 26 F.Supp.2d 963 (E.D.Mich.1998).

In a separate opinion, the court considered motions for partial summary judgment by the university and professor based on Eleventh Amendment sovereign immunity. The U.S. Supreme Court has construed the Eleventh Amendment to prevent citizens from suing their own states in federal court. States, their agencies, and employees sued in their official capacities are thus shielded from suits seeking monetary or retrospective relief. The court found no question that the Eleventh Amendment barred the student's claims against the university for monetary damages, since the university was a state instrumentality and any payment to her would come from the state coffers. The injunctive relief sought by the student was moot since all of her artwork and materials had been returned.

The damage claims against the professor in his official capacity were dismissed, since they would require the payment of state monies. However, the court retained jurisdiction over any claims against him in an individual capacity. The copyright claims against the university and professor for injunctive relief were not barred, but appeared to be moot in view of the return of the student's artwork. The student was required to show cause why this claim should not be dismissed. *Rainey v. Wayne State Univ.*, 26 F.Supp.2d 973 (E.D.Mich.1998).

♦   *A public university in Texas was entitled to immunity in a lawsuit filed by an author who asserted copyright violations for the university's publication of her book without consent. The U.S. Court of Appeals, Fifth Circuit, held that Congress did not have the power to force state entities to submit to federal court lawsuits as a price of doing business regulated by the Lanham and Copyright Acts.*

The author asserted that the University of Houston violated federal copyright law by publishing her book without consent, and violated the Lanham Act by naming her as the selector of plays in another book without her permission. She sued the university in a federal district court, which denied dismissal motions based on the university's claims of immunity. The Fifth Circuit then held that the university had impliedly waived Eleventh Amendment immunity by contracting with the author, because Congress had imposed statutory waivers of immunity in both the Copyright and Lanham Acts.

The U.S. Supreme Court remanded the case for reconsideration under *Seminole Tribe of Florida v. Florida*, 517 U.S. 44 (1996), which held that abrogation of a state's Eleventh Amendment immunity requires an expression of Congressional intent and a constitutionally valid exercise of power. On remand to the Fifth Circuit, the author asserted that the university impliedly waived state sovereign immunity and that Congress retained the power to abrogate state immunity under both federal acts under Article I of the Constitution.

The court held that the *Seminole Tribe* case had rejected the implied waiver theory relied upon by the author. Under *Seminole Tribe*, a state's waiver of immunity cannot be implied simply because the state conducts business in an area subject to federal regulation. **The express provisions of the Copyright and Lanham Acts purporting to require this consent were held outside the power of Congress under Article I.** The court also rejected the author's alternative argument that she had been deprived of property without due process of law by the university's purported violations of federal law.

The author's statutorily-created right to protect her name from misappropriation under the Lanham Act was not a property right protected by the Due Process Clause of the Fourteenth Amendment. **Congress had no power to subject states to federal court lawsuits for Lanham Act violations.** The copyright claim was one for breach of contract, which could not be treated as a procedural due process violation in federal court. The author's theory of recovery amount to a direct end-run around *Seminole Tribe*, and her claims against the university had to be dismissed. *Chavez v. Arte Publico Press*, 157 F.3d 282 (5th Cir.1999).

Subsequently, the Supreme Court decided *Florida Prepaid Postsecondary Educ. Expense Bd. v. College Savings Bank*, 119 S.Ct. 2199, 144 L.Ed.2d 575 (1999) and *College Savings Bank v. Florida Prepaid Postsecondary Educ. Expense Bd.*, 119 S.Ct. 2219, 144 L.Ed.2d 605 (1999). The Fifth Circuit again considered the case and held that the Copyright Remedy Clarification Act was not a valid exercise of legislative authority as applied to the states. As a result, the university was entitled to be dismissed from the suit under the Eleventh Amendment. *Chavez v. Arte Publico Press*, 204 F.3d 601 (5th Cir.2000).

III. PATENTS

A patent is a legally protected property interest that gives the owner the right to exclude others from making, using, selling, offering for sale, or importing the invention covered by the patent. Patents generally run for a period of 20 years from the effective filing date of the patent application. To be patentable, an invention must be useful; it must be new or novel; and it must be non-obvious.

♦   *The Eleventh Amendment bars federal court lawsuits by private parties against states under the Patent Remedy Act and the Lanham Act.*

Recently, the Supreme Court decided two cases involving the same parties and the same dispute. In *Florida Prepaid Postsecondary Educ. Expense Bd. v. College Savings Bank*, 119 S.Ct. 2199, 144 L.Ed.2d 575 (1999), **the Court held that Congress' abrogation, under the Patent Remedy Act, of states' sovereign immunity from patent infringement suits was not constitutional.** Building on its earlier decision in *Seminole Tribe of Florida v. Florida*, 517 U.S. 44, 116 S.Ct. 1114, 134 L.Ed.2d 252 (1996), where it held that Congress does not have the power to abrogate a state's sovereign immunity under Article I of the Constitution, the Court found that Congress had overstepped its bounds. Although patents can be considered property within the meaning of the Due Process Clause, there was no indication here that the Patent Remedy Act had been enacted under the authority of the Fourteenth Amendment. Rather, the legislation was authorized by Article I, and thus improperly removed states' sovereign immunity.

The case arose after College Savings Bank, which owned and marketed a patented investment methodology designed to finance the costs of college education, discovered that the state of Florida was selling a similar product. The bank brought separate actions against the state for patent infringement and false advertising under the Lanham Act. In the patent infringement action, the Court determined that Florida could not be sued without its consent where it had merely engaged in interstate commerce.

In the false advertising action, the Court held that **the Trademark Remedy Clarification Act also did not validly abrogate states' Eleventh Amendment immunity from a suit brought under the Lanham Act.** Although Congress may remove a state's sovereign immunity under § 5 of the Fourteenth Amendment, there must be a property interest involved for it to do so. However, there was no property interest at stake in a false advertising suit under the Lanham Act. Further, the state of Florida had not constructively waived its immunity by engaging in interstate commerce. *College Savings Bank v. Florida Prepaid Postsecondary Educ. Expense Bd.*, 119 S.Ct. 2219, 144 L.Ed.2d 605 (1999).

• *An employee's lawsuit against her former advisor and his company could not succeed, for the most part, because he did not own the patents in which she claimed an ownership interest.*

An employee of the University of Chicago held a Ph.D. in molecular genetics and cell biology. She conducted research there in the alteration of DNA under the supervision of her advisor, who held an endowed chair, a distinguished service professorship in virology at the university. After 14 years, she was allegedly barred from future work in the laboratory and was told that she would be fired if she did not resign. She learned that **the university had patented three inventions involving altered Herpes Simplex Viruses, listing either itself or a subsidiary corporation as the owner of the patents.** She sued the university, the subsidiary, the advisor and a private company co-founded by the advisor which was licensed to use the patents, alleging a number of claims, including that she should have been listed as the sole inventor of one of the inventions, and as a joint inventor on the other two. The advisor and the private company sought to be dismissed from the lawsuit.

The U.S. District Court for the Northern District of Illinois noted that **the advisor was not a proper party to the cause of action regarding patent** ownership because he was not an owner of the patents. Further, **the employee had consented to work for the university under its rules of employment, one of which was that all inventions would be owned by the university.** The court also found that the advisor had no fiduciary duty to the employee regarding the patenting of laboratory discoveries. However, it refused to dismiss the cause of action for conversion against the advisor. There was an issue of fact as to whether the advisor had taken her diagrams, drawings, writings and documentation. Finally, the court dismissed the action against the private company, as it had not authorized any of the acts alleged by the employee. In fact, it did not come into existence until after much of the alleged activity had occurred. Only the conversion claim remained against the advisor. *Chou v. Univ. of Chicago*, 2000 U.S. Dist. LEXIS 2002 (N.D.Ill., 2000).

◆   *Where conflicting evidence was presented to a jury, its award for breach of a licensing agreement was upheld.*

A professor of obstetrics and gynecology at the Medical College of Wisconsin invented a cervical cancer screening procedure and assigned the patent to the college. The college licensed exclusive worldwide rights to market the procedure to a company. Subsequently, the company sued the college and the professor for breaching the licensing agreement, and a jury ruled in its favor, awarding the company $10 million to compensate it for its losses. **The college and professor appealed the amount of the damage award, asserting that the company was a startup business that had never been profitable and that the award of $10 million was speculative. Thus, the award did not meet the standard of reasonable certainty.** The Court of Appeals of Wisconsin affirmed the award. It noted that the company was not a new and untried business venture because there was credible evidence in the record of its history, progress and experience since its inception to justify the award. Since there was sufficient evidence to support the jury's award, the court could not overturn it. *NTL Processing, Inc. v. Medical College of Wisconsin*, 2000 Wisc. App. LEXIS 229 (Wis.App., 2000).

◆   *An engineer working for a university as a graduate student failed to prove that the university fraudulently obtained a patent for his invention.*

A senior design engineer at General Motors became acquainted with a professor at the University of West Virginia while touring the facilities. The engineer subsequently quit his job and entered graduate school so that he could work with the professor. While working in the lab, the engineer reviewed prior art work related to wireless power transmission. After examining a prior art antenna, the engineer came up with a contrawound toroidal helical antenna and reviewed it with the professor. **He was informed by the professor that the university's patent policy paid inventors a 30 percent royalty and that inventors were required to cooperate fully with the university in the patent process.**

The engineer listed the professor as a co-inventor on the Disclosure of Invention form, and both men signed it. They also signed the patent application and assigned all rights in the antenna to the university. Subsequently, the engineer invented an improvement to the technology and notified the university of it. The university later filed a patent application on this improvement without the engineer's signature after it received no response from him upon its request for his cooperation.

Some years later, a lawsuit was filed regarding the patents. The engineer claimed that the university had committed fraud and misrepresentation, and had coerced him into naming the professor as a co-inventor, while the university claimed that the engineer had breached his contractual duty to assign patent rights. The court first found that the statute of limitations barred the engineer's fraud claims against the university because more than two years had elapsed. However, even if they were timely, they could not succeed because they did not establish the elements of fraud; nor could the engineer prove those claims by clear and convincing evidence. The court then found that **the engineer had breached his duty to the university under contract and common law to assign patent rights.** Accordingly, the court ruled in favor of the university in all respects. *Univ. of West Virginia Bd. of Trustees v. VanVoorhies*, 84 F.Supp.2d 759 (N.D.W.Va.2000).

♦   *A university could not modify a patent policy unilaterally to decrease the amount it owed a professor.*

The University of California hired an associate professor to teach and do research in the department of pomology. The professor concentrated his research on the genetics of strawberries. At the time of his hire, the professor signed a patent agreement which provided that employees were required to assign inventions and patents to the university, but that they would be assigned royalties pursuant to the university's patent policy. **The patent policy stated that employees would get 50 percent of the net royalties and fees received from their inventions. Subsequently, the university announced its intention to revise the patent policy,** reducing the percentage of royalties it would pay to inventors. When the professor invented six new strawberry cultivars, he informed the university, which notified him that the inventions would be governed by the revised patent policy. The professor sued the university for a declaration that the original patent agreement was in effect and that he was entitled to 50 percent of the net royalties. The trial court granted him pretrial judgment, and the university appealed.

The California Court of Appeal affirmed the decision for the professor. Because the written patent agreement signed by the professor was a valid contract, the university could not unilaterally modify it. **Even though the patent agreement did not state that the professor would get 50 percent royalties, it did state that the patent policy would be followed.** Further, the patent policy in place at the time of signing declared that employees would receive 50 percent of net royalties. As a result, the patent policy was incorporated into the patent agreement and could not be modified by the university without the professor's consent. The policy was not a mere personnel policy which the university could unilaterally modify. *Shaw v. Regents of the Univ. of California*, 58 Cal.App.4th 44, 67 Cal.Rptr.2d 850 (1997).

♦   *A university held enforceable patents to DNA technology. However, specific claims under one patent were invalid because they did not adequately describe the patentable material, and the other patent was not infringed because the process the defendant used was sufficiently different from the university's patent.*

The Regents of the University of California brought a patent infringement action against a company over recombinant DNA technology. They asserted claims under two patents: the '525 patent and the '740 patent. An Indiana federal court held that the asserted claims of the '525 patent were invalid for failure to provide an adequate written description of the subject matter of the asserted claims. It also found that the company had not infringed the '740 patent, and finally determined that the '525 and '740 patents were unenforceable. The regents appealed to the U.S. Court of Appeals, Federal Circuit.

The appellate court held that **the claims of the '525 patent that the university asserted against the company were invalid.** To fulfill the written description requirement, a patent specification must describe an invention in sufficient detail that one skilled in the art can clearly conclude that the inventor invented the claimed invention. **An adequate DNA description requires more than a reference to a potential method for isolating it; it requires a description of the DNA itself.** Because no sequence information indicating which nucleotides constitute human cDNA appeared in the patent, the specification did not provide an adequate written description of the claims asserted. However, the '525 patent was enforceable. The alleged misrepresentation in the patent application was not material to patentability.

With respect to the '740 patent, the court held that the company did not infringe the patent either literally or under the doctrine of equivalents. Here **the university surrendered coverage of DNA that encoded a fusion protein in order to overcome prior art. Accordingly, it could not now assert that the surrendered subject matter was "within the range of equivalents."** The material used by the company for expressing its fusion protein was not equivalent to the protected materials. However, the '740 patent was also held to be enforceable. The university did not have to submit cumulative prior art to the Patent and Trademark Office. Finding that it had no intent to deceive, the court reversed the lower court decision on enforceability. *Regents of the Univ. of California v. Eli Lilly & Co.*, 119 F.3d 1559 (Fed.Cir.1997).

♦   *A state university could not obtain a dismissal of the lawsuit brought against it to determine the validity of a patent because the act of acquiring a patent requires a waiver of Eleventh Amendment immunity.*

Two companies attempted to negotiate the sale of a limited-use license in a Dynamic Cooling Device technology that would be used in conjunction with a laser skin treatment process they marketed. The University of California, which owned the patent on the technology, granted an exclusive license to another corporation. The two companies sued the university, seeking a legal judgment that the patent was invalid, and the university sought to dismiss the lawsuit on the grounds that it was immune from suit under the Eleventh Amendment.

A California federal court noted that this was not a case like *College Savings Bank* and *Florida Prepaid*, above, where a state was merely engaging in "otherwise lawful activity." Rather, this was a case asserting the invalidity of a patent—an integral part of the patent scheme as a whole. The court stated that the **Patent Remedy Act clearly and unmistakably requires a waiver of Eleventh Amendment immunity upon the acquisition of a patent (with respect to a declaratory suit over the validity of a patent).** Congress could require such a waiver because a patent constitutes a gift or gratuity bestowed by the federal government. Accordingly, the court denied the university's motion to dismiss the suit. *New Star Lasers, Inc. v. Regents of the Univ. of California*, 63 F.Supp.2d 1240 (E.D.Cal.1999).

♦ *A university was entitled to damages for a company's willful infringement of its patents, but it was not entitled to a repatriation order compelling the return of material exported from the country.*

A doctor working with Johns Hopkins University discovered an antigen that appears on the surface of immature stem cells but not on the surface of mature cells. This allowed for the relatively pure suspension of stem cells which could be used for transplantation after radiation therapy. The university applied for and received two patents with respect to this discovery. **Four years later, a scientist at a research center developed a method of physically separating stem cells from mature cells that was similar to the method disclosed in the university's patents.** The scientist formed a company that began to use the method and also developed machines that it sold to be used in conjunction with the antibody to perform the scientist's separation method. The company knew of the university's patents, but obtained an opinion letter, which stated that the claims in the patents were invalid and unenforceable.

In the infringement lawsuit that arose, the U.S. District Court for the District of Delaware held that **the company had infringed on the patents.** A jury then assessed over $2.3 million dollars in damages against the company for willful infringement, and the court ordered the company to repatriate all clones or subclones it had exported from the country. The company appealed to the U.S. Court of Appeals, Federal Circuit, which agreed that the company had infringed the patents, that **the infringement had been willful, and** that **the damages award was proper.** However, it found that the repatriation order was improper, and also found that there was an issue of fact yet to be tried as to whether the claims in one of the patents were anticipated or obvious based on evidence the district court refused to admit. The court affirmed in large part the holding of the district court in favor of the university. *Johns Hopkins Univ. v. CellPro, Inc.*, 152 F.3d 1342 (Fed.Cir.1998).

♦ *The U.S. Court of Appeals, Federal Circuit, vacated judgments for punitive damages of $1 million and total damages of over $44 million in a case filed by the University of Colorado, which sought to hold a laboratory liable for fraudulent nondisclosure and unjust enrichment with regard to a prenatal multivitamin mineral supplement. The district court had improperly looked to state law fraudulent nondisclosure and unjust enrichment claims, rather than to federal patent law.*

The university claimed that its researchers invented the supplement and communicated the invention to a chemist employed by the laboratory. It further alleged that the chemist intentionally omitted the researchers as coinventors in the patent application and that the laboratory's corporate parent concealed the patent from the researchers. The university sued the corporation in a federal district court for fraudulent nondisclosure and patent and copyright infringement, seeking restitution and disgorgement of profits from sales.

Applying state common law rather than federal patent law, the court held that the researchers had invented the supplement and that the chemist was not an inventor. The court found the corporation liable to the university for fraudulent nondisclosure and unjust enrichment, arriving at a total damage award of over $44 million. The researchers were entitled to punitive damage awards of $500,000 each. The court held for the corporation on the copyright infringement claim and the correction of inventorship and equitable patent title claims.

The parties appealed unfavorable aspects of the decision to the Federal Circuit, which found it significant that the researchers made no attempt to patent the supplement and had no patent rights to enforce. The state law claims for fraudulent nondisclosure and unjust enrichment covered a broad range of conduct that did not bear on federal patent policy and were thus not preempted. These claims arose not from an attempt to enforce intellectual property rights, but instead from alleged wrongful use of research results. Nonetheless, the fraudulent nondisclosure and unjust enrichment claims depended on the researchers' status as inventors.

The law of inventorship was developed solely under federal law, and preempted any state law purporting to define such rights. The district court had erroneously looked to state law in reaching its decision that the researchers had invented the supplement, and the Federal Circuit vacated this part of the decision. For the same reason, the district court decision regarding fraudulent nondisclosure was vacated. On remand, the district court would be required to apply federal standards to these questions. The court also took issue with certain findings of fact by the district court, observing that the researchers freely shared their research with the chemist and made no patent application. Moreover, the university was not in the business of manufacturing or marketing prenatal vitamins.

If on remand the researchers were found to be inventors of the supplement, the corporation could only be held liable for the payment required to secure their cooperation in filing required patent documents, an assignment of ownership rights and/or an exclusive license from the university. "In particular[,] the court should consider that university licensing barely existed as of the filing date of the '634 patent in 1981. In fact, the Bayh-Dole Act, which set the stage for modern university licensing went into effect less than six months before the '634 patent's filing date. See 35 U.S.C. § 200 (1994)."

The court vacated the unjust enrichment liability finding of the district court, as well as the award of summary judgment to the corporation on the correction of ownership claim. It also vacated summary judgment for the university on its claim for equitable title. The district court had properly held that the university failed to show copyright infringement and the court remanded the case. *Univ. of Colorado Foundation, Inc. v. American Cyanamid Co.*, 196 F.3d 1366 (Fed.Cir.1999).

◆ *Two scientists employed by a university could sue a licensee for fraud in procuring the licensing agreement and for interfering in their contractual relationships with the university.*

Two California scientists sued their university regents and a patent licensee for a number of claims arising from their invention of a process in magnetic resonance imaging (MRI). The scientists assigned their rights to the invention to the university under patent agreements signed at the beginning of their employment. The patent agreements uniformly required the assignment of inventions to the university in return for the payment to the scientists of half the collected royalties.

The scientists initially disclosed the invention to the university patent office with a form indicating that an employee of the licensee was a coinventor. They then entered into the required assignment agreement with the university, which in turn entered into a license agreement with the licensee. Under the agreement, the licensee paid the university $25,000 for the exclusive right to the patent. **The scientists asserted that the market value of the invention was substantially higher than the $25,000 paid by the licensee, and that agents of the licensee had defrauded the university by grossly underrepresenting its value at the same time they were assuring other parties, including themselves, of its great value.** The scientists sued the university and licensee in a federal district court, asserting 10 causes of action, including a claim that the university had a duty to properly investigate the nature and origin of the invention before entering what they claimed was a grossly one-sided agreement.

The court awarded summary judgment to the university on many of the claims against it, ruling that the scientists could not properly rescind the patent assignment agreement, and that they could not prevail on any of their tort claims. It also held that the university had no contractual obligation to obtain a running royalty from the licensee in exchange for the grant of the exclusive license. The court rejected the scientists' argument that the university's decision to enter into the licensing agreement was arbitrary and capricious, observing that they had themselves disclosed to the university that an employee of the licensee was a coinventor and had never challenged this status.

The court further held that **the university's acceptance of only $25,000 for the licensing agreement was not arbitrary and capricious.** There was evidence that the university's negotiating position was limited by its desire to maintain a research funding relationship with the licensee and that the licensee in turn was unwilling to pay a royalty because of its ownership of the patent to a compound used in the MRI patent at issue. The decision did not reach the other contract-based claims by the scientists against the university, including the claim that it had a contractual duty to the scientists to conduct an inventorship audit and to properly inform itself of the nature and value of the invention. *Kucharczyk v. Regents of the Univ. of California*, 946 F.Supp.2d 1419 (N.D.Cal.1996).

The university then moved for summary judgment on the remaining claims against it, including whether it had a duty to determine inventorship and any obligation to the scientists in granting the license to the licensee. The court denied summary judgment on the inventorship and breach of contract claims. It later denied summary judgment to the licensee to allow further pretrial discovery by the scientists.

Subsequently, the parties filed or renewed various motions, including the scientists' claim that the university had contractual obligations to them under various theories arising from the university patent and assignment agreements and patent policy. The court held that the university patent policy vested the university with substantial discretion when fulfilling its role in the intellectual property system. There was no evidence that it acted in bad faith, and the scientists themselves had failed to submit correct information regarding inventorship. The absence instead supported the notion that the university and scientists were victims of misinformation by the licensee. The university was entitled to summary judgment on the contract claims asserting a duty to investigate the true nature of the invention, make a determination of inventorship, and the invention's true value.

The court granted the licensee's summary judgment motion on the inventorship claim, holding that **the scientists had no standing to contest inventorship, since they had relinquished their rights to the patent when executing the assignment agreement with the university.** Despite dismissal of this claim, they were free to establish in their tort claims that the licensee fraudulently caused them (and the university) to believe that the employee was a coinventor. The licensee was entitled to summary judgment on the contractual breach claims for the same reasons that the university could not be held in breach of contract.

However, the scientists submitted sufficient evidence regarding fraudulent conduct by the licensee to deny summary judgment on two remaining tort claims, so that these issues would proceed for a trial. For example, an employee of the licensee asserted that the patent had great commercial value. In the joint application for a $150,000 research grant between the university and licensee, the licensee asserted that annual revenues arising from commercialization of the MRI patent would yield annual revenues in excess of $280 million. The question of whether the licensee had defrauded the scientists and university could proceed to trial, along with the question of whether it had interfered with the scientists' contractual relationships with the university.

The court found that the scientists were third party beneficiaries to the research funding agreement between the university and licensee, and thus had standing to sue the licensee for breaching the agreement. There was a genuine fact issue as to whether this agreement had been breached, and the licensee was denied summary judgment on this issue. Finally, the court held that the university's patent office director was entitled to summary judgment for alleged constitutional rights violations. *Kucharczyk v. Regents of the Univ. of California*, 48 F.Supp.2d 964 (N.D.Cal.1999).

IV. TRADEMARKS

A trademark, defined at 15 U.S.C. § 1127, is any word, name, symbol or device, or any combination thereof used to identify and distinguish goods, including a unique product, from those manufactured or sold by others, and to indicate the source of the goods, even if the source is unknown. Service marks are identical to trademarks in all respects except that they are intended to indicate the origin of services, rather than goods. Trade dress is defined as the total image of a product, and includes features such as size, shape, color, color combinations, texture, graphics or sales techniques. Although trademark issues arise in higher education, they occur much less frequently than copyright and patent issues.

Section 43(a) of the Lanham Act, 15 U.S.C. § 1125(a), creates a federal cause of action for unfair competition in interstate commercial activities. It forbids unfair trade practices involving infringement of trade dress, service marks or trademarks, even in the absence of federal trademark registration. See, for instance, *Two Pesos, Inc. v. Taco Cabana, Inc.*, 505 U.S. 763 (1992). Under § 43(a), civil liability exists in cases where a person "on or in connection with any goods or services, ... uses in commerce any word, term, name, symbol, or device, or any combination thereof, or any false designation of origin, false or misleading description of fact, or false or misleading representation of fact, which—

(A) is likely to cause confusion, or to cause mistake, or to deceive as to the affiliation, connection, or association of such person with another person, or as to the origin, sponsorship, or approval of his or her goods, services, or commercial activities by another person, or
(B) in commercial advertising or promotion, misrepresents the nature, characteristics, qualities, or geographic origin of his or her or another person's goods, services, or commercial activities..."

According to one court, the "touchstone test" for a violation of § 43(a) is the likelihood of confusion resulting from the defendant's adoption of a trade dress similar to the plaintiff's. See *Original Appalachian Artworks, Inc. v. Toy Loft, Inc.*, 684 F.2d 821 (11th Cir.1982).

❖ *In the following case, the University of Florida was unable to demonstrate a violation of § 43(a) of the Lanham Act by the producer of a commercial study guide because it was unable to prove two of the three elements of a § 43(a) violation. There was no proof that the university had information that was inherently distinctive or that had acquired a secondary meaning, and the information was not primarily non-functional.*

A publishing company hired students to take lecture notes from various courses offered by the University of Florida to produce commercial study guides for sale to other students at the university. The university claimed that this arrangement violated federal copyright law, and it sued the publisher in a federal district court for copyright infringement, false representation of origin and deceptive advertising. The court entered judgment for the publisher, and the university appealed to the U.S. Court of Appeals, Eleventh Circuit. It argued that the district court had improperly denied its motions for judgment on the statutory and common law copyright infringement claims, and that the court erred in directing verdicts for the publisher on the false representation of origin and deceptive advertising claims.

The court held that the university was not entitled to judgment on the copyright infringement claims, since this would require the court to review the propriety of the district court's pre-trial rulings, which did not evaluate evidence that was later presented at trial. The university also failed to demonstrate liability for false representation of origin under § 43(a) of the Lanham Act (15 U.S.C. § 1125(a)). It failed to satisfy the **three elements for § 43(a) liability, namely that (1) the mark sought to be protected is inherently distinctive or has acquired a secondary meaning, (2) the mark is primarily non-functional and (3) the defendant's mark is confusingly similar**.

The university had conceded that the information it sought to protect was functional and nondistinctive, and there was no merit to its argument that it was entitled to Lanham Act protection by satisfying the third element alone. Because there was no substantial evidence that the university's information was both distinctive and nonfunctional, the court affirmed the directed verdicts for the false representation of origin and deceptive advertising claims. *Univ. of Florida v. KPB, Inc.*, 89 F.3d 773 (11th Cir.1996).

♦   *Where an invention was created on university time, with university materials, by employees who were paid to do the work that led to the invention, the employees had no ownership rights to the invention.*

In one of the few cases addressing the issue of ownership rights to an invention, the Supreme Court of North Carolina held that **professors and researchers employed at North Carolina State University did not acquire any interest in a secret process for the use of lactobacillus acidophilus they discovered using resources provided them by the university.** The employees here were hired, among other things, to do exactly what they did. Their invention was created on university time, with university materials, and they were paid to do the work. When they notified the university of their discovery, it was determined that the process was not patentable. A trademark was then obtained and a nonprofit dairy foundation was selected to develop and market the process. Subsequently, the employees sued the university and the foundation to impose a constructive trust on the royalties received. The state supreme court ruled against them. It found that because the university owned the process immediately upon its discovery, the employees never possessed an interest in the process that would allow them to share in the royalties. Further, the university's patent policy did not apply because the process was not patentable. Finally, the university did not owe the employees a fiduciary duty to pay a percentage of the royalties. *Speck v. North Carolina Dairy Foundation*, 319 S.E.2d 139 (N.C.1984).

CHAPTER EIGHT

School Liability

I. NEGLIGENCE

Negligence refers to acts or omissions demonstrating a failure to use reasonable or ordinary care. Negligence may refer to inadvertence, carelessness, or the failure to foresee potential harm. Some overlap exists between negligence and intentional misconduct cases. A pattern of negligence by schools and colleges which shows a conscious disregard for safety may be deemed "wilful misconduct," a form of intentional conduct discussed in Section II of this chapter.

A. Duty of Care

The types of tort lawsuits brought against private educational institutions are usually closely related to the tort of negligence, which has three general components: 1) a duty on the part of the school or school officials to protect others from unreasonable risk of harm; 2) the school's failure to exercise the duty of care appropriate to the risk involved; and 3) an injury or loss caused by such failure.

♦ *A university did not breach its duty of care toward a student by detaining him for only 40 minutes after observing him in an altercation with his girlfriend.*

A public safety officer at a New York university saw a student and his girlfriend shouting at and pushing each other. He asked the student and his girlfriend to accompany him to the university's information center, where the operating manager of the center detained the student for 40 minutes. **The student later broke, and jumped through, a window on the fourteenth floor of a dormitory building. He sued the university for his injuries,** alleging that the university was negligent by only detaining him for 40 minutes. The Supreme Court of New York, Appellate Division, held that the student failed to raise an issue of fact for trial that the university had breached a duty of care to him by only detaining him for 40 minutes or that this alleged breach was a proximate cause of his injuries. *Torri v. Hofstra Univ.*, 688 N.Y.S.2d 634 (App.Div.1999).

◆   *A university owed a student a duty to use reasonable care in assigning her to a practicum location.*

A graduate student in psychology at a private Florida university was assigned to an internship (practicum) at a family services agency which was about 15 minutes away from the university's campus. One evening, while leaving the agency, the student was abducted at gunpoint, robbed and sexually assaulted. She sued the university, alleging that it had been aware of a number of criminal incidents that had occurred at or near the agency's parking lot and that it had breached its duty of care to her by assigning her to an unreasonably dangerous internship site. The university sought to dismiss the case, arguing that it did not owe the student a duty of care because it did not own, operate or control the parking lot where the abduction had taken place. A trial court agreed. The District Court of Appeal of Florida reversed and remanded the case, finding that the university owed the student a duty of care. On further appeal, the Florida Supreme Court affirmed. It noted that **because the university required the student to take the internship, and because it assigned her to a specific location, it also assumed the duty of acting reasonably in making that assignment.** Since the university had knowledge that the internship location was unreasonably dangerous, a jury would now have to decide whether the university acted reasonably in placing the student there. The jury would also have to consider the student's knowledge that the internship site was unreasonably dangerous, and assess fault accordingly. *Nova Southeastern Univ. v. Gross*, 2000 Fla. LEXIS 656 (Fla., 2000).

◆   *Where an RA received a serious injury off campus from a student who had been expelled, she was not entitled to recover from the university for her injuries.*

A student at Marquette worked for the university as a resident assistant (RA). One of her duties was to supervise the dormitory room check-out procedure whenever a student left the dorm. When a summer participant in a nationwide program for disadvantaged pre-college students was expelled from the university for inappropriate behavior, the RA was told to supervise the participant when she checked out of her room. The participant was aggressive and uncooperative during the check-out procedure, and eventually the campus police were called. However, by the time they arrived, the participant had gone. The next night, the RA went to a downtown club where she saw the participant. Although she was uncomfortable, she did not leave. Around midnight, as she was leaving, she noticed that the participant was also leaving. The participant taunted her and then hit her in the face with a broken bottle, causing serious injuries.

The RA sued the university for negligence, and a jury ruled that the university was responsible for 80 percent of her injuries. The Court of Appeals of Wisconsin reversed, noting that **even if the university was negligent, the injury was too far removed from the negligence to warrant imposing liability on it.** Further, it was highly unforeseeable that the university's negligence would bring about the kind of harm that resulted. Also, allowing a recovery here could lead to lawsuits even more remote in time and place. **The RA was not entitled to recover anything from the university.** *Conroy v. Marquette Univ.*, 582 N.W.2d 126 (Wis.App.1998).

♦   *A university psychology professor could be liable for negligently referring a suicidal student where he failed to refer the student to someone qualified in suicide prevention.*

A university student with a history of psychological problems sought the guidance of a professor of psychology who was also a psychologist. The professor discovered that the student suffered from depression and had experienced suicidal fantasies almost since elementary school. He only saw the student three times, pursuant to the university's policy of providing only short-term care, and then gave him a list of four people that he could contact for further treatment. None of them were psychiatrists or specialists in suicide prevention. The student selected a specialist in eating disorders, whom he met with for over two years. However, he then terminated his treatment and committed suicide.

His mother sued the professor for negligent referral and the university on the basis of *respondeat superior* as the professor's employer. The court granted the university judgment as a matter of law, and the mother appealed to the Supreme Court of Rhode Island. The supreme court remanded the case for further proceedings on whether the professor negligently referred the student. **A jury could have reasonably concluded that the professor was negligent in failing to refer the student to someone qualified in suicide prevention** or to someone who could prescribe medication that would reduce his suicidal inclinations. *Klein v. Solomon*, 713 A.2d 764 (R.I.1998).

♦   *Where a university knew of a dangerous condition and failed to fix it, it was liable for injuries resulting from that condition.*

A student at Louisiana Tech University (and her roommate) notified the residence assistant on several occasions that the air conditioner in her dorm room was leaking water onto the floor. Although the university twice attempted to fix the problem, leaks reoccurred within 48 hours of each repair. When the student's mother visited her, she slipped on the wet floor, fell, and hurt her knee. After undergoing surgery, she and her husband sued the university and their daughter for negligence. A trial court found the university 100 percent liable for the woman's injuries. It awarded her over $550,000 and awarded her husband $25,000.

The university appealed to the Court of Appeal of Louisiana, which amended and affirmed the lower court's ruling. First, it found that the student was 25 percent at fault for her failure to warn her mother of the wet floor. Because she had knowledge of the dangerous condition, she had a duty to warn. However, **the university also had knowledge of the problem and had attempted to fix it** twice before. **It had the greater responsibility and thus was 75 percent responsible for the woman's injuries.** The court adjusted the damage award to reflect the percentage of fault, awarding the woman $413,000 and her husband $18,000 to be paid by the university. *Varnell v. Louisiana Tech Univ.*, 709 So.2d 890 (La.App.2d Cir.1998).

♦ *A private university was not liable for negligently hiring or failing to supervise its debate coach who murdered one of his students.*

A student at an Alabama university had been a successful member of the debate team since his freshman year. At that time, the university hired a new debate coach and the team became nationally competitive. During his junior year, the student was assigned a topic for an upcoming debate. After months of research, he participated in a practice debate. His team lost and both he and his coach were upset. Later that evening, the student was murdered in his apartment. The coach was convicted of the murder and sentenced to life imprisonment. The student's parents sued the university and coach, alleging that the coach had been acting within the scope of his employment when he killed their son and that the university negligently hired and failed to supervise him. The university filed a motion to dismiss which was granted, and the trial proceeded against the coach. The parents were awarded $12 million but appealed the decision to dismiss the university to the Supreme Court of Alabama.

The court noted that to be acting within the scope of employment, an employee must be pursuing an act that is incident to his employment or that the employer set in motion. It does not arise simply because the act occurred while the person was in the employment of another but rather, it must be shown that the act was at most only a slight, rather than a radical deviation from the employer's business. Here, **the murder of the student was a radical deviation from the university's business and therefore was not within the scope of the coach's employment.** Even if the coach went to the student's apartment to discuss the practice debate, the murder was nonetheless a radical deviation. It was irrelevant whether the deviation occurred before he went to the apartment or while he was there. The court also held that **it was not foreseeable that the coach would commit a murder while working for the university.** Therefore, the university was not liable for negligently hiring or failing to supervise him. The court affirmed the trial court's decision. *Copeland v. Samford Univ.*, 686 So.2d 190 (Ala.1996).

♦ *A jury found that a private college employee's failure to warn others or call the police upon encountering a man carrying a gun and smelling like alcohol on campus did not result in school liability for negligence.*

A man entered the chapel of a Montana private college where he encountered a priest who was preparing for mass. The man became loud and boisterous. The priest smelled alcohol on his breath and noticed that he had a handgun stuck in the front of his pants. He escorted the man out of the chapel and then returned to conduct mass. The man then entered the college's cafeteria and shot a food service employee, as well as another worker. The other worker died and the food service employee sued the college for negligence. She alleged that the college, through the priest and others who observed the man prior to the shooting, was negligent for failing to warn others or call the police. A jury found for the college, and the employee appealed to the Supreme Court of Montana.

The employee had presented evidence that the college breached its duty to provide reasonable security and a reasonably safe place to work. However, the college had presented evidence that it had never before had a problem with transients on campus, had never had a serious crime occur on campus and that the man did not threaten anyone and did not resist when the priest ushered him out of the chapel. Because conflicting evidence was presented, **it was up to the jury to determine the weight to be given to the evidence and to judge the credibility of the witnesses.** The court affirmed the trial court's decision. *Peschke v. Carroll College*, 929 P.2d 874 (Mont.1996).

❖   *Not only may a student advisor have a duty to control his student, his failure to exercise reasonable care to protect minors potentially at-risk from the student's behavior may lead to liability.*

A psychiatric post-graduate student at a New York medical school was accepted into its division of psychoanalytic training in 1986. He told his advisor-instructor that he was a pedophiliac and that he intended to enter into child psychiatry as a profession. Deeming the information confidential, the advisor never attempted to prevent the student from treating children. When the student allegedly sexually assaulted and threatened a mentally retarded ten-year-old minor whom he had been treating for possible suicidal ideation, the minor suffered severe personal injuries. Several years later, the minor sued the school and the advisor in a Connecticut federal court, alleging that the advisor had negligently failed to control the student or to warn his parents of the student's foreseeable conduct. The defendants moved to dismiss the minor's claims.

First, the district court held that the extended statute of limitations for actions involving the sexual abuse of a minor was not limited to the actual perpetrators of the abuse and therefore applied with respect to the advisor. Second, the court held that the advisor at least arguably had a duty to control the student. **The advisor had official authority over the student and had reason to know that he posed a specific threat to minor patients.** Further, he had reasonable mechanisms to control the student's behavior without compromising the confidentiality of his disclosures. For example, steps could have been taken to "redirect the student's professional development." Finally, the court noted that "a psychiatrist who knows or should know that a patient poses a threat to a victim or class of victims has a duty to warn such victims of such danger." **The advisor should have known that a self-confessed pedophiliac who intended to pursue child psychiatry posed a foreseeable threat of harm to minor patients.** Because both the advisor and the college had failed to exercise reasonable care to protect the minor, the court denied the motions to dismiss. *Almonte v. New York Medical College*, 851 F.Supp. 34 (D.Conn.1994).

❖   *A university did not negligently fail to warn when its representatives were unaware of the harm that could result from experiments it was conducting.*

The U.S. Court of Appeals, Fourth Circuit, upheld a lower court's ruling against a diver who allegedly suffered organic brain damage while participating in a simulated deep diving experiment conducted by a Duke University laboratory. The diver was experienced and held a degree in oceanographic technology. He signed an "informed consent" form which detailed the many risks associated with the experiments. After setting the world record for a simulated deep dive of 2,250 feet, the diver suffered organic brain damage. He sued the university in federal court under various legal theories including fraud and negligent failure to warn him of the program's risks. The district court ruled against him and he appealed. The court of appeals agreed with the lower court that because the participant was a highly educated, sophisticated diver who knew that brain damage could result from the experiments, his fraud claim against the university could not succeed. **Even if the university's representatives had concealed the risks of the experiment from the participant, he could not have been harmed since he already knew of those risks but participated in the experiments anyway**. The court of appeals then determined that there was no evidence that the university's representatives were aware that organic brain damage could result from the experiments. The university could not have been guilty of negligent failure to warn him of the risks. The ruling against the diver was upheld. *Whitlock v. Duke Univ.*, 829 F.2d 1340 (4th Cir.1987).

B. Premises Liability

♦   *A university was not liable for the death of a student who fell off the roof of its natatorium.*

A Louisiana university constructed a roof over its swimming pool. The roof's apex stood 56 feet tall, with both sides sloping down to just a few feet off the ground. After campus police reported that a number of students had climbed the roof while intoxicated, and that several of them had fallen and sustained injuries, university officials discussed whether anything should be done about the roof. However, they decided to take no action because the students who had climbed the roof had all appeared to be intoxicated. Subsequently, a 23-year-old senior who had been drinking (and who had a blood alcohol level of .073) decided to climb the roof on his way back to his fraternity house. After reaching the roof's peak, he slipped and fell, suffering head injuries which resulted in his death less than a week later. His parents filed a wrongful death lawsuit against the university and various state entities.

After a trial court dismissed the case, the Court of Appeal of Louisiana affirmed. It noted that **the danger of falling off a roof is open and obvious to everybody. As a result, the roof was not unreasonably dangerous, and the defendants owed no duty to prevent the student from climbing it.** Because there was no hidden defect or disrepair associated with the roof—that is, it was functioning exactly as a roof is supposed to—it was not an unreasonable condition of the roof that caused the injury, but the student's reckless act of climbing it. The university was not negligent and therefore not liable for the student's death. *Robertson v. State of Louisiana*, 1999 La. App. LEXIS 3489 (La.App.1999).

♦   *When a person was injured after slipping on an icy "fire lane" next to a college residence hall, she could not sue under the state's tort claims act.*

A husband and wife operated a snack bar at a Maine technical college. As part of their arrangement with the college, they were permitted to live in an apartment in a residence hall on campus. While walking to the apartment, the wife slipped and fell on the fire lane adjacent to the residence hall. She contended that the college's negligence caused her injuries, asserting that the fire lane was icy and poorly lit. She also asserted that two faculty members who had been hired by the college to plow and sand roads and walkways had performed their jobs negligently. She maintained that they were independent contractors who were liable even if the college wasn't. She sued the college and the faculty members to recover for her injuries. The defendants sought to dismiss the case against them.

The U.S. District Court for the District of Maine noted that the Maine Tort Claims Act provided that a governmental entity is not immune from liability for negligence "in the construction, operation or maintenance of any public building or the appurtenances to any public building." However, it then decided that **the fire lane was not an appurtenance to the residence hall so as to bring the wife's injury within the scope of the exception from immunity.** Further, the court examined the nature of the relationship between the faculty members and the college and found that the faculty members were not independent contractors. It examined eight factors to arrive at the conclusion that they were employees even though they had separate contracts for the plowing and sanding of roads. The court dismissed the case. *Campbell v. Washington County Technical College*, 1999 U.S. Dist. LEXIS 16842 (D.Me., 1999).

◆   *A Texas university had no liability under the state's tort claims act for sexual misconduct that occurred in a dorm room because the room did not cause the alleged injuries.*

The parents of two minor children sued a Texas state university under the Texas Tort Claims Act after they discovered that **a student had taken numerous pictures and videos of their children in sexually explicit poses. Some of the incidents took place in the student's dormitory room,** leading the parents to allege premises liability as well as vicarious liability (on the grounds that the university knew the student was a pedophile and yet continued to rent him a room). The university sought to dismiss the lawsuit, asserting sovereign immunity as a defense. A state court denied the motion, and the university appealed to the Court of Appeals of Texas.

The court of appeals noted that **the state could be liable for premises liability where a condition or use of tangible real property resulted in personal injury. However, the use of the dorm room here did not cause the injuries to the minor children.** It was merely the site at which the student committed his illegal actions. Accordingly, there was no premises liability for the student's sexual misconduct. Further, even if university employees knew of the student's proclivity towards pedophilia, which the university denied, there could be no liability under the tort claims act because the misuse of that knowledge was not a use of real property as would allow for a waiver of sovereign immunity. The court vacated the lower court's decision and dismissed the case. *Lamar Univ. v. Doe*, 971 S.W.2d 191 (Tex.App.1998).

◆   *In a similar case the following year, a similar result was achieved: no liability for a counselor's sexual assault of two youths.*

A counselor in a summer youth program held at a Texas university raped a participant while they were on a field trip at a hotel. Later that night, the counselor returned to the university and attempted to rape another participant who had not gone on the field trip. This assault occurred in a dorm room. Both participants sued the university to recover for their injuries. The university claimed immunity, while the participants claimed that the use of state money to rent a hotel room or a dormitory room was a use of real or personal tangible property that waived immunity under the Texas Tort Claims Act. The Texas Court of Appeals ruled in favor of the university, noting that **the money used to rent the rooms (and the rooms themselves) did not cause the injuries to the participants. The rooms were no more than the settings in which the attacks occurred.** *Scott v. Prairie View A & M Univ.*, 7 S.W.3d 717 (Tex.App.–Houston.1999).

◆ *A private university could be held liable for negligence even though it did not own the property where a student's accident occurred.*

A private university in New York conducted some classes on the campus of another private college. While attending a university class on the college campus, a student was injured when she slipped and fell on a walkway. She sued both the university and the college in a New York trial court, asserting that both institutions were responsible for maintenance of the premises and that they had breached a duty of care to her. The university moved to dismiss the complaint on the ground that it neither owned nor maintained the premises and therefore owed no duty to the student. The trial court denied the motion, and the university appealed to the New York Supreme Court, Appellate Division. The appellate court affirmed because **the university failed to present documentary evidence conclusively establishing that it had no control over or responsibility for maintenance of the common areas of the college campus.** Even though the university did not own the property where the accident occurred, it still might be liable for negligence. *Smuckler v. Mercy College*, 663 N.Y.S.2d 869 (A.D.2d Dept.1997).

◆ *Although landowners owe persons lawfully on their property a duty of reasonable care, they are not required to be guarantors of safe passage.*

A commuter left her job in Virginia amid freezing rain which had begun only an hour earlier. She traveled by subway to a metro station which led to a plaza owned by a Washington, D.C. private university. When she reached the top of the escalator, freezing rain was coating the concrete, fences and surrounding cars. The commuter began sliding immediately after she left the escalator and ultimately fractured her ankle when she fell on the icy pavement. She received medical treatment for her injuries and filed a negligence lawsuit against the university in the U.S. District Court for the District of Columbia. The university filed a motion for summary judgment. The court held that the university had neither a statutory nor a common law duty to clear freezing rain while the storm was in progress. Although landowners owe persons lawfully on their property a duty of reasonable care, they are not required to be guarantors of safe passage. **Landowners are not responsible for damages caused by their failure to remove snow and ice until a reasonable time has elapsed after cessation of the storm.** Because the university did not have such an opportunity and the rainstorm persisted at the time of the accident, the negligence lawsuit had to be dismissed.

Further, because the plaza could not be considered a sidewalk, the university was not liable under the District of Columbia Snow Removal Statute. The court granted the university's motion for summary judgment. *Battle v. George Washington University*, 871 F.Supp. 1459 (D.D.C.1994).

◆   *A private vocational school had a general duty to exercise reasonable care and not to expose its students to unreasonable risks of injury or harm.*

A student at a Louisiana private vocational school proceeded to a small bathroom to collect a urine specimen for the laboratory instruction portion of one of her classes. Upon entering the bathroom, she tripped and fell over a toilet plunger, and landed on her back. Because she was focused on her classroom duties, she failed to observe the plunger which was occasionally used to prop open the bathroom door. An MRI examination and a CAT scan indicated that she suffered from a herniated disk. The student sued the vocational school in a Louisiana trial court seeking compensation for her injuries. The trial court awarded $12,500 in general damages and $3,835 in past medical expenses, finding that her back injuries were more likely due to the fall than to degeneration. The vocational school appealed to the Court of Appeal of Louisiana, which noted that **the student had to prove: 1) that the school's conduct was the cause-in-fact of the injury, 2) that the school owed a duty of care to the student, and 3) that this duty was breached**. The court further noted that the school had a general duty to exercise reasonable care and not to expose its students to unreasonable risks of injury or harm. Here, given the small confines of the bathroom and that the plunger had been improperly used as a doorstop on other occasions, the trial court's finding of liability was not clearly erroneous. The court of appeal also held that the student was not negligent based on comparative fault principles. The holding of the trial court was affirmed. *Butler v. Eastern College of Health Vocations, Inc.*, 631 So.2d 1254 (La.App.5th Cir.1994).

C. Defenses

Several defenses exist which either protect institutions from liability or reduce institutional liability. Public institutions, of course, are generally protected by sovereign immunity. Under certain circumstances, private institutions may also seek immunity under state charitable immunity statutes. However, the institutions must meet the requirements of the statutes to qualify as charitable organizations. More commonly, institutions defend against liability by demonstrating a student's assumption of the risk or contributory negligence. Statutes of limitations provide an additional defense in lawsuits which have been filed after the specific time period designated in such statutes for filing claims.

1. Immunity

◆   *A university was entitled to qualified immunity where the students suing it could not show that they had been deprived of a property interest in their education.*

Two student athletes at an Illinois state university were accused of raping another student. They maintained that the sex had been consensual, and that the accusation of rape had followed from the refusal by one of them to continue a relationship with the student. One of the student athletes was acquitted of all criminal charges, and the other was never charged. Both were, however, required to appear before a hearing board, where one was expelled and the other was suspended indefinitely. The student athletes sued the university and various officials, alleging that they were deprived of a property interest in their education without due process of law. An Illinois federal court dismissed the case, finding that the university was entitled to qualified immunity because the student athletes failed to show that the university violated a clearly established constitutional right, and also that the Eleventh Amendment barred their suit. They appealed to the Seventh Circuit Court of Appeals, which affirmed. **Even if children have a property interest in attending elementary and secondary public schools, the student athletes had not shown that Illinois state law provided them with a property interest in higher education.** The court also noted that the university, as an arm of the state, was immune from suit under the Eleventh Amendment. *Johnson v. Bd. of Trustees of Western Illinois Univ.*, 2000 U.S. App. LEXIS 418 (7th Cir.2000).

◆   *Two students who were injured while traveling to another college to play a soccer game could not sue their college because of a state law granting the college immunity.*

Two members of a community college soccer team were injured when the van they were riding in was involved in a highway accident. While traveling to another college for a soccer match in a van owned by the community college and driven by an assistant coach, the van blew a tire and the coach lost control of the vehicle, causing it to travel across two lanes of oncoming traffic and to flip several times. The players sued the college and the coach to recover for their injuries. The college claimed it could not be sued, citing a California statute that granted immunity to colleges for field trips or excursions in connection with school-related social, educational, cultural, athletic or college band activities to and from places. The statute provided that **persons taking such field trips or excursions are deemed to have waived all claims against the college or the state for any injuries that might result.** The California Court of Appeal affirmed the trial court's grant of summary judgment in favor of the college. Since extracurricular sports programs are "school-related athletic activities," the trip to the other college was covered by the immunity statute, and the students' lawsuit could not succeed. *Barnhart v. Cabrillo Community College*, 90 Cal.Rptr.2d 709 (Ct.App.6th Dist.1999).

◆   *A graduate student's lawsuit against a public university was barred by the Eleventh Amendment.*

A doctoral candidate at the City University of New York (CUNY) decided to switch his major after completing the required classes and written exams, but before completing his dissertation and oral exam. The history department approved the change, and the student found another professor to advise him. Over a year later, the director of the department notified the student that he would have to take more classes and re-take his major written exam. The student contacted the dean of students, who allegedly stated that he believed the student had been wronged by the history department and its director. However, he never convened a hearing. The student then took a two-year leave of absence, and transferred to another program at another university. He sued CUNY, the dean of students and the history department director (in their official capacities) for money damages, including lost income and tuition, alleging that the director was a political leftist who was sympathetic to the PLO, and that the director had taken wrongful action against him because he was a committed and active Zionist. The defendants sought to dismiss the case under Eleventh Amendment immunity, and a federal court granted their request. **Because the state (and not the City of New York) would ultimately be responsible for indemnifying CUNY, the Eleventh Amendment applied to bar the lawsuit against all the defendants.** *Weiss v. City Univ. of New York*, 1999 U.S. Dist. LEXIS 4833 (S.D.N.Y.1999).

◆   *A university student who was raped after getting into the front seat of a taxi in Mexico could not sue the university that had sponsored her trip.*

While participating in a university-sponsored cultural immersion program in Mexico, a student was raped at knifepoint by a taxi driver. The student sued the university for her injuries, and it sought to dismiss the case, asserting that it was immune from liability. The Court of Appeals of Minnesota ruled in favor of the university. It noted that the university was immune from liability for its discretionary decisions. First, the decision to use host families to provide housing was a discretionary decision. So too was the decision not to provide transportation for students in the program. The court also found that the university had warned the student about getting into the front seat of a taxi. It was not required to do more. **Because the university was not the guarantor of the student's safety, and because its decision to design and construct a program allowing students to be immersed in another country's culture was discretionary, the university was entitled to statutory immunity.** *Bloss v. Univ. of Minnesota Bd. of Regents*, 590 N.W.2d 661 (Minn.App.1999).

◆   *Aside from the Eleventh Amendment, state constitutions also provide immunity.*

A graduate student at an Arkansas university failed to obtain his doctorate in Marketing within the seven-year period allowed by the university. He asserted that the professor under whom he was working caused his failure by acting in bad faith and by giving him an unworkable dissertation topic, and then by giving him inaccurate, arbitrary and false information. He sued the board of trustees of the university, as well as several officials and employees for fraud, among other claims. A state court dismissed his suit on the basis of sovereign immunity under the Arkansas Constitution, and the state supreme court affirmed. **Although a person can sue state officials or agencies to stop bad faith and arbitrary and capricious actions, the student's complaint failed to show that any act of the university was in bad faith or arbitrary.** He acknowledged that the university had the discretion to grant an extension to the seven-year period, and that it did not grant extensions in every case. The court also found that the individual defendants were entitled to immunity. *Grine v. Bd. of Trustees, Univ. of Arkansas*, 2 S.W.2d 54 (Ark.1999).

◆   *The Eighth Circuit addressed immunity issues in the following case.*

A women's resource center director and gender equity coordinator for a college in the Minnesota State Colleges and University System was laid off. She subsequently brought suit against the college, its former president, the agency and the state under Title VII, the Equal Pay Act and the First Amendment. A federal court held that the Eleventh Amendment barred her Equal Pay Act claim, and that qualified immunity protected the college's former president with respect to the First Amendment claim. It also concluded that she failed to show that the layoff was a pretext for discrimination under Title VII. She appealed to the Eighth Circuit Court of Appeals, which first held that **Congress had properly abrogated the states' sovereign immunity in the Equal Pay Act.** It then found that the employee failed to present sufficient evidence to support her assertion that she had been laid off for complaining that federal grant funds were not being spent lawfully on gender equity programs. Further, **the college's rehiring of her shortly after the layoff entitled the former president to qualified immunity on her claim under the First Amendment.** Finally, the court concluded that the employee failed to show discrimination under Title VII. The court affirmed the lower court's rulings except for the Equal Pay Act claim, which it remanded for further proceedings. *O'Sullivan v. Minnesota,* 191 F.3d 965 (8th Cir.1999).

◆   *A Virginia college and professor were not entitled to charitable immunity where the professor was not acting on behalf of a charitable institution at the time he injured a beneficiary.*

A professor at a Virginia college established a program with the Boys and Girls Club of Hampton Roads under which students in the professor's recreation programming class were required to spend six hours observing the children and volunteering at the club. The students were required to return to the classroom, design programs for the children, then implement the programs at the club. The professor went to the club to observe his students and help them out when needed. While he was there observing one day, a student asked him to watch a door leading to the weight room. She was giving a talk on wellness and body conditioning to 13- to 18-year-olds and wanted to keep younger students not involved in the program out of the room. The professor closed the door, amputating the right thumb of a minor who had his hand on the doorframe. The minor sued the professor and the college, who sought to dismiss the action on the basis of charitable immunity. The Supreme Court of Virginia noted that the club was a charity and that the minor was a beneficiary of the club. However, **it refused to award the defendants charitable immunity, finding that at the time of the injury, the professor was not engaged in the work of the charity. Rather, he was carrying out his duties as a professor,** observing a student and acting as a "doorkeeper." The court remanded the case for further proceedings consistent with its opinion. *Mooring v. Virginia Weslayan College,* 514 S.E.2d 619 (Va.1999).

◆   *A university could not claim immunity under the Eleventh Amendment where it voluntarily accepted money under Title IX, but a student suing under that statute must sue within the allotted time.*

A student and former athlete at Alabama State University sued the school under Title IX, making a number of allegations, including that a scholarship she had been promised was taken away because of a significant disparity in the amounts allocated to women's athletic programs as opposed to men's programs. The university sought to dismiss the causes of action, asserting that the student had waited too long to sue and that the statute of limitations had passed. The court agreed with respect to the allegation of a significant disparity between funding in the men's and women's programs. The student could not establish a continuing violation of Title IX such that potentially discriminatory behavior in the past would result in continuing liability. However, the court held that some of the student's claims under Title IX survived. It rejected the university's argument that it was entitled to immunity under the Eleventh Amendment. **By voluntarily accepting federal money under Title IX, the university had waived its Eleventh Amendment immunity.** *Beasley v. Alabama State Univ.*, 3 F.Supp.2d 1304, 3 F.Supp.2d 1325 (M.D.Ala.1998).

◆   *In a New Jersey case, a college student who fainted after viewing the vivisection of a rat was precluded from suing the college under the state's charitable immunity statute.*

A New Jersey college student attended a classroom demonstration of a vivisection of an anesthetized laboratory rat. After the procedure began, she left the lab to go to the bathroom and fainted, suffering injuries in the fall. She sued the college and the professor, alleging that her injuries were caused by their negligence. The defendants asserted that they were immune under the state Charitable Immunity Statute and the Tort Claims Act. The case reached the Superior Court of New Jersey, Appellate Division, which agreed. **The college met the requirements for protection under the Charitable Immunity Statute because it was organized for educational purposes.** Since the student was a beneficiary of the college, she could not sue it under the statute. The court also noted that the professor was entitled to immunity under the Tort Claims Act. *Graber v. Richard Stockton College of New Jersey*, 713 A.2d 503 (N.J.Super.A.D.1998).

◆   *The New Jersey charitable immunity statute provided protection to a religious university in a negligence lawsuit arising from the university's operation of a pub on campus.*

A Catholic university in New Jersey operated a pub on campus solely for students and their guests. The pub was not operated for profit, it was subsidized by the student government association, and its employees were students. A 21-year-old senior at the university went with several friends to the pub and slipped in a puddle that was apparently left when a serving cart was moved. He sued the university in a state trial court seeking to recover for his injuries. The court denied the university's motion for a directed verdict and a jury returned a verdict in favor of the student. The university appealed to the Superior Court of New Jersey, Appellate Division.

On appeal, the court noted that the university had deemed the pub to be part of a student's socialization process and a factor in the development of a well-rounded person. The question was whether the state's charitable immunity statute applied to the university while it was running the pub for students and their guests. **Under the statute, nonprofit corporations, societies or associations orga-**

nized exclusively for religious, charitable, or educational purposes could not be held liable for negligence where the person injured as a result of the negligence was a beneficiary, to whatever degree, of the works of the nonprofit corporation, society or association. Because the student was a beneficiary in some degree of the university while patronizing the pub, the university was entitled to charitable immunity under the statute. The court noted that the fact that the pub had since been replaced by a campus coffee house was not critical to the immunity analysis. Since the university had reasonably concluded that a campus experience ought to include opportunities to mature in an environment enriched not only by study and classes, but by diverse forms of social interchange within the university setting, the student was a beneficiary at the time of his injury, and the university was entitled to immunity. *Bloom v. Seton Hall Univ.*, 704 A.2d 1334 (N.J.Super.A.D.1998).

2. Assumption of Risk

♦   *One who participates in sports can impliedly assume the risks which are inherent in that sport, including negligent instruction and supervision. Moreover, signing a release may absolve a school and its employees from liability.*

A student at a private west coast university enrolled in an introductory scuba diving course. At the beginning of the course he signed a number of documents including an "Affirmation and Liability Release." This document released the outside diving firm teaching the course and the Professional Association of Diving Instructors (PADI), from liability. The student completed the course, became certified, and then enrolled in an advanced scuba class. This class was taught by an adjunct professor at the school. The student once again executed a liability release, this time naming PADI and the university. While with the instructor and two other students, he died of an air embolism as a result of too rapid an ascent from a deep water dive. The mother of the student brought a wrongful death action. She alleged that the instructor negligently caused her son's death and that the university was vicariously liable for the negligence of its agent. The instructor and the school countered with the affirmative defenses of release liability and assumption of risk. They were granted pretrial judgment, and the mother appealed to the Court of Appeals of Washington.

In affirming the trial court's decision, the appellate court determined that though the fall liability release did not name the fall instructor, he was nonetheless included as an employee of the university. The general rule is that a pre-injury release of the employer from liability also releases the employee. **The instructor owed no greater duty of care than the school, which was released by contract from liability**. Next, in addressing the assumption of risk issue, the court noted that one who participates in sports impliedly assumes the risks which are inherent in that sport. The student had the option of not taking the class and he was aware of the dangers. Moreover, **by signing the release he expressly assumed the risks of the sport**. Negligent instruction and supervision were clearly risks associated with being a student in a scuba course and were encompassed in the broad language of the release contract. Therefore, pretrial judgment had been properly granted. *Boyce v. West*, 862 P.2d 592 (Wash.App.Div.1993).

♦   *A university could be liable for a student's injuries from attempting to dunk a basketball if he did not assume the risk of injury.*

A student at Cornell University, while playing in a pick-up basketball game, attempted to dunk the ball. He hit his hands on the rigid rim of the basket and fell to the floor, landing on his wrists and sustaining injuries. He and his parents sued the university for negligence, claiming that rigid rims unreasonably increase the risk to a player who is attempting to dunk a basketball. They asserted that the university should have used break-away rims, which give way on contact. The university moved for pretrial judgment, asserting that the student assumed the risk of injury when he attempted to dunk the ball over the rigid rim. **The student asserted that although he knew that he risked falling after attempting the dunk, he did not know of the increased risk that resulted from a rigid rim.** Because he had never been able to jump high enough to dunk the ball before, he did not know how unsafe it could be on a rigid rim. The U.S. District Court for the Northern District of New York held that the risk of hanging up on a rigid rim was not necessarily one that would be perceived by every adult. As a result, it refused to grant pretrial judgment to the university. *Traub v. Cornell Univ.*, 1998 U.S. Dist. LEXIS 5530 (N.D.N.Y.1998).

♦   *Because football is an inherently dangerous sport, a student could not sue after sustaining injuries in a football class.*

A California college student enrolled in an "advanced football" class, which taught appreciation of football and football strategy. Part of the class was devoted to offensive and defensive drills. These were non-contact drills where the offensive players would try to complete a play, and the defensive players would try to stop that play. Once a pass was caught and the offensive player touched, for example, the play would stop. While attempting to catch a pass, the student was hit in the face by a defensive player's elbow. The defender had no intent to harm, but was rather trying to intercept the ball and inadvertently hit the student. The student sustained injuries and sued the college. After the trial court found that the student had assumed the risk of injury, it dismissed the case. The student appealed. The California Court of Appeal affirmed the lower court's ruling. It noted that there are two kinds of assumption of risk: primary and secondary. Primary assumption of risk occurs when a person participates in an activity that carries an inherent risk of injury, and is a complete bar to recovery. Secondary assumption of risk occurs when a defendant breaches a duty of care to a person, but the person nevertheless knowingly encounters the risk created by the breach. This does not create a complete bar to recovery. Rather, comparative negligence principles are used to allocate fault between the parties. **Here, because the risk of injury was inherent in the sport of football, primary assumption of risk barred any recovery by the student.** *Fortier v. Los Rios Community College Dist.*, 45 Cal.App.4th 430, 52 Cal.Rptr.2d 812 (Cal.App.3d Dist.1996).

♦   *Where a student signed waivers assuming the risk of injury, she could not sue a university after sustaining an injury.*

After signing two waivers of liability and an authorization of medical treatment, an Indiana university student participated in a motorcycle training course for beginners. She drove a motorcycle provided by the university into a tree, breaking her arm. She then sued the university for negligence, including failure to provide appropriate equipment and failure to provide appropriate instruction. A state court granted pretrial judgment to the university, and the student appealed. The Court of Appeals of Indiana held that the waivers were not void as against public policy. Here, **the student had agreed that she assumed the risk of injury by participating in the class.** Further, the university did not owe her a statutory duty that voided the waivers she signed. Because the waivers were valid, the university was not liable for the student's injury. *Terry v. Indiana State Univ.*, 666 N.E.2d 87 (Ind.App.1996).

◆   *A university was not liable for injuries a student sustained while sledding into a parking lot.*

When a rare winter snowstorm hit northern Louisiana, a university student went sledding with some fellow students. While riding on a plastic garbage can lid, the student (on his eighth trip down the hill) collided with the concrete base of a light pole in the football stadium parking lot. He sustained head and back injuries resulting in permanent paralysis from the mid-chest down. He and his parents sued the university and the state for negligence, asserting that the university had encouraged dangerous sledding activities and had failed to put cushions on the light poles. A state court granted pretrial judgment to the defendants, finding that the danger of striking a fixed object while sledding was apparent and obvious. The court of appeal reversed, and the case reached the Supreme Court of Louisiana. The supreme court noted that a number of people had testified that the light poles were visible, and that they had tried to warn the student that he was approaching the pole. **Because the conditions of the property were not unreasonably dangerous, and because the dangers of the light poles were apparent and obvious, the university did not have a duty to protect the student.** Further, the university's encouragement of sledding was that it be done in proper areas and using good judgment. Finally, there was no special relationship between the university and the school that created a duty to protect. The supreme court reversed the lower court decision, and ruled in favor of the university. *Pitre v. Louisiana Tech Univ.*, 673 So.2d 585 (La.1996).

D. Damages

The nature and extent of damage awards generally depends upon the nature of the injury and the conduct of the parties. Compensatory damages serve to compensate an injured party for his or her injuries such as medical expenses or pain and suffering. On the other hand, punitive damages serve to punish the offending party because of the party's wilful and wanton conduct.

◆   *Patients who never faced a medically verified substantial risk of contracting HIV did not suffer recognizable damages.*

Six patients received various treatments from several students at an Illinois private university's dental clinic during 1990 and 1991. In July of 1991, the university sent a letter to the patients informing them that a dental student who provided care to the patients was infected with HIV. While the university stated that it was unlikely that they were infected with HIV, it strongly recommended that the patients be tested for the virus. The patients brought an action for damages against the university and the dental student in an Illinois Circuit Court which dismissed their claim. The patients appealed to the Appellate Court of Illinois, First District, which held that **in the absence of a particularly substantial risk of HIV infection, their reasonable fears were not severe enough to warrant compensation**. Because the patients never faced a medically verified substantial risk of contracting HIV, they did not suffer recognizable damages. Therefore, the court affirmed the judgment dismissing the complaint. *Doe v. Northwestern Univ.*, 682 N.E.2d 145 (Ill.App.1st Dist.1997).

◆   *A community college was liable for injuries sustained when a friend of the basketball coach, driving at the coach's direction, got in an automobile accident.*

The head basketball coach of a Kansas community college recruited an Ohio high school senior to play on his team and invited him for a visit. He asked a friend to pick the student up at the airport. The friend lacked a driver's license and liability insurance, and his car was not registered. He was supposed to drive the student to a hotel in El Dorado, but initially traveled to Hutchinson, where the coach had already taken several other recruits to watch a tournament. When the friend arrived in Hutchinson, he called the coach, who told him to drive the student to El Dorado. On the way there, the friend ran a stop sign and collided with a tractor-trailer rig. The friend died, and the student and the semi driver sustained injuries. They sued the college and the coach in federal court, asserting *respondeat superior* liability (that the friend was the servant or employee of the defendants and that he was acting within the scope of his authority at the time of the accident). The court agreed, and **a jury then found the defendants 90 percent liable, assessing 10 percent liability to the semi driver. The student was awarded over $2 million in damages, and the semi driver received over $270,000.** The defendants then moved for a new trial. While that motion was before the court, they settled their case with the student. With respect to the semi driver, the court denied the motion for a new trial. The award of damages was not excessive. *Foster v. Bd. of Trustees of Butler County Community College*, 771 F.Supp. 1122 (D.Kan.1991).

◆   *An injured student under 21 years of age and unemancipated could not recover damages for medical expenses paid by his parents, although his parents were entitled to bring a recovery suit.*

After a student at an east coast private college fell out the window of his dormitory room and was injured he brought a negligence action against the college in a New York trial court. The jury found him 50 percent at fault and awarded him $2.378 million of which he was entitled to one-half. The incident occurred when he fell five stories to the ground through the sliding sash of his dormitory room window while attempting to open the window. On appeal to the Supreme Court, Appellate Division, the court reversed the findings of the trial court and ordered a new trial. The appellate court found that **the question of negligence was impermissibly taken away from the jury** and that the trial court erred in permitting the student to recover for past medical expenses paid by his parents. The court noted that the parents had the absolute duty to pay the medical expenses of the student since he was under 21 years of age and unemancipated.

Although the parents could have brought an action to recover the expenses so incurred, they did not do so. **The student could not maintain an action on his own behalf to recover expenses incurred by his parents.** Since this issue should not have been part of the damages calculation and because of the error on the negligence question a new trial was ordered. *Radcliffe v. Hofstra Univ.*, 606 N.Y.S.2d 333 (A.D.2d Dept.1994).

♦ *Where a private college was found not to have acted wilfully or wantonly towards the safety of its students, an injured student was not entitled to punitive damages.*

Two intoxicated students threw a smoke bomb under the door of another student's room, causing a fire. The fire resulted in death to one student, and injuries to another. The fire alarm failed to warn the students. A lawsuit was filed in a federal district court charging the school and students with wrongful death and other claims. The suit demanded compensatory relief as well as punitive damages. The school moved for pretrial judgment on the demand for punitive damages. **Punitive damages are available only when the wrongdoer has acted wilfully or wantonly.** The court first examined the dormitory supervision system. The plan included having floor and hall monitors, and occasional meetings with residents on safety and other issues. It was not shown that this system was lacking or that the school acted wilfully or wantonly in the supervision of its students. The next argument was that the lack of a policy forbidding the use of alcohol by anyone less than 21 years of age encouraged the drinking which led to the fire. The school countered that it had relied on Delaware law to handle this question. The court found this to be reasonable. The last argument which would allow punitive damages was that the fire alarm system was inoperative and inadequate because it could not detect smoke or heat. Expert testimony was given that the system was appropriate for the conditions at the school. Therefore, the school was found not to have acted wilfully or wantonly towards the safety of the students. Pretrial judgment was granted for the school on the punitive damages issue. *Sterner v. Wesley College, Inc.*, 747 F.Supp. 263 (D.Del.1990).

II. INTENTIONAL CONDUCT

Schools may be found liable for the intentional acts or omissions of school personnel. Additionally, courts have found schools liable for intentional acts of third parties on or near school grounds. In those cases, courts may hold that the school should have foreseen the potential for misconduct.

A. Teacher Misconduct

Common lawsuits against teachers include intentional infliction of emotional distress, defamation, or sexual misconduct. Often, accusations of inappropriate sexual behavior may result in civil as well as criminal action against the teacher.

♦ *A university student could sue for sexual harassment by an instructor under both Title IX and 42 U.S.C. § 1983.*

An Arkansas university student reported sexual harassment by one of her instructors. After the university fired the instructor, the student remained dissatisfied with the university's complaint resolution process and filed a federal district court action against the university, instructor and certain university officials under 42 U.S.C. § 1983 and Title IX of the Education Amendments of 1972. The student sought injunctive relief and monetary damages under § 1983 and raised several claims under Title IX including strict liability for the instructor's action under the theories of *respondeat superior*, failure-to-train and failure to ensure that the university sexual harassment policy was known to employees. The court dismissed several claims on the basis of Eleventh Amendment immunity and qualified immunity, but refused to dismiss the § 1983 claims for injunctive relief against the university and for injunctive relief and monetary damages against the instructor and university assistant president. The Title IX claims against the university, instructor and officials were also retained.

The university and officials appealed to the U.S. Court of Appeals, Eighth Circuit, which rejected the university's claim that Title IX was an unconstitutional exercise of congressional authority. The act came within Congress' powers under the Fourteenth Amendment. There was also no merit to the claim that § 1983 was preempted by the Title IX claim because the U.S. Supreme Court has held that Title IX enforcement mechanisms are not exclusive. The student's claim for strict liability under the theory of *respondeat superior* was dismissed. However, **she was entitled to pursue her remaining § 1983 and Title IX claims against the university since she had a clearly established right not to be harassed.** The court remanded these claims to the district court. *Crawford v. Davis*, 109 F.3d 1281 (8th Cir.1997).

♦   *If a professor's spanking of a student was sexual in nature, then the university could be liable to the student under Title IX.*

While enrolled in a biology class at a Virginia university, a female student took a make-up examination, which her professor immediately evaluated. After reviewing the exam, the professor told her that her performance was unsatisfactory and invited her to his office to review the test. The professor, after reviewing the test with the student, placed her over his knees and spanked her repeatedly with his hand. He then told her that she could re-take the test the next day, but that she should bring a hairbrush with her because he was going to spank her again, even harder, if she did not achieve a certain score. The student left the professor's office and sought medical treatment for sore buttocks. She initiated criminal and administrative proceedings against the professor, which resulted in the professor's conviction for misdemeanor assault and being placed on probation by the university. Subsequently, she sued the university under Title IX, asserting *quid pro quo* sexual harassment (that she was required to submit to the harassment as a condition of receiving an educational benefit). The university sought a pretrial judgment. The U.S. District Court for the Eastern District of Virginia held that **there were questions of fact as to whether the professor's actions in spanking and threatening to spank the student were sexual in nature. However, there was no question that the university was liable for the professor's actions.** Thus, if the spanking and threatened spanking amounted to *quid pro quo* sexual harassment, the university would be liable. The court refused to grant pretrial judgment to the university. *Kadiki v. Virginia Commonwealth Univ.*, 892 F.Supp. 746 (E.D.Va.1995).

* *When a student settled a slander claim against a college, he could not pursue the claim against the professor who committed the act.*

A sociology professor allegedly ordered a student to leave his classroom, then slandered him in a 30-minute tirade to the remaining students. Subsequently, the student entered into a settlement agreement with the college, which released the college, its officers, agents and employees from any liability for any alleged slander committed by the professor. The release did not prevent the student from suing the professor for actions outside the scope of his authority as an employee. When the student sued the professor for slander, a state trial court granted pretrial judgment to the professor. The Supreme Court of Montana affirmed, finding that **the student was statutorily barred in his suit against the professor by reason of his settlement with the college. A state law provided that recovery against a governmental entity barred recovery against the employee whose wrongful act caused the harm.** *Stansbury v. Lin*, 848 P.2d 509 (Mont.1993).

* *A Louisiana appellate court held a professor liable for defamation and intentional infliction of emotional distress for comments he made to other students about an incident with the defamed student.*

A first year professor at a private Louisiana law school recounted an embarrassing experience during which a female law student fell off her chair in a local nightclub. Upset at the comment, the female law student asked, "why didn't you help me up?" The professor replied, "I ain't picking no slut up off the floor." When confronted by the chancellor, the professor denied calling her a slut. During a subsequent class, the professor threatened to give bad grades to any student who testified against him. Eventually, the professor publicly apologized and the law student was allowed to transfer to another class. She suffered emotional injuries and sued the professor for defamation and intentional infliction of emotional distress (IIED). The trial court held that although defamation had occurred, the law student had failed to prove IIED or loss of reputation and granted her only $1,500 plus interest and costs. The professor appealed to the Court of Appeal of Louisiana. The court of appeal determined that **the professor's statements amounted to defamation** *per se* (on its face). Consequently, the court presumed that **the statements were both false and malicious**. The professor was liable for damages as well as for IIED. Thus, the defamatory comments coupled with the emotional distress justified an increase in damages to $5,000. *Smith v. Atkins*, 622 So.2d 795 (La.App.4th Cir.1993).

* *A university could not be held liable for a professor's "battery" against a woman.*

While at a woman's house as a social guest, a university professor walked up behind the woman and touched her back with both of his hands, mimicking the movement of pressing and releasing the keys of a piano keyboard. He did this to demonstrate the sensation of the movement by a pianist, not to cause any harm. However, the woman sustained injuries as a result of the touching and sued the university under the Idaho Tort Claims Act. The university asserted that it was immune from liability because the touching amounted to a "battery" under the law. The university, as a governmental entity was immune from liability for any injuries arising out of a battery committed by an employee. The case reached the Supreme Court of Idaho, which held that for a civil battery to be committed, there need not be any intent to cause harm; there need only be an act that causes an intended contact with another person that is unpermitted and which is harmful or offensive. **Here, the professor's touching of the woman was without her permission, intentional and, despite intent to the contrary, harmful. As a result, it amounted to battery. The university could not be held liable for battery under the state tort claims act.** *White v. Univ. of Idaho*, 797 P.2d 108 (Idaho 1990).

B. Employee Misconduct

Other school employees such as principals, counselors, or custodians also may be subject to lawsuits based on intentional infliction of emotional distress, criminal behavior, or other misconduct.

♦ *A university instructor's physical assault of a student did not result in school liability because the assault was not in furtherance of the school's business and therefore fell outside the scope of employment.*

A student at a New York university enrolled in a noncredit karate course offered during the summer session. The class was held in the school's physical education building. According to the student, he was told by the instructor to do a reverse push-up. After he refused, believing that it was unsafe, the instructor struck several times. He was taken to the hospital and later sued the school in the Court of Claims for his injuries. The school asserted that it should not be held vicariously liable for the student's injuries because the instructor was not an employee but an independent contractor.

The court noted that under the terms of the employment contract, the instructor qualified as an independent contractor. However, it also considered as evidence the summer session catalog of courses in which the teachers of noncredit courses were referred to as instructors and the teachers of credit courses were described as "Instructor[s], Faculty of Summer Session, SUNY." No statements were given indicating the difference between the two or indicating whether the noncredit course instructors were independent contractors or fulltime faculty members. The court noted that this could reasonably lead students to believe that the instructors of the noncredit courses were employees of the school. However, the court held that it did not need to resolve this issue since the karate instructor's conduct was outside the scope of his employment. **The school did not authorize the use of violence and such actions were not within any discretionary authority given to the instructor.** The assault was not in furtherance of the school's business and therefore fell outside the scope of employment. The school could not be held vicariously liable for such actions. *Forester v. State*, 645 N.Y.S.2d 971 (Ct.Cl.1996).

♦ *A private college did not become liable for a priest's sexual assault of a boy because it was not reasonably foreseeable to the college or hospital that the priest would commit such an act against someone who was neither a student at the college nor a patient at the hospital.*

A priest employed as a campus minister by a private college and as a chaplain at a hospital was accused of sexually assaulting a boy. The priest knew the boy and his family through the boy's school and parish. The alleged assaults took place in the evening at the priest's residence where the boy was staying because of his family's friendship with the priest. The boy was neither a patient at the hospital nor a student at the college. After the assault, the boy's parents sued the college and the hospital, alleging *respondeat superior* liability and negligent supervision. The college and the hospital filed motions to dismiss which the trial court granted. The parents appealed to the Court of Appeals of Ohio.

The court noted that **for an employer to be liable under the theory of** ***respondeat superior***, **the employee's act must be committed within the scope of employment**. This means that it must be calculated to facilitate or promote the business for which the person was employed. The court then discussed the circumstances under which the priest's misconduct could be imputed to his employers. Here, the court held that sexual assault diverted from the straight and narrow performance of the priest's job as it was not reasonably foreseeable to the college or hospital that the priest would commit such an act against someone who was neither a student at the college nor a patient at the hospital. His relationship with the boy was in no way related to his roles as campus minister or hospital chaplain. The court also found no liability under the negligent supervision claim. The trial court's decision was affirmed. *Gebhart v. College of Mt. St. Joseph*, 665 N.E.2d 223 (Ohio App.1st Dist.1995).

♦ *An employee's lawsuit against coworkers for "aiding and abetting" in a sexual assault by another coworker failed because the coworkers' actions were not a direct or deliberate cause of the assault.*

A New York woman employed by a private university as an animal attendant was repeatedly subjected to "rude and vulgar" behavior from the stable attendant. Her coworkers at the university knew of the stable attendant's "demeaning and malevolent attitude toward women" and his history of "hostile physical aggression toward women." After the stable attendant assaulted the animal attendant, she sued the university and two coworkers, alleging that they "aided and abetted" the assault and that they were liable for intentional infliction of emotional distress (IIED). The defendants moved for pretrial judgment which the court denied. They then appealed to the Supreme Court, Appellate Division. The appellate division noted that "merely harboring a dangerous person or giving tacit approval" did not constitute aiding or abetting the assault. Rather, in order to prevail on this claim, the defendants had to "overtly encourage the offensive behavior." Here, **the coworkers' contribution to a hostile work environment could not be interpreted as a "direct or deliberate" cause of the assault**. Therefore, the aiding and abetting charge was dismissed. Further, the IIED claim could not survive because the stable attendant's crude and inappropriate comments were not sufficiently "atrocious and intolerable" to establish such a cause of action. The holding of the lower court was reversed. *Shea v. Cornell Univ.*, 596 N.Y.S.2d 502 (A.D.3d Dept.1993).

C. Third-party Misconduct

Liability for third-party misconduct can arise when someone connected with the school is injured by a third-party while outside school property, or when an individual not affiliated with the school enters school property and injures someone connected with the school. Often, third-party misconduct involves some type of criminal behavior such as physical or sexual assault. Claims against schools arise when students seek to hold the school liable for negligence, alleging that the school failed to provide a safe and secure environment.

◆ *Although a college student was sexually assaulted by two men after consuming alcoholic beverages at an off-campus bar, she could not maintain a suit against the college.*

A 17-year-old college freshman at a four-year private school gained entrance to an off-campus tavern through the use of her student identification card. The bar was named after the college's mascot and displayed college memorabilia. After consuming alcoholic beverages, the student left the bar with two men and was sexually assaulted. A parent of the student sued the college on her behalf, claiming that the college had breached its duty of care toward the student in several respects. The first claim asserted that the school breached a duty to provide a campus environment free from foreseeable harm. The college stressed that the tavern was not on campus grounds, the student's activities were unrelated to her curriculum, and that the college had no knowledge of the potential for assault. The court refused to impose liability under these circumstances. The second claim asserted that the school failed to advise the student concerning state law and the dangers associated with drinking. However, the student's deposition contained an admission of her knowledge of these matters. Further, the court stated that no such duty should be imposed upon a college. The final claim concerned duties associated with **an *in loco parentis* relationship**. This relationship **would place a duty on the college to act toward a student as would a parent.** Although courts have almost universally rejected such a notion, the girl's parent argued that the *in loco parentis* relationship should be required because the girl was only 17 years old. The court noted that such a relationship is not within the expectations of either the college or students. It refused to impose the duty, and all claims were dismissed. *Hartman v. Bethany College*, 778 F.Supp. 286 (N.D.W.Va.1991).

◆ *Although a woman was injured while on a university campus, the court determined that the university's alleged lack of security was not the legal cause of her injuries.*

A California woman was grabbed from behind, stabbed, beaten and then raped while on a university campus. Nearly an hour later, two motorists heard her screams but the assailant fled before they arrived. The woman sued the university for negligence. At trial, her independent security expert found many faults with the security provided by the school. The university's expert testified that the security was adequate. The jury returned a verdict for the woman and she accepted a reduced judgment of $1,288,888. The university appealed to the California Court of Appeal, contending that there was no causal connection between its negligence and the woman's injury. The court of appeal agreed. It assumed, without deciding, that the university breached a duty by failing to provide adequate security to prevent the injury. However, that abstract negligence could not be the legal cause of the woman's injury. Noting that absolute safety was not an achievable goal and that increased security meant increased costs, the court was not willing to make landowners guarantors of their patrons' personal safety. **The court concluded that the causation element "imposed rational limits on liability" and avoided turning a third party (the university) into a vicarious criminal.** Thus, the university's alleged lack of security was not the legal cause of the injury. The lower court holding was reversed. *Nola M. v. Univ. of Southern Cal.*, 20 Cal.Rptr.2d 97 (Cal.App.2d Dist.1993).

♦   *Although a church-operated college owned a parking lot adjoining a state university childcare center, a patron of the center had no special relationship with the college that required imposing liability on the college.*

A church-operated Illinois college owned a parking lot adjoining a state university childcare center. Persons dropping off their children at the center customarily used the parking lot, and the practice was acknowledged by a college official. The college employed off-duty police officers to patrol its campus area, including the parking lot. No serious incidents had been reported in the parking lot and the most serious incident on the campus had involved harassment and bottle throwing by local high school students. However, a patron of the daycare center was abducted from the parking lot at gunpoint after dropping off her child. She was then sexually assaulted and slashed with a knife. She sued the college in federal court for her injuries, claiming that the college had voluntarily undertaken police protection for the parking lot. Her husband also sued for loss of consortium. The court granted the college's motion for pretrial judgment, and the patron and her husband appealed to the U.S. Court of Appeals, Seventh Circuit.

According to the court, Illinois law imposed no duty upon parties to protect third parties from criminal attack. Exceptions existed when there was a special relationship between the parties or when a criminal attack was reasonably foreseeable. Here, the patron had no special relationship with the college as she was not upon college property by invitation or for the benefit of the college. **Although the college had undertaken a duty to protect persons who were lawfully upon its campus, it was not liable for injuries resulting from crimes which were not reasonably foreseeable.** Because there was no evidence that any attack resembling the one suffered by the patron had ever occurred near college property, the abduction was unforeseeable. The court affirmed the lower court's decision. *Figueroa v. Evangelical Covenant Church*, 879 F.2d 1427 (7th Cir.1989).

♦   *Without a specified statutory duty, there was no legal requirement for a school to prevent student injuries on adjacent property.*

A California law school opened its library until midnight for use by its students. Criminal activity had occurred in the immediate area but the school provided no security. The school provided no student parking or lighting. An unknown assailant attacked and stabbed a student about 10:00 p.m. one night. The assault occurred on city-owned property which was adjacent to the school. The student sued the school, arguing that a special relationship existed between the school and its students. He asserted that the school should have taken reasonable, inexpensive measures such as providing additional security or lighting to protect him from foreseeable criminal activities. The student argued that the school had "control" of the sidewalk area and had a duty to assume the responsibility of protecting the area. The trial court held for the school, and the California Court of Appeal upheld that decision. It noted that without a specified statutory duty there was no legal requirement for the school to prevent student injuries on adjacent property. **Mature students were considered "business invitees" whose legal status was not analogous to the relationship between minor school students and their schools.** Hence, **there was no special relationship between the school and its students.** The school had not created the risk and did not control the area where the assault occurred. *Donnell v. Cal. Western School of Law*, 246 Cal.Rptr. 199 (Cal.App.4th Dist.1988).

◆   *An Oregon stockbroker who occasionally used the library at Oregon State University (OSU) was appropriately excluded from campus after OSU officials issued exclusion notices for stalking two students. The U.S. Court of Appeals, Ninth Circuit, held that the stockbroker had no constitutionally protected interest in access to the university and that OSU acted reasonably to protects its students.*

The stockbroker was an OSU alumnus who used the library and attended public events on campus. **An OSU student obtained a temporary protective stalking order against him** in 1993 from a county circuit court prohibiting any contact with her and excluding him from named OSU premises, including the fifth and sixth floor of the library. However, the order did not ban him from campus.

In 1995, OSU security services published a policy providing for written trespass warnings to non-students as a way to protect students, staff and faculty. The policy set forth procedures that included an appeal process for non-students to the manager of security services. **The stockbroker was arrested in the OSU library shortly after publication of the policy, based on continuing complaints against him and the 1993 stalking order.** The arresting campus security employee served the stockbroker with an exclusion notice purporting to bar him from the entire campus.

OSU's campus security manager denied the stockbroker's appeal by letter, which also indicated that the notice expired soon after the graduation of one of the complaining students. Some months later, the manager issued guidelines for use of exclusion orders, which explained that the orders applied to non-students who were considered a danger to others or to property on campus. Another OSU student filed a complaint about the stockbroker with campus security and the security manager immediately issued him a second exclusion notice. The complaining student obtained a temporary stalking protective order from a state court, and law enforcement officers cooperated with OSU security services in the distribution of a safety alert flyer depicting the stockbroker.

OSU's security manager denied a second appeal and later denied the stockbroker's requests to return to campus for three specific events. State police cited him for criminal trespass in violation of the exclusion order, and he sued the security manager and others in a federal district court asserting civil rights violations under 42 U.S.C. § 1983. The court dismissed the case, and the stockbroker appealed to the Ninth Circuit.

On appeal, the stockbroker alleged that the OSU campus was an open public forum and that the second exclusion order violated his constitutional right to due process. The court noted that "[w]hile the OSU campus may be open to the public, it does not follow that the University must allow all members of the public onto its premises regardless of their conduct." Even without rules and regulations explicitly allowing officials to exclude persons for conduct, it was reasonable to infer this authority from OSU's exclusion policy. **The U.S. Supreme Court has recognized that educational administrators need flexibility to carry out their educational missions. Any individual right to use the campus had to be balanced against the university's right to protect its students.** OSU acted reasonably in temporarily excluding the stockbroker from its campus, and he had no constitutional right to campus access that was deserving of due process protections. The court affirmed the judgment for OSU officials. *Souders v. Lucero*, No. 98-35527, 1999 WL 1029498 (9th Cir.1999).

III. INSURANCE

Colleges and universities possess insurance policies, which provide coverage for both first- and third-party claims. Third-party claims generally involve liability policies, and lawsuits against schools for negligence of school employees. Unless an exclusion in the policy specifically exempts a claim from coverage, an insurer may be required to defend and indemnify the school in any lawsuit arising from an injury to a third party. First party claims generally involve property and casualty policies, and direct claims of loss by the school.

◆ *A school's liability insurer failed to demonstrate that the school had intentionally violated the Age Discrimination in Employment Act, which required the insurer to provide coverage for the fired professor.*

A Massachusetts theological seminary fired a 62-year-old tenured professor. The professor was later successful in asserting that the termination was in violation of the Age Discrimination in Employment Act (ADEA) and he was awarded substantial damages. The school then sought payment from its insurer. The insurer refused to pay the school, claiming that it was unlawful to insure against liability resulting from deliberate or intentional wrongdoing. The school sued the insurer in a federal district court, which granted pretrial judgment to the insurer. The school then appealed to the U.S. Court of Appeals, First Circuit. The issue on appeal was whether a termination in violation of the ADEA was uninsurable under Massachusetts law. The court of appeals certified the question to the Supreme Judicial Court of Massachusetts. The court noted that the school may have acted with reckless disregard and been found to have acted "wilfully" while not intending any wrongdoing. The court answered the certified question by stating that a finding of willfulness under the ADEA does not automatically preclude insurance coverage under Massachusetts law. The case was sent back to the U.S. Court of Appeals to continue the appeal. *Andover Newton School v. Continental Cas.*, 566 N.E.2d 1117 (Mass.1991).

On remand, the court of appeals determined that **although the school had intentionally terminated the professor, the insurer had the burden of proving the school had violated the ADEA**. The insurer had failed to meet this burden. The school had not knowingly violated the ADEA. *Andover Newton Theological School v. Continental Cas.Co.*, 964 F.2d 1237 (1st Cir.1992).

♦   *Where an insured board member at a private college made misrepresentations to the board of trustees to obtain a personal advantage for his company, and where the college lost $2 million as a result, the college's errors and omissions policy did not provide coverage for the loss.*

A Texas Christian College purchased a "school leaders errors and omissions" policy that insured it against wrongful acts committed by directors and officers of the school. Subsequently, a member of the board of trustees convinced the board to invest $2 million of its endowment funds in a company that accepted accounts receivable as security for short-term loans. However, he did not disclose that the company had a negative net worth, that he was a 49 percent owner of the company, or that he was also a salaried employee of the company. **When the investment failed, the college obtained the board member's resignation, then sued him and his company for misrepresentation of certain facts and for making false statements.** The college obtained a judgment against the board member for $1.8 million and against the company for $2 million. Unable to collect on the judgments, it sought to collect under its errors and omissions policy. The insurer denied coverage under the "fraud or dishonesty" exclusion and the "personal profit or advantage" exclusion.

A Texas federal court held that the two exclusions applied to bar coverage, and the college appealed to the U.S. Court of Appeals, Fifth Circuit. The appellate court affirmed. It noted that **the exclusion for "any claim arising out of the gaining in fact of any personal profit or advantage to which the Insured is not legally entitled" applied to bar coverage.** Here, the board member clearly gained a personal advantage by his company's receipt of the $2 million in endowment funds from the college. Despite the fact that the board member did not ultimately make a profit, he did gain a personal advantage by his wrongful acts. As a result, the insurer had no obligation to pay out under the policy. *Jarvis Christian College v. National Union Fire Ins. Co.*, No. 98-40965, 1999 U.S. App. LEXIS 31999 (5th Cir.1999).

♦   *A public university in Oregon could not deny health insurance coverage to domestic partners of homosexual employees.*

The Oregon Court of Appeals determined that a public health sciences university violated the state constitution's privileges and immunities clause by maintaining **a practice of denying health insurance coverage to the domestic partners of its homosexual employees.** The case arose after three university nurses applied for insurance coverage for their domestic partners. The benefits manager refused to process the application because the university provided health insurance to spouses, not unmarried partners. After the state employee benefits board upheld the denial of benefits, the nurses sued in state court.

The court of appeals stated that Oregon's employment discrimination statute protected the nurses on the basis of their sexual orientation. However, the university did not violate that statute. Rather, the university violated the state constitution's privileges and immunities clause (which requires governmental entities to make benefits available on equal terms to all Oregon citizens). **Because** homosexuals cannot marry under Oregon law, the university's health insurance benefits were made available on terms that, for gay and lesbian couples, were a legal impossibility. *Tanner v. Oregon Health Sciences Univ.*, 971 P.2d 435 (Or.App.1998).

IV. CIVIL RIGHTS ACTS

♦ *In a 1982 case involving a Florida university secretary's § 1983 lawsuit, the Court stated that there was no purpose in requiring § 1983 plaintiffs to exhaust their state administrative remedies. This was because § 1983 had been enacted in the Reconstruction Era as a response to Congressional perceptions that individual civil rights would be abused by state officials.*

A white female secretary worked for a Florida university. She alleged that during her employment there, she had been passed over for employment promotions, even though she was qualified for the positions. She sued the university in a federal district court under 42 U.S.C. § 1983, alleging gender and race discrimination. The secretary also claimed that the university actively sought to hire minorities and separated applicant files according to race and gender. A panel of the U.S. Court of Appeals, Fifth Circuit, dismissed the secretary's complaint for failure to exhaust her state administrative remedies.

The court then agreed to hear the case *en banc* to determine whether the employee should be required to exhaust her state administrative remedies before she was entitled to file a § 1983 claim in the federal court system. Although the U.S. Supreme Court had on several occasions rejected the argument that a § 1983 action should be dismissed where the plaintiff had not exhausted administrative remedies, the court of appeals held that adequate and appropriate state administrative remedies must be exhausted before a plaintiff could bring a § 1983 action in federal court. The U.S. Supreme Court agreed to hear the case.

The Court considered its rationale in prior decisions, when it considered the policy of exhausting administrative remedies. Administrative remedy exhaustion ensures that the parties attempt a settlement before proceeding to federal court. The Court examined Congress' intent in not specifically requiring exhaustion of state administrative remedies in § 1983 actions. Congress assigned to the federal courts the primary role of securing individual constitutional rights in the years after the Civil War. Section 1983 was passed during the Reconstruction Era in response to state-sanctioned constitutional violations of blacks after the ratification of the Fourteenth Amendment. To now require plaintiffs to go through state administrative processes contradicted this purpose. **Congress had intended that § 1983 plaintiffs be able to choose the federal district courts as the forum for civil rights lawsuits. The Court rejected the policy reasons adopted by the court of appeals for requiring state administrative remedy exhaustion.** It stated that reducing federal court case loads and using state agency expertise in these cases did not outweigh the purposes of § 1983. *Patsy v. Board of Regents*, 457 U.S. 496, 102 S.Ct. 2557, 73 L.Ed.2d 172 (1982).

♦ *Another part of the Reconstruction Era Civil Rights Act is 42 U.S.C. § 1981. Section 1981 states that all persons shall have the same right to make and enforce contracts as is enjoyed by white persons. In 1987, the Court ruled that although originally intended to vindicate the rights of former slaves, § 1981 extended to persons of Arab ancestry and others besides American blacks.*

A private college in Pennsylvania denied tenure to a professor it had employed under a one-year nonrenewable contract. The professor was a Muslim who was born in Iraq but was a U.S. citizen. He claimed that the college had refused to grant tenure on the basis of his national origin and religion in violation of state and federal civil rights laws, including § 1981. The professor sued the college in a federal district court, which dismissed many of the claims because they were too late to meet local statutes of limitations.

The court also dismissed the § 1981 claim, ruling that the act did not extend to the professor. It ruled that § 1981, which forbids racial discrimination in the making and enforcement of any contract, does not reach claims of discrimination based on Arab ancestry. The court stated that Arabs were Caucasians, and that since § 1981 was not enacted to protect whites, an Arab professor could not rely upon the statute. The professor appealed to the U.S. Court of Appeals, Third Circuit. The appeals court affirmed the district court's decision that the professor's Title VII claim was untimely, but reversed its decision regarding the § 1981 claim. The College appealed to the U.S. Supreme Court, which agreed to review only the § 1981 portion of the professor's claim.

In affirming the court of appeals' decision, the Supreme Court noted that **although § 1981 does not use the word "race," the Court has construed the statute to forbid all racial discrimination in the making of private as well as public contracts. It observed that persons who might be thought of as Caucasian today were not thought to be of the same race at the time § 1981 became law.** The Court cited several dictionary and encyclopedic sources to support its decision that for the purposes of § 1981, Arabs, Englishmen, Germans and certain other ethnic groups are not to be considered a single race.

Based on the history of § 1981 the Court reasoned that Congress "intended to protect from discrimination identifiable classes of persons who are subjected to intentional discrimination solely because of their ancestry or ethnic characteristics." If the professor could prove that he was subjected to intentional discrimination because he was an Arab, rather than solely because of his place of origin or his religion, the lawsuit could proceed under § 1981. The court of appeals' decision in favor of the professor was affirmed and the case was remanded for trial. *St. Francis College v. Al-Khazraji*, 481 U.S. 604, 107 S.Ct. 2022, 97 L.Ed.2d 749 (1987).

◆ *The NCAA has been held not to be a state actor by the Supreme Court. In a 1988 Nevada case, the Court concluded that the NCAA did not have the power to discipline a school's coach, and thus could not be liable for sanctions imposed against him.*

Following a lengthy investigation of allegedly improper recruiting practices by the University of Nevada, Las Vegas (UNLV), the NCAA found 38 violations, including ten by the school's head basketball coach. The NCAA proposed a number of sanctions and threatened to impose more if the coach was not suspended. UNLV decided to suspend the coach. Facing an enormous pay cut, the coach sued the NCAA under 42 U.S.C. § 1983 for violating his due process rights. The Nevada Supreme Court held that the NCAA's conduct constituted state action for constitutional purposes. It upheld a Nevada trial court's dismissal of the suspension and award of attorney's fees. The NCAA appealed to the U.S. Supreme Court.

The Supreme Court held that the NCAA's participation in the events which led to the suspension did not constitute state action within the meaning of § 1983. The NCAA was not a state actor on the theory that it misused the power it possessed under state law. UNLV's decision to suspend the coach in compliance with the NCAA's rules and recommendations did not turn the NCAA's conduct into state action. This was because UNLV retained the power to withdraw from the NCAA and establish its own standards. The NCAA could not directly discipline the coach, but could threaten to impose additional sanctions against the school. **It was the school's decision and not the NCAA's decision to suspend the coach.** *NCAA v. Tarkanian*, 488 U.S. 179, 109 S.Ct. 454, 102 L.Ed.2d 469 (1988).

V. VICARIOUS LIABILITY

♦   *A university was held vicariously liable for acts of hazing committed by upperclassmen who were acting as agents of the university, even though the upperclassmen went beyond what they were authorized to do.*

A five-year veteran of the Navy enrolled in the Military College of Vermont of Norwich University under a Navy ROTC scholarship. He lasted for only 16 days, during which he was subjected to, and observed, repeated instances of hazing by upperclassmen. After withdrawing from school, he sued the university for assault and battery, infliction of emotional distress and negligence, asserting that it was vicariously liable for the actions of the upperclassmen. A jury returned a verdict in the student's favor, awarding him almost $500,000 in compensatory damages and $1.75 million in punitive damages. The Supreme Court of Vermont affirmed the compensatory damage award against the university, but reversed the award of punitive damages, finding no evidence of malice on the university's part. **Here, the university had charged the upperclassmen with "indoctrinating and orienting" the student. As a result, this was not a simple case of student-on-student hazing for which the university could not be held liable.** Because the upperclassmen were acting as agents of the university, it had a duty of care toward the student which it breached. The court also found that the nearly $500,000 in compensatory damages awarded by the jury was not clearly erroneous. *Brueckner v. Norwich Univ.*, 730 A.2d 1086 (Vt.1999).

♦   *A university may be liable if it is deliberately indifferent to student-on-student sexual harassment.*

Two female students at the University of Colorado who participated in the Reserve Officer Training Corps program alleged that a fellow student (a higher ranking cadet in the ROTC program) committed acts that amounted to a hostile work environment. When they reported the acts to a superior ROTC officer, he retaliated against them by denying them further opportunities in the ROTC program and subjected them to other acts of sexual harassment. They then reported the harassment to university officials and asserted that the university did not take adequate measures to respond to their allegations. They sued the university in federal court under Title IX, where the university maintained that it could not be held liable because ROTC members were not agents of the university and it did not exercise control over them. The court dismissed the case against the university, and the students appealed to the U.S. Court of Appeals, Tenth Circuit. The court of appeals reversed, finding that the lawsuit should not have been dismissed. Here, **the students had adequately pled that the ROTC program was a university-sanctioned program, that they had been harassed by members of that program, and that the university did not take remedial action when notified of the harassment.** The case was remanded for further proceedings. *Morse v. Regents of the Univ. of Colorado*, 154 F.3d 1124 (10th Cir.1998).

◆   *Where an Army officer who instructed ROTC students was not an agent of a college, the college could not be liable for any negligence on his part.*

A Georgia college student enrolled in a military science Mountaineering Techniques class injured his ankle while practicing rappelling techniques. He sued the college, asserting that the instructor had negligently instructed him, causing the injury. The college maintained that the instructor had not been negligent and that, even if he had, he was not an agent of the college because he was a full-time Army officer who was assigned to the college to teach ROTC courses. The trial court held that the college had the right and authority to control the details of the sergeant's work, but chose not to do so. Accordingly, the sergeant was an agent of the college, which was potentially liable for the student's injury. The Georgia Court of Appeals reversed. It stated that **under the cross-enrollment agreement for the establishment of ROTC instruction, the college did not have the right to control the time, manner and method of the Army's performance.** Because the Army provided the rappelling tower, uniforms, textbooks, ropes and other equipment, and because the training procedures were the Army's, the instructor was an independent contractor rather than an agent of the college. The student's lawsuit was dismissed. *Armstrong State College v. McGlynn*, 505 S.E.2d 853 (Ga.App.1998).

◆   *A university was held vicariously liable for an accidental shooting in the following case.*

Two graduate students at a Louisiana university worked as resident assistants in a dormitory. One of them kept a gun in his room. The other approached a student who was not wearing a shirt in violation of dorm rules, and a verbal altercation ensued. Afterwards, the graduate student who had been in the altercation asked the other graduate student if he could borrow the gun. He then returned to continue the argument. At this point, another student happened on the scene and tried to intervene. The gun discharged, hitting him in the thigh. He sued the university and the other three students to recover for his injuries. A jury found the student who had fired the gun 90 percent at fault, and the other graduate student 10 percent at fault. The court found the university vicariously liable as the students' employer, and the university appealed.

The Court of Appeal of Louisiana examined the issue of whether the resident assistants were acting within the scope of their employment. It found that the trial court could have concluded that they were. **Even though the university prohib-**

ited the possession of weapons on campus, the accident occurred on the university's premises, during the hours of employment while the resident assistants were on duty. Further, the student who discharged the gun stated that it was an accident and that he only brought it with him because he felt he needed protection from a student he perceived as threatening. Because the trial court's finding of vicarious liability was reasonable, the court of appeal refused to overturn it. *Emoakemeh v. Southern Univ.*, 654 So.2d 474 (La.App.1995).

CHAPTER NINE

School Operations

I. STATE REGULATION

A. Residency

◆ *Although a state may validly classify students in its university system as "resident" and "nonresident," the means by which it does so is subject to challenge. In this case, the Court struck down a statute which created an irrebuttable presumption of nonresidency. The Court held that students must be allowed to present evidence rebutting any presumption of nonresidence.*

Connecticut required nonresidents enrolled in the state's university system to pay tuition and other fees at a higher rate than state residents. It also created an irreversible and irrebuttable statutory presumption that if the legal address of a student, if married, was outside the state at the time of application for admission or, if single, was outside the state at some point during the preceding year, the student remained a nonresident as long as the student remained enrolled in Connecticut schools. Two students, one married, one single, who were both residents of Connecticut, challenged the presumption, claiming that it violated the Fourteenth Amendment's guarantee of due process and equal protection. A three-judge district court panel upheld the students' claim and the matter was appealed to the U.S. Supreme Court.

The Court held that **the Due Process Clause does not permit states to deny a student the opportunity to present evidence that the student is a bona fide resident of the state, and thus entitled to in-state tuition rates,** on the basis of an irrebuttable presumption of nonresidence. Such a presumption is not necessarily true and the state had reasonable alternatives in making residency determinations. *Vlandis v. Kline*, 412 U.S. 441, 93 S.Ct. 2230, 37 L.Ed.2d 63 (1973).

♦   *Reiterating the general rule of* Vlandis v. Kline, *above, the Supreme Court, in this case, held that the right to rebut a presumption of nonresidence extends even to aliens with visas living in state.*

The University of Maryland granted "in-state" tuition status only to students domiciled in Maryland, or, if a student was financially dependent on the student's parents, to students whose parents were domiciled in Maryland. The university could also deny in-state status to individuals who did not pay the full spectrum of Maryland state taxes. The university refused to grant in-state status to a number of students, each of whom was dependent on a parent who held a "G-4 visa" (a nonimmigrant visa granted to officers and employees of international treaty organizations and members of their immediate family).

The university stated that the holder of a G-4 visa could not acquire Maryland domicile because the holder was incapable of showing an essential element of domicile—the intent to live permanently or indefinitely in Maryland. After unsuccessful appeals at the administrative level, the students brought a class action lawsuit in federal court seeking declaratory and injunctive relief. The students alleged that university policy violated the Equal Protection Clause. The district court granted relief, stating that the G-4 visa could not create an irrebuttable presumption of nondomicile. The Court of Appeals affirmed.

On appeal, the Supreme Court refused to decide the matter and certified the question to Maryland's highest court, the Maryland Court of Appeals, for a determination. The Court stated that the case was controlled by the principles announced in *Vlandis v. Kline*, above, that **when a state purports to be concerned with domicile, it must provide an individual with the opportunity to present evidence bearing on that issue. Federal law allows aliens holding a G-4 visa to acquire domicile in the United States.** However, the question of whether such domicile could be acquired in Maryland was a question of state law. Since no controlling precedent had been decided by the state's highest court, the Supreme Court declined to rule and certified the question to the Maryland high court. *Elgin v. Moreno*, 435 U.S. 647, 98 S.Ct. 1338, 55 L.Ed.2d 614 (1978).

♦   *Federal law supersedes, or preempts, state law when both deal with the same subject matter and the state law attempts to impose burdens not contemplated by Congress. In the follow-up to* Elgin v. Moreno, *above, the Court struck down a university policy that imposed additional restrictions on an alien's right to acquire domicile in a state and thus qualify for in-state tuition.*

The University of Maryland's student fee schedule policy denied students whose parents held nonimmigrant alien visas (those visas issued to officers or employees of certain international organizations and their families) in-state status, even if they were domiciled in the state, thus denying them preferential fee and tuition schedules. The U.S. Supreme Court found the policy to be in violation of the Supremacy Clause of the U.S. Constitution which states, "This Constitution, and the laws of the United States which shall be made in Pursuance thereof; and all Treaties made, or which shall be made, under the Authority of the United

States, shall be the supreme Law of the Land." The Court stated that the university's policy conflicted directly with the will of Congress as expressed in the Immigration and Nationality Act of 1952. In passing the Immigration and Nationality Act, Congress explicitly decided not to bar nonimmigrant aliens such as these the right to acquire domicile in the United States. **The university's policy denying these aliens "in-state" status, solely on the basis of their immigration status, amounted to a burden not contemplated by Congress** in admitting them to the United States. Thus, the University of Maryland's student fee schedule as applied to these aliens was held to be unconstitutional. *Toll v. Moreno*, 458 U.S. 1, 102 S.Ct. 2977, 73 L.Ed.2d 563 (1982).

◆   *A university could adopt a higher standard of proof for students seeking in-state tuition status.*

An applicant to the University of Vermont College of Medicine was born and raised in Massachusetts. However, he moved to Vermont on June 1, 1994 and obtained employment at the university. Two weeks later, he applied for admission to 23 medical schools, listing his father's Florida residence as his permanent address. In September, he applied to the university's College of Medicine, listing his Vermont address as his permanent one. He obtained a Vermont driver's license, registered his car in the state, and filed his income tax returns in the state. The following year, he was accepted for admission to the medical school as an out-of-state student. When he applied for in-state tuition status, his application was denied. He appealed, and the university used a "clear and convincing evidence" standard to determine that the student was not entitled to in-state status. The case reached the Vermont Supreme Court, which ruled in favor of the university. It noted that **although the "preponderance of the evidence" standard is usually appropriate for administrative proceedings, the university was free to adopt the more stringent "clear and convincing evidence" standard. The student was not entitled to in-state status.** *Huddleston v. Univ. of Vermont*, 719 A.2d 415 (Vt.1998).

◆   *An applicant at a New Mexico medical school could sue to be placed in the next entering class where the school had used her short length of residency to deny her admission.*

In three successive years, an applicant to the University of New Mexico School of Medicine was rejected for admission. At each of her interviews, **her relatively short length of residency was listed as an obstacle to her admission.** The university preferred those who had lived in the state for a longer period of time because it believed they would be more likely to stay in the state and provide needed medical care to underserved areas. She sued the university and a number of officials for injunctive relief and damages, alleging that the residency policy violated her due process and equal protection rights. A federal court held that the residency policy violated clearly established law concerning the fundamental right to travel and that the university could not consider length of residency in future admissions decisions. The Tenth Circuit Court of Appeals reversed in part, finding that the applicant did not have standing to pursue a claim regarding the determination of residency length in future admissions decisions. However, she could pursue her claims for admission under the *Ex Parte Young* exception to qualified immunity. Under *Ex Parte Young*, 209 U.S. 123 (1908), where there is an ongoing violation of federal law, a party may obtain prospective relief against a government official to prevent the official from continuing to violate the law. Accordingly, **the applicant could seek injunctive relief that would place her in the immediate entering class at the university.** *Buchwald v. Univ. of New Mexico School of Medicine*, 159 F.3d 487 (10th Cir.1998).

◆   *Where two students indicated that they were in North Carolina for educational purposes, they failed to show that they were residents for tuition purposes.*

A North Carolina university residence committee affirmed the university's decision to deny two student applications for state residency for tuition purposes. In both cases, the students indicated that their parents resided outside the state of North Carolina, and that the applicants had recently relocated to North Carolina, in part to take advantage of educational opportunities. Both of the applicants held part-time jobs, had recently attended college in other states, obtained North Carolina driver's licenses, and registered to vote. In separate actions, state superior courts upheld the committee's decisions, and the Court of Appeals of North Carolina consolidated appeals by the students. Under state law, both of the students were presumed to have the same domicile as their parents. **Although state law allowed resident tuition for those individuals establishing legal residence in the state for at least twelve months with a bona fide presence in the state, the law presumed that a person's legal residence was with the person's parents.** Both students had failed to rebut this presumption and both had indicated that their presence in the state was related to education. Because this supported, rather than rebutted, the presumption that the students were only present in the state for educational purposes, the superior court had correctly upheld the committee's decision to deny state residency for tuition purposes in both cases. There was no merit to the argument by the students that the university's appeal process violated their due process rights. *Norman v. Cameron*, 488 S.E.2d 297 (N.C.App.1997).

◆   *Where a nonimmigrant student did not seek a change in her status, she could not show that she was a resident for tuition purposes.*

A citizen of Uruguay obtained a nonimmigrant student visa. She moved to Arkansas, where she petitioned a state university for resident status for tuition purposes. The university denied her application, basing its decision on state education department regulations. Under the regulations, a student should be classified as an in-state resident for tuition purposes only if the student establishes legal residence within the state. The regulations further require an applicant to establish a permanent legal home in Arkansas for six continuous months with no present intention of moving outside the state. The student filed a federal district court action against the university and certain officials, seeking injunctive and declaratory relief, plus the amount of nonresident tuition she had paid with interest. The court found that **the student's classification as a nonimmigrant student depended upon her intention to retain foreign citizenship. The student had failed to seek any change in her nonimmigrant status,** and as a result could not form the requisite intent to become an Arkansas resident. Since she could not meet the intent requirement for state residency, the university officials could not have violated her clearly-established rights, and the court granted summary judgment to the university and officials. *Hein v. Arkansas State Univ.*, 972 F.Supp. 1175 (E.D.Ark.1997).

B. Zoning and Land Use

◆ *A nonprofit private music school was entitled to a special zoning exception as a private school.*

The school had been in existence for about 20 years and leased space in a building in the District of Columbia. It operated under a "special exception as a private school" previously granted by the Board of Zoning Adjustment. The school offered individual and classroom music instruction in orchestral instruments, piano, and voice, for students of all ages and abilities. It sponsored recitals in conjunction with public and private schools in the community and was one of only 17 schools in the country accredited as "community music schools" by the National Association of Schools of Music. When it began to outgrow its leased building, it sought to renovate three buildings on a single lot, and to construct an addition to the main building that would house teaching studios, some classrooms, rehearsal facilities, offices and a 300-seat auditorium. The school also proposed to build a 114-space parking lot.

Several neighborhood groups opposed the school's proposals, arguing that the presence of the private school would result in increased traffic and parking problems in the neighborhood, and that the school was not eligible for a special exception because it was not a "private school" within the meaning of the applicable regulation. The zoning board conducted a hearing and granted the requested special exception subject to several conditions, including limits on the number of persons allowed at the school at any given time and on the school's hours of operation. The neighborhood groups sought a reversal of the board's ruling before the District of Columbia Court of Appeals.

On appeal, the neighborhood groups claimed that the school was not a "school" within the dictionary definition of the term and that, even if it was, it was a trade school because it trained future concert professionals for whom music was a livelihood. The court of appeals disagreed. It noted that **the school plainly met the dictionary definition of a "school" as an organized source of education or training as well as a place where instruction was given.** It was also a private school because it was established, conducted and primarily supported by a nongovernmental agency. The court then noted that the school was not a trade school because, although a small percentage of its students might go on to further training, and an even smaller percentage to performing careers, the great majority did not. Accordingly, since the school was not a trade school, it was eligible to be granted a special exception. The zoning board's decision was affirmed. *Neighbors on Upton Street v. District of Columbia Board of Zoning Adjustment*, 697 A.2d 3 (D.C.App.1997).

◆ *An ordinance that prohibited educational uses of property in a historic district owned by a New York private college was struck down as unconstitutional.*

The private college owned property adjacent to its campus which developed into a distinctive, turn of the century residential neighborhood listed on the National Register of Historic Places. The city adopted a zoning ordinance encompassing the property which limited property uses and restricted special permit uses to public utility facilities, substations and structures. All other special uses including educational uses were foreclosed. The college proposed that the ordinance be amended to allow special permit use for faculty offices, administrative offices and homes for visiting dignitaries and guests of the college. The city's Historic Districts Commission and the New York State Office of Parks, Recreation and Historic Preservation both projected that the proposed amendment would have a deleterious effect on the historic preservation of the property. The college then discontinued its pursuit of an amendment and filed a declaratory judgment action in state court against the city, its mayor and city council, seeking a declaration that the ordinance was unconstitutional. The court granted the college summary judgment, and the appellate division affirmed. Appeal was then taken to the Court of Appeals of New York.

The court of appeals noted that **proposed educational uses must be weighed against the interest in historical preservation as well as other legitimate, competing interests to determine how best to serve the public welfare.** Here, depriving the college of the opportunity to have its presumptively beneficial educational use weighed against competing interests, and thereby wholly excluding educational uses from the property, bore no substantial relation to the public welfare. Therefore, it was beyond the city's zoning authority. Moreover, neither the variance nor the amendment process allowed the zoning board to balance a particular applicant's educational use against the public interest in historical preservation. The judgment of the appellate division was affirmed. *Trustees of Union College v. Schenectady City Council*, 667 N.Y.S.2d 978 (Ct.App.1997).

The U.S. Supreme Court examined the Religious Freedom Restoration Act (RFRA) in *City of Boerne, Texas v. Flores*, 521 U.S. 507, 117 S.Ct. 2157, 138 L.Ed.2d 624 (1997), and found the RFRA to be unconstitutional as applied to state actions. The case involved a building permit for the enlargement of a church. It was denied on the ground that the church building was part of a historical district. The Supreme Court held that the church could not use the RFRA to obtain the permit because the RFRA proscribed state conduct that the Fourteenth Amendment did not even prohibit. However, the Supreme Court did not address the question of whether the RFRA was unconstitutional in all respects. It limited its analysis to state actions. Accordingly, the RFRA may still provide protections against federal actions.

◆   *A religious college was required to pay a development fee in order to build an addition. The fee was not a tax for which the college could claim an exemption because it was not compulsory. It was only applied upon development of property.*

A Catholic private college in California acquired an adjacent tract of land in order to build a postgraduate business school and parking structure. The college intended to move its existing business school to the new building, resulting in no increase in students or faculty. Before construction could begin, the college needed a permit which would not be issued unless the college paid a school development fee. Under state statute, any school district can levy a fee against any commercial, industrial or residential development project for the purpose of funding the construction of school facilities. The only exceptions are facilities used exclusively for religious purposes or facilities owned and occupied by agencies of federal, state, or local government. The college paid the fee under protest and then filed a petition for writ of mandamus in state court. The trial court found for the college and the school district appealed to the California Court of Appeal, Second District.

The college argued that the development fee qualified as a tax, which it should not be required to pay as a nonprofit, educational institution. The court agreed that the college was exempt from state taxes because of its status, but found that the development fee was not a tax. It was not compulsory, like a tax, but was imposed only when a property owner decided to develop. Furthermore, **the California Supreme Court has held that exemptions from taxes refer only to property taxes.** The court also found that the development was not going to be used exclusively for religious purposes. The college did not fall into any of the exceptions to the statute and therefore it had to pay the development fee. *Loyola Marymount Univ. v. Los Angeles Unified School Dist.*, 53 Cal.Rptr.2d 424 (Cal.App.2d Dist.1996).

◆   *A Connecticut university seeking to resubdivide 13 acres of land into 40 building lots, and to excavate and fill the land, had to show the town plan and zoning commission that its development plan would not unreasonably destroy natural resources, and that no feasible and prudent alternatives existed.*

The university-owned land was zoned to permit single-family detached dwellings. The university submitted an application with the city's plan and zoning commission to resubdivide the land into 40 building lots. It also filed for a special permit to excavate and fill the land. The commission approved the university's application. A lawsuit was later filed challenging the approval, and several persons who owned land within a radius of 100 feet of the subject property intervened in the action. Specifically, the intervening landowners alleged 1) that the trees and wildlife on the proposed subdivision were natural resources requiring the commission to consider environmental impact; 2) that the proposed subdivision was a cul-de-sac subject to the ten-lot access rule; and 3) that the commission arbitrarily approved the plan despite several regulatory violations. A state trial court ruled for the university, and the Appellate Court of Connecticut affirmed that decision. On further appeal, the Supreme Court of Connecticut held that **even if the trees and wildlife had no economic value, the commission was obligated to consider whether the proposed development would unreason- ably destroy those natural resources, and whether there was any feasible and prudent alternative to the development of the property.** *Paige v. Town Plan & Zoning Comm'n of Town of Fairfield*, 668 A.2d 340 (Conn.1995).

C. School Licensing and Regulation Issues

◆   *New York's Freedom of Information Law required disclosure of animal testing information to a citizen group.*

A citizen group sued the Board of Trustees of the State University of New York under the state's Freedom of Information Law (FOIL) to obtain certain records relating to biomedical research on cats and dogs. Under the Federal Animal Welfare Act, a dealer who provides a research facility with a "random source" dog or cat must furnish the research facility with a certification that includes the name and address of the person, pound or shelter from which the animal was obtained. The citizen group sought access to those certifications under the FOIL, and the records officer at the facility denied the request. A New York appellate court held that the facility was not an "agency" under the FOIL when it maintained the random source certifications because it was doing so to comply with federal law. However, the New York Court of Appeals reversed, finding that the group was entitled to the information. It found that **the facility was an "agency" for purposes of the FOIL because the certifications were being kept in connection with the research conducted by the facility, and that research was fulfilling the state university system's statutory mission—a state governmental function.** Since the board of trustees had not shown that the information being sought was subject to any exception, the FOIL required that the information be disclosed. *Citizens for Alternatives to Animal Labs v. Bd. of Trustees of SUNY*, 703 N.E.2d 1218 (N.Y.1998).

♦ *The Michigan Department of Education could deny a license to operate to the owner of a trade school teaching casino gambling.*

A Michigan resident applied to the proprietary school unit of the department of education for a license to operate a private trade school teaching casino gambling. The board denied his application because gaming was considered criminal behavior in Michigan. The applicant appealed to a Michigan trial court. The trial court reversed, and the board of education appealed to the Court of Appeals of Michigan. The court of appeals noted that public policy did not completely prohibit casino gambling as evidenced by the legislature's decision to legalize millionaire parties and to allow casino gambling on Indian reservations. On further appeal, the Supreme Court of Michigan reversed. It adopted the dissenting opinion from the lower court, which stated that **licensing the proposed school would violate public policy.** If the school were allowed to teach casino gambling, it would be teaching behavior that was currently defined as illegal under Michigan law. *Michigan Gaming Institute v. State Bd. of Educ.*, 547 N.W.2d 882 (Mich.1996).

♦ *A corporation that provided review courses for nursing school graduates had to pay an annual renewal licensing fee for each location at which it operated.*

The corporation offered courses that prepared nursing school graduates for state certification exams. It offered four-day courses at five different locations within the state. The review courses were held in hotel meeting rooms, college auditoriums or hospital conference rooms. The Council for Private Postsecondary and Vocational Education is responsible for administration and enforcement of the Private Postsecondary and Vocational Education Reform Act. The California legislature modified the act to increase the annual renewal fee for nondegree granting institutions from $225 to a range of $600 to $1,200, depending on size. The corporation made a single $1,200 payment but refused the council's request to make a separate payment for each of its course sites. The corporation challenged the council's interpretation of the statute in a California trial court. The trial court found that a separate fee could be charged for each location, and the corporation appealed to the California Court of Appeal, First District.

The issue on appeal was whether each separate site constituted an institution which must pay a fee within the meaning of the statute. Because the corporation's educational sites were 50 miles from corporate headquarters and were held in places such as hotel conference rooms, they were neither branches nor satellites subject to separate annual fees under the act. However, since the legislature provided that each site be inspected by the council, the court inferred a legislative intent to require separate annual fees for each site. The corporation alleged that this interpretation resulted in an arbitrary imposition of fees with no relationship to the actual costs of approving private institutions as mandated by the act. The court of appeal disagreed, ruling that **as long as the council used some "reasonable method" of estimating the administrative costs of the entire program, the council's annual fee interpretation was reasonable.** Thus, the court of appeal required the corporation to pay an annual fee for each site at which it offered its educational services. *RN Review for Nurses, Inc. v. State*, 28 Cal.Rptr.2d 354 (Cal.App.1st Dist.1994).

♦   *Rhode Island was not allowed to require approval of all advertising for proprietary schools prior to publication in the following case.*

The owner of a Newport proprietary hairdressing school challenged the regulations governing proprietary schools in Rhode Island which established a screening system for school advertising. The regulations required all advertising to be approved prior to publication by the Board of Governors of Higher Education. In October 1992, the school filed suit claiming the regulations constituted prior restraint and were overbroad in violation of the First Amendment. In a motion for summary judgment, the federal district court held for the school. The court found that **restrictions on commercial speech must satisfy a three-part test.** First, the commercial speech must concern a lawful activity and not be misleading or fraudulent. Second, the government's interest in restricting speech must be substantial. Third, the regulation must directly advance a government interest and any restrictions must be narrowly tailored to advance that interest. Because the regulations required the approval of all advertisements regardless of their aim or purpose, they failed this final part. *Berger v. R.I. Bd. of Governors of Higher Educ.*, 832 F.Supp. 515 (D.R.I.1993).

♦   *A New York appellate court upheld the denial of a license to a school that had operated illegally.*

A New York private school which had received a warning for improper conduct from the New York Secretary of Education sought to open another facility. The school began operations at an unlicensed facility, and enticed students to enroll with promises of employment. Both of these practices are illegal, but they continued despite orders to desist. Finally, the secretary denied the school a license to operate. The New York Supreme Court, Appellate Division, held that **the secretary may lawfully deny a private for-profit school a license to operate if the secretary has good cause.** The secretary's decision should not be overturned unless it is arbitrary and capricious. The first issue questioned whether the school had received due process. The school in this case had been given an opportunity to refute the authority's findings, and that opportunity was held to be adequate to satisfy the requirements of due process. The court then observed that the school's conduct was clearly unlawful. The license denial was reinstated. *Blake Business School, Inc. v. Sobol*, 575 N.Y.S.2d 955 (A.D.3d Dept.1991).

♦ *A board for community colleges should have provided an occupational school with a hearing prior to terminating the school's license. However, the board's vice president was entitled to immunity in the school's suit for damages.*

A private Colorado occupational school had been licensed to do business by the State Board for Community Colleges and Occupational Educations. A new statute revised licensing requirements, and the school was required to renew its license. The board's vice president rejected the school's application because it had not employed an independent accountant nor had it utilized accepted accounting procedures as required by the new statute. The school filed a 42 U.S.C. § 1983 action in a Colorado district court against the vice president and the board. It alleged that both had failed to provide a hearing prior to terminating the school's license and had failed to provide an impartial tribunal. The school sought damages and injunctive relief requiring the board to restore its license. A trial court determined that neither the board nor its vice president could be sued under 42 U.S.C. § 1983 and dismissed the case. The school appealed to the Colorado Court of Appeals.

First, the court of appeals stated that the board was a state regulatory body that was entitled to immunity from suits for damages. Next, the court determined that **the vice president's failure to grant the school a predeprivation hearing was not a clear violation of its constitutional rights.** The statutes requiring predeprivation hearings were ambiguous and the vice president should have been allowed great latitude in the performance of his discretionary duties. The vice president therefore had immunity on the claim for damages under § 1983. Finally, an arm of the state could be sued for injunctive relief under § 1983. The board's refusal to grant the school a predeprivation hearing potentially violated its statutory rights. On remand, the school could bring suit for injunctive relief. *National Camera, Inc. v. Sanchez*, 832 P.2d 960 (Colo.App.1991).

♦ *Because a cease and desist order amounted to a license revocation, the board that issued the order should have provided procedural safeguards to the school.*

A corporation operated an association of career schools in Florida. These schools were licensed by the Board of Independent Postsecondary Vocational Trade and Business Schools (board). The board became concerned with the school's advertisement practices and issued the school a cease and desist order which prohibited further advertisement, enrollment of students, or acceptance of further tuition payments. The school contended that the board had in effect revoked the school's license without following the required procedural safeguards. The school appealed directly to the District Court of Appeal of Florida. The court noted that the board was clearly granted the discretion to take the actions included in the cease and desist order by a 1989 Florida statute, which did not mandate that the procedural safeguards at issue here be followed. However, other Florida legislation deals directly with revoking or limiting a school's license, and mandates compliance with specific procedural safeguards in the event of an emergency suspension. The school argued that these procedures should be followed because the cease and desist order had the same effect as revoking the school's license. The court agreed. It then turned to whether the board's actions had satisfied these safeguards. The court held that **the board had not set out specific facts showing the necessity of actions, published an evaluation of the fairness of the action, or provided a prompt hearing.** The court granted relief to the school and quashed the cease and desist order. *Allied Educ. Corp. v. State, Dept. of Educ.*, 573 So.2d 959 (Fla.App.1st Dist.1991).

♦   *The state of Florida could not prevent a consulting firm's education division from using the word "college" in its name even though the division did not offer college credit or degrees.*

A division of a management consulting firm maintained classroom facilities and conducted seminars on quality improvement. However, the division, which was called Quality College, did not offer instruction leading to college credit or any academic degree. In July 1985, the Florida State Board of Independent Colleges notified Quality that it could not use the term "college" in its name without prior express authority from the board. The case reached the Florida District Court of Appeal, which observed that the issue was whether the board correctly denied Quality the use of the name "college." The board had interpreted a state statute to mean that only degree-granting institutions which were accredited, licensed, or exempt were eligible to use the word "college." The court ruled that the board's interpretation was wrong. **The board's interpretation prohibited the use of "college" by any other person or entity for any other purpose (such as "Kiddie College" for preschools).** The board's decision was reversed and Quality College was allowed to retain its name. *Phillip Crosby Assoc., Inc. v. State Bd. of Ind. Cols.*, 506 So.2d 490 (Fla.App.5th Dist.1987).

♦   *New York City was not allowed to ban a private educational institution's distribution of free magazines via newsracks because the proposed ban arbitrarily singled out certain kinds of publications.*

A private institution which offered short, nonaccredited courses in New York City sought to distribute its magazine free of charge by way of newsracks placed on city sidewalks. The city contended that the newsracks were unsightly, unsanitary and unsafe. It also asserted that the magazine was "commercial speech," which is entitled to a lesser degree of First Amendment protection, and that the ban on all commercial speech through sidewalk newsracks was constitutional. The New York Court of Appeals observed that the city's arguments missed the central point in the case: **"a government official or employee may not exercise complete and unregulated discretion, in the absence of duly enacted guidelines, ... to decide which publications may be distributed via [newsracks]."** Here, the city's action against the institution was taken without the benefit of any regulatory guidelines. The city's action therefore violated the First Amendment which requires that government action regulating "speech" be undertaken pursuant to clear guidelines which leave little room for arbitrary decisions. The decision to ban the sidewalk magazine newsracks was illegal. *City of New York v. American School Pubs.*, 509 N.E.2d 311 (N.Y.1987).

◆   *A state tuition refund rule was held to be constitutional such that a school could be denied a license renewal for failing to comply with the rule.*

A Florida based correspondence school offered courses of instruction for home study with optional training at its Florida training school. Florida Department of Education rules required a tuition refund policy identical to or more liberal than the refund policy recognized by the U.S. Office of Education. Sanctions for failure to comply with the rule included nonrenewal of licensing. The school operated in several states, maintaining 44 field offices. The field offices utilized 22 separate contract forms to comply with various state regulations while minimizing the tuition refund to dropout students. In each case, the minimum refund corresponded to student domicile state law rather than Florida law. The Florida Department of Education notified the school that it intended to deny its license renewal application for failure to comply with the state tuition refund rule. The Florida District Court of Appeal rejected the school's argument that the refund rule burdened interstate commerce, because **the rule put nonresident students in the same position as resident students concerning tuition refunds**. Since the rule did not burden out-of-state students but placed them on exactly the same footing as Florida students with respect to refunds of prepaid enrollment charges, it was clear that there was no discrimination. Students would no longer be subject to different tuition refunds depending upon their state's law. *Associated Schools v. Dept. of Educ.*, 522 So.2d 426 (Fla.App.1st Dist.1988).

D. Teacher Certification

◆   *A teacher who had been denied and later granted permanent certification could sue the state department of education for her costs and other incidental monetary damages.*

A student received her undergraduate education at a convent school in Lebanon and subsequently passed the National Teachers Exam. She then obtained a Master of Arts degree from Brooklyn College and began working for the completion of a second Master of Arts degree to teach English as a second language. The New York City Board of Education's Board of Examiners granted her a temporary per diem teaching certificate after accepting her credentials. Two years later, when the Board of Examiners was disbanded, the state Education Department became responsible for evaluating teacher credentials. The teacher's temporary license and substitute teacher certificate were renewed for two successive years but when she applied for permanent certification, the department denied her application for failure to submit evidence of a completed baccalaureate degree. As a result, she lost her job with the New York City Board of Education in its bilingual program.

She commenced an administrative proceeding to obtain reinstatement, a credit for seniority status, backpay, health insurance costs and other appropriate relief. The hearing resulted in her permanent certification and reinstatement by the Board of Education. She then brought a motion for an order granting the relief that she had originally sought—seniority status, backpay, medical insurance and attorney's fees. The court found that it lacked jurisdiction to consider those claims against the state and the teacher appealed to the Supreme Court, Appellate Division, which concluded that the lower court should not have dismissed the teacher's remaining claims. Since **the main thrust of the lawsuit had been the review of the department's determination that her convent education was not the equivalent of a baccalaureate degree, and the monetary relief was incidental,** the lower court could hear the entire case. The court remanded the case for a determination of those incidental damages detailed in the petition. *Awad v. State Education Department of New York*, 658 N.Y.S.2d 755 (A.D.3d Dept.1997).

E. Delegation of Police Power

✦   *An Indiana appellate court held that delegating police power to a private religious university did not violate the Establishment Clause.*

Valparaiso University, an independent institution owned and operated by the Lutheran University Association, operated a police department whose officers were appointed by the governing board of the university. After a university police officer arrested and charged a law student with driving while intoxicated, the student sought to suppress the evidence against him by claiming that the exercise of police power by a religious institution was unconstitutional, that the officer had not undergone the required training of officers employed by the state, and that there had been no reasonable suspicion or probable cause to pull him over. The case reached the Court of Appeals of Indiana, which held that **although the university was religiously affiliated, it was not a religious institution within the meaning of the First Amendment.** It was characterized by a high degree of academic freedom and did not subordinate secular education to religious doctrine. **Accordingly, delegating police power to the university did not violate the Establishment Clause.** Further, because the university was not a political subdivision of the state, the officer was not required to undergo the same training as police officers in Indiana. Finally, there was probable cause for the stop. Accordingly, the evidence against the student was admissible, and his conviction was upheld. *Myers v. State*, 714 N.E.2d 276 (Ind.App.1999).

✦   *However, the Supreme Court of North Carolina found that police power could not be delegated to a religious university.*

A North Carolina Baptist University operated a police force consisting of a captain and eight full-time officers. Pursuant to a North Carolina statute, the university's police officers were commissioned as state police officers by the attorney general. When one of the officers spotted a student weaving across the center line of a highway near the university, he arrested the student for driving while impaired. The student later filed suit in state court, alleging that the statute authorizing commission of university police officers as state police officers was unconstitutional, and seeking dismissal of the charge against him. The case reached the Supreme Court of North Carolina, which noted that the statute violated the Establishment Clause. The court noted that **a state cannot delegate an important discretionary governmental power to a religious institution or share such power with a religious institution.** Because police power is an important discretionary governmental power, and because the Baptist university was a religious institution, the state's delegation of its police power to the university was unconstitutional. *State v. Pendleton*, 451 S.E.2d 274 (N.C.1993).

F. Term Paper Services

♦ *One of the nation's largest private universities was unsuccessful in its attempt to hold a number of term paper writing services liable for violating state and federal laws.*

Boston University sought to prevent enterprises that it characterized as "term paper mills" from assisting and encouraging student fraud and cheating on term papers. In 1981, the university obtained a permanent order from a state court against various term paper services. However, it claimed that many students continued to purchase term papers from the services and submit them as their own work in order to fulfill class requirements.

In 1997, the university organized a sting operation to investigate term paper research and writing services, at least one of which was a party to the 1981 action. After obtaining information that at least one of the services offered a student information on how to alter papers to avoid detection and concluding that many services continued to sell papers to Boston University students, the university commenced a federal district court action alleging interference with its educational policies in violation of RICO.

The services responded with counterclaims against the university for RICO violations and abuse of process. The Commonwealth of Massachusetts intervened in the case to address their challenge to the constitutionality of a state law prohibiting the sale of term papers and research materials for submission as original work for academic credit. The services moved for pretrial judgment.

The court rejected the university's RICO claim because it failed to show that a number of distinct entities were engaging in racketeering activities. The services were not distinct entities from their individual owners. It also **refused to apply a Massachusetts criminal statute that prohibits the sale of term papers if the seller has knowledge that they will be submitted for academic credit as original work.** The law created no private right of action to accompany its criminal sanctions.

Because the university's remaining claims could not be aggregated to meet the minimum required amount of $75,000 in controversy for federal jurisdiction, the court refused to consider the state law claims for unfair or deceptive acts or practices in commercial relationships between businesses. The only commercial relationship between the university and the services had been the sting operation, which involved only small payments for term papers. The court awarded judgment to the services. *Trustees of Boston Univ. v. ASM Communications, Inc.*, 33 F.Supp.2d 66 (D.Mass.1998).

G. Desegregation

♦ *Where a state perpetuates policies and practices that can be traced to a segregative system and that have segregative effects, the policies will be considered unconstitutional unless there is sound educational justification for them and it is not practical to eliminate them.*

Mississippi maintained a dual system of public education at the university level—one set of universities for whites, and another set for blacks. In 1981, the State Board of Trustees issued "Mission Statements" to remedy this, classifying the three flagship historically white institutions (HWI) as "comprehensive" universities, redesignating one of the historically black institutions (HBI) as an "urban" university and characterizing the rest as "regional" institutions. However, the universities remained racially identifiable. A federal district court found that state policies need merely be racially neutral, developed in good faith, and not contribute to the racial identifiability of each institution. The court held that Mississippi was currently fulfilling its duty to desegregate. The U.S. Court of Appeals, Fifth Circuit, affirmed. The U.S. Supreme Court granted review.

The Supreme Court held that the district court had applied the wrong legal standard in ruling that Mississippi had brought itself into compliance with the Equal Protection Clause. **If a state perpetuates policies and practices traceable to its prior dual system that continue to have segregative effects, and such policies are without sound educational justification and can be practicably eliminated, the policies violate the Equal Protection Clause.** This is true even if the state has abolished the legal requirement that the races be separated and has established neutral policies. The proper inquiry is whether existing racial identifiability is attributable to the state. Because the district court's standard did not ask the appropriate questions, the court of appeals had erred in affirming the judgment. Applying the proper standard, several surviving aspects of Mississippi's prior dual system were constitutionally suspect. First, the use of higher minimum ACT composite scores at the HWIs, along with the state's refusal to consider high school grade performance was suspect. Second, the unnecessary duplication of programs at HBIs and HWIs was suspect. Third, the mission statements' reflection of previous policies to perpetuate racial separation was suspect. Finally, the state's policy of operating eight universities had to be examined to determine if it was educationally justifiable. *U.S. v. Fordice*, 505 U.S. 717, 112 S.Ct. 2727, 120 L.Ed.2d 575 (1992).

On remand to the U.S. District Court for the Northern District of Mississippi, **the court entered a remedial decree prohibiting the state from maintaining remnants of the prior segregated system** and mandating specific relief in areas of admissions and funding. However, the court refused to order the relief requested by the complaining parties, which would significantly increase the number of African-Americans accepted for regular admission at state universities. The complaining parties claimed that the district court order's reliance on a summer remedial program to boost African-American admissions was inappropriate, and the parties appealed to the U.S. Court of Appeals, Fifth Circuit. The court agreed with the complaining parties that the district court's order affirming the elimination of many remedial courses had to be reconsidered, along with its finding that use of college entrance scores as a criterion for scholarships was not traceable to the illegal system of segregation. The court remanded for clarification the status of a proposal to merge two universities to eliminate unnecessary program duplication, as well as questions of increasing the other-race presence at two HBIs and issues of accreditation and funding. The court affirmed many aspects of the district court decision as consistent with the *Fordice* decision, significantly affirming its decision to maintain admissions standards that ensured educational soundness. *Ayers v. Fordice*, 111 F.3d 1183 (5th Cir.1997).

H. Financial Aid

♦   *In the following case, the Supreme Court stated that federal assistance may be based on compliance with federal laws. The Court held that a statute mandating compliance with the Selective Service System's requirements as a prerequisite to federal aid did not violate the Fifth Amendment's protection from self-incrimination since no student is compelled to apply for federal aid.*

Section 12(f) of the Military Selective Service Act denied federal financial assistance under Title IV of the Higher Education Act to male students between the ages of 18 and 26 who failed to register for the draft. Applicants for assistance were required to file a statement with their institutions attesting to their compliance with the Selective Service Act. A group of students who had not registered for the draft sued the selective service system to enjoin enforcement of § 12(f). A federal district court held that the act was a bill of attainder (a law which imposes a penalty on a group of people without a trial) because it singled out an identifiable group that would be ineligible for Title IV aid based on their failure to register. The district court also held that the compliance requirement violated the Fifth Amendment's privilege against compelled self-incrimination.

On appeal, the Supreme Court rejected the claims that the law was a bill of attainder, and upheld the law. **The law clearly gave nonregistrants 30 days after receiving notice of ineligibility for federal financial aid to register for the draft and thereby qualify for aid.** Furthermore, the bill of attainder prohibition in the Constitution applies only to statutes that inflict punishments on specified groups or individuals such as "all Communists." The Court also held that the denial of aid based on these requirements was not "punishment." The Court stated that **if students wish to further their education at the expense of their country, they cannot expect the benefits without accepting their fair share of governmental responsibility.** Finally, the law did not violate the Fifth Amendment because there was nothing forcing students to apply for federal aid. *Selective Service System v. Minnesota Public Interest Research Group*, 468 U.S. 841, 104 S.Ct. 3348, 82 L.Ed.2d 632 (1984).

♦   *Three students who did not have to register for the draft still had to provide information about why they were exempt in order to qualify for aid.*

Three Boston University theology students who were exempt from Selective Service registration either because of age or gender refused to answer questions about their draft registration status on their applications for federal financial aid. They objected to providing information about their exempt status because of religious principles. They were refused federal financial assistance and sued the university, asserting that their religious freedom and free exercise rights had been violated. A federal court prohibited the denial of aid to the students, and the case reached the U.S. Court of Appeals, First Circuit. The appellate court held that although the Department of Education's regulations were broader than the statute on which they were based, they were not unconstitutional. **Even though the department had other means to acquire the information it sought, the** burden on the applicants to state that they were female or of a certain age (and thus exempt) was minimal. Also, the information being sought was not of a religious nature. Thus, the government's interest outweighed the applicants' interest and required the lower court's decision to be reversed and remanded. *Alexander v. Trustees of Boston Univ.*, 766 F.2d 630 (1st Cir.1985).

I. Procedural Issues

✦ *In 1982, the Supreme Court ruled that a Pennsylvania taxpayer group lacked standing to challenge a governmental conveyance of surplus property to a private religious college. The Court ruled that the group could show no injury to itself or any of its members as a result of the conveyance.*

Congress enacted the Federal Property and Administrative Services Act, 40 U.S.C. § 471 *et seq.*, to dispose of surplus property and authorize its transfer to public or private entities. This statute authorized the education secretary to dispose of surplus real property for schools. The secretary was permitted to take into account any benefit accruing to the U.S. from any new use of the transferred property. In 1973, the secretary of defense and general services administration declared a Pennsylvania army hospital site surplus property. In 1976, **the education secretary conveyed part of the property to a Christian college.**

Although the appraised value of the property was $577,500, the secretary computed a 100 percent public benefit allowance, permitting the college to acquire the property for no cost. **A taxpayer group advocating the separation of church from state learned of the conveyance and sued the college and federal government** in a federal district court, claiming that the conveyance violated the Establishment Clause. The court dismissed the complaint, ruling that the taxpayers lacked standing under the Supreme Court's decision in *Flast v. Cohen*. The U.S. Court of Appeals, Third Circuit, reversed the district court's decision, and the Supreme Court agreed to hear an appeal by the college and federal government.

The Court stated that Article II of the Constitution limited the judicial power of courts to cases and controversies. Litigants were entitled to bring a lawsuit only by showing some actual or threatened injury. Without such a showing, lawsuits were to be dismissed for lack of standing. In this case, the taxpayers had alleged injury from deprivation of fair and constitutional use of their tax dollars. This allegation was insufficient to confer standing in federal courts. Under *Flast*, taxpayers were proper parties only to allege the unconstitutionality of congressional actions under the Taxing and Spending Clause and were required to show that the action went beyond the powers delegated to Congress. **Courts were not available to taxpayers to vent generalized grievances of government conduct or spending. The complained of statute arose under the Property Clause and therefore the taxpayers had no standing to complain about the property transfer.** As the taxpayers had failed to allege any personal injury, the Court reversed the court of appeals' decision. *Valley Forge Christian College v. Americans United for Separation of Church and State*, 454 U.S. 464, 102 S.Ct. 752, 70 L.Ed.2d 700 (1982).

•   *One of the difficulties faced by students and school officials seeking judicial resolution of disputes is the amount of time it takes a case to move through the court system. By the time a case reaches its final appeal, depending on the nature of relief sought, there may well be no reason for the court to decide the issue. In these situations, the case is considered moot and dismissed. In this case, a student sought a final court order mandating admission to law school, but by the time the case reached the Supreme Court it was the eve of the student's graduation. The Court dismissed the case.*

A student applied for admission to a state-operated law school in Washington. The size of the incoming class was limited, and the school accepted less than ten percent of those who applied. The student was among those rejected by the school. **He sued the school, claiming that its policy of giving favorable status to certain minority students in admission decisions discriminated against him on the basis of his race in violation of the Equal Protection Clause** of the Fourteenth Amendment. The student brought suit on behalf of himself and not as the representative of any class. He sought an injunction ordering the school to admit him as a member of the first-year class. A Washington state trial court agreed with his claim and granted the requested relief. The student entered the school and began his legal studies. The Washington Supreme Court reversed and held that the admissions policy did not violate the Constitution. By this time, the student was in his second year.

The student petitioned the U.S. Supreme Court for review and received a stay of the Washington Supreme Court's judgment pending the final disposition of the U.S. Supreme Court. When the case was finally argued before the Court, the student was in his final quarter of law school and the Court determined that the question was moot. The Court stated that since the student had only brought the action for his own behalf and had already been granted the relief he had sought, the controversy between the school and himself was at an end. Furthermore, there was no immediate danger that the student might be subjected to the "gauntlet" of law school admissions again. The Court dismissed the case. *DeFunis v. Odegaard*, 416 U.S. 312, 94 S.Ct.1704, 40 L.Ed.2d 164 (1974).

•   *In 1989, the U.S. Supreme Court ruled that a choice of law in a university contractor's construction contract superseded arbitration rights found in the Federal Arbitration Act. This was because the parties had intended to incorporate state arbitration rules into the contract. As state law controlled, the Court refused to set aside the judgment of the California courts.*

An electrical contractor contracted with a California university to install conduits. The contract contained a clause in which the parties agreed to arbitrate disputes relating to the contract. The contract also contained a choice-of-law clause which stated that it would be governed by the law of the place of the project's location. A dispute arose concerning overtime compensation and the contractor made a formal request for arbitration. The university sued the contractor in a California trial court for fraud and breach of contract. **The contractor claimed that it was entitled to arbitration under the contract and the Federal Arbitration Act (FAA).** The court granted the university's motion to stay arbitration under a California statute which permits a stay when arbitration is the subject of pending court action. The contractor appealed to the California Court of Appeal, which affirmed the trial court's decision. The court of appeal acknowledged that although the contract affected interstate commerce, the California statute applied because of the contractual choice-of-law clause. The California Supreme Court denied the contractor's petition for discretionary review, but the U.S. Supreme Court agreed to hear its appeal.

On appeal, the contractor reiterated its argument that the court of appeal's ruling on the choice-of-law clause deprived it of its federally guaranteed right to arbitration under the FAA. The Supreme Court ruled that **the FAA did not confer a general right to compel arbitration. Rather, it guaranteed the right to arbitrate according to the manner provided for in the parties' contract.** The court of appeal had correctly found that the contract incorporated California law. The FAA was not undermined by the state law which permitted a stay of arbitration. The Court affirmed the court of appeal's decision for the university. *Volt Information Sciences v. Board of Trustees of Leland Stanford Junior University*, 489 U.S. 468, 109 S.Ct. 1248, 103 L.Ed.2d 488 (1989).

II. ACCREDITATION

Regional and other accrediting institutions have been sued by private schools upon withdrawal of accreditation. The general rules emerging from such cases establish that: 1) actions of accrediting institutions do not constitute "state action" triggering due process requirements, 2) a school may maintain a breach of contract lawsuit against an accrediting institution if the institution fails to follow its own rules and procedures, and 3) if an accrediting institution's procedures are fair, its decision to revoke accreditation will likely be upheld.

A. Grants of Accreditation

♦   *Where an accreditation foundation's denial of accreditation was supported by substantial evidence, it did not qualify as arbitrary or unreasonable.*

A college of art and design petitioned the foundation for accreditation of its interior design program. In accord with its rules, the foundation sent a visiting team of interior design educators and practitioners to the college to evaluate its program's compliance with foundation standards and guidelines. The team met with administration and faculty members, students and alumni, and inspected facilities, evaluated course offerings and reviewed student work. The team concluded that the college's program did not meet standards in 12 areas and recommended denying accreditation. The foundation's Board of Appeals affirmed the denial of accreditation. It then remanded the issue back to the trustees for its final decision regarding accreditation status.

The Board of Trustees decided to re-inspect the college's program. The second team, however, turned out to be even more critical than the first one. As a result, the foundation's Board of Trustees unanimously voted to deny accreditation to the college. A Michigan federal court concluded it did not have the authority to conduct a review of the foundation's evaluative decisions. **The Board of Trustees behaved reasonably, and its denial of accreditation was supported by substantial evidence.** *Foundation for Interior Design Education*

Research v. Savannah College of Art and Design, 39 F.Supp.2d 889 (W.D.Mich.1998).

♦ *After an unsuccessful antitrust action in federal court against the American Bar Association, a law school association and an accredited law school, a nonaccredited law school could not sue the same parties again in state court alleging different claims arising from the same set of operative facts.*

A Massachusetts nonprofit, nontraditional law school applied for American Bar Association (ABA) accreditation. Although the school recognized that its practices were contrary to ABA standards, it sought a waiver for each standard that might bar accreditation. An ABA team visited the school, and recommended denial of accreditation. The school unsuccessfully sought administrative appeals, then brought an antitrust lawsuit in a federal district court against the ABA, a law school association, an ABA-accredited law school in Massachusetts, and several individuals. The district court dismissed claims against certain defendants and granted summary judgment to the remaining defendants. The U.S. Court of Appeals, Third Circuit, affirmed.

Next, the school filed suit in a state trial court against the same defendants and three new defendants. The defendants removed the case to the U.S. District Court for the District of Massachusetts, which dismissed several defendants and granted summary judgment to the others. The school appealed to the U.S. Court of Appeals, First Circuit, which addressed the question of whether the state law claims against the ABA and the association were sufficiently related to the causes of action asserted in the antitrust lawsuit to warrant preclusion of the claims. **The school's pending claims, although rooted in Massachusetts law, plainly arose from the same set of operative facts as the antitrust suit. Both suits stemmed from the school's failed efforts to receive ABA accreditation.** Both suits alleged that the ABA and the association orchestrated a long-term scheme to accumulate power and money, and a short-term scheme to deny accreditation unjustly to the school because it dared to oppose their hegemony. Moreover, the factual underpinnings of the two suits were the same, including the same potential witnesses. Finally, it was a reasonable expectation that the two suits would be brought together. Because the school had had an appropriate opportunity to litigate its first set of claims, and conveniently could have brought the second set as part of the same proceeding, the prior antitrust suit satisfied due process concerns. *Massachusetts School of Law at Andover, Inc. v. American Bar Assn.*, 142 F.3d 26 (1st Cir.1998).

♦ *An amendment to Oregon law allowing certain schools in the state to be exempted from requirements that out-of-state schools were not exempted from, was struck down.*

A private Washington university with a branch campus in Oregon was accredited by the Northwest Association of Schools and Colleges (NASC). Following NASC accreditation, the Oregon Office of Educational Policy and Planning (OEPP) continued to review non-Oregon schools every three years. The statute provided that "no school ... shall confer ... any degree ... without first having submitted the requirements for such degree to the [OEPP] and having obtained the approval of the director." However, an amendment exempted

Oregon schools in good standing with the NASC from OEPP review. The university filed suit in an Oregon circuit court, seeking a declaration that the statute violated the Commerce Clause. The circuit court held for the university and severed a portion of the amendment. The court of appeals affirmed, but invalidated the exemption in its entirety. The Oregon Supreme Court allowed the university's petition for review solely on the issue of remedy.

The university contended that the entire amendment had been improperly invalidated. The supreme court disagreed, ruling that the statute as severed was not capable of being executed in accordance with legislative intent. The legislature had intended both to continue the exemption from OEPP authority for Oregon schools that were members of the NASC and to remove the exemption from OEPP authority for out-of-state schools, even if those schools were NASC members. However, the dominant intent of the amendment was to ensure that Oregon branch campuses of the out-of-state schools had the same level of faculty and facilities as their main campuses. **Because a partial severance would subject these out-of-state schools to lesser scrutiny, the court ordered the amendment severed in its entirety.** The court of appeals' ruling was affirmed. *City Univ. v. Office of Educ. Policy*, 885 P.2d 701 (Or.1994).

♦ *Denial of accreditation by an association of schools was not state action that would trigger application of the Constitution.*

The Medical Institute of Minnesota, a private technical school training students for careers as medical and dental assistants, received accreditation from the National Association of Trade and Technical Schools for a five-year period commencing in 1977. In 1983, the institute's application for reaccreditation was denied, and an association hearing panel upheld the denial. The institute then sued the association in federal court, claiming a violation of its constitutional rights. The case reached the U.S. Court of Appeals, Eighth Circuit, which held that the **denial of accreditation was not "state action" that triggered application of the U.S. Constitution. The court also refused to substitute its judgment for the association's with respect to a purely educational matter.** It further noted that although the institute had been given an opportunity to justify its deficiencies, it had been unable to do so. The institute's action could not succeed. *Medical Institute of Minnesota v. NATTS*, 817 F.2d 1310 (8th Cir.1987).

B. Claims of Fraud

♦ *A class of students was allowed to sue an accrediting agency for fraud after the agency extended the accreditation of a school without checking to see if the school met the agency's standards.*

A District of Columbia vocational school applied to an accrediting agency for accreditation in 1985. The agency granted the school an accreditation that was to expire in two years. However, despite areas of concern including curriculum, instructional materials, clarity of the school's mission statement and the school's financial status, the agency granted the school a series of automatic extensions until November of 1988. A number of students who had enrolled during this period began to notice that the school did not carry through on all of its promises. The students filed suit against the accrediting agency in the U.S. District Court for the District of Columbia, alleging that the agency was liable for fraud because it extended the accreditation of the school without any knowledge of whether the school met its standards for accreditation. On cross-motions for summary judgment, the court determined that **the class of students had established a** *prima facie* **case of fraud** under District of Columbia law. The elements of a cause of action for fraud are 1) a false representation, 2) in reference to a material fact, 3) made with the knowledge of its falsity, 4) with the intent to deceive, and 5) on which action is taken in reliance upon the representation. Here, there were issues of fact that precluded the granting of summary judgment for either party. The motions for summary judgment were denied. *Armstrong v. Accrediting Council for Continuing Education & Training, Inc.*, 961 F.Supp. 305 (D.D.C.1997).

◆   *A fraud claim brought by nursing students against a school that had allegedly misrepresented its accreditation status failed where the students could not show that they relied on the school's misrepresentation.*

A Missouri nursing school graduated its first class of students in 1984. The school was accredited by the Missouri State Board of Nursing. It was also a "candidate for accreditation" with the North Central Association for Colleges and Schools NCA). The NCA recommended that the school's brochure state that it was a "candidate for accreditation by the NCA." However, the brochure actually stated that the school "has ... been granted [NCA] candidacy for review status" and that "accreditation for [the school] is expected in 1983." In 1981, a letter from the student services coordinator restated the above-quoted information to the class of 1984. However, the students were not apprised of the NCA accreditation status prior to their graduation and the school was not formally accredited until 1987. This accreditation status did not apply retroactively to the class of 1984. Several members of the class of 1984 filed suit in a Missouri trial court, alleging that the school intentionally misrepresented its accreditation status which limited their job prospects, advanced education and future earning power. The trial court granted the school's motion for summary judgment, and the students appealed to the Missouri Court of Appeals.

The students contended that the school's affirmative statement regarding the likelihood of achieving accreditation legally bound it to disclose all material facts related to its receipt of NCA accreditation. Consequently, they argued, the school's silence on this issue was intentional misrepresentation. The court of appeals rejected the students' appeal. **Although misrepresentation of a material fact by silence may amount to actionable fraud, the students failed to show that they relied on the school's allegedly fraudulent statements in enrolling or remaining enrolled in the program.** Because the students failed to establish the reliance element of fraud, the court refused to address the issue of whether the school had a duty to disclose all material facts related to the anticipated accreditation. The holding of the trial court was affirmed. *Nigro v. Research College of Nursing*, 876 S.W.2d 681 (Mo.App.W.D.1994).

◆   *Where a college catalog did not state that the college was accredited, students who sued for fraud were unable to prove up their case.*

Four students enrolled in an Illinois nursing college. They later discovered that the college was not accredited by the National League for Nursing, Inc. (NLN). The students alleged that the school failed to communicate that it was not accredited, nor did it notify them of the significance of the lack of accreditation. In 1984, the NLN site visitation team began its accreditation process. The NLN denied accreditation to the nursing school and also denied an appeal from the school. The nursing school officials then met with the students to discuss the effect of the nonaccreditation and informed them that they could remain at the school for their final year or they could transfer to another nursing program. However, if the students transferred to another school, they might have to repeat courses. Four students who chose to transfer sued the school and the officers of the school, alleging fraud. The trial court entered a decision in favor of the school. The students appealed to the Appellate Court of Illinois.

The appellate court decided that the evidence clearly showed that some of the nursing students would have entered the school anyway, and many students remained at the school even after discovering the absence of accreditation. Further, the students failed to prove that the omission proximately caused their injury. The appellate court also decided that the students would not have had to repeat their junior years, as **many of the students who stayed at the school were very successful. The catalog was not a misrepresentation since it did not discuss accreditation** and only set forth that students could go on to successful nursing careers after graduation which many students had done. The appellate court affirmed the trial court's decision and ruled in favor of the school. *Lidecker v. Kendall College*, 550 N.E.2d 1121 (Ill.App.1st Dist.1990).

C. Negligence

♦   *Students were allowed to sue accrediting agencies for negligence in the following case. The Higher Education Act did not preempt their lawsuit.*

An Arizona private technical school made certain positive representations to several prospective students about the school's accreditation status as well as the education, jobs and benefits they would receive during school and after they graduated. Based on these representations, the students obtained loans and enrolled at the school. They could not have obtained the loans if the school had not been accredited. The school went out of business prior to the students' graduation, leaving them with thousands of dollars in student loans to repay. The students filed a negligence lawsuit against the accrediting agencies in a U.S. district court, **alleging that they had negligently accredited and failed to monitor the school.** The district court ruled that the Higher Education Act (HEA) preempted the students' negligence lawsuit and held for the agencies. The students appealed to the U.S. Court of Appeals, Ninth Circuit. The court of appeals noted that the HEA did not expressly preempt state common law tort claims against accreditors. It also declined to find an implied preemption. Consequently, the HEA did not preempt the students' claims. Rather, state courts had to decide whether to recognize a cause of action for negligent accreditation. *Keams v. Tempe Technical Institute Inc.*, 39 F.3d 222 (9th Cir.1994).

* *However, the lawsuit for negligence failed when the U.S. Court of Appeals held that the accrediting agencies did not have a duty to the students.*

In a subsequent case, a group of students who had taken out federally guaranteed student loans in order to attend the Arizona technical institute, filed suit against the institute and the accrediting agencies in federal district court. They alleged that the agencies negligently accredited and monitored the institute, causing them monetary damages. The district court dismissed their lawsuit for failure to state a claim upon which relief could be granted, and the students appealed to the U.S. Court of Appeals, Ninth Circuit. The court of appeals noted that to establish a cause of action for negligence under Arizona law, **a plaintiff must establish that the defendant has a duty, recognized by law, to conform to a certain standard of conduct.** This duty can be imposed when both the person to whom the duty is owed and the risk are foreseeable to a reasonable person. The students argued that it was foreseeable to the agencies that the negligent performance of their duties would cause the alleged damages. The court disagreed, finding that the students had not sufficiently shown that the agencies had given them false information. It also found no Arizona cases that recognized a duty of care in this type of situation or held that accrediting agencies owe a duty to students attending the institutions that they accredit. The court affirmed the district court's decision. *Keams v. Tempe Technical Institute, Inc.*, 110 F.3d 44 (9th Cir.1997).

D. Withdrawal of Accreditation

* *A Florida business school was entitled to an injunction to stop an accrediting council from suspending its accreditation where it would suffer irreparable harm if the suspension were allowed and where it was likely to prevail on the merits of the case.*

The school was accredited by a council of independent schools and colleges. The council used a list of criteria in its accreditation decisions. In determining whether to continue accrediting the school, the council conducted an on-site evaluation and found that the school was not in compliance with a number of the listed criteria. Most importantly, less than 50 percent of the school's students had a high school diploma or its equivalent and the number of students enrolled in nonbusiness programs exceeded the number enrolled in business programs. The school failed to adequately explain its noncompliance, the council suspended its accreditation and a review board approved this decision. The school filed an emergency motion for injunctive relief in the U.S. District Court for the Southern District of Florida.

The court noted that its review was limited to whether the council's decision was arbitrary and unreasonable or supported by substantial evidence. Although the school had originally reported that most of its students did not have high school diplomas, it later discovered that the report was wrong because of a computer error and actually less than 50 percent of its students were without a diploma. The school also argued that it believed its cosmetology and nursing programs qualified as business programs based on language in the council's accreditation manual and the practices of other accrediting agencies. Because the school would not receive federal funding and would be closed if it did not receive accreditation, **the court found that it would suffer irreparable harm. This harm outweighed the**

harm that the council would suffer. Based on the evidence, the court also found that the school showed a substantial likelihood of success on the merits. It granted the preliminary injunction and remanded the case for further proceedings. *Florida College of Business v. Accrediting Council for Independent Colleges and Schools*, 954 F.Supp. 256 (S.D.Fla.1996).

♦   *The withdrawal of accreditation by a nonprofit agency was held not to be government action requiring compliance with the Fifth Amendment.*

An Illinois corporation was licensed as a vocational business school by the Illinois Department of Education. The Accrediting Council for Continuing Education and Training is a nonprofit agency recognized by the U.S. Department of Education as a national accrediting agency. The agency accredited the business school for five years but, following subsequent complaints, conducted an on-site examination and revoked the school's accreditation due to financial instability. The school appealed the decision pursuant to agency guidelines, and the matter was reconsidered. However, the withdrawal of accreditation was affirmed. The school appealed to the U.S. District Court for the Northern District of Illinois, alleging a Fifth Amendment due process claim and a violation of common law principles of fundamental fairness.

The school contended that the agency's actions could be attributed to the federal government and therefore required compliance with the Fifth Amendment. The court disagreed. There was not a sufficient nexus between the agency's actions and the federal government. Here, **the agency was a private corporation.** Even if the government promulgated regulations which the agency had to follow and officially recognized the agency, **this was not sufficient state action to require compliance with the U.S. Constitution.** The court also rejected the school's common-law claim. The agency's decision was neither arbitrary, unreasonable nor unsupported by substantial evidence. To the contrary, the agency had provided for a fair appeals process and had applied objectively fair standards. Here, the school's financial position had "substantially deteriorated" and it might not have been able to complete the instruction of all its enrollees. Accordingly, both the constitutional claim and the common law claim were dismissed. The agency's decision was affirmed. *Peoria School of Business v. Accrediting Council*, 805 F.Supp. 579 (N.D.Ill.1992).

♦   *Where a decision to withdraw accreditation was not arbitrary or capricious, a federal court should not have ordered the agency to continue the accreditation.*

The Commission on Occupational Education Institutions (COEI) is part of the Southern Association of Colleges and Schools (SACS). It was set up to accredit postsecondary, nondegree granting institutions. In March 1988, COEI conducted an on-site inspection of a cosmetology school's campuses to determine whether to reaffirm accreditation. After finding various problems (violations of dual accreditation and of refund and disclosure policies, and failure to submit an annual report for 1986) COEI dropped the school's accreditation. Since this was a prerequisite for the school's students' receipt of federal financial assistance, the school brought suit against COEI and SACS to enjoin the disaccreditation. A federal district court issued an injunction preventing SACS from withdrawing the school's accreditation for at least one year, and it further ordered SACS to pay the school's attorney's fees and costs.

During SACS appeal to the U.S. Court of Appeals, Fifth Circuit, five of the school's six campuses closed. The school voluntarily relinquished SACS accreditation for the other campus. This rendered the validity of the injunction moot. However, the court of appeals found that it had to reach the merits of the case because of the question of attorney's fees and costs. The court then noted that **there had been clear evidence that the school had been in violation of the dual accreditation policy set by COEI.** The district court had incorrectly found that COEI's policy language was vague. It should have accorded COEI's accreditation decisions greater deference. Thus, the court reversed the district court's award to the school and held that it was not entitled to attorneys' fees and costs. *Wilfred Academy v. Southern Assn. of Colleges and Schools*, 957 F.2d 210 (5th Cir.1992).

◆   *An accrediting agency did not have to accredit a teaching hospital run by the Catholic church because the hospital did not train future physicians on abortion procedures.*

A teaching hospital followed the guidelines of the Roman Catholic Church. One of the programs offered was in obstetrics and gynecology. This program was cited as deficient by the Accrediting Council for Graduate Medical Education (ACGME) for four reasons. One of those reasons was failure to provide training in abortion, sterilization, and artificial contraception (family planning). This specific deficiency led through probation and hearings to the eventual revocation of the hospital's accreditation. The hospital filed suit in a federal district court, claiming that by forcing a choice between religious principles and accreditation the ACGME violated the hospital's rights guaranteed by the Free Exercise Clause of the First Amendment to the U.S. Constitution.

The court found that the hospital did have a sincerely held religious belief which had been restricted. However, the court found that ACGME had satisfied its burden of showing that it furthered an essential public interest in the least restrictive manner. **Physicians leaving the hospital would be licensed to practice family planning, including abortion, without being trained.** There was no other method by which ACGME could assure the public's interest in safety other than to require the contested training. Also, the procedures followed by ACGME to remove its accreditation fully comported with the Due Process Clause and its standards of accreditation were fair. Removal of the hospital's accreditation was upheld.

On a motion for reconsideration, and a request for an injunction, the court restated its opinion that the school was unlikely to win at trial. It also held that the accreditation requirements did not irreparably or unnecessarily violate the hospital's First Amendment rights. They allowed residents to get training in family planning with an outside institution. Similarly, a loss of accreditation is not irreparable. The hospital was free to modify its program and reapply for accreditation. Next, the court found that accreditation was ACGME's sole function; restraint of that function would surely result in harm. Finally, the court viewed the accreditation requirements of a residency program as a safeguard of the public's interest, which leaned toward denial of the injunction request. The injunction pending appeal was denied. *St. Agnes Hosp. of the City of Baltimore v. Riddick*, 748 F.Supp. 319, 751 F.Supp. 75 (D.Md.1990).

CHAPTER TEN

School Finance

I. PUBLIC ASSISTANCE TO PRIVATE SCHOOLS

Since public schools are financed by a combination of tuition and public grants, finance issues seldom arise in the courts. This chapter addresses the much more common private school finance issues that have reached the courts in recent years.

The Establishment Clause of the First Amendment to the U.S. Constitution prohibits Congress from making any law respecting an establishment of religion. It has been construed by the U.S. Supreme Court as prohibiting direct financial assistance by government agencies to religious schools and colleges. In 1997, the Court decided *Agostini v. Felton*, 521 U.S. 203, 117 S.Ct. 1997, 138 L.Ed.2d 391 (1997), an important private school finance case in which the Court abandoned the presumption that the presence of public employees on parochial school grounds creates a symbolic union between church and state that violates the Establishment Clause. Under *Agostini*, government assistance to private schools must not result in government indoctrination or endorsement of religion. The recipients of government assistance must not be defined by reference to their religion, and the assistance must not create excessive entanglement between church and state.

A. Federal Funding

♦ *In* Tilton v. Richardson, *the U.S. Supreme Court held that the receipt of Higher Education Facilities Act funds by four religious colleges did not violate the Establishment Clause.*

The Higher Education Facilities Act of 1963 contained an exclusion for any facility used for sectarian instruction or as a place of religious worship or any facility which is used primarily as part of a school divinity department. Federal education officials had powers to enforce the statute for a 20-year time period during which they could seek to recover funds from violators. A group of Connecticut taxpayers filed a federal district court action against government officials and four religious colleges which received Higher Education Facilities Act funds, seeking an order against the release of funds to sectarian institutions that used federal funds to construct libraries and other facilities. The court held that the act did not have the effect of promoting religion.

The U.S. Supreme Court reviewed the case and held that the statute had been carefully drafted to ensure that no federal funds were disbursed to support the sectarian aspects of these institutions. **The four colleges named as defendants in this case had not violated any of the restrictions in the statute as they had placed no religious symbols in facilities constructed with the use of federal funds, nor had they used the facilities for any religious purposes.** The was no evidence that any of the colleges maintained a predominantly religious atmosphere, and although each of them was affiliated with the Catholic Church, none excluded non-Catholics from admissions or faculty appointments, and none of them required attendance at religious services. **The receipt of funds by the colleges did not violate the Establishment Clause.** The Court held, **however,** that **the 20-year limit on federal oversight created the potential for religious use of the facilities after the 20 years expired.** Because of the risk of use of the facilities for advancing religion, the court invalidated this portion of the legislation. *Tilton v. Richardson*, 403 U.S. 672, 91 S.Ct. 2091, 29 L.Ed.2d 790 (1971).

♦   *The U.S. Court of Appeals, Second Circuit, upheld federal regulations published under Title IV of the Higher Education Act as representing a reasonable interpretation of the statute.*

Title IV of the Higher Education Act, 20 USC 1091b(a), requires college and post-secondary vocational training schools that receive federal funds for student financial aid programs to establish a fair and equitable policy for refunding unearned tuition and other costs when a student receiving such aid fails to enter or prematurely leaves the intended program. Subsection (b) declares that an institution's refund policy shall be considered fair and equitable if the refund is at least the largest of the amounts provided under state law, the institution's nationally recognized accrediting agency formula, or the statutorily described formula for pro rata refunds.

A regulation issued by the Secretary of Education (found at 34 CFR § 668.22(b)(4)) provided that schools had to deduct "any unpaid charges owed by the student for the period of enrollment for which the student has been charged." Former regulations had put the risk of student nonpayment on the government. A coalition of vocational training schools in New York sought a federal district court injunction against the operation of the regulation. The court granted the injunction, but the U.S. Court of Appeals, Second Circuit, vacated the injunction and stated that **§ 668.22(b)(4) represented a reasonable interpretation of the statute.** The statute set a minimum refund amount but did not bar the secretary from asking for a larger amount. *Coalition of New York State Career Schools Inc. v. Riley*, 129 F.3d 276 (2d Cir.1997).

♦   *A federal district court upheld regulations published by the U.S. Department of Education under 1992 amendments to the Higher Education Act as rationally related to legitimate government interests. The regulations did not violate the Equal Protection Clause.*

The amendments added a new eligibility requirement so that proprietary institutions had to derive at least 15 percent of their revenues from non-Title VII Funds in order to be eligible for participation in Title VII programs. This was intended to attract students based upon the quality of an institution's programs, rather than its offer of federal student financial assistance. The Department of Education proposed regulations that interpreted "revenue" to mean funds received by the institution from tuition and fees plus funds from other activities necessary to the education and training offered by the institution. It further determined that the revenue calculation pursuant to the formula promulgated by the department was to use a cash-based accounting system and was to go into effect about 60 days later. Several private Puerto Rico institutions that relied heavily on Title VII funds filed a declaratory judgment action in a U.S. district court, seeking to prevent implementation of the regulations. The court held a consolidated hearing on the preliminary injunction issue.

The court determined that the department's interpretation of revenue reflected the demand for the institutions' educational services and was not arbitrary or capricious. Further, the department complied with the Administrative Procedure Act by publishing a notice of proposed rule-making and providing interested parties 60 days to respond. Nothing in the law required the department to extend the notice period. Because institutions which cannot meet statutory requirements do not have property or liberty rights under the Fifth Amendment, the regulations did not constitute a taking of these interests. The court also noted that **Congress had a legitimate interest in providing better education by tightening the eligibility requirements for Title VII funds.** Consequently, the **regulations were rationally related to legitimate government interests and did not violate the Equal Protection Clause** of the Fourteenth Amendment. The court denied the institutions' request for an injunction. *Ponce Paramedical College v. U.S. Dept. of Educ.*, 858 F.Supp. 303 (D.Puerto Rico 1994).

B.   State Funding

♦   *For more than a generation, courts have analyzed Establishment Clause cases under the framework established by the U.S. Supreme Court in* Lemon v. Kurtzman. *In recent years, the test has been criticized by legal experts and by members of the Court itself. Nonetheless, the three-part* Lemon *test remains an important one for assessing the validity of government programs under the Establishment Clause and is still routinely applied by the courts.*

In *Lemon v. Kurtzman*, the Court invalidated Rhode Island and Pennsylvania statutes which provided state money to finance the operation of parochial schools. The Rhode Island statute provided a 15 percent salary supplement to parochial school teachers who taught nonreligious subjects using public school teaching materials. The Pennsylvania statute authorized payment of state funds to parochial schools to help defray the cost of teachers' salaries, textbooks and other instructional materials. Reimbursement was limited, however, to the costs of secular subjects which were also taught in the public schools. The Supreme Court evaluated the Rhode Island and Pennsylvania programs using its **three-part test: First, the statute must have a secular legislative purpose; second, its principal or primary effect must be one that neither advances nor inhibits religion, finally; the statute must not foster "an excessive government entanglement with religion."** Applying this test to the two state programs in question, the Court held that the legislative purpose of the programs was a legitimate, secular concern with maintaining high educational standards in both public and private schools. The Court did not reach the second inquiry because it concluded that the state programs failed to pass muster under the third inquiry.

The Rhode Island salary supplement program excessively entangled the state with religion because of the highly religious nature of the Catholic schools that were the primary beneficiaries of the program. The teachers who received the salary supplements provided instruction in classrooms and buildings containing religious symbols such as crucifixes. In such an atmosphere, even a person dedicated to remaining religiously neutral would probably allow some religious content to creep into the ostensibly secular instruction. Similar defects were found in the Pennsylvania program. The Court also observed that in order to ensure that the state-funded parochial school teachers did not inject religious dogma into their instruction, the state would be forced to extensively monitor the parochial school classrooms. This would result in excessive state entanglement with religion. Consequently, **the salary supplement programs were held to violate the Establishment Clause of the First Amendment.** *Lemon v. Kurtzman,* 403 U.S. 602, 91 S.Ct. 2105, 29 L.Ed.2d 745 (1971).

◆   *In* Hunt v. McNair, *the Supreme Court upheld a South Carolina plan which allowed both private and public colleges to use the state's authority to borrow money at low interest rates.*

Hunt v. McNair involved a Baptist college that used state funding to finance the construction of a dining hall. The college had no religious test for either its faculty or students and the student body was only about 60 percent Baptist, the same percentage found in the surrounding community. The Supreme Court found that the college was not "pervaded by religion." **Unlike the situation commonly found in K-12 parochial schools, religiously-affiliated colleges and universities are often not dominated by a religious atmosphere.** The Court concluded that both **the purpose and effect of the state's borrowing program was secular and was therefore constitutional.** The argument that aid to one (secular) portion of a religious institution makes it free to spend more money on religious pursuits was rejected as unpersuasive and irrelevant. If that were the case, the Court noted that police and fire protection for religious schools would have to be cut off as well. *Hunt v. McNair,* 413 U.S. 734, 93 S.Ct. 2868, 37 L.Ed.2d 923 (1973).

◆   *The Supreme Court held that the "secular side" of a college could be distinguished from sectarian programs, making it permissible for a state to provide funding to a religiously-affiliated college, where the assistance goes only to a college's secular side.*

The state of Maryland enacted a program which authorized annual, noncategorical grants to religiously affiliated colleges. The program was challenged by taxpayers who alleged that state money was being put to religious uses by the schools, which had wide discretion in spending the funds. The Supreme Court began its analysis of the Maryland program with the following observation: "*Hunt [v. McNair]* requires (1) that no state aid at all go to institutions that are so "pervasively sectarian" that secular activities cannot be separated from sectarian ones, and (2) that if secular activities can be separated out, they alone may be funded." The colleges involved in this case were not found to be pervasively sectarian even though they were affiliated with the Catholic Church. The Court held that the "secular side" of the colleges could be separated from the sectarian, and found that **state aid had only gone to the colleges' secular side**. It was admittedly somewhat difficult to ensure that the colleges and the Maryland Council for Higher Education would take care to avoid spending state funds on religious activities, but the Court expressed its belief that those entities would spend the money in good faith and avoid violating the First Amendment. *Roemer v. Bd. of Public Works*, 426 U.S. 736, 96 S.Ct. 2337, 49 L.Ed.2d 179 (1976).

♦   *A religiously affiliated private college could receive state funds if it could demonstrate that no state funds would be used for religious instruction or worship.*

A Maryland program provided state funding to private colleges meeting specified requirements. After the U.S. Supreme Court held that the program did not violate the Constitution, see *Roemer*, above, the Maryland Higher Education Commission denied program funding requests by a four-year private liberal arts college affiliated with the Seventh Day Adventist Church on grounds that the college was "pervasively sectarian."

The college sued the commission, alleging that the denial of program funds violated the college's constitutional rights, and the case reached the U.S. Court of Appeals, Fourth Circuit. The appellate court observed that the appropriate criteria for assessing whether an institution is "pervasively sectarian" includes whether the institution requires students to worship, the extent to which religious influences dominate the academic curriculum, faculty and admission processes, and the degree of autonomy enjoyed by the institution in relation to its sponsoring church. Here, the lower court record was insufficient to determine whether the college was "pervasively sectarian." **Even though there was evidence that the college required some students to attend worship and prayer services, this did not compel the inference that the college attempted to indoctrinate students or compromised their academic freedom.** The case was remanded for further proceedings. *Columbia Union College v. Clarke*, 159 F.3d 151 (4th Cir.1998).

♦   *The Supreme Court of Virginia held that a university with a pervasively religious mission could not receive the proceeds of a city bond issue without violating the Establishment Clauses of the U.S. and Virginia Constitutions.*

Liberty University is a private, sectarian institution that is closely related to a local Baptist church. It required all of its students and faculty to comply with clearly spelled out religious requirements. The Lynchburg, Virginia, city council and Industrial Development Authority (IDA) approved the issuance of up to $60 million of Educational Facilities Revenue Bonds in order to assist Liberty University in building and developing academic and administrative facilities in Lynchburg. The validity of the bond issue with respect to both the U.S. and Virginia Constitutions came under question. The IDA filed an action to answer those questions. A Virginia trial court validated the bond issue, and a group of opposing taxpayers appealed to the Supreme Court of Virginia.

The main issue in this case was whether the bond issuance was in violation of the Establishment Clauses of the U.S. or Virginia Constitutions. The First Amendment to the U.S. Constitution states, "Congress shall make no law respecting the establishment of religion." The court turned to a number of decisions in which the U.S. Supreme Court has allowed comparable arrangements for other church-related schools. Those decisions involved schools which imposed no religious requirements for admission or employment, or religious requirements for students or faculty while affiliated with the school. The court contrasted Liberty's policies and found the issuance to be unconstitutional. Liberty had published policies requiring specific church attendance six times per week. Academic freedom was also limited. **The court found Liberty to be "a religious mission" with a "pervasive aim [of] equipping young people for evangelistic ministry." Because of this pervasiveness, the bond issue could only have the effect of establishing religion**. The judgment of the trial court was reversed. *Habel v. Industrial Dev. Authority*, 400 S.E.2d 516 (Va.1991).

◆   *The Wisconsin Court of Appeals held that a lower court would have to hold a trial to determine whether a private religious college could constitutionally receive state aid. It could not otherwise determine crucial issues such as whether the college was "pervasively sectarian."*

Wisconsin legislators provided a $100,000 grant to a private religiously affiliated college for the establishment of an "international center." The college was a nonprofit organization that was required by its articles of incorporation to be run "within the context of theology, philosophy, [and] other teachings and doctrines of the Roman Catholic Church." Also, a religious organization was the sole shareholder of the college, and had complete power to appoint its board of directors and amend or repeal its articles of incorporation. The grant did not further specify the legislature's purpose or whether the activities held in the center would be religious or secular. An assembly of opposed citizens filed suit in a state court against the governor. They sought to reverse the grant, and argued that it violated the First Amendment of the U.S. Constitution as well as Article 1, § 18 of the Wisconsin Constitution.

The trial court found that the grant was unconstitutional on its face, and granted the citizens judgment on the pleadings. The state appealed to **the Wisconsin Court of Appeals which held that whether the purpose of the grant was permissible would need to be determined at trial**. The citizens argued that the college was "pervasively sectarian," such that no state aid would be constitutional. It based that argument on the school's control structure. The school asserted that, despite its legal structure, the day-to-day management was done by a board of trustees of which no more than 30 percent could be members of the religious organization. A trial would resolve these issues. *Freedom from Religion Foundation, Inc. v. Thompson*, 476 N.W.2d 318 (Wis.App.1991).

II. PUBLIC ASSISTANCE TO STUDENTS

The U.S. Supreme Court held in Grove City College v. Bell, *below, that private schools whose students receive federal funds are deemed to be recipients of federal assistance. Therefore, even a college with an unbending policy of rejecting all forms of government assistance was required to comply with federal laws since its students received federal grants and loans.*

A. School Funding Issues

◆   *In* Grove City College v. Bell, *the U.S. Supreme Court held that a private college was a recipient of federal financial assistance, and thus subject to Title IX of the Education Amendments of 1972, because its students received federal grants.*

A private college which had an "unbending policy" of refusing all forms of government assistance in order to remain independent of governmental restrictions was asked by the Department of Education (DOE) to supply "assurance of compliance" with Title IX, which the college refused to do on the ground that it was receiving no federal funding. The DOE disagreed, saying that because the school enrolled large numbers of students receiving federal Basic Educational Opportunity Grants (BEOGs), it was receiving financial assistance for purposes of Title IX. The DOE then cut off student financial assistance based on the college's failure to execute the assurance of compliance. Four students and the college brought suit challenging the termination of financial assistance. **The Supreme Court held that the college was a recipient of federal financial assistance and thus subject to the statute prohibiting sex discrimination. This was so despite the fact that only some of the college's students received BEOGs and even though the college did not receive any direct federal financial assistance.** Thus, the college was obliged to submit assurance of compliance, but only with regard to the administration of its financial aid program, in order for students to continue to receive federal aid. *Grove City College v. Bell*, 465 U.S. 555, 104 S.Ct. 1211, 79 L.Ed.2d 516 (1984).

◆   *In the following case, the U.S. Court of Appeals, Ninth Circuit, held that the Higher Education Act does not confer upon educational institutions a private right of action to sue loan guarantors. However, a school which serviced loans for a large number of minority students had stated a claim against Arizona's designated federal loan guarantor under 42 U.S.C. § 1981.*

The federal government appointed a private corporation as Arizona's designated guarantor of federally funded and mandated student loan programs. The corporation then terminated a private business school's participation in the Arizona loan guaranty program. The school, which serviced a large number of minority students, filed a race discrimination claim against the corporation in federal court, alleging violations of the Equal Protection Clause pursuant to 42 U.S.C. §§ 1981 and 1983. It also alleged that the corporation terminated its participation in the program without a hearing in violation of the Due Process Clause of the Fifth and Fourteenth Amendments. The district court dismissed both claims, and the school appealed to the U.S. Court of Appeals, Ninth Circuit.

The court of appeals held that **the Higher Education Act does not confer upon educational institutions a private right of action to sue loan guarantors.** Congress intended review by the secretary pursuant to the requirements of the Administrative Procedure Act to be the exclusive means for ensuring a lender's compliance with the statutes and regulations. The court also dismissed the school's constitutional claim pursuant to 42 U.S.C. § 1983, ruling that the corporation did not act "under color of state law" as the statute required. Specifically, there was no nexus between the state and the challenged termination, the corporation had no sovereign powers, the HEA expressly provided for private guarantors, and the state did not compel the offensive action. However, the court of appeals reversed the district court dismissal of the constitutional claim pursuant to 42 U.S.C. § 1981. The students here were improperly being prevented from attending a private school. **Because the corporation's alleged discrimination could arguably destroy the school's business and property, the school stated a claim under § 1981.** The trial court ruling was affirmed in part and reversed in part. *Parks School of Business, Inc. v. Symington*, 51 F.3d 1480 (9th Cir.1995).

♦   *A federal district court upheld the inspector general's ability to subpoena documents in student loan cases.*

A private Delaware school was one of the nation's largest recipients of Pell Grants and Stafford Loans. The school underwent what was intended to be a routine audit by the Inspector General. The audit was necessary because there were $54 million in Stafford Loans (federally guaranteed student loans) in default. This represented 46 percent of the total amount outstanding from students who had received loans to attend this school. Concurrent with the audit, an investigation began, involving the FBI and the inspector general. After the audit was completed, the FBI seized documents and computer files as part of a further investigation. This seizure was ruled unlawful and the record of the brief investigation was destroyed. After the records were returned to the school, the inspector general served a subpoena in an attempt to review the documents and files. The school then sued to oppose the subpoena.

The issue in this case involved determining what the inspector general was authorized to subpoena. The school stated that there were so many documents and files called for that it would be unduly burdensome for the school to comply. Additionally, the school objected to some of the specific information requested. The court found that **all of the information asked for in the subpoena was in fact obligatory for the school to maintain and make available to the inspector general.** The school was bound to such duty because of the agreement any school must enter with the Department of Education if the school wishes to become an "eligible school" to receive Pell Grants and Stafford Loans. The court ruled that the school could not object to either the amount or scope of documents requested in the subpoena. The court enforced the subpoena and ordered the school to produce the documents and files. *U.S. v. Teeven*, 745 F.Supp. 220 (D.Del.1990).

B. Grants and Loans for Religious Schools

✦ *In 1986, the U.S. Supreme Court held that the First Amendment to the U.S. Constitution did not prevent the state of Washington from providing financial assistance directly to an individual with a disability attending a Christian college. However, the Supreme Court of Washington then held on remand that the assistance violated the state constitution.*

A visually impaired Washington student sought vocational rehabilitative services from the Washington Commission for the Blind pursuant to state law. The law provided that individuals with visual disabilities were eligible for educational assistance to enable them to "overcome vocational handicaps and to obtain the maximum degree of self-support and self-care." However, because the plaintiff was a student at a Christian college intending to pursue a career of service in the church, the Commission for the Blind denied him assistance. The Washington Supreme Court upheld this decision on the ground that the First Amendment to the U.S. Constitution prohibited state funding of a student's education at a religious college. The U.S. Supreme Court took a less restrictive view of the First Amendment and reversed the Washington court. The operation of Washington's program was such that the Commission for the Blind paid money directly to students, who could then attend the schools of their choice. **The fact that the student in this case chose to attend a religious college did not constitute state support of religion because "the decision to support religious education is made by the individual, not the state."** The First Amendment was therefore not offended. *Witters v. Washington Dept. of Servs. for the Blind*, 474 U.S. 481, 106 S.Ct. 748, 88 L.Ed.2d 846 (1986).

On remand, the Washington Supreme Court reconsidered the matter under the **Washington State Constitution, which is far stricter in its prohibition on the expenditure of public funds for religious instruction than is the U.S. Constitution. Vocational assistance funds for the student's religious education violated the state constitution because public money would be used for religious instruction.** The court rejected the student's argument that the restriction on public expenditures would violate his right to free exercise of religion. The court determined that the commission's action was constitutional under the Free Exercise Clause because there was no infringement of the student's constitutional rights. Finally, denial of the funds to the student did not violate the Fourteenth Amendment's Equal Protection Clause because the commission had a policy of denying any student's religious vocational funding. The classification was directly related to the state's interest in ensuring the separation between church and state as required by both state and federal constitutions. The court reaffirmed its denial of the student's tuition. *Witters v. State Comm'n for the Blind*, 771 P.2d 1119 (Wash.1989).

✦ *The Court of Appeals of Minnesota upheld the Minnesota Post-Secondary Enrollment Options Act (PSEOA), holding that the state constitution does not prohibit government assistance for religiously-oriented institutions.*

The PSEOA allowed eleventh and twelfth grade students enrolled in public schools to take secondary or post-secondary courses for credit at eligible public and private colleges and universities. The state reimbursed participating students for the lesser of the actual cost of tuition and related expenses or an amount derived from a formula representing the school district's actual basic revenue. The Minnesota Federation of Teachers filed a federal district court action against state education officials and 15 private institutions, seeking to enjoin state funding of the private schools under the act. The teachers' federation asserted that the PSEOA violated the establishment clauses of the state and federal constitutions. The court granted pretrial judgment to the state and colleges for claims arising under the U.S. Constitution and dismissed the state law claims without prejudice. The federation commenced a new action in state court based on the state law claims and the court granted pretrial judgment to the officials and colleges.

The federation appealed to the Court of Appeals of Minnesota, which found that **the state constitution does not prohibit government assistance in the form of an indirect or incidental benefit to a religiously-oriented institution, even if it is pervasively sectarian.** Even though payments were made directly to the colleges under PSEOA, the students decided which school they would attend and the statute was neutral on its face. The benefit to the institution was incidental, because only some costs were reimbursed. **The PSEOA did not violate the Minnesota Constitution.** However, the court reversed and remanded the pretrial judgment order concerning the status of Bethel College to consider its alleged sectarian nature as there was an absence of information in the record concerning its use of funds. *Minnesota Federation of Teachers v. Mammenga*, 485 N.W.2d 305 (Minn.App.1992).

On remand, the trial court again entered pretrial judgment against the federation and it appealed to the court of appeals. The court applied a two-part analysis in determining whether the state assistance constituted a prohibited benefit or support of Bethel College. **The assistance would be permissible where the public benefit was indirect and incidental and the school was not pervasively sectarian. In this case, the benefit to the private school was indirect and incidental because it had been designed to benefit high school students, not private colleges.** Students had the choice to attend either a public or a private college under PSEOA. Bethel College separated PSEOA reimbursements from its other funds to ensure that state benefits were used only for nonsectarian purposes. The PSEOA did not violate the Establishment Clause of the Minnesota Constitution, and the court affirmed the trial court judgment. The Minnesota Supreme Court denied further appeal of this case. *Minnesota Federation of Teachers v. Mammenga*, 500 N.W.2d 136 (Minn.App.1993).

C. State Funding

♦   *The U.S. Supreme Court held that the government may show a violation of Title IV of the Higher Education Act without proving specific intent to injure or defraud by a defendant.*

A private, non-profit technical school in Indiana participated in the Guaranteed Student Loan (GSL) program authorized by Title IV of the Higher Education Act. The program required the school to make refunds to the lender if a student withdrew from school during a term. If the school failed to refund loans to the lender, the student—and if the student defaulted, the government—would be liable for the full amount of the loan. The treasurer of the school conferred with the school's owners and initiated a practice of not making GSL refunds. As a result, the school owed $139,649 in refunds. After the school lost its accreditation, a federal grand jury indicted the treasurer for "knowingly and willfully misapplying" federally insured student loan funds in violation of 20 U.S.C. § 1097(a). A federal district court dismissed the indictment because it lacked an allegation that the treasurer intended to injure or defraud the United States. The U.S. Court of Appeals, Seventh Circuit, reinstated the prosecution, and the U.S. Supreme Court granted review. The Supreme Court held that § 1097(a) did not require the specific intent to injure or defraud. **If the government can prove that the defendant misapplied Title IV funds knowingly and willfully, that is sufficient to show a violation of § 1097(a).** The Court affirmed the court of appeals' decision to reinstate the prosecution against the treasurer. *Bates v. U.S.*, 522 U.S. 23, 118 S.Ct. 285, 139 L.Ed.2d 215 (1997).

♦   *A federal appeals court upheld the U.S. Department of Education's subclassification of prisoner students, finding that federal law allowed distinctions between groups of students.*

An accredited for-profit vocational-technical school in Texas entered into an agreement with certain privately operated prison facilities to provide training programs for prisoners. The prisoners were not obligated to provide funding; however, the school received compensation by having the prisoners obtain federal Pell Grants based on the amounts it normally charged nonprisoner students, with an adjustment for the shorter prison programs. The school received a total of about $8.1 million. The U.S. Department of Education determined that because the prisoner students were under no obligation to pay tuition, there was no tuition "charge" that could be offset by a Pell Grant. Also, the school could not include "expenses" since the prisoners did not pay for books or other materials and the state of Texas paid for their living arrangements. Thus, the school was required to reimburse the Department. The school sued the Department, and the case reached the U.S. Court of Appeals, Fifth Circuit.

The Higher Education Act (HEA) defines the tuition and fees component of a student's "cost of attendance" as those "normally charged" at the institution. The Department determined that for prisoner students, to whom the school was required to provide classes free of charge, the tuition "normally charged" was zero. Thus, the school was not entitled to receive reimbursement for tuition in the form of a Pell Grant. The court upheld the Department's subclassification of the prisoner students, finding that the HEA plainly allowed distinctions between groups of students who are normally charged different amounts. **The court held that the school had reasonably and detrimentally relied on the Department's previous interpretation, which indicated that tuition and fee waivers did not affect the "cost of attendance" for Pell Grant purposes, and did not require the school to reimburse the tuition portion of the awards.** However, the school remained liable for reimbursement of the expense allowance portion of the awards. Because the students incurred no expenses, the school was never entitled, nor could it ever have believed it was entitled, to make awards based on those amounts. *Microcomputer Technology Institute v. Riley*, 139 F.3d 1044 (5th Cir.1998).

● *A federal district court refused to dismiss a complaint against the operator of three Pennsylvania vocational schools that was brought by students alleging fraudulent activity under the federal Racketeer Influenced and Corrupt Organizations Act (RICO).*

A Pennsylvania corporation operating three vocational schools admitted two students without high school diplomas or their equivalent. The students obtained federally guaranteed student loans (GSLs) and enrolled in a course to become medical assistants. One student withdrew after six weeks and another completed her course work but the school closed before she could receive any placement services. Federal statutes mandate that schools certify to the Department of Education that students admitted without high school diplomas or their equivalent have the "ability to benefit" from the school's courses prior to receipt of any GSLs. The students sued the school owner in a Pennsylvania federal court under RICO, claiming that the owner had fraudulently certified to the DOE that his schools complied with these requirements when, in fact, these schools were using artificially low cut-off scores on the entrance examinations and thereby qualifying students who did not have the ability to benefit from the school's courses.

The students argued that the school's conduct amounted to a pattern of racketeering in violation of RICO. The school argued that the students' injury was not "by reason of" the allegedly fraudulent conduct and, for this reason, it was not liable under RICO. **The court held that the students stated a RICO claim, ruling that the school's allegedly fraudulent certification of the students which had allowed them to take out federally guaranteed loans could have proximately caused their injuries** (their indebtedness). The students were directly injured, and the court rejected the school's motion for pretrial judgment. *Rodriguez v. McKinney*, 878 F.Supp. 744 (E.D.Pa.1995).

◆ *The New York Supreme Court, Appellate Division, held that the state could review a nonpublic educational institution's certification of a student's eligibility for a state grant.*

A New York private college accepted and certified a group of students who had previously attended a local community college as eligible for state Supplemental Tuition Assistance Program (STAP) grants. The STAP grants provided tuition assistance to New York students whose educational deficits were so great that they would not be considered admissible to a college level program. The state denied the college's request for STAP awards and a New York trial court affirmed the denial. On appeal by the college, the appellate division court held that **the state had both the authority and the obligation to review a nonpublic educational institution's certification of a student's eligibility for a STAP grant.** The regulatory scheme did not contemplate awards to students with successful college experience who had previously received funds pursuant to the Tuition Assistance Program. The appellate court affirmed the trial court's denial of STAP funds. *Touro College v. Nolan*, 620 N.Y.S.2d 558 (A.D.3d Dept.1994).

◆ *A university could not maintain a race-based scholarship program where past discrimination did not justify it.*

The University of Maryland maintained a merit scholarship program open only to African-American students. It alleged that the program redressed prior constitutional violations against African-American students by the university, which had formerly been segregated by law. A student of Hispanic descent attempted to obtain a scholarship under the program, but was denied on the basis of his race. He filed a lawsuit against the university and a number of its officials in the U.S. District Court for the District of Maryland. The court granted summary judgment to the university and the student won reversal from the U.S. Court of Appeals, Fourth Circuit. On remand, the parties again filed cross motions for summary judgment, and the district court again awarded summary judgment to the university.

The case was again appealed to the court of appeals. It determined that the district court had improperly found a basis in the evidence for its conclusion that a remedial plan of action was necessary. It had also erroneously determined that the scholarship program was narrowly tailored to meet the goal of remedying past discrimination. The court had misconstrued statistical evidence presented by the parties and had erroneously found a connection between past discrimination and present conditions at the university. **The reasons stated by the university for maintaining the race-based scholarship—underrepresentation of African-American students, low retention and graduation rates and a negative perception among African-American students—were legally insufficient.** The court reversed the summary judgment order for the university and awarded summary judgment to the student. *Podberesky v. Kirwan*, 38 F.3d 147 (4th Cir.1994), *cert. den.*, 115 S.Ct. 2001 (1995).

♦   *Students who belonged to tribes that were not federally recognized sued the Bureau of Indian Affairs for an order awarding them higher education grants.*

A Bureau of Indian Affairs (BIA) regulation authorized funds for higher education grants and loans to students of one quarter or more degree of Native American blood who enrolled at accredited institutions of higher education. However, this regulation was struck down as invalid in a 1986 decision by the U.S. Court of Appeals, Ninth Circuit. The BIA then adopted a rule requiring students to be members of a federally recognized tribe to be eligible for funds. Two students, who were both five-sixteenths Wintun Indian, were denied higher education grants because the tribe they belonged to was not federally recognized. The BIA's decision was affirmed by the U.S. District Court for the Eastern District of California, and the students appealed to the Ninth Circuit.

The court found that the BIA had violated federal administrative law requirements to publish proposed rules in the Federal Register when announcing new criteria for student loans and grants. Accordingly, it could not use the eligibility criteria it had relied on since the 1986 Ninth Circuit decision. Although the students prevailed on this question, **the court determined that without a properly published regulation, there could be no basis for an order directing the BIA to award higher education grants to the students** as they had requested. The court encouraged the BIA to adopt criteria consistent with federal law tending to exempt the California Indian population from federal recognition requirements. The court reversed the district court decision concerning the validity of the BIA's current criteria and affirmed the denial of injunctive relief. *Malone v. Bureau of Indian Affairs*, 38 F.3d 433 (9th Cir.1994).

D. Student Default

◆   *A Washington, D.C. vocational school student could not obtain discharge of a student loan despite the closing of the school.*

A student enrolled at a Washington, D.C. vocational school. The school informed her that tuition for the program would exceed $5,000 but that the school could arrange a guaranteed student loan (GSL). The student claimed that the school represented its program was accredited, approved by the D.C. Educational Licensure Commission, and certified by the Department of Education (DOE) as an "eligible institution" under the GSL program and the Higher Education Act of 1965 (HEA). She paid a portion of the tuition and received a GSL for the balance. After the school closed, the student sued several defendants in the U.S. District Court for the District of Columbia, seeking to compel the U.S. Secretary of Education to discharge her student loan.

The student argued that the school did not meet the requirements for an "eligible institution" at the time she received her GSL because the school's accreditation had subsequently expired, thereby making the contract voidable as either an illegal contract or a contract based on mistake. The district court disagreed, noting that if accreditation was improperly granted, it is a matter of concern between the school and the DOE, not between the student borrower and the lenders and guarantors. **The student's loan, which was entered into prior to the loss of accreditation, was enforceable.** On further appeal, the court noted that although current federal student loan policy recognizes school misconduct defenses against lenders who have "referral relationships" with for-profit schools, no such remedy existed in 1988 when the student obtained her GSL. Permitting the student to raise the fraud defense against repayment of her pre-1992 loan would subject her lender to risks neither anticipated by it nor intended by the Guaranteed Student Loan Program. *Armstrong v. Accrediting Council For Continuing Education and Training, Inc.*, 168 F.3d 1362 (D.C.Cir.1999).

◆   *A federal district court allowed a Wisconsin student to recover interest and collection fees paid that were not authorized by the federal Fair Debt Collection Practices Act (FDCPA).*

A student enrolled in a Wisconsin private college. Prior to enrollment she was not shown the college handbook which contained information regarding payment of tuition and charges for interest and collection fees. The handbook also stated that outstanding balances were subject to an 18 percent annual service charge. The student failed to make timely payments and the debt was turned over to a collection agency. The college assessed interest charges and a collection fee of 33 percent of the account total. The student made over 60 payments to the college, substantially diminishing the amount owed. However, the debt collector demanded payment in full and sent the student a threatening letter. The student filed a lawsuit against the private college and the debt collection agency, alleging violations of the FDCPA and the Wisconsin Consumer Act. The court held that the **defendants' attempt to collect the collection fees violated the FDCPA.** The student was entitled to recover interest and collection fees paid that were not authorized by law. The private college was also liable for violations of federal and state law. Holding creditors like the college liable for acts of collection agencies they use on a regular basis advanced purposes of fair debt collection statutes: to protect consumers from abusive, unfair or unconscionable collection practices. *Patzka v. Viterbo College,* 917 F.Supp. 654 (W.D.Wis.1996).

❖   *A student who defaulted on his student loans was unable to avoid liability under the Higher Education Technical Amendments (HETA), which eliminated a six-year statute of limitations on actions under prior law.*

A borrower defaulted on several student loans. These loans were assigned to the U.S. Department of Education on November 30, 1976 and on August 20, 1984. After the department sought to collect the defaulted student loans, the borrower filed suit in a U.S. district court alleging that the department's action was barred by the statute of limitations. The district court granted summary judgment to the department, and the borrower appealed to the U.S. Court of Appeals, Ninth Circuit. The court of appeals noted that the Higher Education Act, as modified by the Consolidated Omnibus Budget Reconciliation Act, provided for a six-year statute of limitations, commencing from the date the loan was assigned to the department. However, **the Higher Education Technical Amendments of 1991 (HETA) eliminated the six-year statute of limitations and revived all actions which would otherwise have been time-barred.** Consequently, the HETA revived all student loan collection actions against the borrower. *U.S. v. Phillips,* 20 F.3d 1005 (9th Cir.1994).

❖   *A federal district court rejected a student's due process claims arising from alleged inadequate notice that his loans were in default based on evidence that he knew that his payments were delinquent.*

A student attending a university in Washington, D.C. participated in the Guaranteed Student Loan Program (GSLP) and signed two promissory notes. The student dropped below half-time in January 1990 and graduated in May 1990. He became delinquent after missing his first loan payment in August 1990. However, the student then enrolled in a Texas law school and received a deferment until December 1990. When the student entered the repayment period in January 1991, both the loan servicing agency and the guaranty agency repeatedly and unsuccessfully attempted to contact him. When contact was finally made with the student in June 1991, he was sent a loan deferment form which he failed to return. In July 1991, the guaranty agency paid the amount in default and commenced collection procedures against the student. The student filed suit in a U.S. district court alleging that he received inadequate notice that his loans were in default. The guaranty agency counterclaimed for the amount in default.

The student contended that he was denied procedural due process because the guaranty agency had failed to give him adequate notice of the due date of his first payment. The court disagreed, noting that he was advised of his default status in June 1991. Further, the student had the burden to request a deferment. Here, the student was already delinquent at the time of his first deferment and he then resumed that delinquent status upon his January 1991 repayment period. Since the student was aware that he was delinquent, and that he could obtain a deferment, he had received adequate notice. **The court held that the student was liable for the promissory notes and entered judgment for the guaranty agency.** *Stone v. United Student Aid Funds, Inc.,* 818 F.Supp. 254 (S.D.Ind.1993).

◆   *Because the real purpose of National Health Service Corps (NHSC) scholarships is to encourage health professionals to serve internships, and not to
provide financial assistance to students, a federal district court allowed the
collection of treble damages against a medical student who defaulted on his
obligation to the corps.*

A Texas medical student financed a majority of his education through a
National Health Service Corps (NHSC) scholarship. The scholarship provided
"reasonable educational expenses and a monthly stipend" in exchange for service
in the corps in a location where there are not enough health professionals. A
student serves one year in the corps for each year he or she receives scholarship
funds. If a student fails to fulfill his or her obligation, he or she must pay triple the
amount disbursed. In the student's final year, his professional plans changed and
he elected not to extend the scholarship contract. No scholarship funds were paid
to him during his final year. After he graduated, the Department of Health and
Human Services (HHS) twice sent him a request for deferment so that he could
complete his residency program before fulfilling his obligation in the corps. The
student did not respond and he became liable for $159,369, the trebled scholarship
amount plus interest. The United States sued the student, and the case reached the
U.S. Court of Appeals, Ninth Circuit.

The court of appeals rejected the student's argument that in order to be subject
to treble damages one must receive scholarship funds for the entire four years.
Rather, scholarship obligations were incurred in "single, one year units." **The
student could not escape the previously incurred obligations for each year
that he had received the funds.** If treble damages were not assessed, the
scholarship could be transformed into a standard loan as long as the student
withdrew from the corps before the final year of medical school. This was not the
purpose of the scholarship. **The real purpose was to "overcome a geographic
maldistribution of health professionals."** Thus, in order to effectuate congressional intent, the court imposed treble damages plus interest. *U.S. v. Williams*, 994
F.2d 646 (9th Cir.1993).

III. PRIVATE SCHOOL TAXATION

*The U.S. Supreme Court has infrequently considered federal income tax
cases involving private schools. In Bob Jones Univ. v. U.S., 461 U.S. 574, 103
S.Ct. 2017, 76 L.Ed.2d 157 (1983), it held that private schools must comply with
the strong federal interest against race discrimination and that federal tax exempt
status can be denied to schools maintaining discriminatory policies. More
recently, in* Camps Newfound/Owatonna, Inc. v. Town of Harrison, Maine, *520
U.S. 564, 117 S.Ct. 1590, 137 L.Ed.2d 852 (1997), the Court found no reason why
nonprofit status should exempt a private entity from laws regulating commerce,
including local property tax laws.*

A. Federal Income Taxation

◆   *The U.S. government's strong public policy against racial discrimination was
held sufficient to deny tax exempt status to an otherwise qualified private college.*

Section 501(c)(3) of the Internal Revenue Code (IRC) provides that "corporations ... organized and operated exclusively for religious, charitable ... or educational purposes" are entitled to tax exempt status. The Internal Revenue Service routinely granted tax exemption under IRC § 501(c)(3) to private schools regardless of whether they had racially discriminatory admissions policies. In 1970, however, the IRS concluded that it could no longer grant tax exempt status to racially discriminatory private schools because such schools were not "charitable" within the meaning of § 501(c)(3). In *Bob Jones University v. United States*, two private colleges whose racial admissions policies were allegedly rooted in their interpretations of the Bible sued to prevent the IRS from interpreting the federal tax laws in this manner. The Supreme Court rejected the colleges' challenge and upheld the IRS's interpretation.

The Court's ruling was based on a strong federal public policy against racial discrimination in education. **Because the colleges were operating in violation of that public policy, the colleges could not be considered "charitable" under § 501(c)(3). Thus, they were ineligible for tax exemption. The Court held that in order to fall under the exemption of § 501(c)(3) an institution must be in harmony with the public interest.** It also held that the denial of an exemption did not impermissibly burden Bob Jones' alleged religious interest in practicing racial discrimination. *Bob Jones University v. United States*, 461 U.S. 574, 103 S.Ct. 2017, 76 L.Ed.2d 157 (1983).

B. State and Local Taxation

◆   *Land used by a seminary for recreational purposes and as a buffer zone was exempt from taxation.*

A North Carolina county reviewed several parcels of land owned by a seminary and determined that they were not eligible for tax exemptions because they were not used for educational or religious purposes. After the state property tax commission held that exemptions applied to three parcels, the county appealed. The North Carolina Court of Appeals affirmed the decision in favor of the seminary. **Although the land was used essentially for recreational purposes and as a buffer between the campus and commercial development surrounding the campus, it served to provide and maintain a relaxed campus atmosphere.** Further, the seminary's attempt to rezone one of the parcels for commercial development so that it could sell the land for a profit was a planned future use which did not change the present exempted use of the land. *In the Matter of Southeastern Baptist Theological Seminary*, No. COA98-1440 (N.C.App.1999).

◆   *An office building owned by teaching doctors of Midwestern University did not qualify for real estate tax exemptions.*

The primary activities taking place at the property constituted billing, collection, data processing, accounting, administration, management, payroll and related functions for the physician group. When a state court held that the physician group did not qualify for the "charitable purposes" or "school" exemptions under Illinois law, appeal reached the Appellate Court of Illinois. **Under Illinois law, a property entitled to an exemption must be used exclusively for charitable purposes and owned by a charitable organization.**

Here, the group failed to meet either requirement. The Appellate Court did not allow the group to use its relationship with the university to cast itself as a charitable organization. No patient care, medical research or instructional classes took place on the property. *Midwest Physician Group, Ltd. v. Dept. of Revenue of Illinois*, 711 N.E.2d 381 (Ill.App.1st Dist.1999).

◆   *A university could not claim tax-exempt status for a parking garage or parts of a building leased to for-profit companies.*
    A university owned a four-story building with an attached parking garage, and leased space to five tenants. Two tenants were non-profit organizations and the other three tenants were for-profit companies. The Board of Tax Appeals found that the building and the land under it were exempt from taxation, but the garage and land under it were not. The Cleveland Board of Education filed a notice of appeal, wanting the whole property to be taxed.
    The Supreme Court of Ohio affirmed the Board of Tax Appeals decisions regarding the tax exemption for the space leased by the two non-profit organizations, and the non-tax exempt status of the garage and the land under it. It reversed exemptions given to the university for the space held by the for-profit tenants and vacant areas in the building. **The garage did not qualify for tax exempt status because it was not an essential and integral part of the university's or non-profit tenants' charitable and/or educational activities.** *Case Western Reserve Univ. v. Tracy*, 84 Ohio St.3d 316, 703 N.E.2d 1240 (1999).

◆   *The Commonwealth Court of Pennsylvania held that a college was entitled to exemption from real estate taxes because it was maintained as a public charity.*
    A Pennsylvania educational institution founded by the Presbyterian Church in the 18th century developed into a nonsectarian, private, coeducational four-year college. Students were admitted based on academic qualifications and irrespective of sex, race, color, creed or national origin. No criterion based on financial need was established as a condition of enrollment but if a student was unable to pay the tuition he or she would not be allowed to complete his or her education. The college's board of trustees served without compensation and the salaries of the college's employees were not excessive. Nearly 80 percent of the students received financial aid and the college regularly had an operating loss, although the market value of its endowment fund was over $50 million. The state board of assessment denied the college's application for a real estate exemption. On appeal by the college, a Pennsylvania trial court affirmed the board's decision. The college appealed to the Commonwealth Court of Pennsylvania.
    The commonwealth court held that the college qualified as a purely public charity. It advanced a charitable purpose, donated a substantial portion of its services, and benefited a substantial and indefinite class of persons who were legitimate subjects of charity. For example, the college offered a program to academically underprivileged youth, awarded substantial grants based on academic and financial need to students, enrollment was open and students were admitted pursuant to a nondiscriminatory admissions policy based on merit. The court also held that the college relieved the government of some of its burdens and operated free from the private profit motive. **Because the college was founded and was maintained as a purely public charity, it was entitled to a real estate**

tax exemption. The trial court ruling was reversed. *City of Washington v. Board of Assessment*, 666 A.2d 352 (Pa.Cmwlth.1995).

◆   *The Court of Appeal of Louisiana held that state law does not require private colleges to substantiate their tax exempt status except as set forth by the state legislature.*

A Louisiana church operated a private university that offered a variety of secular undergraduate and graduate programs. The Louisiana Board of Regents notified the university that it had failed to complete and submit the required licensure application and was therefore in violation of state law. Consequently, it sought to close the school. **Although degree granting institutions were generally required to be registered and licensed by the board, institutions granted a tax exemption under the Internal Revenue Code were exempted from these requirements.** Previously such private universities were required to supply only basic information to obtain a license. The state attorney general filed suit in a Louisiana trial court, seeking to enjoin the church's operation of the university based on its noncompliance with the board's procedural requirements. The trial court found that because the Internal Revenue Code does not require churches to obtain recognition of their exempt status, the board was prohibited from requiring the organization to do so. It denied the state's request for injunctive relief, and the state appealed to the Court of Appeal of Louisiana.

The university argued that the board improperly required licensure applicants such as the university to substantiate their tax exempt status. The state countered that it was acting within its implied powers to implement and administer state law when it required the university to do so. It argued that the trial court's interpretation circumvented the law's purpose to put into place a licensure scheme which would ensure the viability of post-secondary, academic degrees. The court of appeals affirmed, however, ruling that the state legislature chose to defer to federal law in this procedural area. **Federal law, pursuant to the Internal Revenue Code, granted churches automatic exempt status without the necessity of paperwork.** Absent a contrary directive from the state legislature, the court refused to read additional requirements into the law. The trial court's ruling was affirmed. *Ieyoub v. World Christian Church*, 649 So.2d 771 (La.App.1st Cir.1994).

◆   *The Commonwealth Court of Pennsylvania held that property owned by the private college in the following two cases was tax exempt because the college was a public charity under state law and the property was regularly used for the purposes of the college.*

A Pennsylvania nonprofit private college owned a house occupied by its grounds crew leader. The college charged the grounds crew leader a discounted rent that averaged about 70 percent of the fair market value. In exchange for the discount, the grounds crew leader agreed to be available on a 24-hour basis to respond to emergencies and nighttime calls. He was allegedly called to campus after hours six times in both 1991 and 1992 for snow and ice removal and to remove fallen tree limbs. The Delaware County Board of Assessment Appeals determined that the house was not exempt from property taxes. On appeal by the college, a Pennsylvania trial court reversed, finding the house exempt from taxation. A local public school district appealed the finding to the Commonwealth Court of Pennsylvania.

Article VIII of the **Pennsylvania Constitution provides that the general assembly can exempt real property of public charities "regularly used for the purposes of the institution."** Section 204 of the General County Assessment Law **exempts all college property "necessary for the occupancy and enjoyment of the same."** The commonwealth court stated that the college need not prove that the property was absolutely necessary to its needs for the exemption to apply. Rather, it was required to show only that it had a reasonable need for the property. Here, emergency personnel were essential to the college community. The grounds crew leader was able to respond much quicker to an emergency than personnel who were living off campus. The college properly chose to forego the additional rental revenues to provide these needed services. Further, the alleged infrequency of emergency situations did not render the house incidental to the college's purposes. **Because emergency services were directly related to the proper functions of the college, the trial court did not err in concluding that the house was tax exempt.** *In Re Swarthmore College,* 645 A.2d 470 (Pa.Cmwlth.1994).

The college also owned a large house designed for entertaining. The college's vice-president for alumni development lived in the house rent free and was not charged for utilities. The house was used for meetings, special events, receptions and to entertain potential donors from whom one-third of the college's yearly income was derived. These events were allegedly an important part of building trust with major donors. The Delaware County Board of Assessment Appeals determined that the house was not exempt from property taxes. On appeal by the college, a Pennsylvania trial court reversed, finding the house exempt from taxation. The Commonwealth Court of Pennsylvania stated that the **college was not required to prove that the property was absolutely necessary to its needs for the exemption to apply. Rather, it was required to show only that it had a reasonable necessity for the property.** Here, the vice-president was required to live in the house, use it to cultivate personal relationships with donors, and utilize it for numerous college functions. **These uses were directly related to the proper functions of the college.** Consequently, the trial court did not err in concluding that the vice-president's house was tax exempt. *In re Swarthmore College,* 643 A.2d 1152 (Pa.Cmwlth.1994).

♦   *The Supreme Court of Iowa upheld tax exempt status for property owned by a private university because it was used solely for the university's purpose of providing Catholic education for its students.*

A private Catholic university in Iowa was organized for charitable, scientific, religious, and educational purposes. The university acquired property adjacent to the campus and converted it into a child care center. The purpose of the child care center was to enable parents of preschool age children to attend the university. Priority admission to the center was given to students, then to faculty, then to the general public. The university vice president, a Catholic priest, was also provided rent-free housing at a location apart from the central campus of the university. This property also served as an office and conference center for the school. The university sought an exemption from general property taxation for both parcels.

The district court held that the child care facility was exempt but that the university vice president's residence was not exempt. The university appealed to the Supreme Court of Iowa.

The supreme court noted the statutory requirements for exemption. First, the **property must be used by literary, scientific, charitable, benevolent, agricultural or religious institutions and must not be operated for profit**. Because the child care facility was nonprofit and the university had a religious affiliation, these requirements were satisfied. Next, the property must be used "solely for its appropriate object." Here, the child care facility was properly used to enable students to attend the university and to enable university employees to further their goal of educating the students. The court also noted that the university vice president was a priest and was therefore "necessary" to further the stated purposes of the university. Consequently, **both the child care facility and the rent-free housing were solely for the university's object of providing an education based on the Catholic religion**. Both properties were exempt from general property taxation. The holding of the district court was affirmed in part and reversed in part. *St. Ambrose University v. Board of Review*, 503 N.W.2d 406 (Iowa 1993).

♦   *The Court of Appeals of Washington held that property owned by a religious order was of an educational nature as that term was defined in Washington law. The college was therefore entitled to exempt the property from state property taxation.*

An order of Benedictine monks established a small liberal arts college in Washington in the late 1800s. The religious order maintained the college in that same location since its inception. In 1985, the Washington Department of Revenue denied the college's application to exempt certain portions of its campus from real property taxation. After several unsuccessful administrative appeals, the college appealed to a Washington trial court.

The land in question was an undeveloped and unmaintained area of the campus which served essentially as a buffer zone. The students and faculty were free to utilize the property for recreational purposes, but the property was also occasionally used for classes. Additionally, religion students periodically entered the property to meditate. The trial court reversed the administrative decisions and determined that the property was entitled to be exempted from real property taxation. The department appealed the adverse decision to the Court of Appeals of Washington.

On appeal, the department conceded that the property was smaller in size than the maximum acreage permitted by statute (to still be eligible for an exemption), and that the property in question incidentally furthered an educational purpose. However, it contended that the exemption was unwarranted because the property was essentially unused, empty land which was not reasonably necessary for achievement of the educational, athletic or social programs of the college. The court found that the utilization of the property was of an educational nature as that term was defined in Washington law.

The purposes of a religious educational institution could be better carried out in a pleasant atmosphere which was conducive to the contemplation of nature than it could be in a crowded urban setting. The court found it significant that several state colleges and universities were also surrounded by green belts and buffer zones. **Since the property had been and continued to be an integral part of the college campus, the application for tax exemption should not have been denied.** The court affirmed the trial court's decision in favor of the college. *St. Martin's College v. State Dept. of Revenue*, 841 P.2d 803 (Wash.App.| Div.2 1992).

APPENDIX A

UNITED STATES CONSTITUTION

Provisions of Interest to Higher Educators

ARTICLE I

Section 1. All legislative Powers herein granted shall be vested in a Congress of the United States, which shall consist of a Senate and House of Representatives.

* * *

Section 8. The Congress shall have Power To lay and collect Taxes, Duties, Imposts and Excises, to pay the Debts and provide for the common Defence and general Welfare of the United States; but all Duties, Imposts and Excises shall be uniform throughout the Unites States;

To borrow money on the credit of the United States;

To regulate Commerce with foreign Nations, and among the several States, and with the Indian Tribes;

To establish an uniform Rule of Naturalization, and uniform Laws on the subject of Bankruptcies throughout the United States;

* * *

To promote the Progress of Science and useful Arts, by securing for limited Times to Authors and Inventors the exclusive Right to their respective Writings and Discoveries;

* * *

To make all Laws which shall be necessary and proper for carrying into Execution for the foregoing Powers, and all other Powers vested by this Constitution in the Government of the United States, or in any Department or Officer thereof.

* * *

Section 9. * * * No Bill of Attainder or ex post facto Law shall be passed.

* * *

Section 10. No State shall * * * pass any Bill of Attainder, ex post facto Law, or Law impairing the Obligation of Contracts, or grant any Title of Nobility.

ARTICLE II

Section 1. The executive Power shall be vested in a President of the United States of America. * * *

ARTICLE III

Section 1. The judicial Power of the United States, shall be vested in one supreme Court, and in such inferior Courts as the Congress may from time to time ordain and establish. The Judges, both of the supreme and inferior courts, shall hold their Offices during good Behaviour, and shall, at stated Times, receive for their Services a Compensation, which shall not be diminished during their Continuance in Office.

Section 2. The judicial Power shall extend to all Cases, in Law and Equity, arising under this Constitution, the Laws of the United States, and Treaties made, or which shall be made, under their Authority; - to all Cases affecting Ambassadors, other public Ministers and Consuls; - to all Cases of admiralty and maritime Jurisdiction, - to Controversies to which the United States shall be a party; - to Controversies between two or more States; - between a State and Citizens of another State; - between Citizens of different States; - between Citizens of the same State claiming Lands under the Grants of different States, and between a State, or the Citizens thereof, and foreign States, Citizens or Subjects.

* * *

ARTICLE IV

Section 1. Full Faith and Credit shall be given in each State to the public Acts, Records and judicial Proceedings of every other State. * * *

Section 2. The Citizens of each State shall be entitled to all Privileges and Immunities of Citizens in the several States.

* * *

Section 4. The United States shall guarantee to every State in this Union a Republican Form of Government, and shall protect each of them against Invasion; and on Application of the Legislature, or of the Executive (when the Legislature cannot be convened) against domestic Violence.

ARTICLE V

The Congress, whenever two thirds of both Houses shall deem it necessary, shall propose Amendments to this Constitution, or, on the Application of the Legislatures of two thirds of the several States, shall call a Convention for proposing Amendments, which, in either Case, shall be valid to all Intents and Purposes, as part of this Constitution, when ratified by the Legislatures of three fourths of the several States, or by Conventions in three fourths thereof, as the one or the other Mode of Ratification may be proposed by the Congress; Provided that no Amendment which may be made prior to the Year One thousand eight hundred and eight shall in any Manner affect the first and fourth Clauses in the Ninth Section of the first Article; and that no State, without its Consent, shall be deprived of its equal Suffrage in the Senate.

ARTICLE VI

* * *

This Constitution, and the Laws of the United States which shall be made in Pursuance thereof; and all Treaties made, or which shall be made, under the Authority of the United States, shall be the supreme Law of the Land; and the Judges in every State shall be bound thereby, any Thing in the Constitution or Laws of any State to the Contrary notwithstanding.

The Senators and Representatives before mentioned, and the Members of the several State Legislatures, and all executive and judicial Officers, both of the United States and of the several States, shall be bound by Oath or Affirmation, to support this Constitution; but no religious Test shall ever be required as a Qualification to any Office or public Trust under the United States.

* * *

AMENDMENT I

Congress shall make no law respecting an establishment of religion, or prohibiting the free exercise thereof; or abridging the freedom of speech, or of the press; or the right of the people peaceably to assemble, and to petition the Government for a redress of grievances.

* * *

AMENDMENT IV

The right of the people to be secure in their persons, houses, papers, and effects, against unreasonable searches and seizures, shall not be violated, and no Warrants shall issue, but upon probable cause, supported by Oath or affirmation, and particularly describing the place to be searched, and the persons or things to be seized.

AMENDMENT V

No person shall be held to answer for a capital, or otherwise infamous crime, unless on a presentment or indictment of a Grand Jury, except in cases arising in the land or naval forces, or in the Militia, when in actual service in time of War or public danger; nor shall any person be subject for the same offence to be twice put in jeopardy of life or limb; nor shall be compelled in any criminal case to be a witness against himself, nor be deprived of life, liberty, or property, without due process of law; nor shall private property be taken for public use, without just compensation.

AMENDMENT VI

In all criminal prosecutions, the accused shall enjoy the right to a speedy and public trial, by an impartial jury of the State and district wherein the crime shall have been committed, which district shall have been previously ascertained by law, and to be informed of the nature and cause of the accusation; to be confronted with the witnesses against him; to have compulsory process for obtaining witnesses in his favor, and to have the Assistance of Counsel for his defense.

AMENDMENT VII

In Suits at common law, where the value in controversy shall exceed twenty dollars, the right of trial by jury shall be preserved, and no fact tried by jury, shall be otherwise re-examined in any Court of the United States, than according to the rules of the common law.

AMENDMENT VIII

Excessive bail shall not be required, nor excessive fines imposed, nor cruel and unusual punishments inflicted.

AMENDMENT IX

The enumeration in the Constitution, of certain rights, shall not be construed to deny or disparage others retained by the people.

AMENDMENT X

The powers not delegated to the United States by the Constitution, nor prohibited by it to the States, are reserved to the States respectively, or to the people.

AMENDMENT XI

The Judicial power of the United States shall not be construed to extend to any suit in law or equity, commenced or prosecuted against one of the United States by Citizens of another State, or by Citizens or Subjects of any Foreign State.

* * *

AMENDMENT XIII

Section 1. Neither slavery nor involuntary servitude, except as a punishment for crime whereof the party shall have been duly convicted, shall exist within the United States, or any place subject to their jurisdiction.

Section 2. Congress shall have power to enforce this article by appropriate legislation.

AMENDMENT XIV

Section 1. All persons born or naturalized in the United States, and subject to the jurisdiction thereof, are citizens of the United States and of the State wherein they reside. No State shall make or enforce any law which shall abridge the privileges or immunities of citizens of the United States; nor shall any State deprive any person of life, liberty, or property, without due process of law; nor deny to any person within its jurisdiction the equal protection of the laws.

* * *

Section 5. The Congress shall have power to enforce, by appropriate legislation, the provisions of this article.

APPENDIX B

Subject Matter Table of United States Supreme Court Cases Affecting Higher Education

Note: Please see the Table of Cases (located at the front of this volume) for Supreme Court cases reported in this Volume.

Academic Freedom

Univ. of Pennsylvania v. EEOC, 493 U.S. 182, 110 S.Ct. 577, 107 L.Ed.2d 571 (1990).

Epperson v. Arkansas, 393 U.S. 97, 89 S.Ct. 266, 21 L.Ed.2d 228 (1968).

Meyer v. Nebraska, 262 U.S. 390, 43 S.Ct. 625, 67 L.Ed.2d 1042 (1923).

Arbitration

Volt Information Sciences v. Bd. of Trustees of Stanford Univ., 489 U.S. 468, 109 S.Ct. 1248, 103 L.Ed.2d. 488 (1989).

Athletics

NCAA v. Smith, 525 U.S. 459, 119 S.Ct. 924, 142 L.Ed.2d 929 (1999).

Attorney's Fees

Webb v. Board of Education, 471 U.S. 234, 105 S.Ct. 1923, 85 L.Ed.2d 233 (1985).

Smith v. Robinson, 468 U.S. 992, 104 S.Ct. 3457, 82 L.Ed.2d 746 (1984).

Civil Rights

Farrar v. Hobby, 506 U.S. 103, 113 S.Ct. 566, 121 L.Ed.2d 494 (1992).

St. Francis College v. Al-Khazraji, 481 U.S. 604, 107 S.Ct. 2022, 97 L.Ed.2d 749 (1987).

Grove City College v. Bell, 465 U.S. 555, 104 S.Ct. 1211, 79 L.Ed.2d 516 (1984).

Rendell-Baker v. Kohn, 457 U.S. 830, 102 S.Ct. 2764, 73 L.Ed.2d 418 (1982).

Collective Bargaining

Central State Univ. v. American Ass'n of Univ. Professors, Central State Univ. Chapter, 526 U.S. 124, 119 S.Ct. 1162, 143 L.Ed.2d 227 (1999).

Compulsory Attendance

Wisconsin v. Yoder, 406 U.S. 205, 92 S.Ct. 526, 32 L.Ed.2d 15 (1972).

Pierce v. Society of Sisters, 268 U.S. 510, 45 S.Ct. 571, 69 L.Ed. 1070 (1925).

Continuing Education

Austin ISD v. U.S., 443 U.S. 915, 99 S.Ct. 3106, 61 L.Ed.2d 879 (1979).

Harrah ISD v. Martin, 440 U.S. 194, 99 S.Ct. 1062, 59 L.Ed.2d 248 (1979).

Corporal Punishment
Ingraham v. Wright, 430 U.S. 651, 97 S.Ct. 1401, 51 L.Ed.2d 711 (1977).

Court Intervention in School Affairs
Epperson v. Arkansas, 393 U.S. 97, 89 S.Ct. 266, 21 L.Ed.2d 228 (1968).

Criminal Activity
Bates v. U.S., 522 U.S. 23, 118 S.Ct. 285, 139 L.Ed.2d 215 (1997).

Desegregation
U.S. v. Fordice, 505 U.S. 717, 112 S.Ct. 2727, 120 L.Ed.2d 575 (1992).
Freeman v. Pitts, 503 U.S. 467, 112 S.Ct. 1430, 118 L.Ed.2d 108 (1992).

Disabled Students
Florence County School Dist. Four v. Carter, 510 U.S. 7, 114 S.Ct. 361, 126 L.Ed.2d 284 (1993).
Zobrest v. Catalina Foothills School Dist., 509 U.S. 1, 113 S.Ct. 2462, 125 L.Ed.2d 1 (1993).
Dellmuth v. Muth, 491 U.S. 223, 109 S.Ct. 2397, 105 L.Ed.2d 181 (1989).
Honig v. Doe, 484 U.S. 305, 108 S.Ct. 592, 98 L.Ed.2d 686 (1988).
City of Cleburne, Texas v. Cleburne Living Center, 473 U.S. 432, 105 S.Ct. 3249, 87 L.Ed.2d 313 (1985).
Honig v. Students of Cal. School for the Blind, 471 U.S. 148, 105 S.Ct. 1820, 85 L.Ed.2d 114 (1985).
Burlington School Committee v. Department of Education, 471 U.S. 359, 105 S.Ct. 1996, 85 L.Ed.2d 385 (1985).
Smith v. Robinson, 468 U.S. 992, 104 S.Ct. 3457, 82 L.Ed.2d 746 (1984).
Irving Independent School District v. Tatro, 468 U.S. 883, 104 S.Ct. 3371, 82 L.Ed.2d 664 (1984).
Board of Education v. Rowley, 458 U.S. 176, 102 S.Ct. 3034, 73 L.Ed.2d 690 (1982).
University of Texas v. Camenisch, 451 U.S. 390, 101 S.Ct. 1830, 68 L.Ed.2d 175 (1981).
Pennhurst State School and Hosp. v. Halderman, 451 U.S. 1, 101 S.Ct. 1531, 67 L.Ed.2d 694 (1981).
Southeastern Community College v. Davis, 442 U.S. 397, 99 S.Ct. 2361, 60 L.Ed.2d 980 (1979).

Discrimination, Generally
Kimel v. Florida Board of Regents, 120 S.Ct. 631, 145 L.Ed.2d 522 (2000).
Texas v. Lesage, 120 S.Ct. 467, 145 L.Ed.2d 347 (1999).
Jett v. Dallas Indep. School Dist., 491 U.S. 701, 109 S.Ct. 2702, 105 L.Ed.2d 598 (1989).

Carnegie-Mellon Univ. v. Cohill, 484 U.S. 343, 108 S.Ct. 614, 98 L.Ed.2d 720 (1988).

School Board of Nassau County v. Arline, 480 U.S. 273, 107 S.Ct. 1123, 94 L.Ed.2d 307 (1987).

Hazelwood School Dist. v. U.S., 433 U.S. 299, 97 S.Ct. 2736, 53 L.Ed.2d 768 (1977).

DeFunis v. Odegaard, 416 U.S. 312, 94 S.Ct. 1704, 40 L.Ed.2d 164 (1974).

Due Process

Gilbert v. Homar, 520 U.S. 924, 117 S.Ct. 1807, 138 L.Ed.2d 120 (1997).

Univ. of Tennessee v. Elliot, 478 U.S. 788, 106 S.Ct. 3220, 92 L.Ed.2d 635 (1986).

Memphis Community School Dist. v. Stachura, 477 U.S. 299, 106 S.Ct. 2537, 91 L.Ed.2d 249 (1986).

Cleveland Bd. of Educ. v. Loudermill, 470 U.S. 532, 105 S.Ct. 1487, 84 L.Ed.2d 494 (1985).

Perry v. Sindermann, 408 U.S. 593, 92 S.Ct. 2694, 33 L.Ed.2d 570 (1972).

Board of Regents v. Roth, 408 U.S. 564, 92 S.Ct. 2701, 33 L.Ed.2d 548 (1972).

Employment

Corp. of the Presiding Bishop of the Church of Jesus Christ of Latter-Day Saints v. Amos, 483 U.S. 327, 107 S.Ct. 2862, 97 L.Ed.2d 273 (1987).

NLRB v. Catholic Bishop of Chicago, 440 U.S. 490, 99 S.Ct. 1313, 59 L.Ed.2d 533 (1979).

Federal Aid

Traynor v. Turnage, 485 U.S. 535, 108 S.Ct. 1372, 99 L.Ed.2d 618 (1988).

Selective Service System v. MPIRG, 468 U.S. 841, 104 S.Ct. 3348, 82 L.Ed.2d 632 (1984).

Bell v. New Jersey and Pennsylvania, 461 U.S. 773, 103 S.Ct. 2187, 76 L.Ed.2d 312 (1984).

Grove City College v. Bell, 465 U.S. 555, 104 S.Ct. 1211, 79 L.Ed.2d 516 (1984).

Valley Forge Christian College v. Americans United for Separation of Church and State, 454 U.S. 464, 102 S.Ct. 752, 70 L.Ed.2d 700 (1982).

Board of Education v. Harris, 444 U.S. 130, 100 S.Ct. 363, 62 L.Ed.2d 275 (1979).

Wheeler v. Barrera, 417 U.S. 402, 94 S.Ct. 2274, 41 L.Ed.2d 159 (1974).

Tilton v. Richardson, 403 U.S. 672, 91 S.Ct. 2091, 29 L.Ed.2d 790 (1971).

Freedom of Religion

City of Boerne, Texas v. Flores, 521 U.S. 507, 117 S.Ct. 2157, 138 L.Ed.2d 624 (1997).

Edwards v. Aguillard, 482 U.S. 578, 107 S.Ct. 2573, 96 L.Ed.2d 510 (1987).

Ansonia Board of Education v. Philbrook, 499 U.S. 60, 107 S.Ct. 367, 93 L.Ed.2d 305 (1986).

Freedom of Speech

Bd. of Regents of Univ. of Wisconsin System v. Southworth, 120 S.Ct. 1346, 146 L.Ed.2d 193 (S.Ct.2000).

Bd. of Educ. of Westside Com. Sch. v. Mergens, 496 U.S. 226, 110 S.Ct. 2356, 110 L.Ed.2d 191 (1990).

Bd. of Trustees of the State Univ. of New York v. Fox, 492 U.S. 469, 109 S.Ct. 3028, 106 L.Ed.2d 388 (1989).

Hazelwood School Dist. v. Kuhlmeier, 484 U.S. 261, 108 S.Ct. 562, 98 L.Ed.2d 592 (1988).

Bethel School District v. Fraser, 478 U.S. 675, 106 S.Ct. 3159, 92 L.Ed.2d 549 (1986).

Wayte v. U.S., 470 U.S. 598, 105 S.Ct. 1524, 84 L.Ed.2d 547 (1985).

Board of Education v. Pico, 457 U.S. 853, 102 S.Ct. 2799, 73 L.Ed.2d 435 (1982).

Givhan v. Western Line Consolidated School District, 439 U.S. 410, 99 S.Ct. 693, 58 L.Ed.2d 619 (1979).

Mt. Healthy City School v. Doyle, 429 U.S. 274, 97 S.Ct. 568, 50 L.Ed.2d 471 (1977).

Papish v. Board of Curators, 410 U.S. 667, 93 S.Ct. 1197, 35 L.Ed.2d 618 (1973).

Grayned v. City of Rockford, 408 U.S. 104, 92 S.Ct. 2294, 33 L.Ed.2d 222 (1972).

Police Dep't v. Mosley, 408 U.S. 92, 92 S.Ct. 2286, 33 L.Ed.2d 212 (1972).

Tinker v. Des Moines, 393 U.S. 503, 89 S.Ct. 733, 21 L.Ed.2d 733 (1969).

Pickering v. Board of Education, 391 U.S. 563, 88 S.Ct. 1731, 20 L.Ed.2d 811 (1968).

Keyishian v. Board of Regents, 385 U.S. 589, 87 S.Ct. 675, 17 L.Ed.2d 629 (1967).

Adler v. Bd. of Educ., 342 U.S. 485, 72 S.Ct. 380, 96 L.Ed. 517 (1952).

Intellectual Property

Florida Prepaid Postsecondary Educ. Expense Bd. v. College Savings Bank, 119 S.Ct. 2199, 144 L.Ed.2d 575 (1999).

College Savings Bank v. Florida Prepaid Postsecondary Educ. Expense Bd., 119 S.Ct. 2219, 144 L.Ed.2d 605 (1999).

Labor Relations

Lehnert v. Ferris Faculty Ass'n, 500 U.S. 507, 111 S.Ct. 1950, 114 L.Ed.2d 572 (1991).

Fort Stewart Schools v. Federal Labor Relations Authority, 495 U.S. 641, 110 S.Ct. 2043, 109 L.Ed.2d 659 (1990).

Minnesota State Board for Community Colleges v. Knight, 465 U.S. 271, 104 S.Ct. 1058, 79 L.Ed.2d 299 (1984).

NLRB v. Yeshiva University, 444 U.S. 672, 100 S.Ct. 856, 63 L.Ed.2d 115 (1980).

NLRB v. Catholic Bishop of Chicago, 440 U.S. 490, 99 S.Ct. 1313, 59 L.Ed.2d 533 (1979).

Abood v. Detroit Bd. of Educ., 431 U.S. 209, 97 S.Ct. 1782, 52 L.Ed.2d 261 (1977).

Maternity Leave

Richmond Unified School Dist. v. Berg, 434 U.S. 158, 98 S.Ct. 623, 54 L.Ed.2d 375 (1977).

Cleveland Board of Education v. La Fleur, 414 U.S. 632, 94 S.Ct. 791, 39 L.Ed.2d 52 (1974).

Cohen v. Chesterfield, 414 U.S. 632, 94 S.Ct. 791, 39 L.Ed.2d 52 (1974).

Private School Funding

Agostini v. Felton, 521 U.S. 203, 117 S.Ct. 1997, 138 L.Ed.2d 391 (1997).

Bd. of Educ. of Kiryas Joel Village School Dist. v. Grumet, 512 U.S. 687, 114 S.Ct. 2481, 129 L.Ed.2d 546 (1994).

Witters v. Washington Department of Services for the Blind, 474 U.S. 481, 106 S.Ct. 748, 88 L.Ed.2d 846 (1986).

Aguilar v. Felton, 473 U.S. 402, 105 S.Ct. 3232, 87 L.Ed.2d 290 (1985).

Grand Rapids School District v. Ball, 473 U.S. 373, 105 S.Ct. 3216, 87 L.Ed.2d 267 (1985).

Mueller v. Allen, 463 U.S. 388, 103 S.Ct. 3062, 77 L.Ed.2d 721 (1983).

Valley Forge Christian College v. Americans United for Separation of Church and State, 454 U.S. 464, 102 S.Ct. 752, 70 L.Ed.2d 700 (1982).

Committee for Public Education and Religious Liberty v. Regan, 444 U.S. 646, 100 S.Ct. 840, 63 L.Ed.2d 94 (1980).

New York v. Cathedral Academy, 434 U.S. 125, 98 S.Ct. 340, 54 L.Ed.2d 346 (1977).

Wolman v. Walter, 433 U.S. 229, 97 S.Ct. 2593, 53 L.Ed.2d 714 (1977).

Roemer v. Board of Public Works, 426 U.S. 736, 96 S.Ct. 2337, 49 L.Ed.2d 179 (1976).

Meek v. Pittenger, 421 U.S. 349, 95 S.Ct. 1753, 44 L.Ed.2d 217 (1975).

Wheeler v. Barrera, 417 U.S. 402, 94 S.Ct. 2274, 41 L.Ed.2d 159 (1974).

Sloan v. Lemon, 413 U.S. 825, 93 S.Ct. 2982, 37 L.Ed.2d 939 (1973).

Committee for Public Education and Religious Liberty v. Nyquist, 413 U.S. 756, 93 S.Ct. 2955, 37 L.Ed.2d 948 (1973).

Hunt v. McNair, 413 U.S. 734, 93 S.Ct. 2868, 37 L.Ed.2d 923 (1973).

Levitt v. Committee for Public Education and Religious Liberty, 413 U.S. 472, 93 S.Ct. 2814, 37 L.Ed.2d 736 (1973).
Early v. Di Censo, 403 U.S. 602, 91 S.Ct. 2105, 29 L.Ed.2d 745 (1971).
Lemon v. Kurtzman, 403 U.S. 602, 91 S.Ct. 2105, 29 L.Ed.2d 745 (1971).
Flast v. Cohen, 392 U.S. 83, 88 S.Ct. 1942, 20 L.Ed.2d 947 (1968).

Racial Discrimination
St. Francis College v. Al-Khazraji, 481 U.S. 604, 107 S.Ct. 2022, 97 L.Ed.2d 749 (1987).
City of Pleasant Grove v. United States, 479 U.S. 462, 107 S.Ct. 794, 93 L.Ed.2d 866 (1987).
Wygant v. Jackson Board of Education, 476 U.S. 267, 106 S.Ct. 1842, 90 L.Ed.2d 260 (1986).
Runyon v. McCrary, 427 U.S. 160, 96 S.Ct. 2586, 49 L.Ed.2d 415 (1976).
Lau v. Nichols, 414 U.S. 563, 94 S.Ct. 786, 39 L.Ed.2d 1 (1974).
Norwood v. Harrison, 413 U.S. 455, 93 S.Ct. 2804, 37 L.Ed.2d 723 (1973).

Recognition of Student Organizations
Bender v. Williamsport Area School District, 475 U.S. 534, 106 S.Ct. 1326, 89 L.Ed.2d 501 (1986).
Healy v. James, 408 U.S. 169, 92 S.Ct. 2338, 33 L.Ed.2d 266 (1972).

Release Time
Zorach v. Clauson, 343 U.S. 306, 72 S.Ct. 679, 96 L.Ed. 954 (1952).
McCollum v. Board of Education, 333 U.S. 203, 68 S.Ct. 461, 92 L.Ed. 649 (1948).

Religious Activities in Public Schools
Rosenberger v. Rector and Visitors of Univ. of Virginia, 515 U.S. 819, 115 S.Ct. 2510, 132 L.Ed.2d 700 (1995).
Lamb's Chapel v. Center Moriches Union Free School District, 508 U.S. 384, 113 S.Ct. 2141, 124 L.Ed.2d 352 (1993).
Lee v. Weisman, 505 U.S. 577, 112 S.Ct. 2649, 120 L.Ed.2d 467 (1992).
Karcher v. May, 484 U.S. 72, 108 S.Ct. 388, 98 L.Ed.2d 327 (1987).
Wallace v. Jaffree, 472 U.S. 38, 105 S.Ct. 2479, 96 L.Ed.2d 29 (1985).
Widmar v. Vincent, 454 U.S. 263, 102 S.Ct. 269, 70 L.Ed.2d 400 (1981).
Stone v. Graham, 449 U.S. 39, 101 S.Ct. 192, 66 L.Ed.2d 199 (1980).
Chamberlin v. Dade County Board of Public Instruction, 377 U.S. 402, 84 S.Ct. 1272, 12 L.Ed.2d 407 (1964).
Abington School District v. Schempp, 374 U.S. 203, 83 S.Ct. 1560, 10 L.Ed.2d 844 (1963).

Residency
Martinez v. Bynum, 461 U.S. 321 103 S.Ct. 1838, 75 L.Ed.2d 879 (1983).
Toll v. Moreno, 458 U.S. 1, 102 S.Ct. 2977, 73 L.Ed.2d 563 (1982).

Elgin v. Moreno, 435 U.S. 647, 98 S.Ct. 1338, 55 L.Ed.2d 614 (1978).
Vlandis v. Kline, 412 U.S. 441, 93 S.Ct. 2230, 37 L.Ed.2d 63 (1973).

School Liability

Gebser v. Lago Vista Indep. School Dist., 524 U.S. 274, 118 S.Ct. 1989, 141 L.Ed.2d 277 (1998).
Regents of Univ. of California v. Doe, 519 U.S. 337, 117 S.Ct. 900, 137 L.Ed.2d 55 (1997).

Sex Discrimination & Harassment

United States (Brzonkala) v. Morrison, 120 S.Ct. 1740 (2000).
Davis v. Monroe County Bd. of Educ., 526 U.S. 629, 119 S.Ct. 1661, 143 L.Ed.2d 839 (1999).
U.S. v. Virginia, 518 U.S. 515, 116 S.Ct. 2264, 135 L.Ed.2d 735 (1996).
Franklin v. Gwinnett County Public Schools, 503 U.S. 60, 112 S.Ct. 1028, 117 L.Ed.2d 208 (1992).
Ohio Civil Rights Commission v. Dayton Christian Schools, 477 U.S. 619, 106 S.Ct. 2718, 91 L.Ed.2d 512 (1986).
Mississippi University for Women v. Hogan, 458 U.S. 718, 102 S.Ct. 3331, 73 L.Ed.2d 1090 (1982).
Cannon v. Univ. of Chicago, 441 U.S. 677, 99 S.Ct. 1946, 60 L.Ed.2d 560 (1979).
Bd. of Trustees v. Sweeney, 439 U.S. 24, 99 S.Ct. 295, 58 L.Ed.2d 216 (1978).

Student Searches

Vernonia School District 47J v. Acton, 515 U.S. 646, 115 S.Ct. 2386, 132 L.Ed.2d 564 (1995).
New Jersey v. T.L.O., 469 U.S. 325, 105 S.Ct. 733, 83 L.Ed.2d 720 (1985).

Student Suspensions

Regents v. Ewing, 474 U.S. 214, 106 S.Ct. 507, 88 L.Ed.2d 523 (1985).
Board of Education v. McCluskey, 458 U.S. 966, 103 S.Ct. 3469, 73 L.Ed.2d 1273 (1982).
Carey v. Piphus, 435 U.S. 247, 98 S.Ct. 1042, 55 L.Ed.2d 252 (1978).
Bd. of Curators v. Horowitz, 435 U.S. 78, 98 S.Ct. 948, 55 L.Ed.2d 124 (1978).
Wood v. Strickland, 420 U.S. 308, 95 S.Ct. 992, 43 L.Ed.2d 214 (1975).
Goss v. Lopez, 419 U.S. 565, 95 S.Ct. 729, 42 L.Ed.2d 725 (1975).

Taxation

Camps Newfound/Owatonna, Inc. v. Town of Harrison, Maine, 520 U.S. 564, 117 S.Ct. 1590, 137 L.Ed.2d 852 (1997).
Allen v. Wright, 468 U.S. 737, 104 S.Ct. 3315, 82 L.Ed.2d 556 (1984).
Bob Jones University v. United States, 461 U.S. 574, 103 S.Ct. 2017, 76 L.Ed.2d 157 (1983).
Mueller v. Allen, 463 U.S. 388, 103 S.Ct. 3062, 77 L.Ed.2d 721 (1983).

Ramah Navajo School Bd. v. Bureau of Revenue, 458 U.S. 832, 102 S.Ct. 3394, 73 L.Ed.2d 1174 (1982).

California v. Grace Brethren Church, 457 U.S. 393, 102 S.Ct. 2498, 73 L.Ed.2d 93 (1982).

Gordon v. Lance, 403 U.S. 1, 91 S.Ct. 1889, 29 L.Ed.2d 273 (1971).

Askew v. Hargrave, 401 U.S. 476, 91 S.Ct. 856, 28 L.Ed.2d 196 (1971).

Doremus v. Bd. of Educ., 342 U.S. 429, 72 S.Ct. 394, 96 L.Ed. 475 (1952).

Teacher Termination

Patsy v. Bd. of Regents, 457 U.S. 496, 102 S.Ct. 2557, 73 L.Ed.2d 172 (1982).

Chardon v. Fernandez, 454 U.S. 6, 102 S.Ct. 28, 70 L.Ed.2d 6 (1981).

Delaware State College v. Ricks, 449 U.S. 250, 101 S.Ct. 498, 66 L.Ed.2d 431 (1980).

Beilan v. Board of Public Education, 357 U.S. 399, 78 S.Ct. 1317, 2 L.Ed.2d 1414 (1958).

Textbooks

Norwood v. Harrison, 413 U.S. 455, 93 S.Ct. 2804, 37 L.Ed.2d 723 (1973).

Board of Education v. Allen, 392 U.S. 236, 88 S.Ct. 1923, 20 L.Ed.2d 1060 (1968).

Cochran v. Louisiana State Board of Education, 281 U.S. 370, 50 S.Ct. 335, 74 L.Ed.2d 1929 (1930).

Transportation

Kadrmas v. Dickinson Pub. Schools, 487 U.S. 450, 108 S.Ct. 2481, 101 L.Ed.2d 399 (1988).

Wolman v. Walter, 433 U.S. 229, 97 S.Ct. 2593, 53 L.Ed.2d 714 (1977).

Everson v. Board of Education, 330 U.S. 1, 67 S.Ct. 504, 91 L.Ed. 711 (1947).

Weapons

U.S. v. Lopez, 514 U.S. 549, 115 S.Ct. 1624, 131 L.Ed.2d 626 (1995).

The Judicial System

In order to allow you to determine the relative importance of a judicial decision, the cases included in *Higher Education Law in America* identify the particular court from which a decision has been issued. For example, a case decided by a state supreme court generally will be of greater significance than a state circuit court case. Hence a basic knowledge of the structure of our judicial system is important to an understanding of higher education law.

Almost all the reports in this volume are taken from appellate court decisions. Although most education law decisions occur at trial court and administrative levels, appellate court decisions have the effect of binding lower courts and administrators so that appellate court decisions have the effect of law within their court systems.

State and federal court systems generally function independently of each other. Each court system applies its own law according to statutes and the determinations of its highest court. However, judges at all levels often consider opinions from other court systems to settle issues which are new or arise under unique fact situations. Similarly, lawyers look at the opinions of many courts to locate authority which supports their clients' cases.

Once a lawsuit is filed in a particular court system, that system retains the matter until its conclusion. Unsuccessful parties at the administrative or trial court level generally have the right to appeal unfavorable determinations of law to appellate courts within the system. When federal law issues or Constitutional grounds are present, lawsuits may be appropriately filed in the federal court system. In those cases, the lawsuit is filed initially in the federal district court for that area.

On rare occasions, the U.S. Supreme Court considers appeals from the highest courts of the states if a distinct federal question exists and at least four justices agree on the question's importance. The federal courts occasionally send cases to state courts for application of state law. These situations are infrequent and in general, the state and federal court systems should be considered separate from each other.

The most common system, used by nearly all states and also the federal judiciary, is as follows: a legal action is commenced in district court (sometimes called trial court, county court, common pleas court or superior court) where a decision is initially reached. The case may then be appealed to the court of appeals (or appellate court), and in turn this decision may be appealed to the supreme court.

Several states, however, do not have a court of appeals; lower court decisions are appealed directly to the state's supreme court. Additionally, some states have labeled their courts in a nonstandard fashion.

In Maryland, the highest state court is called the Court of Appeals. In the state of New York, the trial court is called the Supreme Court. Decisions of this court may be appealed to the Supreme Court, Appellate Division. The highest court in New York is the Court of Appeals. Pennsylvania has perhaps the most complex court system. The lowest state court is the Court of Common Pleas. Depending on the circumstances of the case, appeals may be taken to either the Commonwealth Court or the Superior Court. In certain instances the Commonwealth Court functions as a trial court as well as an appellate court. The Superior Court, however, is strictly an intermediate appellate court. The highest court in Pennsylvania is the Supreme Court.

While supreme court decisions are generally regarded as the last word in legal matters, it is important to remember that trial and appeals court decisions also create important legal precedents. For the hierarchy of typical state and federal court systems, please see the diagram below.

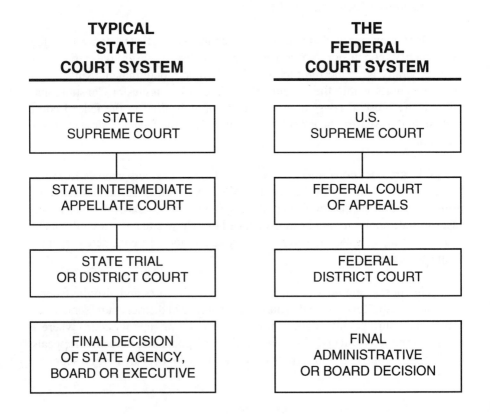

TYPICAL STATE COURT SYSTEM	THE FEDERAL COURT SYSTEM
STATE SUPREME COURT	U.S. SUPREME COURT
STATE INTERMEDIATE APPELLATE COURT	FEDERAL COURT OF APPEALS
STATE TRIAL OR DISTRICT COURT	FEDERAL DISTRICT COURT
FINAL DECISION OF STATE AGENCY, BOARD OR EXECUTIVE	FINAL ADMINISTRATIVE OR BOARD DECISION

Federal courts of appeals hear appeals from the district courts which are located in their circuits. Below is a list of states matched to the federal circuits in which they are located.

First Circuit	— Puerto Rico, Maine, New Hampshire, Massachusetts, Rhode Island
Second Circuit	— New York, Vermont, Connecticut
Third Circuit	— Pennsylvania, New Jersey, Delaware, Virgin Islands
Fourth Circuit	— West Virginia, Maryland, Virginia, North Carolina, South Carolina
Fifth Circuit	— Texas, Louisiana, Mississippi
Sixth Circuit	— Ohio, Kentucky, Tennessee, Michigan
Seventh Circuit	— Wisconsin, Indiana, Illinois
Eighth Circuit	— North Dakota, South Dakota, Nebraska, Arkansas, Missouri, Iowa, Minnesota
Ninth Circuit	— Alaska, Washington, Oregon, California, Hawaii, Arizona, Nevada, Idaho, Montana, Northern Mariana Islands, Guam
Tenth Circuit	— Wyoming, Utah, Colorado, Kansas, Oklahoma, New Mexico
Eleventh Circuit	— Alabama, Georgia, Florida
District of Columbia Circuit	— Hears cases from the U.S. District Court for the District of Columbia.
Federal Circuit	— Sitting in Washington, D.C., the U.S. Court of Appeals, Federal Circuit hears patent and trade appeals and certain appeals on claims brought against the federal government and its agencies.

How to Read a Case Citation

Generally, court decisions can be located in case reporters at law school or governmental law libraries. Some cases can also be located on the internet through legal websites or official court websites.

Each case summary contains the citation, or legal reference, to the full text of the case. The diagram below illustrates how to read a case citation.

case name (parties) case reporter name and series court location

Mangla v. Brown Univ., 135 F.3d 80 (1st Cir. 1998).

volume number   first page   year of decision

Some cases may have two or three reporter names such as U.S. Supreme Court cases and cases reported in regional case reporters as well as state case reporters. For example, a U.S. Supreme Court case usually contains three case reporter citations.

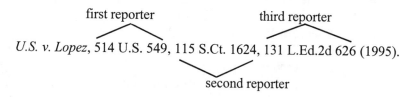

first reporter   third reporter

U.S. v. Lopez, 514 U.S. 549, 115 S.Ct. 1624, 131 L.Ed.2d 626 (1995).

second reporter

The citations are still read in the same manner as if only one citation has been listed.

Occasionally, a case may contain a citation which does not reference a case reporter. For example, a citation may contain a reference such as:

case name   year of decision   first page   year of decision

Porta v. Klagholz, No. 98-2350, 1998 WL 598385 (D.N.J.1998).

court file number   WESTLAW[1]   court location

The court file number indicates the specific number assigned to a case by the particular court system deciding the case. In our example, the U.S. District Court for the District of New Jersey has assigned the case of *Porta v. Klagholz* the case

---

[1] WESTLAW® is a computerized database of court cases available for a fee.

number of "No. 98-2350" which will serve as the reference number for the case and any matter relating to the case. Locating a case on the internet generally requires either the case name and date of the decision, and/or the court file number.

Below, we have listed the full names of the regional reporters. As mentioned previously, many states have individual state reporters. The names of those reporters may be obtained from a reference law librarian.

P.	**Pacific Reporter**	
	Alaska, Arizona, California, Colorado, Hawaii, Idaho, Kansas, Montana, Nevada, New Mexico, Oklahoma, Oregon, Utah, Washington, Wyoming	
A.	**Atlantic Reporter**	
	Connecticut, Delaware, District of Columbia, Maine, Maryland, New Hampshire, New jersey, Pennsylvania, Rhode Island, Vermont	
N.E.	**Northeastern Reporter**	
	Illinois, Indiana, Massachusetts, New York, Ohio	
N.W.	**Northwestern Reporter**	
	Iowa, Michigan, Minnesota, Nebraska, North Dakota, South Dakota, Wisconsin	
S.	**Southern Reporter**	
	Alabama, Florida, Louisiana, Mississippi	
S.E.	**Southeastern Reporter**	
	Georgia, North Carolina, South Carolina,Virginia, West Virginia	
S.W.	**Southwestern Reporter**	
	Arkansas, Kentucky, Missouri, Tennessee, Texas	

F.　　　**Federal Reporter**
　　　　　The thirteen federal judicial circuits courts of appeals decisions. *See, The Judicial System, p. 375* for specific state circuits.

F.Supp.　**Federal Supplement**
　　　　　The thirteen federal judicial circuits district court decisions. *See, The Judicial System, p. 375* for specific state circuits.

U.S.　　**United States Reports**
S.Ct.　　**Supreme Court Reporter** ⟩ U.S. Supreme Court Decisions
L.Ed.　　**Lawyers' Edition**

GLOSSARY

Ad Valorem Tax - In general usage, a tax on property measured by the property's value.

Age Discrimination in Employment Act (ADEA) - The ADEA, 29 U.S.C. § 621 *et seq.*, is part of the Fair Labor Standards Act. It prohibits discrimination against persons who are at least forty years old, and applies to employers which have twenty or more employees and which affect interstate commerce.

Americans With Disabilities Act (ADA) - The ADA, 42 U.S.C. § 12101 *et seq.*, went into effect on July 26, 1992. Among other things, it prohibits discrimination against a qualified individual with a disability because of that person's disability with respect to job application procedures, the hiring, advancement or discharge of employees, employee compensation, job training, and other terms, conditions and privileges of employment. The act also prohibits discrimination against otherwise qualified individuals with respect to the services, programs or activities of a public entity. Further, any entity which operates a place of public accommodation (including private schools) may not discriminate against individuals with disabilities.

Bill of Attainder - A bill of attainder is a law which inflicts punishment on a particular group of individuals without a trial. Such acts are prohibited by Article I, Section 9 of the Constitution.

Bona fide - Latin term meaning "good faith." Generally used to note a party's lack of bad intent or fraudulent purpose.

Claim Preclusion - (see Res Judicata).

Class Action Suit - Federal Rule of Civil Procedure 23 allows members of a class to sue as representatives on behalf of the whole class provided that the class is so large that joinder of all parties is impractical, there are questions of law or fact common to the class, the claims or defenses of the representatives are typical of the claims or defenses of the class, and the representative parties will adequately protect the interests of the class. In addition, there must be some danger of inconsistent verdicts or adjudications if the class action were prosecuted as separate actions. Most states also allow class actions under the same or similar circumstances.

Collateral Estoppel - Also known as issue preclusion. The idea that once an issue has been litigated, it may not be re-tried. Similar to the doctrine of *Res Judicata* (see below).

Due Process Clause - The clauses of the Fifth and Fourteenth Amendments to the Constitution which guarantee the citizens of the United States "due process of law" (see below). The Fifth Amendment's Due Process Clause applies to the federal government, and the Fourteenth Amendment's Due Process Clause applies to the states.

Due Process of Law - The idea of "fair play" in the government's application of law to its citizens, guaranteed by the Fifth and Fourteenth Amendments. Substantive due process is just plain *fairness*, and procedural due process is accorded when the government utilizes adequate procedural safeguards for the protection of an individual's liberty or property interests.

Employee Retirement Income Security Act (ERISA) - Federal legislation which sets uniform standards for employee pension benefit plans and employee welfare benefit plans. It is codified at 29 U.S.C. § 1001 *et seq.*

Enjoin - (see Injunction).

Equal Pay Act - Federal legislation which is part of the Fair Labor Standards Act. It applies to discrimination in wages which is based on gender. For race discrimination, employees paid unequally must utilize Title VII or 42 U.S.C. § 1981. Unlike many labor statutes, there is no minimum number of employees necessary to invoke the act's protection.

Equal Protection Clause - The clause of the Fourteenth Amendment which prohibits a state from denying any person within its jurisdiction equal protection of its laws. Also, the Due Process Clause of the Fifth Amendment which pertains to the federal government. This has been interpreted by the Supreme Court to grant equal protection even though there is no explicit grant in the Constitution.

Establishment Clause - The clause of the First Amendment which prohibits Congress from making "any law respecting an establishment of religion." This clause has been interpreted as creating a "wall of separation" between church and state. The test now used to determine whether government action violates the Establishment Clause, referred to as the *Lemon* test, asks whether the action has a secular purpose, whether its primary effect promotes or inhibits religion, and whether it requires excessive entanglement between church and state.

Ex Post Facto Law - A law which punishes as criminal any action which was not a crime at the time it was performed. Prohibited by Article I, Section 9, of the Constitution.

Exclusionary Rule - Constitutional limitation on the introduction of evidence which states that evidence derived from a constitutional violation must be excluded from trial.

Fair Labor Standards Act (FLSA) - Federal legislation which mandates the payment of minimum wages and overtime compensation to covered employees. The overtime provisions require employers to pay at least time-and-one-half to employees who work more than 40 hours per week.

Federal Tort Claims Act - Federal legislation which determines the circumstances under which the United States waives its sovereign immunity (see below) and agrees to be sued in court for money damages. The government retains its immunity in cases of intentional torts committed by its employees or agents, and where the tort is the result of a "discretionary function" of a federal employee or agency. Many states have similar acts.

42 U.S.C. §§ 1981, 1983 - Section 1983 of the federal Civil Rights Act prohibits any person acting under color of state law from depriving any other person of rights protected by the Constitution or by federal laws. A vast majority of lawsuits claiming constitutional violations are brought under § 1983. Section 1981 provides that all persons enjoy the same right to make and enforce contracts as "white citizens." Section 1981 applies to employment contracts. Further, unlike § 1983, § 1981 applies even to private actors. It is not limited to those acting under color of state law. These sections do not apply to the federal government, though the government may be sued directly under the Constitution for any violations.

Free Exercise Clause - The clause of the First Amendment which prohibits Congress from interfering with citizens' rights to the free exercise of their religion. Through the Fourteenth Amendment, it has also been made applicable to the states and their sub-entities. The Supreme Court has held that laws of general applicability which have an incidental effect on persons' free exercise rights are not violative of the Free Exercise Clause.

Incorporation Doctrine - By its own terms, the Bill of Rights applies only to the federal government. The Incorporation Doctrine states that the Fourteenth Amendment makes the Bill of Rights applicable to the states.

Individuals with Disabilities Education Act (IDEA) - 1990 amendment to the Education of the Handicapped Act (EHA) which renames the act and expands the group of children to whom special education services must be given.

Individualized Education Program (IEP) - Required by the IDEA, it ensures that each student will be given an appropriate education by tailoring the educational program to the needs of the individual student.

Injunction - An equitable remedy (see Remedies) wherein a court orders a party to do or refrain from doing some particular action.

Issue Preclusion - (see Collateral Estoppel).

Jurisdiction - The power of a court to determine cases and controversies. The Supreme Court's jurisdiction extends to cases arising under the Constitution and under federal law. Federal courts have the power to hear cases where there is diversity of citizenship or where a federal question is involved.

Labor Management Relations Act (LMRA) - Federal labor law which pre-empts state law with respect to controversies involving collective bargaining agreements. The most important provision of the LMRA is § 301, which is codified at 29 U.S.C. § 185.

Mill - In property tax usage, one-tenth of a cent.

National Labor Relations Act (NLRA) - Federal legislation which guarantees to employees the right to form and participate in labor organizations. It prohibits employers from interfering with employees in the exercise of their rights under the NLRA.

Negligence per se - Negligence on its face. Usually, the violation of an ordinance or statute will be treated as negligence per se because no careful person would have been guilty of it.

Occupational Safety and Health Act (OSHA) - Federal legislation which requires employers to provide a safe workplace. Employers have both general and specific duties under OSHA. The general duty is to provide a workplace which is free from recognized hazards that are likely to result in serious physical harm. The specific duty is to conform to the health and safety standards promulgated by the Secretary of Labor.

Overbroad - A government action is overbroad if, in an attempt to alleviate a specific evil, it impermissibly prohibits or chills a protected action. For example, attempting to deal with street litter by prohibiting the distribution of leaflets or handbills.

Per Curiam - Latin phrase meaning "by the court." Used in court reports to note an opinion written by the court rather than by a single judge or justice.

Preemption Doctrine - Doctrine which states that when federal and state law attempt to regulate the same subject matter, federal law prevents the state law from operating. Based on the Supremacy Clause of Article VI, Clause 2, of the Constitution.

Prior Restraint - Restraining a publication before it is distributed. In general, constitutional law doctrine prohibits government from exercising prior restraint.

Pro Se - A party appearing in court, without the benefit of an attorney, is said to be appearing pro se.

Remand - The act of an appellate court in returning a case to the court from which it came for further action.

Remedies - There are two general categories of remedies, or relief: legal remedies, which consist of money damages, and equitable remedies, which consist of a court mandate that a specific action be prohibited or required. For example, a claim for compensatory and punitive damages seeks a legal remedy;

a claim for an injunction seeks an equitable remedy. Equitable remedies are generally unavailable unless legal remedies are inadequate to address the harm.

Res Judicata - The judicial notion that a claim or action may not be tried twice or re-litigated, or that all causes of action arising out of the same set of operative facts should be tried at one time. Also known as claim preclusion.

Section 504 of the Rehabilitation Act of 1973 - Section 504 applies to public or private institutions receiving federal financial assistance. It requires that, in the employment context, an otherwise qualified individual cannot be denied employment based on his or her handicap. An otherwise qualified individual is one who can perform the "essential functions" of the job with "reasonable accommodation."

Section 1981 & Section 1983 - (see 42 U.S.C. §§ 1981, 1983).

Sovereign Immunity - The idea that the government cannot be sued without its consent. It stems from the English notion that the "King could do no wrong." This immunity from suit has been abrogated in most states and by the federal government through legislative acts known as "tort claims acts."

Standing - The judicial doctrine which states that in order to maintain a lawsuit a party must have some real interest at stake in the outcome of the trial.

Statute of Limitations - A statute of limitation provides the time period in which a specific cause of action may be brought.

Summary Judgment - Also referred to as pretrial judgment. Similar to a dismissal. Where there is no genuine issue as to any material fact and all that remains is a question of law, a judge can rule in favor of one party or the other. In general, summary judgment is used to dispose of claims which do not support a legally recognized claim.

Supremacy Clause - Clause in Article VI of the Constitution which states that federal legislation is the supreme law of the land. This clause is used to support the Preemption Doctrine (see above).

Title VI, Civil Rights Act of 1964 (Title VI) - Title VI prohibits racial discrimination in federally funded programs. This extends to admissions, financial aid, and virtually every aspect of the federally-assisted programs in which private schools are involved. Codified at 42 U.S.C. § 2000d.

Title VII, Civil Rights Act of 1964 (Title VII) - Title VII prohibits discrimination in employment based upon race, color, sex, national origin, or religion. It applies to any employer having fifteen or more employees. Under Title VII, where an employer intentionally discriminates, employees may obtain money damages unless the claim is for race discrimination. For those claims, monetary relief is available under 42 U.S.C. § 1981.

Title IX - Enacted as part of the Education Amendments of 1972, Title IX prohibits sexual discrimination in any private school program or activity receiving federal financial assistance. Codified at 20 U.S.C. § 1981 *et seq.*

U.S. Equal Employment Opportunity Commission (EEOC) - The EEOC is the government entity which is empowered to enforce Title VII (see above) through investigation and/or lawsuits. Private individuals alleging discrimination must pursue administrative remedies within the EEOC before they are allowed to file suit under Title VII.

Vacate - The act of annulling the judgment of a court either by an appellate court or by the court itself. The Supreme Court will generally vacate a lower court's judgment without deciding the case itself, and remand the case to the lower court for further consideration in light of some recent controlling decision.

Void-for-Vagueness Doctrine - A judicial doctrine based on the Fourteenth Amendment's Due Process Clause. In order for a law which regulates speech, or any criminal statute, to pass muster under the doctrine, the law must make clear what actions are prohibited or made criminal. Under the principles of the Due Process Clause, people of average intelligence should not have to guess at the meaning of a law.

Writ of Certiorari - The device used by the Supreme Court to transfer cases from the appellate court's docket to its own. Since the Supreme Court's appellate jurisdiction is largely discretionary, it need only issue such a writ when it desires to rule in the case.

INDEX